GOWER HANDBOOK
OF SUPPLY CHAIN
MANAGEMENT

(5th Edition)

Dedication

This book is dedicated to my friends and professional colleagues in the global supply chain 'community'.

GOWER HANDBOOK OF SUPPLY CHAIN MANAGEMENT

(5th Edition)

Editor

John L. Gattorna

Assistant Editors

Robert Ogulin

Mark W. Reynolds

GOWER

APL™ is a registered trademark of Accenture
EVA™ is a registered trademark of Stern, Stewart & Co.
CPFR® is a registered trademark of the Voluntary Interindustry Commerce Standards Association (VICS)

Published by
Gower Publishing
Gower House
Croft Road
Aldershot
Hants GU11 3HR
England

Gower Publishing Company
Suite 420
101 Cherry Street
Burlington, VT 05401–4405 USA

John L. Gattorna has asserted his right under the Copyright, Designs and Patents Act 1988 to be identified as the editor of this work.

British Library Cataloguing in Publication Data

Gattorna, John
Gower handbook of supply chain management. – 5th ed.
  1. Business logistics
  I. Title II. Handbook of supply chain management
  658.7

Library of Congress Cataloging in Publication Data

Gower handbook of supply chain management / executive editor, John
    Gattorna. – 5th ed.
      p. cm.
  Rev. ed. of: The Gower handbook of logistics and distribution
    management. 4th ed. c1990.
  Includes bibliographical references.
  1. Physical distribution of goods – management. I. Gattorna, John. II. Gower
  handbook of logistics and distribution management.
  HF5415.7.H33 2003
  658.7′88–dc21

                                                          2002029488

ISBN 0 566 08511 9 (Hbk)
ISBN 0 566 08581 X (Pbk)

Typeset in Palatino by LaserScript Ltd, Mitcham, Surrey

Printed and bound in Great Britain by MPG Books Ltd, Bodmin, Cornwall

5289627

Contents

Acknowledgements

A book of this sheer scope and scale requires the dedicated efforts of many people over the course of a year to complete successfully, so the list of people to whom I am indebted is far longer than I can recognize individually; but they all know who they are. However, a few deserve special mention.

Robert Ogulin and Mark Reynolds, my co-editors, have worked tirelessly to ensure the content and structure of this seminal reference work on the supply chain is as near perfection as is humanly possible.

Carmel McCauley of Future Perfect Communications took the raw individual contributions and has once again produced a comprehensive text, designed specifically for the business reader.

Of course there would be no book in the first place if such a large number of subject matter experts were not prepared to give their time and concentration so unselfishly, despite heavy workloads in their respective 'day jobs'. To all these authors, many of whom are friends and colleagues in Accenture, academia and further afield, I am particularly grateful for producing an outcome we all can be proud of.

The preparation of hundreds of graphics to go with the text was a mammoth task, and here I wish to express special thanks to consultants Sally Cowin and Sarah Z. Kim and to The Design Group at Accenture, in particular Alison Bruniges. In addition, Angela Field helped to improve the overall quality of the text through her tireless research and attention to detail.

The inimitable Fiona Gibson is master-minding the marketing and positioning of this book (the last in a series of three) in conjunction with Gower Publishing – so it is in safe hands. Gower Publishing have, as usual, been a delight to work with throughout the entire project. And finally, a special thank you to Jacqueline Turner, my executive assistant, who has helped me juggle this project along with running a busy supply chain practice during what has been a very hectic year for all of us.

John L. Gattorna
Sydney, December 2002

Foreword

In this book, we are challenging executives to push the boundaries and take supply chain management into a new sphere of activity and opportunity. Although good management is important, leadership in putting new concepts into practice is what truly differentiates the exceptional. We have segmented the book into a three-tier framework of operational excellence, integration/collaboration, and new business models. It invites executives to pursue continuous improvement, moving from one level to the next, always in search of additional growth and value.

I have great empathy for this philosophy, as my own organization is committed to add value for clients at all three levels, and do it simultaneously and expediently, because we manage in a world that operates in real time and knows no boundaries. Indeed, the oft-repeated words used by executives, 'we are not ready for this degree of change', are simply not defensible in today's fast-moving e-world. These very words are tantamount to destroying shareholder value. No stakeholder can afford the ways of the past that produce lacklustre results and have a devastating effect on market capitalizations.

The book also seeks to address the interests of all stakeholders in the enterprise; the ever-important customers, the living organization itself, the employees within, and shareholders, all of which are inextricably linked. Supply chains are no longer a subject for functional specialists; rather, their performance has a great impact on all stakeholders, and often creates competitive differentiation. Creating this dynamic alignment between all four parties, which we first outlined in *Strategic Supply Chain Alignment* (Gattorna, 1998), is something for which we will continue searching.

Simply seeking to improve process is no longer good enough either. Enterprises must now be aiming for the appropriate portfolio of 'execution models' to maximize the value generated along their respective 'value chains'. The key to success is capability; if you don't have the required mix, then you must tap into other sources. Unfortunately, many executives working in the supply chain area are 'experiential' and simply don't know what they don't know. This leads to sub-optimization, because they underestimate the complexities involved in the business, and the corresponding sophistication required to extract maximum value and differentiation from their operations.

Finally, this book is, above all, about transformation, transforming the organization through constant renewal of the corporate 'central nervous system', that is, the supply chain operations within, and the wider value chain connected to suppliers upstream and customers downstream. Managers may recognize that these tasks are quite challenging and not without risks, but change never is and genuine leaders will approach these tasks with passion, for leadership will be the differentiation that leads to greater shareholder value.

Gregory Owens
Chairman & CEO; Manugistics, Inc.
Rockville, MD
November 2002

Introduction and frameworks

John L. Gattorna

This book is designed specifically for senior executives and functional specialists interested in extracting the value embedded in the supply chains of their enterprises. As such, the overarching framework around which all the content is based has two primary dimensions – performance and capability, as depicted in Figure I.1. In particular, we focus mostly on the content around Curve 1: Operational excellence.

The content of this book is based on two primary dimensions: supply chain performance and capability.

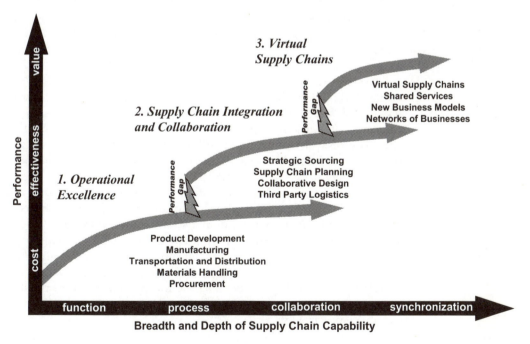

Figure I.1
The supply chain management performance/capability continuum

For completeness we also venture into collaboration content consistent with Curve 2: Supply chain integration and collaboration, and Curve 3: Virtual supply chains, because supply chains must and will progress in this direction.

Indeed, the key message in this book is that concentration on operational excellence alone is no longer sufficient for success because, as depicted in Curve 1, the 'diminishing returns' effect eventually comes into play and performance improvement slows. So, while tackling initiatives along Curve 1, companies must concurrently begin to focus on Curve 2. Along this curve, the potential for performance improvement jumps significantly over Curve 1, by 10–20 per cent, rather than 5–10 per cent. But there is more. With the coming of the e-commerce era, the potential for completely new supply chain operating models (Curve 3: Virtual supply chains) becomes a reality, with the promise, as yet largely unfulfilled, of further quantum improvements in performance of the order of 25–40 per cent.

To navigate through this handbook easily and successfully, an understanding of its structure and content is mandatory.

Part 1: Supply Chains in the Context of Customers and Strategy

Part 1 is designed to stress that 'everything starts at the customer end'.

Part 1 precedes treatment of the performance versus capability framework described above, and is our way of stressing that 'everything starts at the customer end'. The guiding principle here is that of *Strategic Supply Chain Alignment* (Gattorna, 1998) as depicted in Figure I.2.

Chapter 1.1, 'The challenging new operating environment and size of the prize', and Chapter 1.4, 'Operating strategy: configuring segmented supply chains', jointly deal with the world outside the enterprise. In particular, the latter chapter introduces a fundamentally new way of segmenting customers along buyer behavior lines, and sets the scene for later chapters which describe how to respond appropriately to the new operating environment.

Indeed, Chapter 1.2, 'Formulating a supply chain vision', and Chapter 1.3, 'Developing an aligned supply chain operating strategy', are specifically included to demonstrate the second level of the alignment model: strategic response. The trio of chapters, Chapter 1.5, 'Customer relationship management capabilities in a supply chain context', Chapter 1.6, 'The 'impact of pricing on supply chains', and Chapter 1.7, 'Trading terms and customer account profitability', provide important insights into the development and operation of supply chain strategy.

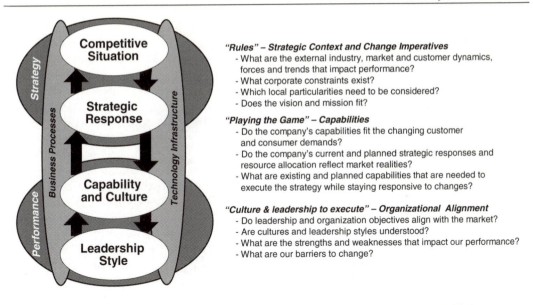

"Rules" – Strategic Context and Change Imperatives
- What are the external industry, market and customer dynamics, forces and trends that impact performance?
- What corporate constraints exist?
- Which local particularities need to be considered?
- Does the vision and mission fit?

"Playing the Game" – Capabilities
- Do the company's capabilities fit the changing customer and consumer demands?
- Do the company's current and planned strategic responses and resource allocation reflect market realities?
- What are existing and planned capabilities that are needed to execute the strategy while staying responsive to changes?

"Culture & leadership to execute" – Organizational Alignment
- Do leadership and organization objectives align with the market?
- Are cultures and leadership styles understood?
- What are the strengths and weaknesses that impact our performance?
- What are our barriers to change?

Source: In Introduction, *Strategic Supply Chain Alignment*, J. L. Gattorna (ed), Gower Publishing, Aldershot, 1998, pp. 1–7

Figure I.2
The Strategic Alignment Model

Part 2: Operational excellence

In Part 2, 12 chapters are devoted to operational excellence, which represents the first and most fundamental curve of the performance versus capability framework introduced earlier. It is in this section of the book that another subsidiary framework, depicted in Figure I.3, has an important role to play.

Operational excellence is the first and most fundamental curve of the performance versus capability framework.

The peak element of the subsidiary framework is comprehensively covered in Part 1; however, the other three layers are the subject of Part 2.

Chapter 2.1, 'Supply chain network optimization modeling', sets out how the static infrastructure of supply chains can be configured to deliver pre-agreed levels of service at minimum cost, that is, an optimal network configuration. Chapter 2.2, 'Supply chain diagnostics', describes tools that can be used as a precursor to more comprehensive network optimization work if so desired.

The operational layer of the supply chain framework contains several chapters. Chapter 2.3, 'Manufacturing strategy for supply chains', is part of manufacturing and distribution operations. Chapter 2.4, 'Six Sigma – improving the quality of business', is closely related to manufacturing and explores how rigorous quality concepts are

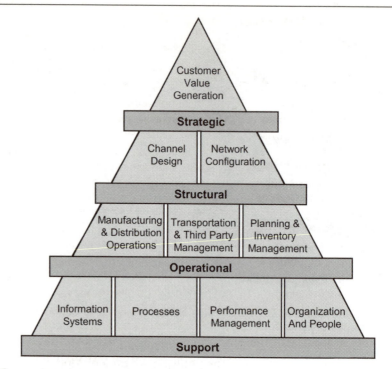

Source: Accenture

Figure I.3
Supply chain strategy framework

making a comeback in supply chain operations. Chapter 2.5, 'Distribution operations – design for excellence', complements the manufacturing chapters with a thorough examination of distribution and facilities design to meet customer needs.

Chapter 2.6, 'Integrated transportation management', is about linking and coordinating all transportation functions; and three chapters, Chapter 2.7, 'Forecasting and demand planning', Chapter 2.8, 'Inventory management', and Chapter 2.9, 'Service parts management', fit into the inventory management space. Chapter 2.12, 'Reverse logistics', is there to remind us that this vexed topic is far from solved in most if not all industries where forward distribution is such a big user of resources and energy. In a world of diminishing resources this is the next big area to come under intense scrutiny.

Chapter 2.10, 'Supply chain financial performance measurement', and Chapter 2.11, 'Supply chain performance measures and systems', both fit in the information management systems space, and provide an invaluable prescription for developing meaningful measures of performance across the entire supply chain.

Part 3: Supply chain integration and collaboration

In Part 3, we move to the second curve of the performance versus capability framework. In Chapter 3.1 'Creating agile supply chains', we emphasize again the connection between the make-up of the marketplace and corresponding behavioral segmentation. The reality is that multiple responses are required in the form of several supply chains with different operating characteristics. In the agile framework we propose that up to four different demand/supply supply chain configurations will possibly exist in any given situation, with some clearly more dominant than others. Figure I.4 depicts this operational reality.

Agility in the market, supply chain planning, sourcing, product development and technology are all part of achieving integration and collaboration.

There follows Chapter 3.2, 'Supply chain structures to deliver value', which provides a general overview of what good supply chains look like. Chapter 3.3 'Supply chain planning', which in many ways is the 'brain' of the supply chain provides an early hint of how quantum improvements in performance can be achieved through design and implementation of the new breed of decision support systems overlaying fundamentally re-designed processes. The two chapters dealing with the procurement of materials (both direct and indirect) – Chapter 3.4, 'Strategic sourcing and procurement', and Chapter 3.5, 'Securing immediate benefits from e-sourcing' – are also included in this part because the potential for large benefits is high

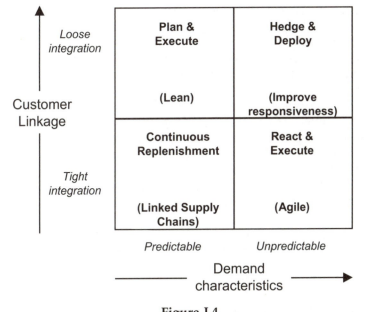

Figure I.4
Demand/supply characteristics that determine supply chain strategic responses

and close to realization. The notion of 'reverse alignment' is new and significant. Two chapters follow, dealing with the emergence of more collaborative behavior in supply chains: Chapter 3.6, 'Industry-level collaboration through ECR', and Chapter 3.7, 'Collaborative product commerce'. The next chapter, Chapter 3.8, 'Integrated fulfilment', is included because it describes the collaborative context for business-critical fulfilment processes. To round off Part 3, we have included a comprehensive treatment of the role of information technology in driving supply chains – Chapter 3.9, 'Information systems strategy for supply chains'.

Part 4: Virtual supply chains

Virtual supply chains offer the greatest potential for improvement through radical transformation of supply chain configurations.

Part 4 takes us to the ultimate level in the performance versus capability framework, where the potential for improvement through radical transformation of supply chain configurations is greatest. This section contains six chapters, the first two of which deal with the impact of e-commerce on supply chains - Chapter 4.1, 'e-commerce and supply chains – breaking down the boundaries', and Chapter 4.2, 'Best-of-breed supply chains'. The following three chapters focus on the emerging area of 'organization transformation' where we introduce the notion of supply chains being an ideal vehicle from which to launch large-scale change within the organization.

Chapter 4.3, 'Supply chains as vehicles for transformational change', aims to deal with the topic at the internal organic level. Chapter 4.4, 'Third- and Fourth-party logistics service providers', goes further and introduces the notion that some type of outsourcing arrangement might be the appropriate solution in cases where previous internal attempts at change have failed. The next chapter is devoted to the critical topic of capabilities in the supply chain, that is Chapter 4.5, 'Emerging requirements for networked supply chains'. Finally, Chapter 4.6, 'Strategic transformation and supply chains', goes yet another step along the continuum, suggesting relatively radical ways to achieve the much desired lift in operational and financial performance. This particular approach also provides new insights into how capability can be built rapidly and the capture of benefits across the supply chain accelerated.

Part 5: Regional and global supply chains

Regional and global supply chain strategies are becoming increasingly prevalent.

Four chapters make up Part 5. Chapter 5.1, 'Globalization and regionalization of supply chains', is an attempt to bring the reader up to speed on the progressive movement towards global and regional supply chain strategies by large multinational organizations. The following two chapters (5.2 and 5.3) refer specifically to the way supply chains are developing in Europe and Asia respectively. Chapter 5.4, The changing face of supply chains in China', focuses specifically on what is happening in mainland China with regard to the development of supply chains to power this rapidly growing economy.

Part 6: Other practical considerations in supply chains

In Part 6, the aim is to sweep up any outstanding issues that might impinge on performance. First and foremost is Chapter 6.1, 'Achieving supply chain alignment through behavior change'; in our view you cannot learn enough about this topic. Chapter 6.2, 'The role of knowledge management in supply chains', promotes the importance of using every avenue of knowledge collection in order to oil the wheels of supply chain operations. Future education requirements for supply chain personnel are put under the microscope in Chapter 6.3, 'Education and skills training requirements in supply chains'. Finally, in Chapter 6.4, 'Building successful consulting relationships', we attempt to answer the question most frequently asked by clients of consultants and trusted advisors: 'Explain where you can add value to our company'. My first reaction in such cases is to explain that 'Do-it-yourself brain surgery' is quite difficult, but usually I am able to convince clients that expert outsiders can bring the content and new perspectives that will deliver benefits at speed, and simultaneously lower risks to the organization.

Knowing how to achieve behavior change, build knowledge and skills, and manage consulting relationships are all part of today's supply chains.

Finale: The future is here at last

In the finale, I attempt to do the impossible by prescribing what supply chains will look like over the next decade. Of course, all this thought projection will be to no avail unless bold leadership of this vital part of industry and commerce occurs. As an optimist, I have to believe that supply chains, which account for over half the assets and operating expenses in most business and have a significant impact on top-line revenue, will finally get the attention of the 'numbers men' in corporations around the world. Huge advances in value creation will occur as a consequence. Let's hope! In the meantime, I trust that all who pick this book up and dip into it, will find it a source of inspiration, however small. If that happens, then our effort in compiling this selection of materials and points of view will have been very worthwhile.

Bold leadership is needed to create the supply chains of the future.

References

Gattorna, J. L. (ed.) (1998), *Strategic Supply Chain Alignment*, Aldershot: Gower Publishing.

Morrison, I., (1996), *The Second Curve – Managing the Velocity of Change*, New York: Ballantine Books.

Part 1

Supply Chains in the Context of Customers and Strategy

Operational performance and sound strategic direction need to be aligned in order to drive out cost and revenue benefits. A paradigm shift has emerged where companies can simultaneously increase services while reducing cost-to-serve, achieving the 'best of both worlds'. Companies that are slow to adopt improved supply chain integration have seen their competitive positions eroded with startling speed. Chapter 1.1, 'The challenging new operating environment and size of the prize', deals with these issues and sets the scene for the following chapters in Part 1. Adopting a concurrent approach by managing multiple initiatives in parallel is designed to unlock value, quickly. The approach is complex to manage, but the results are worth the effort. To achieve world-class performance and maximum shareholder value, supply chain management therefore needs to address costs, revenues and use of capital, simultaneously.

It is apparent that few organizations today have a true vision of the future that guides and directs their strategies every day. Chapter 1.2, 'Formulating a supply chain vision', contends that, for an ideal vision, individuals and organizations must analyse alternatives critically to arrive at the best decision. A vision template is introduced to help executive teams formulate a meaningful, yet practical, vision statement that takes into account customer needs, technology and geography.

Chapter 1.3, 'Developing an aligned supply chain operating strategy', introduces the Strategic Alignment Model, which can be used to align the supply chain with customer needs, thereby reducing over- or under-servicing. Appropriate segmentation allows the supply chain to better align services with buyer values and adjust cultures and leadership styles to improve the ability to deliver value to the customer.

1

Supply chain segmentation describes the nature of customer requirements in terms of how customers want to be serviced. This is an external, behavioral approach to segmenting customers. Chapter 1.4, 'Operating strategy: configuring segmented supply chains', defines how the supply chain will operate in practice. Channel relationships are as much about information and financial flows as they are about the physical facilitation of goods and services. Organizations need to assess the strategic potential and execution risks of new channel options versus that of proven channels, and weigh up short-term cost issues against the potential longer-term benefits of positioning for growth and seizing new opportunities. The design of logistics pathways provides the structure for managing differentiated service levels to different customer segments. Using segment-driven design principles will serve to reduce the complexity of what many organizations have found to be a costly and value-destroying exercise in 'over-customization'.

In Chapter 1.5, 'Customer relationship management capabilities in a supply chain context', the authors discuss how customer-driven enterprises, looking through the lens of the customer, take an outside-in perspective to ensure that their best customers receive consistently differentiated and, wherever possible, personalized service. The challenge of customer relationship management begins with gaining deep insight into customers, then draws on that insight to strengthen supply chain responses – that is, to create more appealing value propositions, products and service delivery mechanisms.

Most traditional supply chain theory focuses on reducing costs and increasing asset productivity. Chapter 1.6, 'The impact of pricing on supply chains', addresses another aspect of future strategy execution. It explains how combining price optimization with new supply chain management tools will drive profit growth.

Chapter 1.7, 'Trading terms and customer account profitability', considers how commercial terms of trade in supply chains can be used to differentiate offerings in a trading relationship. Trading terms can be evaluated based on a superior understanding of the cost-to-serve and the corresponding profit contribution of particular accounts.

The challenging new operating environment and size of the prize 1.1

John L. Gattorna

The new operating environment for supply chains can be likened to a maze; the task for management is to find a way through this maze with optimal allocation of resources. Managers have no easy path to follow, as the Supply Chain Maze picture below depicts.

Two particular forces are at work in the evolving operating environment for supply chains. On the one hand, new technology is enabling the more rapid adoption of true supply chain integration (SCI) within companies and collaboration across the supply chains of multiple companies. But on the other, this wider access to technology brings with it additional complications that make it part of the problem as well as part of the solution. By 'technology' we mean the convergence of

The real challenge is to improve the capabilities across supply chains significantly in order to drive out cost and realize revenue benefits – fast.

computing, communications and content technologies, all of which combine to enable the efficient exchange of supply and demand information. So despite the open access to new technology and the increased availability of information, which are the lifeblood of supply chains, relatively few companies on the global scene have improved their integration and collaboration capabilities. The real challenge is to improve the capabilities across supply chains significantly in order to drive out cost and realize revenue benefits – fast.

Indeed, the whole paradigm has changed dramatically, as depicted in Figure 1.1.1.

A paradigm shift has emerged where companies can simultaneously increase service while reducing cost-to-serve, thus achieving the 'best of both worlds'.

The traditional view was that increasing customer service levels was costly. However, we now know that if companies truly understand customer buying behaviors they can reallocate existing resources, rather than increase resources, as is so often assumed. They can then improve alignment with customers to the extent that a new paradigm is possible. We call this the 'best of both worlds', where service profile increases simultaneously with a reduction in cost-to-serve. Realization of this paradigm shift is the essential challenge for supply chain executives in the new millennium.

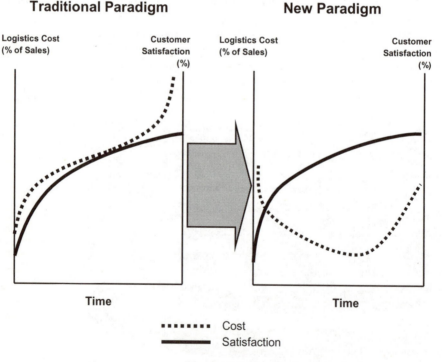

Figure 1.1.1
The cost/service paradigm shift

Table 1.1.1

Impact of the e-economy on supply chains

Supply chain domain	Traditional economy characteristics	e-Economy characteristics
Develop products and services	• Standard products • Mass market/uniform • Optimized stand-alone functionality	• Informated products • Individualized products and services • Optimized value-add overall network performance
Generate demand	• Mass communication • Supply push (extrapolated forecasting) • Vertical market structures • One segment – one channel (market, sell)	• 'One-to-one' relationship • Demand pull (real time demand management) • Hybrid markets • One segment – many channels (market, sell)
Fulfill demand	• One segment – one channel (fulfill, service) • Make to stock • Supply chain • Decreasing returns	• One segment – many channels (fulfill, service) • Make to order • Value network • Increasing returns
Plan and manage the enterprise	• Physical enterprise • Industry-based strategy formulation • Command and control	• Virtual enterprise • Dynamic strategy formulation • Alliance building

The so-called e-economy is projected to be twice the size of the industrial economy in the US, as a percentage of gross domestic product (GDP), by 2006, according to Marvin Zonis & Associates. The world is certainly changing, because the distinctive characteristics of the new e-economy will have a significant impact on supply chains, as summarized in Table 1.1.1.

Winners and losers

Companies that can quickly adapt to the new operating conditions and evolve to stay aligned with emerging conditions will dominate the marketplace, as they will achieve both operational efficiency and revenue enhancement. Operational efficiency will mean reduced costs, shorter process cycles and better communications. Revenue enhancement will mean improved customer service, increased responsiveness and differentiation. The quantum of benefits achieved will increase with the degree of integration and collaboration as depicted schematically in Figure 1.1.2.

Slow adopters of improved supply chain integration have seen their competitive positions eroded with startling speed.

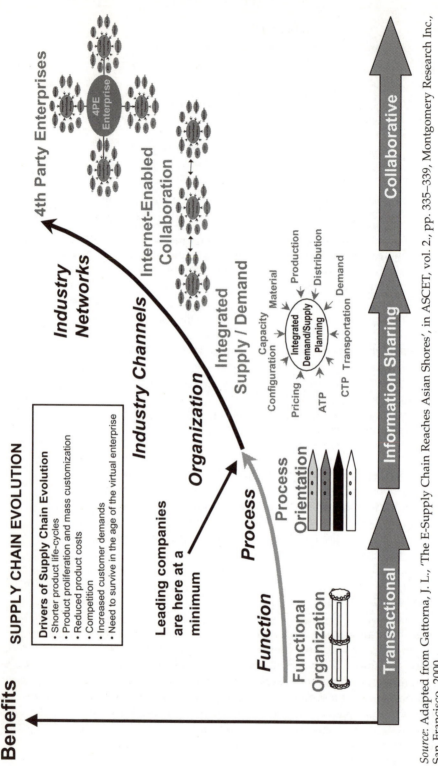

Figure 1.1.2
Supply chain evolution

Source: Adapted from Gattorna, J. L., 'The E-Supply Chain Reaches Asian Shores', in ASCET, vol. 2, pp. 335–339, Montgomery Research Inc., San Francisco, 2000

Table 1.1.2
Winners and losers in the PC market (market share)

Year 1995		Year 1998		
1.	Packard Bell NEC	1.	Compaq/Digital	← Succeeding at SCI
2.	Compaq	2.	Dell	← Direct masters
3.	Hewlett-Packard	3.	IBM	
4.	Apple	4.	Hewlett-Packard	← Adopting SCI fast
5.	Gateway 200	5.	Gateway	← Direct, like Dell

Source: Accenture

Unfortunately, despite the business benefits at stake, relatively few companies have achieved the desired level of supply chain integration. There are several reasons why. Most have focused on business survival rather than business improvement and sought cost reduction through process improvement alone. They have mistakenly pursued enterprise resource planning (ERP) solutions as the 'silver bullet', become bogged down in Y2K issues and, generally, focused on the short term.

Undoubtedly, the slow adopters of improved supply chain integration have seen their competitive positions eroded with startling speed, such is the nature of the new operating environment. This is well illustrated by the marked changes that have taken place in leadership of the personal computer market in the United States in recent times, as illustrated in Table 1.1.2.

ERP as a solution 'for all times'

Many companies have had a very one-dimensional response to their increasingly unforgiving operating environment. They have focused on cost reduction and improving internal efficiencies, using ERP as the ultimate 'solution'. As Beth Enslow (1999) of the Gartner Group describes, 'an ERP application delivers the disciplined data processes, global control, and management oversight that many enterprises need to manage their myriad business processes. By bringing financial, distribution, and other business functions into balance, enterprises contain their operations and save money by being more efficient'. Depending on the degree of process re-engineering undertaken, cross-industry experience shows a consistent picture of effort-driven benefits, as outlined in Table 1.1.3. Unfortunately, too many companies have erred on the conservative side and not enjoyed the returns available through a more fundamental review of business strategy and corresponding processes to stay aligned with the evolving operating environment. In this respect, many companies have actually gone backwards, as evidenced by their financial results.

Companies that have gone beyond simply 'replacing' their legacy systems and transformed their processes have accrued far greater business benefits.

Table 1.1.3
Typical benefits by nature of business change

	'Systems replacement'	'Re-engineered'	'Transformed'
Benefit category	No fundamental business changes	Key processes re-engineered	Processes and organization aligned with strategy
Revenue uplift	0	1–3%	5–10%
COGS reduction	0–1%	1–2%	3–8%
Overhead reduction	0–1%	1–2%	3–5%
Inventory reduction	(30)–5%	5–20%	25–50%

Source: Accenture

However, ERP solutions are inherently limited in their decision support capability, and this is something that many companies seemed not to understand as they set out on a sometimes expensive path to 'replace' existing legacy systems. The results shown in Table 1.1.3 amply demonstrate the significant difference in potential benefits between simply 'replacing' systems compared to an approach that seeks to fundamentally transform the way business is done.

ERP systems should be regarded as a foundation and overlaid by new processes and corresponding layers of systems capabilities.

Clearly, the way forward is to think of ERP systems as the foundation, overlaid by new processes and corresponding layers of systems capabilities, all of which combine to provide the degree of supply chain integration necessary to cope with the new operating environment. Figure 1.1.3 depicts how this would look.

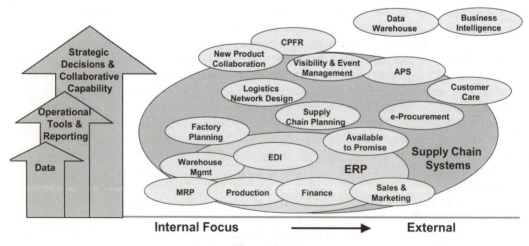

Figure 1.1.3
A layered view of systems

Concurrent approach

As the operating environment has become more complex, many companies have taken the view that the way to cope is to simplify things by dividing up the problem. In practice this means attacking the problem in a piecemeal and linear way. The paradox is that this 'experiential' approach is the worst possible way to handle increasing complexity because of the inherent interdependencies in modern business. The best way forward in these circumstances is to adopt a concurrent approach which, although seemingly more difficult to manage, will produce significantly better results. This is another example of Ashby's (1956) 'Law of Requisite Variety' at work, where variety is a measure of complexity of the system. To adapt to an external environment, organizations must incorporate complexity. The key to this approach is aggressive management of multiple initiatives in parallel in order to extract value from the business, quickly. We call this 'speed to value'.

Adopting a concurrent approach by managing multiple initiatives in parallel can unlock value quickly. The approach is complex to manage, but the results are worth the effort and the risk.

The advantages of this approach are that time to value is significantly decreased, planning and implementation are combined, the momentum for change is increased and knowledge transfer and learning are encouraged. On the other hand, the parallel approach is complex to manage and requires increased sophistication and competent resources in order to succeed. A relatively large investment of resources is required upfront, but the results are well worth the effort.

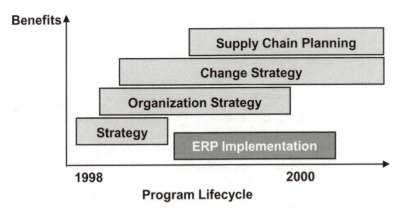

Figure 1.1.4
Speed to value – a parallel approach

Shareholder value – the final prize

To achieve world-class performance and maximum shareholder value, supply chain management needs to address costs, revenues and use of capital.

Supply chain management is at the heart of the changing business environment and instrumental in gaining shareholder value, as indicated in Figure 1.1.5. In order to achieve this gain, organizations must simultaneously address costs, revenues and use of capital. Too often, executives use the supply chain to address costs only.

However, companies will need to work on all three aspects of the supply chain: operational excellence, supply chain integration and virtual supply chains, the three component curves of the model outlined in the Introduction. Simultaneously working in these three areas will extract maximum shareholder value and gain the attention and support of senior 'C'-level management. In doing so, world-class performance will be achieved and the operating environment finally tamed.

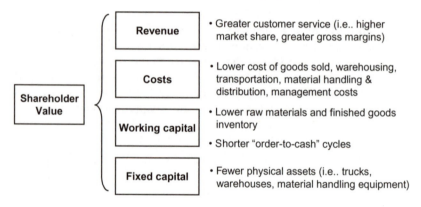

Figure 1.1.5
Delivering shareholder value

References

Ashby, W. R. (1956), *An Introduction to Cybernetics*, London: Chapman & Hall.

Enslow, B. (1999), *The Myth of ERP Inventory Management for Field Service*, Gartner Group, Stamford CT.

Gattorna, J. L. (1977), *The Effects of innovation on Channels of Distribution*, unpublished doctoral thesis, Cranfield School of Management, Cranfield University, Cranfield, UK.

Gattorna, J. L., (2000) 'The E-Supply Chain reaches Asian Shores', in ASCET, vol. 2., pp. 335–339, Montgomery Research Inc., San Francisco, 2000.

Formulating a supply chain vision

1.2

John L. Gattorna and Ming Tang

As Kurt Lewin, one of the founders of organizational theory, once commented: 'There is nothing more practical than a good theory.' For business leaders seeking to optimize their operational performance, a similar principle holds true: every organization needs an unambiguous concept of its business and a clear view of how it wishes to position itself in the marketplace. We call that 'vision'.

Few organizations have a true vision of the future that guides and directs their activities every day.

Indeed, many organizations purport to have a 'vision statement', variously called a charter, mission, credo, principle or philosophy statement. However, relatively few have a true vision of the future state the organization wants to attain – a future that guides and directs the organization every day. Like a golfer hitting a good putt as described by Floyd (1989), companies need to visualize their future first, before executing their strategies.

Vision is also something that leaders need to share with the rest of the organization and use to galvanize the energy of people around specific courses of action to drive the organization towards its goals. Put simply, the vision is the picture on the front of the jigsaw puzzle box and the pieces inside are the day-to-day units of work performed across the organization. Both are critical to realizing the full picture.

Ideally, vision is something that comes from the top of an organization, filtering down through the various levels of business units and across functional areas. In turn, each of these organizational units defines its own vision or purpose within the boundaries of the broader corporate vision, so that all statements are mutually reinforcing.

However, there is a problem. Developing a meaningful vision is paradoxical in that, while it appears to be a simple task, it is in fact exceedingly difficult to do well. Why is this so? Mainly, the difficulties arise because people see the world differently, as depicted in the sketch below.

11

"But why have an inside?
We'll never use it"

Reproduced with permission

Our aim in this chapter is to explore the intricacies involved in formulating a vision statement, and then to apply the process for formulating a corporate vision to developing a specific vision for the supply chain. We have provided examples to illustrate how organizations have defined their supply chain vision.

'Vision' defined

For an ideal vision, individuals critically analyse alternatives to arrive at the best decision. They do not engage in 'group think'.

The vision statement is a qualitative, albeit philosophical, statement that embodies a long-term view of what the organization is, or is striving to become. In effect, it is a 'what do we want to stand for?' statement, and in that sense may be thought of as a boundary or positioning statement.

The way the vision is 'pitched' is important. For example, if there are too many differing views on what the vision should be, a fragmented perspective of the organization's future is created, as depicted in the 'Vision 1' picture.

If, on the other hand, those involved in setting the vision are overly rigid in what they see of the future, then 'group think' can occur, where the group's main concern is to force consensus. Janis's (1972) analysis of President Kennedy's decision to invade Cuba at the Bay of Pigs showed the danger of such thinking. Members of the Cabinet did not want to challenge the reasoning of such a strong leader, and instead preferred to show support during the crisis. See the 'Vision 2' picture.

For an ideal vision, individuals critically analyse alternatives to make the best decision, and in the process are prepared to challenge each other. They do not engage in 'group think'. Ultimately, they reach a common area of agreement.

Reproduced with permission

'Vision 1'   **'Vision 2'**

The ideal vision statement should be creative, yet it should also be realistic, so that it is broadly within reach. The vision should encompass the aims and aspirations of the organization in terms general enough to allow adaptation to changing circumstances, but specific enough to have an impact on the behavior of everyone in the organization. In other words, the vision must 'ring true' to people at every level in the organization, so that they can interpret the vision down to the level of their respective roles and jobs.

Unfortunately, most vision statements are of the 'motherhood' variety, destined for the inside covers of annual reports and designed to stroke shareholders; but otherwise of no practical use. We are advocating the creation of a meaningful statement, unique to the organization or unit concerned, and made up of words that really do influence the behavior of executives at all levels.

Constructing a vision statement

The task of formulating a vision statement is quite daunting. Certainly, it is achieved rarely by taking executives away on a weekend retreat to debate the future of the organization. Our experience over years of empirical work with top management teams is that a template is required when embarking on this undertaking. This, combined with a facilitated real-time environment, is the only way to achieve a meaningful, yet practical, vision statement. We have developed a vision template through working with hundreds of management teams over a decade; it has four components as indicated below, all of which are essential.

A vision template is a useful tool to help executive teams develop a meaningful, yet practical, vision statement.

1. Contextual

The first component of our vision template is the context within which the particular organizational unit is operating. Leaders need to consider the role or unique contribution that the unit makes to the larger organization. The idea is to test whether or not the business unit has an ongoing role within the parent organization. In many cases, organizations struggle to pass this first hurdle and consequently doubt is cast on long-term viability from the outset. Typically, the internal contributions of supply chains will be in terms of cash generation; working capital reduction; ownership of the pipeline through which products move to market; and custodianship of the inventory.

2. Business definition

Customer needs, technology, and geography define the boundary of a business.

In the second component, the organization needs to describe clearly what the business of the organization is now and is likely to be in the future. Too many vision statements fail at this point because they describe the business in terms of what the organization does from day-to-day – and that may change.

However, there is only one way to describe the business or boundary of the organization, and that is in terms of the needs the organization has set out to satisfy, for both internal stakeholders and external customers. If organizations follow this method, their definition of the business will remain constant over time. Contrary to popular opinion, the fundamental needs of customers do not change over time; only the way organizations go about satisfying those needs. That usually has something to do with the ever-changing technology landscape. However, technology and geography, combined with customers' needs, also may be used as part of the 'boundary' definition.

So, the vision statement can be thought of as a 'boundary' or 'positioning' statement, as depicted in Figure 1.2.1.

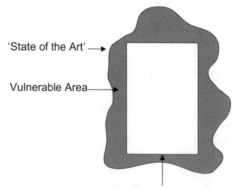

Figure 1.2.1
A vision statement and its boundary

The empty space between the organization's own 'boundary' and that of 'state of the art' practice represents an area of potential vulnerability where a competitor may go to gain a competitive edge. In today's turbulent operating environment, the 'state of the art' boundary is moving away from organizations at an accelerating rate. The area of vulnerability is therefore growing progressively and will continue to do so unless organizations develop plans to follow, or at least stay close to, this expanding boundary.

The vision an organization adopts will vary in color and personality, depending upon the behavioral characteristics of the market segments it services and the impact this has on the internal sub-cultures. Four possible variations of vision, depicted in Figure 1.2.2, are: 'Taking stock', 'Reaching out', 'Exploiting internal resources' and 'Exploiting the market'.

This view is consistent with the strategic alignment concept that we use to anchor all our supply chain work. It is also consistent with our view that organizations have supply chains plural, rather than one supply chain as envisaged by previous writers on the topic. To understand this better, think in terms of several conveyor belts running inside an organization, all at different speeds and with different operating characteristics. The same product can travel down any conveyor or pathway.

3. Distinctive competence

Distinctive competence is the third component of our vision statement template and is perhaps the most difficult to understand and operationalize. Internal to the organization, distinctive competence attempts to identify the essential skills, capabilities and resources that underpin current and future success. It involves identifying those

Distinctive competence is what an organization does best: it is not easy to copy or emulate.

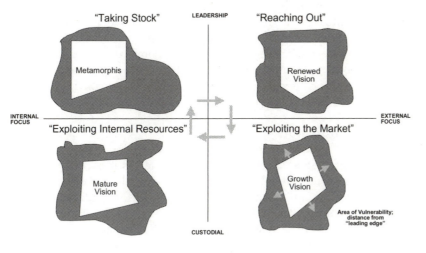

Figure 1.2.2
The four different flavours of vision

things that the organization does particularly well compared to competitors in the same business domain. Generally, a true distinctive competence is not easy to copy or emulate in the short to medium term.

Clearly, you must look for potential distinctive competencies among an organization's strengths. In our experience, most organizations lack this 'silver thread' or 'essence' running through the business, and this is one of the reasons why they are seemingly always struggling to achieve differential advantage in the marketplace; distinctive competencies underpin differential advantages. If the conclusion is that no such unique competence exists, then try to define what competence you want to build and start the long process of growing it organically within the business. If, in the rare case, a genuine distinctive competence is uncovered, nurture and develop it further. Unfortunately, there have been many cases over the last few decades where distinctive competencies have been ignored and lost through neglect, very often as an outcome of mergers and acquisitions. In such situations, the business cases on which the mergers or acquisitions were approved are unlikely to be ever realized.

A defensible distinctive competence, according to Quinn, et al. (1990) in the *Harvard Business Review*, usually derives from outstanding depth in human skills, logistics capabilities, knowledge bases, brand loyalty and other intangibles that competitors cannot easily replicate, and which lead to demonstrable value for the customer. In any event, distinctive competencies can either be grown organically over time or bought as part of an acquisition, albeit with due care in the latter case. The most difficult distinctive competencies to compete against are those that are qualitative rather than quantitative, for example a company's culture or tacit knowledge. In both examples, the competence is deeply embedded in the organization and almost impossible to unbundle and extract.

Finally, unlike physical assets, Prahalad and Hamel (1990) observed that a distinctive competence can be used simultaneously in several applications; does not wear out; and can be combined in various ways to create new opportunities. Indeed, a distinctive competence can be used to screen or filter any new opportunities being considered and, in this way, it helps the organization to maintain focus.

4. Future indicators

Future indicators give the vision statement a dynamic character because they involve major strategies, which may change over time.

This final component in the vision statement template is designed to give the overall statement a dynamic character as it is the only component of the four that is likely to change materially from year to year. Future indicators are designed to provide a sense of future direction and the initiatives likely to be pursued in the medium term. In effect, future indicators are a catalog of the organization's major strategies and are important enough to be included in the vision statement. Over time, the organization will modify these directional statements gradually as it weaves a path through its operating environment.

This, then, completes the template. As indicated, the 'personality' of the organization is best captured in the flavor of its vision statement, and the flavor should ideally reflect the dominant logic of the operating environment. At least four flavors of vision statement are possible, and the one chosen will be embedded eventually in the predominant culture of the organization. The four flavors are shown in detail in Figure 1.2.3 (refer also to Figure 1.2.2).

Acid test of an effective vision

An effective vision has several important defining characteristics. It must be evolutionary rather than static. The value system it represents must be both implicit and explicit. It is never perfectly achievable – there is always some stretch and tension between what is and what can be. Above all, it is an energizing force, clear and consistent, passionate, and inspirational. However, two acid tests can be applied that will leave no doubt as to whether or not the vision will be a genuine moving force in the life of the organization.

An effective vision will be energizing, evolutionary, passionate, and consistent.

Internal acid test
Organizations should not be able to remove their company or business unit name from the top of the statement, replace it with a competitor's name and have it still make sense! Their particular statement should be unique to their organization, just as personalities are varied and individual. To test if the vision is working, individual executives in the organization should be able to compare their day-to-day activities with the vision and assess whether or not they are working inside the boundary. If they are within the boundary, they are contributing to the attainment of the organization's objectives. If they are clearly outside the boundary they are probably wasting resources.

External acid test
An organization should be able to go into its usual marketplace, mention the category of goods or services involved, and the customer should have instant recall as to the best supplier in that market. Ideally, the customer will choose the organization's name. If so, the company has succeeded in the best possible way to operationalize its vision.

Communicating the vision

The vision statement, once developed, is a 'call to arms' for the rest of the organization, and as such should be communicated widely. Each senior manager involved in the formulation of the vision should conduct at least a half-day briefing session with his or her direct reports. In preparation for this vital session, each key word or phrase

The vision must be communicated widely and consistently, so that everyone will act and react as planned.

Leadership

"Taking Stock"		"Reaching Out"	
Contextual	• Revitalization – prepare for next growth phase • Providing a springboard for change in strategy	**Contextual**	• Creating new market/Technology edges • "Pathfinder" contribution
Business Definition	• Exploring partnerships internally (teamwork) and externally (channel relationships) • Beginning the search for next vision /boundaries of business	**Business Definition**	• Redefining needs • Push business boundaries out • New technologies • Close the gap between current vision and the ideal (vulnerability)
Distinctive Competence	• People, relationships, loyalty, commitment • Service mentality	**Distinctive Competence**	• Technology • Creative design – new product development
Future Indicators	• Close gap between current position and ideal distinctive competence	**Future Indicators**	• Close gap between current position and ideal distinctive competence

Internal Focus _____ **External Focus**

"Exploiting Internal Resources"		"Exploiting the Market"	
Contextual	• Profit maximization • Optimizers • Cash cows	**Contextual**	• Provide growth momentum for the larger organization • Resources focused here • Tomorrow's "cash cow"
Business Definition	• Optimization of resources • Aggressive utilization of internal efficiency • Exploring processes and methods to improve efficiencies • Value for money	**Business Definition**	• Exploit known market opportunities • Aggressive outward vision • Penetrating markets by refining segments/niches (squeeze the lemon)
Distinctive Competence	• Process efficiencies • Logistics, optimization of resources (physical & info) • Low cost producer	**Distinctive Competence**	• Marketing skills and knowledge of market / consumer logic • Financial resources
Future Indicators	• Close gap between current position and ideal distinctive competence	**Future Indicators**	• Close gap between current position and ideal distinctive competence

Custodial

Figure 1.2.3
Content of the four vision types

of the vision should be extracted and given an agreed meaning for use in this and similar sessions that cascade down through the organization.

In this way, the managers put a consistent interpretation on the statement so that everyone will act and react as intended. At the end of this education process, it is possible to shorten the statement for practical purposes to a paragraph, and ultimately to a one-line slogan. However, the hard work must be done to embed the required level of understanding of the vision down through the organization *before* a slogan is engaged. Unfortunately, many organizations try to short cut the process and end up with a fancy but empty slogan.

Examples of supply chain vision statements

The supply chain groups of several large organizations in Asia Pacific have developed vision statements for their supply chains. The statements illustrate the depth of thinking involved in formulating a vision. While they might look relatively long at first, remember that once the hard graft of formulating a statement is done and the vision has been internalized by those involved, the statement can be shortened. Through this process, people will think of the full weight and content of the longer statement when they see the slogan. The names of the companies involved in the examples below have been changed

Supply chain vision statements illustrate the depth of thinking involved in formulating a vision.

Alpha Department Stores' supply chain vision

The supply chain function within Alpha Department Stores is the custodian of the pipeline that links customers with suppliers. The Supply Chain function is charged with the professional management of those considerable resources that participate in the complex task of moving merchandise through the pipeline, that is facilities, systems, personnel and capital. The actual merchandise in the pipeline remains the 'property' of the merchandise function, but we are the *facilitators*. In effect, Supply Chain is an internal contractor, which has the potential to influence significantly the Department Stores Group's overall profit by optimizing the service–cost equation.

The Supply Chain function has several 'stakeholders', and in meeting their respective needs we effectively define our business. For example:

Suppliers: look to Supply Chain to fulfill elements of the strategic partnership arrangements entered into with the Merchandise function for the purpose of achieving mutual profitability.

Merchandise function: is an internal client that requires Supply Chain to shorten the strategic lead times that inventory is in the pipeline to stores. Management of this lead time has tremendous leverage on the group's overall profitability. We collaborate with merchandise personnel at the interface with suppliers, and manage the Merchandise on their behalf from that point on.

Stores function: is another internal client which requires Supply Chain to deliver merchandise to every store according to previously agreed service levels, and in some cases to arrange final delivery to, and installation in, customers' premises. We also liaise with stores on a range of matters that affect the management of merchandise, such as packaging, price marking, allocations, storage, facilities design and handling practices at the back door.

We liaise with *Marketing* in regard to promotional campaigns, packaging and other special conditions that influence the flow of merchandise. Finally, it is our ultimate aim to contribute to customer satisfaction by collaborating with all internal functions, as well as suppliers. Our scope of operations is Asia Pacific.

Supply Chain owns the methodologies and procedures that facilitate the cost-effective flow of merchandise from suppliers to stores and on to customers. These methodologies include leading-edge physical and information systems, supported by a customer orientation among all our personnel. Because we are responsible for the operation of such a comprehensive network of facilities, we can make things happen.

For the future, the Supply Chain function intends to develop and implement a blueprint for quantum change that will take Alpha to the forefront of supply chain practice in department stores, worldwide.

To achieve this we must institute and manage major changes in the way we currently do things. Our task is to ensure that no competitor outperforms Alpha in a supply chain sense; that stock in the 'pipeline' is managed expeditiously, and that the entire supply chain (including the supplier component) comes under our influence – all of which adds up to a competitive advantage for Alpha at the point of sale.

We are determined to realize most, if not all, of the potential savings available through improved supply chain practices. For this reason, measurement systems and corresponding standards will be established along the supply chain. Technology will be applied as appropriate in the form of hardware and software. In regard to the latter, optimization models and other decision support systems will be a priority, as will electronic links with suppliers. We are mindful that Supply Chain manages major elements of the Group's assets and as such we will seek to ensure acceptable rates of return on these investments. As an additional incentive, we propose to operate the function as a profit center, servicing our various stakeholders to pre-arranged service levels for a predetermined cost-to-serve.

Apex World Wide Express Logistics' (AWWEL) vision

AWWEL exists to enhance and complement Apex Airways' current business, and to tap new emerging opportunities in the international express distribution market. Apex Airways is committed to expanding its service offering to selected customers and AWWEL has an important role in this expansion program. In the process, AWWEL will increase Apex Airways' sophistication – which will have a positive spin-off on the core business, increase competitiveness, build customer loyalty and contribute to corporation profits. However, it is important that Apex customer management remains fully cognizant of the impact that the logistics operation may have on existing network facilities and other key resources servicing the core business.

Our business is to facilitate the cost-effective, time definite movement of product through customers' supply chains, worldwide. In this, we effectively reduce the risk and complexity for our customers, thus allowing them to focus on their respective business(es). For our part, it is essential that we gain an in-depth understanding of customers' business and adopt a consultative selling approach, supported by advanced decision support technology, when formulating appropriate response(s). Such an approach will be able to change the 'rules' in the marketplace and dilute the current preoccupation with transport rates.

We have a truly global company at our disposal, providing an international network of express shipping, pick-up and delivery capabilities, interconnected with a reservoir of local knowledge about individual country-markets worldwide. We also have an adaptive culture, capable of flexible responses to customers' needs and a desire to access further competencies relevant to our business (for example, relationship management of other suppliers of specialist services in the supply chain).

For the future, it is important that we position WWEL in that part of the overall third party logistics services spectrum which best protects and leverages our evolving core competencies. This will involve careful market segmentation and, ultimately, selection of customers with genuine international requirements – which we feel we can meet within specified resource limitations – and whose products have handling and market characteristics, which align with our capabilities. Development of our logistics services portfolio will be evolutionary, consistent with our experience curve. It is important that we avoid the 'over customization trap', and instead develop a portfolio of standard service products which are capable of being combined in unique ways to satisfy the individual needs of our customers.

In that it is likely that we will necessarily have to enter into and play the lead role in developing strategic relationships with key suppliers, we should continue to develop our sourcing and relationship management skills.

Getting to the vision

It is important to round off our thinking on corporate vision in general, and supply chain vision in particular, by addressing ways of operationalizing the words The work that needs to be done is illustrated in Figures 1.2.4 and Table 1.2.1. Figure 1.2.4 provides a spatial perspective of the journey and outlines the four guiding principles involved in getting to the vision: business-led, segmented, cost-aware and integrated operational strategies.

Table 1.2.1 explains at a high level the specific actions that must be executed in order to move from 'today' to 'tomorrow's vision' under the four guiding principles. Decisions, for instance, need to shift from being based in functional silos to being based on their total impact on the supply chain. Senior managers should move their focus from 'one-size-fits-all' processes to, instead, tailoring processes and policies to customer segments. Organizations should end the lack of accessibility to costs and achieve a common understanding of total costs. Interactions too need to move from being primarily transactional to integrated processes based on shared information.

In addition to the actions in Table 1.2.1, a whole raft of change management initiatives are needed to modify the existing sub-cultures in the business so that people faithfully deliver the vision and its constituent strategies. Chapter 4.3 discusses this subject in detail.

Once the leadership team understands the vision, it is important to encompass the vision in a slogan or phrase. This encapsulation is vital

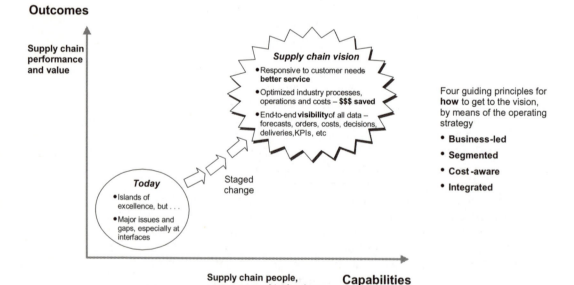

Figure 1.2.4
Moving from today's supply chain to tomorrow's

Table 1.2.1
The impact of supply chain vision

	Supply chain vision		Impacts
	From	To	What it means
Business-led	• Decisions made in functional silos based on local goals • Information hard to get	• Decisions based on total supply chain impact • Data transparency – one version of the truth	• Current rules are changed in terms of when, how and who makes decisions • Decisions to be based on agreed service levels, total supply chain costs and profitability
Segmented	• Management by 'one-size-fits-all' processes • Services and costs not always what customers want	• Processes and policies tailored to segments • Customer offers maximize profitability and growth	• Processes and policies for planning, delivery and inventories aligned to meet the needs of each segment and manage product flow • Responsive organization to match customer and segment needs
Cost-aware	• End-to-end costs not readily accessible • Difficult for local initiatives to improve overall supply chain	• Common understanding of costs • Coordinated approach to supply chain optimization	• Cost and delivery information made visible • Minimize total supply chain cost rather than just local costs
Integrated	• Interactions are primarily transactional • Conflicting objectives at interfaces	• Integrated processes based on shared information • Consistent, agreed performance measures and accountabilities	• Management of end-to-end processes rather than functions • Agreed governance structure to guide decisions • Performance measures used to drive improvements

to enable communication of the vision in a way that drives action, enthusiasm and ownership. The simplification of the message is best done with a small senior team who can distill the meaning into a communicable phrase and then develop it further into a slogan.

The importance of a slogan to focus people's efforts around a common vision should not be underestimated. The right slogan can have a big impact, internally and externally. The slogan for Avis Car Rental is a good example of a simple, effective phrase. 'Avis – We Try Harder' communicates the customer focus of the organization and helps to channel internal activities to consider the customer impact.

Conclusion

Jack Welch succeeded in aligning the action of GE's business units with a single, powerful vision.

Developing a unique vision for the enterprise is exceedingly difficult, but it must be done and done well. An insight into how difficult even the best leaders find this task can be gleaned from Jack Welch, the former CEO of General Electric. In his book *Jack* (2001), Welch talks about the need for a vision with a powerful message. He emphasizes the message needs to be characterized by simplicity and clarity as these qualities bring the words to life and influence everyone's behavior across the organization. Jack's vision for GE to become 'No. 1 or No. 2 in every business we are in' met these criteria, but he still struggled for some time to communicate the vision across GE's 42 strategic business units. The results are on record for all to see. Welch turned GE into the most valuable company in the world, and he achieved this by ensuring that every management action across GE during his reign was 'aligned' with a single, powerful vision.

References

Floyd, R. (1989), *From 60 yards in – How to master Golf's short game*, New York: Harper and Row.

Janis, I. (1972), *Victims of groupthink*: psychological study of foreign policy decisions and fiascoes (2nd ed.), Houghton Mifflin, Boston.

Prahalad, C. K. and Hamel, G. (1990), 'The Core Competence of the Corporation', *Harvard Business Review*, (May/June), pp. 79–91.

Quinn, J. B. et al. (1990), 'Beyond Products: Service-based strategy', *Harvard Business Review*, (March).

Welch, J. (2001), 'The Vision Thing', *Jack: what I've learned leading a great company and great people*, Headline Books Publishing, London, pp. 105–120.

Developing an aligned supply chain operating strategy

1.3

Ming Tang and John L. Gattorna

Organizations today need to be able to design and implement flexible and responsive supply chains to maximize their value in dynamic markets. However, many business leaders face a quandary in how to do this, given that so many supply chain strategies are available. Effective supply chain strategies must be aligned with corporate or business unit objectives. The advantage of aligning supply chain strategy to business strategy is that it can increase revenue, reduce costs and improve competitive advantage. The opposite is true for a misaligned operating strategy; it usually results in value destruction through the pursuit of misdirected initiatives.

The role of the supply chain operating strategy in the delivery of business goals is shown in Figure 1.3.1. The operating strategy is driven by business strategy and is focused on delivering against a vision for the supply chain. At the outset, business strategy is developed in response to market conditions, with the objective of maximizing business goals. The business strategy will at the highest level determine how the organization competes in the marketplace. This may imply one or several of a multitude of possible strategic positions, ranging from a high-service value proposition to targeting niche markets to the mass market distribution of a mature lifecycle product. The supply chain strategy starts with the business value proposition to customers, and shows how the supply chain can contribute to achieving business goals.

This chapter describes the initial formulation steps in developing a leading-edge supply chain strategy. We look at the key components of an aligned strategy, the issues that need to be resolved, and the frameworks used to understand customer segments and define the strategic response. The goal is to achieve alignment between business strategy and a supply chain operating strategy to ensure that business objectives are met and value creation is sustained. An aligned supply

An aligned supply chain strategy can increase revenue, cut costs and boost competitive advantage.

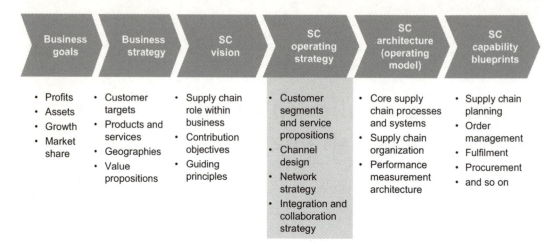

Figure 1.3.1
The pivotal role of supply chain operating strategy

chain operating strategy defines the appropriate supply chain capabilities required to meet customer needs consistently in the most cost-effective manner. Ultimately, it will determine the organization's success in achieving its business goals of profitability and sustained growth.

Components of an aligned operating strategy

Components of a strategy are interdependent. The market should be used to indicate anchorage points for alignment.

A supply chain strategy that is aligned with business strategy has four major components:

- achieving alignment with business objectives, using vision and guiding principles
- achieving alignment with the market, through effective segmentation of customers
- defining the strategic response through appropriate customer service propositions, supported by a cost-to-serve analysis, and
- designing the strategic response in terms of how the supply chain will operate. This topic is covered in more detail in Chapter 1.4, 'Operating strategy: configuring segmented supply chains'.

As these components are interdependent, organizations need to develop each by keeping clear alignment principles in mind. They can do this by using the market to indicate the 'anchorage' points for alignment.

Achieving alignment with business objectives

Organizations can seek to achieve alignment with business objectives by first using their overall business vision to formulate a supply chain vision and then developing guiding principles to drive the operating strategy.

Chapter 1.2 looked at how to formulate a supply chain vision and transform the vision into reality via manageable steps and measurable outcomes. The importance of having a vision with clearly defined outcomes should not be underestimated as it is key to an effective operating strategy. In many ways, the operating strategy provides the pathway, that is, it describes the planned approach to achieving a given vision. A critical step is to develop a set of guiding principles from the vision. The guiding principles should encompass the desired outcomes from the business vision and are used as the reference point to direct the formulation of specific strategic responses.

An operating strategy for the supply chain should define the organization's response to market conditions. The strategy should identify differentiated service propositions for various customer groups in terms of channel options and priorities. It should provide the framework for formulating roles, responsibilities and collaboration requirements with channel partners, and develop the cost-optimized physical supply chain configuration required to facilitate the delivery of the customer value proposition. In doing so, organizations will have developed a framework that guides day-to-day decision making, relationship management of suppliers and customers, focused operating model development, and the direction for short- and long-term capability building.

Research across a variety of industries suggests that despite significant investment in supply chain change programs, there is generally little alignment between the business strategy, the marketplace and supply chain initiatives. Consequently, organizations are pursuing an unaligned set of initiatives that deliver a fragment of the value that would be possible otherwise. Most organizations are unable to articulate an explicit supply chain strategy, meaning that it either does not exist or is confused with broader business strategies. Little evidence exists to suggest that many organizations have consciously aligned supply chain strategies that help them to focus and drive their change programs.

A major barrier appears to be a lack of recognition among senior managers of the need to formalize supply chain objectives. In the face of short-term shareholder pressures, executives often wish to move directly to capability building. This desire is exacerbated by a deficiency in management skills and experience in leading the development of strategy. The result can be organizational paralysis at the perceived immensity and cost of the task to formulate an operating strategy in the face of current operating complexity and new technologies.

Differentiated service propositions should be identified for various customer groups.

The Strategic Alignment Model can be used to align the supply chain with customer needs.

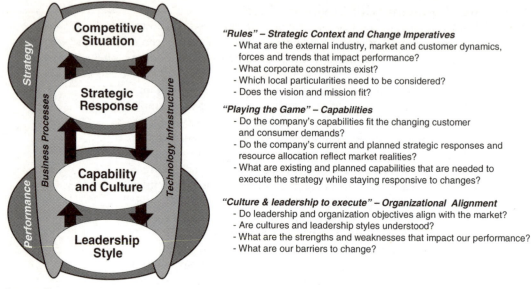

"Rules" – Strategic Context and Change Imperatives
- What are the external industry, market and customer dynamics, forces and trends that impact performance?
- What corporate constraints exist?
- Which local particularities need to be considered?
- Does the vision and mission fit?

"Playing the Game" – Capabilities
- Do the company's capabilities fit the changing customer and consumer demands?
- Do the company's current and planned strategic responses and resource allocation reflect market realities?
- What are existing and planned capabilities that are needed to execute the strategy while staying responsive to changes?

"Culture & leadership to execute" – Organizational Alignment
- Do leadership and organization objectives align with the market?
- Are cultures and leadership styles understood?
- What are the strengths and weaknesses that impact our performance?
- What are our barriers to change?

Source: Gattorna, 1998

Figure 1.3.2
The Strategic Alignment Model

One way of focusing senior managers' attention on the need for a robust operating strategy is to demonstrate how the operating strategy will directly align the supply chain with customer needs using the Strategic Alignment Model (Figure 1.3.2). The model provides a compelling logic to developing a strategic response to the market. The strength of the model lies in the way it shows the interaction between the formulation of strategy and its execution by addressing the internal capabilities and leadership elements required to deliver a given strategy. Overall, the Strategic Alignment Model seeks to improve the alignment between markets, strategy, culture and leadership. Several levels of alignment need to be considered in developing and delivering an operating strategy: both market alignment and alignment of internal capabilities.

Achieving alignment with the market

Market alignment ensures appropriate levels of service for customers, reducing over- or under-servicing.

The market comprises the structure, conditions, dynamics and competitive intensity in a given industry. For the supply chain to operate effectively, organizations need to understand how the market operates and what buyer behaviors are driving the dynamics of the market. By understanding buyer values, organizations will be able to establish clear responses to buyer needs and thereby create value for the customer. This approach enables the supply chain to offer differentiated service offerings, automatically reducing the likelihood of over- or underservicing customers. Achieving market alignment overcomes one of the major pitfalls of driving a supply chain strategy, and that is, treating all customers as equal through a primary focus on reducing costs or building service satisfaction.

Effective segmentation

Understanding the market and the inherent buyer values is a critical aspect of developing an effective operating strategy. The insights derived from buyer values are used to drive segmentation of the supply chain, and the process used to enable differentiation of service levels to different groups of customers. Segmentation allows the supply chain to better align services with buyer values. The result is a framework that enables simplification of processes and appropriate resource allocation. Alignment against the supply chain segments offers benefits of more cost efficiency and a focus to create supply chain responses that support revenue generation through enhanced customer satisfaction and competitive power.

> *Segmentation allows the supply chain to better align services with buyer values.*

Allocating customers to supply chain segments provides organizations with the basis for developing tailored supply chain offerings. This approach results in organizations being able to fulfill customer requirements with less effort. Cost savings can be achieved by removing the unnecessary overservicing that occurs through operating a 'one-size-fits-all' supply chain. By understanding what is critical to the customer, organizations can redesign processes and thereby provide a level of service that better matches customer needs.

Customer segmentation is often used by sales and marketing managers. However, the sales and marketing approach to segmentation is usually based on a classification of customer attributes according to internal values such as customer size, strategic value, volume and customer profitability. Such segmentation often pays little regard to the true cost of servicing each customer group. Groupings of customers into Gold, Silver and Bronze are often developed, with the assumption that Gold customers require the highest level of servicing and Bronze customers the lowest. Sales and marketing segmentation usually focuses on the importance of the customer to the organization rather than the alignment of service with the buyer values associated with each customer product combination.

> *Supply chain segments help to identify the type of supply chain required to align and respond to customer needs.*

The concept of supply chain segmentation is very different and is based on an assessment of how customer buyer values have an impact on the way they interact with the supply chain. Supply chain segments help to identify the types of supply chains required to respond to customer needs.

Supply chain segmentation can be achieved by using a buyer value framework to map customers against a series of given buyer value descriptions, as shown in Figure 1.3.3. The PADI taxonomy used in Figure 1.3.3 is derived from the work of Ichak Adizes (1983) who defined four quadrants of different buyer values:

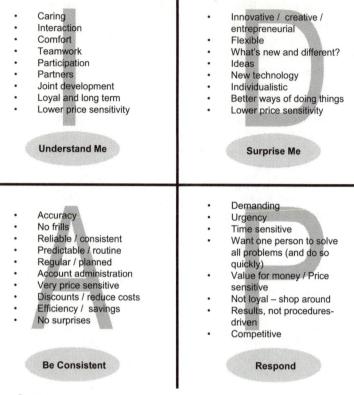

Source: Gattorna

Figure 1.3.3
PADI buyer value framework

P – Production
A – Administration
D – Development, and
I – Integration

The nature of customer requirements is derived by asking a series of structured questions with a cross-section of sales, marketing, customer servicing and logistics groups. The questions are designed to elicit information on the drivers of customer behavior and the nature of demand. Based on this information, organizations can configure the supply chain to focus on delivering against buyer values.

The process for deriving answers to the questions is best done in a workshop environment, where the group is asked to describe several types of customers. The questions act as a prompt to deriving behavioral characteristics. Example questions are listed below:

• What type of relationship do you have with the customer?
• How predictable is the customer?

- What is the relative importance of price to the customer?
- Are new technologies, services or products important?
- Does the customer seek or value teamwork?
- Is timing a critical issue?
- How does the customer share information?
- How does the customer assess our performance?
- How demanding is the customer beyond wanting reliability of supply delivered consistently?
- How unique are the customer's needs?

The answers to these questions are used to map the customers against the dimensions of the PADI buyer value framework. When mapping a customer it is important to remember that in practice any given customer will have characteristics in each of the four quadrants. However, one or two dominant characteristics will always drive their behavior. The mapping exercise will elicit clear customer groupings, with these groupings effectively forming the supply chain segments. The buyer values driving customer behavior are mostly dependent on the type of product or service being purchased. And, the same customer can appear in more than one segment, depending on a changing situation.

Any given customer will have characteristics in each of the buyer value segments.

For example, a retail customer will have different expectations and different requirements for the delivery and supply of fresh foods compared with shelf-stable produce. Deliveries of fresh foods may need daily replenishment at fixed times and possibly shelf-level merchandising. In contrast, a commodity packaged item such as sugar may be adequately serviced by inventory-level triggered replenishment. The PADI framework allows segmentation to be focused on supply chain requirements. Segmentation, therefore, enables the organization to focus on designing responses to these groupings with appropriate service requirements.

Using this framework to segment customers, organizations will find that all customers can be allocated to three or four distinct segments, at most. The final number of segments can be determined by following the guiding principle that each segment should be distinct, sizeable and actionable. Distinctiveness is important because the strategy is to use segmentation to drive the design of specific supply chain responses that satisfy the unique needs and characteristics for each segment. The segments must also be actionable in the sense of having sufficient critical mass and executable service value propositions.

Defining the strategic response

The next step in developing an aligned operating strategy is to define the appropriate supply chain responses to satisfy each segment. This process requires the development of distinct service propositions to service each segment. The detailed descriptions of segment characteristics are used to define clear strategies to meet buyer needs.

Identifying the characteristics of customer segments helps to define clear strategies to meet buyer needs.

Table 1.3.1
Customer segments for a global dairy ingredients company

Segment	Dynamic	Consistent	Collaborative	Flexible
Segment description	Rapid response to unpredictable supply and demand conditions	Consistent response to largely predictable demands	Close working relationships for mutual gain	Supplier-led development and delivery of new ideas
Segment characteristics	• Uneven demand • Commodity relationship • Urgent delivery requirements • Opportunity focus • Ad hoc source of supply • Low loyalty, impersonal • Price awareness, commercial deals based on pragmatism	• Predictable demand within contract • Regular delivery • Efficiency focus • Multiple sources of supply • Price sensitive	• Mostly predictable demand requiring regular delivery • Mature and/or augmented products • Primary source of supply • Teamwork, relationship focus • Joint customer/ supplier initiatives	• Unpredictable demand • Flexible delivery • Innovation/ solution focus • Augmented products and services • Low price sensitivity, good margins • Rapid change • Management of IP

The characteristics of each segment are refined and clarified within the organization to define the buyer values in such a way that they describe the nature of the demand and the type of customer service expectations. Table 1.3.1 shows the characteristics of different dairy ingredients customers of a global food manufacturer.

The characteristics were used to define the type of customer servicing strategy that creates value for the customer without inherent overservicing. The servicing strategy also embraces the type of organization sub-culture and leadership style that is required to deliver the customer servicing strategy and so enables true alignment of the market, servicing strategy and organization capability to respond.

To illustrate how the framework is used, the Dynamic customer segment in Table 1.3.1 can be described as: 'rapid response to unpredictable supply and demand conditions'. The segment description is used to characterize the nature of the demand, that is, an uneven offtake that requires rapid response once the order has been agreed. The Dynamic segment customers are typically contract customers in the commodity dairy ingredients market; they primarily buy in an opportunistic manner when market conditions dictate needs.

The segment characteristics describe the buyer values as well as the nature of the demand:

• uneven demand

- commodity relationship
- urgent delivery requirements
- focus on opportunity / deal
- ad hoc source of supply
- low loyalty, impersonal and
- price awareness with commercial deals based on pragmatism.

The customers in this segment buy based on specific needs, requiring suppliers to be responsive to product- and delivery-related issues. The customers place value on paying the 'right' price based on a dynamic supply base. Their priority is to gain responsiveness and flexibility to buy on an ad hoc basis rather than to foster a stable supply base and build long-term relationships.

Segment characteristics of this type demonstrate how some organizations can reduce customer satisfaction by implementing a generic strategy across the customer base. For instance, a strategy to increase customer service through relationship-orientated collaboration would not be considered beneficial by customers in the Dynamic segment. These customers would be more responsive to a strategy that drives performance in terms of delivery and flexibility to match requirements rather than high levels of customer interaction. The buyer values show a desire for responsiveness, with low interaction and low supplier dependency.

Operating characteristics or guiding principles for managing the segment can be developed based on the values of the segment. Examples of appropriate operating characteristics for the dynamic segment are:

Customer values can help to determine the appropriate operating characteristics for each segment.

- processes with more human intervention to ensure flexibility
- action and results orientation to identified opportunities
- mechanisms to support growth objectives
- wider distribution of responsibilities and considerations in the organization and
- mechanisms to increase responsiveness assessment and action against opportunities.

The operating characteristics can be used to define an appropriate strategic response for this segment. For example, the Dynamic segment would benefit from a response that enables hedging and deployment strategies to build and improve responsiveness. In addition, the operating characteristics are used to guide the hard configuration of the network and are integral with channel design and development of logistics pathways. The characteristics are, therefore, pivotal to driving alignment of cost-to-serve for each segment. They help to focus on what is valued by the customer and therefore guide the design and reconfiguration of channels and pathways to serve the segment more effectively.

Aligning culture and leadership style can improve the ability to execute strategy.

The ability of the organization to execute the strategy is supported by aligning the cultural and leadership styles of the organization with the market segments. The Strategic Alignment Model can be used to define the appropriate sub-cultures and leadership styles. For example, the sub-culture and leadership style that will support the Dynamic segment are defined below:

Sub-culture

The sub-culture of the organization responsible for the Dynamic segment must be characterized by a team that is outward looking, tries to ensure that the facts to support decisions are up to date, and can apply the facts quickly to enable a fast assessment of opportunities. Characteristics include:

- a focus on external market expansion
- productivity
- responsiveness
- deploying mechanisms to improve stability and
- guidelines orientation

Leadership style

To create this sub-culture requires a leadership style that provides sufficient flexibility and encourages a positive direction towards maximizing profit. Characteristics include:

- practical approach
- cost awareness
- leading by objectives
- plans for profitability, and
- a focus on what is important, maintaining a clear view of the big picture.

By using the segment characteristics in this way, it is possible to define differentiated servicing without over- or underservicing the customer. We will extend this theme in Chapter 4.3, 'Supply chains as vehicles for transformational change'.

Conclusion

The logic and role of the supply chain are linked intricately with delivering value to the customer.

Organizations seeking to deliver value to the customer need to consider the benefits of aligning their operating strategy for the supply chain to overall business strategy and the marketplace. By using this approach, executives will discover that the logic and role of the supply chain are linked intricately with delivering value to the customer, making it possible to drive better customer service while reducing operating costs. The principles of strategic alignment also provide an added benefit by considering the ability of the organization to deliver the strategy. This ensures alignment between the strategy itself and organizational capabilities, culture and leadership style. By applying a 'check and balance' for the operating strategy, the alignment framework ensures that the final strategy is aligned with the organization's capabilities and meets the increasing needs of customers.

The final component in developing an aligned operating strategy involves designing the most appropriate strategic response, so that the configuration of the supply chain is aligned with the supply chain segments. This topic is covered in Chapter 1.4, 'Operating strategy: configuring segmented supply chains'.

References

Adizes, I. (1983), *How to Solve the Mismanagement Crisis*, Santa Monica, CA: Adizes Institute.

Adizes, I. (1979), 'Organizational Passages: Diagnosing and Treating Life-Cycle Problems in Organizations', *Organizational Dynamics*, vol. 1.8 (no. 1).

Chorn, N. H. et al. (1990), 'Bridging Strategy Formulation and Implementation', unpublished paper presented to the 10th Annual International Conference of the Strategic Management Society, Stockholm.

Gattorna, J. L. (1991), 'Alignment and the Concept of Strategic Fit', *Strategy Spotlight*, vol. 1 (no 1), Sydney: Gattorna Strategy.

Gattorna, J. L. (ed) (1998), *Strategic Supply Chain Alignment*, Gower Publishing, Aldershot, pp. 1–7.

Jung, C. G. (1995), *The Structure and Dynamics of the Psyche*, New York: Pantheon.

1.4 Operating strategy: configuring segmented supply chains

Geoffrey Thomas and Ming Tang

Supply chain segmentation describes the nature of the customer's requirements in terms of how the customer wants to be serviced. This is an external, behavioral approach to segmenting customers.

Perhaps the most strategic area of business in the next decade will be channels of distribution: the complex commercial arrangements involving the array of different parties bringing products and services to consumers or other end users. As firms vie for competitive advantage, traditional channels of distribution are coming under increasing scrutiny, driven in many cases by new options presented by e-commerce, increasing inter-firm collaboration, and the development of true supply chain networks. Similarly, the consolidation of legacy or newly acquired manufacturing and distribution facilities remains important because of its potential impact on capital expenditure. Determining the optimal channels of distribution, product logistics flow paths and supporting network infrastructure are important ingredients to configuring a supply chain to deliver business objectives.

A prerequisite of any supply chain configuration review is a fundamental re-think of the way supply chain management segments its customers. This ensures that channel alternatives, logistics flow paths and facilities will be designed, evaluated or optimized within a framework that ensures that positive supply chain outcomes translate to desired business outcomes. Customer segmentation provides the anchor for design and performance requirements for all supply chain configuration components and represents the starting point of the journey to achieve improved alignment between the marketplace and the firm's response to that marketplace. As discussed in Chapter 1.3, segmentation has two distinctly different dimensions which are often confused.

Customer segmentation describes the value of the customer to the firm in terms of size and profit contribution. This is an internal view of the customer and is used to guide marketing and selling effort. Logistics, or supply chain, segmentation describes the nature of the customer's requirements in terms of how the customer wants to be serviced. This is an external, behavioral approach to segmenting customers and is used

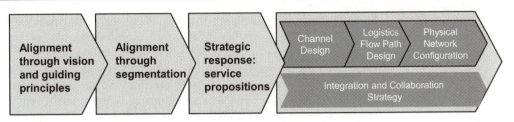

Figure 1.4.1
The strategic response of supply chain operating strategy: configuring the segmented supply chain

to design a fulfilment system that is capable of delivering different service levels at correspondingly different costs-to-serve.

It is the completion of the latter segmentation that forms the starting point for the design approach described in this chapter, that being, configuring an already segmented supply chain.

Designing the strategic response

As described in Chapter 1.3, configuring the supply chain represents the final element in the development of an aligned supply chain operating strategy. Effectively, it delivers the appropriate strategic response by shaping the fabric of the supply chain. This strategic response means developing an optimal day-to-day operational and relationship framework that supports the requirements of each of the customer segments of the supply chain. As such, designing and then implementing the response invariably involves undertaking a complex, long change program of significant and varying scope. However, several fundamental building blocks support this framework and shape our discussion in this chapter:

The strategic response defines how the supply chain will operate in practice.

- channel design
- logistics flow path design
- physical network configuration and
- integration and collaboration strategy.

Channel design

Channel design, a major component of supply chain configuration, involves structuring the value chain so that it meets value propositions for the product or service end user. In this sense, channel design defines the scope of the configuration effort. Most often driven by sales and marketing, but now more closely linked to supply chain initiatives, channel design considers the intermediaries required for the flow of goods or the performance of services.

Channel relationships are as much about information and financial flows as they are about the physical facilitation of goods and services.

In doing so, it also addresses the individual roles and relationships between the institutions, agencies and establishments. As such, channel relationships are as much about information and financial flows as they are about the physical facilitation of goods and services; they exist both to satisfy and to stimulate demand for the product or service. They also span the full spectrum of supply chain relationships, from purely transactional interactions to strategic collaborative relationships.

The major determinants of channel design are the buyer values of each customer segment, the organization's value proposition for the segment, as determined by its business strategy, and the required capabilities of the organization when compared to its intermediaries. Formulating an effective channel design requires an organization to have a deep understanding of customer-driven logistics in dynamic markets and an insight into the influence of potential channel partners. Examples of channel design options are shown in Figure 1.4.2 below.

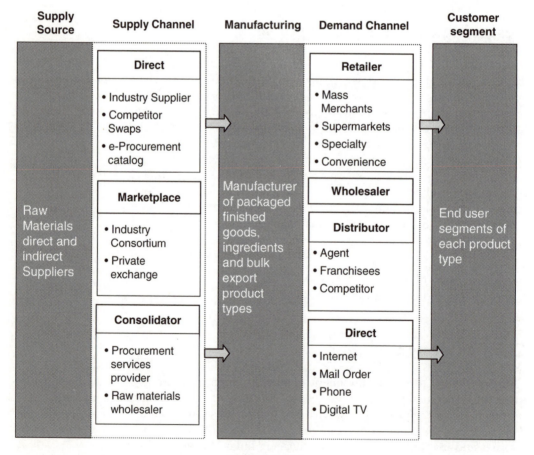

Figure 1.4.2
Examples of channel design options

Channel design should be focused on understanding the value-added impact of meeting customers' needs. Organizations have to understand the supply chain segments, assess how their requirements are changing and develop the leading practices to meet their needs. In this context, an effective channel design strategy must address several questions:

- What kinds of value-adding services and activities must be performed to meet the buyer values of customer segments and align with business strategy?
- Which of these services can the originating organization best perform?
- Which intermediaries are in the best position to perform the balance of those value-adding activities and services and how much will it cost?
- Finally, what is the optimal channel structure that creates competitive advantage by offering a superior value proposition at lower execution cost?

Design issues and steps
Any methodology for channel strategy execution should include several essential steps to ensure a consumer-driven channel design that is aligned to business strategy.

Step 1. Analyse current and competitor channel design
The organization's initial step in gaining knowledge of customer segments should be to analyse its existing channel design and that of competitors and other industries. By conducting data analysis and some benchmarking of competitors, the organization needs to answer the following questions:

The output is effectively a gap analysis that either supports or suggests the need to refine or reconstruct the current channel design.

- How effective is the current structure in delivering the desired value proposition to each customer segment?
- How much value is being added to the product/service package by each channel participant and is each aligned to the overall proposition?
- How much does it cost for each value-adding step performed by intermediaries and what commercial arrangements are in place?
- What is the overall cost-benefit equation for intermediaries when compared within and across industries?
- Does the current structure support future technologies and sustained growth through new service offerings opportunities?

The final output of this step is effectively a gap analysis that either supports or suggests the need to refine or reconstruct the current channel design.

Step 2. Develop options for channel design

Organizations need to assess the strategic potential and execution risks of new channel options versus those of proven channels.

Developing options for channel design is the most creative step in the process. Organizations need to develop alternatives based on a set of predefined requirements ranging from assembly, storage and delivery, selling, advertising, promotion, warranties, insurance, customer service, order processing and customer intelligence that are to be delivered to distinct levels and cost constraints. The major issues involved are: industry concentration, maximizing coverage versus a few select channels, product make or buy decisions, service insourcing versus outsourcing, the product lifecycle stage, end-user loyalties and desired channel control.

More recent trade-off issues will involve exploring new channels options such as e-marketplaces or value networks. Organizations need to assess their strategic potential and risks of execution versus those of proven channels. With a focus on customer needs, the options development should be guided by the objectives of achieving:

- growth and new service offerings
- insulation from competitors via customer loyalty
- clear value propositions with well-defined roles and responsibilities for each intermediary
- economic application of channel resources and
- use of the best intermediaries for each value creation element.

Step 3. Evaluate and select channel design option

Organizations need to weigh up short-term cost issues against potential longer-term benefits of positioning for growth and seizing new opportunities.

The final step is to evaluate and select the most appropriate channel design option. This step involves determining the short- and long-term costs and benefits of each option and the fit with organizational and existing industry constraints. Essentially, the short-term cost-benefit equation revisits several of the questions in Step 2. However, organizations need to weigh these against the longer-term benefits of strategic positioning for growth, new service offering opportunities and insulation from competition that guided option development in Step 3.

The analytical basis of this step is often termed a cost-to-serve analysis, which is conducted for each customer segment and channel combination. The second evaluation factor is to test if the channel design 'fits' with the organization's culture and management. Is the organization averse to taking risks? What are the irrational constraints? What are the limits that need to be adhered to in order to succeed in implementation? Most industries also have historical barriers, some of which are translated into regulations that define strict performance requirements around distribution that the future channel structure must deliver.

Logistics flow path design

Logistics flow paths, also termed logistics pathways, are defined as the generic pathway of nodes, comprising plants and distribution facilities, and linkages, the transportation modes and routes, that a product undertakes from point of origin to customer segments. Pathways are often confused with the channels previously discussed. However, they are quite distinct in that channel structure defines the type and composition of intermediaries used to facilitate a product's movement from point of origin to end user, while logistics pathways describe physical movements and processes, as shown in Figure 1.4.3.

The design of logistics flow paths provides the structure for managing differentiated service levels to different customer segments.

The design of logistics flow paths provides the structure for managing differentiated service levels to different customer segments. The design should answer the critical question of how many 'internal' supply chains an organization needs to manage. The design output should also help to determine the supply chain configuration by answering the following questions:

- Which product groups can be combined synergistically into a generic logistics flow path that can be managed distinctively and monitored to meet customer segment-aligned service and cost objectives?
- What are the requirements of these logistic flow paths in terms of volumes, levels and locations of manufacturing and distribution facilities?
- What is the flow path inventory positioning that determines the processing in these facilities? For example, make to order versus make to stock; safety stockholding versus flow-through operations.

Design issues and steps

Logistics flow path design is dependent on defining customer segments and developing appropriate service propositions to respond to each segment, as discussed in Chapter 1.3. This segment-driven approach to flow path design overcomes the false simplicity of a 'one-size-fits-all' approach and provides the organization with the ability to sustain the required service levels in a cost-effective manner.

A segment-driven approach to flow path design gives an organization the ability to sustain the required service levels in a cost-effective manner.

For the purpose of flow path design, different factors shape the analysis and outputs of customer segmentation and service propositions. These can be divided conveniently into two groups: logistics operational complexity and customer logistics sophistication.

Logistics operational complexity

Logistics operational complexity is comprised of several sub-categories that would drive the segmentation outcome:

- Customer demand profiles. Typically, the category defines ordering characteristics and includes factors such as demand volatility, regularity of orders, order frequency and order size.

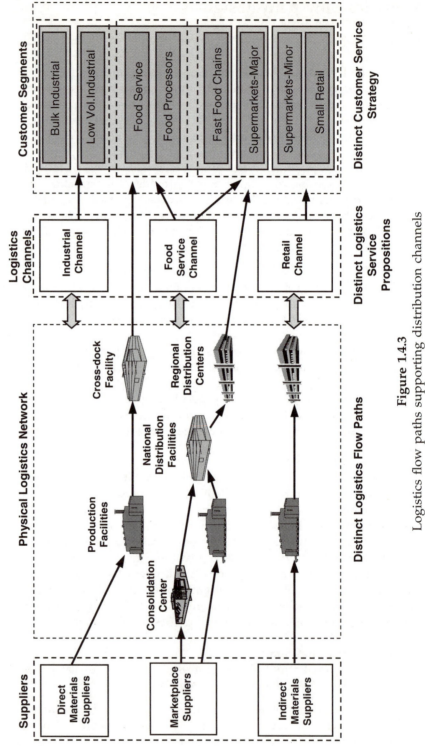

Figure 1.4.3
Logistics flow paths supporting distribution channels

42

- Supply issues. Factors such as number of supply points, lead times and seasonality affect segmentation.
- Product characteristics. Segments are influenced by the complexity in physical handling, such as bulky or hazardous goods, shelf life and temperature control.

Detailed analysis of these characteristics will provide an understanding of the operational alternatives for slicing the product portfolio into synergistic chunks that organizations can manage distinctively throughout the supply chain. These logistically determined product groups will often require different processing, routing, modes of transport or inventory positioning as they pass through the network. It is thus the identification of these logistics product groups that provides the constraints for flow path alternatives.

Customer logistics sophistication

Similarly, the characteristics falling within the customer logistics sophistication group would have determined the appropriate customer service responses to satisfy each segment. These characteristics include:

- sophistication of required information linkages
- approach to collaborative planning
- degree of focus on supply chain optimization
- focus on pricing of services
- response time
- quality requirements
- level of performance required across all products
- delivery windows and
- floor-ready packaging requirements.

They will further refine the flow-path alternatives but, more importantly, provide clear performance objectives for each flow path.

Predictably, an appropriate mix and weighting of the above factors largely determines the final design of the flow paths and is typically influenced by the organization, its industry, product portfolio and target market. Design is also often influenced by an organization's positioning along the value chain. A manufacturer with a small number of influential customers would tend to prioritize sophistication of customer requirements above logistics operational complexity factors. In contrast, a grocery and general merchandise retailer offering consistent store-front service to consumers with a small-volume Internet trade would likely prioritize logistics operational complexity in shaping its flow path design.

To take this retailer as an example, within logistics operational complexity, the product characteristics may be shelf life and temperature control; customer demand profiles would be product velocity, demand volatility; supply issues would be lead times for

An effective flow path design should challenge traditional divisions and maximize the opportunities for synergies across manufacturing, distribution facilities and transport infrastructure.

off-shore manufactured product. Flow path design could result in the following distinct flow paths:

- Dry grocery items: high velocity, high service level, requiring varied temperature control. Uses several composite-temperature, regional flow-through distribution facilities close to store demand, and fast-flow product from vendors to stores.
- General merchandise: low velocity, lower service level. Uses safety stock held in one central national distribution facility, conventionally picks these products and then cross docks them through regional facilities to stores.
- Seasonal lines: longer lead time. Uses consolidation in third-party facilities to accommodate peak short-term volumes, and cross-dock these through regional facilities to stores as required.
- Internet grocery business: low volume, high service level, requiring temperature control. Uses urban fulfilment centers to consolidate orders, and hold safety stock, order pick product and deliver direct to consumers.

These generic flow paths become the internal supply chains that the retailer will manage according to quite different performance requirements; however, they still meet the expectations of its customer base, both store-front and the Internet segments. In summary, an effective flow path design should challenge traditional merchandise-based divisions and maximize the opportunities for synergies across manufacturing, distribution facilities and transport infrastructure. It should be recognized that flow path management principles also provide a framework for development of the required business architecture for the supply chain, because core process, system and organizational capabilities will be implied for each distinctive flow path.

Physical network configuration

The multitude of network variables, with differing levels of network configurations and potential sensitivities, highlights the complexity associated with network configuration.

Logistics flow path design provides the directional requirements as to levels and volumes of facilities, their operational intent and product ranging. The critical next component is the complex optimization modeling analysis required to answer the numerous data trade-offs involved in arriving at the optimal network. This is termed physical network configuration. The detail of network optimization modeling is covered in Chapter 2.1, 'Supply chain network optimization modeling', but the key points regarding operating strategy are discussed here.

The major issues in any optimizing exercise are the number and levels of network variables that need to be scoped as part of the network configuration. Current networks are becoming increasingly complex. Most traditional manufacturer-to-retailer channel configurations have supported an intermediate level of warehousing to meet required lead times. Often a concentrated sourcing and dispersed demand region involves several tiers of distribution in order to balance transportation and inventory costs effectively. Many of the difficulties involved in developing a network configuration lie in the interrelationships between the network parameters, manufacturing, warehousing, inventory, transportation, purchasing and customer service.

Decreasing one element, such as the number of warehouses, increases others, such as transportation and inventory levels, and may have an impact on customer service. The multitude of network variables, with differing levels of network configurations and potential sensitivities, highlights the complexity associated with network configuration. Figure 1.4.4 below depicts this situation.

The physical network configuration exercise will be required to answer the following types of questions:

- How many levels of distribution facilities are required, such as national or regional?
- How many manufacturing and distribution center facilities are required, and where should they be located?
- Which customer and product groups should be served from each facility?
- What should be the capacity of each manufacturing plant?

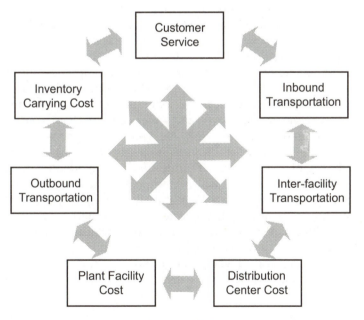

Figure 1.4.4
Network configuration trade-off elements

- What is the appropriate level of inventory for each distribution facility and the mission, stocking or flow-through of each?
- What transportation modes should be used for each network linkage?
- Should all or any part of the organization's network within the channel be operated by a third party?

Design issues and steps

The use of a network model enables organizations to conduct a cost-to-serve analysis for specific logistics flow paths and alternative network configurations to support the supply chain segments.

In order to derive an optimized configuration, it is best to design a network optimization model that will enable the development of strategic options for the network. The use of a network model enables organizations to conduct a cost-to-serve analysis for specific logistics flow paths and alternative network configurations to support the supply chain segments.

The optimization modeling problem will involve taking inputs in terms of cost and volume information from the main network parameters, and simultaneously taking into account the existing interrelationships between these parameters to derive the optimal configuration. Due to the complexity associated with such an optimization, any complete network configuration undertaking will require the use of specialized network modeling tools. An exception may be use of sophisticated spreadsheet modeling in a single-tier limited product range operation; however, the advantages of the new breed of network optimization modeling tools is compelling in almost all situations.

Essentially, network modeling tools re-create the supply chain network as a mathematical model of each of its parameters. The modeling function uses linear and mixed integer programing techniques to represent the trade-offs that occur between each parameter as one or more of them are changed. Optimization of the network is defined as the best possible balance between these parameters, minimizing network operating costs while simultaneously meeting service level and other supply chain constraints. Once configured to the network, the tools put immense analytical power at the disposal of business users by enabling a thorough examination of many 'what if?' questions, often identifying many counter-intuitive solutions, which is impossible to do manually. The best of breed are now relatively easy to adapt to market dynamics, as well as quick to update the affected variable and recalculate the optimal solution. A recent trend is to not only to outsource a network modeling tool for a single network evaluation, but to acquire the software license and develop the in-house skills as an ongoing capability to address network extensions due to changing market conditions.

Six steps in network modeling optimization

The essential steps involved in a network modeling optimization exercise are typically as follows;

Step 1. Determine data requirements. This step involves determining the best groupings of products, customers and suppliers that form the basis of data consolidation. Data consolidation is critical as modeling is based on the extrapolation of representative samples. Typical data elements are forecasted sales growth, manufacturing fixed and variable costs, distribution center fixed and variable costs, transportation costs, cost of goods sold and inventory holding costs.

Step 2. Establish the requirements and constraints to be applied to the modeling exercise. This involves determining conditions such as transport capacity and store receiving capability, and customer service levels applicable to the current network.

Step 3. Configure the modeling tool. This step requires integrating the cost and volume data into a mathematical logic model that represents the parameters of the network.

Step 4. Validate the model. This requires running a base-case model that represents the current network configuration, and accurately reflects the existing supply chain cost structure using current financial data.

Step 5. Allow the model to optimize the network by conducting iterations to determine economies and diseconomies of scale, existing and future capacities of facilities, remove validation constraints and build capacities and economies into the model.

Step 6. Model to determine the viability of potential business scenarios that imply changes to existing network parameters. Scenarios therefore have predetermined conditions and situations rather than unconstrained optimization. Valuable input to these scenarios would be provided by the directional thinking on product combinations and facility roles delivered in logistics flow path design.

The output of the physical network configuration will be the optimization of total network costs against predetermined service-level constraints for each supply chain segment.

The output of the physical network configuration will be the optimization of total network costs against predetermined service-level constraints for each supply chain segment, considering:

- fixed and operating costs for manufacturing plants and distribution centers
- inventory carrying costs
- transportation costs and
- cost of goods.

Ideally, building a network optimization model should precede and indeed be a major input to any supply chain operating strategy.

Integration and collaboration strategy

The final component of configuring the supply chain involves determining how to integrate information internally and how to collaborate with suppliers and customers. This step occurs concurrently with the building blocks of configuration, as discussed, and is influential in determining their outcomes. In an integration and collaboration strategy, organizations need to consider the information flows between each supply chain entity to reduce the duplication of effort and distortions between demand and supply chains. The integration of information helps to drive a more effective, responsive and flexible supply chain. Organizations also need to achieve collaboration with customers and suppliers. In doing so, they can transform the focus of supply chain activity from cost-effectiveness to offering new customer value propositions.

The key imperative for success in enabling integration and collaboration is the ability to obtain skills and achieve geographic reach and critical mass – without necessarily growing organically. Integration of information requires an information systems architecture that can support external interfaces; the convergence of data standards to create a single platform through the Internet has made this much easier.

An integration and collaboration strategy should include:

- An integrated map of the business architecture needed for the future state that the organization wants to attain. The map shows the required capabilities to manage the business and, for each capability, it defines the business processes, organization roles, responsibilities and behaviors, key performance measures and the systems needed to enable the new processes. The business architecture provides a blueprint of the change required and helps to define the applications architecture and the organization change plan to move towards the future state. An overall business architecture is critical to an aligned operating strategy as it enables the implementation of the strategy and helps to define the value approach for integration.
- Value chain analysis. An analysis of the value chain is critical input, as described earlier, as it will capture the appropriate integration and collaboration points internally and externally with suppliers and customers. The analysis should be used to identify key value drivers and provide an assessment of how to improve value chain competitiveness by enabling the following six success factors:

  - operational excellence and continuous improvement – developing a view on the type of partners of choice to accelerate internal capability
  - extending reach into customers and suppliers
  - compressing the supply chain, aiming to have fewer physical assets using supplier and/ or customer networks. This may

require developing new business models and relationships with third-party suppliers
- creating flexibility and agility, using the configuration of the value chain to improve overall responsiveness, such as the creation of industry stocks
- price optimization, using dynamic pricing to control demand and optimize flows and utilization across supply chains and
- defining where to compete. This may include the creation of new e-marketplaces with other industry bodies to maximize the value chain.

Conclusion

Configuring the segmented supply chain represents the final component of achieving an aligned operating strategy. Effective supply chain configuration requires building on the business alignment platform established through customer segmentation and customer service propositions. Using segment-driven design principles – and focusing on the core building blocks of channel design, flow path design, physical network configuration, integration and collaboration strategy – will serve to reduce the complexity of what many organizations have found to be a costly and value-destroying undertaking. The important outcome, an optimal configuration, will provide the organization with an operational and partnership framework that facilitates delivering the desired business performance, cost-effectively and across multiple interfaces of supply and distribution.

Using segment-driven design principles will serve to reduce the complexity of what many organizations have found to be a costly and value-destroying undertaking.

References

Gattorna, J. L. (1991), 'Pathways to Customers – reducing Complexity in the Logistics Pipeline, *Strategy Spotlight*, vol. 1 (no. 2), Sydney: Gattorna Strategy.

Gattorna, J. L. (1991), 'Taking the "ing" out of Marketing: Creating Market-Focused Organizations', *Strategy Spotlight*, vol. 1 (no. 2), Sydney: Gattorna Strategy.

1.5 Customer relationship management capabilities in a supply chain context

Stephen F. Dull, David N. Morris, Timothy Stephens and Mark T. Wolfe

Differences in executing CRM capabilities account for roughly half the difference in financial performance between top and average performers.

Supply chain practitioners have for a long time calculated the cost to serve customers: to meet their requirements better and to optimize the supply chain. This optimization has traditionally focused on improving the processes to deliver product to customers in the most cost-effective way. But managing customer relationships today offers opportunities that go far beyond cost containment. In convincing the customer to buy in the first instance, companies can use that first interaction to develop a strong long-term relationship, based on a deep understanding of the customer's requirements and the company's ability to deliver.

It was the legendary Philadelphia retailer John Wanamaker who uttered that now famous management complaint: 'I know half the money I spend on advertising is wasted; the trouble is, I don't know which half.' The problem, extended to the broader marketing environment, is as old as commerce itself: there has never been an objective, reliable way to predict how – and how much – proposed investments in attracting and retaining customers will affect profit.

Until now, that is. An ambitious study completed by Dull *et al* (2001) establishes for the first time the strong link between excellence in a company's overall interaction with customers – what we call customer relationship management, or CRM – and financial performance. Our research shows that companies that have not invested in developing specific CRM capabilities are leaving millions of dollars in profit on the table.

In fact, differences in executing CRM capabilities account for roughly half the difference in financial performance between top and average performers. Companies that enjoy the highest profitability in their industries are those that have invested in developing a very specific set of CRM capabilities – revealing, for the first time, the capabilities that contribute the most to the bottom line.

Looking through the customer's lens

What Accenture calls customer relationship management can be defined as the holistic and methodical approach to identifying, attracting and retaining a company's most valuable customers through a set of capabilities which in turn must also be integrated into supply chain processes in order to achieve their objectives.

The challenge of CRM begins with gaining deep insight into customers, then drawing on that insight to strengthen customer offers.

The concept has evolved considerably over time. Today, in truly customer-driven enterprises, it would be more accurate to say that the approach is about customer–managed relationships.

Customer-driven enterprises look through the lens of the customer, taking an outside-in perspective to ensure that their best customers receive consistently differentiated and, wherever possible, personalized service. This, in turn, increases market share, the share of the customer's business and the total value derived from those customers over their lifetime. This adds up to considerable customer equity, the new measure of value that emphasizes the relationships that companies build with their customers.

The challenge of customer relationship management begins with gaining deep insight into customers, then drawing on that insight to strengthen customer offers, that is, to create more appealing value propositions, products and services. It also involves enhancing customer interactions through superior sales and service as well as strong personal relationships.

These core capabilities rely on equally important underlying strengths. A high-performing organization needs people who are skilled in customer care and has the relevant technology and the ability to operate in new integrated ways through partnerships, alliances and e-commerce initiatives.

Research findings

Customer relationship management is a misnomer. It implies that companies have significant control over customers – over what they buy, from whom, when and how. However, customers are increasingly in charge, especially in the emerging e-world. Customers have an enormous amount of information at their pointing-and-clicking fingertips and they use it to make purchasing decisions. They have many more options and they take advantage of those options to get the best products, services, prices and performance. In the business-to-business arena, the e-explosion is expected to be more than five to ten times the size of that in the consumer market.

A company could add more than US$1 million per year to pre-tax profit as a result of improving its CRM capabilities, the research found.

Accenture's CRM Capabilities Research Study surveyed close to 500 executives, representing over 250 companies across 6 industries (chemicals/communications/forest products/electronics and high technology/retail and pharmaceuticals), including separate sections on marketing, sales and service. Executives completed questions relevant to their area of responsibility; the 430 questions in the survey covered a range of strategy, process, technology and human performance issues, and were designed to score how well the responding business unit performs on various CRM capabilities.

The extensive survey found 21 individual capabilities that, regardless of industry, could add more than $1 million per year to pre-tax profit, given appropriate performance improvements. For 70 per cent of those capabilities, the benefit exceeds $5 million per year (Figure 1.5.1). For example, if a $1 billion company improves its CRM performance from average to high in either customer service or motivating and rewarding people, its return on sales could improve by as much as $13 million.

Some executives will read this list and smile knowingly, as many of the capabilities look all too familiar. Hiring and retaining the right people. Customer service. Key account management. Segmentation. Advertising. Aren't these, and other capabilities on the list, basics done by every customer-attentive company? Maybe, but probably not. While the terms are familiar, the capabilities they describe are growing more complex and are largely interrelated. Creating the most value and impact to financial performance depends on how many capabilities a company executes and how well it executes them.

While the terms are familiar, the capabilities they describe are growing more complex and are largely interrelated.

Improving performance can have a significant financial impact: a 10 per cent improvement across all CRM capabilities can improve

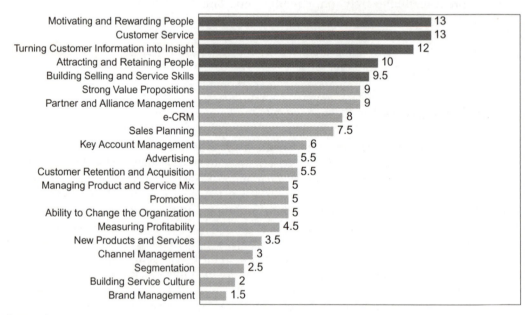

Source: Accenture

Figure 1.5.1
Impact of moving from average to high performance ($m for a $b company)

returns by about $40 to $50 million per year for a typical $1 billion company. Greater returns, up to $120 to $150 million, are likely for more aggressive efforts (a 30 per cent improvement), and there is always room to improve – even for high performers.

To help companies make the decisions required to invest their CRM dollars wisely, Accenture mapped the 21 most profit-adding capabilities identified in the research to our framework for the customer-driven enterprise. Made up of five key areas, this model shows the relative impact of specific capabilities and capability areas on pre-tax profit (see Figure 1.5.2). For example, if a $1 billion business unit moves from average to high performance in customer interaction capabilities, it could have an impact on pre-tax profit by up to $40 million per year.

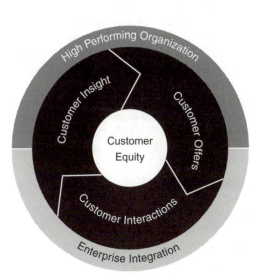

	$ millions
Customer Insight	**25**
• Turning Customer Information into Insight	12.0
• Customer Retention and Acquisition	5.5
• Measuring Profitability	4.5
• Segmentation	2.5
Customer Offers	**19**
• String Value Propositions	9.0
• Managing Product and Service Mix	5.0
• New Products and Services	3.5
• Brand Management	1.5
Customer Interactions	**40**
• Customer Service	13.0
• Sales Planning	7.5
• Key Account Management	6.0
• Advertising	5.5
• Promotion	5.0
• Channel Management	3.0
High Performing Organizations	**40**
• Motivating and Rewarding People	13.0
• Attracting and Retaining People	10.0
• Building Selling and Service Skills	9.5
• Ability to Change the Organization	5.0
• Building Service Culture	2.0
Enterprise Integration	**17**
• Partner and Alliance Management	9.0
• e-CRM	8.0

Source: Accenture

Figure 1.5.2
Relative impact of specific CRM capabilities

Improving capabilities from average to high in each area can improve return on sales for a $1 billion company by the amount indicated.

Deepening customer insight

Just gathering customer information within different company functions will provide a limited view of the potential of the customer relationship. A total view is needed.

Customer insight is an ongoing process that applies a fact-based understanding of customer needs, expectations and value potential to tailor customer offerings and interactions.

Accenture's research study asked executives questions relating to:

- customer segmentation
- measuring profitability
- the costs of customer acquisition and retention
- how technology is used to gather information about customers, including data mining and data warehousing
- how companies analyse customer behavior and
- how information is shared across different parts of the company, including the development of processes to do so.

Many companies collect vast amounts of information about customers – function by function. The sales department knows customers' buying history, characterized in terms of volume, pricing and purchases. Distribution knows their delivery needs and fulfilment history. The marketing and service organizations know their product needs and past service issues. However, this fragmented pile of information cannot build real customer insight.

Therefore, just gathering customer information within different company functions will provide a limited view of the potential of the customer relationship. At best, it is a 'point in time' understanding of that customer. New technologies today allow the creation of a total

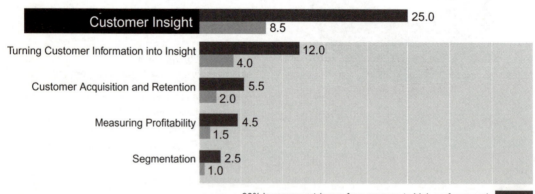

Source: Accenture

Figure 1.5.3
Impact of performance improvement – customer insight ($m for a $b company)

view of the customer that combines data about the customer from external sources and delivers it on a continuous real-time basis. This customer insight, which helps identify patterns of customer behavior, is needed to develop attractive products and services and woo the customer to purchase them, again and again. Deep customer insight can inform a host of marketing, selling, and service decisions that, in turn, shape resource commitments and day-to-day operations in the marketing, sales and service organizations.

Recognizing the competitive advantage represented by customer insight, the most profitable companies studied, across industries, are already using technology to gather the right information about customers and turn it into true customer insight (see Figure 1.5.3).

The research showed that the secret of success lies in technology – its ever-increasing power to collect data, analyse it to synthesize insights and then share those insights with everyone in the organization whose work touches customers.

Transforming customer information into insight

A key challenge is collecting, accessing and integrating customer data, no matter where and how it is collected and where it is stored, then making this information useful to the organization. While a few visionary companies have been building customer data warehouses for almost two decades, only recently have these warehouses become prominent features of the data landscape.

A key challenge lies in making the customer data useful to the organization. Some top-performing companies share the information with channel partners.

Today the declining costs of collecting, storing, manipulating and distributing customer data are encouraging companies of all types to follow the visionaries' lead. Some are compiling any number of data records for a single customer to understand product history, likelihood of the customer buying multiple products and most promising promotional opportunities.

Some of the top-performing companies in the study even share information with channel partners outside the organization. This practice has become a primary way to differentiate companies within the communications industry, to the benefit of market leaders. The common basis of understanding helps everyone work together, to better serve the needs of individual customers.

Measuring customer acquisition and retention

The ease of accumulating, accessing and analysing data invites companies to ask themselves 'how are we doing?' But by what means do companies measure success? Best practice companies look at the lifetime value of individual customers and the potential value of underspending segments. Accordingly, such companies take a multi-dimensional view of success.

They look not only at customer attraction, but also at retention and defection. While most companies devote significant budget to tracking acquisitions, few measure retention or defection.

Ironically, the research finds that some companies squander precious time and resources in assessing how they are doing. These companies repeatedly invent administrative measures and checks, but never act on the results. The moral of the story: measure judiciously and act quickly on the results.

Measuring profitability

Profitability data was the only type of data that consistently showed up as having strong value in all of the industries studied.

The research revealed that one of the hallmarks of highly skilled CRM leaders is that they have an excellent grasp of just where and how they make money. CRM leaders have rich, reliable and easy access to profitability by product, customer, geography and channel, enabled by modern information systems. They can more easily get a detailed handle on revenue and costs at even the transaction level.

Moreover, CRM leaders also use their technology to integrate information on purchase patterns, product usage, customer needs and other data. Armed with this integrated view, leaders make better-informed decisions to balance customer preference and profit.

Laggards are those whose often outdated systems produce limited data that few trust, and only after great manual intervention or 'massaging' of the data. As analysing the data is so difficult and time-consuming, such efforts tend to be episodic at best. Thus, the organization does not develop the skills of adequate analysis or informed decision making that its more strongly equipped peers are honing.

Simply put, the availability, or lack thereof, drives the use of profitability data. The study explored the use of many types of data, but profitability data was the only type that consistently showed up as having strong value in all of the industries studied. In fact, moving from average to high performance in measuring profitability is worth $4 to $5 million in added returns for a $1 billion business unit.

Seems obvious? Perhaps. But most executives understand the difficulty of getting from where they are to anywhere close to top performance. Often, new systems require significant investment, not just to plug in, but to get an organization up to speed and to change all the processes that depend on the systems. Now, however, the added benefit can at least be quantified when these systems are part of an integrated CRM skill-building agenda, and can provide added impetus to the debate over whether to invest.

Seeing the forest for the trees: customer segmentation

High-performing companies make deliberate choices about which customers they will and will not serve and the level of service they will offer each group.

The research showed that understanding customer segments, as well as individual customers, is important. Leading companies across industries not only understand segment profitability and the economics of acquiring, retaining and losing attractive segments – they have perfected this art. Further, they make disciplined decisions on which customers to serve more, less or not at all, and how to personalize service effectively, yet cost-efficiently.

Many companies collect the data needed to support segmentation, but fail to analyse or act on it. Those that do so, however, will be positioned to deliver the kind of personalized, targeted service that keeps customers satisfied and loyal, which in turn helps build profitability. What separates average companies from the highest performers is not the segmentation itself, but the actions that are taken as a result. High performers use segmentation to make deliberate choices about which customers they will and will not serve and the level of service they will offer each group. Those choices often are based on a careful assessment of customer acquisition and retention costs.

Having well-defined customer segments also helps companies identify more desirable prospective customers. By identifying the attributes of 'best' customers, companies can proactively seek these attributes in prospects.

Customer offers: giving customers what they want

The customer offers capability area is all about providing the most appealing products and services to customers. Leading companies draw on customer insight to shape and refine offers and, thus, enhance the customer's interactions with the company.

Leading companies draw on customer insight to shape and refine offers and, thus, enhance the customer's interactions with the company.

In the CRM Capabilities Research Study, executives were asked questions relating to developing new products and services, managing product/service mix, value propositions and brand management.

Companies that do not apply customer insight to the design of products and services have missed the boat. From the customer's perspective, products and services are at the core of the customer interaction. Therefore, smart companies take a disciplined approach to developing products and services, predicated on two fundamental beliefs:

- A customer makes purchasing decisions based on perceptions of value – and often the degree to which the fundamental product and service is tailored to the needs of the individual customer, which creates the foundation of loyalty.
- A customer's total experience with the company, not with a single product or service, ultimately determines loyalty. Thus, everything that touches the customer must work together to produce customer value.

These beliefs lead more profitable companies to focus on four key capabilities, as outlined in Figure 1.5.4.

Together, these practices generate significant value for a typical $1 billion business unit – over $6 million by enhancing capabilities by a modest 10 per cent. By moving from average to high performance, a business unit can add as much as $19 million to pre-tax profit.

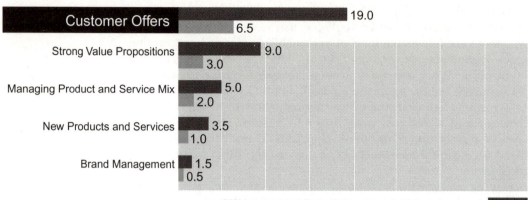

Customer Offers — 19.0 / 6.5

Strong Value Propositions — 9.0 / 3.0

Managing Product and Service Mix — 5.0 / 2.0

New Products and Services — 3.5 / 1.0

Brand Management — 1.5 / 0.5

30% improvement (move from average to high performance):
10% improvement (moderate improvement, for any level of performance):

Source: Accenture

Figure 1.5.4
Impact of performance improvement – customer offers ($m for a $b company)

Creating compelling value propositions

A value proposition is a promise – one the company makes to customers about which benefits it will deliver for a given price.

Value proposition has become one of the most popular phrases in the business lexicon. For many companies, a value proposition is nothing more than the slogan that flashes across its web site or the tagline that adorns every TV commercial and print advertisement.

But a real value proposition is much more than a clever phrase. Best practice companies realize that a value proposition is a promise – one the company makes to customers about which benefits it will deliver for a given price. These companies further realize that the real power of a value proposition lies in using it to guide the short- and long-term actions of employees as they go about serving customers. Unleashing that power requires:

- at the strategic level, clarifying the promised benefits and the customer's experience to inform decisions regarding quality, product lines, distribution, pricing and the like
- at the tactical level, giving front-line employees the understanding of the company's promise, which equips them to respond consistently and to make decisions quickly. Technology increasingly puts key customer information at employees' fingertips, but the value proposition guides its interpretation.

A strong value proposition is an informed value proposition. It rests on:

- clear facts about how to balance customer needs with profit needs
- deliberate choices of how to compete, where to excel and where to match competitors.

An exclusive focus on customer needs usually is a formula for making no money. Securing customers' profitably is the winning formula, and everyone in the company must understand that value proposition. Sales and marketing typically do, but if operations, service and technical support are not equally informed, they are unlikely to deliver as expected.

A winning value proposition need not beat the competition on every count. In fact, parity claims can be as important as superiority claims, even for a segment of one, which is typically the key account. For a given customer, parity performance on a wide range of basic needs is the price of admission.

Failure to be at least at parity can be dangerous. It complicates customer trade-offs. A company may deliver superior service, but if quality is less consistent than that of competitors, many customers may see no reason to buy and the business likely will not be as large or as profitable. High performers understand and apply the discipline of setting explicit goals for parity and superior performance.

This discipline pays off in financial and market performance. Poor performers across industries tend to operate with a cynical, commodity mindset. They are certain that differentiation is impossible, that competitors enjoy insurmountable advantages (like low-cost operations or a global supply network), that basic fixes cannot work or that the magic bullet awaits discovery somewhere else.

High-performing companies look at the world through a different lens. Their execution of very basic marketing, sales and service activities is meticulous. Even in cut-throat industries battered by oversupply, they discount a little less steeply and a little less frequently. Their margins show the impact.

Managing product/service mix

High performers maximize margins by continuously managing their product and service mix. Low performers typically have not done detailed cost-to-serve analyses nor integrated it into actions that enrich mix.

Information technology provides powerful support, making it easy to track and measure profitability at the product and service level, customer level and even transaction level. Such easy access to data looms especially large in mix management, which requires hundreds of small decisions – for example, aiding the up-selling or cross-selling initiative of a customer service agent. Individually. it may not add much per transaction but, in aggregate, marginally profitable customers can become more attractive.

e-CRM moves at speed up the profit ladder

Despite its infancy, e-CRM is in the top third of the most profit-adding CRM capabilities, ahead of traditional value drivers such as segmentation and channel management.

The rapid growth of e-commerce has accelerated the importance of technology as a key to success in managing customer relationships. E-CRM is what we describe as using electronic channels to market to, sell to and serve customers, both directly and with channel partners. Our research highlights that, despite its infancy, e-CRM is in the top third of the most profit-adding capabilities identified in the research. E-CRM came out ahead of more traditional drivers of value such as segmentation and channel management.

What is adding the most value today consistently across industries is the ability to transact business over the Internet:

- The ability to share product and other information with customers and channel partners via the Internet is a foundation e-CRM skill that has a high correlation with profit.
- The basic ability to take an order also adds to profit.
- In the early adopting industries, leveraging advanced e-CRM technologies that make information-intense and complex purchase decisions easier, faster and more tailored to customer needs has strong payback.
- High technology is also realizing the first real pay-off on e-CRM selling tools, like configurators, which provide inexpensive, tailored selling expertise to help customers configure products online and dramatically reduce return rates and invalid sales orders.
- The ability to finalize transactions through electronic bill payment contributes to additional value.

One major caveat: while completing transactions over the Internet is highly correlated with richer profit, more is not necessarily better. In high technology and chemicals, for example, there is a negative correlation with higher Internet sales and profitability. We believe this reflects two phenomena we are observing in the market today. First, the current limitations of the types of product and service that can be sold over the Internet. Second, the concerns about the extent to which the Internet might contribute to the commoditization of the sale. As a result, companies have tended primarily to move less complex products and commodities over the Internet. This does not mean that Internet transactions are less profitable, however. These products, by definition, typically have a lower margin.

Overall, the message is clear: early adopters are winning customers, sales and increasing profit by steadily building their e-CRM capabilities. Laggards are threatened not just by the direct competition of better-enabled competitors, but by the increasing profit margins these leaders will be able to leverage in the future. We believe the early adopters have a lead in terms of building deeper relationships with their customers and profiting from this advantage. These e-Interactions provide them with an opportunity to get more insight about their customers' needs and set up stronger barriers against competition and new entrants. We fully expect the overall measured impact of e-CRM on profit to grow to the top of the list as one of the most differentiating and value-adding CRM capabilities in the marketplace.

Conclusion

CRM focuses on understanding customers and developing the right products and services to attract and retain them. This is achieved through organizations collecting information at every customer touchpoint and using this insightful information to develop the right products and services to meet the customer's requirements. However, simply understanding the customer's requirements is not enough: everyone that touches the customer, from sales to delivery, must work together to produce customer value. Consequently, understanding the cost-to-serve customers, that considers the entire value chain rather than just the front or back ends, is the key to delivering the right value proposition to customers and the factor that will truly differentiate companies in the future.

Reference

Dull, S. F. et al. (2001), 'How much are Customer Relationship Capabilities really worth? What every CEO should know', Accenture White Paper.

1.6 The impact of pricing on supply chains

Greg Cudahy

Most traditional supply chain theory focuses on reducing costs and increasing asset productivity.

Virtually all supply chain professionals have been educated and directed to address a simple business paradigm: forecast customer demand; plan inbound supply, production and distribution; and fulfill demand by executing against the supply plan. In recent years, event management technologies have been introduced that allow individual companies and, in theory, the entire supply chain to be more responsive by identifying supply–demand imbalances and execution problems and focusing management attention on these difficulties.

Yet, despite this added technology, unexpected demand peaks or valleys have typically been addressed through one or both types of capacity available to the supply chain professional: production assets or inventory. Most supply chain theory, and the technology that supports it, focuses on reducing the costs of responding to these unexpected demand transients and increasing the productivity of the assets used across the supply chain – while maintaining revenue generation.

Unfortunately, using only these two levers to address unexpected demand swings has its limitations. Inventory and productive capacity can only be ramped up or down so fast. This is particularly true as we enter a truly global economy where goods are frequently produced far from their ultimate point of consumption. Furthermore, even where the physical capability exists to respond to unexpected short-term demand swings, the cost may be prohibitive or the risk to customer satisfaction may be exceptionally high. This shortcoming of traditional supply chain theory and practice is becoming ever more apparent as companies deploy more sophisticated supply-side technologies and economic and competitive pressures become that much more stringent.

The future of strategy and execution lies in combining price optimization with new supply chain management tools.

The solution to this problem is the future of supply chain strategy and execution in the 21st century: bringing together the two historically separate disciplines of demand influence and demand responsiveness. The field of pricing and revenue optimization (PRO) is being combined with traditional and emerging supply chain management techniques to create an entirely new management space, with breakthrough value opportunities across a variety of industries.

In this chapter, we will define this management domain, known as enterprise profit optimization (EPO), and provide practical case examples. In addition, the chapter will discuss how adding a third value lever – revenue enhancement – to the long-established value levers of cost reduction and asset productivity drives significantly increased shareholder value.

The promise of enterprise profit optimization

The logic and aim of EPO is easy to describe: the simultaneous optimization of the supply and demand sides of a business. In a sense, the long history of performance improvements at different points along the value chain have always been moving toward this goal implicitly – the maximizing of the return from assets through end-to-end optimization. The development and continued evolution of supply chain management solutions has provided the means for pulling the supply side value lever. The advent of pricing and revenue optimization solutions has provided the means for pulling the demand side value lever. Now, their convergence in enterprise profit optimization is helping companies drive profitable growth through the simultaneous optimization of the supply-side and demand-side functions – both within a company and throughout its trading network.

EPO is driving profit growth through the convergence of supply- and demand-side solutions.

Combining the proven power of cost reduction solutions with the revolutionary breakthroughs of emerging pricing and revenue optimization tools, EPO integrates disparate parts of the value chain, helping companies improve operational efficiency and achieve profitable growth simultaneously. EPO looks across the entire enterprise to enhance profitability. When mismatches of supply and demand occur – as they always do – they should not be viewed strictly as a supply chain problem or a pricing problem, but rather as an opportunity for EPO.

How EPO evolved

To understand the full potential of EPO, it is helpful to understand how it is evolving from the convergence of cutting-edge supply chain management techniques and new methods for pricing optimization. The story of supply chain management needs little retelling. Using successive generations of information technology, manufacturing and operations executives cut costs, reduced cycle times, enhanced manufacturing efficiency, brought ever-higher levels of service to customers and made mass customization a reality.

Innovative technologies are giving companies the global visibility and clarity needed to make intelligent decisions.

With the advent of the Internet, managers applied these technologies to make both intra- and inter-enterprise manufacturing more efficient. In addition, by using Internet-based collaboration technologies, companies could interact with their suppliers, customers and other trading partners more effectively.

Today, innovative technologies are linking trading partners via the Internet and transforming linear supply chains into intelligent marketplaces. By adding intelligence to forecast sharing, procurement, order fulfilment, trading partner analytics, and logistics, and by enabling real-time collaboration, these solutions give a company's trading network the global visibility and clarity needed to make intelligent decisions.

The story of pricing and revenue optimization is less familiar. Using advanced mathematical algorithms, PRO techniques apply differential pricing strategies and the smart allocation of capacity in order to match supply with demand. The primary goal is to maximize revenue and profits from available capacity and assets. By segmenting the market and predicting the buying behavior of each segment, PRO determines what differing segments are willing to pay for what goods or services and optimizes pricing and product availability accordingly.

Airlines have been employing these techniques for years. Following airline deregulation in the United States in 1979, airlines were forced into a world of unrestricted competition and fare wars. To survive, leading airlines developed and refined 'yield management' – the practice of deciding how many seats to sell at what prices and when. 'Yield management' soon became 'revenue management,' with the sharper focus on revenues that the change in terminology suggests.

The US airline industry doubled seating and cut costs by one third using PRO techniques.

Using historical sales information to allocate some seats to price-sensitive, low-paying leisure travellers, while holding others for time-sensitive, high-paying business travelers, airlines continually aim to produce the optimal product mix of variously priced seats. In this way, they squeeze the highest possible revenue from the fixed capacity of each airline flight. Widespread use of these techniques has produced dramatic improvements throughout the industry. In 1984, US airlines sold only 60 per cent of their seats. By 1998, passengers filled more than 71 per cent of all seats, the highest occupancy rate for US carriers since the 1940s. During that time, airlines doubled seating capacity and cut the cost of air travel by one third.

Recent years have brought further significant advances. Information technology has continually improved demand forecasting – an essential element of revenue management. A far more dynamic marketplace, including the world of e-commerce, in which prices can be adjusted instantaneously, has brought new flexibility to pricing. Most recently, new and ever more mathematically sophisticated software applications have made it possible to optimize prices in order to balance the likelihood of winning business with maximum contribution to profit. Therefore, 'pricing and revenue management' has become 'pricing and revenue optimization', reflecting these powerful new advances.

From airlines, PRO spread to other reservation industries such as hotels, car rentals and cruise lines, producing impressive gains in revenue and profits. More recently, non-reservation industries such as electronics manufacturing and distribution, express package delivery, telecommunications and broadcasting have used PRO to enhance profits quickly. PRO is now spreading to manufacturing industries such as automotive, office equipment, durables and industrial equipment.

Influencing demand: a primer for the supply chain professional

Improved management of pricing and margins is one of the fastest and most cost-effective way to increase profits. That was the conclusion of a pioneering study by McKinsey & Company as long ago as 1992 in the *Harvard Business Review*. Examining the economics of more than 2400 companies, Harn *et al* (1992) concluded that a 1 per cent improvement in price creates an improvement in operating profit of 11.1 per cent. By contrast, 1 per cent improvements in variable cost, volume and fixed cost produce profit increases of 7.8 per cent, 3.3 per cent and 2.3 per cent respectively. As the McKinsey researchers note, given the enormous gains in profit from even the smallest gains in price, there is no company that cannot improve.

New PRO technology has the potential to increase revenue by between 4 and 8 per cent annually.

Yet, organizations have often neglected this clear path to growth. The value of pricing and margins was misunderstood, the data requirements appeared overwhelming and the tools for effectively managing such a path did not exist. Now, however, a new generation of packaged software has moved PRO from the realm of largely customized solutions to become the next widely available 'killer application'. In fact, it is estimated that this new PRO technology has the potential to generate revenue increases of between 4 and 8 per cent annually.

The PRO process

Introducing a pricing and revenue optimization system involves four basic steps:

PRO is not about competing on price – it is about maximizing value from products and capacity.

Step 1. Segmenting the market. Using historical transaction data, a company develops statistically relevant micro-market segmentation based on customer buying behaviors.

Step 2. Calculating customer demand. Powerful pricing software predicts how a customer or micro-segment will respond to products and prices based on the current state of the market and other conditions.

Step 3. Optimizing prices. Based on the predicted customer response, the PRO systems determine which prices to offer to which customers for each product through each channel in order to maximize a particular profit objective, market share or other strategic goals. It recommends the optimum prices – not the lowest prices – to achieve these goals.

Step 4. Recalibrating prices. Based on the actual results of optimization actions, the system continually recalibrates forecasting and optimization models.

Once such a system becomes part of a company's operations, ongoing price targeting helps to maximize its revenues. As introducing a PRO system does not require changes to the company's asset base, the cost of implementation is minimized and the majority of savings become profit.

It is important to understand that pricing and revenue optimization is not about competing on price – it is about extracting the maximum value from a company's products and capacity. In fact, for companies weary of the death-spiral of cut-throat price competition, PRO can provide a way out. The key lies in understanding where and how to pull the price levers to realize the gains available through the fine tuning of pricing to customer buying behaviors.

Addressing specific pricing challenges

PRO solutions can address critical pricing challenges such as list pricing, customized price quotes and promotion and incentive pricing. In all these challenges, the aim is to ensure that the right products are

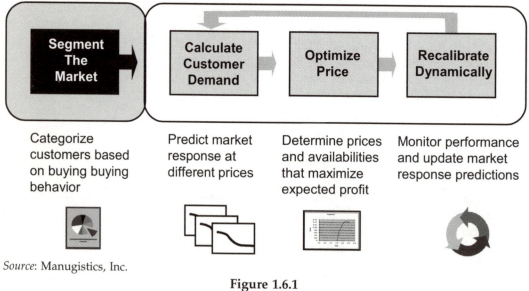

Source: Manugistics, Inc.

Figure 1.6.1
The four-step PRO process

offered to the right customers, through the right channels, at the right price in order to maximize profit or achieve other strategic goals. When these specific solutions are combined with supply chain management solutions, the result is simultaneous and reciprocal optimization of the demand and supply side of the supply chain.

Price list optimization

In any setting where prices can be changed in response to market conditions, intelligently managing price lists offers a rich opportunity for increasing revenues and maximizing profits. However, it is no easy task. Managers must factor in numerous complex variables – product availability, shifting demand, competitor price reactions, production costs, market share objectives, customer buying behavior and other conditions. Moreover, they must do it on a monthly, weekly or even daily basis for different products, customer segments and distribution channels.

PRO solutions for price list optimization calculate optimum prices that reflect and exploit the changing conditions of markets, distribution channels and customer segments, as well as the changing conditions of inventory and production capacity. The solutions can handle such calculations for thousands of products and update prices daily, if desired.

Price list solutions calculate optimum prices based on market conditions and internal inventory and capacity.

Drawing on immediate information about market conditions and internal inventory and capacity, such solutions use advanced statistical and mathematical models to adjust prices continually and rigorously. In doing so, the solutions help companies to:

- respond to changing customer demand – adjusting for seasonal purchasing patterns, introduction of competing products or other influences
- respond to changes in product availability – increasing prices for company- or industry-constrained products, reducing prices in anticipation of possible oversupply, and avoiding expensive 'fire sales' of distressed inventory
- meet and beat competition – ensuring that potential competitive threats are considered in all pricing recommendations
- meet strategic objectives – considering sales and margin targets or other goals in select pricing actions
- maximize return over product life cycles – adjusting prices to reflect new product market strength, product maturity or perishability
- capitalize on market segment differences – optimizing price based on unique price elasticity and brand premium for multiple customer segments and
- coordinate channel prices – customizing prices through different channels to reflect differences in cost-to-serve, market preference and volume or margin limitations of each channel while achieving strategic distribution goals for each channel.

By leveraging actual sales and transaction data, such solutions help to develop pricing strategies for products, customers and market segments that maximize profit in a repeatable, objective manner that is easy to validate and monitor.

Frequent and accurate supply chain inputs can enable enterprise profit optimization.

With frequent and accurate inputs from supply chain applications, price list optimization can then move into the realm of enterprise profit optimization. Such supply chain inputs enable the pricing solution to determine optimal prices more precisely, based on product availability. In turn, predictions of sales volumes become key inputs for increasing the accuracy of supply chain planning. The entire organization is unified around the common goal of offering the right products to the right customers, through the right channels and at the right price.

Price quotation optimization

PRO solutions set the optimum price for a quote by predicting the customer's response.

Few decisions are as complex as optimally pricing bids. The customized quotation must include just the right combination of products, options, and services, while generating an attractive profit. In addition, it must take into account the trade-off between maximizing profit and winning the maximum number of deals. Getting those complex calculations right can significantly increase revenue and profits. Getting them wrong can reduce the profitability of the contract or the chances of winning the business in the first place.

Unfortunately, few companies have reliable, repeatable methods for developing optimal quotes. In pricing contracts, companies typically set prices using fixed margins or some combination of static market guidelines. Using those guidelines, salespeople often discount inconsistently or rely on guesswork, rather than mathematical algorithms, to determine individual customer prices. Despite the best of intentions, tens of millions of dollars are lost daily due to such unsupported pricing decisions.

For customized price quotations, PRO solutions set the optimum price for a quote by predicting what the customer's response to that tender will be. Advanced statistical methods are used to strike the right balance between the probability of winning the bid and its total contribution to profit.

Pricing low will increase the chances of winning the deal, but delivers little or no profit. Conversely, pricing high will ensure that the deal is profitable, but the chances of winning in a competitive market will be reduced. Price quotation optimization helps identify the point where profitability and the win rate are in the desired balance. For each custom quotation, the solution systematically integrates market information cost information, and customer information, as well as other variables, to determine the target price – the most effective price for optimizing profitability.

Price quotation optimization can also operate at the portfolio level to help to ensure that each individual product or service in the portfolio is both competitively and profitably priced. The probability of winning the business and the profitability of the complete set of products and services in each deal can also be determined. The profit contribution of each individual product and service is traded off to establish a win probability and predicted profitability for the entire deal.

Price quotation optimization can also build strategic objectives such as market share growth, profit targets or production capacity utilization into the calculation of the target price. For example, it can establish what it may cost to 'buy' market share by pricing lower, or how a 'skim' pricing strategy could result in a predictably lower deal win rate and market share.

In developing customized price quotations, it is also crucial to remember that not all customers value the same bundle of products or services equally – some will pay less, others more. Price quotation optimization gauges a customer's willingness to pay, segmenting the market along such dimensions as customer type, size, product category, current supplier, region and many other statistically significant variables. Using this segmentation, it forecasts the market response to price changes for each important market segment – before a price quotation is submitted to a potential customer. This market response capability not only captures the price sensitivity for each segment, but also captures the brand preference given to products in a given bidding situation. The solution sets optimal prices for each deal to maximize the probability-weighted profit.

Price quotation optimization captures the price sensitivity and brand preference for each customer segment.

At the time of a quotation, it is necessary not only to provide a price but also to promise delivery. Price quotation optimization can be used with supply chain 'commit' applications to ensure that a company makes promises it can keep – profitably. Such supply chain applications help to provide accurate, reliable, real-time promises to customer requests by performing a comprehensive availability check of inventory, production, materials, manufacturing scheduling, distribution and transportation and then immediately allocating resources consistent with strategic goals. In addition, if the supply chain tool can check configuration, substitution and delivery alternatives, it is possible to respond immediately to customer requests, boosting customer loyalty while optimizing supply chain allocation.

Price quotation optimization can also be used in conjunction with supply chain planning, demand and strategy software to help to ensure that supply chain planning and optimization are based on accurate demand forecasts. In arriving at optimal customized bid prices, price quotation optimization generates a probability-weighted demand forecast – product volume multiplied by the probability of winning the business – that can then be fed into supply chain applications. Such timely, statistically sophisticated information is crucial for matching supply with demand, making optimal trading network and design decisions, and maintaining an enterprise-wide plan for the business.

Profitable promotions management

Few companies can predict the effectiveness of their promotional spending.

To generate incremental revenue or expand market share, companies spend hundreds of billions of dollars annually in promotional discounts, rebates, cash incentives and subsidized financing. Most of those companies operate in a complex pricing environment, with numerous promotional campaigns targeting a range of products and multiple segments and channels. Not surprisingly, few companies are able to predict accurately the overall effectiveness of their promotional spending.

PRO promotions management solutions forecast the result of a promotion program before committing to a promotional strategy. They test promotional scenarios and forecast results to help companies to develop and target effective promotions for each product, customer segment and distribution channel. Such solutions are designed to determine an optimal allocation of promotion and incentive dollars to help enhance profitability, while simultaneously meeting such strategic objectives as protecting or expanding market share, entering new markets or rewarding valued customers.

PRO solutions can forecast increases in sales volume and revenue, enabling an optimal promotions strategy.

Using historical data and market response models, a strategy tester enables analysts to explore any promotional pricing scenario and forecast its expected outcome. It can model various promotional campaign alternatives, factoring in customer price elasticities, competitive response, inventory availability and strategic objectives. By forecasting which promotion will generate the largest increases in sales volume and incremental revenues and best achieve strategic objectives, it can help enable an optimal promotional strategy.

To determine an optimal promotional offer, an analyst develops and defines 'what-if?' promotion scenarios. Using historical data and market response models, the strategy tester then compares the various scenarios by:

- calculating incremental profit and revenue and associated cost for various promotion alternatives
- predicting promotional impact on virtually any combination of promotion types, targeted products, segments, and channels
- identifying the impact of promotions on inventory, and
- measuring cross-product cannibalization and cross-channel dilution.

These calculations enable the analyst to select easily the most effective promotion for meeting specific business objectives. Once the promotional campaign is under way, results are fed back into the system to help to fine-tune future campaigns.

PRO promotions solutions can provide information on incremental demand from promotional activities to supply chain management applications in order to coordinate supply and demand planning better. Such coordination can act as an early warning system, predicting future demand and alerting executives to supply chain problems, such as oversupply, that might be addressed by a promotional program. The optimal promotion can then be combined with the baseline forecast to drive supply-planning optimization, helping match supply with demand in a more cost-efficient manner. By unifying promotions planning with supply chain optimization in a continuous loop, it is possible to achieve an ever tighter and more efficient synergy that simultaneously helps to enhance profitability and reduce cost.

Beyond supply chain improvement

Historically, demand has been treated by supply chain executives as a given that the supply chain should fulfill as effectively as possible. Supply chain initiatives usually aimed to cut costs and improve customer service. While this approach produced significant gains in supply chain efficiency across many industries, it is inherently limited by its disconnection from the demand side of the business. Powered by the new ability of PRO to influence demand, supply chain improvement can move beyond its inherent limitation and toward simultaneous optimization of prices, revenues and supply chain cost.

PRO is powering companies to optimize simultaneously for prices and supply chain costs.

The unique potential of PRO helps companies to answer difficult questions on price, capacity and profits.

Broadly, enterprise profit optimization can improve supply chain efficiency through four iterative steps:

Optimizing prices

Using powerful pricing optimization applications and techniques, a company can determine the optimal prices at which to sell its products and services. This optimization may be done quarterly, monthly, weekly, nightly, or even on an order-by-order basis. The company may also generate only one price for each product or decide to generate prices for each channel, order type (such as large versus small, guaranteed versus non-guaranteed) or customer segment.

Optimal prices are based on a variety of appropriately weighted factors in a complex environment, including demand, price sensitivity, competitive threat, costs and strategic objectives. In addition, pricing can now take into account the latest information about inventory position and available product capacity, which is provided from the operational side of the company through supply chain applications. Thus, in the initial pricing optimization, EPO simultaneously harnesses both demand and supply information and converts it into insight to enhance profit on both sides of the supply/demand equation.

Stimulating desired demand

Through offline and online selling channels, the optimal prices are communicated to the market, converting the predicted demand into confirmed orders at the desired margin, revenue or market share targets established during the price optimization.

Optimizing fulfilment

The confirmed orders are captured and routed through the fulfilment system, where supply chain applications optimize manufacturing, supply and transport. Customer commitments are fulfilled in the most efficient, cost-effective manner. Of course, this is the objective of any well-run supply chain. However, in an EPO environment, the resulting efficiency and profitability at this stage have already been enhanced by the initial inclusion of supply chain information in determining optimal prices.

Reoptimizing prices

As transactions occur and orders are delivered, the results are used to update the underlying forecasts and price sensitivity parameters while the latest product availability and cost information from the supply side are fed back into the system.

The cycle begins all over again with the reoptimization of prices and another cycle of optimizing profitability across the entire enterprise.

The potential for enterprise profit optimization to optimize prices and supply chain processes simultaneously provides many unique capabilities. For example, it enables a company to answer such questions as:

- How should we price our products to make best use of our manufacturing capacity, raw materials, storage and distribution capabilities?
- What is the optimal price at which we should commit to an order? And at what price should we be willing to walk away from the business?
- What is the most profitable method of fulfilling the order?
- Should we delay or reject an order in anticipation of more profitable future customers?
- How should we price contracts for large customers, large suppliers and other trading partners – balancing those commitments against our capacity and other commitments?
- What is the least expensive way of stimulating demand when sales are lagging (for example, below plan or when a competitor has reduced its price) or specific sales objectives must be met (for example, end of quarter) or the pipeline cleared (for example, for a new product introduction)?
- What is the optimum range for negotiating a profitable price? and
- How should our prices be adjusted for specific strategic objectives such as market share targets, competitor positioning, Wall Street expectations and other goals?

All companies want to increase efficiency, reduce costs, increase profits and deliver customer satisfaction. By tightly integrating pricing actions and supply chain actions, EPO provides companies with the tools they require to achieve those goals quickly and effectively. Such companies gain the ability to:

- maximize revenue from existing inventory
- maximize revenue opportunity on excess inventory
- stimulate demand to maximize throughput consistently
- enhance margin across the network
- enhance profit across channels and segments
- manage product life cycles effectively
- respond rapidly to competitor actions
- respond rapidly to changes in market demand
- reflect strategic objectives such as increasing market share, protecting market share and maintaining brand image, and
- improve supply chain efficiency by smoothing demand through pricing.

Case studies

Automaker uses PRO to enhance revenue
One of the largest automobile manufacturers in the world sells millions of units annually to commercial fleet customers in North America. Traditionally, the company fuelled its sales and profits by running assembly lines near capacity for its most profitable automobiles. Until recently, the automaker negotiated incentives or competitive price allowances customer by customer. However, the company lacked a systematic process for targeting and consistently pricing across its commercial fleet business. The challenge was to win as much commercial business as possible, while maintaining appropriate profit margins and reinforcing strategic goals.

The company implemented a software solution for pricing and revenue optimization to manage competitive price allowances for its commercial fleet sales business. By predicting how each customer would react at a given price point in a given situation, the solution created more revenue from existing and future customers and helped companies to win more customers and increase profit margins.

Using advanced statistical methods to strike a balance between the probability of winning the business and its total contribution to profit, the software systematically integrated market information, cost information, customer information and other variables to determine optimal pricing recommendations. The PRO solution is forecast to provide an annual increase of 3 to 5 per cent of North American fleet sales. As most of the benefits flow directly to the bottom line, the increase in revenue will have a larger corresponding impact on profit.

Price quotation optimization in express package delivery

One of the world's leading express package delivery companies must evaluate more than 100 000 commercial contracts per year. To each of these customers, the company offers a price for a mixture of package delivery services at a forecasted volume. Customers come in all shapes and sizes – from 'Mom and Pop' operations to the largest corporations in the world. Each customer expects a customized pricing structure and each varies in ways that dramatically affect the profitability of a contract.

Historically, the sales force submitted contracts, based on a fixed rate table, to the local, regional or corporate sales offices. Bids were calculated using general guidelines, but neither the company nor the industry could determine how changing the profit margin as little as 1 per cent might influence the likelihood of winning the bid. It was equally difficult to determine which contract offers were profitable and which were not. In an increasingly complex marketplace, where profitability was more important than ever, the company implemented a price quotation system that helped to maximize the probability of winning bids, while supporting strategic goals, enhancing customer loyalty and maintaining profit margins.

The solution's sophisticated statistical methodology, as well as its ability to incorporate price and non-price objectives into calculations, has allowed the company to:

- calculate the cost of serving each customer or market segment
- assess accurately the profit impact of each potential contract
- find the desired balance between market share and profit margin
- capture win/loss and competitive pricing information to refine future bids
- achieve more cost-effective customized pricing and
- redefine sales productivity measures.

The company can now forecast what bid price will achieve the company's strategic and profit objectives. In addition, the company can take even greater advantage of the specialized customer knowledge of account executives; and the executives are free to offer discounts within fixed margins. As the results of every bid are fed back into the pricing model, the company also improves its chances of winning the next contract.

By striking a balance between the likelihood of winning a contract and attaining the largest profit margin, PRO has helped the company remain profitable, hold the line on prices and increase sales. As a result, the company has been able to:

- streamline the bid process
- increase customer and sales force satisfaction

- increase revenue by three to five per cent, and
- anticipate increased profits of several hundred million dollars per year.

Conclusion

As cost improvements become harder to find, today's overriding business challenge is to find profitable ways to drive top-line growth and improve bottom-line performance. Enterprise profit optimization addresses both sides of the equation simultaneously. Companies that adopt this revolutionary approach will gain operational, organizational and strategic benefits that will be hard for their competition to match.

Companies that simultaneously optimize demand and supply will discover a powerful new source of value.

Operationally, such companies can regularly and consistently apply assets and resources toward increasing revenue. Organizationally, they can become much more responsive to customers. Strategically, they can maintain and extend their position by increasing their ability to deliver quality products by rapidly responding to changes in demand and to competitor initiatives. By driving unprecedented returns through the simultaneous optimization of the demand-side and supply-side of their enterprises, these companies will lead the way to this powerful new means of value creation.

Reference

Harn, M.V. and Rosiello, R. (1992), 'Managing Price, Gaining Profit', *Harvard Business Review* (September–October), pp. 84–94.

1.7 Trading terms and customer account profitability

Cameron H. Hall

Determining the commercial terms of business relationships.

During the 1990s, many organizations successfully reduced their cost structures. Senior managers implemented initiatives such as business process re-engineering, shared services organizations and the outsourcing of non-core activities to improve their efficiency and effectiveness. Their success has led to debate about whether single organizations have any scope left to reduce costs. Today, companies are seeking value through focusing on the relationship between trading partners. Trading relationships can be both operational and commercial, and cost control opportunities exist within both.

Operationally, a major step forward in constraining costs and increasing effectiveness lies in the ability to reduce costs involved in the inter-enterprise supply chains. However, companies have tempered their enthusiasm for this source of cost control with the recognition that all parties in the supply chain must share in the benefits. Some organizations are inevitably more advanced in their approach to operational improvement and are able to extract greater benefit. Commercially, trading partners are seeking to have an impact on the net price paid for goods and services, most often through putting pressure on the trading terms for purchases. Where an imbalance of power exists between a buyer and seller, trading terms can reflect margin erosion and, most often, the erosion occurs within the seller or the supplier.

Understanding the cost-to-serve is the first step in managing a profitable trading relationship.

Given these trends, companies that understand the true costs associated with serving each customer are at a strategic advantage over their competitors. The suppliers who can incorporate their understanding of the cost-to-serve into their commercial relationship with their customers are better positioned to manage their customers to achieve profits. Achieving this advantage is not easy. The challenge for suppliers is to develop a customer profitability mechanism that captures and reports discrete costs of doing business that can be integrated into the regular price and trade terms negotiations. To achieve this, the supplier must understand the underlying drivers of customer cost and develop a means to measure the outcomes. The supplier must develop and embed in the organization an approach to negotiate, monitor, measure and report the agreed costs to enable proactive action if required. Suppliers must recognize that the owners of costs, driven by customer behavior, may not be those who traditionally manage customer accounts. The impact of supply chain-related costs on customer profitability requires a broad perspective in the management of customers for profitability.

Understanding cost drivers using activity-based costing

ABC analysis approach

The first step required to incorporate customer account profitability information into the trade terms between businesses is to understand the profitability of the customer. To accomplish the breakdown of the financials, activity-based costing (ABC) is required. For many years, managers have used ABC to develop a better understanding of product costs. The application of ABC has also evolved into a management approach designed to understand the costs of an organization. This evolution can be seen in three stages:

An ABC analysis breaks down the financial and cost structure.

Stage one was the allocation of resource (cost) to products based on headcount. In manufacturing environments, accountants traditionally allocated the overhead costs such as supervisory, quality control, engineering and maintenance to the firm's products, using a single arbitrary allocation basis such as direct labor hours. This was an appropriate approach when direct labor costs comprised the majority of expenditures and indirect costs were a minor expense.

Stage two was the allocation of resource (cost) to products based on activities. ABC uses a two-step process to achieve this: identifying the resources consumed by activities and identifying the activities consumed by the products.

Stage three in the evolution of ABC was a derivation of the second. This was where the resources are allocated to products and customers based on activities driven by customers and consumed by products. The result is a cost per product per customer. As ABC matured, supply chain practitioners found that not only did ABC provide more accurate cost and profitability measurement, but the activity information is useful for understanding processes as well. This led to the development of the process view or activity-based management.

The analysis of all costs associated with the customer must start with the process of managing the customer, a process that has two parts. First, the business must manage the customer relationship. Companies can use a framework (plan, execute and evaluate) to guide the

Costs are analyzed on a strategic and relationship level as well as on an operational level.

management of the customer towards predetermined objectives. The typical style adopted by the customer relationship manager includes a strategic and relationship focus. An example of this process exists in the Australian Fast Moving Consumer Goods (FMCG) industry where a manufacturer conducts regular 'category team' meetings. The functions represented at these meetings include Sales, Manufacturing, Distribution, Marketing, Finance and New Product Development. Input from each function results in a common and understood plan for the category. One of the objectives of this process is to develop customer management plans within the context of the category. One member (the representative from Sales) is charged with the coordination of the plan with the customer using input from other team members (such as manufacturing and distribution). At the end of a predetermined period, the group evaluates performance against the original plan. Second, managers must understand the operational process involved in customer orders being received, accepted and delivered against. In another example, the department responsible for capturing customer orders for despatch is also responsible for the measurement of compliance to certain terms such as 'quantity buying'. As part of this approach, the processes for demand fulfilment are documented and communicated to the sales function and eventually to the customer. This helps communicate the cost impact associated with non-compliance by the customer.

To understand the relevant costs applicable to a given customer, businesses should document the steps in these processes, the people involved, the technology and the assets used. This analysis must include the exceptions to the process caused by certain customer behavior. These must also be costed. Using the process approach will allow supply chain managers to choose which processes and behaviors they seek to encourage and those they want discouraged. It also enables managers to identify the relative scale of the costs for each process.

Tools and techniques

At all times during the analysis, the level of detail should be considered. Excessive levels of detail caused many ABC exercises to fail in the past, stalling the program and demotivating the people involved. The business should see the benefits from any analytical project within a reasonable timeframe in order to justify the investment. A good 'rule of thumb' on the appropriate level of detail is that if managers are 80 per cent confident that the detail is sufficient to achieve the results, then going into greater depth will result in diminishing returns.

For many businesses, ABC can still be done on spreadsheets for one-time only studies. Over time, 'best-of-breed' software vendors have developed software with improved functionality. Applications have approached ongoing systems, but usually with quarterly reporting frequencies. Managers have found developing ABC systems difficult due to the number of data sources and the effort required collecting and managing the data.

During the last few years, the focus of software providers has turned to the integration of their software to existing systems. Recently, enterprise resource planning (ERP) vendors have also entered the market. The specialist software vendors still have a functionality advantage, while the ERP packages also offer better integration to core financials and operational systems. Both software vendor types offer a practical solution for understanding multi-dimensional cost and account profitability across the enterprise. Importantly, the decision to use software or spreadsheets will depend on the complexity of the business, its customer landscape, the capabilities of personnel and the desire to use the analysis in an ongoing fashion, perhaps for uses other than the redesign of trading terms.

Not only does the analysis of customer account profitability provide the answer to many questions regarding profitability, but it also creates a solid foundation for the management of trading terms with customers. Without ABC in place, firms will find it difficult to create corporate governance models using balanced scorecards, and other performance measurement and accountability techniques. As well, forecasts, budgets and long-term plans will be much more realistic with the understanding provided by ABC.

Developing a measurement approach

Select the appropriate measures

The incorporation of cost-to-serve into trading terms is a sound principle for supply chain managers to adopt. In general, the management teams of the highest performing companies allocate funds to the opportunities that offer the highest possible shareholder returns in the long term. These managers control the allocation of funds because they can identify where and how the funds are spent and located. They typically know which sales opportunities are the best from a margin perspective and which might appear sound but consume too many resources.

Selecting the appropriate measurement approach has to consider diverse factors.

An understanding of these high-resource consuming customers is a critical component to align the terms of trading successfully with account profitability. The subtlety exists when determining the extent to which management time is consumed in measuring the details of cost. Managers can expend significant time and effort on creating a raft of measures in extraordinary detail using the most sophisticated tools available. Alternatively, they can select one or two key measures deemed to be a fair representation of true cost and collect them manually. The approach depends on the reliability of the information collected, its likelihood of significant change over time and the likely impact on the final terms outcome, as discussed below. The impact on the terms outcomes is derived from the ability to implement the desired outcome, the ability of the customer to influence the measure and the scale of the data collected.

Reliability of information

Information reliability is critical in determining what measures to select. During the 1990s many Australian corporations invested in ERP systems. One of the benefits of these systems includes the ability to generate increased reliability in management information. Many ERP systems impose a discipline on personnel charged with data entry. This has resulted in an increase in the reliability of data.

Stability of cost structures

Managers should take into account the likelihood of a change in the structure and nature of costs when selecting measures. A stable cost profile is more likely to result in measures that will be applicable for some time. An unstable cost structure that can result from acquisition, growth, competition or significant industry change will typically require a more frequent evaluation of the measures. However, if the structure is not likely to change over the course of the period of the trading terms, then additional assessment and review will not be required.

Considering customer capabilities

The ability to implement the trading terms outcomes must be considered. Investing in measuring certain cost factors is not pragmatic for companies if their use will be limited to internal reporting. The measures must be easily explainable to the customer, they must make sense to the customer, they must demonstrate equity in the evaluation of cost and they must be auditable. In many cases, customers will seek to conduct their own evaluation of the measure. This should be encouraged if the measure is deemed as non-sensitive from a commercial perspective by the supplier's management team.

Supply chain managers should also keep in mind that the measure must be something that the customer can influence in their trading relationship with the supplier. If customers cannot influence the measure then it will be difficult to convince them to align the trading terms structure to it. Managers should consider the degree of difficulty for the customer to implement any changes required to improve the results of the selected measure. They should consider the likely cost borne by the customer in influencing the results of the measures selected. Finally, the timeframe required to make a change must also be taken into account. If the cycle takes many months to change the results of a performance measure, it will have limited impact on the motivation of the customer to do so. Ideally, the best measures should be easily influenced by the customer at no explicit cost, within a timeframe of less than one month.

Dependability of measurement

The scale of the impact must be considered. While the sum total of all cost drivers has an impact on the total cost-to-serve of a customer, the parts must be considered separately when selecting measures for input into trading terms. The measure should be a stand-alone metric. As such it should be of sufficient size to make a visible impact on the trade terms between the businesses. For example, the cost of handling a manual order (say $100) might amount to one hundred times that of an electronic order (say $1). The annual number of manual orders placed (say weekly, to 52) might amount to a significant number when compared to the automatic order. But if the average order size is large, say $550,000 for a $28 million per year customer, then the method of order handling becomes less relevant, at 0.018 per cent of sales.

Critical success factors in using cost drivers to negotiate terms

The analysis of cost drivers and the development of measures is an essential element on developing terms linked to account profitability. However, the discipline of embedding the analysis and measures into the terms negotiation process is an essential element. This is the part of the process where many organizations fail. Managers can apply some critical success factors to reduce the risk of failure in this endeavor.

To implement requires strong leadership, diversity and cross-functional skills.

Executive leadership

The leadership of senior managers is the most critical success factor in embedding cost drivers into trading terms. The nature of pricing between businesses is a critical component in the determination of shareholder value. Typically, a small number of customers may combine to make up a large proportion of total sales revenue. A loss of a customer could be catastrophic in terms of profit stability. Reduced margin from a customer can also be severely detrimental to the stability of profit.

In most cases, the most appropriate level of management involvement is the most senior manager (managing director or chief executive officer). Without this level of management commitment to the process, it will find difficulty in gaining the appropriate level of management priority. The leadership displayed by the senior executive must also be highly visible internally and demonstrate a willingness to act decisively. This will encourage the best results from the process of embedding change in the negotiation cycle.

Cross-functional teams

In large organizations, the 'ownership' of the trading terms often resides with a single group. The function charged with sales performance is often the group that controls the terms negotiation with customers. In most organizations, the sales function is charged with this responsibility. The sales division often contains personnel charged with conducting numerical analysis of various customer-related metrics, ranging from sales forecasting through to cost analysis. Terms that reflect true cost-to-serve will often contain costs outside the scope of the sales area. The collection and analysis of such costs can become an inhibitor in the collection and incorporation of them into the terms negotiation process. Therefore, the team with control over the terms must be convinced of the rationale for incorporating cost drivers into the terms.

Difficulties can arise in achieving this. The performance metrics of the sales team can preclude cost factors outside the control of the sales function. Indeed, sometimes a high-revenue customer might also be a high-cost customer. To introduce terms that reflect the high-cost nature of the business might even run counter to the objectives set for the sales division. It is critical that the objectives of the sales group are aligned with achievement of true customer profitability. Measures and objectives will need to be changed to reflect this. Once the sales division is committed to the rationale for terms that reflect customer profitability, then the framework can be embedded into the negotiation process.

Diverse skill requirements

A broad range of personnel needs to be involved in the redesign of terms. The activity requires analytical skills, legal knowledge, supply chain knowledge and finance and negotiation skills. Also, a healthy dose of pragmatism is required to ensure that the process does not stall. Careful selection of functional representatives must consider not only skills but, in larger organizations, a perception of equitable functional representation. The process must include all planned communications and representations to the customer. Clearly, when redesigning trade terms, the nature of the relationship with the customer will dictate the degree of involvement due to the commercial sensitivity. Some corporations seek to involve customers intimately. Others have chosen to stop all high-level communication with customers during the process of redesigning the framework.

Usually the best result will be achieved from an intensive effort. Businesses often task small project teams with the responsibility for the redesign of trading terms according to cost drivers. The team should report to the senior executive as sponsor. The approval process should include some representation from the senior sales executives; however this should be balanced with representation from other senior functional representatives such as finance, supply chain, marketing and legal. An implementation trap can occur when the approval process is heavily weighted towards the sales executives.

Without changes to functional and even personal objectives, the 'approvers' can imprudently become the 'implementers'. The team tasked with the analysis and redesign need to address the question with rigorous guidelines and scope. The best results tend to come from teams that are small, focused, working full-time on the problem and are from the operational side of the business. Often large corporations tend to build centralized corporate teams for problem resolution; and these teams can lack credibility with the sales and supply chain personnel in the business.

Implement a trading terms framework

A new trading terms framework can be designed from 'first principles'. This approach starts with the development of a set of guiding principles. The current trading terms can be disregarded except for regulatory constraints and a new approach devised. This approach is often required when incumbent trading terms structures fail to account for cost-to-serve. This approach is relevant for businesses where management deems the current terms to have become unworkable, unstable and costly to the business.

New trading terms must be simple, easily communicated and monitored regularly.

Clearly, an evaluation of the current trading terms is essential to come to such a conclusion. This analysis should include an assessment of the degree of compliance to terms, their cost trend over previous years and the rationale for application of customers to specific levels. An alternative approach is to start with the incumbent trading terms framework and make alterations to it. This approach carries significant risk where the power in the trading relationship rests with the customer. Often it can result in the inclusion of an additional allowances or discounts without the commensurate reduction or elimination of another. The degree to which trading terms require an overhaul is a key management decision.

Choose simple measures

The measures developed must be incorporated into the new trading terms framework. The best results are achieved by choosing simple, unambiguous measures that can be easily shared with the customer. It is also imperative that a process is conducted to monitor the effectiveness of the measures. The means for doing this should be part of the project team's brief. The selection of appropriate personnel for this task is also an important step. Most often, an individual's job description of professional performance measures needs to change to reflect the new role. A feedback loop must exist to ensure rapid response to changes in customer behavior that affect the cost-to-serve. The feedback mechanism such as regular meetings, e-mail or memo is dependent on the culture of the organization.

Compliance limits should be established. These will set the scope for allowable deviation to agreed customer behaviors without a formal response by the supplier. For example, if a customer is granted a 5 per cent discount on the basis that 90 per cent of the orders received are in full-pallet configuration, then the supplier must decide on the non-compliance cut-off point for escalation of a problem. The escalation procedure should be defined to ensure the best possible result.

Regular reviews of terms

The management team need to decide on the frequency of review and the frequency of changes to the trading terms. However, these are often driven by the typical negotiation cycle. In many cases, the broader organization can be leveraged in the process of terms redesign. To do this can increase the focus and involvement in compliance monitoring. Furthermore, the supply chain function can often resolve a potential cost problem prior to escalation given the nature of the operational and often collaborative link to the customer. Indeed, failure to involve the supply chain function can result in failure to manage trading terms and customer account profitability, as the supply chain is expected to deliver the value created.

Most often, supply chain managers need to conduct all of this work simultaneously. The redesign of trading terms framework needs to drive the cost-to-serve, yet the cost-to-serve analysis is of little relevance if it is not actionable. The ability to reduce costs in the firm's supply chain will remain critical to sustainable performance. As businesses increasingly seek to collaborate in their supply chains, the ability to convert cost performance into commercial arrangements will become increasingly important. Businesses need to adopt a structured approach to the process of incorporating customer account profitability into trading terms frameworks and negotiations.

A case example

To illustrate the selection of an appropriate set of cost-to-serve measures, an example is the case of a large Australian FMCG company. The company, which supplies the grocery channel with food products from many distribution points, sought to develop a trading terms framework that was built on a cost-to-serve foundation. The method of distribution was warehouse-to-warehouse pallet units on road transport. Logistics cost would fluctuate if the method were unexpectedly altered due to some action by the customer.

For example, if a customer chose to place an order for less than a pallet of product, then handling costs would be incurred by the manufacturer. One of the measures selected was the percentage of cartons ordered in full-pallet configuration. The company had recently implemented a large-scale ERP system and was for the first time able to generate reliable logistics performance data in an automated fashion. The data produced used electronic data interchange (EDI) order information to generate a profile of a customer's order patterns.

The nature of the business was such that this handling cost would remain a significant component for the near future. The ability to use the measure was accepted as the cost-benefits were clear, compelling and easy to outline to a customer. The ability of the customer to influence the result was high. Notably, other measures such as ratio of full truck orders were rejected on this basis in the analysis. Finally, the scale of the impact was judged sufficient to incorporate into the trade terms framework.

Conclusion

Companies that can understand their cost-to-serve and build that into their commercial relationships with their customers are best positioned to achieve competitive advantage. Managers need to develop an appropriate measurement approach that reflects the nature of their trading relationships. Many factors should be considered; however perhaps of most critical importance is the ability of the customers to change their behaviours to reduce supply chain cost. Only then can the supplier make alterations to the commercial relationship that reflect the operational supply chain costs. Finally, in implementation, sustainable results are more likely from the use of simple measures, with compliance limits reviewed in line with the standard negotiation timeframe and the collaborative involvement of the supply chain management function.

Reference

Gattorna, J. L. and Walters, D. W. (1977), 'Customer Account Profitability – the Next problem for Physical Distribution Management', *Retail and Distribution Management*, vol. 5 (no. 3), May/June, pp. 49–52.

Part 2
Operational Excellence

With the increasing complexity of supply chains, it becomes even more important to make the right decision about establishing a physical network infrastructure and optimize its performance. Chapter 2.1, 'Supply chain network optimization modeling', introduces modeling methodologies and solutions as part of a comprehensive decision support system (DSS).

The following Chapter 2.2, 'Supply chain diagnostics', addresses the need for the supply chain to be assessed in a structured, disciplined way to identify actionable opportunities that will deliver sustainable improvements in performance. A basic diagnostic frame-work is introduced to facilitate results on an accelerated timeline compared to that of a more traditional assessment project.

Many product-oriented businesses have to get their manufacturing right, because it is where they have the most complexity, costs, assets and inertia. Promising manufacturing strategies emerge despite the isolation of manufacturing from the needs of customers and the rest of the business. Chapter 2.3, 'Manufacturing strategy for supply chains', elaborates on the new network environment where existing require-ments are the starting point and new network factors add further layers of complexity to the design task.

It is in manufacturing where Six Sigma had its roots and was transformed from a simple quality measurement tool to a breakthrough business excellence philosophy spanning the entire organization and beyond. Chapter 2.4, 'Six Sigma – improving the quality of business', describes four phases for improvement, each designed to find the drivers of measures that organizations care about and that they can control.

Outside the shopfloor, warehousing and distribution design, Chapter 2.5, 'Distribution operations – design for excellence', includes people, processes, equipment, information technology and facilities. The concepts for effective operations begin with creative thinking about solutions to operating challenges.

A company has to understand the vision for successfully managing transportation under an integrated, holistic strategy. Neglecting transportation management capabilities leads to significant operational inefficiencies. Chapter 2.6, 'Integrated transportation management', aims to introduce a new paradigm that recognizes the importance of transportation in the supply chain, from the viewpoints of both customer service and cost management.

Another area of supply chain operations is the management of demand and supply plans. Chapter 2.7, 'Forecasting and demand planning', discusses the challenges of accurate forecasting and planning and describes the effects of inadequate demand plans – poor service, excess inventory, poor production efficiency and increased costs.

Many may argue that inventories are undesirable and should be eliminated from the supply chain entirely. The fact remains that organizations require inventory in order to operate effectively, and ensure the smooth operation of their business on a day-to-day basis. Chapter 2.8, 'Inventory management', describes the tools and methods of effective inventory management. Case studies provide examples of companies that recognized the criticality of managing inventory and identified how inventory can improve both operational and financial performance.

Equipment vendors have long regarded after-sales service as a necessary evil at best. However, after-sales service is rapidly moving on to the boardroom agenda of today's major manufacturers. Chapter 2.9, 'Service parts management', discusses the reasons for having a service management capability. It outlines the benefits of service parts management systems and explains different methodologies for service parts planning.

Assessing the role of the supply chain is an important aspect of performance measurement. Chapter 2.10, 'Supply chain financial performance measurement', describes how to quantify both tangible benefits such as cost savings or intangible gains such as reduced lead times and changed culture, and forms a basis for decisions. The importance of profitability and efficiency ratios in driving supply chain performance is highlighted.

In Chapter 2.11, 'Supply chain performance measures and systems', the emphasis is on operational performance. The chapter discusses existing management frameworks that have been defined to facilitate communication, guide and direct behaviors within the organization, foster improvement and assess positioning and operational capability.

Chapter 2.12, 'Reverse logistics', takes a comprehensive look at product flows from the point of consumption back to the point of origin, and identifies opportunities to recapture value or ensure proper disposal.

Supply chain network optimization modeling

2.1

Stephen N. Wagner, Jamie M. Bolton and Linda Nuthall

'If you cannot measure it, you cannot manage it' is a familiar adage for managers seeking to improve their business performance. What they may not realize is that the same principle holds true for the supply chain. Companies need accurate measurement in order to design, execute and manage complex supply chains. Unfortunately, most organizations do not understand the cost-to-serve for the essential components composing a supply chain and, thus, have no way to assess alternative approaches accurately to improve performance.

With increasing complexity of supply chains, it becomes even more important to measure and optimize performance.

Designing and executing an effective and efficient supply chain is an extremely difficult undertaking. For many companies, this entails the simultaneous managing of inbound material and components, the location and design of manufacturing/processing operations (which may be multi-staged) and outbound distribution of finished goods to customers. This process would be formidable in a stable environment. Today, short product cycle times, significant fluctuations in energy and other resource costs, outsourcing opportunities, shifting demographics and rapid technological innovations related to products and process improvements (among many other factors) make management of the supply chain a staggering undertaking.

Why bother? We bother because:

- the benefits of a well-managed supply chain are significant, with many companies often saving up to 20 per cent of total supply chain costs, and
- the result of a poorly managed supply chain can be economic ruin.

Network optimization models (NOM) provide a means of not only describing and measuring the performance of all key operating characteristics within a supply chain, but also of selecting the optimal materials sourcing, facility infrastructure, processing activity and flows throughout the chain as per various estimates of future demand, costs, capacities and other external and internal factors. Used correctly, such models provide an accurate assessment of risks and rewards under a wide range of likely future operating environments. This information allows management to make well-informed and intelligent decisions on supply chain management issues.

While providing tremendous insight into operating structure and characteristics, network optimization models are only a tool used within the broader context of general supply chain design and management. Indeed, most of the topics discussed within this book are applicable to the successful utilization of NOM within planning and operations.

Network optimization model overview

Network optimization modeling uses mathematical algorithms to provide decision support.

Network optimization models are a class of mathematical programing models formulated to represent conveniently all the activities occurring within the supply chain. In the most simplistic sense, a supply chain network can be viewed as a collection of nodes and arcs (or links), with suppliers, facilities and markets representing nodes that are linked together with transportation arcs. Raw materials, work-in-process and finished products 'flow' through the network, selecting the right combination of facility/process activity that will minimize total costs while abiding by all facility, process and arc capacities and constraints. This network is graphically displayed in Figure 2.1.1 below.

Suppliers
The level of model detail, especially for modeling processing activities within facilities, has been greatly expanded in many NOM packages. In Figure 2.1.1, the solid boxes represent processes and the solid circles represent resources. The model allows a choice between alternate processes, given multiple production 'recipes' that consume or create

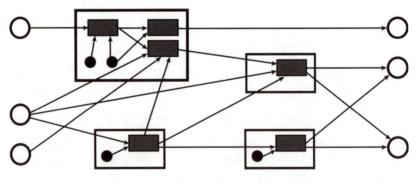

Figure 2.1.1
Network optimization model processing and product flows

multiple resources and multiple products. As opposed to earlier systems, many of the modern NOM systems allow definition of real-world cost and capacity elements such as stepped costs, fixed costs and economies of scale. Further, many packages allow for the optimization of profit, using piece-wise demand elasticity curves, in addition to cost minimization, and support optimization of multiple-period models, which may include inventory build-up or depletion considerations.

From a different perspective, Figure 2.1.2 reviews the model components defined within an advanced NOM system. The model is segregated into three levels of activity:

- *raw materials sourcing* includes the definition of costs and capacities for raw material products or components, and the transportation costs by mode to each of the processing facilities
- *manufacturing and/or processing activity* includes the transformation of raw materials into finished goods, which may entail numerous sequential product transformations. Multiple recipes may be

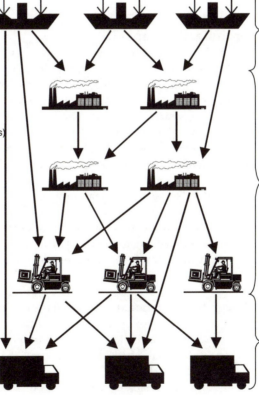

Raw Materials Sourcing
- Product Grouping
- Min/Max by Supplier
- Cost per Volume Level
- Arc Capacity by Link / Mode
- Arc Cost by Flow Volume

**Suppliers,
Supplier Arcs**
(by Mode)

Manufacturing / Processing
- WIP/FG Product Grouping
- Facility Cost & Capacity
- Process Lines (within Facilities)
- Resources (global / within Facilities)
- Recipes (within Process Lines)
    - Alternative selection
    - Resource & Product BOM
    - Variable Cost
    - Min / Max Capacity
- Arc Capacity by Link / Mode
- Arc Cost by Flow Volume

**Facilities, Processes,
Resources, Inter-
Facility Arcs**
(by Mode)

Demand Fulfilment
- Customer Grouping to Markets
- Demand Forecast (point demand)
- Elastic Price Curves /
  Shortage Cost
- Arc Capacity by Link / Mode
- Arc Cost by Flow Volume

**Markets,
Market Arcs**
(by Mode)

Figure 2.1.2
Network optimization modeling components and flows

defined for process lines/activities within a plant to utilize one or more products and/or resources in the production of one or more products and/or resources

- *demand fulfilment* includes either satisfying a fixed demand forecast (by product/market combination) to minimize total cost or optimally determining the market demand volume per price elasticity curves to maximize profit.

Figure 2.1.2 reflects the actual model constructs available in a top-of-the-line strategic and tactical NOM and the constructs that can be included within a customized model. When a NOM is executed, recipe volumes are optimally selected to minimize total costs, or maximize total profit per demand fulfilment criteria, while abiding by all minimum and maximum capacity constraints. This may result in shutting down facilities and/or process lines to avoid fixed operating costs and/or invest in new or expanded facilities, process lines and resources.

The level of sophistication of network optimization modeling solutions varies significantly.

Recent advances in network optimization models and computer technology have resulted in three distinct paths set by major package vendors and advanced users of NOM models:

Stand-alone advanced strategic and tactical supply-chain optimization capability

Offered by a handful of generally smaller NOM packages (in terms of both sales and cost), the stand-alone capability allows automated selection of facility and process infrastructure by including a rich set of strategic-level model constructs. These models include non-linear (integer) constructs such as fixed costs, shutdown costs, conditional minimum operating levels, stepped costs, operating policy constraints, economies of scale (on both nodes and arc flows) and other factors that require a more advanced model solution technique known as mixed integer programming. These problems are much more difficult to solve than linear programing problems and thus require model components to be summarized into product groups, vendor groups, geographic markets, and model periods. A few NOM vendors have developed custom model formulations that drastically reduce the solution time for large-scale mixed integer programming problems.

Integrated operational supply chain optimization

This capability is offered by many of the major ERP and supply chain suite providers and allows optimization of daily operational decisions at an individual stock keeping unit (SKU) level. To solve these gargantuan models, the vendors have limited, or eliminated, the integer model constructs with the focus of optimizing the flows within the current facility and process infrastructure. Integer model constructs include fixed operating costs, shutdown costs and stepped investment costs for facilities, processes or resources. Integrated optimization models *are solved* using commercial software packages that are tuned to efficiently solve large-scale linear programing models.

Custom-built operational and strategic/tactical planning optimization

Created due to both the limitations and costs of the packages listed above, this capability provides the ability to address unique and complex supply-chain business issues with optimization models. Modern mathematical programming (MP) 'languages' allow for the straightforward creation of complex NOM systems by skilled users. This approach is often taken for analysis of problems outside the domain of strict supply chain NOM models, or in cases (quite frequently) where some very key aspects of a firm's supply chain cannot be adequately described by currently available NOM packages. However, the 'canned' translation of model language equations into MP model input often foregoes the ability to utilize custom model formulations, and thus model solution times may be longer than either cumbersome handcrafted approaches or advanced NOM packages.

Due to the improved quality of many of the available supply chain modeling packages, their increased descriptive capability of supply chain issues, and their mature data input and results analysis capabilities, most firms now use pre-defined NOM packages.

Use of NOM for strategic and tactical supply chain modeling

Strategic and tactical supply chain modeling is the classic area where NOM tools are employed. The network optimization model can be developed to mimic, at a summarized but operationally accurate level, the flows and processing activities along a firm's total supply chain, including purchasing, inbound transportation, manufacturing/processing, inter-facility flows and flows to end markets. Given capacities, costs and demand volume, the model will select the best sourcing and processing locations and activity to minimize costs while satisfying demand (or, in the case of limited resources or materials, maximize profit per variable demand curves).

The NOM can be developed to mimic, at a summarized but operationally accurate level, the flows and processing activities along a firm's total supply chain.

However, technically creating a model of the supply chain network for a firm is perhaps the easiest piece in the overall design of the strategic supply chain network. The supply chain design 'process' can be viewed as four distinct stages, with the creation of the initial NOM framework as only one task within the second stage. These stages are listed overleaf and shown schematically in Figure 2.1.3.

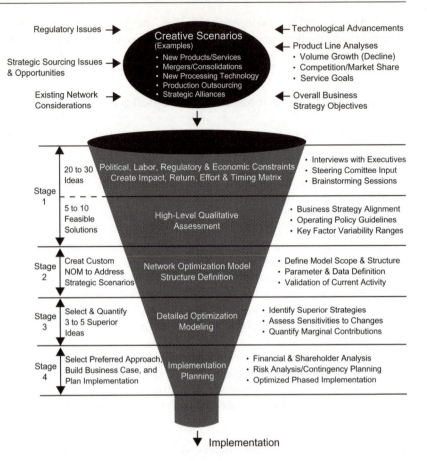

Figure 2.1.3
The four-stage process in designing network optimization models

1 identify supply chain scenarios to model
2 design and build the NOM to evaluate the scenarios
3 evaluate each scenario in light of uncertain future costs, volumes and other internal and external factors and
4 define a future supply chain operating vision, guidelines and detailed implementation plans.

Stage 1 – identify supply chain scenarios

The purpose of Stage 1 is to identify a wide range of alternative operating scenarios to manage the supply chain. This process requires creative thinking, an in-depth understanding of leading-edge supply chain practices, sound business judgment and a thorough under-standing of internal and external influences to the firm. In the first part, scenarios are not critiqued, but listed as potential approaches and positioned for their potential impact on the firm, expected return, implementation effort, and timing.

The second part of Stage 1 provides a qualitative assessment of the general aspects of each of the proposed ideas and limits the list to between five and ten viable approaches. These approaches are aligned to business strategy, viewed to be operationally sound and have the potential for high returns. Any operating policy guidelines and ranges for key unknown future events (such as projected ranges for overall demand, fuel costs or any other factors key to the business) should be specified for these test scenarios.

Stage 2 – design and build the NOM

The NOM structure must be created to address the strategic and tactical issues of the firm and be designed to model the identified scenarios. This process is reviewed below:

Given the supply chain scenarios to test as developed in Stage 1, a generalized model operating structure is defined, and vendor / product / market aggregations are established that will accurately represent actual operations.

For a recent operating period, a model is created using historical shipping transactions appropriately aggregated into model groups. The current cost and capacity is defined for all entities (facilities, processes and resources) and for transport arcs between entities. Processing activity at each entity and product flows between entities are constrained to match historical activity. This fully constrained model is called a *validation model*, and is used to establish a baseline for alternative scenarios and to verify the accuracy of the model data and constructs.

The baseline validation model constraints are relaxed across all arcs and process levels, but all current facility and process configurations are forced to be active. This *constrained optimization model* provides some short-term direction for raw material sourcing, realignment of market assignments to facilities and general levels for processing lines. This model is also a future or potential baseline given the adoption of the guidelines provided by the model.

In Stage 3, model data are updated and expanded as required to address alternative supply chain approaches and sensitivities to ranges of important factors, as reviewed above. This may entail adding potential future facility sites or new process lines (per investment requirements) or a host of other entities that are viable alternatives per the scenario issues. The NOM will optimally utilize each available entity within the supply chain to achieve the lowest cost/highest profit solution. Generally, 100 to 200 *scenario models* will be run to assess fully the viable supply chain configurations given uncertain future business conditions.

A flow diagram, shown in Figure 2.1.4 below, reviews the process of creating an initial model and for developing and testing alternative model scenarios.

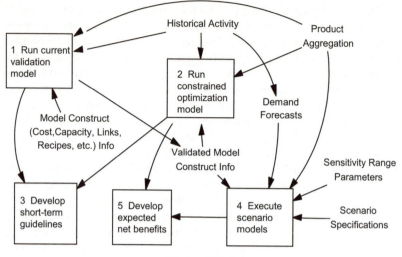

Figure 2.1.4
An initial model for testing alternative scenarios

Stage 3 – optimize model scenarios

The purpose of Stage 3 is to quantify the expected returns under each of the viable scenarios developed within Stage 1. The general strategy is as follows:

- for anticipated future volume and cost levels, model each of the approaches to understand relative differences between the approaches
- for the three to five approaches viewed as superior, execute models that reflect various levels of demand and cost to understand the sensitivities of the models to changes in these factors
- for likely investment or facility closure decisions, run models to display the marginal costs/benefits for each key action.

This model execution strategy is a managed process for developing insight into the costs, performance and network configuration of alternative supply chain designs. However, rather than being 'cast in stone', this process is somewhat iterative and is directed by the output of previous model runs. A steering committee, which includes key managers from all operational areas, actively participates in the dynamic selection and fine-tuning of NOM models.

Stage 4 – determine future supply chain vision

In Stage 4, the purpose is to assess the information regarding alternative supply chain configurations, the sensitivity of these configurations to various changes in demand, costs and other key data, and marginal costing for specific key business information. This information includes cost and volume activity information for all entities within the supply chain (suppliers, supplier links, facilities, processes, resources, facility links, market links market demand/revenue).

In addition, unique outputs produced by optimization models, called *shadow prices*, provide additional insight into the characteristics of the management of the supply chain.

Shadow prices are calculated whenever some minimum or maximum constraint is imposed within a model. Shadow prices reflect the marginal cost of incurring the next/previous unit of volume above a minimum constraint or below a maximum constraint. For example, if a minimum required demand is defined within a model, the shadow price defines a marginal cost (considering all supplier, production and transportation costs) to serve a particular market. This is the true cost-to-serve for a market. Similarly, if a facility is constrained and is used to capacity, the shadow price represents the opportunity cost of additional savings per each additional unit of capacity. Shadow prices also define the true cost of bottlenecks and are a valuable means of identifying and prioritizing operational constraint areas.

The breadth and depth of model runs provides considerable insight into the risks and rewards of alternate supply chain configurations. There will be many selections (facilities, processes and so on) that the models will consistently choose given the ranges of future model inputs that are tested. These consistent selections are known as 'anchors' and are the basis for the formulation of an implementation plan. Additional model runs may be required to formulate a complete vision around the future supply chain.

Once a future vision is defined and confirmed (see also Chapter 1.2, 'Formulating a supply chain vision'), detailed implementation plans must be developed to realize this vision. As it may take two to three years to implement the required changes to optimize the supply chain network fully, the NOM can be used to define efficient intermediate supply chain networks, which provide an optimized phased implementation plan. Changes to the network may include building new manufacturing or distribution facilities, closing existing facilities, installing new processes or any other of a myriad of potential changes.

Use of NOM for operational modeling

A large number of companies have interjected network optimization models successfully into their detailed operational planning. The primary focus of these models is to determine the optimal utilization of resources and processes on a daily basis, understanding the costs and capacities of facilities, processes and resources, inventory holding/acquisition costs, transportation costs and so on. Operational models generally optimize daily or weekly activity down to a SKU level. Many of the models are able to address economies of scale and stepped costs at various production levels. The output of these models

The NOM can be developed to determine the optimal utilization of resources and processes on a daily basis.

is forwarded to other operational planning system components to create production schedules, raw material requisitions, and finished goods shipment requirements in the least-cost manner possible.

Operational NOM systems are focused on operational issues in the supply chain, and not on tactical and strategic investment decisions. They are mentioned here to clarify their role in contrast to the more general strategic and tactical NOM systems, which they closely resemble. Operational NOM packages are generally very cumbersome and inadequate when addressing strategic and tactical business issues.

Complementary decision support systems

The NOM needs to be integrated with other information systems.

Strategic and tactical NOM systems are designed to accurately mimic and optimize aggregated flows throughout a supply chain network. These aggregations generally include product, market and supplier classifications and time periods. For example, a strategic NOM for a retailer with 150 000 products, 4000 retail outlets, and 10 000 vendors may include 150 product groups, 200 store clusters and 500 vendor clusters, aggregated over four three-month quarters.

The supply chain flows, though, are very much dependent on the underlying operational support systems, which will control ordering methods and may also define optimal shipping methods. In addition, the vastness of a company's product offerings, suppliers, and customers may require analytical aid to aggregate into sound groupings.

- *Simulation models* can provide an effective role in understanding some of the cost and capacity relationships within firms. These relationships may include inventory requirements and shipping costs under various levels of service, effective capacity under significant daily volume variability and many other areas. The level of detail capable by a simulation model, and the ability to assess and/or make complex logical choices, allows very close replication of the underlying business processes. Indeed, simulation models can be constructed to replicate the logic of the underlying operating systems (such as order requisition and inventory management systems) and can accurately represent activity under higher or lower volume levels or under alternative business rules. In this way, simulation models may be employed to develop cost and capacity relationships at a higher level of detail for the subsequent use within a NOM. This functionality is displayed in Figure 2.1.5 below.
- *Statistical methods* (such as regression models, cluster analysis, forecasting methods and summary statistics) can also be utilized to define relationships for use within a NOM. Regression models of transportation rates based on mileages (using logarithmic transformations) have proven to be exceptionally accurate in practice and allow very straightforward definition of model transportation costs.

Cluster analysis may aid in developing product groupings for very large numbers of products, especially if a wealth of data is available for classification purposes. Analysis of variability of demand, seasonality, forecasting methods and econometric methods may provide insight on drivers and levels of demand.

- *Geographic information systems* may provide significant help in aggregating supplier sources and markets from a geographic perspective. Advanced packages include clustering algorithms to accomplish these tasks somewhat automatically. In addition, the thematic mapping of demand concentrations and current facility shipping activity provides a visual aid for suggesting alternative facility location and mission.

- *Vehicle routing models (VRM)* select the cheapest way to move freight, given a wide range of modal choices (truckload, LTL, rail, air, ship and so on), carrier contracts, time requirements and shipping best practices. Best practice approaches to using trucks include truckload/stop-off (where truck routes are assigned to reduce shipment costs by simultaneously building full loads and limiting vehicle mileage), use of pooling locations (where smaller, local loads are aggregated to larger shipments) and continuous routing (where loaded trucks may pick up additional cargo en route, again increasing vehicle use and lowering costs). Companies currently using VRM should define the effective NOM origin/destination rates based on optimized VRM results. These results should be extrapolated, where possible, to other model routes required as options by the NOM but not currently utilized. The interplay between NOM and VRM is reviewed in Figure 2.1.5.

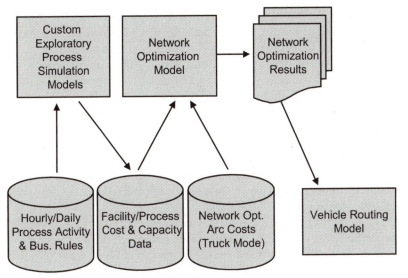

Figure 2.1.5
NOM/VRM/simulation model integration

The accuracy of the NOM model in replicating expected operating activity under any given optimized supply chain configuration is the key for the credibility and actual use of the NOM model. Complementary decision support systems (DSS) models and tools may be extremely valuable to accurately defining NOM model parameters and data.

Guidelines for selecting and implementing NOM capability

Before selecting a commercial off-the-shelf (COTS) package, managers should have a clear understanding of the issues and anomalies of the current supply chain to be modeled and of the alternative operating scenarios to be tested.

This section reviews some general guidelines for implementing strategic and tactical NOM capability within an organization. As touched on earlier, a large number of commercial off-the-shelf (COTS) packages exist for optimizing the supply chain. Some of these models are designed for efficient use in an operational environment; other packages are specifically designed to address general strategic and tactical issues arising in most companies.

Unfortunately, an understanding of the capabilities and features of these competing packages is extremely limited. Some attempts have been made in the past to compare these packages, but they have failed to address some of the more important features within the packages, and these studies are very outdated. Thus, this section will highlight features and functionality key to successfully creating a NOM to address strategic and tactical supply chain issues.

Before selecting a COTS package, managers should have a clear understanding of the issues and anomalies of the current supply chain to be modeled and the alternative operating scenarios to be tested. The NOM should be able to accurately describe (at an appropriate level of detail) all of the controllable activities that are performed within the supply chain. It should also be able to model potential alternative issues and the investment required to implement those issues.

The analysis of the supply chain for a paper manufacturer, for example, may include: a) harvesting of trees, b) transportation to mills, c) debarking and slashing of logs, d) conversion to pulp (or acquisition of pulp from third party sources), e) conversion to paper grade, f) trimming/finishing to rolls, and g) shipment to customers. This process may exist at ten or so mill locations in North America, each containing one to three paper machines, to support a North American customer base. All the activities are constrained somewhat, with the potential to increase (per investment) or shift capacity for some activities within some of the mills.

The network optimization model to assess the paper manufacturing operation must be able to model six to seven echelons of processing activity, stepped investment costs, recipe processing for alternative blending of pulp by paper grade and so on. If a COTS package cannot be found that addresses all of the key operating characteristics, then a user must weigh the cost and time required to modify a package, create a NOM from scratch (generally, using one of the advanced MP modeling languages), or formulate a more simplistic model to match the COTS capabilities versus the functionality, and credibility, afforded by a more accurate model.

Selection criteria

Given the clear understanding of supply chain business issues to be addressed by a NOM, the selection criteria to evaluate strategic and tactical COTS packages are listed below, in order of importance:

- *Model functionality and features.* The NOM tool needs to be able to model accurately the costs and capacities of key business processes. These may include variable costs, fixed costs, shutdown costs, conditional minimum operating levels, stepped operating and investment costs, economies of scale (for processing costs and transportation flow volumes), sole sourcing requirements and other operating policy constraints. Most of these issues require integer modeling constructs which are much more complex to efficiently model and solve.

  For businesses with very seasonal production, network optimization models should be able to model multiple periods low, peak (and normal) simultaneously and be able to consider inventory build-up requirements. Multiple period models can also be effectively used to evaluate multi-year implementation or growth / decline strategies. All of these issues can be addressed by a NOM. The ability (and individual need) of a particular COTS package to address these issues will vary widely.

- *Model creation and execution ease of use.* Companies must address two primary areas: the initial creation of a model and the maintenance of the many scenarios that will be run over the course of a modeling engagement.

  A NOM is defined logically by a large number of input data categories and types. The model may include a large number of tables or files to define a single scenario. A COTS package should have some capability to manage all of the files across multiple scenarios, including features such as logging a description of the scenario, copying an existing scenario to a new scenario.

  Large, complex supply chains may include one million or more data elements defined across various files. COTS packages should include the ability to interface to files that were programmatically created and should include utilities (such as arc generation) to aid in this process. Unconstrained, spreadsheet-like data grids are required to define information, including cut, copy, paste and sort operations.

- *Ease of model debugging / problem resolution.* Large, complex models may initially be ill-defined, or may not be feasible to solve (for example, not enough production capacity to satisfy required demand). The COTS package should allow for means to debug an initial model effectively. Automated debugging methods can considerably shortcut the model debugging time, taking minutes or hours to correct a model instead of days or weeks.

- *Reporting and visualization capabilities.* Supply chain NOM output addresses all of the functional areas within a supply chain across numerous scenarios. The COTS package should include a rich set of reporting capability across all functional areas at various levels of detail. The supply chain solutions can be effectively visualized through the use of thematic maps. Maps should display flow volumes and volume activity at suppliers, facilities, and markets. Some COTS packages allow on-line display of model results within the input data grids. This is useful in providing an understanding between input data elements and model activity. Some packages also create model results databases that span multiple scenarios and aggregate major model cost elements. Such a capability would allow functionality as Online Analytical Processing and graph creation across multiple model results.

- *Operating system environment.* A strategic and tactical NOM model is typically (and most conveniently) run on a stand-alone basis on a high-powered personal computer. This platform provides full dedication of the processor to the problem at hand and is more responsive to interactive graphics display and other interface areas. Many of the NOM tools designed to address operational issues are server-based and are generally much more cumbersome and considerably less portable.

- *Model execution speed and efficiency.* The NOM must be able to solve efficiently the mathematical programming model that it creates. The differences in effective model formulation (which can significantly improve solution times by tenfold or more), custom solution techniques and/or choice of commercial solvers will vary considerably across COTS packages. These variances can result in substantial differences in the ability and solution speed for large-scale mathematically programed problems.

- *NOM implementation cost.* The cost of NOM COTS packages will vary considerably from $5000 to more than $500 000. COTS packages that have an operational focus will tend to cost considerably more. Solid strategic and tactical focused COTS packages are priced in the $75 000 to $125 000 range, with systems of generally lesser modeling capability priced under $50 000. The cost for consulting to aid in initial development of a NOM can range considerably, according to the extensiveness of the supply chain, and may be many times the price of the NOM package itself.

A four-step process

Given the wide variance in NOM COTS package capability, a four-step process should be used in selecting a NOM software tool:

Step 1. A functional requirements document should be prepared addressing specific and general capabilities required for the NOM tool per the unique requirements of the enterprise. These include modeling functionality, ease of use and output capability (reports, maps, graphs, comparative scenario databases and so on) as reviewed in more detail above.

Step 2. Potential providers of NOM tools are available from several sources, including the Accenture-sponsored ASCET web site <www.ascet.com> and the Council of Logistics Management <www.clm1.org>. Vendors that are viewed as potential sources of NOM packages should be sent the functional requirements document.

Step 3. Based on the responses from the questionnaire, sample model scenarios should be sent to a small set of NOM vendors that, on paper, demonstrate their ability to address the supply chain modeling issues. These models can be very small (and defined within an Excel workbook), but should address all of the salient issues involved in modeling the supply chain.

Step 4. The top two to three vendors should be asked to demonstrate their model for final selection, (based on NOM capability and the ability to solve the sample model, level of required customization, level of support and other factors as above). This will allow full appreciation of actual ease of use and model output capabilities that would be difficult to discern simply from the questionnaires.

Some final thoughts and perspectives

The use of a network optimization model within the strategic and tactical design of a firm's supply chain can provide extraordinary financial gains. These gains are achieved through the identification of:

- an optimally integrated facility, process and resource infrastructure
- size per investment opportunities, raw material availability and expected product demand elasticity
- position considering the location of supply sources and markets and the cost of local labor, energy and other resources, and
- optimal product flow (raw material, work-in-process and finished goods) guidelines defined through the supply chain infrastructure to achieve the highest possible return to the firm.

The key components to utilizing a NOM successfully include a well-thought-out and executed scenario analysis methodology and a model that accurately addresses all major scenario issues. Scenarios are conceived to test potential alternative supply chain designs, each operating under varied estimates of demand and other key future factors. Development of these scenarios requires a deep understanding of the business, best practice supply chain knowledge, a dash of creativity and a lot of common sense. In some cases, complementary DSS models, such as vehicle routing, simulation or statistical models may be required to define expected efficiencies, capacities, and costs under new process methods not yet implemented in practice (and thus unavailable to measure).

The scenario results provide significant insight into both the operation of a firm's supply chain network and the sensitivities to fluctuations of demand and key costs. This insight allows management to select a vision for future supply chain design. Around this vision, the NOM allows creation of effective contingency plans and also an optimal phased implementation plan (which may span several years).

Advances in processing technology, large-scale solution technology and the general quality of many of the current NOM COTS packages provide unprecedented supply chain modeling capability. However, NOM COTS packages vary considerably in functionality, and only a few packages are capable of addressing complex strategic and tactical supply chain issues (especially across large networks). Indeed, even these systems may not address all of the key supply chain issues, requiring extension to an existing NOM package or the development of a custom NOM using an advanced MP modeling language. An in-depth understanding of a firm's NOM requirements and a careful matching of those requirements with the functionality of a NOM package are needed in order successfully to implement NOM capability within a firm.

Overall, a very low percentage of companies are currently using NOM within the strategic and tactical design of their supply chains. Part of this is due to the complexity of the underlying mathematical models, which is foreign to most users who cannot conceive that such a tool is possible. Another reason is the failure of many NOM COTS packages to accurately address key supply chain issues, resulting in limited use and reliance on model results, and a lack of credibility for NOM packages in general.

However, the bottom line is that the prudent use of a network optimization modeling system can significantly reduce a firm's cost-to-serve, and allow pricing economics that could not be matched by the firm's competition. As firms within an industry adopt NOM practices, there will be an increased need for their competitors to follow suit, to the benefit of the whole industry, and the economy in general.

Reference

Shapiro, J. F. (2001), *Modeling the supply chain*, Pacific Grove, CA: Duxbury/Thomson Learning.

Supply chain diagnostics

2.2

Douglas W. Allvine and Trevor Gore

A company's real core capability lies in its ability to design and manage the supply chain to maximize advantage in a market where competitive forces may change at lightning speed. With supply chain costs often accounting for 75 per cent of a typical company's operating budget, organizations cannot afford to spend months waiting for lengthy assessments of the supply chain. But several challenges exist for companies looking to improve on this situation.

Effective diagnosis can speed up supply chain assessment and help to ensure that improvements are successful.

Often, the first challenge is simply to determine how to go about rapidly and effectively assessing the supply chain to develop the best improvement initiatives. What can operational and supply chain managers do to make sure they end up with a high-quality, actionable plan? The questions can be endless. Using an organized, efficient and effective diagnostic approach can accelerate the assessment process and make a large difference to the success of improvement initiatives proposed. This chapter focuses on providing managers with some basic guidelines to conduct supply chain diagnostics.

Introduction

The idea behind the term 'supply chain diagnostics' is that organizations might perform a diagnosis on their supply chains for the same reason that a doctor might perform a diagnosis on a patient. People typically visit a doctor for three reasons: 1) for a routine check-up; 2) when demonstrating unhealthy symptoms; or 3) if there is a serious problem or emergency. Regardless of the reason, the doctor quickly assesses the patient's situation, tries to identify any problems (current or latent) and ultimately develops a solution to ensure ongoing well being. Organizations that can apply the same diagnostic method to their supply chain are typically successful at

A supply chain diagnostic is a structured, disciplined assessment of the supply chain.

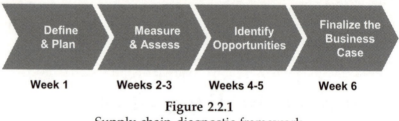

Figure 2.2.1
Supply chain diagnostic framework

implementing and sustaining healthy improvements across their supply chains.

What is a supply chain diagnostic?

Simply, a supply chain diagnostic is a structured, disciplined assessment of the supply chain (fully evaluating symptoms). It is designed to identify actionable improvement opportunities (to prescribe a remedy) that will deliver sustainable improvements in a company's performance (that will return the patient to health). There are four phases to a diagnostic:

- *Phase 1.* Define and plan the diagnostic. The primary objective is to understand the project goals clearly and to scope, structure and organize the diagnostic accordingly.
- *Phase 2.* Measure and assess current supply chain performance. The primary objective is to collect the necessary data and compile the results to develop an initial assessment of the current environment.
- *Phase 3.* Identify improvement opportunities and value. During the identification phase, the information is analysed and interpreted to determine where performance gaps exist, to begin quantifying opportunities and develop alternatives for addressing opportunities.
- *Phase 4.* Finalize the business case. The cost and benefits are documented and the implementation plan is developed in this phase.

Together, the four phases form a basic diagnostic framework to help organizations to effectively assess and ultimately improve their supply chains, as Figure 2.2.1 illustrates. This approach allows for an accelerated timeline compared to that of a traditional assessment project. The supply chain diagnostic effort generally takes around six weeks to complete, but the time will vary depending upon the scope and scale of the project.

Why conduct supply chain diagnostics?

A supply chain diagnostic should connect supply chain capabilities to business objectives.

Supply chain diagnostics provide an effective, structured means to assess the supply chain and build a powerful case for supply chain improvement. Successful diagnostics can address the changing role of the supply chain in an enterprise strategy. The organizational relationships, processes and assets that make up the supply chain have become a key source of competitive strategy, differentiation, cost reduction and revenue lift. Companies that genuinely wish to improve their supply chain must be able to diagnose their supply chains effectively in order to make correct, sustainable changes.

A good supply chain diagnostic should deliver a cost-benefit analysis to underpin a supply chain-driven transformation. This typically includes:

- assessing today's supply chain capabilities
- identifying potential future capabilities
- quantifying and prioritizing a list of supply chain opportunities
- estimating business benefits for selected opportunities and
- recommending next steps for implementation and value capture.

In the end, a supply chain diagnostic should connect supply chain capabilities to overall business objectives.

What findings should be expected?

While diagnostic projects all yield different outcomes, some issues commonly recur.

Often companies have weak key performance indicators (KPIs) and take a functional rather than process view of their business.

Almost without exception, companies key performance indicator (KPI) systems have significant weaknesses. Ideally, KPIs should be holistic, balanced and aligned across the organization so that they drive all parts of the business to common strategic goals. While this sounds fundamental to any business, in actual fact it is a rarity. As a direct consequence, the effort required to source comparative information across the various sectors of a business is significantly increased.

Perhaps the most common error is for organizations to measure what they can measure, rather than what they should measure. An example of this is measuring truck departures as a means of assessing customer service, when what matters to the customer is product arrivals, in full and on time. Another example is using warehouse issues as a surrogate for actual demand, with inevitable 'bull whip' consequences and sales opportunities going unrecognized.

Related to the KPI problem is the issue of taking a functional view of operations rather than a process view. KPIs tend to be focused on functional performance rather than process outcomes. The result can be a sales department focused on customer service and consequently intent on delivering from stock, while the distribution department is accountable for stock on hand, has a cost focus and aim to minimize stock. This lack of alignment across the supply chain can be a cause of much inefficiency.

In addition, few supply chain operations regard the cash collection process as part of their remit. A major driver of working capital is the cash-to-cash cycle time, the time from which money is paid to suppliers for raw materials to when it is collected from customers in payment for goods and services. Yet, few organizations measure it, even though supply chain operations have by far the major influence on the length of the cycle time. Ultimately, the only difference between finished goods stock (often a supply chain accountability) and accounts receivable (commonly a finance responsibility) is where the goods are located, so it makes sense to take a holistic view of the process.

Conducting the diagnostic

Phase 1 – define and plan the diagnostic

Defining and planning the project objectives is the most important phase of any diagnostic.

For a diagnostic assessment to be successful, an organization needs to define and plan the project objectives sufficiently *before* starting. This is the most important phase in any diagnostic. Without proper planning, the diagnostic team will fail. The major steps in this phase include determining the project scope and approach and developing a data collection strategy.

Understand goals and expectations

Discuss goals and expectations with project owner   The project owner or sponsor will be the champion of the diagnostic effort. This person needs to understand what the concerns are, what is perceived to be 'broken', which areas are 'in' and which are 'out' of focus, the expected deliverable, and the anticipated timeframe. Before appointing the project owner, senior executives need to define the project objectives and identify the 'soft spots' that need to be investigated fully.

Conduct research and develop initial observations and hypothesis   Often the primary focus of the diagnostic can be drawn from discussions with the project sponsor or from the charter set for the diagnostic team. In addition to reviewing the goals developed by the sponsor, managers need to ask questions about trends in the business and the industry, current supply chain capabilities, the likely value of improvements, and the capacity for the organization to change. Such questions will allow the diagnostic team to develop 'going-in' hypotheses for the project.

Determine scope and approach

The scope of the diagnostic needs to be within organizational constraints.

At this point the business should have a good idea of what the diagnostic is about, areas of focus and sponsor expectations. The next tasks are to define the project details, create the project team and develop a project communication plan.

Define project details and work plan   Defining the scope in more detail will help to reveal specific parts of the assessment, including:

- finalizing the start date and timeframe for completion
- developing a plan outlining interim tasks and milestones
- identifying and securing involvement from non-core team participants
- defining data requirements
- hypothesizing on the business's and project's capacity for change
  around the organizational structure, technology, strategy and
  processes, and
- finalizing the scope, such as specific areas of the supply chain
  (planning, purchasing, logistics and so on), plants, divisions and
  regions.

An important aspect of finalizing the scope is to determine how much
of the organization can be effectively assessed, based on constraints
such as timeframe, resource availability, sponsorship influence,
change capacity and budget. The scope needs to be manageable in
order to support a successful effort.

Define team resource requirements   A core diagnostic team will typically
consist of four to six people. The success of the project will depend
heavily on the insights drawn by the team from cross-functional,
trans-supply chain information. The team, therefore, needs to contain
several highly skilled and experienced supply chain practitioners. If
radical change is anticipated, the team members should be either
highly respected or able to build their credibility rapidly. Plans for
dramatic change need to be delivered by the right person to win
support.

The core team will comprise four to six people with roles based on their expertise and influence.

The core team consists of those individuals whose primary
responsibility will be to execute the diagnostic; each team member
will fulfil a particular role based on their expertise and influence, as
outlined in Table 2.2.1. Extra input can be gained by appointing part-
time members to the team, including content experts, process experts,
customers and suppliers.

Table 2.2.1
Diagnostic team

Team member	Role
Sponsor	The project champion. Overall accountability but limited detailed involvement. Part-time.
Manager	Change leader. Responsible for day-to-day management. Full-time.
Analysts	Team members. Conduct diagnostic alongside the manager. Full-time.
Systems Analyst	Responsible for extracting and providing all required data. Part-time, although high participation early in the project.

Develop a communication strategy   Creating a communication strategy for diagnostic participants is another important activity when defining the diagnostic. The first and simplest task is for the sponsor or lead executive to deliver a memo introducing the project. The memo should communicate, to all those to be affected, what is going to happen; it should stress the importance of the assessment initiative and highlight their involvement.

A second task when defining the communications strategy is to develop a simple plan that can provide periodic status updates during the diagnostic. Short, simple status meetings are the main component of any such plan. The audience will not only be leaders within the company, but all those who can or will be affected by the assessment.

Develop data collection plan and tools

Data is the 'fuel' that drives any diagnostic. A well-planned and well-executed strategy for collecting data is critical to getting a diagnostic off to a good start. Three main types of data need to be collected in any diagnostic. One type of data is quantitative data, which typically consists of process-driven, numerically based data that can be used to calculate performance, document a process and conduct analysis.

The other two types of data are qualitative in nature. One type is interviews and site visits with essential people across the length and breadth of the supply chain. The second type involves conducting surveys or questionnaires. All three types together can form a powerful database to help the project team analyse the supply chain and build a fact-based case for change. Each type is described in more detail below.

Quantitative data collection   An important step in defining any diagnostic is developing a preliminary plan of what to measure, how to measure it and how to interpret the results. Like any complex system, the supply chain presents a multitude of opportunities for enhanced performance. Organizations will need to create a data collection request and collect the desired quantitative data at the start of the project. Potentially, the data collection might need to start before the diagnostic team's full mobilization due to the long lead times involved.

Determining what metrics to collect data on and how to interpret them is complicated and requires detailed discussion. Usually, existing metrics are not aligned with what the organization is trying to achieve. The diagnostic team can often find that a gap exists between supply chain operational measures and the company's strategic objectives.

A good guide to the metrics to collect can be deduced by answering how value is created in the organization. Identifying what high-cost and high-benefit activities the business undertakes will immediately shift the focus to areas of greatest value. Saving 15 per cent of a large cost item will always deliver more than saving 15 per cent of a small cost item.

The completed data requests must allow senior managers to calculate KPIs and conduct detailed analyses that address the focus areas. In the end, these analyses should relate supply chain operational performance and financial outcomes to the organization's business strategy.

Supply chain surveys   Surveys, or questionnaires, are a simple yet effective way to collect individual perceptions around the supply chain and company performance. Surveys also provide diagnostic teams with the ability to reach a large, broad audience in a very short period. Survey questions can concentrate on many different aspects of the supply chain. Questions might address relationships between entities, both within the organization, such as purchasing to manufacturing, and between the business and its partners, such as purchasing to suppliers.

A large discrepancy often exists between the perceptions of an organization and its suppliers.

Procurement KPIs	Supplier Program Definition	Supplier Rationalization	Materials Rationalization	Supplier Selection & Addition	Supplier Certification	Supplier Relationship Management	Supplier Performance/Compliance	Organization Management	Need Identification (MRP)	Requisition	Receiving (Goods & Services)	Inventory Management	Invoice Processing/Remittance	Data & Systems Management	Performance Management
Average Purchase Cost per Unit									X	X	X				X
Average Time to Payment												X	X		X
Certified Suppliers	X	X	X	X	X	X	X	X							X
Raw Material Inventory Turns	X	X	X			X	X		X	X	X	X			X
Raw Material Stockouts			X	X			X		X	X	X				X
Perfect Orders	X	X		X	X	X	X				X		X		X
Average Procurement Cycle Time		X		X	X	X	X		X	X	X				X
Cost of Reorder	X	X	X	X	X	X	X		X	X	X	X			X
Cost of Quality	X	X	X	X	X	X	X	X			X	X	X		X
Dollars Spent on Contract Maintenance	X		X	X	X	X	X								
EDI Transactions per Supplier	X	X		X	X	X	X			X			X		
Inventory Accuracy									X	X	X	X		X	X
Invoice Errors													X	X	X
Invoices per Supplier	X	X		X	X	X	X						X		X

Source: Accenture

Figure 2.2.2
Sample KPIs

Questions might also focus on how organizations compare to leading practices. The survey questions and objectives can be framed in a variety of ways. A common misconception is that a supply chain diagnostic is about collecting a 'bunch of facts': emphasizing quantity over quality. However, organizations must deal with perceptions and feelings, sentiments and capabilities, and trust and confidence in the practitioner before they can try to solve the quantitatively defined problem.

With surprising frequency, surveys can uncover a large discrepancy between the perceptions an organization has of itself and the perception suppliers have of this organization. Senior managers will have to dispose of that discrepancy before they can discuss the issue with staff and customers. It is amazing how often business partners believe they are each contributing the information that the other side needs, when in fact assessments often reveal quite the opposite. Executives have to determine whether the discrepancy is exposing a relationship or perception issue before they can attack the factual issues. Either way, a solution is required.

Survey participants range from key executives across the organization to people in the extended supply chain of suppliers and customers. Surveys can be distributed manually but the best, simplest and fastest way is to use the Internet. Numerous sites on the Internet do nothing else but host Web-based surveys, such as that shown in Figure 2.2.3. The cost of the surveys is surprisingly low, they are professional and simple to learn, their development time is only a couple of hours and the results are captured immediately.

Interviews should be well planned and conducted with people from each important area.

Interviews and site visits   Talking to key representatives across the supply chain and capturing their perspectives is critical to any supply chain diagnostic. A few simple guidelines can make the interview process more successful. First, the diagnostic team should be selective about who to interview. Interviews are valuable but also very time-consuming. The team should try to interview at least one person from each key area. Group interviews can be successful; however, some individuals may not be forthcoming if their peers or superiors are present.

Second, plan for the interviews. Developing an interview outline or plan and incorporating data from the survey (if available) is extremely beneficial. And third, schedule interviews as early in the process as possible. Usually, initial interviews should be completed very early in the diagnostic process. The project sponsor should set up the meetings to ensure interview participants understand the importance of their involvement.

How to tell when Phase 1 is completed

The diagnostic team has finished Phase 1 when the members know what they are going to do, how they are going to do it, what data

My company has a formal sales and operations planning process to develop a single, consensus driven forecast that is supported by management.

○ Strongly Disagree	○ Disagree	○ Agree	○ Strongly Agree	○ Don't Know

Our inventory deployment processes accurately reflects service level requirements and relevant storage and truck receiving/shipping constraints.

○ Strongly Disagree	○ Disagree	○ Agree	○ Strongly Agree	○ Don't Know

My company takes advantage of transportation load-shipping opportunities with distributors and suppliers.

○ Strongly Disagree	○ Disagree	○ Agree	○ Strongly Agree	○ Don't Know

My company proactively communicates transportation delivery issues to customers/distributors (e.g. late deliveries).

○ Strongly Disagree	○ Disagree	○ Agree	○ Strongly Agree	○ Don't Know

My company effectively utilizes transportation technology in planning and executing deliveries.

○ Strongly Disagree	○ Disagree	○ Agree	○ Strongly Agree	○ Don't Know

| ‹Back | Next › | Save |

Source: Accenture

Figure 2.2.3
Web-based survey example

they need to collect and from where. Importantly, the project sponsor needs to support the team's approach. The team also needs to have communicated the project goals to all those likely to be affected. At this point, a team member should be able to deliver an 'elevator speech' about the project to a colleague, capturing the project's key messages within the time taken to ride between floors. The acid test for moving to the next phase is when the colleague says 'I know'.

Phase 2 – Measure and assess current performance
It is time to execute on the diagnostic plan laid out in the first phase. Two main steps make up this phase. The first step is to gain a good understanding of the current supply chain, which often includes measuring performance and establishing a baseline to compare against improvement targets. The second step is to begin assessing current performance. How well is the organization really doing? What specific issues and opportunities are there? Phase 2 should deliver a fact-based, more accurate profile of current performance and position the diagnostic team for identifying opportunities for improvement in Phase 3.

Phase 2 should deliver a fact-based performance profile of the supply chain.

Measure and understand current supply chain

The diagnostic team will start by collecting and processing the data from the quantitative data request, interviews and site visits and completed surveys. Many items should be considered when trying to establish a baseline for performance:

- review existing business and IT strategy
- develop 'as-is' process overviews for key areas
- conduct additional industry or competitor research
- identify any similar or conflicting initiatives that might be going on simultaneously and
- determine required benchmark information and collect as required.

As this information is being collected, the team should document results and start to summarize findings.

Assess current performance

The review of performance should identify opportunity indicators.

It is important to conduct an 'as-is' review of the supply chain and establish a baseline for the diagnostic. As the team reviews the business's current performance it should identify various opportunity indicators and start to formulate initial business situation observations. Some examples might include: 'Communication is breaking down between our organization, our contract manufacturer, and suppliers (forecast updates, lifecycle data).' and 'No clear accountability exists for overall inventory and service levels (functional silos).'

In addition to creating these supply chain observations, the diagnostic team should also:

- calculate KPIs for current performance
- develop a supply chain profile, including current volumes, flows and capacities and
- compare current practice to leading practices, as suggested in Figure 2.2.4. below.

At the conclusion of this phase it is a good idea for diagnostic teams to review their 'going-in' hypotheses on improvement opportunities and update if appropriate.

How to tell when Phase 2 is completed

The diagnostic team has finished this phase when it truly understands the current performance of the supply chain. The team needs to have reconciled any aspect of performance being shown by KPIs with the 'hearsay' from within and, if necessary, from without the operation. The team has done a good job when, in an elevator conversation, a member can explain the shortcomings about a particular part of the operation that the team has discovered, typically where the problem had not been visible. The colleague responds 'I always knew something was odd there. I'm glad you've worked out what it is.'

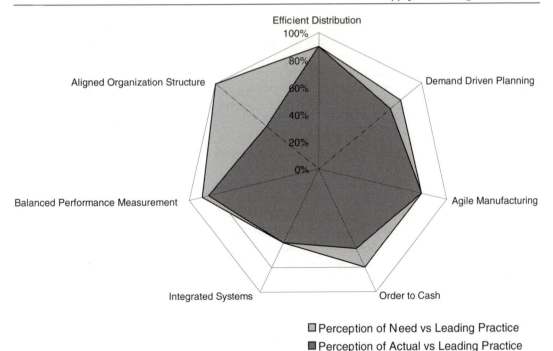

Efficient Distribution
100%

80%

60%

40%

20%

0%

Aligned Organization Structure

Demand Driven Planning

Balanced Performance Measurement

Agile Manufacturing

Integrated Systems

Order to Cash

☐ Perception of Need vs Leading Practice
■ Perception of Actual vs Leading Practice

Figure 2.2.4
Perceived versus actual supply chain effectiveness

Phase 3 – identify improvement opportunities and value

At this point, the diagnostic team understands the current performance of the supply chain and where the issues and opportunities lie. The next phase consists of conducting more focused analyses around specific opportunity areas, defining and quantifying the value that can be gained through improving and developing the improvement strategies.

Analyse supply chain capabilities and performance

The diagnostic team should analyse the collected data and identify performance trends. The level of detail and complexity of analysis will vary from one focus area to the next. Analysis can be as simple as measuring performance and comparing it to a target level or benchmark or as complex as testing particular hypotheses developed by the team.

The level of detail and complexity of analysis will vary from one focus area to the next.

Some examples of detailed analyses include: procurement spend analysis, customer/product segmentation analysis and comparison, and transportation mode analysis. Regardless of the level of detail pursued, it is important to have some comparative data for the opportunity areas, such as internal performance goals and targets, leading practices and benchmarks. The team can compare current performance to guide it further in identifying opportunities.

Nothing is 'good' or 'bad' unless by comparison

When conducting any analysis it is also important to recognize that certain knowledge or expertise may not exist in the core diagnostic team. Successful diagnostic teams often use external experts to provide valuable assistance in identifying, assessing and summarizing opportunities. As the team completes its analysis, it should be developing conclusions on opportunity areas.

Define and quantify value

The team needs to define the best value opportunities, prioritize them, then look for alternatives.

Ultimately, the team wants to define the benefit and value that it can achieve by improving the company's supply chain performance. Team members can start by comparing current supply chain performance with desired performance targets and benchmarks. As they assess the different performance gaps they should also review the degree of change required to close the gaps and to start to model and summarize the financial implications of doing so. The team should start thinking about which opportunities provide the best value and prioritize opportunities into high, medium and low.

Develop improvement alternatives

After completing the analysis and quantifying the value of closing the performance gaps, the team should begin to summarize value-creating alternatives by assessment area, such as by function or business unit. Again, this may be a point where the team needs to use supply chain or industry experts to assist in developing the correct improvement strategies. The diagnostic team should work towards developing a consolidated list of opportunities. It is always a good idea to conduct brainstorming sessions to confirm the improvement hypotheses.

How to tell when Phase 3 is completed

At the conclusion of this phase the team should have a summary of findings by process area, a list of improvement strategies, potential updates to performance targets and an updated perspective on the potential financial benefits. When a team member bumps into the colleague he or she last met in the elevator, the colleague should have arrived at the same improvement opportunities as the diagnostic team.

Phase 4 – finalize the business case

Information should be translated into a clear message and an actionable plan.

By Phase 4, the diagnostic team should have a good understanding of the supply chain opportunities, the value that can be gained from the opportunities and an estimate of the change effort required. It is important to take this information and turn it into clear messages and an actionable plan. The three main steps in this phase are: define the solution in enough detail to explain what the team is proposing; summarize the financial benefits; and roll everything together into a single business case.

Define the solution

The business case should be able to answer questions such as: 'What are you proposing?', 'Why are you proposing it?', 'How are you going to do it?', 'Where and when is it going to happen?'. All the team's previous assessment work should be used to help to define answers to these types of questions.

Several other influences need to be taken into consideration when defining the solution. As mentioned earlier, an organization's willingness and capacity for change need to be taken into account when developing an action plan. The team needs to determine how much change the organization and the project charter will allow. The team needs to take into account the diagnostic project's strategy as well as people, process and technology capacity.

One effective way of organizing and presenting the improvement strategies is to divide the opportunities into 'quick hit', short-term, medium-term and long-term projects, according to the type and extent of the change needed, as Table 2.2.2 shows.

Summarize the financial benefit

The team needs to be able to answer the primary question in the minds of the executives who will be giving the 'go ahead' on the project recommendations: 'What is the value? What does it mean to our organization financially?' The diagnostic team might already have a good idea of what the value is from Phase 3. However, when calculating a final figure it is often helpful to develop 'to-be'

Table 2.2.2
Characteristics of different improvement projects

Improvement project	Duration	Characteristics
Quick hit	1–6 months	Provides 'immediate' benefits. Typically easy to implement. Often, quick hits can be as simple as a process or policy change. Quick hits can also be temporary solutions put in place until larger, more strategic improvements can be implemented.
Short-term	Less than 6 months	Includes pilot efforts identified in the supply chain diagnostic. Often includes process, policy, and organization changes. May also include minor technology enhancements.
Medium-term	6–18 months	Often consists of significant organizational change of one or more key supply chain components. Can include additional rollouts of piloted efforts. Can also include large-scale technology improvements.
Long-term	More than 12 months	Strategic and large in nature. Often includes changing the way an organization approaches the supply chain. Can be the large-scale change that allows organizations to maximize their supply chain and differentiate themselves from their competitors.

performance targets to quantify the value potential of achieving the improved performance.

The team can also tie these financial improvements back to the balance sheet and income statement to show true impact to shareholder value and return on net worth. Accounting personnel can be helpful to present the financial projections in line with the organization's normal accounting standards. Some diagnostics may be expected to present findings using accounting tools such as net present value (NPV) or Economic Value Add^{TM} (EVA^{TM}). The team should balance that level of detail with expectations.

Finalize the business case

A compelling business case will ensure the diagnostic team crosses the finish line.

A 'formal' business case helps tie all the different opportunities together into consolidated improvement strategies and a single vision. Along with including project summaries and the projected benefit, the team will also need to include a high-level implementation plan. The plan should consider the approach, timing, resource requirements, expected cost and benefits timeline and other basic information required for the project. The danger of preparing a poor business case is that it can stop the diagnostic team short of achieving its goals. However, a compelling business case will ensure the team crosses the finish line!

How to tell when a diagnostic is successful

The team members will know they have conducted a successful diagnostic when every time they get into the elevator different managers regularly 'buttonhole' them, wanting to know when the improvement initiatives in their area will kick off. Even arriving at their intended floor does not quell the managers' zeal.

The references to elevator conversations may appear somewhat flippant. However, in real organizations they can be a true measure of how well executives and diagnostic team members spread the messages and create both the will and, hopefully, the capability to change. If the team reaches the end of the project and faces a major 'selling' job to garner support for the initiatives, it has failed. The team's report will be doomed to collect dust on an office shelf, irrespective of the quality of the recommendations.

Conclusion

A diagnostic establishes a fact-based case for change.

A successful supply chain diagnostic will build a powerful business case for why an organization should change its approach to the supply chain. Whether the improvement is as complex as implementing new supply chain systems or as simple as changing supplier relationships, an organization will mitigate the risk of failure by undertaking a supply chain diagnostic. A diagnostic will speed the organization to achieve benefits because it establishes a fact-based case for change.

By dealing with an agreed system of metrics, the diagnostic will work because people support it and because the resulting data do not lie. By following the four phases outlined in this chapter, an organization will be in a better position to create sustainable change. The system of metrics will be tied to business objectives and will continuously guide improvement. Speed-to-benefit, risk mitigation and sustainability; these are not rocket science but organizations can achieve extraordinary business results by adopting effective supply chain diagnostics.

2.3 Manufacturing strategy for supply chains

Mark Reynolds

Many product-oriented businesses have to get their manufacturing right, because it is where they have the most complexity, cost, assets and inertia.

Manufacturing strategy has always been at the forefront of supply chain strategic thinking and fundamental to its successful application. Many conveniently forget that the peak of the industrial era saw manufacturing lead the supply chain out of the dark ages. The principles developed in manufacturing have taken most of a century to be applied to other logistical areas. As early as 1926, Henry Ford was achieving cash-to-cash cycle times of four days, driven largely by his use of continuous-process thinking to develop superior techniques in production line manufacturing. His contemporaries, however, were stuck in 'batch think' and still making deliveries by horse and cart or canal barge, unconcerned that they were taking weeks or months to cycle their working capital.

The concepts of low or no inventory, lean manufacturing, Just-In-Time and quality management took another 50 years for businesses to adopt. Just-In-Time and 'kanban', where the consumption of a unit triggers the replenishment of the space that it occupied, has yet to reach most supermarkets. Out-of-stocks at the shelves, the only place where it counts, typically ranged from 8 to 11 per cent on a normal trading day, according to an out-of-stock study by ECR Australasia (2001). All too often we find that supply chain integration and performance diminish rapidly with distance from manufacturing.

For many product-oriented businesses, manufacturing is where they have the most complexity, cost, assets and inertia, so they must get it right. A profound and practical manufacturing strategy helps do this by describing what manufacturing must do to support the present and future competitiveness of the business – and its supply chains. This chapter will primarily canvas the middle ground of manufacturing, comprising companies that repetitively produce discrete products that are neither high-volume process commodities, such as oil, beer, steel or paper, nor uniquely engineered, custom creations like satellites, oil platforms or industrial plants. The scope of manufacturing strategy for the middle-ground companies covers:

- manufacturing's strategic positioning and contribution to business value – the manufacturing mission
- interfaces between manufacturing and product development, sourcing, distribution, sales and marketing
- required manufacturing capabilities, today and in the future
- manufacturing resources and infrastructure, particularly facility roles, assets and production technologies and
- key performance measures.

Considered in isolation, apart from the supply chain, manufacturing deserves a good mark for its advances over recent years. A balanced report would say 'tried hard, performed well'. The most under-recognized achievement of discrete product manufacturers during the economically stable decades since 1950 has been to play a major part in raising the sophistication and lowering the cost of industrial and consumer products to an astonishing degree. Contemplate the design, features, finish, performance, safety and durability in a BMW or a Hyundai today compared with the basic engineering and comparatively high prices of 1940s cars. Now do the same mental comparison with machine tools, telephones, toys, home appliances, housewares and practically any other product.

Today's level of product excellence reflects the complexity and effectiveness of the networks of design, supply, production, quality and service that are often taken for granted. We have reached an age when almost every supplier makes great products and the basis of competition is shifting to the supply chain level. The reality that this creates for many manufacturing businesses is the need to take hard decisions about the ongoing role of manufacturing. Is manufacturing still a core capability and the bedrock of the business as it might have been 10 or 20 years ago? Or is manufacturing something that is now so commoditized it should be contracted out to supply partners while the core business focuses on brand management and distribution channels?

The critical questions to be addressed by this chapter are therefore:

- what's different about manufacturing strategy in the new world of supply chain networks?
- how should you build a manufacturing strategy aligned with your supply chain networks?

The old, narrow view of manufacturing

Promising manufacturing strategies emerged despite the isolation of manufacturing from the needs of customers and the rest of the business.

For many decades, manufacturing has typically existed as an island of specialized capability surrounded by manual interfaces, with neither the processes nor technologies to support any form of collaboration, integration or synchronization upstream or downstream. Yes, work-arounds were developed and wonders were performed with clever card systems and elegant planning techniques but, on the whole, manufacturing strategy was narrowly defined. The standard answer was to manufacture in long runs at minimum cost and let distribution grumble about the resulting inventories. Strategy could have easily become a synonym for game playing around the twin gods of cost-minimization and facility utilization, leading to sterile propositions such as: 'How can we justify buying new machines when we can keep old ones going at low cost?' or 'You can't have that product for another month – its economic batch quantity determines we only make it four times a year'.

Slowly, promising manufacturing strategies emerged despite the isolation of manufacturing from the needs of customers and the rest of the business. Companies achieved startling successes in high-volume environments, such as the Toyota Production System (TPS) and lean manufacturing principles in the automobile industry. Equally, remarkable improvements were made in the responsiveness of jobbing plants by paying close attention to quick changeover techniques and the arrangement of machines and operators into cellular workgroups. The standardization of many products in recent years encouraged the growth of sub-contract manufacturers, to the point where some fields of manufacturing became little more than assembly of the subsystems bought in from specialized makers. Where the finished product largely comprised bought-in sub-assemblies, such as personal computers or microwave ovens, some businesses reached the point of asking whether their manufacturing strategy had become one of elimination.

The new network context

The new network environment is an AND-AND world where all the old requirements are the starting point and new network factors add further layers of complexity to the design job.

What's different about manufacturing strategy in the new world of supply chain networks? Essentially, it is the need to bring new factors into the value equation – integration, collaboration and even synchronization far beyond the boundaries of manufacturing. In addition, companies need new technologies to enable the supply chain linkages. It is worth remembering that the basic requirements for manufacturing strategy have *not* changed. There is still the same need for rigorous analysis and searching assessment of options to find the solution that does the best job of delivering high-quality, low-cost products from safe, reliable operations that meet customer and business needs. The new network environment is an AND-AND world where all the old requirements are the starting point and new network factors add further layers of complexity to the design job.

Let's look at an example. 'Swing plants' are a neat manufacturing strategy for the fashion industry in Europe and North America. Asian plants have significant cost advantages, as long as orders are large and lead times are long. Using Asian plants to make-to-forecast for a whole season brings the initial purchase cost right down, but invariably means stock-outs of the most popular garments and expensive write-downs of the sizes and colors that do not sell to expectations. The solution? Companies bulk order the core requirements from Asia and use local higher-cost swing plants to supply specific sizes, colors and styles in response to retailer demands. Two distinct manufacturing strategies are employed to achieve a superior supply chain outcome. The quick response strategy for the swing plants requires much tighter integration and collaboration with distributors and retail customers, so their manufacturing planning and execution capabilities are differently specified, with swing plant operations geared around short-run agility.

Clearly, manufacturing strategy is subservient to bigger strategic goals. Business strategy should drive the development of a supply chain operating strategy, which in turn determines the role of manufacturing amongst other functions. In a perfect world, each business would have a well-articulated supply chain operating strategy, as set out in Chapter 1.4. See also Figure 2.3.1 below. Unfortunately this is not always the case, so the development of manufacturing strategy should begin by reviewing what needs to be known about the supply chain and the business.

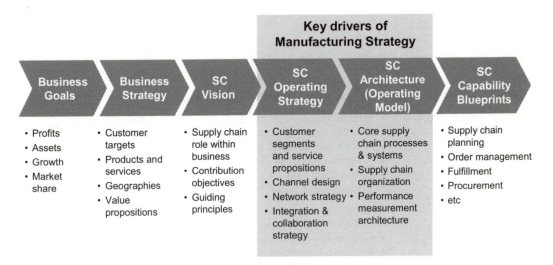

Figure 2.3.1
Drivers of manufacturing strategy

How should you build an aligned manufacturing strategy?

The manufacturing strategy grows in precision and clarity through five steps, as the key issues are driven down to meaningful detail.

We propose a five-step approach to building a manufacturing strategy aligned with the supply chain network. Each step delivers critical outputs and provides data and decisions for input to the next step. The manufacturing strategy will grow in precision and clarity with each step, as the key issues are driven down to meaningful detail. This five-step framework, shown in Table 2.3.1, is a general one for application to a wide range of industries, so it needs tailoring to each

Table 2.3.1

Five steps to building a manufacturing strategy aligned with the supply chain network

Steps	Considerations	Critical outcomes
1. Determine alignment with network and segment needs	• Competitive positioning – the network business model • Supply chain operating strategy – customer segments and their needs, and channel strategy • Product presentation requirements differentiated by segment	Alignment with business needs
2. Define make-to-order versus make-to-forecast profile	• Product family characteristics and lifecycles • Demand and supply variability • Process, production technology and capacity realities • Lead times, volumes and inventory deployment needs • MTO/MTF by product groups	Performance definition
3. Decide make/buy mix and develop manufacturing assets	• Sourcing options • Network partner capabilities • Make/buy mix • Logistics network optimization • Required manufacturing facilities, people, processes and technologies	Manufacturing capabilities
4. Develop effective network partnerships	• Strategic sourcing • Collaborative mindset • Shared performance measures • Aligned incentives • Information sharing • Network technologies	Linked network capabilities
5. Deliver operational results	• Time compression • Collaborative product design • Synchronized planning and execution • Optimum customer outcomes • Minimum total cost • Continuous change and growth	Efficient synchronized operations

particular industry and business by intelligent selection of the decisive issues. There is little value in mindless analysis and documentation of things that do not make a difference. Instead, focus on the differentiating points that will create sustainable advantage.

These steps provide a logical sequence for thinking through an externally focused manufacturing strategy. The depth and effort put into each step will vary by company. A newly established start-up will need to work through each step in depth. On the other hand, managers of established manufacturing businesses already have a detailed understanding of their own performance requirements (Step 2), and are well aware of their manufacturing capabilities (Step 3). Their choices will be to focus more attention on Step 1 (supply chain alignment) or Step 4 (network capabilities) before evaluating their performance against targets in Step 5 (synchronized operations). Their thinking may well lead back to a critical review of Steps 2 and 3, seeking better answers than those inherited or empirically applied to date. For instance, many a manufacturer has benefited from rigorous optimization modeling of their logistics network along the lines detailed in Chapter 2.1.

Let's explore each step in detail.

Step 1 – determine alignment with network and segment needs

A manufacturing strategy of long-term value must be built upon a deep and accurate understanding of the basis of supply chain competitiveness, including a forward view of how supply chain competitiveness is changing. Such understanding is necessary because manufacturing capabilities normally represent a substantial commitment and are not easily changed once put into place. The network business model must be understood at a level sufficient to answer the hard questions about EVA^{TM} and sustainability over a five- to ten-year horizon. What is the basis of value delivery and competition at the supply chain level? Is it lowest cost? Advanced technology? Customized products? Instant availability? Installation services? What are the implications for manufacturing?

Businesses must have a deep and accurate understanding of the basis of supply chain competitiveness before proceeding with manufacturing strategy.

To breathe life into the concept of supply chain alignment from a manufacturing perspective, consider the implications of a trend towards mixed-SKU 'rainbow' pallets in the grocery industry. Under what conditions might mixed-SKU pallets be produced at the manufacturing stage rather than picked and assembled at extra cost in distribution centers? Alternatively, consider the production scheduling, filling and packing implications of the remarkable innovation in product delivery created by a leading US water treatment supply company. Instead of delivering chemicals in traditional drums with associated handling, safety and labor requirements, the company offered its customers exchange service units already filled with chemicals for safe and simple usage. They rapidly captured market share and increased sales by 65 per cent, more than justifying the capital investment in the stainless steel delivery units and the infrastructure for their transport and refilling.

Analysis and quantification of such alignment issues should start with the supply chain operating strategy, or in the absence of this, with definition and sizing of customer segments and their current and future needs, as set out in Chapter 1.4. Customer segment volumes and service requirements, projected into the future will become a substantial data set, which gains another dimension when channel design considerations are added. The result should be a tabular definition of future product delivery requirements by channel, service level, value delivered and critical product presentation factors such as packaging, configuration and so on.

The aim of Step 1 is to set out a fact base defining the supply chain basis of customer value. The step quantifies the characteristics of product delivery that will meet the present and future needs of each supply chain segment and channel, without considering current manufacturing, distribution or third-party constraints. Big new ideas like Nalco's Porta-Feeds should be highlighted at this stage.

Step 2 – define MTO versus MTF profile

The aim is to define a practical balance between MTF and MTO, while considering what aspects can be postponed and outsourced to third parties.

The second step assesses the realities of product family characteristics and production technologies alongside the dynamics of demand and supply to determine how to achieve product delivery and assess the impact on inventory deployment and distribution. The aim is to define a practical balance between make-to-forecast (MTF) and make-to-order (MTO), while considering what aspects can be postponed from the manufacturing process and become the responsibility of distribution or third parties. The final outcome of this step is a scope and performance definition for manufacturing, in considerable detail. Completion of this step should define the required manufacturing approach (along the MTF to MTO spectrum) and tabulate responsiveness measures for each product family and lifecycle stage, to support the product delivery requirements established in Step 1. Many assumptions also will be documented regarding the capabilities that must be provided by other parts of the supply chain and the completeness of information integration required for manufacturing to reach the expected standard of supply chain responsiveness. Another valuable output will be the inventory holding implications by product family and channel.

Some businesses have obvious goals. Winning strategies through the 1980s and 1990s for traditional MTF businesses like the car industry have been to follow the lead of Toyota. They have gone 'lean' with high-volume production of sub-assemblies and at the same time pushed the boundaries of production and information technology to get close to MTO on finished vehicles. The prize is enormous. Success in breaking the car industry paradigm of making countless vehicles that customers do not want and then discounting them deeply to move the dead stock has the potential to save the industry billions of dollars. But the prize is still out of reach despite remarkable achievements in flexible production, examples of which include units of one, instant paint color changes and tight synchronization with Tier 1 suppliers. These and many other achievements are still not enough to address the overwhelming network and product complexity that has limited MTO in the car industry to small-scale or pilot efforts. We are likely to see the first examples of truly integrated MTO from European and US car makers around 2005 to 2008, more than a decade after serious efforts were launched to change the industry's manufacturing and marketing paradigm.

The spectrum of possibilities from MTF to MTO is very broad, providing one reason why successful strategies for one industry have often failed in another. The key is to get the business model right for the market while configuring manufacturing for competitive advantage. Dell Computer has done so famously by developing its build-to-order model to the point where its assembly plant inventories are as little as two hours usage. To do this, a superbly synchronized web of third-party logistics activities, both inbound and outbound, surround Dell's assembly plants. Dell is a commonly quoted example simply because it has done an exceptional job of refining the build-to-order manufacturing model as part of its customer-focused business strategy.

The full spectrum of manufacturing models covers six broad options. The mixed models address the realities of lifecycle and promotional considerations, which require the same product to be MTF to initially fill the channel then shift to MTO as it fades in the market. The options are:

1 pure MTF producers like magazine printers, toy factories and low-price clothing makers
2 seasonal MTF/variable supply businesses like fruit canners and wine makers
3 mixed MTF/MTO producers of chemicals, consumer goods and foods
4 MTF/configure-to-order manufacturers like the most advanced car makers
5 pure MTO or BTO assembler/manufacturers like Dell Computers
6 engineer-to-order makers, typically in construction, aerospace and defence.

Step 3 – decide make/buy mix and develop manufacturing assets

Answering the question 'What should be made where, when and by whom?', will define the location and evolving role of each manufacturing facility.

Given the directional choices and the fact base now assembled in Steps 1 and 2, what proportion of product supply should be contributed by manufacturing, and what proportion by third parties? In other words, what is the make/buy mix? Answers to this question begin at a high level. They can be driven down to component-by-component detail in the case of complex machinery like diesel engines for which analytical make/buy methodologies are commonly used to optimize sourcing of every part.

Keeping the focus on strategy and staying above component level, this is the stage at which sourcing options, network partner capabilities and the geographical realities captured in logistics network models must be brought to a conclusion. Answering the question 'What should be made where, when and by whom?', will define the location and evolving role of each manufacturing facility over the strategic planning horizon. From each facility role definition, the required manufacturing capabilities must be derived, in terms of assets, people, processes and technologies. These are aligned with the product delivery and performance data from Steps 1 and 2. In parallel, companies should also generate similar levels of definition around the required capabilities and performance of third parties, be they transport providers, distribution center operators, component suppliers or second-source makers of products.

Make/buy decision-making has been developed to a high art in some industries by including everything from business strategy to component costing within its scope. Such breadth is not necessary if Steps 1 and 2 have properly addressed the bigger supply chain issues, allowing this step to focus on production-specific tradeoffs that primarily relate to capacity, cost, flexibility and capital investment.

Businesses should be guided in their make/buy decision-making by the product and process maturity, which largely determines what is possible. Car companies were not able to outsource complete braking systems to suppliers such as Bosch and PBR until almost all the technical and performance issues around disk brakes, brake pads and ABS systems had been resolved and standardized. Doing so eliminated braking performance as a differentiator between mass-market car makers. Leading-edge products and new manufacturing processes usually require intensive in-house supervision or difficult and costly efforts to achieve supply chain integration. On the one hand, there is an understandable preference to 'make' in these cases. On the other hand, commodity products and mature, proven components should cause few integration challenges. Therefore, they require careful analysis of scale economies, capital investment, operating costs, capacities and reliability at minute levels of detail to arrive at the best 'buy' or 'buy some' decisions.

After deciding what is to be 'made', organizations can narrow their attention to each manufacturing facility and determine the capabilities that each plant must have to meet performance needs throughout the planning horizon. With all the details of products, delivery formats and performance expectations at hand, the operational experts can enjoy the challenge of applying their kit of tools and techniques to minimize cost, waste, time, energy and inventories in the production facility. Numerous textbooks provide exhaustive coverage of product, process and manufacturing improvement techniques for application at this stage. Given good judgment and a sufficient but disciplined budget any production engineer worth his or her salt could devise a way to make things more cleverly and efficiently. The challenge is to do so sustainably, in other words to build ongoing capability.

Organizations can focus on building the ongoing capabilities of each manufacturing facility according to the planning horizon.

The most obvious element of manufacturing capability is the production machinery and equipment, especially big-scale capital-intensive assets like chemical process plants, around which tends to grow a culture of process efficiency, volume maximization and facility utilization, not always aligned with supply chain needs.

The next most obvious manufacturing capability is that represented by the people, their culture and their years of ingrained knowledge. Anyone who has established a greenfield plant in a developing country or in a rural area lacking a long history of manufacturing knows how slow and painful is the process of building a production culture, even with leadership from a substantial number of imported experts. People capability is a slow-growing asset requiring careful nurturing and stewardship to develop performance and pride. The pay-off is in the hard numbers of safety, yield, process stability, continuous improvement and reliability.

The least problematic manufacturing capabilities are the ones you can buy – enabling and connecting technologies. More and more standardized solutions are emerging for process control, manufacturing execution and the linkages with planning, scheduling and ordering systems. The days when real-time shop-floor control systems did not talk to batch-oriented business systems are largely gone, and we should now expect seamless integration between supply chain plans and manufacturing outputs. See Chapter 4.5 for more extensive treatment of supply chain capabilities.

Step 4 – develop effective network partnerships

With the knowledge that manufacturing can no longer be an island, the new strategy should be developed to this stage on the assumption that a partnership approach will prevail. The organization should be looking at jointly developed, aligned processes and performance measures, supported and enabled by network technologies that connect manufacturing upstream and downstream. Despite plenty of proof of their value, there are some major challenges in making these a reality.

A partnership approach should underpin the strategy development, including jointly developed, aligned processes and performance measures.

A few industries, mainly high technology, have well and truly overcome the technical challenges of integrating design management with manufacturing. This is particularly the case with complex engineered products like aircraft, cars and computers where aggressive targets for product performance and speed to market can only be met by live links between design and production. The best design-production teams can now leap-frog traditional physical prototyping stages and slash months out of development cycles by going straight from computer models to production tooling, in many cases by means of electronic collaboration between team members scattered around the world in different time zones, connected only by their modeling software.

Industries with less extreme demands on product performance will usually direct the partnership effort towards either customer alignment or strategic sourcing. A good example of the customer alignment case is the packaging industry. Makers of high-volume packaging for the food and consumer packaged goods industries suffer particularly badly from the 'bull-whip syndrome'. They are at the tip of the whip and often experience drastic ups and downs in orders and delivery off-takes, making crisis response an essential, but costly, skill. The sudden ups and downs usually come without any warning because the downstream supply chain has traditionally allowed packaging companies no visibility of changes in demand or levels of inventory of the goods wrapped in their packaging.

From their relatively powerless position in the supply chain, packaging companies have struggled to improve their alignment and collaboration with customers. Economically viable technologies did not exist until the end of the 1990s to support sharing of demand planning information. In Europe, packaging companies were early participants in collaboration pilots and CPG (consumer packaged goods) e-marketplaces in Europe, the US and Australia. What they were after was reliable demand planning information to better stabilize their production schedules, and they were willing to share the significant cost savings with their customers.

Alignment and collaboration means much more than sharing demand data. The needs of customers must be understood and appropriate strategic responses developed.

In reality, alignment and collaboration mean much more than sharing demand data, and some packaging suppliers led the way in more fully understanding the needs of their customers and the required strategic response from their own manufacturing sites. An example was a large Australian packaging manufacturer that conducted an extensive customer alignment review with their biggest customers, summarizing customer service requirements on the matrix shown in Figure 2.3.2. To their surprise, practically all their large customers were envisioning 'value plus' or 'integrated operations' relationships, and simply lacked the cost-effective processes and technology to put a collaborative approach into effect. The will was there but not the way.

The things that could be tackled by the packaging company and their customers during the waiting period before effective CPG

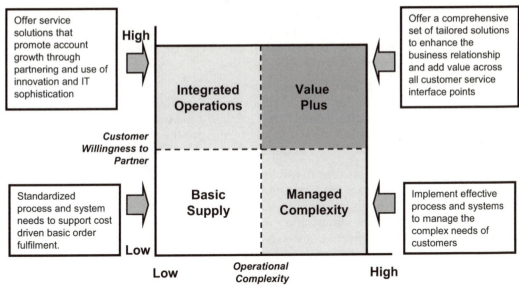

Figure 2.3.2
Customer service matrix

e-markets or industry-standard processes are adopted to enable true collaborative planning were identified as:

- excellence in enterprise-level demand and supply planning
- a collaborative mindset
- shared performance measures and aligned incentives
- regular information sharing, manually if necessary, and
- use of low-cost supply chain visibility tools, especially those available as a service from others such as third-party logistics providers.

All of these initiatives have some impact on manufacturing strategy.

So, a sound strategy for network partnering and for manufacturing in the networked world is a necessity. The strategy must allow for quite long timescales where collaborative infrastructure does not currently exist, and plan for a different manufacturing environment and a culture with fewer crises, when the links are in place and working.

Step 5 – deliver operational results

Step 5 is really about execution and at first glance may appear out of place in an approach to strategy formulation. It is included in the framework because 'execution as strategy' is becoming a notable factor in the success of agile businesses in a fast-changing world. The shrinking timeframes that all businesses are experiencing make it hard to stand back and take the time to develop strategic answers in a linear, logical sequence. Instead the world is driving us towards a more experimental approach that recognizes the value of learning from experience.

Strategy must be alive and growing, developed as part of a learning process embedded in the organization.

In the manufacturing context this insight means that strategy must be alive and growing, developed as part of a learning process embedded in the organization. The essentials of the 'execution as strategy' approach include:

- act faster than your competition
- define and utilize your critical capabilities
- iteratively launch and manage experiments
- measure the results, capturing benefits and lessons, and
- view failures as part of the learning process.

The operational results that must be delivered are well known – optimum customer outcomes at minimum cost, usually achieved through the sound principles of time compression, waste elimination and synchronization with supply chain partners. Soundly based measurement, analysis and review are essential to prove that the results are being achieved and to contribute data on issues and opportunities for further development of the manufacturing strategy.

Conclusion

Manufacturing companies are responding to and prospering from their supply chain roles, despite the challenges.

In this chapter we have discussed the sort of outwardly oriented approach to manufacturing strategy that must be followed by any manufacturer playing a part in a complex supply chain network. We have identified the key differences between the old view of manufacturing and its new supply chain role. We have provided some examples of the ways in which manufacturing companies are responding to and prospering from their supply chain roles, despite the challenges. For more information on single-company or single-facility manufacturing improvement strategies there are many sources. The Six Sigma business philosophy provides a particularly comprehensive approach, compatible with the networked world of today, and is described in Chapter 2.4.

References

'A Guide To Efficient Replenishment and Reducing "Stock Outs" Within The Grocery Industry' (April 2001), ECR Australasia, <www.ecr.australasia.org.au>.

Holweg, Matthias and Pil, Frits K. (2001); 'Successful Build-to-Order Strategies Start With the Customer', MIT, *Sloan Management Review* (Fall).

Moozakis, C. (2002), 'Nissan Wants To Be Like Dell – Automaker Says It Can Achieve Build-To-Order Via The Web In 18 Months, Experts Are Skeptical', *Internetweek* (8 January).

Six Sigma – improving the quality of business

2.4

Richard D. Schleusener and Andrew J. Berger

The evolution of quality

On 16 May 1924, a young engineer at Bell Telephone Laboratories named Walter Shewhart wrote a memo to his superiors suggesting that they adopt a process called statistical process control. Shewhart's work was the start of the quality movement, as organizations know it today.

Both Juran and Deming believed that only management could influence the majority of quality problems.

Many years later, shortly after World War II, General Douglas MacArthur, the commander of the US occupation forces in Japan, was charged with leading an effort to rebuild Japan's economy after the devastation of the war. MacArthur worked with manufacturers in Japan to address quality problems and created training for managers, part of which included Shewhart's methods of quality control. Dr W. Edwards Deming, a colleague of Shewhart's who had trained 31 000 people in the US on quality control techniques, delivered the training.

Another American, Dr Joseph Juran, was also invited to help improve the quality of Japanese industry. Juran applied the Pareto Principle for quality problems, which states that 20 per cent of problems cause 80 per cent of quality issues. By focusing on solving the vital few problems using project-by-project improvement, instead of attempting to address the many trivial problems all at once, significant progress could be made to improve quality. Both Juran and Deming believed that only management could influence the vast majority of quality problems.

Under Deming and Juran, Japan's application of these techniques dramatically improved quality. In the 1970s, Japanese car manufacturers experienced a breakthrough because they knew how to manufacture fuel-efficient cars cost-effectively that Americans needed at a time of severe gasoline shortages. These high-quality cars made inroads into the US automobile market. A documentary of Deming's work in Japan made and broadcast in 1980 – 'If Japan Can, Why Can't

Table 2.4.1
Comparison of quality level to cost of poor quality

Sigma level	Defects per million opportunities	Cost of poor quality (% of sales)
2	308 537	
3	66 807	25–40%
4	6210	15–25%
5	233	5–15%
6	3.4	<1%

We?' – sparked enormous interest in understanding and applying quality methods. The approach that came to be known as total quality management (TQM) was embraced by corporate America as a way to improve the level of quality and the competitive position of their products and services.

In the early 1980s, Motorola coined as well as trademarked the term 'Six Sigma', an extension of TQM, and used it as a new framework to improve quality. Motorola applied the methodology to its products and found it could improve cost structures by removing the rework required when quality problems were present. Table 2.4.1 shows the cost benefits of achieving higher levels of quality. The name 'Six Sigma' itself applies to the ambitious statistical target of achieving no more than 3.4 defects per one million chances.

This chapter outlines the Six Sigma methodology and describes how it has proven to be successful in different sectors of the economy, in different organizational cultures, in different countries and in organizations with varied goals and objectives. Six Sigma provides a useful management framework for today's supply chain executives to consider when seeking to improve the quality of supply chain performance.

The Six Sigma difference

Six Sigma was transformed from a simple quality measurement tool to a breakthrough business excellence philosophy.

Six Sigma was elevated from the shop floor to the boardroom when the former CEO of General Electric, Jack Welch, announced in 1996 that he planned to lead GE to become a Six Sigma company by 2000. Even today, GE lists Six Sigma as one of its four key thrusts as an organization and says Six Sigma continues to realize savings in the billions of dollars. GE is currently taking Six Sigma outside the borders of manufacturing process control and applying the methodology to interactions with suppliers and customers.

In addition to GE, industry leaders such as Motorola, ABB and Allied Signal (now Honeywell) were among the first companies to use the Six Sigma framework as an operating strategy. Motorola saved more than $2 billion in less than three years when it first deployed Six Sigma. Allied Signal saved more than $1 billion in its first two years of deployment, while ABB saved just under $1 billion within the first year. Institutions like the Six Sigma Academy have helped many companies in the manufacturing, energy, service, financial services and health care industries to implement Six Sigma.

The definition of Six Sigma has evolved as a result of the way these major companies deployed and fine-tuned Six Sigma in their organizations. ABB required Six Sigma efforts to be linked directly to the bottom line. Allied Signal's deployment required that financial results be demonstrated in a short timeframe. GE's experience highlighted the need for organizational focus for the effort.

Dr Mikel Harry and Richard Schroeder, ex-Motorola executives, were responsible for creating the unique combination of change management and data-driven methodologies that transformed Six Sigma from a simple quality measurement tool to the breakthrough business excellence philosophy it is today.

In their book *Six Sigma: The Breakthrough Management Strategy Revolutionizing the World's Top Corporations* (1999), Harry and Schroeder suggested that Larry Bossidy, Allied Signal's CEO, and Jack Welch took risks expending resources on deployment because they were unsure if they would realize the returns from the investment. Today that risk is minimal because companies that have deployed Six Sigma have provided a strong track record of quantifiable benefits and tangible results.

Organizations need to focus their managers as well as use tools correctly to realize the full benefits of Six Sigma.

Harry and Schroeder believed the difference between TQM and Six Sigma is a matter of focus. 'Total quality management programs focus on improvements in individual operations with unrelated processes', they said. 'The Six Sigma architects at Motorola focused on making improvements in all operations within a process, producing results far more rapidly and effectively.'

A strength of Six Sigma compared to TQM is Six Sigma's sustainable use of tools. Institutions like the Six Sigma Academy train deployment 'champions' – the middle managers who develop and support the implementation of Six Sigma. The Academy also describes different levels of expertise that are needed within organizations to sustain the benefits of Six Sigma.

'Master black belts' (MBBs) are the individuals with significant analytical expertise and Six Sigma experience. MBBs require extra training in the in-depth use of the quantitative tools, and training in group processes to lead teams successfully. Typical 'black belts' have a two-year tenure, so more waves of training will be needed if Six Sigma is deployed in an ongoing way. MBBs need training experience and some understanding of adult learning theory to teach new waves of black belts effectively.

While the Six Sigma methodology uses the same set of tools described in total quality management, there are distinct differences between the application of TQM and Six Sigma. Six Sigma practitioners would suggest TQM applications fail in a way that does not happen with Six Sigma. If the tools are similar, what is the difference? What are the characteristics of Six Sigma that allow for a greater contribution to meeting an organization's goals and objectives?

One reason Six Sigma works so well is its disciplined approach to applying quantitative tools. Using statistics to see through the fog of variability is a critical step in intervening in a process; it will make the process run more reliably with less variability. In contrast, relying solely on experience to design interventions rather than data-based approaches leads to potentially faulty solutions. It is important to note that these tools – used both in TQM and Six Sigma – are necessary but not sufficient to realize significant savings. Organizations need to achieve management focus as well as the correct use of tools to realize the full benefits of Six Sigma.

Four steps: measure, analyse, improve and control

The Six Sigma methodology involves a four-step process: measure, analyse, improve and control. The four phases are designed to use data to find the drivers of aspects of performance that organizations care about and that they can control. The first phase, measure, is designed to quantify current performance of an aspect of the business that is important to the overall goals and objectives of the organization. The key measure, usually the measure of a desired business outcome, is denoted by a 'Y' in Six Sigma terminology, and can be regarded as an outcome, or effect of a process. An analysis is conducted on the way that the outcome/effect is measured to verify that the measurement data collected reflects the true performance of the process. In many cases, faulty collection of data can obscure a process's true performance. In addition to quantifying how well the process runs currently, tools are used to identify any potential drivers, or causes of that outcome/effect. These drivers or causes are called 'Xs' in Six Sigma terminology.

In the analyse phase, statistics are used to determine true causal relationships between the potential drivers and outcomes (cause and effect relationship) to determine which of the Xs really influence the Y. This phase helps sort out the causes (Xs) that are true drivers of the system (cause a real effect by changing the outcome (Y)) from those that just have a correlation to a change in outcome. This step is important because implicit in it is the change from using 'woolly data', hearsay and anecdotes, to the use of hard, factual, rigorous information to guide decision-making. At the end of the analyse phase, a short list of Xs that are true drivers of Y are identified to use in the next phase. This means that we have established true causal relationships.

In the improve phase, the short list of causes (Xs) are manipulated in a systematic way to develop a model, a mathematical equation, that describes how much the causes influence the outcomes (Y). The goal is then to use the Xs, which managers can control, to control the Y.

In the control phase, a system is put in place to hold the gains. Control schemes are designed to keep the outcome (Y) well within the specifications required by the customer of the process. Organizations reach the Six Sigma levels of quality when they control the outcome such that they see only 3.4 defects per every million opportunities.

However, using the tools alone is insufficient to realize the significant gains available to an organization. The organization needs to have management support and focus also occurring in concert with the data-driven answers to the concerns being addressed. One lesson learned from the Six Sigma deployments at Allied and GE is that the companies' underlying focus on using the methodology was a major way of meeting their organizational goals and objectives. For instance, to support the efforts of the project teams, the companies put significant resources behind the training of the teams and gave them sufficient time to deliver results.

The deployment challenge

Six Sigma is a change initiative at its core. Any large change effort in an organization is difficult. Michael Fullan (1993) from the University of Toronto said planned change was not the cumulative development of a comprehensive strategy, rather, it was 'one damned thing after another'. Fullan's comments highlight the difficulties in deploying Six Sigma: there are no guarantees of success. Complex change strategies teach that there is no one right answer or one right way. A template that describes how to deploy any program in a rigid way is destined to fail. Instead, an organization should implement a strategy of learning, benchmarking and testing during the deployment to ensure it embraces and exploits all opportunities available.

Learning, benchmarking and testing should occur throughout deployment to ensure all opportunities are captured.

Once an organization has decided to deploy Six Sigma, it needs to determine the scope of the deployment. What business units will the effort be focused in? What geographic locations? What types of business will start the effort? What is the goal of the initiative? Will benefits be in the form of hard financial savings? Will projects address customer satisfaction issues? Potentially, the effort could be focused at increasing revenues. A front-end decision is made in the deployment to help define the organization needed to support the effort.

The organization needs to identify what the financial targets of the effort will be. They will determine who needs to be trained and establish a timeline for when the training will take place. Personnel to support the effort will be identified and contacted, and plans for transition into Six Sigma roles made and executed. Once the personnel and targets are in place, the organization needs to determine a set of guidelines to identify potential projects for applying Six Sigma.

The projects should be prioritized and the supporting resources identified to help Six Sigma personnel make progress on the projects. Extra resources will include people to work on the project teams, financial resources for necessary travel, and backfill resources if a decision is made to replace people who will be doing full-time improvement work with Six Sigma. In addition, logistical support from human resources is required to define job expectations and career paths of Six Sigma participants, to develop reward and recognition schemes, and to create an infrastructure to support change initiatives.

The efficient deployment of Six Sigma will ensure Six Sigma thinking is fully integrated into the DNA of corporate culture.

The information technology group needs to think through how to provide necessary computing power and database accessibility. Finance needs to develop a framework to quantify the savings realized on any project, and develop a process for verification of project success. The communications group needs to develop an ongoing communications plan, from rollout of the initiative through sustainability efforts. The logistics of executing the training needs to be addressed, and Six Sigma policies and procedures developed and a deployment scorecard created.

Once the infrastructure has been put in place, the fun work begins. After training, the project champions will develop a portfolio of projects and create a queue so that once one project has been executed, the next will be addressed. They will also develop a process for communicating success stories so that essential learnings are distributed across the organization. A process needs to be developed to review projects. Financial results and other measures on the deployment scorecard also need to be tracked.

As outlined, the deployment process requires a substantial effort by many people. An efficient process is an important contributor to the success of the deployment, while a haphazard effort is likely to lead to haphazard results. The Six Sigma Academy has described particular characteristics for deploying Six Sigma that are necessary to achieve sustainability. These characteristics, described below, are designed to support the full integration of Six Sigma thinking into the DNA of the corporate culture.

Competence

Six Sigma black belts, green belts and champions need to be well versed in the application of the quantitative tools. They need to have an understanding of the process that allows for probing questions of the project teams to ensure that the methodology is being followed appropriately. This training requires significant investment, but the returns are also significant. It is important that statistical capability is diffused throughout the organization to remove any mystique from statistical thinking. Everyone should understand Six Sigma and the rationale for using the methodology. Ideally, both suppliers and customers need to understand the fundamental concepts as well.

Commitment

Visible and ongoing top-down leadership is needed for a successful deployment of Six Sigma. Organizational leaders should not only lead the deployment, but also believe that the process will help them meet their goals and objectives. Such belief will encourage others in the organization to adopt Six Sigma and change the way business is done. Recognition programs for individuals and teams should be designed and adjusted to support the effort. The results from Six Sigma projects should be aimed at key objectives and the results should be tracked.

Managers need to be trained in Six Sigma tools. Leaders need to believe in how Six Sigma can deliver their objectives.

Communication

A good Six Sigma communication plan begins with a clear definition of the methodology so that everyone has a common understanding of the initiative. The plan must include two-way communication of the deployment timetable, opportunities and achievements. Project status, progress reporting, and financial results should be a part of the company's management program.

Results

To achieve tangible results, the organization must create quantitative goals for the deployment, such as to become a 4.5 sigma division within a year. A goal such as 'meeting or exceeding customer expectations' may be too nebulous to measure progress. Enabling data-driven approaches to Six Sigma deployment is also critical, so tracking progress toward the goal on these measures is important. Six Sigma initiatives should support strategic needs. Successes should be visible and publicly recognized. Projects should support the need for a continuous flow of successes, while at the same time champions need to remain pragmatic and accountable for their results.

Organizations need to set quantitative goals for the deployment and use the right tools to address the specific problems.

Incremental change can occur by tweaking a process and trying harder. If the goal is to create significant change, it is important to change the way work is currently done. Performance should show an improvement in results that is discontinuous. Setting stretch goals can help because they create the need to do work differently, as long as there is a process to support realizing the stretch goal.

Use appropriate tools

The problems being addressed should define the appropriate tool set. The company should not require that every project uses a certain tool. Instead, it should encourage a diversity of applications of the Six Sigma methodology. In this way, the organization will avoid a 'purity' problem – that there is only one right way to proceed.

Company organization

Silo-busting should be a key priority during the deployment of Six Sigma. Rummler and Brache (1995) say the important work of an organization is to manage in the white spaces of the organization chart.

Self-sufficiency

An organization deploying Six Sigma needs to develop internal capability. That means that performance plans include developing Six Sigma capability, recognizing and rewarding internal training skills, and focusing on developing and rewarding the presence of skills in the workplace.

Integration

Six Sigma works just as well in the service and transaction world as it does in manufacturing. In addition, companies are now learning how to use Six Sigma to support revenue improvement with projects that address effective sales processes. Programs that are already supporting the organization in meeting goals should be integrated with Six Sigma, not thrown out.

The quality program needs to be established so that it addresses what is important to the business. The quality program should never stand alone. According to Mikel Harry *et al* (1999), organizations should be concerned about the quality of business, not the business of quality. Everyone needs to play a role in a successful Six Sigma deployment, not just a quality department. Reward systems need to be designed to support the framework of improving quality necessary for the entire business.

Applying Six Sigma to non-manufacturing areas

The next Six Sigma frontier will be in non-manufacturing areas such as sales and marketing, where processes can be improved and savings made.

The Six Sigma Academy reports that each Six Sigma project in manufacturing typically realizes about $250 000 in savings. The academy's experience also shows that projects in non-manufacturing areas are realizing savings of more than $300 000. It is believed that non-manufacturing areas have less experience in applying quantitative tools, so there is more 'low-hanging fruit' – and hence more financial savings – available.

All work is a process, whether it is making widgets or providing a service. Six Sigma is about process execution excellence, so intuitively the methodology should support improvements in other areas. Successful Six Sigma projects in service areas such as Human Resources include reducing the time it takes from when a requisition is submitted for a new employee until the person is hired and in place. Other examples include processes for salary, promotion and compensation. The Finance area can also use the Six Sigma approach to address the amount of time it takes to close the books, shorten the average time of accounts receivable or reduce errors in accounts payable. The data-driven techniques of Six Sigma can be used to improve the operation of each one of these processes.

In addition to typical service work, Six Sigma can be applied to 'art form' processes as well. An example would be a sales process.

Determining key drivers for closing sales could provide significant savings. As an example, customer contact may be a critical component of closing a sale. What the data can help determine is whether or not customer contact needs to be a golf outing or just a site visit.

A vast body of Six Sigma knowledge and experience exists today, as it applies in manufacturing. However, there is an increasing number of Six Sigma examples in traditional service industries such as financial services and healthcare. The next Six Sigma frontier will be in non-manufacturing areas such as sales and marketing. The goal will be to weave excellence into the fabric of business. The typical approach will be to look at an existing process and determine where errors occur and put processes in place to reduce or eliminate the errors. Another opportunity to apply Six Sigma thinking is in the area of design, of both products and processes.

Design for Six Sigma is a process that looks at customer expectations and uses quantitative tools to create a product or process that meets customer requirements. The tools look at environmental factors that unfavorably influence a process and then determine ways to define the process so that environmental factors have no effect. A common example most people can all relate to is a gas pump. Since drivers never want to make the error of putting leaded gasoline into an engine needing unleaded gas, the nozzle for leaded gas is made too large to put into an unleaded tank. That is a simple example of one way to work with a process to prevent errors from occurring.

Integrating Six Sigma with other improvement tools

Six Sigma is a process that supports an organization in meeting their goals and objectives. Six Sigma should not necessarily replace any other improvement initiatives. Constancy of purpose was a cornerstone of TQM, and should be in place with a Six Sigma initiative as well. If an organization has developed lean capability, is Class A MRPII, has ISO registration in hand, has used business process re-engineering, or any of several business improvement initiatives, the question to ask is whether or not there is consistency between that initiative and Six Sigma. Typically, Six Sigma can support the other initiatives.

Typically, Six Sigma can support other business improvement initiatives.

Six Sigma focuses on reducing variability and eliminating defects while lean is about eliminating waste and achieving single piece flow. Single piece flow requires high reliability and high quality, so the initiatives go hand in hand. MRPII requires that an organization identify customer needs and has high-quality order fulfilment. Six Sigma is a process to reduce errors, and can certainly support an MRP effort. ISO requires a documented process to address quality, and Six Sigma offers a specific process to review customer needs and address quality problems. Business process re-engineering offers a way to understand what the key business processes are. For Six Sigma to help an organization to meet its goals and objectives, it is important to look at the entire business process and focus Six Sigma resources in the appropriate places.

Applying new technologies to Six Sigma

Software today gives process experts access to statistical methodology, helping them to analyze data better.

The power of quantitative tools is exponentially greater in the hands of a process expert. When outside experts such as statisticians look at data summaries, they can draw appropriate conclusions and support a team in addressing problems. When a process expert looks at data summaries, they see things that external experts do not have the insights to look for. Process experts know the unusual occurrence that happened the day the data was collected; they know when the data is not representative of typical experience. Process experts today are also assisted by software to help them access statistical methodology. The ability to apply and think with statistics is infinitely easier today than it was 15 years ago.

In the same way, other examples of technology allow access to people who traditionally did not have access. Software is available to explore potential solutions to the design for Six Sigma problems that are apparently in conflict. Software can also act as a library for revisiting the tools that were covered in training. Internet-based programs exist to share information from successful projects so that improvements made in one area can be applied throughout a company.

The more people know and understand Six Sigma, the more powerful its application in a company. e-Learning provides a way to share the methodology, but also to share success stories and bring energy to an organization to sustain its change efforts.

Conclusion

The lessons pressed by the masters of TQM are still important to those implementing newer improvement strategies such as Six Sigma. One of Fullan's (1993) lessons of change is that connection to a wider environment is critical. The best organizations learn externally as well as internally. Applying best practices from three generations of quality and process excellence experts, Shewhart, Deming and Juran, and now Harry and Schroeder, contributes to continuously improving upon the strategies and tactics to achieve breakthrough results in business excellence.

References

Fullan, M. (1993), *Change forces*, New York: The Falmer Press.
Harry, M. J. and Schroeder R. (1999), *Six Sigma: The Breakthrough Management Strategy Revolutionizing the World's Top Corporations*, Doubleday.
Rummler, G. A. and Brache, A. P. (1995), *Improving Performance – How to manage the white space on the organization chart*, 2nd edition, Jossey-Bass.

About Six Sigma Academy

Six Sigma Academy is the pre-eminent, global consultancy creating transformational change at industry-leading corporations worldwide. Six Sigma Academy works with corporations to transfer knowledge to potentially thousands of employees, who in turn remove variation, reduce waste and increase efficiency and quality in the everyday processes of their business. Founded in 1994 by Dr Mikel Harry and Richard Schroeder, Scottsdale, Arizona-based Six Sigma Academy offers a full range of services, as well as a suite of customized software tools, to help companies achieve breakthrough results including profitability, client satisfaction and employee satisfaction. Web site address: www.6-sigma.com.

About Continuous Innovation Culture

Continuous Innovation Culture is a leading provider of Six Sigma project software founded by Andrew Berger. The company has a unique platform for helping project sponsors, managers and teams to record and share key data, reviews and results on Six Sigma projects. The software helps to cut project and training costs, improve project tracking and to improve the effectiveness of Black Belts and Green Belts. Web site address: www.ci-c.com.

2.5 Distribution operations – design for excellence

David R. Olson

Executives need to reassess and adjust distribution capabilities if they wish to pursue supply chain operational excellence.

Warehousing and distribution center operations are the pivot points for product and information flows between sources of supply and customers. To achieve operational excellence, organizations must have the capability to execute their distribution operations efficiently and effectively. Such a capability can meet customer needs and supply chain requirements, while minimizing costs and maximizing return on capital. However, too many organizations assume that distribution operations designed for the early 1990s are still adequate. Some believe that outsourcing means they also outsource their risk to a third party. Others are ignoring the business reality of extended supply chain networks, where collaboration is changing the role of some distribution operations and placing new requirements and performance expectations on others.

To retain a competitive edge in such a dynamic environment, it is critical that supply chain executives understand that significant changes in business requirements create correspondingly new and different operating requirements. If they choose to pursue supply chain operational excellence, they need to reassess and adjust distribution capabilities periodically. This chapter explores how organizations can ensure they have warehousing capability and a capacity for operational excellence. Using a holistic perspective, the chapter outlines a proven approach to develop new distribution centers and upgrade existing ones. It explores the depth and breadth of the warehousing business process and presents a four-phase approach for developing and implementing an effective distribution operation.

Warehousing or distribution center operations

Is it a warehouse or a distribution center? Of course, that depends. People commonly use the term 'warehouse' to describe a place where goods are stored until they are needed or distributed. Distribution centers are places where goods are consolidated from geographically dispersed sources of supply and shipped to geographically specific sources of demand. Today, the terms 'store-room', 'stock-room', 'depot', 'warehouse', 'distribution center', 'sequencing and mixing center', 'logistics center', 'customer service center' and 'transportation hub' are used to describe similar operations throughout the supply chain. They have a common purpose, but vary widely in ways that are key to the design of distribution operations. This chapter will use the term 'warehouse' in the general sense to represent all these operations and the term 'warehousing' for the collective business process that receives, stores, selects and ships products.

Warehousing is pervasive throughout the supply chain, despite recurring predictions of its decline.

Warehousing is pervasive throughout the supply chain, despite recurring predictions of its decline. Its future is guaranteed by such realities as natural phenomena, distance, geography, the commercial need for profit, consumer demand, and a truly global economy. Fundamentally, its role in the supply chain can be defined in a single word: *availability*. Having the right material, in the right quantity, in the right place, at the right time in the right condition is often dependent on the age-old business process of warehousing. At the core, a warehouse does four things:

- takes control of materials from others – receiving
- protects the materials until needed – storage
- selects materials required by its customers – picking, and
- transfers control of the material for delivery to the customer by others – shipping.

In reality, many more processes may be performed within a given warehouse operation. The extended core processes are an expanded list of the four primary functions and include cross docking, cycle counting and returns processing. The postponement processes serve to reduce the number of stock keeping units (SKU) that must be managed in a warehouse by storing components in their simplest form. They represent processes formerly done upstream that have migrated into the warehouse and include kitting, packaging, labeling and light assembly. The custom services originate with a customer's requirements and represent the movement upstream of processes once done downstream of the warehouse operation. They include such processes as price ticketing, label hanging, sequencing, shipping compliance labeling and construction of retail store displays.

A holistic, four-phase approach

People, processes, equipment, information technology and facilities are all addressed through each phase of a distribution operation.

Developing and implementing a warehouse operation is a journey best managed in phases. The actual number of phases will vary according to budget, timing and funding authority, but a successful program will involve four major phases: needs assessment, concept design, detailed design and implementation. This chapter focuses on the most creative phase – concept design.

Each of the components of a warehouse operation – people, processes, equipment, information technology and facilities – are addressed within each phase, but at increasing levels of detail and specificity. Typically, organizations fund each phase separately, requiring executives to sign off as the milestones are accomplished and the succeeding phase is planned and proposed. Each phase refines the accomplishments of the previous stage and readies the organization for achieving the next step. The overall effect is to minimize risk to the organization for the investment in planning and preparation.

Phase 1 – needs assessment

A needs assessment can be triggered by several events or business needs. A network optimization study could find that changes are needed to a company's distribution network, requiring substantial changes to the number, location, and/or mission of existing warehouses. A company might decide to outsource or 'in-source' part or all of its warehousing requirements. An organization might also experience 'pain' in its warehouse operating performance, typically due to out-dated methods and inadequate capacity, and decide that it needs to improve its distribution performance substantially.

The needs analysis will document the need for change and communicating the need to all stakeholders.

Regardless of the trigger, the assessment of distribution operations needs top executive support at the start of the process. Once this is secured, supply chain executives can establish a team to conduct a mini-design project. The initial team comprises a project sponsor and key operating staff, as well as content experts as needed. Their first task would be to document the need for change and communicating the need to all stakeholders, clearly and effectively. Through interviews, observations and high-level quantitative analysis, the team would document strengths and weaknesses of the current operation. By doing this, they would identify opportunities for improvement.

A comprehensive needs analysis would include the documentation of:

- capacity shortfalls
- gaps between best and existing practices
- expected improvements in key performance indicators
- potential ranges for costs and savings
- business and supply chain requirements that mandate change and
- a budget and a plan for concept design.

Phase 2 – conceptual design

Conceptual design of a warehouse operation is a big job and is best undertaken in a team environment. In fact, at least three teams are useful. The core team is the design team, comprising content experts for warehousing operations as well as operating personnel. The team requires a 'go to' information technology person to facilitate data collection. The second, expanded team would include stakeholders in the warehousing operation, including representatives from supply chain management, inventory management, customer service, human resources and information technology. The project sponsor would provide advice and act as an ongoing sounding board.

Three teams are needed: the core design team; the expanded stakeholder team; and the steering committee.

The third team would be the steering committee, chaired by the project sponsor, and including members of executive management including supply chain, information technology, procurement, inventory management, marketing, sales and operations. At the conclusion of the needs analysis, the mini-design team would submit their proposal to the steering committee for approval before proceeding. Typically, the steering committee would provide review and feedback while making decisions to move the process forward once milestones are accomplished. They would also ensure that adequate resources were available for the project.

As described below, the conceptual design phase comprises four tasks: defining future operating requirements, conceptualizing the operation, facility planning and preparing for detailed design and implementation.

Defining future operating requirements

The aim of this step is to develop an operations model that can be used as a tool for conceptualizing and evaluating alternatives. The team would start by collecting information that is readily available within the organization or from its supply chain partners. Primary sources include the needs assessment report, interviews with steering committee members, historical operating data, and the organization's business plan and supply chain operating strategy. The team could use the information to establish a profile of current operations and then use growth factors – from the business plan and marketing and sales forecasts – to develop the future operating profile.

The team would prepare a profile of current operations, then use growth forecasts to develop a future operating profile.

Developing future requirements encompasses two facets: storage requirements and throughput requirements. Storage requirements are the future peak and average amount of inventory, expressed in physical handling units, for which the warehouse must provide storage capacity. Throughput requirements are the peak and average materials handling activity for which the warehouse operation must provide capacity.

First, future storage requirements need to be assessed in order to design the reserve and fast pick storage areas. Standard materials handling units will include pallets, cases, and other containers that have a specific length, width, and height. Estimating the future storage requirements encompasses the following tasks:

Two tracts are needed: requirements for future storage and future throughput.

- profiling the current inventory in terms of units on hand, inventory turns, seasonality factors and physical characteristics including container size, and quantity for each SKU in today's inventory
- adjusting the current inventory levels for planned changes over the planning horizon, including changes in inventory turns and growth in sales per SKU. The result is a frequency distribution: the number of existing SKUs that will require the space represented by standard handling units, and
- adjusting the handling unit frequency distribution for SKU growth over the planning horizon.

Second, throughput requirements are needed for both inbound and outbound processes. Data can be sourced from activity reports for each sub-process as well as transaction level history from receiving reports, customer orders, and shipping manifests. The inbound and outbound throughput requirements are needed to design the yard, receiving and shipping processes. They include trucks, loads, and lines processed per day. It is useful to classify each metric by carrier class (truckload, less than truckload and parcel), handling unit, whether the shipment is a live delivery or a dropped trailer, and whether the goods are floor-loaded, crated or palletized. This information also would be used to determine the equipment and staffing levels required to perform the work.

For both inbound and outbound throughput requirements current levels of activity are used to estimate future levels by:

- defining current peak and average levels of activity
- defining the relevant growth factors, such as customer, stock keeping unit, sales per SKU, and inventory turns. These values should be obtained from inventory management sales and marketing planners, and
- estimating the future peak and average levels of activity by growing their current levels according to growth factors.

Conceptualizing the operation

Conceptual design begins with creative thinking about solutions to operating challenges.

Several approaches are popular that lead to a conceptual design. 'Visioning' or 'imagineering' can be described as the unconstrained and creative process that leads to the ideal solution. However, without a rigorous requirements definition and analysis, visions designed by committees are little more than a loose collection of opinions and compromises. When used effectively, vision development is followed by a more practical process of alternative development and evaluation, and results in a practical solution to warehousing challenges.

The process flow as illustrated below in Figure 2.5.1 is typical, but many variations exist. When cross-docking applies, goods may move directly from the receiving buffer to shipping staging. If the warehouse operation processes returns, once the shipment is accepted

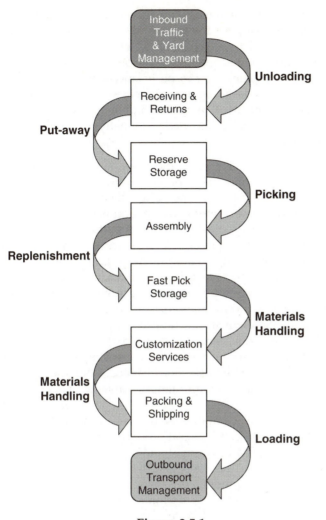

Figure 2.5.1
Warehouse operations flow

from a carrier, it is processed in a dedicated area for check-in and evaluation prior to being placed in the put-away staging area. Not all goods may have a reserve storage location, and not all may have a dedicated fast-pick storage location. Saleable goods may be stored generically and require assembly processes either before or after order picking. Certain types of order picking do not require consolidation, whereas others require sortation systems for order assembly. In addition, different customers will have differing requirements for special services.

Ideally, inbound traffic is managed and a yard management system exists for inbound flow control. The yard management system is used as a locator system for trailers that are stored outside the building. It assists in warehouse management and scheduling and sequencing the receiving process. Likewise, the outbound transportation management system may be used to select carriers, schedule pick-ups, plan the loading of carriers, and sequence the picking process.

An iterative, fact-based approach to process design can balance practicality and creativity.

Practicality and creativity can be balanced by using a fact-based approach to process design and improvement. The general approach outlined below is iterative in nature and requires skills in process re-engineering and a deep knowledge of materials handling, storage, and control systems.

- *Establish the baseline.* Typically, the baseline represents the current method of operation. The process flow, space requirements, equipment, staffing levels, operating schedule, information technology, performance metrics and operating costs define it. The baseline process is used as a point of departure for the next step.
- *Conceptualize the future process.* Here the focus is on improving the process by simplifying requirements, eliminating unnecessary steps, combining others, rectifying performance gaps and applying best practices including information technology support. The result is the ideal process flow diagram, annotated to highlight changes relative to the baseline at the sub-process level.
- *Design the process components.* Each process can be considered as a tradeoff of resources and objectives. Investment and automation can be traded for labor costs. For instance, storage equipment can be traded for space and throughput capacity can be traded for service levels. As the design team weighs competing objectives, the conceptual design components are developed. These include workstations in receiving, special processing, packing and shipping, as well as storage and material handling equipment.

  For each process the team needs to determine the types and quantities of equipment, the process flow and layout, the description of the operations, preliminary budgetary cost estimates, staffing levels and control system requirements. Receiving workstations might be designed for processing single SKU loads, mixed loads and parcel packages. Storage equipment might include a variety ranging from small load to large load, static to dynamic, floor storage to rack storage. Likewise, handling equipment includes industrial trucks, mechanical assist devices, conveyors and a variety of automated equipment.
- *Evaluate the conceptual design.* The team would compare the baseline with the concept of operations using qualitative and quantitative factors. The factors should be relevant to the performance gaps and business requirements identified in the needs analysis and requirements definition and are tailored to the situation. Space constraints might put a premium on space efficiency. Throughput and schedule demands might put a premium on high-surge capacity. Capital constraints might require a high return on

investment. A high-level, cost-benefit analysis of each process component will ensure the overall design meets financial objectives.

- *Review and refine design as needed.* A review of the design by content experts, operations personnel and the steering committee might offer a new and useful perspective or operating consideration. It will certainly lead to broad understanding and acceptance of the conceptual design.

This example of a fact-based approach to design encompasses all of the processes relevant to a warehouse operation. Other issues also need to be considered during the conceptualization of design; and these are specific to different warehousing processes. Such issues include yard management receiving and shipping; the put-away process; storage system design; order picking to fulfill customer requirements; and custom services.

Facility planning

The next stage of conceptual design involves facility planning. It translates the building blocks developed during conceptual process design into a blueprint for building design. Like process design, it can be an iterative process and can involve the following steps.

Facility planning translates the building blocks developed during conceptual process design into a blueprint for building design.

- *Personnel planning* is simply a summary of the staffing required for each of the processes of design and conceptual design as well as estimates of the clerical, supervision and managerial staff that will be required for the future operation. The team needs to determine the peak and average staffing levels.
- *Space planning* is the process of coupling the concept space requirements with the necessary personnel and equipment maintenance services. These may include break areas, lunchrooms, lockers, training facilities, conference rooms, offices, communications and information technology spaces, and industrial truck battery changing and charging areas. If the concept design is space-constrained, it will also be necessary to adjust the total space, or reconcile the gap. Strategies for adjustments include the use of high-rise storage methods, mezzanines for low-bay processes, and off-site storage for reserve and slow moving items. In addition, seasonal and non-core activities may be outsourced to a third party.
- *Block layout planning* is the process of selecting the best strategy for laying out the warehouse operation. If there are site constraints, they need to be identified, prioritized and considered relative to the placement of trailer storage, employee parking, entries and exits, and the location of receiving and shipping docks. Once the docks are located, the flow of materials will be prescribed. In fact, multiple flows may exist, including those for handling cross-dock-items, returns processing, normal warehousing. A 'U'-shaped flow features receiving and storage stocks located on the same side of the building, which works well when materials are shipped in the same

form as they are received. A cross or 'X'-shaped flow is used typically in a flow-through environment, with the space between receiving and shipping used for short-term storage and consolidation of shipments.

The team needs to develop several alternatives and select the best based on criteria that includes flexibility, modularity, expandability, and efficiency considerations (such as minimizing travel distances and congestion areas).

- *Materials handling systems concept design* is done after block layout planning because only now would the team understand the number of handling moves and the distance traveled between process areas. The moves as well as functionality such as sortation constitute the functional requirements of a materials handling system. The kinds of materials handling systems found in warehousing operations will range from industrial trucks to automated guided vehicles, conveyors, trash removal systems and sortation equipment. Unless expertise exists within the design team, it is highly advisable to gather support from the vendor community for automated handling system conceptual design. The result of this step will be establishing the number and type of handling equipment, the space requirements, and budgetary cost estimates. These are in addition to the handling and storage equipment previously identified.

- *Detailed layout planning* is the final step within the facility-planning task. At this point, the team would have defined virtually all layout requirements. Ideally, scaled layout drawings for each component are assembled within the context of the block layout plan. As a detailed layout plan takes shape, the team should specify certain building construction features and the architect and engineers should agree. These include column spacing and approximate sizes, clear heights, dock leveler sizes and locations, task lighting zones, trash disposal doors, security features, and the type of fire suppression equipment including sprinklers. Finally, the various workstations are located and their utility requirements are specified for the benefit of the architect.

Moving the conceptual design towards implementation

The objective of the final stage of conceptual design is to manage risk, both internal and external.

To complete the conceptual design phase, the team must prepare for the next phase. At a minimum, this would entail developing a strategy for implementation, developing a plan for detailed design and implementation, documenting the business case and securing executive support. The objective is to manage risk. Typically, the degree of risk increases with the degree of change required and the complexity of the design. Risks can be focused internally and externally.

The primary internal risk is the lack of buy-in, which results from a lack of understanding, a lack of involvement in the process and inadequate communications. These issues are important at all levels.

The team will need to ensure buy-in to the change by operations personnel, cross-functional support staff and the executive steering committee. The primary external risk is that the organization lacks the capability to implement the plan without disrupting customer operations. Two approaches should be used to mitigate this risk: develop and adopt a time-phased strategy and develop and execute an effective training program.

The implementation strategy defines the approach to implement the concept design. A phased approach is natural and generally advisable. A 'big bang' implementation should be avoided, except where the design entails minimal process change and the operation is relatively straightforward. The team should start by identifying business segments that are defined by a subset of products shipped and a sub-set of the customers that are served. Then select one that represents the least business risk for a pilot demonstration. The demonstration will be used to gain confidence throughout the organization. Upon its successful completion, subsequent segments are sequenced into the new operation. The timing of the pilot and rollout of subsequent segments is critical. Ideally, peak seasons should be avoided and periods of low inventory are good times to relocate operations.

The project plan translates this implementation strategy into an action plan. It includes the tasks, their relationships, the timing and the resources required through the detailed design and implementation phases.

Phase 3 – detailed design

Once the concept design is approved, three design work packages are developed to provide details of the design. These operate in parallel during the implementation and comprise:

Three interrelated work packages expand the concept design into detailed specifications.

- *process* – including space, equipment, staffing, organization, performance management and process layout
- *information technology* – execution systems including warehouse management systems (WMS), transportation management systems (TMS) and yard management systems (YMS) and relevant interfaces
- *facility* – including architectural and engineering design (this may be started during concept design for significant new construction to compress lead times).

Clearly, all three are interrelated and close coordination is needed. The basic steps for each are the same but they demand different skill sets. The timing is dependent on the design specifics, but generally, the approach involves:

- reviewing and refining the concept design for each warehouse function
- developing functional specifications for items to be procured
- soliciting proposals from pre-qualified suppliers

- selecting the best equipment vendors, control system suppliers, general contractors, system integrators and project managers
- conducting a functional design of the execution systems and the architectural/engineering design for the facility
- procuring all equipment and develop training tools, and
- preparing a detailed implementation plan and obtaining steering committee approval to proceed.

Phase 4 – implementation

During the implementation phase, the three tracks continue in the build, test and start-up modes. The typical results of this phase include:

- owners' acceptance of the new facility, if any
- the delivery, installation, and acceptance of material handling equipment
- the building, testing and training for execution systems
- the development of job descriptions, operating procedures, performance measurement tools and organization structure
- the training of all staff in new processes, equipment use, and use of execution systems, and
- the acceptance of the new operating design by operating personnel.

Another ingredient necessary to move the concept design towards implementation is a business case. Invariably, a business case will be required to obtain the funds needed for the project. Thankfully, the team has already done much of the work to provide the content for the business case report. The conceptual design has included estimates of the costs and benefits and these have driven the design team towards an economically justifiable design. However, additional costs include those predicated on the implementation strategy and the timeline leading to full start-up. The form of the business case will vary from company to company, but it will generally include several important elements:

- a narrative that defines the mandate for change. This section was developed mostly during the needs assessment phase
- the 'bottom-line' impact of the conceptual design. Using commonly accepted financial performance measures, the cost-benefit analysis is presented
- the 'top-line' impact of the conceptual design, comprising anticipated improvements in customer service performance as well as increases in capacity to enable the support of future growth projections
- a discussion of the risk of not implementing the conceptual design, and
- a discussion of the risks involved in implementation and the plans for mitigating those risks.

Finally, the design team and project champion must confirm executive support for the design and the plan. If the four-phase approach has been followed, this process would have started during the needs assessment and would have been ongoing. Meetings with the steering committee have confirmed the need, clarified expectations, defined constraints, established urgency and endorsed the team composition. However, at this critical juncture a formal review is needed to empower the project team. Often the steering committee heightens its focus and sensitivity to the project at this time.

Therefore, it is a good idea to minimize surprises by providing a draft document to the committee members for their review prior to each meeting.

Conclusion

The design of distribution operations is a big job. The team that is assigned to this task should consider it tantamount to 'going to war', in the sense that it is very difficult to do on a part-time basis. A high level of effort and focus is needed from all involved. Supply chain executives should be wary of the 'cookie cutter' approach to warehouse operations design, where one operation design after the other is cut and all look the same. Just as all organizations and their requirements are different, all warehousing operations have to be different. Businesses may have a similar mix of SKUs in their operations, but their storage requirements, throughput volumes and customer demands can be very different. A comprehensive, four-phase approach will ensure the appropriate mix of resources for the operation and the highest return on investment.

Organizations pursuing supply chain excellence need to start planning for the growing complexity of warehousing.

Organizations wishing to achieve supply chain excellence need to start planning for the growing complexity of warehousing. Supply chain integration is becoming a reality, with the virtual organization and the extended enterprise operating nationally and globally. Warehousing arrangements are changing from 'pallet-in' and 'pallet-out' flows to hybrid operations that include a mix of individual items, cases and pallet flows in and out of the operation. Postponement and light assembly processes are migrating to the warehouse operation, while disintermediation is also occurring, with an increase in in-store-direct and customer-direct shipments. Finally, the use of third-party logistics providers is growing because of the extra security, control and information technology expertise the providers can offer. In this ever-changing logistics environment, supply chain executives will gain substantial advantages by achieving a superior capability in distribution operations.

2.6 Integrated transportation management

Brooks A. Bentz

A company has to understand the vision for successfully managing transportation under an integrated, holistic strategy.

Transportation is a vital component in every economy and a critical link in the supply chain of most companies. The robust growth of technology and the advent of e-commerce has done little to change the fact that 'stuff' still has to get picked up and delivered.

New and emerging Web-based technology is enabling much greater capability for improving supply chain management, including transportation services. The extent of the impact this will have on organizations worldwide is untold. Some predict it could be the next great leap in industrial development, as revolutionary as internal combustion engines replacing steam for locomotion and digital technology replacing analog for communications.

Regardless, improving capabilities in supply chain execution will change radically the way business is conducted, which also means change in the way transportation service is managed. Historically, the transportation of product has been regarded as an ancillary function, of little or no central importance. More recently, efficient transportation has been seen to be an essential determinant in competitive advantage. Summarizing this thinking into a series of actionable steps, and successfully implementing those steps, will result in world-class performance.

The underlying premise is that companies moving product – inbound from suppliers and vendors and outbound to customers and end users – require two core competencies:

- understanding the fundamentals of transportation and having a broadly accepted vision of the role transportation plays in the enterprise, and
- having capabilities for executing successfully against the vision and strategy. This has several sub-requirements:

    - an actionable operating plan

156

- a clear set of performance metrics that define success, and
- the enabling technology for monitoring and reporting results accurately so that management can adjust or correct problems as needed.

These competencies are not new. However, what distinguishes this approach is the concept of integrated transportation management – where all transport functions are linked and coordinated in much the same way as manufacturing processes. Broadly applying these concepts in the supply chain arena improves operating efficiency, cost and, ultimately, service to customers.

Transportation of raw materials, semi-finished and finished goods in the United States typically accounts for more than half of all logistics costs, as shown in Table 2.6.1 below.

Multiple modes exist for moving product, giving companies an array of options to achieve the optimum blend of service and price. However, companies must also have the appropriate vision, supporting strategy and enabling technology to achieve superior performance. They need to be equipped and their managers and staff trained to execute an integrated transportation strategy. Those seeking optimum solutions achieve a competitive edge over those who do not.

Neglecting transportation management capabilities results in operational inefficiencies.

Transportation is the glue that connects and holds supply chain partners together, be they retailers, manufacturers or any number of other players.

The challenge arising from this is straightforward. Senior managers typically focus on their core business, which is the area of their greatest expertise and where they feel most comfortable. During the 1990s, a groundswell of re-engineering projects emerged, most of which focused on making the core business leaner and more efficient. Components of the business viewed as ancillary were left out of major re-engineering projects, with the result that companies frequently overlooked, forgot or ignored transportation.

Now that the intense focus on re-engineering has subsided, many management teams are looking at new ways for achieving additional

Table 2.6.1
US domestic logistics costs (2000)

	Amount (US $bn)	% of total logistics cost
Transportation	$ 580	58%
Warehousing	$ 80	8%
Administration	$ 40	4%
Inventory carrying costs	$ 300	30%
Total logistics costs	$1000	

Source: International Warehouse Logistics Association

benefits. Improving the effectiveness of transportation management is fertile ground. Left unmanaged, transportation can become an unseen competitive liability. Costs can spiral out of control and poor performance can have unpleasant ripple effects across the supply chain, disrupting production, inflating inventory and alienating customers.

Erratic service can cause departments and managers in other areas of the business to mistrust the reliability of the supply chain. This, in turn, leads to unwanted side effects, such as disproportionate inventory safety stock and re-handling or re-shipping of product. Finally, for many customers, the only window to their supplier is through the delivery mechanism. Unacceptable or shoddy performance reflects directly on the management and reputation of the selling organization.

What, then, is the best way forward? Developing a comprehensive vision and strategy for how transportation should function within the broader enterprise is an essential first step. Socialization of the important facets of transportation's effect on supply chain execution and education of constituents relying on transportation execution will go a long way toward improving overall supply chain performance.

A core presumption when assessing most business practices is that good execution will have a positive impact on shareholder value, as shown in Figure 2.6.1. Transportation pulls at several levers that have an impact on shareholder value.

Not all of these value levers fall into the cost reduction category, as one might imagine. Service differentiation and improved reliability and predictability are also essential contributors to improving value.

Drivers of transportation management excellence

Transportation of product, whether inbound to distribution centers, stores or manufacturing facilities, or outbound to customers or other end users is a fundamental building block of the supply chain. Misunderstanding or overlooking transportation can frequently result in higher costs, poor service and greater levels of inventory than are necessary. Two compelling reasons exist for improving transportation management. The first relates to market competition, the second to serving customers.

Market competition

Transportation management is a competitive differentiator.

Very few businesses have no competitors for their products. When two or more companies compete in a specific market, excellent transportation management and service often makes the difference between success and failure.

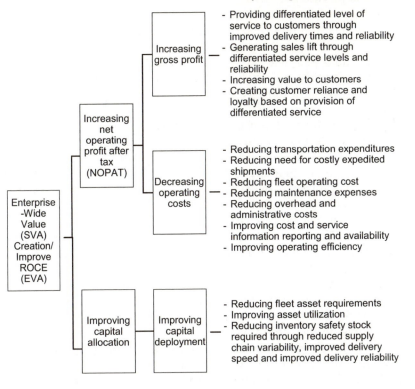

Figure 2.6.1
Transportation impact on shareholder value

Say two companies are both competing for the same customer. Company 'A' manages transportation as though it was a competitive weapon; Company 'B' simply passes its cost on to the client. With all else being equal, the company that understands how to use transportation effectively will be able to out-maneuver its competitor or simply improve its internal supply chain. This will not overcome poor management of other parts of the enterprise, but it enhances the ability of a well-run franchise in a competitive environment.

In this example, Company 'A' is able to offer a variety of services (rail, intermodal, truckload, less than truckload, and parcel/package) tailored to its client's service and price requirements because it understands the customer's logistics needs. Company 'A' also helps its client improve margin and service with the right mix of mode and price. Company 'B' pays no attention to specific customer logistics needs. It simply ships orders as they are received by whatever mode seems to make sense at the time, adding the cost (and perhaps a mark-up, as well) to the cost of goods.

This strategy is short sighted. It may work in the short term, with customers who are unsophisticated in their buying practices. In the longer term, though, customers will surely become increasingly more advanced in making their supply chains more efficient and will cull vendors and suppliers who do not share this philosophy. The smarter, long-term strategy is true collaboration between the parties on transporting product the most efficient way possible, thereby achieving a win for both. Built-in inefficiencies eventually rebound, to the detriment of those who attempt to perpetuate them.

Serving customers – a client example

Collaborative approaches lead to improvements in service and cost across the supply chain.

During the late 1980s, I ran a third-party logistics (3PL) company that delivered retail merchandise from a distribution center in Atlanta in the United States to a large number of stores in Florida. We won the contract because we developed a solution that the client initially viewed as counter-intuitive.

The client had been obtaining optimum transportation economics by scheduling two and three stops for 45-foot rail trailers, and employing intermodal service to several railheads in Florida. The disadvantage lay in the service, not from a typical transit time standpoint, but rather in their inability to meet their customer stores' requirements. Our client had scheduled all deliveries for 8 a.m. every day. While this was not difficult to attain on the first stop, it was impossible on the second or third stop.

Our solution was to build a fleet of 28-foot, high-cube pups and load one store per trailer. When the train arrived, the drivers would pull a set of doubles out of the railhead, dropping one at the first store, and live unloading the second trailer at the next stop before returning with the empties. At first, this ran counter to our client's instincts because it increased freight costs. However, the change more than doubled on-time performance (within 15 minutes of 8 a.m.), from 45 per cent to more than 98 per cent.

Why was this important? Our client used store labor to assist in the unloading of inbound merchandise. The staff members also applied price stickers and put the product on the shelves. Obviously, these people could not be unloading, pricing and stocking while simultaneously serving customers. The 8 a.m. delivery time was designed for enabling completion of these tasks before the stores opened at 10 a.m. Surveys had also told the client that customers would avoid aisles where stocking was occurring during store hours, which reduced sales.

The engineered solution cured most of these problems for an entire network of stores, but it was only possible because our client had a clear vision about what they were trying to accomplish. This vision transcended the simplistic goal of reducing transportation expenses and extended to a broader view of the supply chain, enabling the right solution to be implemented for our client and their customers.

Challenges in transportation management

The majority of organizations that rely on transportation in some form or another have a fragmented or disconnected way of managing their requirements and those of their customers. The most common form of disaggregation lies between inbound and outbound transportation. Most companies focus whatever effort they expend on managing outbound shipments to their customers, but almost universally overlook managing inbound transportation from their vendors and suppliers in a way that coordinates with other transportation activities.

The company with the superior transportation service and economics should take the lead in a truly collaborative relationship.

This effectively eliminates any synergy that may be generated by matching inbound and outbound requirements to produce backhauls or continuous moves. This sub-optimizes carrier performance, which in turn, drives costs higher than they might otherwise need to be.

One of the challenges is, 'who *should* control the freight?' Large companies that use leading-edge transportation management organizations typically seek to control freight because they have invested the time and effort into building core carrier programs and leveraging their volume. In this way, they achieve the best service at the best price. Potentially conflict can occur between a large supplier managing its outbound flow and a large customer seeking to gain control of its inbound flow to improve its economics. Clearly, they cannot both exercise control over the same business, but they can certainly collaborate. Generally, the party with the best supply chain economics should be managing the movement of product.

Collaboration between the supplier and end user will produce the best value. One obstacle is the use of freight routing and scheduling as a profit center or mechanism for improving margin. True collaboration involves sharing information between supplier and customer, with the objective of deriving the best overall supply chain solution.

A more granular problem faced by many organizations is the failure to segregate the transportation spend by mode within the company so that mode shift opportunities are not readily apparent, nor are they readily achievable. Even in companies where this is not the case, managers often view modal choices in a static rather than dynamic way. This means movements that are determined to be rail always go by rail, and movements allocated to truck always go by truck and so on, without regard to how shifting delivery requirements might permit more economical routings.

Inbound transportation is often embedded in the cost of goods and is managed, if at all, by a separate part of the organization, such as purchasing. Delivery economics are therefore difficult to assess and more difficult to manage. Scheduling is frequently driven by factors that do not take transportation economics into account, which almost inevitably drives the total landed cost higher. An example might be an order for newsprint that should move by rail, but which often goes by truck because the purchase is not made sufficiently in advance due to poor forecasting and order management.

Even in cases where it makes sense for the supplier to control the freight, an understanding of the transportation economics and modal trade-offs is important for optimising price and service. The over-riding challenge is obtaining timely and accurate information that enables informed and beneficial choices, rather than simply doing it 'the way we've always done it'.

Enabling technology

Probably the largest single challenge facing companies attempting to streamline and improve their supply chains is enabling technology: 'What should we have, what should we buy, what should we build, what should our capabilities be, how do we install it, how do we configure it, how do we use it to get optimum results?' There are many questions.

The competitive advantage of the future will not be in having the cheapest rates or the trailers with the biggest cube or, for that matter, any of the results of the conventional thinking of the past. The competitive advantage of the future will stem from the ability to select or design, implement and execute decision support technology that will provide the best information for managing customers, inventory, costs and service.

Much of the vision for this technology falls under the label of 'Pipeline Visibility' or 'Supply Chain Visibility,' which includes event management and intelligent messaging.

Pipeline Visibility can be simply defined as the ability to view and manage the flow of goods, documents, services and funds through all supply chain nodes and links from order to cash, supported and facilitated by the appropriate decision support technology.

Global supply chains have moved beyond theory to reality; however, uncertainty, bottlenecks and poor information typically lead to extended lead times and inflated inventory, producing higher operating costs. Without decision support technology, pipeline visibility is not feasible and supply chain optimization is more guesswork than science. In such instances, curing supply chain problems must be done opportunistically, rather than systemically. Solutions are conceptually simple, but operationally complex and time-consuming to execute.

The three core functions that Pipeline Visibility deals with are product visibility, event management and performance management (Figure 2.6.2).

The challenge, and the beauty, of these kinds of capabilities is the ability then to manage the supply chain more holistically. This means, for example, a buyer of retail merchandise is able to view all of the product, by SKU, that he or she 'owns', be it on the dock at the vendor, at the outbound consolidator, or in-transit via ship, plane, truck or train.

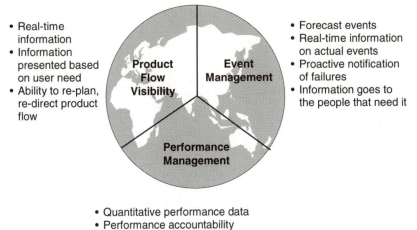

- Real-time information
- Information presented based on user need
- Ability to re-plan, re-direct product flow

- Forecast events
- Real-time information on actual events
- Proactive notification of failures
- Information goes to the people that need it

- Quantitative performance data
- Performance accountability
- Continuous performance improvement opportunities

Figure 2.6.2
Pipeline visibility

This allows for event management, corrections to repetitive bottlenecks and problems, and provides the capability for changing allocations and distribution 'on the fly' in a real-time environment.

Modern global supply chains are manifestly more complex and require robust decision support technology in order to manage them effectively (Figure 2.6.3).

What to track and measure is as important as how to do it. Monitoring all of the individual transactions across a supply chain is technologically feasible but operationally impractical. The art in the science is in carefully configuring the supply chain and defining what is important to measure and what to do with the information, once it is produced.

The objective is to develop a model of the supply chain or, in some cases, multiple supply chains that illustrates the key links and nodes, and the elements to be watched and measured. Identifying the specific links and nodes, whether they are labeled critical path elements or predictive markers, or something else, is a vital part of the work.

This is what will, when tripped by an alert, tell the monitoring party that not only has an event occurred improperly or has not occurred as scheduled, but based on that occurrence, the plan, as designed, will fail to meet schedule. This provides the greatest opportunity to turn a problem into a solution and proactively take corrective steps, rather than reacting to a missed deadline and trying to make up lost ground with an event that has already happened.

Utilizing this capability for providing leading-edge customer service and differentiating oneself from competitors, even in a commodity business, can be a significant competitive advantage.

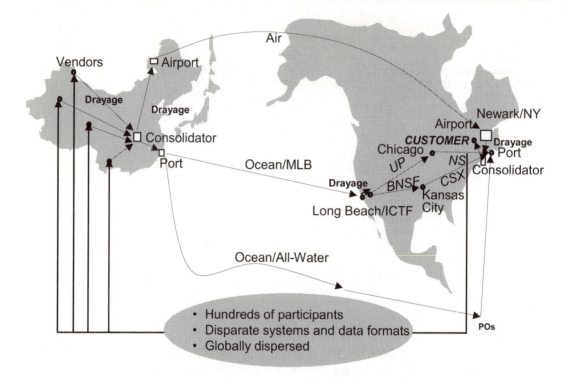

Potential Supply Chain Participants

- Manufacturers
- Freight Forwarders
- Consolidators
- De-consolidators
- 3PLs
- 4PLs
- Customs Houses

- Terminals
- Carriers
  - Ocean
  - Air
  - Truck
  - Rail
  - Barge

- Warehouses
- Distribution Centers
- Retail Outlets

Figure 2.6.3
Complexity of global supply chains

This makes the understanding, design and configuration of the supply chain vital elements in optimizing the transportation of product across a complex network.

Enabling technology, then, is not only a better glue for holding the supply chain together, it is also the tool set for elevating operating and performance effectiveness to a whole, new level (Figure 2.6.4). This becomes the single biggest element in gaining the upper hand in a competitive landscape.

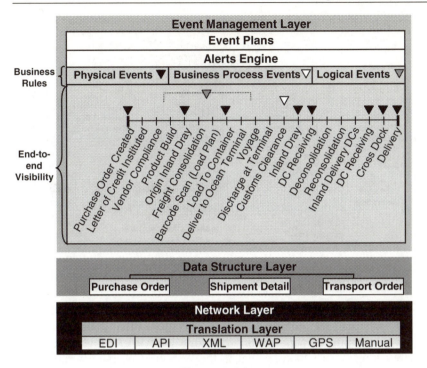

Figure 2.6.4
Supply chain applications architecture

Integrated transportation management

The concept of integrated transportation management simply seeks to bring focus and coordination to a related series of similar events so that by doing so, service to customers, both external and internal, is improved and costs are reduced. Developments in enabling technology, particularly Web-based technology is on the cusp of facilitating large-scale changes in supply chain management.

Historically this has not been possible. Companies often managed transportation in an ad hoc way and they focused any developments in technology on other parts of the business, such as manufacturing and accounting.

Transportation, represented by dark and light arrows in Figure 2.6.5, is embedded throughout the supply chain, moving product from vendors and suppliers to retailers, manufacturers and distributors and eventually to end users and customers. Integrating these related, but often disparate, operations has been historically infeasible. The advent of Web-enabled technology provides new visions of how supply chains can be integrated, how collaboration among trading partners can drive out costs and improve efficiency, and how carriers can also benefit from improved supply chain functionality entirely possible.

The goal now is to introduce a new paradigm that recognizes the importance of transportation in the supply chain from a customer service and cost management standpoint.

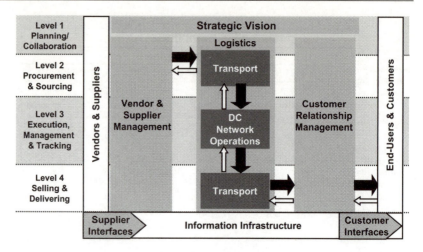

Figure 2.6.5
The supply chain footprint

For supply chain managers, these exciting possibilities also raise key questions about the role of transportation. What does the process for integrating transportation functions look like? How is it done? How long does it take? What is the benefit? Companies can take a series of specific and related steps to achieve superior supply chain integration, service improvement and cost reduction.

Much of transportation management is transactional in nature, which makes documenting process improvements and benefits easier to substantiate than less explicit elements of business operations. The approach shown in Table 2.6.2 outlines steps that will help an organization gain better control of its costs and produce better service for its customers.

Best practices are an approach to gauge performance in transportation management.

In addition to these steps, organizations can improve their performance further by assessing whether they are achieving industry best practice in their transportation management. Many transportation practices are common across a wide spectrum of businesses and industries. Observing and emulating industry leaders can identify opportunities for improvement and provide a short cut to creating a high-performance organization (Table 2.6.3).

Transportation best practice offers a tool for gauging organizational performance, and measuring the gap between the organization as it is today and the organization it wants to be in the future.

The companies that improve their transportation management can increase their profitability, improve asset utilization, reduce capital commitments, and enhance service commitments. Assessing, analysing and incorporating these companies' best practices enables others to gain these same benefits.

Organizations wishing to become world-class performers need to remember that best practice management is only a tool and not a

Table 2.6.2
Integrated transportation management efforts and benefits

Initiative	Timing (Months)	Benefits
Inbound transportation management	3–12	5–25%
• vendor conversion (prepaid – to collect)		
• vendor conversion (expanded backhaul)		
Outbound transportation management	6–12	3–15%
• carrier rationalization		
• automated load tendering		
• automated tracking and tracing		
• automated carrier performance reporting and management		
• freight bill audit and payment		
Carrier management	Ongoing	3–8%
mode selection and optimization	Ongoing	5–15%
Network optimization	Periodic	5–15%
Strategic transportation procurement	6–12	3–20%
• contract standardization and simplification		
• holistic RFP/bid		
• carrier rationalization		
Enabling technology	12–18	5–20%
• supply chain visibility and event management		
• TMS		
• Routing and scheduling		

Table 2.6.3
Lifecyle of transportation management projects

Development	Characteristics
World-class organization	• Pace setters in optimization and automation technology • Aggressive in setting and enforcing standards for quality • Assets managed integrally with business units • Manage transportation network holistically • Exception-based management versus transaction management • Active use of performance metrics with customers and carriers • Partnerships with suppliers and carriers to meet customer needs
Quality-service focused organization	• Technology used to track utilization • Effort to maximize use of assets • Adopting quality and service measurements • Rely on low-risk 'tried and true' programs • Peak coverage ensured by adequate fleet size • Relationships with suppliers solid, but at arm's length • Decision support systems to evaluate cost and service trade-offs
Developing organization	• Basic technology only • Beginning to develop service requirement specifications • Rudimentary quality and service measurements (manual processes) • Gradually experimenting with new programs • Gradually moving away from 'old-line' practices
Basic organization	• Base decisions primarily on cost or service alone • Generally unwilling to take risks • Traditional operating methods prevail through the organization • Quality, service, and the cost not considered simultaneously • Reluctant in partnering with service providers • Little or no understanding of relationships linking service requirements, quality and cost • Few or no processes to track quality, performance and cost

'silver bullet' solution. Senior managers will have to apply stringent requirements and give full commitment to their goal. Best practice is also not a static target as best practice by its very nature constantly changes. Organizations need to be prepared to maintain ongoing vigilance and a preparedness to change if they are to become world-class companies.

A final source of improvement is technology. Information technology is increasingly becoming a crucial instrument used by world-class companies to improve and optimize transportation management processes. The Internet is playing an emerging role in how companies provide the infrastructure to manage transportation strategies, operations and administration.

The overriding and constant trade-off is between service quality and the cost of providing that service. The ability of senior managers to exercise judgment and take account of customer requirements in this decision process is critical. World-class service may be defined as next-day delivery, which is achievable for high-priority documents, but financially and operationally impractical for 100-ton cars of grain and unacceptable for the transportation of human organs and tissue. Sorting out complexities such as this is one of the essential functions of management and illustrates clearly why a transportation vision is so necessary.

One of the interesting conundrums faced by those responsible for engineering transportation services is that, while enabling technology in the supply chain arena has advanced rapidly, very few companies

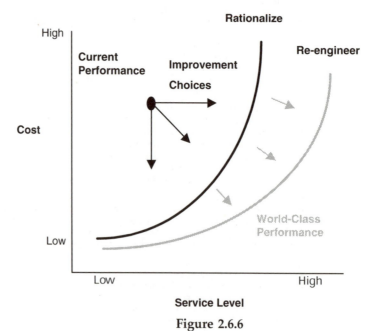

Figure 2.6.6
Requirements to manage transportation at world-class levels

are able to analyse cost and service trade-offs from a supply chain standpoint (Figure 2.6.6). Most can do so from a transportation cost standpoint (for example, one-day service is $20; two-day service is $10). Factoring in other related elements is profoundly more challenging: impact on inventory and safety stock, warehouse handling costs and timing, store receiving, document processing and so on.

How does all of this come together and how should each initiative be prioritized? Each company has its own distinct profile, needs, ability and appetite for execution. A representative schematic in Figure 2.6.7 depicts various initiatives and their respective ease of implementation and value to the enterprise.

The challenge facing each organization is the ordering and prioritizing of those initiatives viewed as desirable to undertake. Formulating the comprehensive vision and strategy is the first step.

Asking a series of key questions helps provide a sense of direction in terms of how to proceed.

- Can executives articulate the supply chain, logistics or transportation vision and strategy?
- Are you technologically enabled for providing pipeline visibility and intelligent messaging?

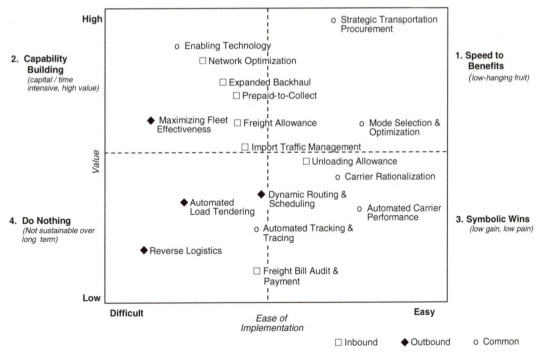

Figure 2.6.7
Impact of transportation initiatives on business goals

- Do you have defined and measurable performance criteria for key supply chain functions?
- Do you have the right mix of carrier and service options?
- Do you know your transportation costs, and are they in line with those of world-class companies?
- Do you receive superior service?
- Are your customers clearly defined and segmented with respect to transportation service requirements?
- Has your company taken advantage of the asset reductions and cost advantages provided by global 3PLs?
- Do your trading partners collaborate or coordinate with you on transportation issues and capitalize on innovation opportunities?

Other questions may arise, stimulated by the dialog generated by this self-examination. The goal is to have a clearly defined and actionable mission with measurable outcomes.

Conclusion

The role of transportation in the context of superior supply chain execution is a critical one. Much like an army in the field, the troops of which cannot accomplish their mission without a continuous supply of ammunition, food and medical supplies, corporations cannot serve customers without adequate transportation service. How well they execute this service, whether it be from the standpoint of adequate supply from vendors or delivery to end users, revolves around the ability to design, acquire, produce and deliver the right transportation service.

That transportation service is a fundamental requirement is a given. Employing it, by using an integrated, holistic strategy linked to broader corporate objectives, is where management excellence can lead to strategic competitive advantage. Using this concept of transportation as a strategic competitive weapon will be the coming trend in improving supply chain execution and facilitating supply chain excellence.

Forecasting and demand planning 2.7

Scott F. Githens

Poor accuracy in demand planning can cause widespread disruption, poor customer service and increased costs to organizations. Conversely, organizations that develop high-quality demand plans will benefit from meeting customer needs swiftly and cost-effectively. This chapter reaffirms that a demand plan is an essential business tool for most organizations and outlines the attributes that underpin an effective and accurate demand planning capability. Leading practices in the areas of statistical forecasting, promotions management, causal event management and demand plan integration are proposed. If implemented, these simple yet comprehensive steps will increase the quality of an organization's demand plan and help it to build a stronger, more accurate customer response capability.

An accurate demand plan is an essential business tool for most organizations.

Why a demand plan?

Forecasting versus demand planning

The requirement to produce a demand plan is a reality for almost all organizations involved in providing physical products to satisfy customers' needs. However, most organizations producing a demand plan believe that their demand plan is not as accurate as it should be.

Before delving further into demand planning, it is important to clarify the difference between a forecast and a demand plan (Figure 2.7.1). A forecast is a statistically based initial estimate of future demand. A demand plan is an estimate of future demand derived by a consensus-driven review and approval of the forecast. In effect, a forecast is subject to several planning and verification processes to generate the demand plan.

A demand plan is an estimate of future demand derived by a consensus-driven review and approval of the forecast.

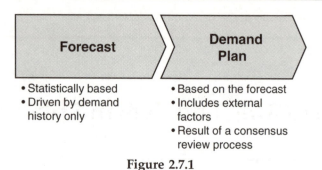

Figure 2.7.1
Difference between a forecast and a demand plan

Reasons for an accurate demand plan

Most organizations need to have an accurate and valid demand plan.

The rise of Just-In-Time (JIT) in the 1980s and more recently the Quick Response (QR) philosophy led many organizations to believe that spending time and money generating an accurate demand plan would be no longer needed. It is debatable whether JIT as a philosophy ever really promised this outcome. In hindsight, a misunderstanding of JIT is probably more to blame for this belief than a fundamental failure in JIT itself. However, with all the sophisticated technology to support real-time business in the 21st Century, we are unable to escape from the fact that most organizations need to have an accurate and valid demand plan. A number of reasons support why this is the case.

An accurate demand plan will help to: deliver product within customer lead times; deploy the right quantity of the right product; make sound operational decisions; and ensure financial planning reflects reality.

- *Lead time imbalances.* The customer service lead time – the time that a customer is prepared to wait between ordering and receiving a product – is often a far smaller interval than the lead time required by the organization to produce or distribute the product. Quite simply, it takes companies longer to create and deliver a product than the customer is prepared to wait for it. Organizations have spent vast amounts of money reducing the difference between these two intervals.

  Actions have included modifying production processes to reduce production lead times and moving operations closer to customers to reduce distribution lead time, as illustrated in Figure 2.7.2. While these have often been successful, they are seldom successful enough to reduce the difference in lead times to zero. Consequently, a demand plan that tries to ensure that a product will be available so that it can be delivered within the customer's service lead time is still required.

- *Marketing management.* The maturity of many industries today means that the only way many organizations can grow is through increasing their market share. Promotions and other marketing events are major ways that organizations seek to do this. While marketing events can be quite effective, they are often expensive and if badly planned, they will have little impact on growth.

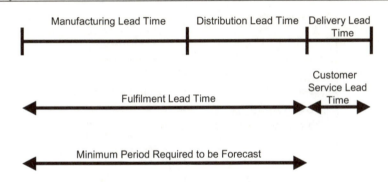

Figure 2.7.2
Lead time imbalances

Organizations need to look no further than Sony's promotion of PlayStation 2, when customer demand far outstripped supply, to see what can happen if the impact of promotional events is underestimated. An accurate demand plan is essential for making decisions about deploying the right quantity of the right product, at the right time, to the right location.

- *Medium-term operational planning.* The capital-intensive nature of many operations, coupled with the long lead times needed to transport products in a global supply chain, mean that purchasing decisions need to be made now in order to meet customer needs in the medium term. An accurate demand plan is essential to allow sound decisions to be made.
- *Financial planning and budgeting.* All organizations are required to produce regular financial plans and budgets. Without an accurate demand plan it is likely that the continued correlation and relevance of these budgets to actual operational conditions will be poor.

Implications of poor demand plans

Poor demand planning can have an adverse effect on an organization's performance. In the United States, Nike attributed a 33 per cent shortfall in its estimated 2000–01 earnings to poor demand planning (Wilson, 2001). Some of the major impacts of inadequate demand plans include unsatisfactory customer service, excess inventory, poor production efficiency and increased distribution costs, shown in Figure 2.7.3.

Inadequate demand plans can result in poor service, excess inventory, poor production efficiency and increased costs.

- *Poor customer service.* Without a sound demand plan, it will be difficult for an organization to understand its customers' future requirements. In addition, without such an understanding, it is likely the organization will have insufficient stock to satisfy its customers' orders. If a demand plan is poor, then customer service levels are likely to be correspondingly poor.

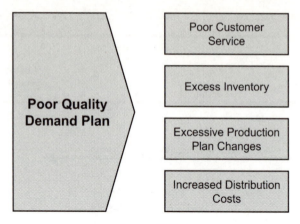

Figure 2.7.3
Implications of a poor-quality demand plan

- *Excess inventory.* If an organization has an approach to setting safety stock based on demand plan error, then the levels of safety stock required to achieve the desired customer service level will be correspondingly high. A poor demand plan will lead to high levels of safety stock, thus increasing the investment of capital tied up in inventory.
- *Excessive production changes.* An organization could have to make last-minute changes to production schedules in order to respond to customer demands quickly. While agile factories are a worthwhile goal, managers need to balance the cost of production inefficiency due to changes caused by unforeseen customer demand with the profit generated by customer orders. An accurate demand plan allows organizations to keep a more stable and efficient production plan, while still meeting customer demand.
- *Increased distribution costs.* Express or rapid deliveries outside the normal distribution process might be needed to respond to customer demands. This leads to excessive distribution costs and, in many cases, the removal of any profit the organization was likely to gain from the customer's order. An accurate demand plan will allow organizations to deploy products to meet customer orders with minimal express or expedited deliveries.

The actual costs being incurred due to poor quality in the demand plan depend very much on an individual organization's circumstances. It is worth noting, however, that in many cases the payback period for the implementation of a Tier-1 demand planning tool such as Manugistics or i2 demand planning modules is measured in months, rather than years.

Leading practice demand planning

The achievement of an effective and accurate demand plan is not as difficult as many organizations think. Quality demand plans are underpinned by particular attributes in forecasting, promotions management, causal event management, demand plan integration and performance measurement. In many cases, demand plan attributes do not require high investment in technology. Often the causes of a low-quality demand plan are more attributable to poor process and coordination rather than a lack of technology.

Low-quality demand plans are often caused by poor process and coordination rather than a lack of technology.

Leading practice statistical forecasting

The ability to generate an accurate demand plan starts with the ability to generate a valid forecast. If the demand plan is based on a poor forecast, then it is likely to fail at the outset. Organizations can take several steps, shown in Figure 2.7.4. and outlined below, to help to ensure that they embark on demand planning with a valid forecast.

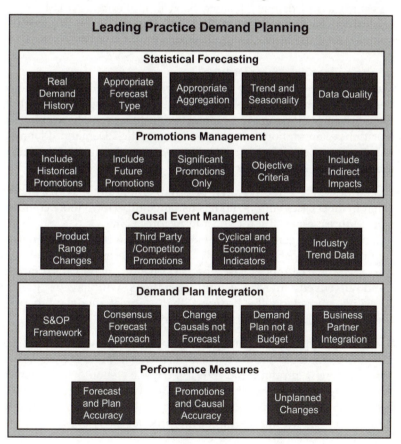

Figure 2.7.4
Leading practice demand planning

Real demand history

The customer's original order should be the history on which the forecast is based.

In most cases, a forecast is a model of the future based on data about the past. For this model to be valid, it must be based on valid history. Forecasts, therefore, should be based on real demand. From a demand planning perspective, it is irrelevant if the customer's order was not filled. The customer's original order should be the history on which the forecast is based as this ensures that the customer's demand will be predicted next time.

Some organizations that do not accept backorders or have customers who do not accept backorders use invoice history instead of demand history. This removes the upward distortion in order history caused by customers ordering multiple times to satisfy the one requirement. While effective in the short term, this method will not capture a backorder at the time of original demand and thus next time is again likely to result in a backorder. A more effective long-term approach is to use real demand. If real demand is captured the situation is reversed – each customer order is captured, leading to an overestimation of demand history. Next time the forecast is likely to overestimate customer demand. This will result in no backorders and thus over time the forecast should stabilize.

Use the appropriate forecast type

A large number of different forecast types or methods are available. These range from very simple models, such as averaging, through to quite sophisticated proprietary algorithms, such as the Lewandowski algorithm – an option within the Manugistics Demand Planning module. Two principles need to be understood when determining what forecast method to use:

The best forecasts will be based on simple models, and the right information and integration.

- Keep it simple – the research of Spyros Makridakis (1998) shows that in most cases simple models usually outperform more complex procedures, especially for short-term forecasting.
- Concentrate on getting the right information and integration, not on getting the most theoretically correct forecasting engine. An average forecast model based on good history, good causal factors and effectively integrated into operations will have a greater positive impact on the business than a great model with poor history, poor causal factors and poor integration.

Based on these principles, an organization should review the aspects that differentiate a product from a forecast perspective. When assessing a new product, the forecast database should be reviewed for its applicability with the forecast types being used. An organization should confirm the validity of this initial assessment at regular intervals during the life of the product to ensure the forecast type is still applicable.

To minimize workload, it is appropriate to use forecast accuracy as an indicator of which products need to be assessed. If the forecast is

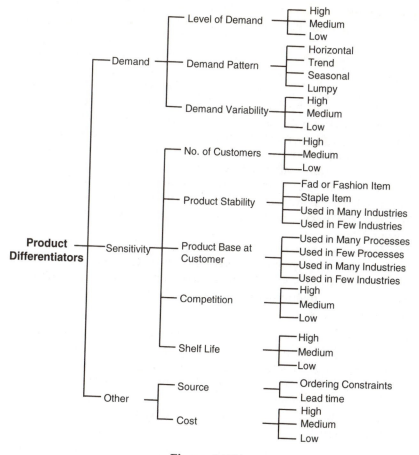

Figure 2.7.5
Product differentiators

accurate, the product does not need reassessment. If the forecast is poor then one of the causes may be a change in the product differentiators. Part of the investigation of poor forecast performance is to confirm that the initial assumptions made on these product differentiators is still valid (Figure 2.7.5).

Use the appropriate level of aggregation and time horizon

A forecast generated at a higher level of aggregation will be more accurate, on average, than forecasts generated at a lower level. For example, forecasting sales of 375ml cans of Coke at the local corner store is not likely to be as accurate as predicting sales of 375ml cans of Coke across all corner stores in Sydney. The individual fluctuations at the store level tend to balance each other out at the aggregated level. Likewise, a forecast for an event happening in the near future is likely to be more accurate than the forecast for an event in the distant future.

Organizations should forecast at the highest levels of aggregation possible. How high to go is a trade-off between achieving accuracy at the highest and lowest levels.

For example, the forecast for sales of 375ml cans of Coke for Sydney for next week is likely to be more accurate than for the same week next year.

The implications of these principles are clear. First, organizations should forecast at the highest appropriate level of aggregation, which will depend upon an individual organization's situation. Generally, the decision as to how high to go is a trade-off between improved accuracy experienced at the higher levels versus the loss of granularity of the demand plan obtained at the lower level. For example, a forecast of all products sold by an organization should be quite accurate; however, a forecast at this level cannot be included in the master production schedule, as the schedule requires a view at the individual product level. In most cases, the appropriate level is somewhere in between the lowest and highest levels available, as illustrated in Figure 2.7.6.

Organizations should aggregate history then distribute the forecast among the lower levels using a variety of tools.

Second, organizations should aggregate history, generate the forecast at the aggregated level and then distribute the forecast among the lower levels rather than forecasting at the lower levels only. The method of distribution depends on the tools available; however, the basic options are:

- distribute the forecast based on the volume of history that the lower level item contributes to total history
- distribute the forecast based on the volume of forecast that the lower level item contributes to total forecast (only an option if you also generate a forecast at the lower level) or
- use a manual split based on, say, a percentage or hard number breakdown.

Third, organizations should aim to reduce lead times so that the forecasts only have to be prepared for as short a time horizon as possible.

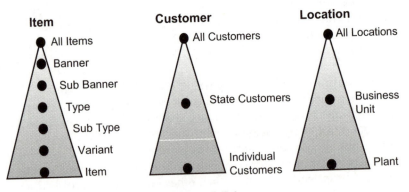

Figure 2.7.6
Illustrative aggregation options

Include realistic trend and seasonality impacts

A forecast comprises three basic components, as shown in Figure 2.7.7

- trend – the overall direction of the forecast (either positive, negative or flat)
- seasonality – a regular repetitive pattern within the forecast (such as an increase in sales in summer or a peak in sales at the end of every month)
- noise – the changes within the demand that occur randomly and cannot be forecast.

An accurate forecast needs to have the right level of trend and seasonality included within the model. As external factors change, it is important that the trend and/or seasonality aspects of the model are updated.

An accurate forecast will include the right level of trend and seasonality in the model. The forecast will be updated as external factors change.

Manage the data quality

The quality of the statistical forecast is only as good as the quality of the data upon which it is based. Care and resources need to be committed to ensuring that accurate and complete sets of data are captured and maintained within the forecasting application. The person responsible for developing the demand plan should be the 'owner' of the forecast database and responsible for the quality and integrity of the data within it.

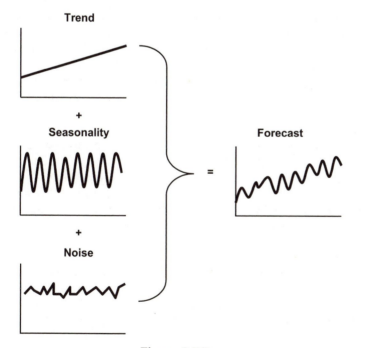

Figure 2.7.7
Forecast components

Leading practice promotions management

While a quality forecast is a good basis for a demand plan, the forecast needs to be modified for external activities that will have an impact on the demand for the product being forecasted. In many consumer packaged goods industries, an organization's own promotions and marketing can have one of the biggest impacts on the accuracy of the forecast. However, with the appropriate level of information management and integration, promotional events can be managed into the forecast and demand plan so that they actually add to the accuracy of both. The actions described below need to occur to ensure that this integration of promotional events into the forecast and demand plan takes place.

The impact of promotional events needs to be integrated into the forecast and demand plan so that the accuracy of both is improved.

Ensure past promotional events are included in history

The history database is likely to include demand figures that have been affected by past promotional events. An organization needs to ensure that any valid promotional events that had a significant impact on the history data are included in history so that the forecast model does not extrapolate the sales impact of that event into the future. This can be done by actually modifying history to remove the promotional impact. However, the recommended way is to 'mask' history so that the original data is not lost, rather a modified number is used in the forecast calculation.

Past, future and indirect promotional events should be included in the forecast history and demand plan.

Ensure future promotional events are included in the demand plan

The accuracy of the demand plan is dependent upon the information about future promotional events included in the forecast. It is essential that future promotional events be included in the demand plan such that the demand plan reflects the impact of these future events. If these events are not included then the accuracy of the demand plan will be reduced.

Only include significant promotional events

A promotional event should be included in the forecast or demand plan if it has a significant impact upon the history or demand plan. Some promotional events have such a small impact that they are not worth including. However, the person preparing the forecast or demand plan should still be informed of these events so that they can determine if the events are worth including.

Base the impact of the event on objective criteria

The impact of each promotional event on the forecast should be based upon objective criteria such as history of similar event's. The actual impact of past events upon the demand plan should be assessed against the estimated impact to build up an accurate database of event impacts. The marketing or sales estimate of an event's impact is only the initial element. The demand plan leader should have the final say on the forecasted impact of the event.

Include the impact of indirect promotional events
Promotional events seldom have an impact on only the actual product promoted during the actual timeframe of the event. Some indirect impacts of promotional events include:

- Bringing forward or cannibalizing future sales of the product being promoted as customers buy to take advantage of the savings. An example is a supermarket buying two months' worth of stock in month one to take advantage of a promotion and then buying little or no stock in month two.
- Lower sales or cannibalization of similar products in preference to the promoted product. For example, a promotion of a 25 per cent bigger Mars Bar may reduce sales of standard size Mars Bars and also sales of Dove Chocolate as people opt to buy the promotional Mars Bar.
- Increased sales of products that are complementary to the items actually being promoted. For example, a sales promotion for razors can lead to an increase in demand for the razor blades to fit that razor.

The indirect promotional impacts also need to be included in the forecast history and demand plan to ensure the accuracy of the demand plan.

Leading practice causal event management
Adding an organization's own promotional events into the demand plan will help increase the accuracy of the plan. However, while promotions are often seen as the major causal events that affect a forecast, several other causal events also need to be included in the demand plan.

A variety of causal events need to be included in the demand plan to improve accuracy further.

Changes in product range
The impact of new products or discontinued products can have an impact on the accuracy of forecasting for similar products. For example, if Coca Cola decides to discontinue supply of the 600ml bottle of Coke it is likely to increase sales of the 370ml and 1.25l bottles of Coke as customers are forced to buy a different size. Such events need to be included in the demand plan for all relevant products.

Competitor and third-party promotions
Promotional events that affect the accuracy of a forecast and demand plan are not limited to those run by the organization itself. Competitor promotional events can have a big impact on sales. For example, a promotion by Sanitarium for Wheat Bix can reduce the sales of Goodman Fielder's Vita Brits.

Promotions by competitors and third parties can have a big impact on sales.

In addition to competitor activity, third-party promotional events can also have an impact on sales. For example, if Woolworths is promoting Vita Brits then it is logical that the quantity of Vita Brits that

Woolworths orders from Goodman Fielder will also change. Any significant instances of competitor or third-party promotional events need to be included in the forecast or demand plan in a similar way to the organization's own promotional events.

Include relevant cyclical and economic indicators

In many industries, economic conditions can have a significant impact on sales. Often, economic data are available that will allow the impact of these economic conditions to be assessed and included in the demand plan. For example, CSR may use housing start data provided by the Australian Bureau of Statistics to predict the medium-term trend in sales of building materials used in domestic house construction. Data of this type should be incorporated into the demand plan to ensure that trend and/or seasonality of the demand plan is more accurately modeled.

Include long-term industry trend data

The overall trend of growth in some industries is quite marked and can add value to a demand plan. For example, the consumption of beer in Australia is trending down, with drinkers moving to wine and spirits in preference to beer. Thus any demand plan over the medium to long term that shows significant growth in beer sales needs to be assessed against this fact. Before accepting such a demand plan, the specific reasons why the company might achieve growth need to be validated. Such reasons may include cannibalization of existing brands or expected gain in market share at the expense of a competitor. This type of data should be included in the demand plan and used to validate the reasonableness of the demand plan being put forward.

Leading practice demand plan integration

Companies must have the capability to add new data to their demand plan and integrate an updated plan into their processes.

A forecast can be transformed into a valid demand plan by adding information about an organization's own promotions, competitor and third-party promotions, economic data and seasonal events. However, organizations can find it difficult to facilitate effectively the addition of all this data in a timely manner. They can also face problems in effectively integrating the resultant demand plan into the organization's other planning and execution processes. Typically, the most successful organizations are those that adopt some of the following steps:

Use a sales and operations planning (S&OP) framework to integrate demand with supply

A formal S&OP framework provides the structure, process and tools to help to ensure that the demand plan is effectively integrated with the other planning and executions processes in the organization. The S&OP is also the correct forum to sign off the final demand plan. Such a framework also provides the right forum to address many of the issues encountered in gathering and adding the promotions, competitor and third-party promotions, economic data and seasonal events.

Use a consensus-forecast approach to solve issues before the S&OP meeting
Gathering all the necessary data for the demand plan is too big a task to be managed informally. Organizations should adopt a formal, consensus-forecast approach that incorporates the following:

- a process that details how to obtain the causal information and who is responsible for obtaining it
- simple templates and tools to communicate this information efficiently to the person responsible for updating the demand plan, and
- guidelines on how to resolve disagreements on what adjustments should be made to the demand plan (including guidelines on what decisions are required to be escalated to S&OP for resolution).

Change the causal factors, not the forecast. A fundamental principle of leading practice demand planning is the sanctity of the forecast model. The forecast is normally generated using an objective model, and by adding various causal factors and data, the forecast is transformed into the demand plan. The transformation occurs as the forecast is modified by the expected impact of these various causal factors or by adjustments to the model used to generate the forecast. It is not valid simply to adjust the forecast manually to make the numbers appear correct. If this is required, then it is a symptom of either a forecast model that needs adjustment or an inappropriate use of causal factors.

It is not valid simply to adjust the forecast manually to make the numbers appear correct.

An example best illustrates this principle. Assume an organization's demand plan for next month is 200 units below that required and its forecast model is valid. The organization cannot simply decree that the forecast must increase by 200. The company must perform some external act to increase demand by 200. Thus, an event such as a promotion should be added to the demand plan to increase volume by the required 200 units. If this principle is not maintained, then the demand plan rapidly becomes a management wish list of future sales rather than an accurate model of what can be expected given the demand history and known events.

The demand plan is not the budget
Following from the above principle, the demand plan is not the budget. A budget may be used to set the desired sales targets, and these targets may then be compared with the demand plan. If a significant gap exists between the two numbers, then the organization should adjust its demand plan by adding or modifying causal events.

Integrate demand plan processes with appropriate business partners
Significant business partners should be involved in generating the demand plan to facilitate the gathering and validation of data on third-party promotional events. In addition, organizations can gain significant benefits through the greater visibility of future customer requirements. Integrating the development of demand plans does not have to be a high-technology solution. It can be as simple as significant customers e-mailing their forecast for consideration within the demand plan development process.

Leading practice performance measures

The demand plan process should be measured to ensure it is effective, adding value and improving whenever possible.

The development of a demand plan is like any other business process in that process effectiveness should be measured to ensure the process is effective, adding value and all opportunities for continuous improvement are recognised. From a demand plan perspective, the following areas need to be measured.

Forecast and demand plan accuracy
The accuracy of the forecast and demand plan should be captured at essential points in the development process. The major points of accuracy include the:

- initial statistical forecast – to assess the quality of the model or algorithm being used to generate the forecast and if required make any adjustments
- demand plan after promotions are added – to assess the quality of the promotional data being added and
- final demand plan – to assess the quality of the final demand plan.

Promotions and causal event accuracy
The accuracy of the promotions and causal events added to the forecast should be measured. When the actual demand data are available, the estimated impact of the event should be compared with the actual impact. This allows similar future events to be assessed more accurately and thus the demand plan to be more accurate after future similar events.

Unplanned changes
The number of unplanned changes to downstream processes such as production and distribution that can be attributed to poor demand plan accuracy should be captured. The organization needs an overall view of the effectiveness of the demand plan, including the costs of a poor demand plan. The results often surprise and, in some cases, are more than enough to build a significant business case to improve demand plan capability.

Improving demand plan accuracy

The reality of a demand plan is that it will always be wrong. Random variation and inherent inefficiency across an extended supply chain mean that it is impossible to increase demand plan accuracy beyond a certain level. Nevertheless, organizations must strive to understand and minimize as many causes of error as possible so that they can improve the effectiveness of their demand plan. While improving their demand plan capability on the one hand, organizations should be also implementing strategies that either reduce their reliance on aspects of the demand plan or have an impact on the inherent variability of that demand plan. Such strategies should include:

To complement demand plan capability, organizations should also implement strategies to reduce their reliance on aspects of the demand plan.

- Lead-time reduction. By reducing the lead time of the fulfilment process, the actual demand plan used to execute does not have to look as far into the future, and thus should be more accurate than a demand plan looking further out. An example of this is a postponement strategy used by Benetton. The clothing manufacturer originally used a manufacturing process that colored the cloth before assembling the clothes. This meant that each garment had a demand plan for each color of each style and the production of the garments was based on this demand plan.

  Reducing lead times means the demand plan does not have to look as far into the future.

  As demand in clothing is quite seasonal, Benetton needed to begin production early to build up enough stock for the coming season. This meant that Benetton had to get its demand plan right for each color and style months in advance. However, Benetton modified this process so that the garment was made without color, before being warehoused. The garments were then colored just before shipment. Thus, the new demand plan for determining what color to produce only had to predict demand days, or a few weeks, in advance rather than months ahead. This short-term demand plan is more accurate, and therefore, less stock should be needed to maintain the required service level (Figure 2.7.8).

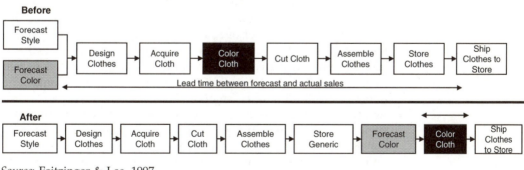

Source: Feitzinger & Lee, 1997

Figure 2.7.8
Postponement

- *Demand aggregation*. By aggregating separate demand into one higher level demand, the accuracy should improve. An example of this is the direct customer delivery model used by department stores and white goods manufacturers. Floor stock of white goods in many department stores is display only. The actual stock used to satisfy customer orders is kept at the manufacturer's or distributor's warehouse and shipped directly to the customer who orders at the department store. This means that the demand plan for white goods from each department store is aggregated to the DC level. The individual demand variances across stores will tend to balance each other out at the DC level, leading to a more predictable demand at the DC. This requires less safety stock to maintain the same service level than would be required if stock was maintained at the department store. The inventory savings more than cover the additional delivery costs incurred with this model.

Demand management

Many causal events can be used to manage demand proactively so that the demand actually becomes more predictable.

As detailed in this chapter, a forecast needs to have several causal events added to it to transform it into an accurate demand plan. In most cases, organizations see these events as external factors that need to be added to the forecast in a reactive way, so that the forecast will reflect reality more closely. However, many of these causal events can be used to manage demand proactively so that the demand actually becomes more predictable. The aim is to modify or remove external factors that lead to lumpy demand. The smoother the demand is, the easier it is to forecast. Examples of causal factors or external aspects that can be used in this way include:

- *Terms of trade*. By changing terms of trade from a calendar-based payment term to a fixed period of time after purchase, organizations can remove the incentive for customers to buy early or late in the month to gain a longer period before payment is due. This tends to smooth demand over the month rather than have demand lumped at certain times in the month.
- *Sales force incentives*. Sales people are most often rewarded for achieving a certain level of sales within a set period, an example being a target set by month. This often manifests itself in demand lumped towards the end of the month. By including a component in the incentive program that discourages lumpy demand, the demand profile should be smoothed.
- *Promotions*. Products that are promoted in a non-regular and variable manner are difficult to forecast. By running regular and consistent promotions or, even better, by removing promotions and just incorporating an everyday low price, the demand pattern can be smoothed.

Conclusion

Many organizations are settling on a demand plan that has a far lower quality than they could actually achieve. The actions required to improve demand plan quality are not reliant on high technology solutions or complex or difficult processes. Simple and effective action can be taken in the short term to improve quality. Companies can embark on leading practice statistical forecasting to improve the validity of their forecast that forms the basis of their demand plan. They can manage their own promotions and marketing better, and take account of other causal events, to improve their forecast accuracy. Organizations can also take steps to reduce their lead times, aggregate demand to the highest level possible, and help to remove external factors that disrupt smooth demand processes. By taking these simple but comprehensive steps, organizations can improve their demand plan quality and produce a positive impact on their company bottom line.

Simple and effective action can be taken in the short term to improve demand plan quality.

References

Abbott, H. L. (1993) 'Forecasting for Inventory Control' in the CPIM Master Planning Reprints, : American Production and Inventory Control Society.

Berger, A. J. and Gattorna, J. L. (2001) *Supply Chain Cybermastery*, Aldershot: Gower Publishing.

Feitzinger, E. and Lee, H. (1997) Mass Customization at Hewlett-Packard: The power of postponement, *Harvard Business Review*, Jan/Feb 1997, pp. 116–121.

Gattorna, J. L. (1998) *Strategic Supply Chain Alignment*, Aldershot: Gower Publishing.

Makridakis, S. and Wheelwright, S. C. (1998) *Forecasting – Methods and Applications*, 3rd edn, Wheelwright and Hyndman:

Plossl, G. W. (1985) *Production and Inventory Control Principles and Techniques* 2nd edn, New Jersey: Prentice-Hall.

Vollman, T. E. et al. (1997), *Manufacturing Planning and Control Systems*, 4th edn, New York: Irwin/McGraw-Hill.

Wallace, T. F. (2000) *Sales & Operations Planning*, T. F. Wallace and Company: Ohio.

Wilson, T., in *Internet Week* (23 July 2001), <www.internetweek.com>.

2.8 Inventory management

Geremy J. Heath and Alister Danks

Organizations require inventory to ensure the smooth operation of their day-to-day business. However, inventories can have adverse effects and disguise issues.

Inventory management is an essential process for all parties engaged in supply chain activities, from the procurement of raw materials through to the delivery of finished goods. The effective execution of this process has a major influence on both the financial and operational performance of an organization.

While many may argue that inventories are undesirable and should be eliminated from the supply chain, the fact remains that organizations require inventory in order to operate effectively and to ensure the smooth operation of their day-to-day business. Notwithstanding the critical importance of inventories, companies have to keep in mind that inventories can also cause adverse effects and often disguise other underlying issues in the supply chain. Managing inventory can be both a complicated and critical process given the conflicting business objectives that can occur within an organization and across multiple enterprises.

To provide a clear understanding of inventory management, this chapter will look at how inventory can improve both operational and financial performance. We will consider why companies hold inventory and what types of inventory exist in the supply chain. The objectives of holding inventory are analysed and how these might conflict across an organization. We also consider how much inventory supply chain executives need to hold and how they can reduce this amount. Finally, we outline some examples of leading practice in inventory management.

Why hold inventory?

In a perfect world raw materials would be delivered in any quantity, at any time, with 100 per cent on-time delivery. Production plants would never break down and companies would achieve 100 per cent product quality each time. Plants would always have sufficient capacity, while both upstream and downstream production processes would run together in perfect sync. Perfect forecasts would allow products to be shipped just-in-time, with production quantities exactly equal to demand. Delivery trucks would never break down, stock would never be damaged and staff would never be sick or go on strike. Sound ideal? The reality, however, is far different: companies are continually faced with variability and uncertainty throughout the entire supply chain.

Inventory is a variable resource providing the buffer to ensure businesses continue to run smoothly amidst the uncertainty that exists throughout the supply chain.

How, then, do businesses overcome this variability and uncertainty? The answer is inventory. Inventory is a variable resource providing the buffer to ensure businesses continue to run smoothly amidst the uncertainty that exists throughout the supply chain. Without inventory, customers would be subjected to poor product availability, long lead times and delays and a reduced choice of product variety.

From a company's perspective, inventory gives greater flexibility to operate a business efficiently, providing a lever to balance the customer service, cost and operational objectives. Purchasing large quantities of raw materials in bulk may result in a discounted price from suppliers. Running longer production runs may result in reduced production and changeover costs. Holding inventory in warehouses located closer to the customer may reduce delivery lead times and lower transportation costs. However, the trade-off for each of these examples is increased inventory and higher inventory holding costs. The key is for businesses to adopt inventory levels and deployment strategies that will optimize both the operational and financial performance of the company, while satisfying customer expectations. There is no-'one-size-fits-all' approach; each business requires its own solution to satisfy its own set of objectives.

Types of inventory throughout the supply chain

Different types of inventory are used throughout the supply chain; each type enables a company to operate smoothly and provide end users with an uninterrupted supply of products. By tracing the supply chain events, from the acquisition of raw materials to the final delivery of finished products, the classification of each inventory type becomes clear.

Each type of inventory enables a company to operate smoothly and provide end users with an uninterrupted supply of products.

Raw materials

Raw materials are any material inputs acquired externally by a company for use in the manufacturing process and include manufactured products from other suppliers. Companies often buy large quantities of raw materials to reduce purchase and transportation costs.

A number of large automotive manufacturers have managed to reduce raw materials requirements by locating their suppliers close to the production plant. This results in reduced and more reliable delivery lead times, which in turn reduces the manufacturer's safety stock requirements. The closer proximity of the supplier to the production plant also allows smaller more frequent deliveries through reduced transportation distances and costs.

Work-in-process

Once raw materials leave the inventory stockpile and begin transformation through the production process, they are work-in-process (WIP). The amount of WIP differs greatly from industry to industry and depends on the production process being employed. Reducing the manufacturing lead time will reduce the amount of WIP, while also improving a company's ability to react quickly to changes in demand.

A common mistake made by organizations is to base incentives around production utilization for individual job stations in the production process. The result is high levels of WIP and an inability to react to fluctuating demand. In order to reduce WIP, raw materials should be fed into the production process only at the rate of the slowest process. The slowest process is often called a bottleneck. Only by increasing the capacity of the bottleneck are companies able to increase the overall throughput of production.

Semi-finished goods

Storing stock as semi-finished goods rather than finished products can help companies build to customer specifications and reduce the risk of obsolescence.

Raw materials that have been processed, fabricated or assembled into intermediate parts or sub-assemblies, and temporarily re-stocked for later use in the production process, are known as semi-finished goods. This differs from raw materials, as it is not acquired from external suppliers, and differs from finished goods, as it is not in a sellable form.

Dell Computer stores the majority of its stock as semi-finished goods, with the finished product not assembled until a firm customer order is received. This type of manufacturing process is referred to as assemble-to-order, and allows Dell to reduce its inventory requirements, while maintaining a large range of configurable end products built to the customer's specification. Given the large number of end configurations and short product life cycles for personal computers, holding the product in a finished good state would result in a large range of products with a high risk of inventory obsolescence.

Finished goods

A finished good is an item that can be sold to a customer and may be either a completed item or a repair part. Companies hold finished goods inventory where the customer's expectation is to have the product available immediately. Finished goods held at storage locations or in transit throughout the distribution network may also be referred to as distribution inventory. Finished goods are often held in storage locations closer to customers in order to reduce delivery lead times and minimize transportation costs.

MRO inventory

MRO is the familiar acronym used for maintenance, repair and operating supplies. All companies, not just manufacturers and distributors, require MRO inventory to operate their business effectively on a day-to-day basis. MRO goods are often low-cost, high-volume products and include items such as stationery, spare parts or even the coffee for the office coffee machine.

The objectives of holding inventory

Inventory may assist in achieving several objectives across multiple functions in an organization. While inventory decisions are primarily driven by operational objectives, they also have a significant impact on a company's financial performance.

The key is for inventory decisions to maximize a company's financial and operational performance, contributing to the overall economic value of the business.

Figure 2.8.1 highlights the important drivers of economic value creation for a business and how each is affected by inventory decisions. Profitability and capital expenditure (invested capital) are the two biggest drivers of this value. Profitability is driven by revenue and costs, while capital expenditure is driven by both working and fixed capital. To ensure a company's financial and operational performance is maximized, a cross-functional focus is essential. The key is not to minimize costs for specific business functions but rather to focus on maximizing the overall economic value of the business.

Generally, any type of inventory, be it raw material, work-in-process or finished goods, contains two components that must be considered when evaluating inventory decisions, that is cycle stock and safety stock (Figure 2.8.2).

Cycle stock represents the stock required to satisfy demand between replenishments. This is inventory's most fundamental function and is driven by the frequency of inventory replenishments. Decisions on replenishment quantities and frequencies have an impact across multiple functions in a business, with each function having its own set of objectives (Table 2.8.1).

The second major component of inventory is safety stock. Safety stock is the additional stock required to satisfy product availability (service levels) by providing a buffer against supply chain variability.

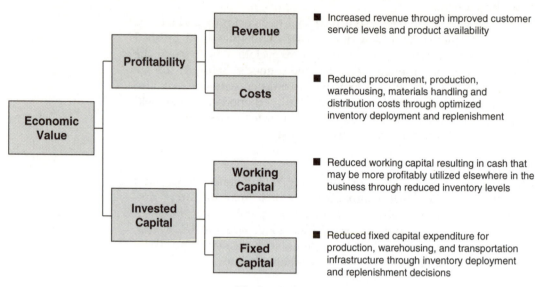

Figure 2.8.1
Benefits of effective inventory management

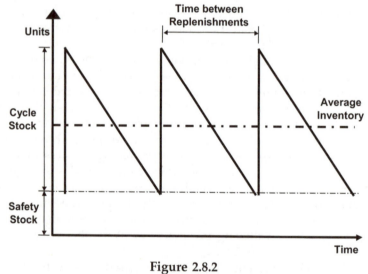

Figure 2.8.2
Inventory sawtooth diagram

High levels of variability in an organization's supply chain results in a need to hold high levels of safety stock. Likewise, high service level requirements also contribute to the need for holding large buffer stocks. Again, conflicting objectives between departments result in different behaviors when considering the level of safety stock to hold (Table 2.8.2).

Table 2.8.1
Functional objectives for cycle stock

Functional area	Primary objectives	Key drivers	Outcome
Purchasing	• Minimize purchasing costs	• Volume discounts for large order quantities • Transportation discounts for large shipment quantities • Reduced order processing costs through less frequent ordering	• High levels of cycle stock
Production	• Minimize production costs • Maximize plant utilization	• Long production runs to reduce set-up time and maximize production efficiency	• High levels of cycle stock
Finance	• Improve cash flows • Minimize costs	• Minimize inventory levels to release working capital tied up in the business • Minimize costs for each function	• Optimum levels of cycle stock
Sales and marketing	• Increase sales volume • Maximize market share	• Large product mix to capture sales from a broader customer base • Provide customers with new product designs to capture sales and market share	• Lower cycle stock through increased production changeover due to larger product portfolio

Table 2.8.2
Functional objectives for holding safety stock

Functional area	Primary objectives	Key drivers	Behavior
Production	• Reduce production stoppages • Maximize plant utilization	• Need to maintain steady and continuous flow of materials through the plant to reduce production stoppages	• High levels of safety stock throughout the production process
Finance	• Improve cash flows • Maximize revenues	• Minimize inventory levels to release working capital tied up in the business • Ensure adequate availability to capture customer sales	• Optimum levels of safety stock
Sales and marketing	• Increase sales volume • Maximize market share	• Provide high levels of product availability (service levels)	• High levels of safety stock

While there is always a desire to maintain high service levels, large safety stock requirements are ultimately driven by high variability in both supply and demand. The need to hold high levels of safety stock is a strong symptom of underlying process issues, which contribute to high variability in the supply chain. The key to improving service levels, while reducing safety stock requirements, is to identify the causes of variability in the supply chain and take action to reduce them.

Achieving optimal inventory levels

The inherent fear of stocking out means that executives are often overly conservative in their safety stock decisions.

Stocking out of a product will result in a lost sale and potentially a lost customer. For this reason the need to carry enough stock to satisfy demand is critical.

In many organizations, the notion of a stock-out is very much a worst-case scenario, to be avoided at all costs. This mentality also exists for production, where stocking out of raw materials would halt the production process. For many industries, a raw materials stock-out is often more catastrophic than the stocking out of finished goods. For example, running out of coal at a coal power station would result in an entire plant shutdown and large financial losses.

Companies use safety stock as insurance to protect themselves against stock-out situations; the safety stock provides a buffer against supply chain variability. The inherent fear of stocking out means that executives are often overly conservative in their safety stock decisions, resulting in large amounts of safety stock being held throughout the supply chain. Many executives base their decisions on gut feel and previous experience, rather than what is actually required.

At the same time, if a product is to stock out, a lack of inventory is identified as the immediate culprit. In order to avoid a stock-out situation occurring in the future, safety stock levels are increased. Over time customer service levels are maintained, however inventory levels continue to climb. The reason for the increase in inventory is increased supply chain variability.

Extra inventory provides a short-term fix for maintaining service levels, but conceals the underlying issues.

This increase in variability is often within the control of a company, and is a result of deteriorating process performance. Extra inventory provides a short-term fix for maintaining service levels, but at the same time conceals the true underlying issues.

High inventory levels are a symptom of poor supply chain performance. A common analogy used is that of water covering the jagged sea floor, as shown in Figure 2.8.3. Similarly, inventory is often used to cover up poor supply chain performance. When faced with product shortages, a lack of adequate inventory is generally identified as the problem. Little consideration is given to the source of variability and uncertainty responsible for the shortage. For a business to maintain high service levels, with lower levels of inventory, it must

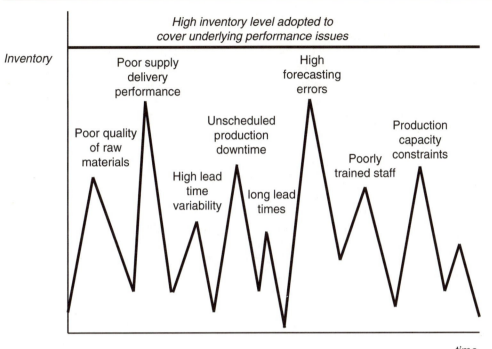

Figure 2.8.3
Inventory used to cover poor supply chain performance

first focus on removing the sources of variability and uncertainty within the supply chain rather than disguise poor supply chain process performance with high buffer stocks.

So, how much inventory should a company hold? The answer is, enough to satisfy demand between replenishments (cycle stock) while also providing a buffer (safety stock) against the variability and uncertainty that exist in the supply chain.

While many companies may wish to embark on inventory reduction programs, very few would feel comfortable adopting a trial and error approach of lowering inventory levels to uncover underlying problems. This approach would undoubtedly lead to stock-out situations and potential lost sales or, even worse, lost customers.

For this reason a two-step approach should be used when attempting to reduce inventory and improve levels of service. The first step is to eliminate excess stock by reducing inventory to satisfy service levels based on current levels of variability and stock replenishment frequencies. As previously mentioned, the approach of most companies to stocking out means that high levels of safety stock are held throughout the supply chain. Safety stock levels are usually higher than required to satisfy desired service levels. Going back to our analogy, the first step represents lowering the water to just cover the highest rock.

Companies should hold enough inventory to satisfy demand between replenishments while also providing a buffer against variability and uncertainty.

The next step is to focus on identifying and eliminating the root causes of high inventory. High variability drives up safety stock requirements while long replenishment periods result in large cycle stocks. Again back to our analogy, this phase is about removing the rocks under the surface allowing the water to be dropped to new low levels. Businesses wishing to sustain ongoing improvements need to focus their efforts on improvement programs that will reduce supply chain variability. Remember, a stock-out is not necessarily due to a lack of inventory but rather excess variability and uncertainty within the supply chain.

Software packages can enable companies to statistically calculate optimum safety stock requirements and lower inventory to levels that satisfy service needs.

Few companies, however, would feel comfortable blindly reducing inventory levels to expose underlying supply chain issues. So the question remains: how much inventory should a company hold to adequately satisfy desired service levels? The answer can be obtained through statistical analysis. Leading supply chain planning vendors such as Manugistics, i2 and SAP now offer software packages that statistically calculate optimum safety stock requirements. The requirements are based on historical supply chain variability, replenishment frequencies and desired service levels. These software tools allow businesses to complete safely the first step of lowering inventory to levels that satisfy service needs.

Once the first step of eliminating excess inventory is completed, a company may next focus on reducing the variability that drives the need to hold high levels of safety stock. Companies setting safety stocks based on gut feel and previous experience will not fully benefit from supply chain improvements that reduce variability and lower safety stock requirements such as improved forecast accuracy. Generally, the inherent fear of stocking out overrides confidence in the improved forecasts. However, statistical safety stock levels would immediately reduce stock levels as a reduction in the historical demand variability would have a direct impact on the calculated safety stock requirement.

As described in Case study 1 below, Accenture has developed a custom-built inventory modeling and decision support tool called the Inventory Rebalancing Model (IRM) to assist clients in addressing stock levels in a consumer packaged goods environment by adopting statistical modeling techniques.

The basic analytical principles of inventory management are well documented and have not changed at all over the years. Two good references are the forerunner to this book, *Handbook of Logistics and Distribution Management* (Gattorna, 1994), and *Fundamentals of Logistics* (Lambert et al.; 1997).

Examples of leading practice in inventory management

Companies can take a variety of steps to optimize their inventory holdings and eliminate excess stock holdings. However, no one method can be prescribed for all companies, since each company has particular characteristics that influence its situation and opportunities for improvement. Such characteristics include number of stock keeping units, uniqueness of product, length of production runs, breadth of distribution network, customer behavior, degree of influence with customers and suppliers, sophistication of information systems and management culture. However, by studying examples of leading practice we are able to identify initiatives and opportunities that can be applied to a range of companies.

No one method for managing inventory can be prescribed, since each company has particular characteristics that influence its situation and improvement opportunities.

The case studies below show how:

- a leading fast-moving consumer goods (FMCG) company used a custom-built inventory modeling and decision support tool to recommend statistically generated safety stocks and offer improved decision support capabilities for a large number of stock keeping units
- a global mobile telephone manufacturer implemented a supplier logistics center to introduce vendor-managed inventory and collaborative information sharing with its suppliers, as a key component of achieving a lean supply chain
- a global dairy company leveraged a redesign of its organizational structure and simple inventory models to improve the visibility of inventory costs and facilitate effective decision making and
- a regional oil company used statistical modeling to change the operating practices of country-based management across the region and release more than $100 million in savings.

Case study 1 – Inventory Rebalancing Model for a leading FMCG company

With its market share under threat, and its local brands being eroded, this national FMCG company intensified its focus on core brand rejuvenation, new product development and the premium market segment. Competitive threats in the market put pressure on the company to upgrade the quality of its national supply chain operations, while improving customer service without adding new costs.

Accenture developed a custom-built inventory modeling and decision support tool to assist the company in reducing inventory levels while improving service levels.

Accenture worked with the company to identify the most pressing supply chain issues. Pre-eminent among these were forecasting accuracy, inventory fluctuations, and discounting and write-offs of aged and surplus stock. The supply chain processes were not sufficiently integrated or enabled by the underlying transaction system, nor was there adequate information to support key supply chain decisions. Overall, there was an opportunity to improve performance to support customer service requirements better.

While a two- to three-year change program was put in place to provide leading processes and systems in supply chain planning, customer management and enterprise transaction management, an immediate solution was required to solve the inventory issues.

Accenture developed a custom-built inventory modeling and decision support tool to assist the company in reducing inventory levels while improving service levels. The Inventory Rebalancing Model statistically calculates optimum inventory levels based on historical supply and demand variability, replenishment frequencies and desired service levels. The tool compares statistically generated inventory levels with an organization's actual inventory levels to identify inventory reduction opportunities. As its name suggests, the IRM does not only identify reduction opportunities, it also identifies and recommends increased inventory levels for products that require additional inventory to satisfy desired service levels.

The IRM was used first as a diagnostic tool for assessing and quantifying inventory reduction benefits and then as an interim planning solution until the organization was ready to implement and commission integrated decision support software provided by i2 Technologies. The organization reduced inventory levels by $7 million, allowing it to capture financial benefits of lower inventory early. The improved forecast accuracy achieved by the IRM resulted in reduced safety stock requirements and consequently had a direct impact on the bottom line. It also helped to quickly introduce the concept of statistically calculated safety stocks to the business and these were then integrated into demand and production planning process with the new system.

The powerful 'what if?' modeling capabilities embedded in the model allow users to alter replenishment frequencies, service levels and forecast accuracy to assess the impact that each of these variables has on a company's inventory requirements. New inventory requirements and the associated reduction opportunities are generated based on entered values. The tool was extremely useful for quantifying the impact that changes in replenishment frequency, service level and forecast accuracy would have on inventory levels. Accenture has since used the tool on several client engagements around the world to identify inventory reduction opportunities achievable by adopting statistical safety stock. A sample of the application is shown in Figure 2.8.4.

The statistical safety stock algorithm used in the model is based on the exponential approximation of normal density. More information on the algorithm may be found in Johnson et al. (1995).

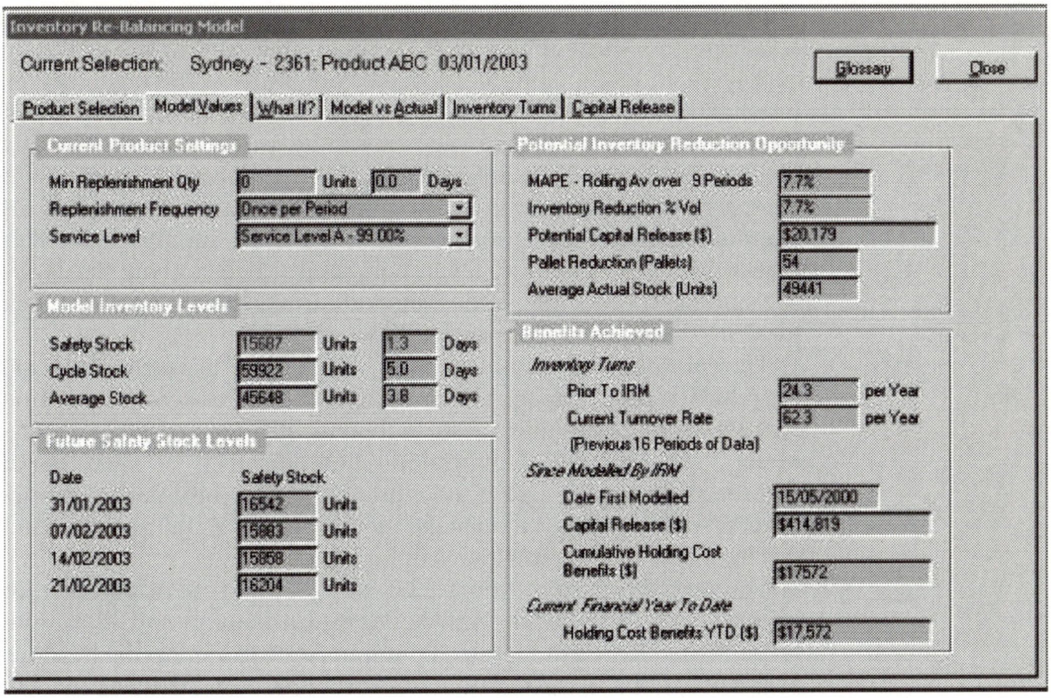

Source: Accenture

Figure 2.8.4
Accenture's Inventory Rebalancing Model (IRM)

Case study 2 – achieving a lean supply chain at a global mobile manufacturer

In 1997, this global mobile telephone manufacturer saw significant challenges in the increasingly competitive cellular telephone market. Its marketplace was changing from a technology-driven 'under supply' market, to a consumer-driven 'quick response' market with fast shifting and increasing consumer demands, shortened product lifecycles and lower selling prices. The company realized it needed to become a leaner, more efficient, globally integrated organization.

The company, together with Accenture, launched its 'time-to-customer' program to define and implement a new supply chain strategy, business model and enabling systems. Manufacturing processes were converted from 'make-to-forecast' to 'make-to-customer order' and direct customer shipments (drop shipments) were introduced, resulting in a positive impact on customer service levels. Delivery accuracy improved to nearly 100 per cent, inventory levels decreased by up to three weeks, the number of very satisfied customers tripled, work-in-progress levels fell by as much as 85 per cent and manufacturing yields increased significantly.

The supplier logistics center manages an Internet-based information system, which provides transaction, status and forecast information to all relevant parties.

In addition to addressing manufacturing and distribution processes, achieving the lean supply chain required attending to the upstream supply chain and looking outside the four walls of the organization. Integration with suppliers was needed to combat the 'bullwhip effect' (Lee, et al. 1997), which had been caused by multiple interfaces along the supply chain. Poor information sharing, long lead times and inaccurate forecasts were causing ever-increasing fluctuations as demand signals moved from consumers up the supply chain. This caused increased inventory levels and handling costs along the chain, sub-optimal production and transport arrangements and frequent material shortages at the mobile phone plant.

The solution was to implement a supplier logistics center (SLC) to introduce vendor-managed inventory and collaborative information sharing with its suppliers. An independently managed SLC warehouse was established within a short distance of each major manufacturing plant across the world. A global third-party logistics partner was introduced to manage the warehousing and transport and facilitate a neutral interface to the suppliers.

The suppliers own the material in the SLCs and are responsible for keeping their stock levels between agreed minimum and maximum levels. When the manufacturing plant makes a call-off to the SLC, the SLC manager picks the required number of parts and delivers them to the plant. Call-offs are made up to six times per day (24-hour operation) by one of three methods. Materials which are used frequently are held in a staging area within the plant from which production personnel pick what they need for production. Whenever the stock levels reach a minimum level, a kanban signal is sent to the SLC to request replenishment at the next scheduled delivery. Materials which are used less frequently are ordered for specific production runs. In addition, where possible, a trolley system is used to deliver a set of materials required for a particular production process directly to the production line. Each four hours, the partially empty trolleys are removed and replaced by a trolley replenished with a standard number of units of each component. In each of these call-off processes, the ownership of the inventory transfers from the supplier to the manufacturer at the time that the materials leave the SLC.

The SLC manages an Internet-based information system, which provides transaction, status and forecast information to all relevant parties. Suppliers can access the system to view their current inventory levels, assess short-, medium- and long-term forecasts and determine the replenishment required to keep the inventory levels between the pre-determined minimum and maximum levels. The system also links to the manufacturer's system, which determines the call-off requirements and records the amount of material delivered each time. This record is then consolidated each month and a self-billing invoice is transmitted automatically to the supplier.

Together with its 'make-to-customer order' manufacturing and direct customer shipments, the supplier logistics centers will ensure that the manufacturer achieves a lean supply chain. Raw materials inventories have been cut dramatically, down to less than one-day coverage in many cases, while at the same time materials availability has been improved. Transparency in the supply chain has been increased, with all parties having access to the latest forecast.

Suppliers are able to schedule their deliveries to optimize their production and transport arrangements. The amount of materials handling at the plants has been reduced dramatically and space created for additional production capacity. Finally, procurement and finance personnel have been freed up from tedious ordering and invoicing processing.

Case study 3 – global dairy company addresses unusual inventory problem

With a production capacity that it cannot control, this dairy company had an unusual challenge. The company makes milk powder, cheese, cream and protein ingredients and exports them around the world. Set up as a cooperative owned by dairy farmers, the company must process all the milk that is produced every year. While customer demands are largely steady during the year, the production peaks during the summer months and drops over winter. The duration of the production period also varies depending on the weather. As Figure 2.8.5 shows, the variables make it very difficult to forecast the amount of milk produced in one season and have confidence about when production would resume in the next season.

With large peaks in production, it was difficult to forecast the amount of milk produced in one season and have confidence about when production would resume next season.

Due to the large peak in production and a demand that is largely steady, the company builds up large inventories to help it survive during the non-production or 'carry-over' period. This incurs a significant expense due to the cost of holding the inventory over an

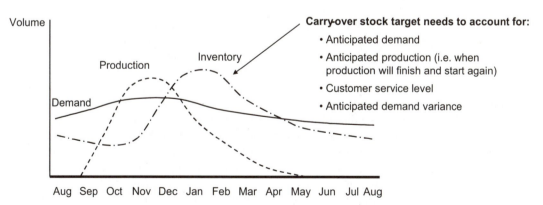

Figure 2.8.5
The impact of the production peak and long carry-over period

extended period, and the use of additional third-party warehousing to store the peak of the inventory.

The global supply chain director of the cooperative recognized the importance of 'integrating marketing with manufacturing to create the platform to drive performance improvements and extract maximum value from the farm-to-customer value chain'. Accenture worked with the company to develop and realize a new supply chain strategy that aligns the way that they supply product to meet the needs of their different customer segments efficiently. The organization redesign and a capability improvement program were based around the segmentation approach that separates the more predictable portion of the business from the rest. See also Chapter 1.3 for more details.

The supply chain organization design included establishing an optimization manager and site supply chain structure. The site supply chain managers (based at each of the major processing sites) were aligned directly to key customers in different locations across the world. The alignment allows them to establish collaborative relationships and work together to match supply and demand efficiently, to improve customer service levels and decrease inventory costs. The optimization manager on the other hand has a team of planners who look across the production sites and across the product classes to optimize the matching of supply and demand at a company level.

Inventory management had previously been inhibited by poor information availability, limited confidence in the data that were available, different approaches to managing inventory in each part of the supply chain and the lack of a formal decision making process. In fact, it was very difficult to see where the problems were because reports generated at the product class (group) level were hiding the issues at the individual product specification level. Some 'specs' had high inventory levels, while others were too low, causing poor customer service levels. To resolve this, a sales and operations planning (S&OP) forum was established to be chaired by the optimization manager. Some simple inventory models were also developed to improve the visibility of inventory costs and facilitate effective decision making at the S&OP forum. In parallel, a longer-term initiative was started to build more sophisticated advanced planning systems to achieve the next level of information transparency and easy access to decision support tools across the supply chain.

The inventory model was developed at the product specification level to determine the target inventory at each month of the season.

The inventory model was developed at the product specification level to determine the target inventory at each month of the season. Business rules were built in to allocate product to high-priority customer segments before 'opportunistic' segment customers. Assumptions were also made about when the new season's production would start and how much variability of supply to incorporate. Inventory holding costs were included to support important decisions such as whether to hold inventory over the carry-over period for a given customer demand, or trade it on the spot market prior to the carry-over period. This was particularly powerful in saving the holding costs for components of demand that represented only 'opportunistic' segment customers that had uncertain demand.

The model was developed using a Microsoft Excel ® spreadsheet workbook into which the initial production and demand data was downloaded from the legacy production planning system. The data was then analyzed, with algorithms built into the model, to calculate the target inventory level at the end of the carry-over period and then work back to determine the safety stock and cycle stock requirements each month. To calculate the safety stock requirements over the long carry-over period, a 'replenishment interval adjustment factor' (RIAF) was introduced. The RIAF theory was developed originally by Plossl and Wright (1985) for a manufacturing environment where some products were not produced every period. However, it also applied in this situation where there was no production over several months in winter and spring. The theory says that the amount of safety stock required to satisfy demand variability over X production periods is less than X times the amount of safety stock required to satisfy demand variability within each production period. This is because the demand variability in one direction during one period may be cancelled out by a variability in the opposite direction in the next period (that is, the events are not entirely independent).

The model gave a clear set of data for each specification, which was presented graphically and in a table, in either dollars or tons. This provided visibility of the inventory position looking forward and the impact of the detailed allocation decisions made by the production planners. The data showed the surplus stocks positions where the projected inventory levels were more than the minimum required to meet the anticipated demand and demand variability of the priority customer segments. A hit list was generated automatically to identify the five to ten specifications with the highest surplus stock positions (representing 80 per cent of the total surplus of a product class with over 100 specifications) and provide information required to analyse different potential scenarios. Objective decisions could then be made as to whether to trade the surplus stock early (potentially at a lower price) or incur the holding cost and sell the stock at a later date to opportunistic customers.

Achieving results with the model required articulating clear roles and responsibilities, communicating the dollar benefits of using this approach and facilitating the decisions through the S&OP process. The model was run before the monthly pre-S&OP meeting in which managers representing sales, production planning, product mix and manufacturing met to review initial demand and supply plans. The key improvement opportunity areas were identified in this initial meeting so that robust cost-benefit analysis could be completed prior to the S&OP meeting itself where trade-off decisions could be made based on the support provided. The inventory model became integral to this process because it provided transparency to the inventory position and presented the dollar cost of different production and demand scenarios.

Case study 4 – inventory reduction at a regional oil company

Faced with increasingly demanding customers, limited growth in consumption, increased operating costs from environmental require-ments and increased competition from competitors across Asia, this regional oil company recognized the need to address the cost and efficiency of its supply chain. Working with Accenture, an inventory reduction project was designed to free up cash and cut costs via better process effectiveness, accurate data and quality end-to-end planning, to reduce the inventory held across the region.

The initiative needed to address several key issues including:

- no overall view of inventory levels across the supply chain due to multiple fragmented systems and unclear ownership
- inconsistent performance calculation and reporting
- minimal use of traditional analytics to calculate the required safety stock levels, and
- country-based managers who were reluctant to accept alternative approaches to reduce inventory.

The solution was to introduce new inventory management processes, statistical analytical models, one common supply chain language, standardized and relevant KPIs and a change management approach to ensure acceptance of the changes. Phase 1 of the solution was developed through a four-step approach conducted over three to four months in each of nine countries.

Step 1 focused on identifying the opportunity to reduce inventory across refineries, terminals, in-transit vessels and pipelines. Customer and supplier requirements were profiled through questionnaires and interviews, inventory processes were reviewed and inventory data was analysed to produce 'sawtooth' graphs showing how the inventory levels actually fluctuate day by day.

This provided the inputs required to develop an operating vision in Step 2. Workshops with management were conducted to gain consensus on the gaps to best practices and discuss improvement opportunities.

These were translated into an action plan in Step 3. Detailed inventory models were developed and standard processes were adapted to the local requirements. One of the keys to success was a robust inventory analysis model, which allowed the inventory to be visualized as cycle stock, buffer stock, safety stock and heels (stock below the draw-off). Specific analytical techniques were used to optimize each component – driving the total inventory down. The model revealed that stock replenishment was occurring before reaching safety stock levels, replenishment cycles were being driven

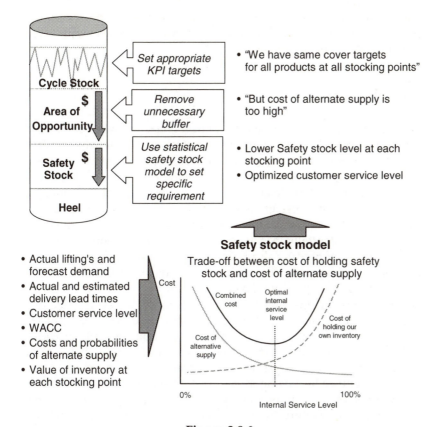

Figure 2.8.6
Key components of the statistical modeling approach

by ship utilization and excess buffer stocks which were being held 'just in case'. New safety stock analysis was conducted to extend to the traditional analysis of inventory holding cost versus service level to encompass the cost of alternate supply (from other companies' refineries and terminals). As shown in the graph in Figure 2.8.6, the resulting optimal internal service level could be met at a far lower cost than relying on internal sources alone.

The final step involved planning and kicking off the implementation of the solutions. A business case was developed and execution plans detailed and costed. A key element of the execution involved bedding down the benefits of the modelling through new processes, roles and responsibilities and performance reporting that was tied back to the inventory goals and applied consistently across countries to facilitate comparison and encourage continual improvement.

The first phase of the inventory reduction initiative resulted in more than $100 million in savings from reduced inventory, including a 15 per cent saving in refineries and 20 per cent in marketing and distribution. Customer service, fleet utilization and transport costs were also improved. Most importantly, the new processes and performance measures ensured that these improvements were sustained over the longer term.

Conclusion

A balance has to be achieved between carrying too much or too little stock if inventory decisions are to contribute to value creation in a business.

Supply chain executives face a significant challenge when it comes to managing inventory. They need to maintain a reasonable level of inventory to provide a safety zone to guard against large variations in demand throughout the entire supply chain. Poor inventory management can result in long lead times, poor product availability, unhappy customers and, at worst, cause stock-outs of raw materials or finished products and lost sales. However, maintaining too high inventory levels will substantially increase holding costs and, in some industries, create the risk of product obsolescence. A balance has to be achieved if inventory decisions are to contribute to value creation in a business.

Achieving an optimum level of inventory can help executives achieve cost savings, deliver quick response to ever-demanding customers, and improve sales. Companies need to hold sufficient inventory to satisfy demand between replenishments while providing a buffer against variability throughout the supply chain. Some companies are introducing inventory reduction programs supported by an inventory modeling and decision support tool to calculate optimum safety stock requirements. Others are redesigning their organizational structure and inventory models to improve visibility of costs, and changing their operating practices or implementing supplier logistics centers with vendor-managed inventory and information sharing. Leading companies understand the way that inventory management can improve customer service without adding new costs, giving their business a competitive advantage.

References

Gattorna, J. L. (1994), *Handbook of Logistics and Distribution Management*, 4th edn, Aldershot: Gower Publishing.

Johnson, E. M. and Davis, T. (1998), 'Improving Supply Chain Performance by using order fulfilment metrics', *National Productivity Review* (Summer).

Johnson et al. (1995), 'Expressions for Item Fill Rate in Periodic Inventory System', *Naval Research Logistics*.

Lambert, D. M. et al. (1997), *Fundamentals of Logistics*, McGraw-Hill.

Lee, H., et al. (1997), 'The Bullwhip Effect in Supply Chains', *Sloan Management Review*, **38** (3), Spring, pp. 93–102.

Plossl, G. W. and Wright, W. (1985), *Production and Inventory Control: Principles and Techniques*, 2nd edn., Prentice Hall.

Service parts management

2.9

Olaf Schatteman and Jonathan Wright

Having the right part at the right place and at the right time is absolutely fundamental to a service network's ability to satisfy customers and hence ensure their continued loyalty. Service parts planning requires both a completely different mindset and a radically different tool set from mainstream manufacturing.

According to United States company Bancorp, the spare parts market represents $700 billion and 8 per cent of US gross domestic product. Research from Bain & Company indicates computer and high-technology hardware makers spent nearly $17 billion on service parts logistics worldwide in 1999, and they claim the figure is growing by 6 per cent annually.

After-sales service, long regarded by equipment vendors as a necessary evil at best, is today rapidly moving on to and up the boardroom agenda of major manufacturers. The reasons are not hard to find.

Manufacturers of even the most sophisticated equipment are finding their products becoming increasingly commoditized and are consequently experiencing steady downward pressure on prices and margins. After-sales service offers an opportunity to break out of that cycle by increasing differentiation between manufacturers of essentially similar products and, making a virtue of necessity, to develop new sources of revenue in their own right. Many manufacturers find that margins for services can top 40 per cent, whereas margins for finished goods top out at around 13 per cent, according to industry estimates.

Customers also have been driving the trend, demanding increasingly sophisticated service packages as adjuncts to, or even components of, their initial purchases. The result is a dramatic expansion in the range and sophistication of service offerings, backed by service level agreements (SLAs) incorporating penalties for substandard performance.

After-sales service offers manufacturers an opportunity to differentiate themselves and develop new sources of revenue.

With these trends, this chapter discusses the implications for organizations if they fail to develop a superior service planning capability. It outlines the benefits of service parts management systems and explains some different methodologies for service parts planning.

Implications of service capabilities

The fact that after-sales service offers manufacturers opportunities both to differentiate their products and to develop additional revenue streams means there is also a downside. Poor service will inevitably translate into losses of future sales when manufacturers are offering broadly similar variations on a plain theme. In this situation, the customer has few incentives to retain its supplier. The financial penalties for non-compliance with an SLA may well be the least of the long-term costs of failing to satisfy customer expectations.

Conversely and perhaps paradoxically, all the evidence suggests that customers whose problems are solved promptly and efficiently become as much as 50 per cent more loyal, even compared with those whose equipment gives no trouble at all. With the cost of selling to a new customer generally reckoned to be as much as eight times greater than selling to an existing customer, the potential for service to enhance or to blight a manufacturer's future prospects cannot be overestimated.

Given the growing recognition of the vital role of after-sales service, how are providers reacting? In spite of the efficiencies gained by the implementation of solutions for enterprise resource planning (ERP), customer relationship management (CRM) and supply chain management, the service arena has remained a neglected part of the organization, often viewed as a necessary evil, a cost center and certainly not a profit center. Granted, components of today's CRM solutions provide effective call management and customer response systems, and some supply chain management solutions are looking at adding some service functionality. However, they both fall short of addressing the actual delivery of service.

Although companies can now deliver goods just-in-time, they often fail to deliver service as effectively. Several of the ERP and supply chain vendors have more recently realized this gap in their products' capabilities and started to attack this market with takeovers, alliances and proprietary developed software. In essence, manufacturing systems focus on the day-to-day, reacting to events to drive the process through the organization. On the other hand, planning systems, and service parts planning systems in particular, are by their nature proactive, attempting to identify and fulfill future needs. Specifically manufacturing executives and their manufacturing tools such as ERP see inventory as an evil to be minimized. To a service organization, however, it is the *sine qua non*.

Even the best service engineer, arriving on site well within the time stipulated by the SLA, is helpless if the part that is required to effect the repair is not available. The optimal inventory needs to be held across the supply chain so that one of the hundreds of parts is available or, in the case of an aircraft, one of the hundreds of thousands required. Such planning requires not simply the modification of existing manufacturing tools, but the provision of an entirely new set of tools specifically aimed at service parts planning. However, this does not mean that all parts need to be kept in stock, just in case. Usually, companies without sophisticated parts management systems are not able to determine which parts to stock where, and end up with too many of the wrong parts in the wrong place while missing the ones they need.

Service parts planning systems may have to handle hundreds of thousands of different parts to support both current and discontinued products.

Even within the planning discipline, service parts planning poses radically different problems from, for example, planning for consumer finished goods. The latter can draw on vast amounts of data to forecast demand levels and plan production of, for example, beverages, but they only have to handle a relatively small number of different stock items. By contrast, service parts planning systems may have to handle hundreds of thousands of different parts with a relatively small amount of historic data, not just to support current products, but products that are no longer manufactured. Details of parts planning methodologies will be discussed later in the chapter.

That volume complexity is compounded by the need to provide a network of support both nationally and internationally. Stock must be maintained and controlled right down to the level of the individual technician's car or van. And added to that is a third level of complexity introduced by the population of installed equipment being supported on a maintenance, repair and overhaul basis. Not only are parts being distributed to the field but equipment and sub-assemblies are coming back for repair and return to stock. Few conventional finished goods systems are required to handle such 'reverse logistics'!

The benefits of effective service management

Clearly, ensuring that appropriate levels of inventory are maintained is fundamental to the success of any after-sales service operation. The service specialist will weigh the benefits against the potential cost, not just of failing to meet service level agreements, but also of the engineer or technician having to make a return visit to complete a repair. Reducing 'returns-to-fit' will translate directly into reduced staffing to meet a given service level. On top of having the right inventory, companies need several other capabilities to deliver service effectively and efficiently in order to guarantee both service cost reductions as well as increased customer satisfaction that in turn can possibly lead to extended loyalty and revenues. Insights into those capabilities are provided below.

Apply sophisticated planning mechanisms

Manufacturers increasingly need to take well-informed decisions about the level and profile of their service parts inventory.

Determining what is the appropriate level of service parts inventory and the distribution of that inventory through the service network until recently has been based largely on an amalgam of intuition and experience. With manufacturers increasingly competing on the quality of their service networks, the need to take well-informed decisions about the level and profile of the service parts inventory also has become apparent. The service organizations need tool sets that will enable them to understand the trade-off between the inventory levels they must maintain and the SLAs that they are entering into. Conversely, they also need to be able to ensure that the individual SLAs do not demand inventory levels, which make it impossible to provide the service on a profitable basis.

Although some manufacturers have developed their own bespoke systems to address certain aspects of service parts planning, tools that are capable of addressing the entire service parts supply chain are few and far between. They must be capable of taking into account, for example, the population of equipment being supported, be that for a single technician supporting, say, ten photocopiers, or a regional facility supporting a number of aircraft. For each part they must then be able to consider a host of criteria including usage over time, historical failure rate by part, MTBF (mean time between failures) and MTTR (mean time to repair) and the age of the population as it affects failure rate and obsolescence. It must allow these criteria to be compared against, for example the cost of inventory, the cost of obsolescence of that inventory, the cost of return visits and the cost of lost business. In addition, it must be able to do so for potentially hundreds of thousands of parts, a task that would be quite impossible to handle manually.

Even then there may be other overriding criteria – on the one hand, the part may be so expensive as to make it impossible to stock locally, on the other the penalty attached to the SLA may be such as to demand it being stocked irrespective of that cost.

While the data to support such decisions can be gathered at a regional or national level and then applied to the individual stock points, the tool must at the same time be capable of handling considerations of micro strategy, as shown in Figure 2.9.1. For instance, what is the likelihood of an individual technician or facility being confronted by a failure of a given component while it is out of stock due to an earlier failure and awaiting replenishment? Is the risk tolerable in the light of the SLA? The tool must also be able to handle more mundane considerations for each component. How big is the

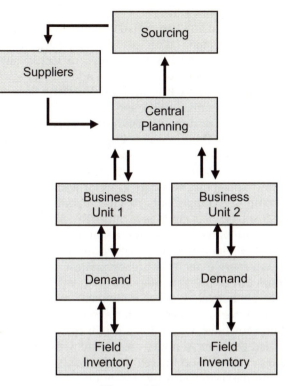

Figure 2.9.1
Aspects of service strategy

technician's van? Will the component fit in it? Is it too fragile to be continually bounced around the country? Is it subject to special shipping conditions, which might prevent rapid replenishment of stocks? Will it be affected by customs restrictions if shipped across international frontiers?

Application of a service parts 'algorithm', based on historical data or, where such data is not yet available, on assumptions which can be subsequently modified in the light of experience, has the potential to improve service performance dramatically and hence service revenue. In the majority of cases, the manufacturer also frees up substantial amounts of capital, which can be redeployed elsewhere by optimizing the distribution network. A service operation maintaining inventory comprising 100 000 different items has only to achieve a 10 per cent reduction in overall stock levels by adjusting the profile to reflect the actual requirement to release capital running into millions of dollars. Small wonder that pioneering manufacturers are realizing that there is nothing to be gained by compromising on service parts planning and every advantage in moving straight to the leading edge. However, this is not always the case and the costs of not having the part needs to be weighed against holding inventory.

Service parts logistics

Logistics partnerships between electronics companies and 3PLs are aiming for cost savings, rapid response times, operational excellence and measurable results.

Third-party logistics providers (3PLs) often handle the actual physical distribution and transportation of service parts. The distribution structure includes a forward flow to numerous service sites as well as large amounts of moving stock locations, and a reverse logistics loop with returns being sent back to multiple locations depending on the service requirements and the demand pattern of service parts. Given this complexity, transportation costs can be a significant component of the service delivery. Therefore it is important to determine the right composition and structure of the distribution network. 'Milk runs' are often used to deliver parts and pick up the returnable broken parts. At the same time, speed can be a critical factor with medical equipment, high-end computer components or vital manufacturing parts. Some 3PLs have realized this and have taken a step beyond 'last-mile' handling of spare parts. Some providers in the US even guarantee the ability to reach 88 per cent of business addresses in the US within two hours through more than 200 warehouse sites.

One innovative copier company developed a pan-European distribution system in close collaboration with multiple 3PL providers. The providers have spare car keys for every field service technician's van; and the vans have a default overnight parking location. The 3PL providers visit the vans at night, drop off new replenishment or low-urgency parts, and pick up the returnable broken parts that have been placed on the passenger seat by the service engineer. This system is mainly managed from a central European stock location for normal replenishment, combined with several regional forward stock locations for critical, large, heavy, expensive or fragile parts. To be able to set up such systems, tight integration with logistics service providers is essential. Continuous update of service technicians' details, spare part order status, and closed loop quality and quantity checks must be available to manage this kind of capability effectively.

Another example of tight collaboration with a 3PL is Sun Microsystems and DHL. Sun launched a plan in 2001 to reinvent its repair logistics supply chain to achieve 90 per cent cycle-time reduction in three years and cost reductions of 50 per cent in two years, with no loss of service. With international carrier DHL as its 3PL partner, the Asian subsidiary of Sun Microsystems Inc. designed a system that delivered a needed part to the repair location in one to two hours. From 52 locations, DHL has to deliver the part to Sun's customers within 2 hours. Under certain conditions it can source the part from anywhere: even purchasing is an option. The entire process is traceable online in real time. They report reduced cycle times of 52 per cent and costs down almost 35 per cent, and achieved on-time delivery levels of 99.7 per cent. The Sun–DHL logistics partnership illustrates the goals of electronics companies and 3PL providers: cost savings, rapid response times, operational excellence and measurable results. While many electronics companies still prefer to keep some complex logistics functions in-house, Sun is tightening its relationships with 3PL companies.

Also in the automotive industry, initiatives are being launched. Ford and Cat Logistics have formed a software alliance to develop a logistics information system to increase the speed at which service parts are delivered to the market. The new system, in combination with 21 new distribution centers and daily restocking of dealer inventories, should reduce order-to-delivery times for service parts by 80 per cent and also reduce shipping and handling damage to parts.

Provide visibility of inventory

Visibility of inventory is a critical component of delivering the service promise. With numerous, often moving, stock locations and parts continuously going forward and others coming back to central warehouses, this poses a real challenge to service providers. Bar coding and the widespread use of scanners coupled with mobile data communication devices throughout the service parts supply chain, is an effective way of providing real-time or near-time visibility across the chain. This information should be used when despatching engineers to jobs where definite or likely replacement parts are known. But the information is also crucial for replenishment and forecasting processes. It can also provide field engineers with a much better view of their, and their team members' car stock. This way they do not have to worry about knowing what is in their van, which will save the provider time and money. It also gives companies the opportunity to track closed loop inventory to prevent missing parts in the chain.

Inventory information helps to provide real-time visibility in the supply chain, essential to replenishment and forecasting.

Sharing information across the supply chain

Pioneering companies in such areas as electronics and computing are applying these techniques and extending their reach by, for example, exploiting e-commerce to collaborate and share information with suppliers, the supplier's supplier, customers and even with competitors. For example, the need to hold inventory far forward or even on the customer's own site may provide opportunities to share the risk and the cost of maintaining very high levels of availability. Similarly, competitors in the aviation industry are already seeing opportunities to collaborate by sharing holdings in spare parts, reducing their individual surplus inventory and hence reducing costs without compromising their competitive stance. Such opportunities also abound across the computer and communications sectors where an already high commonality of parts is continually increasing. The emergence of business-to-business (B2B) marketplaces and exchanges, while in no way changing the fundamentals, provides yet another tool for the sharing of information. These e-marketplaces allow a more effective flow of information to suppliers and better control of inventory at every level, from supplier to end user.

Competitors are sharing their holdings in spare parts, reducing their surplus inventory and cutting costs.

Innovative service models

The consequence of such innovative thinking is a range of new models for the service network. A leading manufacturer of mobile phone handsets, for example, broke the repair-return loop that previously had phones returning for repair from across Europe to Scandinavia, by holding stocks of commonly used parts at retailers. Not only has this drastically cut costs but also the approach has increased retailer loyalty by turning what had been a costly chore into a valuable new source of revenue.

Similarly, innovative thinking is now being applied in the automotive industry where lack of profitability among dealers and their consequent resistance to holding stocks of parts is demanding the urgent development of a new model for service and service parts.

Companies that are well advanced in applying leading-edge techniques in service parts planning are already finding that information generated in service can be fed back into the rest of the organization to create a virtuous circle of innovation. Thus, for example, sales teams begin to realize that the added complexity introduced through product customization imposes additional costs on after-sales service; in effect cost-to-service becomes a fact in cost-of-sale and design-for-service becomes an element in design-for-manufacture.

Preventative maintenance

Similarly, the incorporation of self-diagnostic capabilities into equipment has the potential to enhance the value of the product to the customer, and reduce costs and increase revenues for the service organization. The self-diagnosis involves identifying the components that have failed or those that have not yet failed but will do so shortly, and then alerting the service organization by telephone or the Internet. When fed directly into planning and inventory systems, this information can improve parts planning.

For example, most multifunctional office devices (combining a copier, facsimile and printer in one machine) are able to send usage and status information via the Internet to the manufacturer's service center. A technician that happens to be in the same postcode area can be dispatched to carry out some preventative tasks – provided he has the parts. Taking the self-diagnosis concept even further is BNSF, the first US carrier to test Sky-Eye, a low-orbit satellite that tracks instrumented, multilevel train cars. Sky-Eye reads movements – acceleration, longitudinal, vertical, and latitudinal – in real time. If it sees an event that exceeds parameters, it can check for securement, monitor car health, car maintenance and track maintenance. It has a cost-effectiveness not seen with other technologies.

Failure analysis

The next step in moving the service parts management function to world-class capabilities is the use of defect spare parts that have been returned to the manufacturer to analyse reasons for failure. In the airline industry, for example, Boeing may know how many of a certain part are being used on 727 aircraft around the world. But Boeing does not know how a specific airline has deployed its planes, such as how many planes are flying across salt water and whether that is affecting parts. If the airlines share that information with one another and the manufacturer, failure-rate information could be incorporated into parts designing. The ultimate value proposition is to get the design information so that nothing ever breaks during the contractually guaranteed lifetime. Some technology providers are trying to bridge that data content gap between manufacturers and operators with content-driven e-commerce platforms for the support chain. This is described in more detail in Chapter 2.12, 'Reverse logistics'.

Currently, more companies are providing customer self-diagnosis using knowledge management tools, thus making it easier for customers to repair their own equipment in many cases. This calls for more visible and reliable parts inventory information and parts ordering capabilities as well as online interactive capabilities to help the customer manage through the process.

Collaboration between service companies and manufacturers about the failure of parts could improve parts design and performance.

Future outlook

Sound service parts management is one step towards a more advanced service capability; complete enterprise service management (ESM) is the next step. ESM provides a comprehensive approach to managing the complete service arena and is the means by which many companies can now turn their service organizations into profit centres. A natural extension of ERP, CRM and supply chain management systems, ESM comprises the complete set of collaborative, cross-enterprise processes required to plan and deliver service. ESM provides the tools to optimize the service operation while minimizing the cost and maximizing the service delivered. Once a company has mastered these capabilities it can start to expand its service offering to other product categories. In the United Kingdom for example, consumers can get a service contract for all their white goods with British Gas.

Another critical development is the rise of third- and fourth-party asset management or service management models. They provide services that are a natural progression from improving the first-time fix rate to owning the machine or service uptime, as illustrated in Figure 2.9.2. The third- and fourth-party providers can be expected to capture a greater share of the service market in the future. Many manufacturers simply find they either lack the scale or the competency

ESM comprises the complete set of collaborative, cross-enterprise processes required to plan and deliver service.

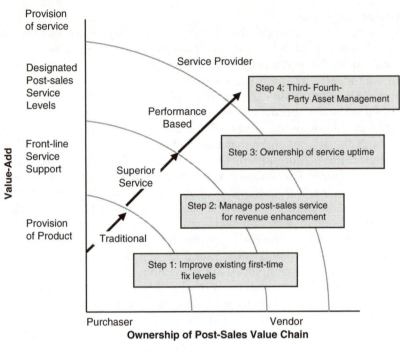

Provision
of service

Designated
Post-sales
Service
Levels

Front-line
Service
Support

Provision
of Product

Value-Add

Service Provider

Step 4: Third- Fourth-
Party Asset Management

Performance
Based

Step 3: Ownership of service uptime

Superior
Service

Step 2: Manage post-sales service
for revenue enhancement

Traditional

Step 1: Improve existing first-time
fix levels

Purchaser   Vendor
Ownership of Post-Sales Value Chain

Source: Accenture

Figure 2.9.2
Service management continuum

to support their products through their life cycle and, therefore, the companies outsource service provision to a specialist provider. Simultaneously, the use of certain common components in, for example, the electronics and high-technology industry can actually stimulate shared service models, while improving costs and providing greater serviceability to clients.

Conclusion

New approaches to service parts management will be creating opportunities for superior performance.

Pioneering companies across the manufacturing industry are realizing that service parts management is fundamental to their drive to make service a key differentiator in an increasingly commoditized world. Not only are they putting parts planning higher on their corporate agenda, they are recognizing that this capability requires a totally different mindset from that required for the management of mainstream manufacturing operations. Vendors today can face downtime costs of up to $20 000 per hour; one day without a photocopier may be just acceptable but two means the loss of a major customer. In this era, managing service parts inventory by reducing it to the point where it hurts is simply no longer an option. Today the best performing companies are introducing new business models into the service arena. Just as third-party logistics providers have been changing supply chain operations, new approaches to service parts management will be creating opportunities for superior performance.

References

Anonymous (2001), 'Cat and Ford to develop logistics software system', *Peoria Journal Star* (1 December).

Harreld, H. (2002), 'Keeping an eye on all your parts', *Infoworld* (7 January).

Krizner, K. (2001), 'Service parts logistics takes on critical role', *Frontline Solutions* (January), p. 13.

Morton, R. (2001), 'The last mile – smoothing bumps at the end of the road', *Transportation & Distribution* (June).

Nairn, G. (2001), Survey FT–IT – 'Spare parts are grounded – Supply chains and inventory levels', *Financial Times* (2 May).

Richardson, H. (1998), 'Service parts: Reaching the highest level', *Transportation & Distribution* (September) pp. 39–49.

Wright, J. et al. (2001), 'Greater than the sum of parts', *Logistics Europe.*

2.10 Supply chain financial performance measurement

David Walters

Assessing the role of the supply chain in emerging new business models is an increasingly important aspect of performance measurement.

Supply chain management, as with any business activity, aims to contribute to generating revenues and profits and, in doing so, invariably attracts costs. Financial performance measurement can help organizations to measure their activities effectively and develop a detailed understanding of the way the supply chain has an impact on each important component of the bottom line.

An obvious consideration, but one typically overlooked, is the level of involvement within an organization. This is important because the performance measurement of any strategic activity requires quite different metrics to the measurement of operations and support. Another consideration concerns the organization's understanding of supply chain management. This also, arguably, is the outcome of a strategic versus operational contribution. A third and increasingly important aspect, is to view the supply chain within its context and its role in emerging new business models. To do this effectively requires a *prospective mindset*, where an organization understands its role in a changing business environment and considers how to take advantage of these changes. Consequently, performance measurement is taken into the field of 'what do we need to be and to do to remain profitable and therefore competitive?' and to consider; 'how well are we achieving customer satisfaction *and* resource utilization goals?'

The nature of the changes to the business environment can be seen from the shift of emphasis in corporate reporting. For example, in recent years the notion of 'value' has become increasingly important. The 1980s saw the emergence of shareholder value as a corporate imperative and, by the mid-1990s, customer value. By the end of the 1990s stakeholder value emerged as a 21st century issue, with relationship management a critical driver in the supply chain context. Another important consideration, which has developed out of the importance of partnerships and relationship management, is the changing nature of asset structure and ownership.

In this chapter, we start by reviewing the use of traditional accounting data as financial performance metrics. Financial reports such as the income statement, balance sheet and cash flow statements can be used to determine and measure financial performance using ratio analysis and models. We also look at current and future trends, and consider both transitional and prospective financial performance measurement approaches. The changing business environment has had a major impact on not only what financial performance is measured but asks that alternative financial structure scenarios be considered prior to strategy decisions being determined.

Why measure performance?

'Why measure performance' is an obvious question, but is often not asked by even the largest of organizations. There are many reasons for this. Performance data is essential for improvement initiatives, process management, and competitive positioning effectiveness and enhancement, as Keebler and Durtsche (1999) describe. Data are also necessary in diverse initiatives such as managing organizational change, monitoring customer satisfaction and controlling the effectiveness of supply chain performance within strategic objectives.

Performance measurement can quantify both tangible benefits such as cost savings or intangible gains such as reduced lead times and changed culture.

While performance improvement is often quantified in terms of tangible benefits such as quality, cycle time and delivery, identifying 'cross-functional gains' is also important. Care must be exercised when measuring financial performance as the structure of typical measurement metrics may in themselves pre-condition the responses they invoke. King (1993) identifies two quite different types of cost savings, which point to some of the challenges for financial performance measurement posed for supply chain managers. 'Green savings' are real cash savings visible in accounting systems, such as procurement and labor savings, which could be reinvested outside the company. 'Blue savings' are indirect and usually not visible, such as reduced need for space, reduced lead times or changed culture. Customers benefit from these savings, but they are *not* real cash savings that can be reinvested. In some respects they are qualitative rather than quantitative, requiring further analysis before the quantitative implications can be identified.

One issue relevant to supply chain managers is whether efficiency is the best basis for performance management systems today. Bredrup (1995) says that efficiency dominates performance measurement in most organizations; the measurement systems are driven by financial data sourced from accounting systems. While this once enabled performance from different activities to be aggregated, it now inhibits the measurement of process management performance.

Bredrup infers that traditional accounting-based performance measures result in green savings. However, the real benefits are accrued from blue savings, which are often the result of a continuous improvement process. They accumulate over time and can be transformed either into customer benefits or company benefits, such as real cost savings. In this way, performance measurement then becomes essential to:

- justify investments and effort in the improvement process
- manage the improvement process and ensure compatibility, and
- manage the transformation process from blue to green savings, such as cost savings that have long-term, strategic benefit for an organization.

Using traditional accounting data

Supply chain management decisions can influence corporate profitability in three areas: operating costs, influence on sales and role in investment.

The insights into performance measurement offered by Bredrup and others are helping to drive innovative new approaches. However, many, if not most, organizations still use conventional accounting data to monitor the financial performance of business functions. Supply chain executives, therefore, need to consider the role and effectiveness of traditional approaches.

Decisions on supply chain and logistics management can influence corporate profitability in three broad areas:

- the level of participation of supply chain management activities in the operating costs: the proportion of total operating cost that logistics absorbs
- influence on sales, and
- role in investment.

Any changes in the level of participation of logistics within the business should be undertaken either if overall effectiveness can be improved, or to reduce the level of input received to achieve a maintained level of output.

Operating costs may be reduced by:

- minimizing inventory handling and eliminating non-productive handling
- removing bottlenecks within the distribution system
- optimizing the number of warehouses and other stock-holding locations
- eliminating activities and intermediaries which/who do not add value to the overall activity
- using group leverage (purchasing power) to minimize transport and other purchased services costs
- regarding suppliers' transport costs as variable with the potential for cost reduction

- removing delays caused by documentation flows and eliminating unnecessary document transfers
- considering suppliers' (and carriers') lead times as a component for overall lead time
- seeking to improve human and capital resource productivity increases
- optimizing vehicle utilization to minimize delivery costs, and
- eliminating errors and thereby reducing the 'total' costs of correction.

Sales revenues generated may be influenced by:

- developing a customer-led approach: a customer service strategy
- minimizing out-of-stocks for given levels of inventory
- communicating information on stock and lead time availability within the business and to customers
- minimizing lead times for 'standard item' orders, and
- maximizing selling space versus stockholding space.

Investment performance may be improved for inventory holding by:

- reducing system lead times
- improving the accuracy of forecasting
- eliminating obsolete and excess inventory
- improving delivery reliability, and
- reducing re-order quantities.

The investment performance of fixed assets may be improved by:

- optimizing the number, size and location of facilities and transportation fleet and equipment, and
- evaluating the actual 'return on investment' generated and considering service alternatives.

Given that managers are aware of the structure and content of these instruments, detailed discussion of each is unnecessary. However, a review of the impact of supply chain and supply chain management decisions can be useful in supply chain financial performance measurement.

The influence of supply chain on the income (profit and loss) statement

To increase sales revenue a company may well adjust its discount policy based upon volumes purchased. To do so effectively requires a detailed knowledge of costs involved in processing and handling customers' orders. Customers may also respond positively to 'customized' service packages. Companies can research customer expectations and views on aspects of service and use these to build exclusive service offers. Figure 2.10.1 shows the revenue and cost components of the income statement together with some of the possible decisions that a company may make when considering a

Supply chain managers need to consider the revenue and cost impacts of offering special service packages. Developing relationships with suppliers can reduce the cost of goods sold.

Revenue and Cost Components	Company Decision/ Competitive Variable	Supply Chain Variable
Sales Revenue *Less*	• Price x Volume • Discounts • Customer service packages	• Customer Account Profitability • Customized service offer(s) vs generic service
Cost of Goods Sold	• Sourcing and procurement • Manufacturing • Selling and sales administration • Distribution • Depreciation (Asset management)	• SCM (Inbound) Nominated suppliers, ECR • Materials management ERP, JIT • SCM (Outbound) • Order management ⎫ • Transportation ⎬ EDI linkages between suppliers and customers • Inventory management ⎭ • "Unitization" economics • Facility utilization and management
≡ *Equals*		
Operating profit *Less*		
Interest expenses	• Inventory carrying costs, facilities etc.	• Inventory locations and volumes • Leasing vs ownership to release capital for use elsewhere in the organization and to enhance flexibility
≡ *Equals*		
Contribution		

Figure 2.10.1

The influence of logistics on the profit and loss account

competitive stance. The influence that may be extended by the supply chain function is shown alongside the competitive variable.

Keebler and Durtsche (1999) provide an excellent example of how Owens and Minor, a surgical supply distributor, operates a 'cost track' program that allows customers to determine which services they need and at what cost. Instead of having to pay a negotiated percentage for distribution, a customer may elect selected services and meet only those costs. Owens and Minor use activity-based costing to determine the actual costs of service. By working with customers to optimize services *and* costs, both partners benefit.

Cost of goods sold may be influenced by working with nominated suppliers to develop long-term relationships that result in improved product quality *and* supply chain management efficiencies. As Figure

2.10.1 suggests, EDI linkages and the broader applications of Web-based technology can reduce 'time spans' and therefore inventory levels throughout the supply chain. The Internet-based buying organizations currently being established in the automobile industry on a global basis can be expected to have a dramatic effect on cost of goods sold. The result of these applications will have a similar impact on interest expenses as working capital costs are lowered throughout the supply chain.

The influence of supply chain on the balance sheet

Supply chain decisions also influence the asset and capital structure of the firm. Figure 2.10.2 identifies those logistics variables that may influence competitive decisions. Thus fixed assets may be influenced by the own-or-lease options, these being logistics infrastructure items. Current assets involve decisions on desired levels of liquidity, and here the influence of supply chain management may be very significant. Figure 2.10.2 shows three important aspects of cost-effective logistics management. Inventory service levels will, if they are excessively high, reduce the level of liquidity through unnecessary stockholding. Accurate order processing and handling will ensure that complete orders reach customers within prescribed lead times, thereby permitting prompt invoicing and cash collection.

Supply chain decisions influence fixed and current assets and the availability of capital.

Balance Sheet Components	Company Decision/ Competitive Variable	Supply Chain Variable
Fixed Assets Property, plant and equipment	• Own or lease distribution facilities	• Warehousing, transportation, customer service and information systems

Current Assets
 	
Cash, receivables and inventory
	• Liquidity	• Inventory availability
		
		• Order management
		  - accuracy
		  - reliability

Current Liabilities Trade creditors and overdraft		• Procurement policy management
Shareholder's Funds Share capital reserves	• Return to the shareholders • Optimal cost of capital and return on capital employed	• Use of specialist services to release capital for investment in the core business areas thereby increasing profitability and productivity

Figure 2.10.2
The influence of logistics on the balance sheet

Logistics, as a function, competes with each of the other functions in the firm for investment funds. It is often possible to produce acceptable levels of service without owning the means by which the service is 'delivered'. Consequently, supply chain management should be aware of the 'overall' issues, and evaluate alternatives offered by third-party providers.

Again, the application of information management technology can be seen to have an impact on the balance sheet. Non-essential fixed assets (such as warehousing and transportation facilities) may be reduced in size, thereby releasing capital for re-investment. Working capital management will be facilitated by the impact of technology and disciplines discussed earlier. As a result, shareholder value can only improve with the influence of supply chain managers.

The influence of supply chain on the sources and applications of funds (funds flow) statement

Analysing the sources and applications of funds can be used to observe the effect of current activities and evaluate alternative scenarios.

The sources and applications, or funds flow, statement is a means by which a company can identify how its activities influence the structure of the assets and capital of the business over time. Figure 2.10.3 illustrates the supply chain variables that create these changes. As can be seen, each of the variables has been mentioned in both the income statement and balance sheet discussions.

This analysis can be used to observe the effect of current activities and evaluate alternative scenarios. Clearly, an objective for any

Cash Flow Components	Supply Chain Variable
Changes in Working Capital (+/-)	
Inventory Customer credit Supplier credit	• Optimize stockholding – lower inventories reduce the need for working capital • Efficient logistics reduces payment cycles • Efficient use of "negative working capital" has a beneficial impact for corporate liquidity
Changes in Fixed Assets (+/-)	
Facilities Systems	• Using service companies to undertake non-core processes releases capital to be applied in processes that generate competitive advantage
Exchange variance	• Match materials flows with currency valuation • Offset fluctuations effects by locating manufacturing and distribution in countries offering positive exchange rate differentials

Figure 2.10.3
The influence of logistics on cash flow

business is to restrict its use of funds to the levels of funding available. Thus a projection of alternative situations can provide management with a range of potential structures, results *and* an objective view of the funding alternatives.

Finally, in Figure 2.10.4 the overall impact of logistics variables can be seen on the return on capital employed, or return on investment. This shows the influence of logistics on margin management and asset management that together are a measure of the return (earnings) on investment (fixed and net current assets) in the business.

It is often helpful to explore cash flow characteristics on two levels. At an operational level the concern is focused on changes in operating profit and depreciation (this is the typical accounting view of cash flow) together with changes (+ or −) in operating working capital. This measure identifies the impact of efficiencies realizable from supply chain management innovations.

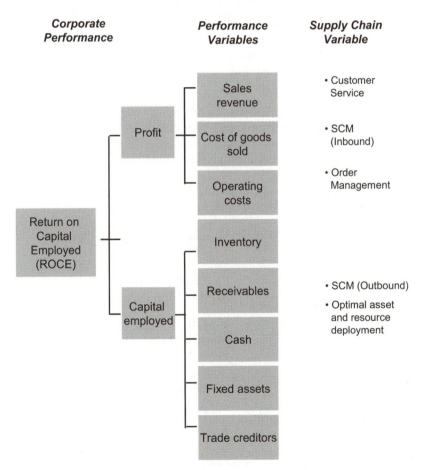

Figure 2.10.4
Impact of logistics on corporate financial performance

At a strategic level, cash flow is influenced by changes in working capital and fixed capital decisions that are influenced by strategic marketing and operations decisions concerning future revenues and service expenditures. These influences are shown as Figure 2.10.4.

Ratio analysis

Information provided by the income statement and the balance sheet may be further evaluated using ratio analysis. The purpose of the analysis is to monitor the planned activities of the business using the relationships identified. The Du Pont Chemicals Company first demonstrated the usefulness of ratio analysis. Du Pont developed a hierarchy of ratios based upon the simple relationship between margin management and asset management.

For a detailed analysis of a business, a series of ratios may be constructed. Several approaches are available and all consider the important performance characteristics of a firm. Typically, they are grouped to show specific characteristics of performance and represent:

- profitability ratios
- operating (efficiency) ratios
- financial structure ratios and
- investment ratios.

Of these, profitability and efficiency ratios have importance for supply chain management decisions and particularly reflect the impact of logistics on the business. Financial structure is important, but the supply chain manager's interest is an indirect one.

Profitability ratios

Five profitability ratios are important:

$$\text{Return on sales ROS (\%)} \quad = \quad \frac{\text{Profit}}{\text{Sales}} \quad \text{(carefully defined)}$$

$$\text{Asset turnover} \quad = \quad \frac{\text{Sales}}{\text{Net assets}}$$

$$\text{Return on assets ROA (\%)} = \frac{\text{Profit}}{\text{Net assets}}$$

$$\text{Financial gearing} \quad = \quad \frac{\text{Net assets}}{\text{Equity}} \quad \begin{array}{l}\text{(alternatively: Debt/} \\ \text{equity ratio)}\end{array}$$

$$\text{Return on equity ROE (\%)} = \frac{\text{Profit}}{\text{Equity}}$$

As mentioned, the Du Pont approach linked ratios and activities as a component in its control process. The relationship between margin management and asset management may be expressed as follows:

$$\frac{\text{Profit}}{\text{Sales}} \times \frac{\text{Sales}}{\text{Assets}} = \frac{\text{Profit}}{\text{Assets}}$$

At least one measure of shareholder value can be developed from this relationship by considering corporate funding:

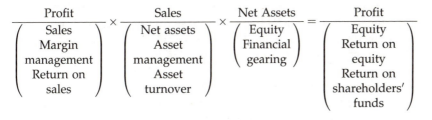

Efficiency ratios

Three efficiency ratios may be influenced by logistics decisions, particularly by effective supply chain management, and each involves aspects of working capital (net current assets). They are a measure of how effectively an organization manages its procurement and inbound materials flows, its stocks of raw materials, work-in-progress and finished goods, and its physical distribution (that is, order processing, handling and delivery) to ensure it can invoice promptly and collect its outstanding accounts.

Procurement ratios

$$\text{Purchase turnover} = \frac{\text{Purchase per trading period}}{\text{Trade creditors}}$$

$$\text{Days stock held} = \frac{\text{Trading period (in days)}}{\text{Purchase turnover}}$$

Inventory ratios

$$\text{Inventory turnover} = \frac{\text{Cost of goods sold}}{\text{Inventory}}$$

$$\text{Inventory cover} = \frac{\text{Trading period (in days)}}{\text{Inventory turnover}}$$

Receivable ratios

$$\text{Receivables turnover} = \frac{\text{Credit sales}}{\text{Accounts receivable}}$$

$$\text{Days' credit allowed} = \frac{\text{Trading period (in days)}}{\text{Accounts receivable turnover}}$$

Each set of ratios enables the organization to consider alternative targets for levels of accounts payable and receivable and inventory levels. There are other issues to be considered. One issue concerns service to customers, and here care should be taken not to affect adversely the availability levels of core products. Another issue relates to other costs (such as transportation and order communications) that may be affected by such changes. If these do not increase appreciably then clearly the option is both economically and 'politically' viable in the context of supplier and customer relations.

Financial structure ratios (gearing decisions)
An important decision for financial managers concerns the amount of long-term debt an organization should carry. Financial management wisdom suggests there is a combination of equity and debt that is optimal; it is the equity/debt combination that reduces financial risk to an optimal level *and* maximizes return from a taxation point of view. To explore the impact of gearing decisions the extended Du Pont ratio is revisited:

$$\underbrace{\frac{\text{Profit}}{\text{Sales}}}_{\substack{\text{Profitability}\\\text{management}}} \times \underbrace{\frac{\text{Sales}}{\text{Net Assets}}}_{\substack{\text{Productivity}\\\text{management}}} \times \underbrace{\frac{\text{Net Assets}}{\text{Equity}}}_{\substack{\text{Financial}\\\text{management}}} = \underbrace{\frac{\text{Profit}}{\text{Equity}}}_{\substack{\text{Return on}\\\text{shareholders'}\\\text{equity}}}$$

This is a useful relationship because we can use it to evaluate current performance levels in context with each other *and* we may also pose 'what if?' questions. Consider the following example:

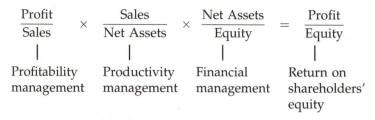

$$\frac{\text{Profit}}{\text{Sales}} \times \frac{\text{Sales}}{\text{Net Assets}} = \frac{\text{Profit}}{\text{Net Assets}} \times \frac{\text{Net Assets}}{\text{Equity}} = \frac{\text{Profit}}{\text{Equity}}$$

$$\frac{80}{800} \times \frac{800}{400} = \frac{80}{400} \times \frac{400}{200} = \frac{80}{200}$$

$$10\% \times 2 = 20\% \times 2 = 40\%$$

Supposing the company disposes of its logistics infrastructure. We can evaluate the impact on the return on equity. In disposing of the logistics infrastructure we release, say, $150 million. However, we will find that our margins decrease because there is now an additional expense for the purchase of outside distribution services. However, unless the capital is applied to the core business we cannot expect overall margins to improve. With these assumptions included the result may be:

$$\frac{\text{Profit}}{\text{Sales}} \times \frac{\text{Sales}}{\text{Net Assets}} = \frac{\text{Profit}}{\text{Net Assets}} \times \frac{\text{Net Assets}}{\text{Equity}} = \frac{\text{Profit}}{\text{Equity}}$$

$$\frac{90}{800} \times \frac{800}{250} = \frac{90}{250} \times \frac{250}{200} = \frac{90}{200}$$

$$11.25\% \times 3.2 = 36.0\% \times 1.25 = 45.0\%$$

Clearly, this example is a simplified view of such a situation. If the capital released is re-invested into brand/reputation development and/or product/service development to strengthen the company's value positioning and competitive advantage strategy, revenue increases are expected. These together with margin improvements should improve the return to shareholders:

$$\frac{\text{Profit}}{\text{Sales}} \times \frac{\text{Sales}}{\text{Net Assets}} \times \frac{\text{Net Assets}}{\text{Equity}} = \frac{\text{Profit}}{\text{Equity}}$$

$$\frac{130.5}{900} \times \frac{900}{400} \times \frac{400}{200} = \frac{130.5}{200}$$

$$11.5\% \times 2.25 \times 2.0 = 62.25\%$$

The example suggests that by re-investing the capital into core capabilities the profitability and productivity performances show improvements. Capital is released and redeployed and the supply chain management role is changed from one of managing dedicated logistics assets to one of coordinating supply chain relationships. This is a commonplace situation for many organizations.

Investment ratios
Investment ratios indicate the relative success of an organization, by measuring profit performance against market-established measures such as earnings per share, price earnings ratio and others such as dividend and interest cover. In most organizations these are remote from supply chain managers but, as has been demonstrated, can have a major impact on their management role.

Alternative supply chain structures can have an influence on these cost elements and the differential service performance that is available may have an impact on revenues generated. Therefore, we should consider the implications of decision alternatives on the value delivered to the shareholder.

However, there are disadvantages in using standard accounting data for measuring supply chain performance. One obvious problem is that the data are collected for financial reporting and are not specific to supply chain management performance. A second problem follows from this. It concerns timing, availability and cost. While both functional and period financial statements are typical features of management control data they may be of limited use to a supply chain activity that is predominantly outsourced across a number of organizations. This problem is addressed later in this chapter.

Creating value for the shareholder

Shareholder value is measured in several ways. Some proponents of the concept use a measure based upon current levels of profitability and share price, together with a measure of the return on equity spread, that is, the return generated less the cost of the equity capital. Negative measures suggest that rather than creating value the business is destroying it, and clearly positive values are adding value.

An alternative measure of shareholder value is based upon a discounted present value of the revenues likely to be generated by a strategy option. While this is financially oriented it is focused on future activities and outcomes and does present an opportunity for the firm to evaluate supply chain options, customer service alternatives and any significant influence they may have on the cash flows.

The shareholder value analysis has a number of stages. They are relatively simple and follow the accepted methods of investment appraisal;

- estimating the cash flows net of fixed and variable costs, taxes and investments in fixed and working capital
- obtaining the discounted value of the profit stream by applying the cost of capital for the business as the discount rate, and
- estimating the residual value of the business unit.

The total shareholder value is then the sum of the present values of future cash flows and residual values less the market value of any debt associated with that element of the business.

A transitional perspective

Shareholder value analysis and strategic analysis

The driving concept behind EVA is the idea that management is accountable for capital expenditure and resources use, therefore a 'return' is expected.

The increased emphasis on corporate responsibility to shareholders resulted in a focus on shareholder value management. Academic interest emerged in the early and mid-1980s with an increasingly pragmatic focus appearing in the 1990s. A number of models appeared. Space restricts a detailed review of how EVA (economic value added) and MVA (market value added) are used to explore the interface between shareholder value management and stakeholder value management. Figure 2.10.5 identifies EVA components and Figure 2.10.6 identifies MVA components.

EVA measures value by comparing published profit with managements' use of capital within the business. A 'cost of capital' is derived that reflects gearing and capital, includes tangible items (such as property, equipment and so on) and intangible items (such as 'brand values', R & D and management development costs, developed to reflect future, rather than current benefits). The driving concept behind EVA is the idea that management is accountable for capital expenditure and resources use, therefore a 'return' is expected. EVA is

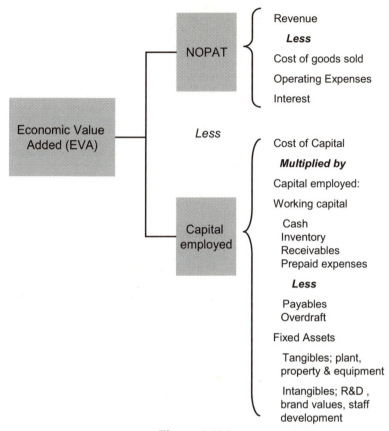

Figure 2.10.5
Component factors of the EVA model

very effective at senior management levels where it has been linked to executive remuneration. Put simply, EVA is:

Economic value added = Operating profit (after tax) (for period) less cost of capital (for period, that is weighted average cost of capital multiplied by total capital employed for that period).

An alternative model is the approach taken by MVA, which links the shareholder value created by company share price performance relative to capital employed. MVA is a simpler calculation. It uses the market value of a company's shares, adds debt and deducts the capital employed. A positive residual result implies value has been created, a negative value suggests value has been destroyed. MVA is:

Market value added = Market value of share issued: (at current prices), plus Corporate debt: long- and short-term debt (loans, overdraft and accounts payable), less Capital invested in the business (equity capital, retained earnings and the share premium account).

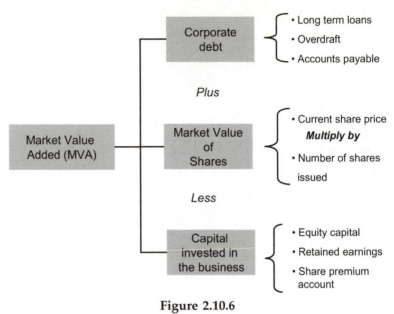

Figure 2.10.6
Component factors of the MVA model

Both EVA and MVA have been criticized because they overlook the future value of income streams. It could be argued that by using current share prices MVA is assuming the market has taken a view on future prospects. EVA is more difficult. It could be assumed that there is an element of the market's view of future prospects in the cost of capital 'charged' to a company and used by it in the calculation of its cost of capital.

The role of EVA in influencing supply chain decisions

Shareholder value planning can be incorporated into the supply chain strategy development process.

Value and competitive advantage are compatible concepts. A value-based competitive advantage can be established by identifying those benefits, or attributes, which offer vendors an opportunity to increase the attractiveness of their market offer to their target customers, or which offer customers 'real' benefits.

To explore the operations strategy and shareholder value interface in more detail the EVA model is expanded. Figure 2.10.5 identified the basic components of the EVA model; operating profit details and capital charges – the cost of all aspects of capital employed by the business in order to achieve the operating profit.

Essentially, we are concerned with three strategic management activities: those decisions that relate to the profitable performance of the business, decisions that ensure a positive net present value of current and future cash flows, and those that ensure the productive use of the assets representing the capital employed.

Using Figure 2.10.7, we can expand upon the model components. We have the assumed shareholder value criteria of: capital gain (from the growth of share prices); dividend payments, and economic cash flow (the positive NPV of current and future income streams). The EVA model does not consider economic cash flow explicitly; however, it can be assumed to be an implicit feature of the model. Without positive cash flow, the organization will neither meet its operational commitments of payment for resources, nor will it meet strategic requirements for fixed and working capital expansion as opportunity appears.

Shareholder value planning can be incorporated into the supply chain strategy development process. Shareholder value expectations provide a framework for identifying marketing strategy options that are considered together with those for manufacturing and supply chain management. The process is iterative at this stage as alternatives for a competitive advantage stance are evaluated together with the capital investment and working capital requirements for alternative strategies.

The process involves financial management assessment of risk, return and alternative capital structures.

The investment requirements for a caretaker/consolidation and productivity strategy (and the risk profile) are lower than those for

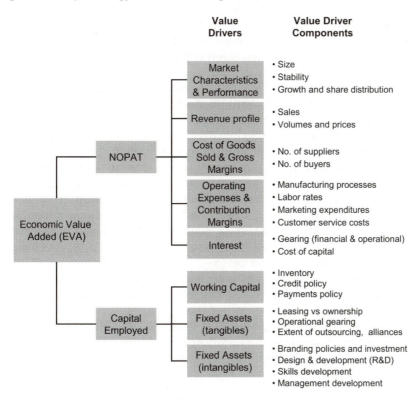

Figure 2.10.7
Details of the EVA model

innovator/product-market growth alternative supply chain infra-structure strategies. The implications of risk can be addressed in the consideration of capital structure for the financing of additional assets. This will be expressed as a higher cost of capital as the 'market' perceives the risk of a highly geared asset intensive strategy compared with the implications of low gearing and the reduced interest commitments.

An example

Capital employed is reduced by almost one third and the ROCE shows an impressive improvement from 25 per cent to 33.3 per cent.

The case study that follows has been developed using an anonymous company. The values given are based upon expected performance levels, which, together with those for fixed assets and networking capital and interest rates, are reliably based estimates.

The company manufactures 'standard' industrial products and at the time of the case study was profitable with a 20.7 per cent ROS and 25 per cent ROCE. The board of directors was under pressure to increase this performance by its larger, institutional, shareholders. They too, being pension funds, were being pressured for better performances from their portfolios.

A review of potential performance outcomes based upon a comparison of two supply chain management options is shown as Table 2.10.1. Using Figure 2.10.7, the financial performance outcome may be estimated by considering the structural alternative and the impact this will have on fixed assets and working capital and of course on the operating (NOPAT) margin.

In the case given as Table 2.10.1, the company's operating margin is reduced by the impact of distribution service expenses of $25 million, resulting in a reduction of the margin to 10.0 per cent.

However, the value of tangible fixed assets is reduced by the sale of the logistics infrastructure, resulting in $300 million. The outsourcing alternative offers lower inventory costs due to improved EDI applications, which also has an impact on accounts receivable. A similar effect was expected on payables with the impact of EDI systems, and by working closely with fewer suppliers, a benefit offered by the EDI systems. As a result, capital employed is reduced by almost one third and the ROCE shows an impressive improvement from 25 per cent to 33.3 per cent.

The 'market's' view of risk is reviewed. Lower gearing and capital commitment reduces perceived risk and this is reflected in a lower cost of capital.

The cost of capital required to generate the NOPAT is, as a consequence, less due to the lower capital value and the lower cost of capital. As a result, the EVA generated for the shareholders is increased significantly.

Table 2.10.1

Using EVA to evaluate the contribution of supply chain management
to shareholder value

$ million	Current: Corporate owned Infrastructure		Option: Outsourced Infrastructure
Sales	3500		3500
COGS			
Materials			
Labor			
Services			25
Overhead			
Tax			
NOPAT ($%)	375 (10.7%)		350 (10.0%)
Fixed assets	1200		900
Tangibles	900	600	
Intangibles	300	300	
Current assets	600		300
Current liabilities	300		150
Working capital	300		150
Total capital employed	1500		1050
ROCE %	25%		33.3%
Weighted average cost of capital %	15%		12.5%
$ Cost of capital to generate NOPAT	$225		$131.25
EVA: Value generated for shareholders	+ $150		+ $218.75

The virtual supply chain: a value perspective

In the fourth annual global survey of CEO opinion, Maitland (2001) in
the *Financial Times* suggested: 'the ability of companies to deliver
value to shareholders and consumers is a deciding factor'. CEOs were
asked to name companies that best delivered on specific value areas,
including value for consumers and value for shareholders. CEOs put
Microsoft, GE, Sony, Toyota, Wal-Mart and McDonald's in their top
ten.

The inconsistency between CEO and customer views of value highlights a major problem in defining value.

A separate survey of consumer value by the *Financial Times*
revealed that major points of difference emerged between the CEOs
and customers. The public took a subjective view of consumer value
and rated General Motors and Volkswagen very highly. 'Personal ties
to the company,' the *Financial Times* reported, 'are one of the two main
reasons they give for their nominations. The other is quality and

reliability.' The consumer view of value appeared to be based on trust: 'large, high-profile companies inevitably offer consumer value'.

Notable by their omission are Dell and Amazon.com. This apparent 'inconsistency' highlights a major problem in defining value. It also suggests that the paragons of value creation and delivery are not rated as highly as they may consider they deserve to be.

Some interesting issues are exposed by this survey. The fact that customer value delivery and shareholder value are seen as separate and distinct is a cause for concern. Customer and other stakeholder satisfaction are inextricably linked; if customer response is poor because their perception of value is low, then customer loyalty will also be poor. Consequently, profitability, productivity and cash flow, three important shareholder value drivers are directly linked to customer value satisfaction and, therefore, to the performance of the business.

The current perception of 'customer value' is slowly being tempered into a meaningful commercial concept.

The current perception of 'customer value' is slowly being tempered into a meaningful commercial concept. This is important for supply chain and logistics management decision-making. Some authors argue that value that is being provided by logistics is not being measured and sold. The potential for much higher inventory turnover, and therefore lower inventory carrying costs, is not being explained to intermediary and business-to-business stakeholders. As customers place demands on suppliers for more value-added services, it is becoming increasingly important to be able to measure the value of these services in terms that are meaningful to the customer.

Slywotzky and Morrison (1996) suggest that customers not only have specific benefits they find necessary to their operations but that they are willing to pay a price premium to obtain them. The arguments follow a familiar theme: in order to justify a price premium the customer benefits, such as an improvement in inventory turnover, lower inventory holding costs and the potential for lowering fixed costs (warehousing and transport) must be identified and demonstrated as *financial benefits* to the customer. Furthermore, it is equally essential for these 'value drivers' to be costed by the supplier. Clearly, unless the receipts from providing these customer value driver benefits are less than the cost of providing them, there is no point in pursuing a strategy that includes them.

Added value is the 'key measure of corporate success', providing both a proper motivation and measure of corporate achievement.

Kay (1993) introduces the concept of added value as 'the key measure of corporate success' and defines this as the difference between the (comprehensively accounted) value of a firm's output and the (comprehensively accounted) cost of the firm's inputs. In this specific sense, adding value is 'both proper motivation of corporate activity and the measure of its achievement'. Kay calculates added value by subtracting from the market value of an organization's output the cost of its inputs:

Added value = Revenues less wages and salaries, materials, capital costs

He suggests that added value is a measure of the loss that would result to national income and to the international economy if the organization ceased to exist.

Added value in this context includes depreciation of capital assets and also provides for a 'reasonable' return on invested capital. Calculated this way added value is *less than* operating profit, the difference between the value of the output and the value of materials and labor inputs and capital costs. It also differs from the net output of the firm: the difference between the value of its sales and material costs (not labor or capital costs). Kay's measure of competitive advantage is the ratio of added value to the organization's gross or net output:

$$\frac{\text{Competitive}}{\text{Advantage}} = \frac{\text{Revenue} - (\text{Wages} + \text{Salaries} + \text{Materials} + \text{Capital costs})}{\text{Wages} + \text{Salaries} + \text{Materials} + \text{Capital costs}}$$

These are viewed as comparisons of added value to either gross or net output. Kay's added value is similar to the concept of the producer's surplus in micro-economics but has the additional benefit of being able to be calculated from accounting data. However, it should be said that inaccuracies are likely if direct comparisons between organizations are made on a one-off basis. Local accounting practices differ and accounting statements therefore are not strictly comparable due to differing procedures and practices. But longitudinal comparisons are worthwhile, particularly over periods of three to five years when input/output and added value/output ratios may be compared.

Kay's model may be illustrated and Figure 2.10.8 depicts two possible outcomes: one (a) shows a successful organization making a positive added value. In Kay's terms, it must be remembered that added value is greater than operating profit because it includes a return on capital; therefore, it *may not* be profitable. The (b) organization represented has difficulties; wages and salaries and capital costs are greater than revenues. Figure 2.10.9 suggests the added value structure of a value chain. At the raw materials (primary production) stage, materials costs are a low proportion of total input costs, but as value is added by successive processes, materials costs become significantly more important as do the capital costs of inventory financing.

Kay's (1993) view of added value measurement focuses on the operating activities of the firm in contrast to the usual financial statements which emphasize the return to its investors, and as such offers an operational aspect of performance measurement required in a value chain context. Furthermore, as different firms, in different industries, at different locations in the value chain will perceive very different 'value creation' opportunities (and therefore structures), added value measures offer the facility of 'locating' the point in the value chain where the added value *and* the competitive advantage benefits are most appealing.

Measures of added value offer the facility of 'locating' the point in the value chain where the added value and the competitive advantage benefits are most appealing.

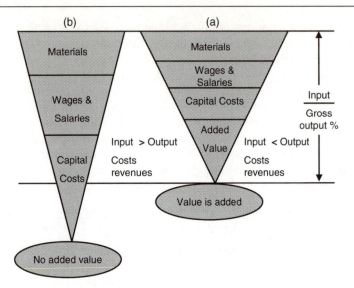

Source: Adapted from Kay, 1993

Figure 2.10.8
Added value perspective

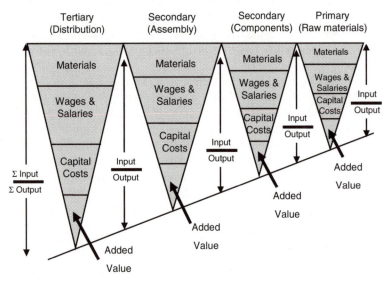

Source: Adapted from Kay, 1993

Figure 2.10.9
Stages in the value added chain

Kay uses the model to explore corporate strategy issues on the basis that: 'Corporate success derives from a competitive advantage which is based on distinctive capabilities, which is most often derived from the unique character of a firm's relationships with its suppliers, customers, or employees and which is precisely identified and applied to relevant markets.'

He asks: 'Did it make sense for Benetton to move into retailing, and was it right to decide to franchise most of its shops to individual franchises? What segment of the motor car market was most appropriate for BMW?'

He questions the measurement of success and performance, suggesting size, a firm's sales, its market share and its value on the stock market as options typically used together with a 'rate of return': this can be measured as return on equity, on investment or on sales. Other measures commonly used include growth, productivity, and increased earnings per share or the price earnings ratio. Kay argues that while these measures are aspects of successful performance the *key measure of corporate performance is added value*, that is the difference between the (comprehensively accounted) value of a firm's output and the (comprehensively accounted) cost of the firm's inputs.

Business relationships are crucial and Kay argues that the added value statement is not simply a means of looking at financial consequences. It describes the set of relationships that constitute the firm. In the virtual supply chain model, its role can be extended beyond relationship management to include both knowledge management and technology management. The flexibility of the model enables any options to be considered. In particular, a model of the industry, or the sector, that explores these components from the perspective of alternative formats can result in identifying the preferable location of the firm within the industry or sector value chain and which capabilities should be sought from external suppliers. Furthermore the qualitative or 'soft' aspects of customer service relationships also influence added value. For example, the Owens and Minor example described earlier shows how the customer relationship may be both reinforced *and* leveraged, resulting in increased revenues because of the customer perceptions of the added value delivered by the company.

The virtual organization and the virtual supply chain

Parolini (1999), like others, has identified the trend towards a 'new enterprise model'. Parolini suggests that connectivity costs associated with data collection and dissemination, controlling and coordinating transactions together with greater economic environmental turbulence have led to the disaggregation of 'vertically' integrated business structures. As a result, competition increasingly takes place between networks and value creating systems.

Most agree that a new economic model exists where a 'visionary' seeks to create a more effective business model, which typically involves:

Typically, a new economic model exists where a 'visionary' seeks to create a more effective business model, identifying core processes and focusing on core capabilities.

- identifying core processes and viewing these as interorganizational rather than intraorganizational
- a focus on core capabilities

- a supporting infrastructure that facilitates integration
- a view that the customer is an integral part of the 'value chain' and a major stakeholder
- an interorganizational performance planning system
- an emphasis on processes rather than functions
- distributed assets
- flexibility in product service delivery
- communication, cooperation infrastructure linkages, and
- synchronized networks that create virtual organizations.

The implications for the supply chain and supply chain management are significant. A focus on core capabilities suggests that the case for specialist operations is even more essential if shareholder and customer value are both to be maximized. The need and the ability to participate in more than one value chain, or value-creating system, is a competitive necessity. The acceptance of the 'interconnected company' and the need to unbundle the existing organization and rebundle it into more competitive structures is also a competitive necessity. A retreat from the functional silo mentality towards an interorganizational process perspective will facilitate leaner and more flexible operations.

The concept of value has shifted

Parolini argues value should be considered as the net value created by the 'system', the net value received by end user customers and the net value acquired by value-creating partners.

In recent years the concept of value has become accepted to be different between the value a customer attributes to a product or service and the cost of acquiring the value. Parolini argues that for the purposes of strategic analysis, and therefore (it follows for the supply chain), value should be considered as the net value created by the 'system', the net value received by end user customers and the net value acquired by value-creating partners.

Thus, end user customer gross value reflects the benefits expected/received less the costs associated with post-purchase operating and maintenance activities. The net value is the difference between the value customers attribute to a product and the price actually paid. The total price paid corresponds to the total revenues received by the value-creating partners. Therefore, the net value acquired by the value chain partnership is the difference between the total price end users have paid to the value chain partnership and the costs they have incurred in creating the value.

Parolini reminds us of the need to classify value in terms of: improving customer product-service performance or reducing costs. These may be 'economic' or real for business-to-business customers and 'psychological' for business-to-consumer customers. They may be 'qualifying' (competitive necessities) or 'determining' (competitive advantage) facilitators.

- Whether or not they are controlled by the end user or a value-chain partner: this is becoming significant as end users become involved in customizing product and service design.

- Whether costs are borne before during or after the time of purchase. This aspect is important for supply chain decisions. Depending upon where profit is made, that is, from the 'product' or from support services; so the implications for service policies will vary. If after-sales service is responsible for profitability it follows that service performance must match customer expectations.

An added value based model for financial performance measurement in the supply chain: a value chain approach

The added value concept can be applied to plan and monitor supply chain performance. To do so requires a shift of perspective to take some of the qualitative aspects of supply chain services expectations into consideration. It also requires management to understand the role of demand management.

Working in partnerships results in more specific and manageable value propositions and increases the returns to the value-chain participants.

Typically, the supply chain is coordinated by manufacturing companies or dominant resellers who use in-house manufacturing or distribution facilities to achieve market-based objectives such as market share volumes and customer penetration. Demand chain management shifts the emphasis towards 'customization' – directing product and service offers towards specific customers or customer groups sharing particular characteristics. Organizations prefer to outsource rather than own processes that facilitate and deliver value if it is clearly cost-effective and cost-efficient to do so. The incentive to integrate supply and demand chains is large – it provides more opportunities for enhancing and creating customer value. Working in partnerships results in more specific and manageable value propositions and increases the returns to the value-chain participants.

Modifying Kay's added value model

Kay's added value model can be applied to this approach. Some small modifications are required but none that conflict with the efficacy of the original model.

As discussed earlier, Kay proposed that corporate success (or failure) is a function of the added value that is created not only for the individual firm but also for the 'value creating' network or chain structure that evolves to create end user customer satisfaction. Kay describes this as an added value chain.

Figure 2.10.10 depicts such a structure, simplifying the value or supply chain in order to simplify the explanation. It also makes an assumption concerning the relationships existing in the structure – the manufacturer is the 'visionary' in the chain.

The basic model proposed by Kay has been modified such that wages and salaries are included with materials and components. This is a matter of expediency and simplifies graphical presentation. The inclusion of supply chain services is another modification and a 'trade-off' facility (the vertical double headed arrow) between supply

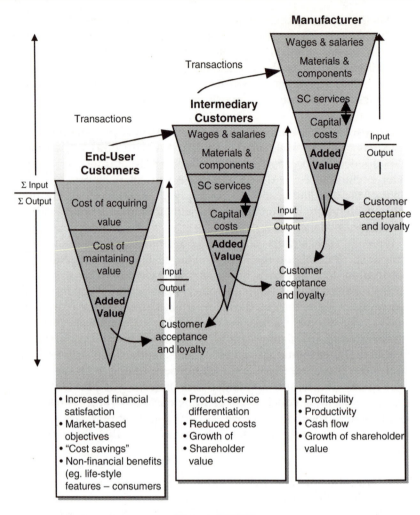

Figure 2.10.10
Modifying Kay's added value chain

chain services and capital costs is also included. The diagram suggests a basic capability difference between 'manufacturers' and 'intermediary customers', that is that the manufacturers' core capabilities are design, development and manufacturing, where the intermediaries are stronger in providing supply chain services. The 'end user' model is based upon the argument that added value is realized only when the combined costs of acquiring and maintaining the value benefits are less than, or equal to, the perceived value of the benefits delivered. The model functions through a series of transactions that result in the realization of the added value expectations of each of the participants. The added value expectations proposed in Figure 2.10.10 are generic; clearly, these will vary depending upon the industry.

The added value expectations of each stakeholder cannot be realized unless they all achieve their added value goals. For the 'manufacturer' these comprise the financial objectives of targeted profitability, productivity and cash flow. Growth is an assured objective throughout the added value chain. The market-based or market-acceptance objective comprises the qualitative aspects of positioning and relative competitive advantage, together with a market (segment) volume objective. Shareholder objectives, ROI, ROE and an EVA/MVA performance reflect an optimal level of performance that is achievable only through cooperative participation with other members of the added value chain. See Figure 2.10.11 below.

The added value expectations of each stakeholder cannot be realized unless they all achieve their added value goals.

Intermediary customers' added value expectations include both product and service characteristics. Accordingly, managers in manufacturer supply chains have a role in developing an understanding with materials and components suppliers to ensure cost-efficient materials management of inbound production materials components. Concern with the 'global' aspects of added value (the inbound as well as the outbound characteristics) is likely to improve aggregate added value (input/output) as well as the individual added value.

The interaction of 'product' and 'service' can be seen at the 'intermediary' level of the added value chain. Added value that impacts on differentiation or reduced costs is delivered through the time, quality, variety and service performance features. Customer loyalty, a feature that dominates the transactions process, is a measure that has implications for both parties. For the 'manufacturer' it has a bearing on costs, quality and security (of supply): it follows that trust is a primary issue for concern because it is the basis on which the other characteristics depend.

End user customer added value is often qualitative and therefore difficult to measure. However, as Parolini contends, it is important to distinguish monetary and non-monetary costs (those connected with the space and time concerns of the purchaser). 'This distinction can be rich in interesting hints for a company that is wondering how to increase the absolute net value given to its customers.'

Measuring the financial performance of added value

Effective supply chain management performance needs to be measured in financial terms. The (earlier) use of conventional accounting data typically provides partial data. The reason for this deficiency is that supply chain performance is not the primary purpose of the accounting system. Hence, while helpful information may be an output it must be remembered that it is a secondary output and consequently could be misleading or may not report the full financial consequences of a supply chain decision or event.

The added value model permits a cause and effect approach to be taken. Figure 2.10.12 suggests an added value approach. The basis of

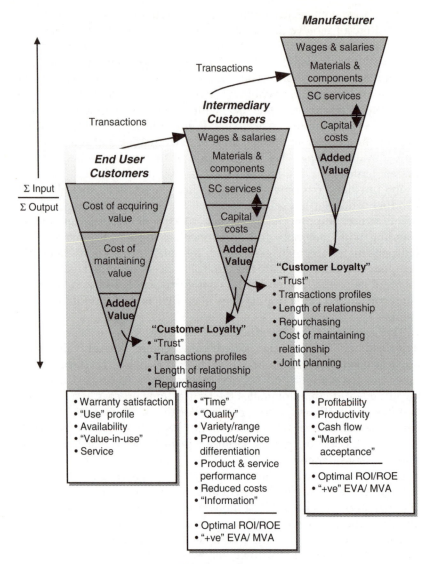

Figure 2.10.11
Added value expectations in the value chain

the model is to identify the *added value performance criteria* of customers (as individuals or as customer segments) and to 'translate' these in terms of the *added value components to be delivered*. The criteria required by customers should be reflected in added value tasks for the supply chain.

Given that supply chain management is a component process in the overall task of managing customer satisfaction it follows that having identified the *value delivery activities* the costs of performing these

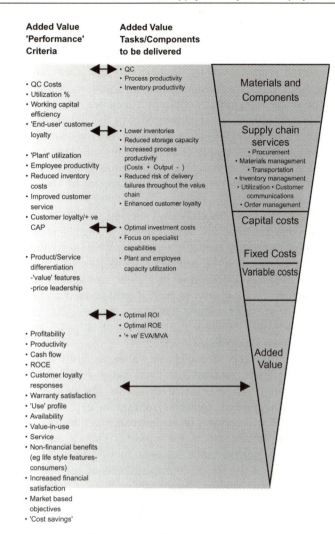

Added Value | **Added Value**
'Performance' | **Tasks/Components**
Criteria | **to be delivered**

Figure 2.10.12
Added value in the supply chain; added value performance monitors
in a B2B channel

should be identified and established as ongoing bench marks or
performance criteria. Some of the more obvious generic criteria are
suggested in Figure 2.10.12.

The primary purpose of an added-value approach should be to
identify important customer criteria and develop performance
measurements that reflect these. By adopting the added value concept
performance criteria can be developed that can be used for planning
and control. Furthermore, they may be applied to customer-specific
situations and extend the usefulness of customer account profitability
models.

Conclusion

The more recent focus on value for both, the shareholder and the customer, possibly has even more significance for supply chain management.

In this chapter we have reviewed current, transitional and future-oriented approaches to financial performance measurement of the supply chain. Traditionally, conventional accounting data have been used to develop supply chain performance data and such methods are still applicable today. The influence of the supply chain can be seen on the income statement as it increases revenue, for instance, and on the balance sheet as supply chain decisions influence the asset and capital structure of an organization. Accounting data can be used in ratio analysis and models to reveal the impact of the supply chain on a business.

New business models and trends in the market, however, are changing the way the supply chain is regarded and measured. The focus of corporate management on shareholder value has seen the rise in popularity of EVA and MVA as methods to measure shareholder value. The shift to value has clear implications for supply chain managers, as they seek to gain a value-based competitive advantage through strategic management activities. A case example of a manufacturer showed the impact of supply chain management alternatives on an EVA model.

The more recent focus on value as both a shareholder and a customer issue possibly has even more significance for supply chain management. In essence it broadens the concern into stakeholder value management. To accommodate the expanded set of interests, we outlined Kay's concept of added value as a more accurate measure of corporate achievement. We modified Kay's added value model to develop a performance measurement model that monitors value delivered *and* the financial implications of supply chain performance. Such a future-oriented approach enables a better assessment of the contribution of the supply chain to company value in a changing, partnership-based market environment.

References

Bredrup, H. (1995), 'The Traditional Planning Hierarchy', in A. Rolstadas, ed., *Performance Management: a Business Process Benchmarking Approach*, Chapman and Hall (February), Boca Raton, Fl.

Day, G. (1999), *The Market Driven Organization*, New York: The Free Press.

Day, G. and Fahey, L. (1990), 'Putting Strategy into Shareholder Value Analysis', *Harvard Business Review* (March/April).

Gale, B. (1994), *Managing Customer Value*, New York, The Free Press.

Gattorna, J. L. and Walters, D. W. (1996), *Managing the Supply Chain: a Strategic Perspective*, London: Macmillan Press.

Kay, J. (1993), *Foundation of Corporate Success*, Oxford: OUP.

Keebler, J. S. and Durtsche, D. A. (1999), 'Keeping score: measuring the business value of logistics in the supply chain', Council of Logistics Management.

King, A. M. (1993), 'Green dollars and blue dollars: the paradox of cost reduction', *Journal of Cost Management*, **7**(3).

Lambert, D. M. and Burduroglu, R. (2000), 'Measuring and Selling the Value of Logistics', *International Journal of Logistics Management*, Vol. 11 (no. 1).

Maitland, A. (2001), 'World's Most Respected Companies', *Financial Times* (17 December).

Naumann, E. (1995), *Creating Customer Value: The Path to Customer Advantage*, Cincinnatti: Thompson Executive Press.

Parolini, C. (1999), *The Value Net: A Tool for Competitive Strategy*, Chichester: Wiley.

Rolstadas, A. (1995), *Performance Management*, London: Chapman and Hall.

Slywotzky, A. and Morrison D. J. (2000) 'How digital is your business?', New York: Random House.

Webster, F. (1994), *Market Driven Management*, New York: Wiley.

2.11 Supply chain performance measures and systems

Linda Nuthall

The supply chain has attracted much boardroom attention over the last decade. Senior executives have started to recognize the true value that the supply chain can deliver if they approach it holistically and strategically. As a result, organizations are now endeavouring to implement end-to-end supply chain solutions rather than simply 'improving' their logistics functions without considering the upstream and downstream impacts. For many organizations, the key challenge in moving to a supply chain operational strategy lies in successfully identifying and implementing a measurement system that steers action towards achieving supply chain goals overall. Developing an integrated system of performance measures across the organization is critical to delivering successful supply chain performance.

Performance measures in the supply chain

Performance measures provide a management framework, facilitate communication, direct behaviors within the organization, foster improvement and assess positioning and operational capability.

Performance measurement systems fulfill a variety of purposes in today's supply chain organizations. Outlined below are the five main reasons organizations introduce performance measures.

First, performance management systems provide an effective management framework. They enable managers to compare their organizational performance with the performance of competitors or partners and to identify the gap between the target achievements and actual progress. Knowledge of these gaps helps to establish the need to change and provides the organizational tension necessary to drive change. Performance measures used at the business unit or division level contribute significantly to making decisions on resource allocation and investment.

With managers today facing an increasingly broad range of issues and problems, performance measurement systems help to prioritize

248

time and resources. A well-structured and defined system will systematically expose problems and their causes, providing management with a framework for informed decision making. In the absence of such a framework, managers could make decisions based on unsupported assumptions and biases, creating a high-risk environment.

Second, performance measures facilitate communication throughout the organization. They provide a mechanism for 'top-down' communication, enabling executives to communicate the strategic intent of the company through all levels of management and to operations. This helps to align business objectives at all organizational levels and to align performance measures with those objectives.

Performance measurement systems also provide a mechanism for 'bottom-up' communications. In this way, managers gain a good understanding of operational processes, which increases their ability to manage them. Performance measures also enable managers to provide comments to individuals, to guide and improve their performance. Sharing performance results throughout an organization not only provides workers with a view of the 'broader picture', but can also provide them with a sense of accomplishment, competence and control.

Third, performance measures play a determining role in people management by directing the behavior of the members of an organization. When people know the criteria on which their performance is being measured, and perhaps rewarded or penalized, it follows that their behavior will be such as to enhance the outcome of these measures. Compensation and performance measurements are crucial in not only communicating management's goals, but also in driving the behavior that enables the company to achieve those goals.

Performance measures are used to direct and motivate.

Fourth, an effective system will do more than steer behavior; it will foster innovation and improvement. Performance measures help to create an environment in which people are encouraged to look for, recognize and pursue innovative improvement opportunities. Rather than simply monitoring people's work, performance measures must show areas of improvement and potential improvement. In this way, performance measures actually encourage innovation and problem solving, and ultimately foster a culture of continuous improvement.

Fifth, performance measures help organizations to assess their competitive positioning and operational capacity. Some of the most motivating measures are those that focus on potential performance rather than actual. If consistent, performance measures enable organizations to make comparisons over time, between divisions or sites, with competitors or other industry players. Indeed, even when operating procedures vary, comparisons of results may highlight the potential benefits of alternative methods and approaches. Once this information is available, management has the opportunity to explore

Performance measures are used to improve operational efficiencies.

the implications of introducing such methods into their particular operations. Benchmarking measures were developed to fulfill this role.

The imperative for getting it right

Performance measurement systems have potentially tragic dysfunctional effects if used unwisely. At the other extreme, they can be the key to an organization's success. Providing conflicting or too many performance measures is likely to result in a lack of conviction in decision-making, dissatisfaction among employees, and consequent poor performance.

While suitable performance measures provide the foundation for informed decision-making, improper performance measures can lead to organizational paralysis by effectively disguising critical issues and warning signs. 'Good' performance measures have several distinguishing characteristics:

- they are directly related to objectives and strategies
- they must be understandable but not underdetermining
- they must be meaningful
- they vary between locations and customer segments
- they change over time, and
- they provide fast feedback.

Directly related to objectives and strategies

In order to assess whether an organization is working towards its corporate objectives, supply chain performance measures must be directly related to these business goals. The process of goal alignment must persist throughout the company to ensure no part of the organization is working at cross-purposes. Performance measures should not only reveal the degree of achievement of the overall objectives, they should also provide managers with information on how well a strategy is being executed and on the appropriateness of the strategy itself.

A performance measurement system is comprehensive if it captures all the relevant constituencies, perspectives and stakeholders of the process. Three basic dimensions of performance should be included to provide a well-balanced picture: customer satisfaction, internal efficiency and financial results.

Understandable but not underdetermining

Supply chains are becoming increasingly complex in terms of their configuration and operations and their purpose. Performance measures need to reflect these complexities in order to be realistic, but must be simple enough to be understood. If performance measures are too simplistic, they underdetermine the process of consideration. If they are too convoluted, they will not be used. To motivate people, the measures must be relevant to people's jobs and to the company's objectives.

Meaningful

In some cases, companies can unnecessarily overcomplicate performance measures, rather than search for understandable, yet realistic measures for truly complex operations. A performance measurement system is only useful if it provides management with focus and direction for the appropriate course of action.

Consider an organization that adopts a measure for customer service that combines orders delivered late, customer returns, average backorder age and invoice error rate. If all these components are quantified, weighted and combined into one measure, say a ratio, then it is highly likely this ratio will have no meaning. Indeed, in order to understand the measure and use it to prompt action, the user will need to reduce the measure to its individual components.

Such a ratio could be a useful way to summarize the organization's customer service achievements. However, due to the inherent offsetting effects of individual elements, trends and other important signals may easily be hidden. Overall, many composite measures lack tangible meaning, are difficult to understand and can mislead management decisions. Only performance issues that are significant to the company operations should be measured, and these should be measured directly.

Vary between locations and customer segments

This characteristic is particularly important in large organizations that have multiple products and services, categories, markets, customer segments and locations. The dynamics of the operating and market environments vary depending not only on these factors, but also on the company's strategic responses to these factors.

Due to the alignment of operational performance measures with the actionable points of strategies, measures will undoubtedly vary between locations, and across customer segments. Alternatively, the same aspects of operations may be measured but in different ways or with a different focus or level of importance placed on them. Performance measurement systems must be flexible enough to recognize and deal with these differences.

Change over time

An organization changes its operating strategies over time in accordance with successes and failures of past strategies, new technologies and operational advances, new products and markets, changing customer requirements and behaviors, and changing corporate objectives. Given the need for performance measures to be aligned with business objectives, it is logical that performance measures must therefore change over time.

Provide fast feedback

With growing pressure on lead times and leaner supply chains comprising increasing numbers of specialist organizations, the importance of detecting and resolving problems quickly is escalating. Performance measures must therefore provide fast, if not immediate, feedback to the appropriate people to facilitate prompt corrective action.

Comparing performance measurement systems

Traditional measures – how do they stack up?

Supply chains are changing and accounting-based performance measurement approaches are not suitable in many new contexts.

The term 'traditional' refers to the management accounting approach to performance measurement. Budgeting, standard costing, overhead absorption, and transfer pricing are all elements of this approach, as are return-on-investment (ROI) calculations, earnings per share, cash flow projections, and forecasting. While some authors debate whether the fundamental principles of management accounting have changed since the 1930s, it is incontestable that supply chain methods used by leading organizations have changed significantly. Supply chain managers, therefore, need to decide if traditional performance measures are suitable for modern organizations. Some of the problems that arise from using traditional measures in today's supply chains are outlined below.

Distorting costs and issues

Traditional cost allocation methods can lead to a distortion of costs due to a changing pattern of cost elements in organizations. The labour component of overall costs – traditionally the basis for overhead allocation – is decreasing significantly due to vast technological advancements. Other examples include the blurring of the distinction between direct and indirect costs, and the fact that the traditional cost elements – labour, material and overheads – no longer emphasize the right issues.

Distortion also occurs because performance measures based on traditional cost accounting data do not provide the right kind of information to management, they do not capture the required depth and breadth of issues, and they underdetermine issues within operational companies.

Irrelevant to objectives and day-to-day operations

Criteria that typically appear in the objective statements of today's supply chain organizations include quality, reliability, flexibility, innovation, lead times, cost, and customer service and satisfaction. With the dubious exception of cost, dubious for the reasons addressed above, none of these factors can be directly measured or monitored using traditional performance measures.

Furthermore, traditional performance measures do not drive down to measure-specific actions and are therefore viewed as irrelevant to day-to-day operations. In other words, traditional performance measures do not directly reflect the actionable points of operating strategies, and therefore do not provide essential feedback regarding the execution of these strategies.

Inflexible

Consistency, not flexibility, is inherent in the design and timing of traditional performance measures. Indeed, an essential feature of management accounting is the standardization of measurement and reporting. This standardization is in direct conflict with the requirements of performance measures to vary between locations and over time as market conditions, strategic responses and accompanying actions change. It is therefore unlikely that adopting a standard set of measures over multiple locations will assist supply chain managers. The very nature of management accounting also makes it unlikely that frequent changes can be made in the system of measures.

Fast and continuous feedback is a critical characteristic of modern management. Not surprisingly, traditional management accounting performance methods attract significant criticism. Monthly or quarterly financial reports frequently reach the appropriate people too late to be useful.

Misdirecting management decisions

As cost variances are the outcomes of issues – not the drivers – controlling against these signals could lead managers to manage the symptoms rather than the cause. This issue links back to all the traditional performance measurement problems discussed. If measures are not tied to the actionable points of strategies, management is not provided with the information required for intelligent decision-making. Inappropriate measures can cause managers to act so as to improve the numbers rather than in the best interests of the organization.

In defence of financial measures

Many of the shortcomings of traditional management accounting measures have come about not from the measures themselves, but from their misuse or misapplication. Organizations often attempt to use their traditional measures in ways for which they were never designed. The limitations and actual meanings of these measures are not well understood or acknowledged.

Despite the movement away from traditional performance measurement, there is still a need or place for financial measures and cost data, primarily for external reporting and comparison purposes. Most importantly, the cost accounts and the financial accounts must be integrated and consistent.

In the absence of an optimal mix of specific financial and non-financial indicators applicable to all organizations, each must find a balance of measures, which it views as sufficient for the management of its own operational activities. The critical success factor is to identify and adopt a balance of traditional and non-financial measures that suits the organization at that particular time.

Advanced methodologies

New approaches to performance measurement have emerged. Supply chain management needs to understand the alternatives.

The last decade has seen the introduction of several frameworks and methodologies for the development of performance measurement systems. Much of this development has been driven by the recognized need to find an alternative to traditional, management accounting performance measurement approaches. This section examines a select number of these frameworks and considers their robustness, logic and useability.

The performance pyramid

Strategy and operations management are linked in the 'performance pyramid'.

The performance pyramid was first developed by A. S. Judson (1991) and later improved by Cross and Lynch (1995), as shown in Figure 2.11.1. With company vision forming the apex of the pyramid, the model works on the basis that strategy and operations are linked by the translation of objectives from the top down and the implementation of measures from the bottom up.

The performance pyramid has five levels, each one representing a different level within the organization. The first is the corporate level,

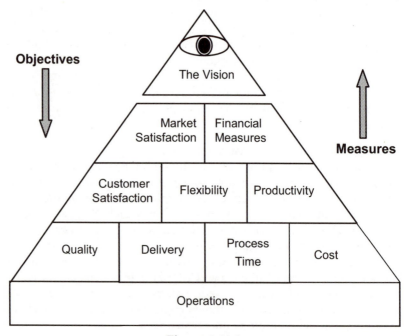

Figure 2.11.1
The performance pyramid

where the overall company vision is determined. The second level represents the business unit where success is typically defined in terms of reaching short-term profitability goals and longer-term goals for growth and market share. The translation of these objectives into tangible measurements begins in the third level of the pyramid.

This third level represents the business operating system and is defined as all activities, policies, procedures and supporting systems that are required to implement a particular business strategy. There is, therefore, a different business operating system for each strategy that is introduced in order to achieve the business unit level objectives. For example, there would be one business operating system for new product introduction and another for customer order fulfilment. Departmental measurement and control start at this level.

The objectives of a business operating system are defined in terms of customer satisfaction, flexibility and productivity. Customer satisfaction represents how the customers' expectations are managed, flexibility addresses the responsiveness of the operating system and productivity represents the management of resources, including time.

These objectives are then further translated to provide a clear foundation for specific operational measures. The fourth level of the performance pyramid contains four principal criteria for local operating performance: quality, delivery, process time and cost. Quality represents meeting the established target values for customer requirements. Delivery represents the on time delivery of products or services to the customer or user. Process time represents the time taken for completion of the operation from the time of the request to do so. Cost represents the excess resources used to achieve the quality and delivery customer requirements.

The measures concerned with quality and delivery are external measures. They are visible and important to the customer. The measures concerned with process time and cost are internal, critical to the ultimate success of the operation. It is vitally important to understand both the behavior of the criteria and how they interact. By the shared objectives at the business operating system level, the dependencies between the criteria can be recognized and communicated. This acts as a guidance system that should self-adjust continually to the changing requirements of the business.

The fifth level of the performance pyramid represents the supporting operational measures. Once the customer service objectives have been set at the business operating system level and the key measures developed at the local operational level, all departments involved in the delivery of products or services must be identified. Measures that represent successful hand-offs between the departments can then be developed. These measures force the departments to focus not only on how effectively each department or group operates, but also on improving the performance of the whole system rather than risking sub-optimization.

Cross and Lynch's performance pyramid offers a clear breakdown between the different levels of the organization and a clear distinction between the business operating system objectives and the determinants of these objectives. However, while it is important to recognize these differences, the breakdown structure of the performance pyramid is questionable in its logic. For example, the pyramid structure dictates that two components make up customer satisfaction: quality and delivery. However, time, indeed flexibility, are also components of customer satisfaction. Similarly, cost belongs on the third tier of the pyramid as an objective output, the determining components being time and asset management.

The balanced scorecard

The 'Balanced Scorecard' provides a holistic view of the corporation's performance.

Kaplan and Norton (1996) developed the balanced scorecard in 1992. Like the performance pyramid, it was developed to provide a comprehensive framework that translates an organization's strategic objectives into a coherent set of performance measures. The scorecard, shown in Figure 2.11.2, considers organizational performance from four viewpoints: the customer perspective the financial perspective, the internal business perspective and the innovation and learning perspective.

The scorecard's measures are grounded in the organization's strategic objectives and competitive demands. Managers select a limited number of measures that are critical to the achievement of goals from each of the four perspectives. The framework was designed to help focus managers on the strategic vision of the organization. The balanced scorecard considers current and future success, internal and external criteria, and financial and non-financial measures. The balance of the set of measures should reveal the trade-offs between the performance measures and guard against sub-optimization.

An important feature of the balanced scorecard is that it is not a template that can be applied to businesses in general. Different market situations, product strategies, and competitor environments require different scorecards. In fact, the scorecard was developed to be implemented at an individual business unit level – one with its own customers, channels, production facilities and financial performance measures.

Like the performance pyramid, Kaplan and Norton's balanced scorecard has the positive feature of incorporating both internal and external perspectives, and financial and non-financial measures. However, it does not offer clear distinctions between the various levels within an organization, and it does not distinguish between output and determinant measures. In addition, no four of the perspectives encompassed in the scorecard are necessarily included in the objective statements of all levels or divisions in an organization. This would necessitate the need to manipulate the company's agreed objectives in order to 'fit' the framework.

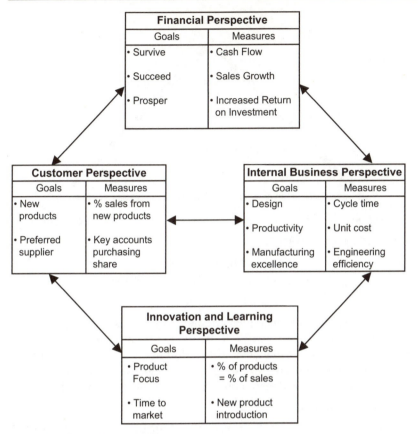

Source: Kaplan & Norton, 1996

Figure 2.11.2
The balanced scorecard: examples of goals and measures for different perspectives

A further issue arises from the fact that the balanced scorecard has been designed for use at an individual business unit level. It makes no provision for comparison between business units, nor is there a mechanism for aggregating measures for management across business units. For managers to examine the performance of the organization as a whole, therefore, they must examine every scorecard from all business units.

Integrated performance measurement
Dixon et al. (1992) put integrated performance measurement forward as a framework and process for developing and deploying performance direction. The framework (Figure 2.11.3) emphasizes the relationship between an organization's strategy, its actions and its measures. Effective organizations maintain congruence along each side of the three dimensions.

The 'Integrated performance management' framework emphasizes the relationship between strategy, corresponding actions and measures.

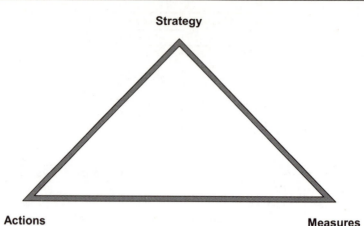

Strategy

Actions   **Measures**

Source: Dixon et al, 1992

Figure 2.11.3
Integrated performance measurement

Integrated performance measurement is not based on a general set of uniform measures, rather it refers to the process of acquiring knowledge of performance and employing it at each step in the strategic management cycle. The strategic management cycle, developed by Shank (1989), consists of the following four steps:

- *Step 1.* Formulate strategies.
- *Step 2.* Communicate those strategies throughout the organization.
- *Step 3.* Develop and carry out tactics to implement the strategies.
- *Step 4.* Develop and implement controls to monitor the success of the implementation steps and hence success in meeting the strategic objectives.

Integrated performance measurement works on the assumption that organizations do not have precise knowledge of future goals, only that they make judgments regarding the general direction in which they should move. Strategies, actions and consequently measures are changed as new information is gathered. The integrated performance measurement process therefore embraces the spirit of continuous improvement by the continuous addition and deletion of measures.

Dixon et al. argue that their approach has been designed to help people learn how to be more effective in achieving strategic objectives by emphasizing the relationship between an organization's strategy, its actions and its measures. However, it neglects to assign measures against the goal outputs themselves. The risk, therefore, is that while successful execution of strategies is monitored, the suitability of the strategies to the overall objectives is not. The process is suitable for feature measures pertaining to specific strategic initiatives, but not to the development of a set of core, high-level supply chain operational output measures.

Scorecard for logistics

Christopher (1998) developed a scorecard for logistics based on the principles of Kaplan and Norton's balanced scorecard. The framework consists of a four-step process:

Step 1. Articulate the logistics and supply chain strategy.
Step 2. Determine the measurable outcomes of success.
Step 3. Determine the processes that impact these outcomes
Step 4. Identify the drivers of performance within these processes.

The 'scorecard for logistics' considers supply chain strategy, processes and drivers that lead to measurable outcomes.

The logistics and supply chain strategy should articulate how these operations will contribute to the overall achievement of the corporate goals. Christopher suggests that the measurable outcomes of success of such a strategy typically fall into the groupings of better, faster, cheaper. Figure 2.11.4 shows a translation of these outcome groupings into more meaningful operational results, and the processes that lead to these outcomes.

The triad of goals incorporates the external, customer-based perception of performance in terms of total quality of service, and the internal perception of performance in terms of resource and asset utilization.

In the fourth step, the specific activities that drive performance within each of the processes are identified. These activities are the basis for the derivation of the key performance indicators at the operational level. Christopher suggests using a cause and effect analysis to aid in their identification.

In proposing the scorecard for logistics, Christopher says the triad of interconnected goals – better, faster, cheaper – is almost universal in its desirability. The distinguishing value of the logistics scorecard, however, is the four-step process for developing measures at both the objective output level and the operational determinant level. This process is considered to have merit due mainly to its logic, its flexibility and its ease of use. It provides valuable guidance for identifying key

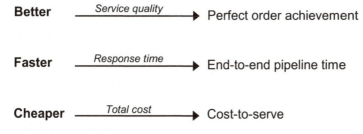

Source: Christopher, 1998

Figure 2.11.4
Creating the logistics scorecard

performance measures as well as the supporting operational measures, without the constraints of a pre-designated structure.

Dashboard metrics

'Dashboard metrics' allow executives to take 'the pulse of operations' at any time.

The dashboard concept, developed by Tyndall (1998), essentially refers to 'a few key metrics that define and measure the pulse of operations'. In this framework, the metrics fall into four categories: operational cost, time and response, profitability and margins, and customer service. Table 2.11.1 shows an example of dashboard metrics.

The creators of the dashboard metrics concept focus on three key messages:

1   too many overly complicated metrics will not lead to success
2   the suggested five to seven metrics used should be easily collated, and
3   the suggested five to seven metrics used should be monitored in as real time as possible.

Tyndall et al. do not provide guidance for identifying measures, nor do they address the issue of objective output measurement as opposed to operational determinant measurement. However, the four categories based on cost, time, profitability and service incorporate all of the key perspectives of supply chain management.

Perhaps not surprisingly, three of the four categories line up with the key objectives put forward in Christopher's framework. Better, faster, cheaper – customer service, time and response, operational cost. The fourth category, profitability and margins, is important in the

Table 2.11.1
Metrics dashboard

Operational cost	Time and response	Profitability and margins	Customer services
• Total delivered cost by product/ customer	• Total supply chain cycle time	• Operational margins by product/ channel	• Customer service levels by segment, channel
• Days sales/ inventory and levels	• Order to (delivery cycle time)	• Net operating profit after tax	• Perfect orders
• Excess and obsolete inventory	• Response time to customer requests and orders	• Return on total supply chain assets	• Order-fill rates
• Backlog and shortages	• Manufacturing cycle time	• Cash flow metrics	• On-time delivery
• Days payable			• Delivery to customer request

Source: Adapted from Tyndall, 1998

context of overall supply chain management, but perhaps not so relevant when the focus of management is on the operational component of supply chain.

A holistic framework for performance measurement

The new performance management framework for the supply chain aims to guide the identification of performance measures so that no crucial element is omitted, while being flexible enough to accommodate various objectives and strategies.

There are two phases to adopting this framework. The first deals with the overall supply chain objectives. Figure 2.11.5 shows the supply chain core measures quadrant. All of the measures in this quadrant must be grounded in the high-level objective statement for the supply chain. The components of a statement of objectives should include both internal and external perspectives. The framework enables managers to distinguish between the objectives of effectiveness and efficiency, measures of outputs and determinants, and measures of forward targets and past achievements. The overview of this quadrant should make visible any trade-off effects, as well as improvement opportunities.

The second part, shown in Figure 2.11.6, follows the same logic as the first, but it focuses on special projects or strategic initiatives which are launched in order to further the achievement of the overall supply chain objectives. Once an initiative has reached its goals, the measures in this quadrant will have met acceptable or target levels. They would

A holistic framework for supply chain performance measurement considers effectiveness and efficiency aspects simultaneously.

Core Measures – Supply Chain Statement of Purpose		Effectiveness		Efficiency	
		Objective	Measure	Objective	Measure
	Outputs				
	Determinants	Objective	Measure	Objective	Measure

Figure 2.11.5
Supply chain framework – core measures quadrant

		Effectiveness		Efficiency	
		Objective	Measure	Objective	Measure
Feature Measure	**Strategic Initiative Outputs**				
	Actionable Points Determinants	Objective	Measure	Objective	Measure

Figure 2.11.6
Supply chain framework – feature measures quadrant

then be deleted to make way for new 'feature measures' that reflect the focus of new initiatives.

The four-step process introduced in Christopher's scorecard for logistics methodology can be used in both phases of this framework, the only minor adaptation being that in Phase 1, step one would refer to the supply chain and logistics objectives or goals, rather than to a strategy adopted to achieve these goals. This process guides managers in identifying the most appropriate measures for their particular supply chain.

Step 1
Phase 1:   Articulate the logistics and supply chain objectives.
Phase 2:   Articulate the logistics and supply chain strategy.

Step 2
Phases 1 and 2:   Determine the measurable outcomes or determinants of success.

Step 3
Phases 1 and 2:   Determine the processes that have an impact on these outcomes or determinants.

Step 4
Phases 1 and 2:   Identify the drivers of performance within these processes.

Steps 3 and 4 should be used to identify key performance measures for all supply chain operations. After all, a supply chain is a cross-functional process with the ultimate goal of fulfilling customer requirements. Therefore, all sub-processes will have an impact on at least one of the high-level objective outcomes.

The value of the high-level set of performance measures to management is severely constrained if it is not supported by a system that allows root-cause identification of problems and detailed analysis of trade-offs at different levels within the organization. The system needs to reinforce the understanding of, and confidence in, the high level measures.

Reporting structure and process

Data collection begins at the most detailed level of the organization's operations: at each discrete activity level. Measurement should be built up from this base, through the various stages of aggregation, to the high-level measures that provide an overall view of the supply chain and logistics operations. The information is effectively constructed and communicated using a hierarchical format where meaningful causal relationships exist between the metrics for each level of the hierarchy.

Organizations with a complex network, often born of a series of mergers, wide product ranges and a large variety of logistics issues, often find there is too much data for managers to analyse, interpret and ultimately use in decision-making. The wealth of information becomes an obstacle to effective management rather than an asset. These organizations in particular require a formal performance management system. It is crucial that information is reported on a need-to-know basis from each level in the organization wherever possible. Performance measurement should be provided in a format that highlights by exception in order to facilitate data interpretation and analysis.

Exception reporting requires definition of the parameters of what constitutes acceptable, standard, or normal performance. The reporting process should then allow performance to flex within this pre-established tolerance without attracting unnecessary management attention. The process must make known any measure that shows unacceptable variances so that the appropriate action can be taken. This approach to performance measurement reporting uses data reduction to ensure that management attention is focused where it is most needed.

Reporting frequency should also correspond to a need-to-know basis. The closer staff members are to the operation being measured, the more frequent is the requirement for reporting and reviewing. At the discrete activity level, for example, reporting should be frequent if not continuous, but for senior managers, monthly standard reporting will likely suffice. Naturally, these should be supported by feature reports to expose exceptions.

Drill down from the core measures

The holistic performance management framework described earlier incorporates a four-step process to guide organizations in identifying the right set of measures for their supply chain operations. Step 3 – determining the processes that have an impact on outcomes, and Step 4 – identifying the drivers of performance within these processes, are useful to identify the supporting, drill-down system of measures.

As all logistics processes affect at least one core measure (Step 3), a systematic procedure for identifying the drivers of performance is necessary (Step 4) to ensure there are no omissions or duplications in the performance management system. The recommended cause and effect approach, using root-cause identification trees, facilitates the breakdown of the problem into manageable parts. Such an approach helps to identify which functional areas should be 'hand-off' in an organization and highlights the potential 'knock-on' effects that particular events have throughout the end-to-end logistics process.

Once the root-cause identification trees have been developed and agreed throughout the organization, appropriate measures can be derived for all critical points in the drill down. Measures can be assigned to each node in the tree diagram; however, the scenarios represented along each branch will vary both in likelihood and in importance. While many of the measures may not be 'key' to the day-to-day running of the organization, it is still advisable that the data be collected and stored, to enable detailed investigation when required. Clearly, not every measure must be reported every month. As proposed earlier, data reduction, through tolerance parameter setting, facilitates exception reporting.

The root-cause identification trees can also be used as checklists to ensure that proper process accountabilities, data ownership, and evaluation measures are established. By tracing the various root causes of problems through the tree, it becomes clear how many individuals or functional groups impact upon each outcome stage. Measures used for evaluation, therefore, must be carefully chosen in line with an individual's area of control and influence. If one person's success or failure relies directly on the success or failure of another, the evaluation performance measures must also reflect this relationship.

The drill downs of cost measures are simply the cost data broken down into various components. The most important point to note here is that the data will need to be examined in various forms for various purposes. For example, the data breakdown may be required by its functional components for trade-off and re-engineering analysis, by product category for product profitability analysis, by customer or customer type for customer profitability analysis, or by some combination of these. A system that provides the flexibility to cut and slice the data in these different ways, at different levels of detail, will provide the greatest value to management.

Key success factors

The right measures in the right place
In assigning performance measures, it is important that due consideration is given to the appropriate scope of the measures and the level of control. This issue was briefly mentioned above in relation to performance evaluation measures. The other imperatives for this approach are that it provides the means for an effective feedback and response mechanism. If measures are made visible at the wrong level within the organization, the response will be delayed until the information reaches the right person or level, with the right authority to act or instruct.

Out with the old
Many organizations have the problem of too many performance measures; too many that are obsolete and too many that are not consistent. Often this is the result of numerous performance measurement initiatives where new measures are introduced without discarding the old. When an organization is implementing a new performance measurement approach, they must abandon the old system.

One way to justify this apparent offloading of possibly long-standing measures is to examine rigorously all existing measures in the context of the entire new system and discard, with articulated reason, those that no longer fit or serve a purpose. The justification of corrective action is also critical in terms of people management as there is often significant resistance and criticism associated with the implementation of a new performance measurement system due to people's inherent aversion to change.

Rubbish in – rubbish out
No matter how well designed the measures and the reporting structure, the value comes from the integrity of the information provided: its accuracy and timeliness. In implementing a new performance measurement system, an organization must establish a formal enterprise-wide program of data ownership, accuracy, integrity and accessibility. Confidence in the performance measurement system is essential for employee motivation, and operational capabilities quickly break down without accurate data.

Define the purpose of the system
A performance measurement system satisfies a specific need: how to improve operational performance. It should therefore be independent from the accounting system the company uses for external reporting. The difference in the purpose of the two systems must be clearly communicated to all parties involved in order to avoid mixed and conflicting messages, and confusing issues of priority.

Conclusion

A new, holistic framework for performance management has been proposed to ensure performance measures are integrated across the organization and support overall corporate objectives. The recommended methodology for identifying and implementing a measurement system is equally applicable to any organizational structure. The time and effort required to develop both the system of measures and the enabling information systems is likely to be substantial; however, the benefits should more than justify the expense. This is particularly true of today's large, often complex, multinational organizations. An effective measurement system is critical to future success.

References

Ballantine, J. and Brignall, S. (1996), 'Interactions and trade-offs in multi-dimensional performance management', research paper No. 247, October 1996, Warwick Business School Research Bureau: Working Paper.

Christopher, M. (1998), *Logistics and Supply Chain Management: Strategies for Reducing Cost and Improving Service*, 2nd edn., London: Prentice Hall.

Cross, K. F. and Lynch, R. L. (1995), *Measure Up!: Yardsticks for Continuous Improvement*, 2nd edn., Oxford: Blackwell Publishers.

Dixon, J. R., Nanni, A. J. and Vollmann, T. E. (1992), *New Performance Challenge: Measuring Operations for World-Class Competition*, Dow Jones-Irwin/Apics Series in Production Management, Illinois.

Judson, A. S. (1991), *Changing Behavior in Organizations: Minimizing Resistance to Change*, Cambridge, MA: Blackwell Publishers.

Kaplan, R. S. and Norton, D. P. (1996), *The balanced scorecard: translating strategy into action*, Boston: Harvard Business School Press.

Nanni, A. J. and Vollmann, T. E. (1992), *New Performance Challenge: Measuring Operations for World-Class Competition*, Dow Jones-Irwin/Apics Series in Production Management, Illinois.

Shank, J. K. (1989) *Strategic Cost Analysis: The Evolution from Managerial to Strategic Accounting*, New York: McGraw Hill.

Tyndall, G. R. (1998), *Supercharging supply chains: new ways to increase value through global operational excellence*, New York: Wiley and Sons.

Reverse logistics

Olaf Schatteman

2.12

A critical area of the supply chain is reverse logistics. Traditionally defined as the process of moving product from its point of consumption through channel members to the point of origin to recapture value or ensure proper disposal, this chapter uses a more holistic definition. Reverse logistics includes activities to avoid returns, to reduce materials in the forward system so that fewer materials flow back, and to ensure the possible reuse and recycling of materials.

Reverse logistics moves product from the point of consumption to the point of origin to recapture value or ensure proper disposal.

Returns can affect every channel member from consumers, retailers and wholesalers to manufacturers. Returns are caused for different reasons depending on who initiates them – end consumer, wholesaler or retailer and manufacturer – and on the nature of the materials involved – packaging or products. Reusable packaging is becoming more and more common, especially in Europe where manufacturers are required to take back packaging materials. This chapter will focus mainly on reverse supply chain for products.

The size of reverse logistics is considerable. According to Stock et al (2001), reverse logistics costs are as high as 4 per cent of total logistics costs, which amounts to an estimated \$35 billion in 2001 for the US alone. Consumers cause most product returns. According to a survey of 311 logistics managers in the US in 1998, average consumer returns across retailers are 6 per cent. Table 2.12.1 shows the return percentages for different industries.

Characteristics of reverse logistics

The reasons for returning products can be distinguished by where the returns initiated. Listed below are the main return reasons for each supply chain partner.

Table 2.12.1
Percentage of returns by industry

Industry	Percentage
Book publishing	10–30%
Magazine publishing – special interest	50%
Computer manufacturers	10–20%
Direct to consumer computer manufacturers	2–5%
Apparel	35%
Mass merchandisers	4–15%
Auto industry (parts)	4–6%
Internet retailers	20–80%

Source: Adapted from Dawe, 1995

Customer not satisfied

Consumers may take advantage of a money-back guarantee, have problems with product installation or return a product because it is faulty.

Most manufacturers and retailers allow customers to return products if they do not meet their demands within a predefined period. Money-back guarantees are standard practice for most direct sales channels. Consumers and retailers will sometimes abuse the return policies of manufacturers. Consumers wanting to try a new product will sometimes abuse the 'not satisfied, money-back' guarantee and simply return the product within allotted return period and receive their money back.

Installation or usage problems

Some customers experience problems with installation or usage of their recently acquired products. They perceive the product to be defective, while the reason for dissatisfaction is actually caused by difficult set-up or installation procedures or unclear instructions. This is a common problem in the computer industry where in some categories such as CD-ROM drives, return rates of 25 to 40 per cent are not uncommon. Complicated installation procedures and a lack of clear and simple instructions exacerbate the issue.

Warranty claims

Defective products or parts can be sent back to retailers or the manufacturer for repair. Products might either be dead on arrival, not working according to specifications or cosmetically damaged. This could happen either to the retailer or the end consumer. Alternatively, products might break down during the course of their life cycle. If the product is still within the warranty period extended by the manufacturer customers might return their product to the manufacturer or if that period has expired, customers could take up other options such as taking the product to a specialist repair center.

Faulty order processing

Both end consumers and retailers can experience shipping problems. Products need to be delivered in full and on time or customers can make claims against manufacturers and return (part of) their shipment. Examples of delivery problems are incomplete shipments or missing parts, wrong quantities, wrong products, duplicate shipments and untimely delivery, which can cause the customer to miss out on the intended use of the product.

Shipping problems, unsold stock, the end of a life cycle or serious product flaws can prompt the return of a product.

Retail overstock

Manufacturers can provide resellers with the luxury of returning unsold stock. This is a common practice in the book industry, for example. Retailers that need to make their accounting figures look good for the end of quarter or month will sometimes send significant amounts of unsold stock back for credits, only to reorder it again after the end of a financial period.

End of product life cycle or product replacement

Once a product has reached the end of its lifecycle, many manufacturers want to get it out of the retailers' shelves as soon as possible to prevent sales cannibalization of the new version. This means that the old products have to be disposed of. Manufacturers either have to take the stock back, based upon the conditions agreed with the retailers, or the latter need to dump the old version quickly.

Manufacture recall programs

Serious flaws in a product can lead to a recall, instigated either by the manufacturer or a government agency. Common recalls appear in the automotive, pharmaceutical, and the toy industry. Aside from the safety issues in such situations, getting the discredited product out of circulation and into designated storage centers as soon as possible is a crucial part of damage limitation strategies. It is a grim deadline that any company would prefer not to have to meet, but many do. The US Consumer Product Safety Commission in 1999 reported 304 corrective actions involving over 75 million consumer product units of various types that either violated mandatory safety standards or presented a substantial risk of injury to the public.

Other complications

The green factor

New environmental laws are being enacted worldwide and more stringent compliance to these laws is required. The laws are often accompanied with serious financial implications. The few managers who implemented reverse logistics in the past usually did so because it was environmentally responsible. Today, the green factor has evolved to a bottom-line issue. In the past once a product left the

Environmental and economic considerations have led to manufacturers taking their products back at the end of their lifetime.

manufacturer's factory doors the responsibility to dispose of the product also disappeared. However, legislation in Europe and in the US is changing, sometimes even making manufacturers responsible for disposal of the product at the end of its life cycle, such as in Germany.

Previously manufacturers could easily dispose of products in a landfill; today there are strict environmental regulations as to how much and what can be dumped. Certain hazardous materials such as chemicals and heavy metals are banned from disposal in landfills, while other products are banned because they can be recycled and therefore should not take up valuable landfill space. Landfill costs have also increased steadily. These environmental reasons along with economic considerations cause a growing number of manufacturers to take their products back at the end of their lifetime.

Electronic commerce

The emergence of selling via the Internet has led to many companies focusing on their reverse logistics capability; with the rise of electronic business channels, there has been a significant increase in consumer returns. Some electronic retailers estimate that up to 50 per cent of their goods sold on the Internet are returned. e-commerce has propelled the amount of returned products to levels demanding every executive's attention.

For electronics and high-technology products, electronic retailers report return percentages in certain product categories of up to 80 per cent. Any manufacturer not paying attention to reverse logistics is basically siphoning profits from the bottom line. With online transactions growing fast, independent analysts, Gartner and Jupiter Media Metrix, expect overall returns to increase drastically over the next few years. The emergence of e-business does not only pose a threat but also an opportunity to improve the total cost of returns. New business models also allow companies to redesign their entire reverse logistics capability in their own and their customer's favor. How this can be done will be discussed later in this chapter.

Shorter product life cycles

Product life cycles of many products, especially in the electronics and high technology industry have reduced drastically. This has led to advanced supply chains to move product out to customers with minimal stock, because obsolescence rates are high and the value of finished goods inventory of computer equipment loses up to 12 per cent per month. Equally important, therefore, are the speed and cycle time with which returned products can be turned around. This will have a tremendous impact on the company's bottom line. Very few companies, however, appear to be giving the manufacturer inventory visibility on returned items. Manufacturers often only learn when the products hit the unloading docks at their warehouses.

Complex and underdeveloped area

The traditional view, however, is that reverse logistics adds no value to the supply chain and places retailers and manufacturers under additional financial pressure. The state of awareness and development of reverse logistics is analogous to that of inbound logistics 10 to 20 years ago. Where firms once only concentrated on physical distribution and gave little attention to inbound materials management, so, too, do many organizations give little attention to reverse logistics. This is demonstrated by the fact that there are few dedicated resources in charge of managing the entire returns process.

When logistics managers suddenly have to throw their supply chain into reverse, they face all kinds of problems.

Many departments own a piece of the process, customer service, logistics, operations, accounting and sales. Behind every returned-goods transaction are complex inventory control, information management, cost accounting and disposal processes. It especially becomes complex in the pharmaceutical industry where returns management is placed under strict regulations of drug enforcement bodies. Organizations handling returns must be licensed and are subject to audits. When there are discrepancies between what a pharmacist claims has been returned and what the manufacturer received investigative procedures take place and parties can be fined.

Another key issue is that most supply chains are specifically designed to go forward. When logistics managers suddenly have to throw their supply chain into reverse they face all kinds of problems that have not been accounted for in the logistics system. This is especially the case with recall programs. When a company does not have the right solution or does not have a plan at all, it could lead to serious problems, particularly if the consumer's safety is involved.

Dr R. Dawe (1995) has described a number of symptoms that indicate whether a company could have a problem with its reverse supply chain. They are: returns arriving faster than processing or disposal; large amount of returns inventory held in the warehouse; unidentified or unauthorized returns; lengthy processing times; unknown total cost of the returns process; and customers losing confidence in the repair process. Supply chain executives recognizing any of these symptoms should find some ways to alleviate their organization's problems in the next section.

Attacking the returns challenge

The volume and the method of processing returns drive the total cost of returns. Companies can reduce the costs associated with returns considerably through a number of different ways and even use their capabilities as a competitive weapon. The most important levers an organization can use to make their returns work best are outlined below. Companies can change the way they are organized to manage returns, alter the way they process returns, use advanced technology

Companies can use their returns process capabilities as a competitive weapon.

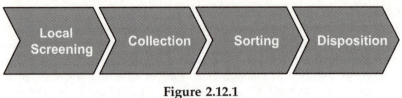

Figure 2.12.1
Four key steps in the returns process

to process more efficiently and to prevent returns or ultimately outsource their entire returns supply chain.

Improving the process

The four key steps involved in a returns process are local screening, collection, sorting and disposition, as shown in Figure 2.12.1.

Local screening

Screening products at the point of collection helps to ensure correct decisions are made and excessive costs are avoided.

Local screening is done at the point of collection of the returned products. Often products enter the supply chain that should not enter in the first place and cause unnecessary transportation, administration and handling costs. In an ideal reverse supply chain, products are screened at the point of collection according to specifications of the manufacturer. Disposition, however, changes based on the product (or its version), the vendor and the retailer. Therefore, complex decision mechanisms need to be maintained to allow disposition of product based on customer agreement on a product-by-product basis. With the ubiquitous presence of the Internet plenty of opportunities exist to do this in a cost efficient and effective way. This will be discussed in more detail in the Technology section.

A good example of effective local screening is the process implemented by Nintendo, the video game manufacturer. Nintendo rewarded retailers financially for registering the product and name of the purchaser at the time of sale. This allowed the retailer and Nintendo to determine when the warranty of a product had expired and also whether the product was returned within the allotted time window. To facilitate this process, Nintendo designed special packaging with a see-through opening for retailers to scan the product serial number when the product was sold.

Another example of innovative local screening is a global copier manufacturer in Europe. It provided its field service technicians throughout Europe with a scanner connected to a handheld device, which determined if technicians had to return their defective spare parts to a central location in Europe for repair or refurbishment or whether they could dispose of the parts locally. On top of the system they worked with colored stickers that indicated the destination of the part to facilitate processing. They were able to reduce half the amount of parts returned through the system, which resulted in significant transport savings.

Collection

There are many different ways to collect the products that are destined to enter the reverse supply chain. Retailers often have to send their return products back to their suppliers' different warehouses throughout the country. Different processes need to be set up to facilitate timely processing of these returns. This can often be very complicated and confusing for both retailers and manufacturers as they are dealing with multiple parties, many of whom are concentrating on getting products out to the customer, rather then back to the source.

Different systems are needed to process returns, particularly because of the complexity of the process and the multiple parties involved.

Many companies have trouble running a logistics system in forward, let alone running one in reverse in parallel at the same time. Some companies have set up central collection centers for collecting and sorting returns, which have proven to be very effective. Ford in the US, for example, is now using one single carrier to handle all its returned spare parts. Simultaneously, it has provided the dealers with one single 800 number for all their issues with returned parts. Subaru of America has gone one step further: it has outsourced the entire returns collection to Roadway Express' reverse logistics subsidiary, Rexsis. The dealers call one toll-free number regardless of the issue and Roadway Express handles all inquiries.

Sorting

Some large retailers have been using centralized return centers (CRCs) for many years. They have selected centralized return centers dedicated to handle their entire reverse logistics operations. The advantages of using centralized return centers are numerous. When a company dedicates an entire facility, organization and system to optimize the handling of returns, benefits arise from a whole range of areas. Some of the key benefits are: efficiency can increase as employees occupy positions full-time and can focus on handling returns only, experience in the sorting process will help employees make better and quicker disposition decisions, and cycle times will improve, resulting in better asset recovery and higher customer satisfaction. GM in the US, for example, has in cooperation with UPS centralized its parts return center. Dealers once returned parts to some 200 locations, which was very confusing. Today all returned parts – 30 000 a month – go to the Orion facility.

CRCs are often more efficient and result in better asset recovery and higher customer satisfaction.

In any case, whether it happens in a centralized way or not, sorting is a crucial step in the reverse logistics process because employees make decisions on what ultimately happens to the returned product. Complex business rules underlying these decisions need to be updated continuously and designed so that employees can implement the rules easily. Use of bar code scanners connected to a database that contains those business rules speeds up the process and avoids judgmental errors. Information technology is a key in this process and will be discussed in more detail later. In the near future use of radio frequency (RF) tags can automate this process even further. RF tags are already used on expensive products, however their current price does not yet allow them to be applied to mass consumer goods.

Disposition

Three ways to dispose of product can be distinguished: sell as-is, repair or reuse (part of it) and ultimately dispose of the product. Some key activities within each of these categories are:

- Sell as-is:
  - resale (as new)
  - sell via outlet or discount store
  - e-auction, and
  - sell to secondary market
- Repair or reuse:
  - repair
  - refurbish or remanufacture
  - modify and
  - recycle
- Dispose:
  - scrap
  - donate (to charity), and
  - dispose in secure manner (for example, certain drugs).

Disposition should be done to maximize the value of reclaimed goods or dispose of the goods in the most cost-effective way. Below are some innovative ways leading practice companies have adopted to improve the disposition of their returned items.

Create profit centers

Some companies have gone as far as to create profit centers around their returns process. This focuses the organization on maximizing the prices they will get for the goods by exploring innovative ways to sell their returned goods. Manufacturers refurbish the product and auction it through the Internet or redeploy it to, say, outlet stores. A key problem in selling returned goods is price setting. Experts in sales and marketing techniques usually set prices for new products. Returned goods prices are frequently determined through negotiation.

However, one thing organizations need to watch out for when reselling their returned items in general, and in particular when setting up profit centers around returns, is cannibalization; the returned goods channels can potentially steal clients away from the primary products and channels. A clearly defined channel and pricing strategy needs to take this into account. More brand-sensitive companies for example will take back returns to keep them from being sold through alternate channels, and then sell them in their own highly profitable outlet stores. In the publishing industry, some publishers have contracts with certain authors that prohibit their titles going to alternate channels to protect their 'brand' name.

e-auction
To obtain the highest prices for returned items, some service providers have set up capabilities to coordinate returns and help manufacturers recoup some of their costs by reselling returned goods on Internet auction sites. One example is ReturnBuy.com, a Virginia-based company in the US that serves the high technology and computer industries. The company uses an Internet-based yield optimization technology to resell goods online. It claims it enables its customers to obtain a much higher price for the goods than through the average liquidator. Another example is the industrial automotive industry, where some manufacturers have set up B2B web sites where customers can buy second hand equipment or certain spares from each other, negotiating on the web site. The selling customer then simply ships the equipment or part directly to the web site buyer.

Change to leading practice organizational structure
One way of dealing with reverse logistics is to segment the supply chain into separate forward and reverse organizations. If a logistics organization deals with both forward and reverse product flows, the focus will predominantly be on forward product logistics. Often physical constraints, such as the number of docks and processing space in distribution centers, can limit an organization's capability to effectively handle both logistics flows. When executives have to make decisions around shipping new product out versus processing returned goods, the decision is usually made in favor of the first.

Segmenting the supply chain into separate forward and reverse organizations can improve efficiency.

As mentioned, the creation of profit centers around the returns process is a way of maximizing the value from returned products. Estée Lauder has, after a very successful reverse logistics project, created a $250 million product line from its return goods flow, now representing the third most profitable product line within the company. Centralized return centers have also proven to be a successful way for companies to handle returns more quickly and efficiently. Cost savings most often are realized in labor, due to scale and dedication, and transport, due to consolidation of freight.

Outsourcing is another way of effectively organizing the returns process. Several leading manufacturers and retailers, such as Compaq, Thomson, Target and 3M, have very successfully outsourced their returns processes to competent, dedicated solution providers. Ultimately, companies such as Dell have taken structural steps to avoid the majority of returned products by developing a build-to-order or configure-to-order operating model, which addresses the underlying issues of why returns occur in the first place. These business models are, however, not applicable to every industry or product.

Implement state-of-the-art information technology

Collecting the right information to allocate and accurately calculate debits and credits is crucial for manufacturers and distributors.

Not many leading software manufacturers offer specialized capabilities to handle reverse logistics. The maintenance, repair and overhaul functions in enterprise resource planning (ERP) suites from vendors such as Baan, Great Plains and Oracle provide some support for reverse logistics processes. A number of specialized companies have developed packages to deal with returns. While integration with back office functions remains an issue, the widespread use of Internet technology has substantially improved the way different supply chain partners can communicate with each other. Online return capabilities and electronic processing of returns drastically increase the speed with which returns can be handled, increase customer satisfaction and can reduce costs by more than 400 per cent. According to the Gartner Group, electronic handling of returns costs $4.05 versus $25 if the return is handled by a call center. Information technology should be used in every step of the reverse logistics process, from local screening right through to disposition.

In the local screening process, customers and retailers can simply go to the manufacturer's website, search by stock keeping unit (SKU) or order number to identify the product to be returned, and check its return parameters to see if it can be returned and how to do it. For example, the customer can enter the details of the return on the web site and drop the product in a specified location such as the local post office. If the software can also capture the reason for return, it can determine disposition up front, cutting transportation costs and processing time.

Collection is also simplified as manufacturers have a much better understanding in advance of how many products are to be returned and where they are located so that freight can be combined. An example of a sophisticated solution is Return Valet by catalog retailer Spiegel Inc. In cooperation with Newgistics and local post centers, Spiegel has developed a capability where customers can return their mail-ordered product to a local post office. The clerk validates and checks the return procedure online, prints a receipt with credit amount and sends the product back to Spiegel's distribution center, which issues the credit when the product arrives. Collecting the right information from customers and retailers in order to be able to allocate and accurately calculate debits and credits is crucial for manufacturers and distributors.

If product return information is entered into a system at point of return and matched with the product's bar code or product number, it will considerably ease matching and issuing of credits before sorting the goods. Managing returns online can contribute significantly to this process by, for example, using screens that force customers to enter required data, so receiving companies can keep track of required information to process returns quickly and accurately. In the disposal process, as described earlier, Internet technology can also contribute by providing online auction services to maximize revenues from returned goods. Alternatively it can be used to connect to third party logistics providers to arrange for a quick and proper pick-up of returned products and transport to their next destination.

In the central sorting process, information technology helps employees in the complex decision making process of final destination of the returned product. The computer maintenance company DecisionOne, for example, uses Kirus software, which includes its customers' (Compaq, Dell, Sun) own decision rules for deciding whether to repair, disassemble for parts, redeploy or scrap returned products.

Finally new information technologies can be used to analyse return reasons and provide valuable information to prevent future returns. The next section will deal with this topic in more detail. Many companies are, however, still developing proprietary software to manage their reverse logistics process. Price of available systems and cost of integrating existing packaged systems is often mentioned as a reason for their internally developed systems.

Analyse to prevent returns

Root-cause analysis should be at the heart of every reverse logistics system. A return goods management system provides a window into manufacturers' faults. Companies need to look beyond the processing of returns to reduce their reverse supply chain cost. The real benefit comes from sharing information with design, production, packaging and other departments on such things as what products are coming back and why they are coming back. This way reverse logistics systems can nip return problems 'in the bud'. Companies that concentrate solely on improving returns processes will miss significant cost saving opportunities. A good reverse logistics system includes proper data collection and effective reporting. To understand a consumer's reason for returning a good, companies must collect structured and consistent data concerning the reason for the return and the product and its condition. With this information, trends should be analysed in individual products and consumer segments to determine root causes.

Analysing data on why customers return goods can provide insight into faults and help to reduce reverse supply chain costs.

Mitigating the front-end process by providing front-end customer service and technical support can also help companies reduce returns. Some manufacturers, for example, ask customers for a serial number of their printer when they order cartridges to ensure they receive the correct types. Another good example is Sharp consumer electronics. At one time at least half of the products returned were in perfect working order. To counter this they added simple but effective elements to their reverse logistics program. Through analysing return reasons Sharp could significantly reduce its VCR returns by making products easier to set up. Now, for example, the clock on the VCR is set automatically, the owner's manual has been simplified and customers are encouraged to call a prominently displayed toll-free number when they have installation problems.

Outsource the returns process

Outsourcing of the returns process is also occurring on a more frequent basis and seems to be an alternative to avoid high investments in reverse logistics e-capabilities. Manufacturers such as Compaq, Dell, Cisco and 3M and retailers such as Sears have outsourced the handling of the reverse flow of goods. These companies decided the handling of returned goods was not a core competency and saw significant benefits in taking the flow of returned goods out of their distribution centers and placing it into the operations of outsourcers. These outsource suppliers have become specialists in managing the reverse flow of goods and can achieve economies of scale. They are often in a much better position to handle the returned goods and can provide value-added services such as refurbishment.

Successful reverse logistics projects

Throughout this chapter many companies have been named that have engaged in one way or another successful reverse logistics projects. A good example of a complete reverse logistics program is a project by cosmetics manufacturer Estée Lauder. The firm used to dump $60 million of its products into landfills each year, destroying more than a third of the name brand cosmetics returned by retailers. Estée Lauder made a small investment of $1.3 million to build its proprietary reverse logistics system of scanners, business intelligence tools linked to an Oracle database. The company has apparently recovered its investment in the first year through reducing labor and other costs.

Estée Lauder has reduced its production and inventory levels through its increased ability to put returned goods back on the market and the availability of better data on the reasons for returns. In the first year Estée Lauder was able to evaluate 24 per cent more returned products, redistribute 150 per cent more of its returns, reduce the destroyed products from 37 per cent to 27 per cent and save about $0.5 million in labor costs. After implementation, Estée Lauder even considered making the system commercially available through a consulting firm that could serve as a reseller of the software.

When companies decide to embark on a reverse logistics project they can leverage knowledge, tools and processes from other successful projects such as Estée Lauder's, to prevent them from reinventing the wheel. Together with specialist service providers in the reverse logistics arena, significant improvements can be made to reduce costs, improve customer service and increase revenues.

Conclusion

The economic demand for reverse logistics capabilities is driven by two different factors; first, companies are starting to realize the economic value of sound returns management, and second, legal environmental developments are requiring manufacturers to be fully responsible for products over their entire life cycle. Online retailing and shortening product life cycles, mainly in the electronics and high technology sector, have increased the pressure to build strong capabilities in this area, or to outsource the handling of reverse logistics flow. Organizations currently have many opportunities for improving the way they manage their returns, from improving the process and using more sophisticated software to changing the organization or outsourcing the entire process. Smart executives will be looking to capture the value that is locked within the reverse supply chain.

Organizations have many opportunities for improving the way they manage their product returns.

References

Atkinson, H. (2001), 'Moving Faster', *Reverse: The Journal of Commerce* (23 April).

Blumberg, D. F. (1999), 'Strategic examination of reverse logistics & repair service requirements, needs, market size, and opportunities', *Journal of Business Logistics*, vol. 20 (no. 2), pp. 141–159.

Dawe, R. L. (1995), 'Reengineer your returns', *Transportation and Distribution* (August).

Dugan, J. L. (1998), 'Boldly Going Where Others are Bailing Out', *Business Week* (6 April).

Electronic Commerce News (2001), 'It's reverse logistics, stupid', *Electronic Commerce News* (28 May).

Koller, M. (2001), 'Service eases return process', *Internetweek* (10 September).

PR Newswire (2001), 'Retailers unprepared to re-sell growing number of goods returned online' (10 May).

Richardson, H. (2001), 'Logistics in reverse', *UMI Industry Week* (April).

Stock, J. R. & Lambert, D. M. (2001), *Strategic Logistics Management*. 4th edn. Boston, MA: McGraw-Hill/Irwin.

Part 3

Supply Chain Integration and Collaboration

Part 3 shifts the focus from operational excellence to supply chain integration and collaboration. We believe this will be the area of most benefit in the foreseeable future and one with which the supply chain practitioner needs to become the most familiar.

Chapter 3.1, 'Creating agile supply chains', describes the two goals of agility and leanness to be pursued by organizations today. Agility means achieving a rapid response on a global scale to constantly changing markets, and leanness being about doing more with less. Martin Christopher describes how supply chain strategies can marry the benefits of both 'lean' and 'agile' philosophies.

Chapter 3.2, 'Supply chain structures to deliver value', provides approaches for configuring supply chains, with an emphasis on selecting supply chain partners that complement company objectives. The structure of supply chains is also particularly relevant as technology continues to enable supply chain improvements and markets expect supply chains to increase shareholder value.

Chapter 3.3, 'Supply chain planning', introduces advanced intelligence to the discussion of how businesses must operate in an increasingly complex and volatile environment. The authors elaborate on the fact that supply chain planning presents a real competitive advantage as it enables companies to maximize collaborative relationships in the supply chain to drive optimal planning decisions across organizational boundaries. The chapter describes the fundamental elements of supply chain planning and provides a historical overview of the convergence of all the elements in today's integrated planning software suites.

Chapter 3.4, 'Strategic sourcing and procurement', addresses how purchasing has evolved over the last few decades. Purchasing decisions are in many ways now more complex than they used to be and the days of just selecting the supplier with the lowest quoted cost are over. As organizations strive to differentiate themselves from their competitors, they must look to alternative methods to cut cost and improve services. The chapter discusses how procurement professionals can achieve procurement excellence and secure a competitive advantage for their organization. It provides frameworks, and concepts and tools to enable strategic sourcing.

Chapter 3.5, 'Securing immediate benefits from e-sourcing', picks up the powerful combination of logistics and e-commerce in procurement. The authors introduce a new form of procurement termed 'dynamic trading' and discuss how a buying organization can use emerging e-sourcing technologies to achieve the best possible outcome – speedily and effectively. Particular techniques discussed are reverse alignment and e-auctions.

Chapter 3.6, 'Industry-level collaboration through ECR', explores the issues behind sub-optimizing behavior in supply chains and describes collaboration at the industry level among trading partners and competitors. An example shows how the grocery industry has tackled the breaking down of the walls of mistrust between channel partners to allow the focus of their joint activities to become one of delighting the consumer, and doing so more profitably.

Chapter 3.7, 'Collaborative product commerce', describes a business capability that captures processes, technologies and competencies across dispersed locations and organizations to accelerate and achieve fast and efficient product development across the supply chain. The chapter introduces information systems that capture and manage innovative processes, emerging technologies and the competencies of all product team members.

Chapter 3.8, 'Integrated fulfilment', is a business practice that has regained attention in the context of new Internet-based business models. While traditional approaches to fulfilment often have been overly focused on the physical flows of goods or on optimizing the technology, the authors describe the next level of fulfilment best practice. At this level, the supply chain is viewed as a series of events that must be managed to meet customers' expectations for product delivery and achieve excellence.

Chapter 3.9, 'Information systems strategy for supply chains', rounds off Part 3 by emphasizing the importance of technical and applications architectures in supply chains. Many successful firms have used information technology to support their business strategies and these companies have realized opportunities to enhance their supply chain.

Creating agile supply chains

3.1

Martin Christopher

Continuous change is not a new phenomenon for supply chain managers. However, the rate, scale and unpredictability of change in today's business environment are seriously challenging supply chains that are based on best practice of the 1990s. Significant barriers exist – both within a company and between its upstream and downstream partners – to achieving the level of responsiveness needed across the whole supply chain.

Agility means achieving a rapid response on a global scale to constantly changing markets.

Supply chain professionals of the new millennium will have to contend with the challenges posed by the fact that markets are turbulent, and changing rapidly and unpredictably. Ever greater rates of technological innovation in products and processes are needed, as are shorter product life cycles. Mass markets are fragmenting into niche markets, while product standardization is being replaced by the demand for 'mass customization'. Customers are looking for the delivery of complete 'solutions', comprising products and services. And all of these have to be achieved at less cost!

To meet these challenges, organizations need to adopt a new operating paradigm. This chapter describes how a key factor is the creation of an agile supply chain on a worldwide scale. Agility means rapid strategic and operational adaptation to large-scale, unpredictable changes in the business environment. Agility focuses upon eliminating the barriers to quick response, be they organizational or technical. Organizations that achieve agility achieve responsiveness from one end of the supply chain to the other.

What is agility?

Agility and leanness are different. Leanness is about doing more with less. Agility means flexibility and effectiveness.

Agility is a business-wide capability that embraces organizational structures, information systems, logistics processes and, in particular, mindsets. A key characteristic of an agile organization is flexibility. Indeed, the origin of agility as a business concept lies in flexible manufacturing systems. Initially it was thought that the route to manufacturing flexibility was through automation to enable rapid change (through reduced set-up times) and thus a greater responsiveness to changes in product mix or volume. Later, this idea of manufacturing flexibility was extended into the wider business context and the concept of agility as an organizational orientation was born.

Agility should not be confused with 'leanness'. Leanness is about doing more with less. The term is often used in connection with lean manufacturing to imply a 'zero inventory', just-in-time approach. Paradoxically, many companies that have adopted lean manufacturing as a business practice are anything but agile in their supply chains. The car industry in many ways illustrates this conundrum. The origins of lean manufacturing can be traced to the Toyota Production System (TPS), with its focus on the reduction and elimination of waste.

While the lessons learned from the Toyota principles have had a profound impact on manufacturing practices in a wide range of industries around the world, the benefits of lean thinking have been restricted mostly within the four walls of the factory. Thus, we encounter the paradoxical situation where vehicle assembly is extremely efficient with throughput time in the factory typically down to 12 hours or less, yet inventory of finished vehicles can be as high as two months' of sales. And still, customers have to wait for weeks or even months to get the car of their choice!

While leanness may be an element of agility in certain circumstances, by itself it will not enable the organization to meet the precise needs of the customer more rapidly. *Webster's Dictionary* makes the distinction clearly when it defines lean as 'containing little fat' whereas agile is defined as 'nimble'. Table 3.1.1 contrasts the main characteristics of the two philosophies.

A lean approach makes sense in certain conditions, in particular where demand is predictable and the requirement for variety is low and volume is high. In fact, these are the very conditions in which Toyota developed its lean philosophy. However, problems arise when the philosophy is implanted into situations where demand is less predictable, the requirement for variety is high and, consequently, volume at the individual stock keeping unit (SKU) level is low. Surprisingly, these characteristics are more typical of the Western automobile industry, which suggests that firms may have been misguided in their attempts to adopt a lean model in conditions to which it is not suited.

Table 3.1.1
Characteristics of lean and agile strategies

	Lean	Agile
Primary focus:	Efficiency	Effectiveness
Product features:	Standard	High variety
Product life cycle:	Long	Short
Order winners:	Cost	Time
Supply chain emphasis:	Economies of scale	Flexibility
Capacity utilization:	Level scheduling	Deploy buffer capacity
Supplier selection criteria:	Price and quality	Speed, flexibility and quality

Figure 3.1.1 suggests that the three critical dimensions of variety/variability (or predictability) and volume determine which approach – agile or lean – makes greater sense.

Agility might, therefore, be defined as the ability of an organization to respond rapidly to changes in demand, in terms of both volume and variety. The market conditions in which many companies find themselves are characterized by volatile and unpredictable demand. Hence the increased urgency of the search for agility.

Agile businesses can respond rapidly to changes in demand, both volume and variety.

A further factor that has an impact on decisions about supply chain strategy is the total end-to-end lead time of supply. It is a paradoxical feature of many supply chains today that for all the focus on time compression, lead times are often longer than before. One major

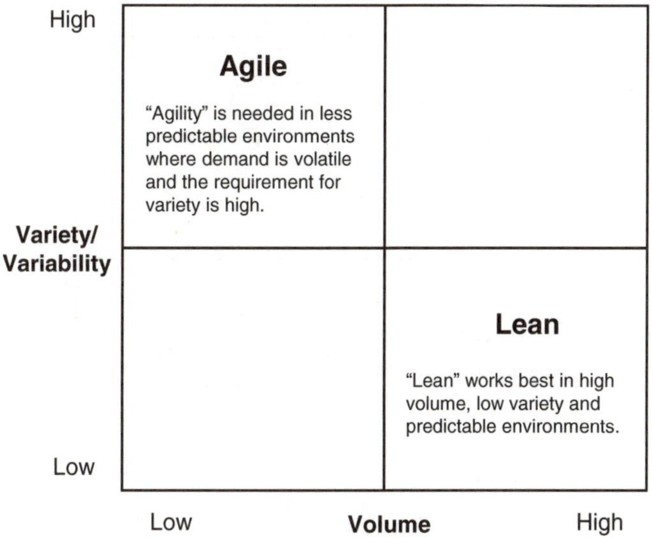

Figure 3.1.1
Agile or lean?

reason for this is the widespread move to off-shore sourcing and manufacturing. Products that used to be sourced or manufactured on a local-for-local basis now often travel halfway around the world as companies seek lower costs of purchasing or manufacturing. Clearly, if total pipeline times are extended, then there will be an impact on the potential responsiveness of the system.

The lead time of re-supply should be compared against the predictability of demand. Obviously if supply lead times are short and demand is predictable then the situation is rather different from a situation of unpredictable demand with long lead times!

Figure 3.1.2 suggests some of the alternative supply chain options that might apply in the context of different demand and supply characteristics.

Unpredictable demand calls for agile solutions, with a focus on time compression and quick response.

Briefly, considering each quadrant of the matrix in turn, we can see how the characteristics of supply and demand combine to influence the choice of supply chain strategy. The bottom left hand corner presents few problems for the supply chain planner: lead times are short and demand is predictable. Here the risk is low and hence a strategy of continuous replenishment and 'make-to-rate' supply can be adopted.

At the other extreme, in the top right-hand corner of the matrix, supply lead times are long and demand is uncertain. Here the first priority should be to seek ways to compress time in the pipeline. The second priority should be to explore opportunities for 'postponement'. The idea of postponement will be explored in more detail later but essentially it involves holding inventory in a generic form, in the fewest locations, and only finishing or finally configuring the product once real demand is known.

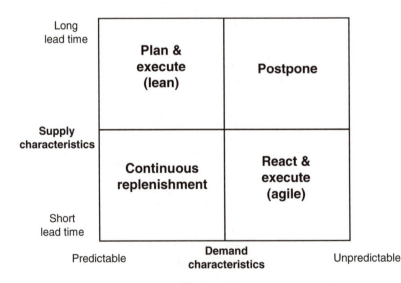

Figure 3.1.2
Demand/supply characteristics determine supply chain strategy

Finally, the two other corners of the matrix, top left and bottom right, suggest 'lean' and 'agile' solutions respectively. As lean solutions are possible, where demand is predictable organizations can make decisions against forecasts with little risk. Conversely, conditions of unpredictable demand call for agile solutions and hence the focus has to be on time compression and quick response.

Creating hybrid strategies

'Lean' and 'agile' are not mutually exclusive concepts. Ideally, organizations should seek to create hybrid supply chain strategies that marry the two philosophies to achieve the most cost-effective solution. Three strategies combining lean and agile ideas are described below.

Supply chain strategies can marry the benefits of both 'lean' and 'agile' philosophies.

Using the 80:20 rule

Many companies manufacturing or distributing a range of products will find that the Pareto law will apply and they can exploit the law to determine supply strategy. Typically, an analysis of the business will show that the 80:20 (or similar) rule holds. In other words, 80 per cent of total volume will be generated from just 20 per cent of the total product line. The way in which these 20 per cent are managed should probably be quite different from the way the remaining 80 per cent are managed.

It could be argued, for example, that, on the one hand, the top 20 per cent of products by volume are likely to be more predictable and hence they lend themselves to lean principles of manufacturing and distribution. On the other hand, the slow-moving 80 per cent will be less predictable typically and will require a more agile mode of management. Figure 3.1.3 suggests one generic way in which supply chain strategies may be devised for the predictable 20 per cent and the more volatile 80 per cent of products.

In this case, it is suggested that the volume products can be made to forecast ahead of demand. The focus should be on achieving efficiency and cost-minimization and seeking economies of scale in procurement and manufacturing.

However, the slow-moving 'tail' of the distribution, which may be as much as 80 per cent of the range, needs to be managed differently. Forecasts will be needed still, but they will be aggregated to enable capacity to be planned; execution at the item level will be against actual orders. Wherever possible, if inventory is held at all, it should be as modules, sub-assemblies or generic materials to enable maximum flexibility. Paradoxically, although demand for these items may be low, they should be given priority in the production schedule to enable agility. In some instances, different manufacturing solutions may be appropriate, such as achieving flexibility through automation and set-up time reduction.

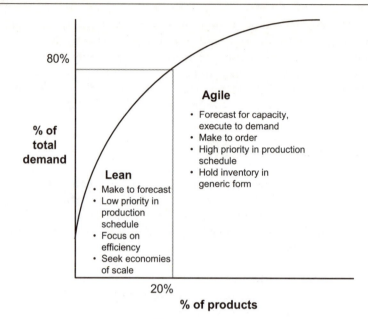

Figure 3.1.3
The Pareto distribution

The role of the 'decoupling point'

The decoupling point is the point at which real demand penetrates upstream in a supply chain.

A major problem in most supply chains is the limited visibility of real demand. As supply chains are often extended, with multiple levels of inventory between the point of production and the final marketplace, they tend to be forecast driven rather than demand driven.

The point at which real demand penetrates upstream in a supply chain may be termed the decoupling point. Previously, this idea has been termed the 'order penetration' point. However, the issue is not how far the order penetrates, but how far real demand is made visible. Orders are aggregations of demand, often delayed and distorted due to the actions and decisions of intermediaries. On the other hand, demand reflects the ongoing requirement in the final marketplace in as close to real time as possible.

The decoupling point should also dictate the form in which inventory is held. Thus, demand at the top level of Figure 3.1.4 is penetrating right to the point of manufacture and inventory is probably held in the form of components or materials. At the other extreme, demand at the bottom level is only visible at the end of the chain. Hence, inventory will be in the form of finished product. The aim of the agile supply chain should be to carry inventory in a generic form – that is, standard semi-finished products awaiting final assembly or localization. This is the concept of 'postponement', a vital element in any agile strategy, and one of the eight Supply Chain Principles.

Postponement, or delayed configuration, is based on the principle of seeking to design products using common platforms, components

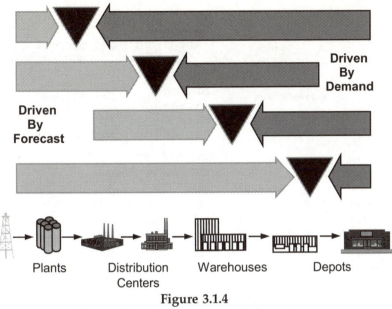

Figure 3.1.4
Decoupling points: a strategic inventory

or modules, but postponing the final assembly or customization until the final market destination or customer requirement is known.

Postponement strategy has several advantages. First, inventory can be held at a generic level so that fewer stock keeping variants are held and, hence, less inventory in total. Second, because the inventory is generic, its flexibility is greater, meaning that the same components, modules or platforms can be embodied in a variety of products.

Postponement can reduce inventory, increase flexibility, improve forecasting and enable mass customization.

Third, forecasting is easier at the generic level than at the level of the finished item. This last point is particularly relevant in global markets where local forecasts will be less accurate than a forecast for worldwide volume. Furthermore, the ability to customize products locally means that a higher level of variety may be offered at lower total cost, enabling strategies of 'mass customization' to be pursued.

The challenge to supply chain managers is to seek to develop 'lean' strategies up to the decoupling point but 'agile' strategies beyond that point. In other words, by using generic or modular inventory to postpone the final commitment, it should be possible to achieve volume-oriented economies of scale through product standardization. The flow of product up to the decoupling point may well be forecast driven; after the decoupling point it should be demand driven, as shown in Figure 3.1.5.

Importantly, there are actually *two* decoupling points. The first is the one already described: the 'material' decoupling point where strategic inventory is held in as generic a form as possible. This point ideally should lie as far downstream in the supply chain and as close to the final marketplace as possible. The second is the 'information'

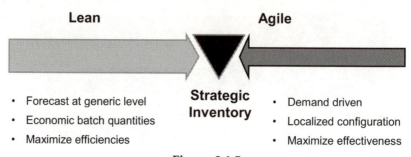

Lean **Agile**

Strategic Inventory

- Forecast at generic level
- Economic batch quantities
- Maximize efficiencies

- Demand driven
- Localized configuration
- Maximize effectiveness

Figure 3.1.5
A hybrid supply chain strategy

decoupling point. This should lie as far as possible upstream in the supply chain – it is in effect the furthest point to which information on real final demand penetrates. By managing these two decoupling points, organizations can create a powerful opportunity for creating an agile response.

Separation of 'base' and 'surge' demands

Base demand can be forecast based on history and met through lean procedures.

Other hybrid strategies that organizations have employed with success rely upon separating demand patterns into 'base' and 'surge' elements. Figure 3.1.6 highlights this distinction. Supply chain managers can forecast base demand using history, whereas they typically cannot forecast surge demand in this way. Base demand can be met through classic lean procedures to achieve economies of scale whereas surge demand is provided for through more flexible and, probably, higher-cost processes.

Strategies such as these are being employed increasingly in the fashion industry where the base demand can be sourced in low-cost countries and the surge demand 'topped up' locally, nearer to the

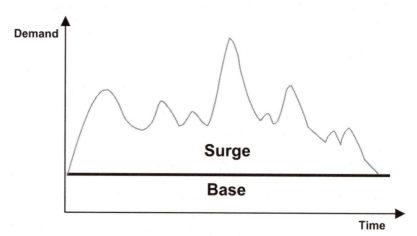

Figure 3.1.6
Characterizing demand through sales history

Table 3.1.2
A contingency approach to supply chain strategy choice

Hybrid strategies	Appropriate market conditions and operating environment
Pareto/80:20 Using lean methods for the volume lines, agile methods for the slow movers.	High levels of variety; demand is non-proportionate across the range.
Decoupling point The aim is to be lean up to the decoupling point and agile beyond it.	Possibility of modular production or intermediate inventory; delayed final configuration or distribution.
Surge/base demand separation Managing the forecastable element of demand using lean principles; using agile principles for the less predictable element.	Where base level of demand can confidently be predicted from past experience and where local manufacturing, small batch capacity is available.

market. Although the unit cost of manufacture in local markets will be higher than sourcing in low-cost locations, the supply chain advantage can be considerable. Alternatively, arrangements can be made for dealing with both 'base' and 'surge' demands either by separation in space (via separate production lines) or in time (by using slack periods to produce base stock). This contrasts with the lean concept of 'level scheduling'. The increased use of contract manufacturing and third-party logistics service providers is evidence of the search for flexibility during uncertain demand.

While these three strategies are complementary rather than mutually exclusive, it is likely that each may work better in certain conditions. A suggested set of appropriate conditions for the application of the three hybrid strategies is presented in Table 3.1.2.

The three lean and agile hybrid strategies confirm that the real focus of supply chain re-engineering should be on seeking ways in which organizations can achieve the appropriate combination of lean and agile strategies.

An integrated approach to supply chain design

Organizations can search for agile solutions to supply chain design through a systematic evaluation of market requirements and supply side characteristics. It is useful to consider the foundations for the creation of appropriate supply chain strategies drawing upon both the lean and agile methodologies. Figure 3.1.7 suggests a three-level framework summarizing the enablers for an agile supply chain.

Conventional views on manufacturing strategy, supplier relations and distribution have to be challenged to achieve real agility.

In this integrative model, Level 1 represents the important principles that underpin the agile supply chain, rapid replenishment and postponed fulfilment. Level 2 identifies the individual programs such as lean production, organizational agility and quick response that must be implemented in order for the Level 1 principles to be achieved. Level 3 specifies individual actions to be taken to support Level 2 programs, for example time compression, demand visibility and waste elimination. Not all the characteristics shown in Figure 3.1.7 may be necessary in any one specific market/manufacturing context, but it is likely that the agile supply chain will embody many of these elements. What is certain is that much of the conventional wisdom concerning manufacturing strategy, supplier relations and distribution will have to be challenged if real agility is to be achieved from within the supply chain.

Rapid replenishment, for example, requires agile suppliers, organizational agility and a demand-driven supply chain. Similarly, postponed fulfilment enables the adoption of lean production principles up to the decoupling point supported by agile capabilities

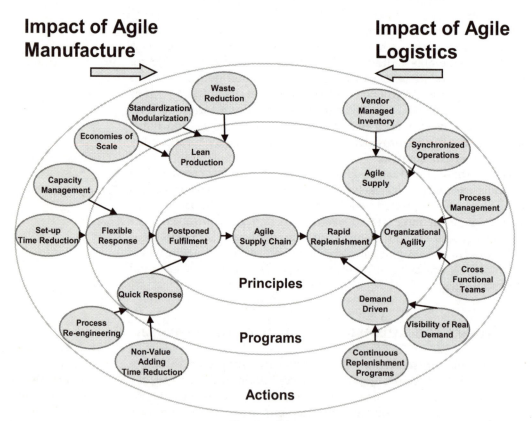

Figure 3.1.7
An integrated model for enabling the agile supply chain

beyond that point. Nor must organizational issues be forgotten, since they may be the single biggest barrier to effective change.

Creating an agile supply clearly requires a number of significant changes to the status quo. Supply chain managers today need also to be change managers – not just managing change within the organization, but managing change in the way that relationships between organizations are structured. The trend towards the creation of the 'virtual' organization, while likely to help achieve agility, also requires a high level of coordination and management.

One way to achieve this coordination is to make use of a 'pipeline integrator' or, as they have sometimes been termed, a fourth-party logistics service provider (4PL^{TM}). These organizations make use of their expertise and knowledge of managing global supply chains to ensure that even in complex networks a more agile response can be achieved.

A 4PL can achieve an agile response in complex global networks.

An example is the Hong Kong-based company Li & Fung. Originally it was a trading company that sourced and distributed products on behalf of its principals. Over the years Li & Fung has developed specific expertise and skills in managing and coordinating supply chains. For example, Li and Fung, on behalf of US retailer 'The Limited', will order undyed yarn from the yarn supplier, book weaving and dying capacity at fabric manufacturers' facilities, and schedule manufacturing capacity at garment factories – all in advance of the actual requirement being known. As The Limited gets a clearer view of the requirement for actual styles, colors and sizes, then Li & Fung will issue precise orders and manage the entire supply chain.

To be truly agile, a supply chain must possess several distinguishing characteristics, as Figure 3.1.8 highlights.

First, the agile supply chain is *market sensitive*: the supply chain is capable of reading and responding to real demand. Most organizations are forecast driven rather than demand driven. In other words, because they have little direct feed-forward from the marketplace by way of data on actual customer requirements they are forced to make forecasts based upon past sales or shipments and convert these forecasts into inventory. The breakthroughs of the last decade in the form of efficient consumer response (ECR) and information technology to capture data on demand, direct from the point-of-sale or point-of-use, are now transforming the organization's ability to hear the voice of the market and to respond directly.

An agile supply chain has four characteristics: it is market sensitive, virtual, network based and process aligned.

Second, the use of information technology to share data between buyers and suppliers is creating, in effect, a *virtual supply chain*. Virtual supply chains are information based rather than inventory based.

Conventional logistics systems are based upon a paradigm that seeks to identify the optimal quantities and the spatial location of inventory. Complex formulae and algorithms exist to support this inventory-based business model. Paradoxically, we are now learning that once visibility of demand is achieved through shared information,

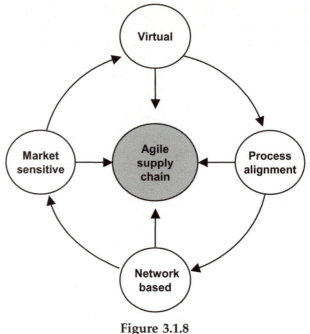

Figure 3.1.8
The agile supply chain

the premise upon which these formulae are based no longer holds. Electronic Data Interchange (EDI) and now the Internet have enabled partners in the supply chain to act upon the same data, that is real demand, rather than be dependent upon the distorted and noisy picture that emerges when orders are transmitted from one step to another in an extended chain.

Shared information between supply chain partners can only be fully used through *process alignment*, the third characteristic of agility. Process alignment means collaborative working between buyers and suppliers, joint product development, common systems and shared information. This form of cooperation in the supply chain is becoming ever more prevalent as companies focus on managing their core competencies and outsource all other activities. In this new world, a greater reliance on suppliers and alliance partners becomes inevitable and, hence, a new style of relationship is essential. In the 'extended enterprise' as it is often called, there can be no boundaries and an ethos of trust and commitment must prevail. Along with process alignment comes joint strategy determination, buyer-supplier teams, transparency of information and even open-book accounting.

The fourth ingredient of agility is the idea of the supply chain as a confederation of partners linked together as a *network*. Today individual businesses no longer compete as stand-alone entities but rather as supply chains. Organizations are now entering the era of 'network competition'. In this era, the prizes will go to those who can better structure, coordinate and manage their relationships with partners in a network where each member is committed to better, closer and more agile relationships with their final customers. In today's challenging global markets, the route to sustainable advantage lies in being able to capture the respective strengths and competencies of network partners to achieve greater responsiveness to market needs.

Conclusion

Managing the global supply chain requires a level of agility and responsiveness several magnitudes greater than that required in the old model of 'local-for-local' manufacturing. Increasingly, organizations will need to develop a business model that recognizes that competitive advantage is created through managing the supply chain as a single entity rather than through fragmented, locally focused decision-making units.

Achieving agility across the entire supply chain will give companies a global competitive advantage.

For the near future, leadership in global markets will belong to those organizations that exhibit greater agility than their counterparts. These companies will have the ability to adapt rapidly to large-scale, unpredictable changes in the competitive environment. The agility of these supply chain leaders will be from one end of the supply chain to the other, and in that way, they will secure a global advantage over their competitors.

3.2 Supply chain structures to deliver value

Michael G. Mikurak and Jonathan D. Whitaker

Companies today can select supply chain partners and adopt a strategy to complement their corporate goals.

The business environment in North America has become increasingly competitive in recent years, with markets becoming ever less tolerant of companies that do not regularly create measurable value. In response, companies have been engaged in an intensive search for value inside their organizations and have a desire to refocus all aspects of their operations to align with their overall corporate strategies. This has led to a re-evaluation of the role of supply chains. Traditionally, supply chains were seen only as a cost to be minimized; with this re-evaluation, supply chains are being tied to overall company strategy and their potential to create value in ways other than cost reduction is being recognized.

Two related trends have facilitated this effort to derive value from supply chain structures. First, new information technologies are simplifying collaboration and synchronization between supply chain partners. Second, firms today can provide deep capabilities in narrow portions of the supply chain, partially because of these technologies. Organizations are now able to develop and coordinate portfolios of supply chain partners due to these trends. Companies can select the optimal set of partners and quickly establish a well-integrated supply chain that complements their overall strategy. These supply chain alliances can also be quickly dissolved and reconstituted to meet evolving market needs.

As companies have come under increasing competitive pressures, they have often turned to the shareholder value framework to examine their operations (see Figure 3.2.1). Supply chains structures have been developed that can have an impact on most shareholder value levers.

While the ideal is to have a positive impact on all these levers simultaneously, in practice this is not achievable. In this chapter we have identified six typical supply chain structures that affect most of the shareholder value levers; we will discuss their respective merits

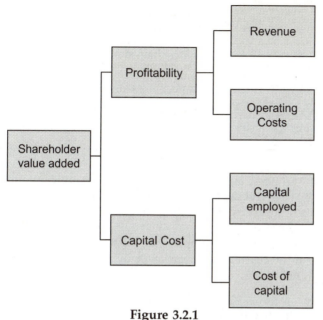

Figure 3.2.1
Shareholder value framework

and their alignment with overall corporate strategy. Collaboration and cooperation between different stages of the supply chain is also essential to the ability to deliver value. We will discuss some of the recent developments in information technologies that have simplified this collaboration, as well as some of the obstacles that remain.

Value-generating supply chain structures

Traditionally, supply chains structures have had a strong cost focus. However, as organizations have viewed supply chains increasingly as sources of competitive advantage, attention has moved towards configuring supply chains so that they have an impact on different levers of company value. We have identified six major supply chain structures:

Supply chains can be configured to have an impact on different levers of company value.

- The *omnipresent* supply chain enhances revenue through pervasive product availability and increasing unit volume.
- The *channel-focused* supply chain enhances revenue by providing value to channel partners who can affect unit volume.
- The *consumer customized* supply chain enhances revenue by providing enhanced value to the consumer and increasing revenue per unit.
- The *operational agile* supply chain enhances revenue by rapidly addressing emerging market needs and capturing first mover margins.

Table 3.2.1
Strategies for enhancing revenue

Revenue layer	Supply chain strategy
Unit volume	Omnipresent Channel-focused
Revenue per unit	Consumer customization Operational agility Speed-focused

- The *speed-focused* supply chain enhances revenue by providing product faster and capturing a 'freshness' premium, and affects the capital employed by minimizing inventory investments locked in the supply chain.
- The *logistics optimization* supply chain affects both the operating cost lever and the capital employed lever by seeking to minimize total supply chain costs.

Revenue enhancing strategies

Supply chain structures can be focused on increasing unit volume or revenue per unit.

Organizations can enhance revenue through either increasing the number of units sold or boosting the average revenue per unit. Two supply chain structures are focused primarily on increasing unit volume. Three are focused mainly on revenue per unit; one of these, the speed-focused supply chain, can also be used to address the capital charge value lever (see Table 3.2.1 above).

The omnipresent strategy

Strong, brand-driven companies benefit most from omnipresent supply chains.

The omnipresent strategy is focused on achieving pervasive product availability; it links well with a mass-market, brand-focused corporate strategy. The omnipresent supply chain ensures that a product is available wherever and whenever desired. Therefore, it supports the corporate goal of wide product availability, reinforces marketing efforts, and helps to capture consumer mind share.

A good example of a company using this supply chain strategy is Coca-Cola. Coke has explained its strategy as 'to be within an arm's reach of desire', and it has designed its supply chain accordingly. In order to meet this universal goal, Coke operates several supply chains reaching consumers through a variety of channels, for example: groceries, club stores, mass merchants, convenience stores, bars and restaurants, vending machines and events. All of these consumer-facing channels have different supply chain characteristics and different cost structures. Coke's goal is to make sure that whenever a consumer is thirsty, Coke is there.

Organizations employ the omnipresent supply chain to draw or pull products through the distribution channel. The food and packaged goods industries use this strategy the most since it ties in well with strong, brand-driven companies. In addition to Coca-Cola, Starbucks and McDonald's also use this strategy.

Outside the food and consumer goods industries, information technology company Intel has started to pursue an omnipresence strategy, targeted more at personal computer value chain participants than at end consumers. By developing the 'Intel Inside' brand, Intel moved towards a branded product that would benefit from pervasive product placement. Intel's move into both motherboards and complete personal computer systems develops omnipresent placement across all stages of the value chain. Only pressure from its current channel partners convinced Intel to ease off this strategy.

Extra supply chain costs can be offset through increased sales and adding a premium for a market-leading brand.

The omnipresent strategy has two major drawbacks. First, operating a pervasive supply chain entails high costs. Second, managing multiple and potentially conflicting channels involves additional complexity and organizational stress. Companies can offset the extra supply chain costs by generating increased sales and by charging a premium for a market-leading brand. However, the increased complexity of managing a portfolio of supply chains remains a challenge for companies choosing this strategy, although the use of coordinating software tools can reduce this difficulty. The cost and complexity issues make this strategy most effective for large, resource-rich companies that are market leaders.

Channel-focused strategy

The channel-focused strategy seeks to provide products on terms attractive to the selling channel. The channel then takes on the responsibility of selling the product. The channel-focused strategy seeks to push goods through the channels. Channel-focused producers will typically have strong relationships with their channel partners, but they provide relatively little insight or information about the end consumer because of their lack of consumer contact. This strategy is cost- and service-based and requires an efficient and effective supply chain to meet the expectations of the channel. Typically, channel-focused companies will work closely with their partners to determine the best allocation of supply chain responsibilities among the participants, minimizing total cost and providing necessary services.

Strong relationships with partners and an efficient supply chain are needed to make a channel-focused strategy work.

Cott Cola is an example of the channel-focused strategy. Cott has focused on developing private label beverages for several large customers. Instead of investing in a brand, Cott has developed strong logistics and manufacturing capabilities that are flexible enough to provide the level of service its customers require. Since it does not spend on developing and maintaining a brand, Cott can afford to price below branded competitors and still ensure that retailers earn a greater margin on Cott products than on branded competitor products. This strategy has enabled Cott to survive and even expand its market share in a highly concentrated market dominated by powerful brands.

Electronics companies can also benefit from a channel-focused strategy.

The electronics industry also employs the channel-focused strategy, with several companies manufacturing equipment to be sold under a partner's brand. The situation in this industry is less stable than in Cott's case since another manufacturer typically re-brands the electronics equipment, adding another player at the same stage of the value chain. This leads to a desire on the part of the actual manufacturer to develop the relationships and expertise to allow it to displace its partner. For example, Acer employed a channel-focused strategy to manufacture laptop computers for several companies. However, Acer has used its market and channel knowledge to develop its own brand and enter the market under its own name. Likewise, Toyota's suppliers will pack parts and place them in a sequence to Toyota's specifications to ensure their products are selected over their competitors'.

In order to be successful with this strategy, a channel-focused company must maintain an efficient and flexible supply chain. Since the main goal for such a company is to provide an attractive offer to its channel partners, the organization must tailor its supply chain to that purpose. Usually this requires a strong cost focus combined with a high degree of flexibility.

Consumer customized strategy

Consumer customizers are typically strong in customer relationships and will target consumers individually.

The consumer customization strategy attempts to use supply chain capabilities to enhance the value received by the consumer. Companies are able to charge a premium for the value they provide, increasing the average manufacturing unit price. Consumer customization is closely aligned with mass-customization strategies. Companies employing this strategy have core competencies in customer relationships and customer intimacy.

Typically, consumer customizers will target consumers at an individual level. In order to serve this finely differentiated market, the supply chains for these companies usually practice postponement to the greatest extent possible. The companies often sell directly to customers rather than working through traditional middlemen, so that they can control the consumer experience and hold the final value-adding stage of the supply chain. Consumer customizers normally will assemble consumer-specific orders and provide a variety of options in supply chain service to meet the needs of different consumer service levels.

Examples of companies using this strategy include Dell Computer, amazon.com and Lands' End. Dell produces most of its consumer volume only after receiving a confirmed order, enabling it to offer a wide degree of consumer choice without having to maintain inventories of many different configurations.

Companies face several difficulties in using this strategy. First, addressing individual consumers involves higher supply chain costs. In Dell's case, the advantages of the direct model in terms of inventory investments and reduced obsolescence have greatly outweighed the costs; amazon.com, on the other hand, is having difficulty generating a sufficient margin to recover the costs of developing a distribution network. Second, consumers are becoming increasingly concerned about the confidentiality and use of the information collected through this sales method.

Operational agile strategy

The operational agility strategy focuses on developing a capability to react nimbly and to reconfigure characteristics of products and the supply chain to meet emerging customer needs. Companies using this strategy focus on capturing the premium for being early to market. Typically, companies using an innovation strategy supported by an operational agility strategy consider product development and consumer insight to be core strengths.

Companies using an operational agility strategy are normally innovative product developers and prefer to outsource many supply chain functions.

Many companies using this strategy outsource whatever supply chain functions they can, preferring to concentrate their efforts on product development and marketing. They typically have developed strong relationships with a broad portfolio of potential supply chain partners. Partners are then selected to participate in individual projects depending on their specific capabilities.

This concept is well established in the electronics industry where a large number of contract manufacturers and semiconductor foundries are available as partners. Cisco is a good example of a company using this approach. Its 'networked supply chain' concept enables Cisco to communicate and share information rapidly with a large network of suppliers and partners. Information is distributed to partners with essentially no delay, allowing for rapid reactions by all the partners in the chain.

Adaptec also employs this strategy, although in a narrower way than Cisco. Adaptec, a designer and marketer of computer interfacing equipment, has decided not to invest in its own semiconductor fabrication plant and instead has contracted fabrication to Taiwan Semiconductor Manufacturing Company (TSMC). Using software, Adaptec has been able to coordinate the information flow with TSMC to the point where it has achieved turnaround times as good as or better than their estimates for owning their own manufacturing facility. This has enabled Adaptec to concentrate on the parts of the value chain where it has an advantage – design and marketing.

While outsourcing portions of the supply chain can simplify the execution of an operational agility strategy, it is not necessary. Wausau Paper is an example of an integrated company using the agility strategy. Although a medium-sized player in an industry that favors scale, Wausau has developed capabilities to rapidly determine customer needs, develop products that will meet those needs and manage the supply chain to deliver quickly to those customers.

Wausau Paper rapidly meets customer needs and is prepared to exit a business once margins shrink.

For example, after discovering that a major customer was suffering from rising pulp prices, Wausau developed a paper that used less pulp. Wausau also offers superior customer service through its distribution system, which ships about 75 per cent of items within 24 hours – far faster than the industry average. When margins are reduced, Wausau is willing to move on. Despite being the original provider of paper to 3M for Post-it Notes, Wausau chose to exit the business when other paper companies entered the market and margins shrank.

The operational agility strategy requires a willingness and a capacity to be innovative, so that companies develop new products and processes for new markets. In the case of companies that own their own infrastructure, they need to be able to refocus their infrastructure quickly, and adapt, or replace the infrastructure as needed. Typically, the companies will need to accept higher costs in order to maximize flexibility. In industries where third-party contract partners are available, the use of an agility strategy requires tight information links and a great deal of expertise in managing a changing network of partners.

Speed-focused strategy

Providing products faster to consumers enables speed-focused companies to charge premium prices.

The speed-focused supply chain strategy seeks to earn a premium by providing the consumer with a product that is newer or fresher than the competition's. This supply chain strategy ties in well with company strategies focusing on customer service.

Caterpillar's spare parts business is an example. The quickness of post-sales support is often cited as one of the two most important factors in the decision to purchase heavy construction equipment. Caterpillar promises its customers to provide 'parts within 48 hours, or the parts are free'. To meet this commitment, Caterpillar has developed a parts supply chain combining sophisticated inventory management with superior transportation management. When required, Caterpillar can find a spare part stored in dealer inventory, anywhere in the world, and manage the transportation to get the spare to the user, anywhere in the world, within 48 hours. The investment in this capability is offset by the value customers place on this service, which enables premium pricing of the spare part as well as providing a marketing advantage for the equipment.

An interesting variation of the speed strategy has been the use of freshness dating on products that are not very perishable – such as beer. By emphasizing freshness and educating the consumer on the desirability of freshness, domestic producers have capitalized on the relative speed of their supply chains compared to imported brands.

In order to use this strategy effectively, collaboration throughout the supply chain is essential. The product needs to be tracked and managed throughout its progression along the chain to the final consumer. For a company selling through traditional channels, there is the additional risk that employing a speed strategy, and heightening consumer awareness of freshness, increases vulnerability to competitors selling directly.

Cost management strategies

In contrast to revenue-enhancing supply strategies, the logistics optimization strategy primarily works the cost lever of the value framework. This strategy focuses on reducing overall supply chain costs, allowing higher margins at lower selling prices.

Logistics optimization strategy

Logistics optimization is the most traditional supply chain strategy. It seeks to lower overall supply chain costs, including operating costs and capital costs, through operational effectiveness and efficiency. Companies with a lower-cost supply chain gain greater pricing flexibility. This strategy ties in well with cost-driven or low-pricing strategies.

Logistics optimization seeks to lower overall costs and gives companies greater pricing flexibility.

To address operating cost issues, this strategy focuses intensely on continuous improvement and efficiency. For capital assets, the focus is on maximizing utilization. Companies using this strategy use sophisticated processes and information systems to manage the supply chain flow and to minimize the current assets deployed, such as inventory. Long-term assets are managed carefully to ensure that the infrastructure is sufficient to meet demand growth without the risk of overinvesting.

Industries with relatively bulky products or products that compete on price have generally employed this strategy from necessity. Some good examples can be found in the resources industries. Pulp and paper companies, for instance, traditionally have managed a portfolio of transportation alternatives in order to minimize the total cost of their supply chain. This has usually involved transportation mode management to ensure that the mode selected is appropriate for the product at a given stage of production.

For example, fiber is transported typically by low-cost transportation modes such as water or rail to a paper mill, where the bulk is reduced and value increased. From the mill, product is shipped usually by rail or truck to converting facilities where bulk is further reduced and value increased. The final leg of shipment to the customer is usually by truck. Thus, as the value of the product increases, there is a trade-off between transportation and inventory costs.

Additionally, at a gross level, paper mills and other primary manufacturing facilities are physically located close to raw material sources, such as fiber, water and power, to reduce costs. Converting facilities are located closer to the customer to provide better service. As a logical next step, paper companies are starting to establish dedicated converting facilities producing packaging material next to their customers.

Companies are reducing transport costs but also seeking to increase service for their customers.

Coal producers are also completely focused on efficiency. They often locate power plants as close as feasible to the point of coal extraction and primarily use the lowest cost forms of transportation such as rail and barge.

A good example of a company outside the natural resources sector with a logistics optimization strategy is Wal-Mart. Wal-Mart's distribution system operates with relatively small instore inventories, which are replenished almost continuously from regional distribution centers. This hub-and-spoke structure enables Wal-Mart to reduce total supply chain costs. For example, the structure allows Wal-Mart to more accurately forecast usage at an aggregated, regional distribution center level and enables vendors to ship in bulk quantities to the distribution center. These cost savings allow pricing flexibility. As an added advantage, the hub-and-spoke distribution system supports an extensive store network.

In order to be successful with an optimization strategy, all partners of the supply chain must understand the strategic intent. Companies pursuing this strategy must collaborate with their partners to invest in appropriate infrastructure and at the appropriate point in the chain. Information sharing is crucial to ensure that all partners can react to a consistent picture of the market. Continuous improvement and operational excellence are also requirements for all partners in the chain.

Capital management strategies

Speed and optimization strategies both have an impact on capital.

In addition to their impact on revenue and cost, the speed and optimization strategies both have a significant impact on the capital employed by a company.

Logistics optimization strategy

The logistics optimization strategy attempts to deliver lowest total cost performance across the supply chain. A company employing this strategy will need to trade off the cost of investment in additional infrastructure with the incremental efficiency improvements that can be gained. This strategy thus has an impact on the operating cost lever and the capital employed lever simultaneously.

Speed-focused strategy

Another use of the speed-focused strategy is to affect the capital employed lever. The corporate objective is to move product through the supply chain as quickly as possible in order to minimize capital investment in inventory. This typically applies to industries where the value of the product is very high or where the product lifecycle is very short. Where a company seeks to gain a premium for the freshness of its product, the speed strategy is more appropriate as a tool for revenue enhancement, as discussed earlier.

Many electronics companies use a speed strategy to minimize capital employed. For example, companies typically ship semiconductors by air from fabrication facilities in order to minimize inventory investment and to minimize the amount of inventory at risk of obsolescence if an improved product is introduced.

For example, Dell Computer's supply chain shows characteristics of the speed strategy as well as the consumer customization strategy. Dell requires suppliers to maintain inventory at a supplier hub, located adjacent to the assembly facility, and assembles to order. Since suppliers own the inventory at the supplier hub, completed systems are shipped immediately, and the assembly process is fast and efficient, Dell maintains nearly no inventories. Thus, employing a speed strategy contributes to Dell's negative working capital position.

Dell gains additional advantages from the speed strategy; downstream channel latency is close to zero due to Dell's direct sales model. The reduced latency relative to a traditional channel allows Dell to introduce new products faster, as the channel does not need to be stocked. This enables the maximization of the new product premium. Furthermore, as new products are introduced, Dell does not have a channel full of obsolete products that must be discounted.

Facilitating technologies

With the collaboration and synchronization between a network of partners critical to maximizing many of the new supply chain strategies, the development of facilitating technologies has been a key to supporting this trend. These technologies facilitate the exchange of information and the development of tighter relationships and alliances between supply chain partners.

New technologies enable information exchange and closer relationships.

We can use the framework shown in Table 3.2.2 to classify the degree of collaboration in these relationships.

Currently, companies achieve the second level of collaboration, information sharing, relatively easily. The state of the art is to develop capabilities in the third category.

Network computer manufacturer Cisco is one of the leaders in collaboration and synchronization. Cisco's concept of the 'networked supply chain' allows all its partners to have access to the same information. Planning functions are integrated with the development of a single forecast, daily transmission of build requirements, and immediate pass-through of real demand signals to all supply chain partners. Order fulfilment is also streamlined, purchase orders and invoices have been eliminated, payments are based on shop floor activities, and configuration checking and testing are done using Cisco processes on supplier lines. Finally, product data systems are integrated, allowing engineering change orders to be managed online.

Cisco is extending the concept to move further into collaborative decision making. Adding constraint-based planning and scheduling across the supply chain are among the developments, as well as joint

Table 3.2.2

Level of collaboration in supply chain relationships

Relationship type	Definition	Data exchanged
Transactional	Basic transactions within a buyer–seller relationship are automated. Primarily procurement-oriented.	Information required to execute a purchase: – purchase orders – invoices – transfer of funds
Information sharing	Information is shared by a buyer or seller either before or after a purchase is made. Sharing of information is on a FYI basis only.	Seller may provide: – order status – product prices/descriptions – quantities available Buyer may provide forecast of needs.
Collaborative	Information is jointly developed by the buyer and the seller. Involves joint processes and decision-making criteria and measurement Information is often strategic or proprietary in nature.	Jointly developed operations and planning information, including: – product designs – future product plans – forecasts – fulfilment processes

capacity planning. Eventually, design collaboration will be included in the tool set.

Challenges to collaboration include motivation, the effort required to scale, and potential conflicts of interest.

In attempting to develop these extended capabilities, Cisco is breaking new ground. However, Cisco has substantial challenges to overcome in achieving tighter collaboration, and these revolve around motivation, the effort required to scale, and potential conflicts of interest.

First, motivation; it is not always easy to define the strategic motivation for developing a collaborative relationship. Companies can use the relationship to extract concessions from weaker supply chain partners. For example, Dell has tried to develop collaborative relationships with suppliers but has often reverted to using its advantage to extract concessions.

Second, the effort required to scale collaborative relationships to include a large fraction of suppliers and customers is substantial. Many companies have developed collaborative relationships with a small number of highly trusted and favored partners. For a small number of close partners, deploying additional resources to manage the relationship has not been difficult. It becomes an issue if this level of integration is to be extended across a significant portion of the customer or supply base. This scale problem leads to an interesting phenomenon known as the 'collaboration paradox'. To feasibly collaborate at scale, the mechanics of the interaction must be so low touch and frictionless that the interaction becomes transactional or information sharing in nature.

The third, and perhaps most formidable, obstacle to closer collaboration is the conflict of interest involved. By collaborating, companies are trying to optimize their operations on a global basis, for the common good. Global optimization often implies local sub-optimization; individual companies in a supply chain alliance will have to accept reduced value in order to increase the total value to the entire alliance. However, the management of each company is obligated to seek to maximize that company's value – not that of the entire alliance.

Even in situations that are less drastic, individual companies will often revert to win–lose behavior. Companies can minimize the contributions of supply chain partners while overestimating their own contributions. Disagreements often arise over how to measure joint gains and how these gains should be shared.

Conclusion

Recent demands to improve performance have encouraged companies to customize their supply chains to fit their overall corporate goals. Historically, supply chains have been perceived as a cost to be minimized; current thinking recognizes that supply chain structures can be tuned to address most of the levers of corporate value.

Market and technology trends will ensure supply chains become better tools to deliver shareholder value.

As supply chains have been customized and fine-tuned, companies have increasingly recognized the value of integrating closely with their supply chain partners. The development of sophisticated technology to share data and support collaboration has facilitated integration. Despite the development of supply chain tools, issues of strategic objectives, management complexity and conflicts of interest between partners raise questions about the level and depth of collaboration that is achievable between separate entities.

New specialized companies have also emerged to provide services in narrow segments of the value chain, driven by a new demand for such capabilities and the technology to enable collaboration.

Driven by these trends, supply chains will become more efficient, better focused and better aligned with overall corporate goals. Supply chain alliances will collaborate more closely, using technological tools to share information and integrate their operations, at least until some equilibrium is reached between collaboration and individual interests. The market for supply chain capabilities will continue to develop and specialized players will emerge to compete in narrow niches of the chain. The power of these trends will ensure supply chains increasingly become better tools for delivering shareholder value into the future.

3.3 Supply chain planning

Dennis Theis, Craig Millis, David Kennedy and Mark Pearson

Real competitive advantage in a complex business environment is determined by the ability to leverage collaborative relationships in the supply chain to drive optimal planning decisions across organizational boundaries.

While tactical and operational planning could be relatively straightforward for those few businesses that operate in a simple and stable environment, the majority of businesses operate in an environment that is becoming more complex and volatile. Achieving excellence is made even more challenging by the need to integrate and collaborate with supply chain partners. In this environment, businesses and whole supply chains beyond a single company's boundary are increasingly dependent on their ability to respond quickly to customer demands and their ability to utilize assets more flexibly and efficiently.

Real competitive advantage, therefore, comes from being able to leverage collaborative relationships in the supply chain to drive optimal planning decisions across organizational boundaries. The current trends toward much closer collaboration between supply chain partners, process synchronization across multiple enterprises, and flexible information sharing across the supply chain can be expected to continue for many years. The improvements to the bottom line of the companies involved are worth the effort. However, the trend towards collaborating and sharing with partners up and down the supply chain needs to be underpinned with good supply chain practices in-house. The old adage of 'get your own house in order first' has never been so true than in the context of supply chain best practice.

This chapter describes the fundamental elements of supply chain planning and the history of the convergence of these elements into the integrated planning suites we see on the market today. Further, the chapter will explore current trends in supply chain planning, the practicalities of making it work, as well as consider how several industries have responded to these challenges with the development of collaborative supply chain planning capabilities. Finally, we will examine the emergence of a new role in the supply chain – the Kingmaker – before closing with a closer look at the benefits to be derived from collaborative supply chain planning.

Overview of supply chain planning

A company's supply chain includes all functions required to develop a product, buy the materials required to manufacture it, make the product and ship it to its customers. These functions need to be planned to quickly and flexibly react to increasingly complex demands from customers. Therefore, supply chain planning covers all planning activities necessary to operate effectively across the supply chain. As shown in Figure 3.3.1, these activities include:

A supply chain includes all functions required to develop a product, purchase materials, and make and ship a product to customers. All need to react to customer demand quickly and flexibly.

- *Strategic network modeling.* Physical infrastructure in the supply chain is optimized through the selection of appropriate sourcing, manufacturing, warehousing and distribution options to ensure that supply chain performance targets of cost and customer service are met.
- *Customer collaboration.* A mutually agreed demand plan is created through collaboration with customers (and customers' customers) on expected demand, available supply and relevant market intelligence.

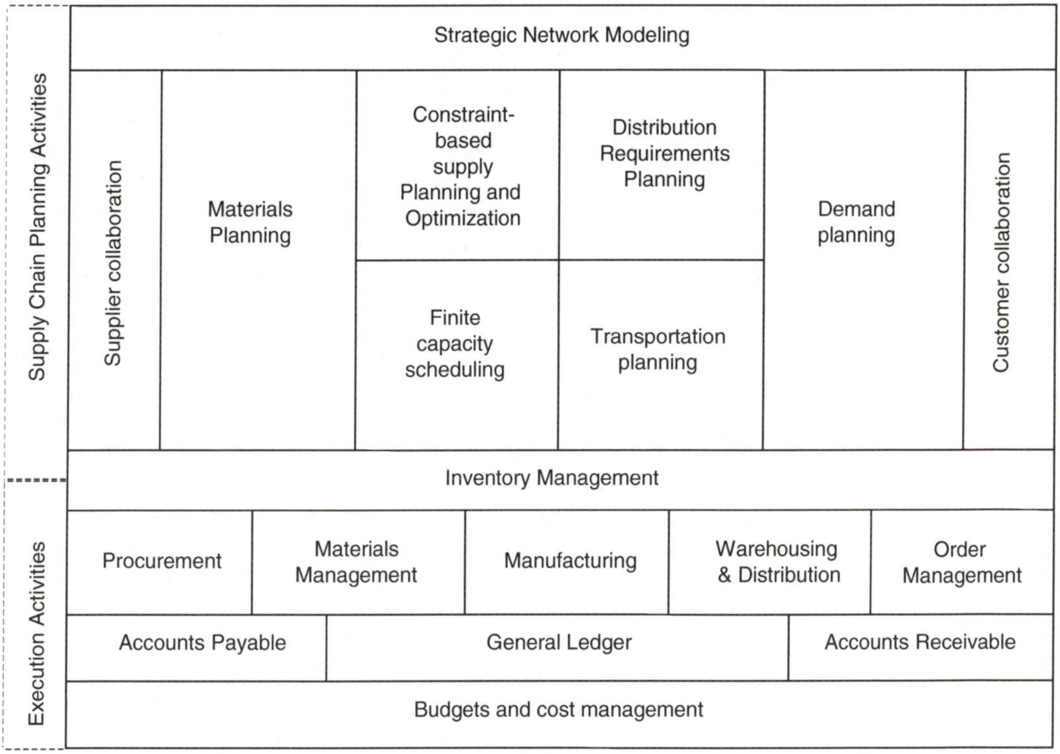

Figure 3.3.1
Supply chain planning activities

- *Demand planning*. A statistical forecast of customer demand is created, based on sales history, seasonality and trends and enhanced through the addition of market intelligence.
- *Distribution requirements planning*. Planned movements of goods are created based on anticipated customer demand, which is derived from the agreed demand plan, and taking into account inventory stocking policies and current and projected inventory levels at each stocking location.
- *Transportation planning*. The distribution requirements plan is translated in actual loads by sea, air, rail or truck (as appropriate for each lane). Loads may be optimized for lowest cost, highest utilization, shortest distance or other targets and put out to tender to third-party logistics (3PL) providers.
- *Constraint-based supply planning*. An optimal supply plan is created, based on anticipated demand and considering any material or capacity constraints and other supply chain characteristics (such as make-versus-buy options; manufacturing strategies; inventory stocking policies; and sourcing, manufacturing and distribution lead times). The utilization of the supply network is optimized towards cost, flexibility and customer service level based on the input from the demand plan
- *Finite capacity scheduling*. A detailed production plan is created at plant level to meet the supply plan, taking into account capacity and material constraints at the plant and other plant-level factors.
- *Materials planning*. A time-phased materials plan for procurement processes and call-off schedules needs to be synchronized to ensure a balanced materials flow. Materials arrival times and availability need to support the overall plan and objectives.
- *Supplier collaboration*. A mutually agreed plan for supply of raw materials is created through collaboration with (possibly) multiple tiers of suppliers.

Additional activities that are tightly related to supply chain planning include sales and operations planning, where consensus supply and demand forecasts are created between all main functions that have an impact on the supply chain. They include marketing, key account management, production planning, distribution planning, materials management, and finance. The effectiveness of order management as the customer-facing execution activity depends on how well agreed supply plans, customer orders, requests, and existing deliveries are integrated. Any informational inefficiencies result in unfilled customer orders and potentially lost sales. Due to the complex nature of such supply chain networks, from distribution to customers and warehouses to raw materials delivery, emerging supply chain planning solutions allow monitoring and event management to better handle exceptional cases.

Evolution of supply chain planning

Supply chain planning, in one form or another, has existed for many years although it has been seen traditionally as a distinct activity from other areas of enterprise planning and execution. Over the years, supply chain planning evolution has benefited from developments such as business process re-engineering and the massive strides forward in technology. Today, supply chain planning is often indistinguishable from core business planning in many companies – even to the extent that many companies consider supply chain to be a core competence and source of competitive advantage over their rivals.

Today supply chain planning is often indistinguishable from core business planning in many companies.

The solution perspective

A convenient way to classify enterprise planning and execution activities is in terms of the solutions that have been developed to support them. As fast as advancements in information technology have allowed, software application vendors have been developing solutions to meet business needs. As recently as a decade ago there were six distinct categories of planning and execution solutions, focused on the activity they were intended to support, namely:

- enterprise resource planning (ERP), including materials requirements planning (MRP)
- supply chain planning (SCP)
- order management systems (OMS)
- warehouse management systems (WMS)
- manufacturing execution systems (MES), and
- transportation management systems (TMS).

In recent years, however, the distinction between supply chain planning and other areas of enterprise planning and execution has become blurred as application vendors have aggressively tried to offer a wider range of functionality. Today we see that although many 'best-of-breed' solutions still prosper, many activities that were previously managed using a point solution (say, warehouse management) can now be performed using an ERP system.

Many activities that were previously managed using a point solution can now be performed using an ERP system. New categories of solutions further confuse the picture.

Further, we have seen the emergence of new categories of solution such as:

- customer relationship management (CRM),
- supplier relationship management (SRM), and
- supply chain event management (SCEM).

These new solutions further confuse the picture as many of them offer overlapping functionality with existing categories of solution.

For clarity, the map of currently available categories of solutions is summarized as shown in Figure 3.3.2. Although point solutions for order management, warehouse management, manufacturing execution

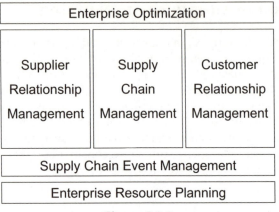

Figure 3.3.2
Enterprise planning and execution solution map

and transportation management do still exist and continue to do well, they have been subsumed into the broader categories of CRM, SCP, SRM and ERP in this diagram.

A new and interesting development is the emergence of enterprise optimization solutions that are focused on overall optimization of the enterprise. At present, the full scope of this category of solution is unclear but it will become better defined as the market leaders further develop their offerings. Currently, solutions in this category focus on a range of activity from basic performance management to enterprise-wide profit optimization.

As the evolution progresses, the lines of demarcation between these concepts blur. A key value proposition exists in the ability to plan and re-plan in (near) real time and evaluate multiple 'what if?' scenarios before selecting and deciding on any one plan. This means companies will be able to react to an event within the supply chain execution that calls for a re-optimization of the plan. For instance, the failure of a truck to arrive at a distribution center may call for the plan of another truck to be changed. Available-to-promise connections are already being made to connect order entry within CRM with real-time planning engines.

The technology perspective

The complexity of optimizing, or even considering, all the variables is well beyond any number of collective brains.

Referring back to Figure 3.3.1, the approaches to the supply chain planning activities suggested fall into three main categories and, correspondingly, three main supporting technologies.

This association of activity and technology has happened through the evolution of supply chain planning sophistication. Decision support given by supply chain planning, under the above scope, is a significant problem to solve. The complexity of optimizing, or even considering, all the variables is well beyond any number of collective brains. Even if it were possible, the time taken to come to a

Table 3.3.1
Enabling supply chain technology

Supply chain planning activities	Underpinning technology
Constraint-based supply planning Distribution requirements planning Transportation planning Finite capacity scheduling Supply optimization Order promising/allocation Strategic network modeling	Memory-resident planning engines
Demand planning Sales and operations planning	Online analytical processing
Customer collaboration Supplier collaboration	Internet

recommendation, would mean that the situation would now be passed, making the suggested decision irrelevant. It is recognized that the human brain can deal with up to only seven variables. Beyond that the natural response is to break the problem up into manageable chunks, solve and then try to piece it back together again to arrive at a solution for the original problem. Indeed, this is the way that the approaches to supply chain planning have evolved over time. Moreover, the supporting technology has evolved this way through the decades.

The planning perspective

Supply chain control in the 1950s started with simple order point replenishment and economic order quantity. It was unsophisticated: the problem was not considered as a whole. But, who cared? There was always enough on order or in inventory to go around and cover for any ill-planned sales order or other supply chain disruptions.

In the 1970s, materials requirements planning recognized the whole problem and it did exactly what any logical problem-solving mechanism that could not cope with the enormity of the problem would do, and broke it down into its constituent parts. Working at an item, work order or purchase order level, it did manage to produce a time-phased (supply chain) plan based on fixed, predetermined lead times. But, because of the need to break the problem up, when the plan was viewed as a whole again, it was deemed infeasible. For example, if an item was required tomorrow, and it took two days to make, then it should have been started yesterday or all the work orders summed at that point in time meant three of these machine tools were needed and only one was available. In addition, the technology available at that time was database-based, and hence suffered from the constraints surrounding input/output and read/write protocols and took inordinate amounts of time to come to a planning decision.

In the 1970s supply chain planning was broken up into several parts. By the 1980s manufacturing resources planning conceptually overlaid a process discipline.

Then came a fix – not to solve the original supply chain planning problem, but to make the results of breaking up the problem and reforming it into a whole more palatable to managers and users alike. In the 1980s, manufacturing resources planning (MRP) came into vogue and conceptually overlaid a process discipline that included feedback loops. This enabled the process to react to the finite capacity issue and for a performance measurement framework to be set up to allow managers to monitor and control compliance to the process. Instead of breaking up the supply chain planning problem into an item level, several intermediate levels were considered first, such as business planning, sales planning and production planning. This was still database-driven and took great time and effort to create the supply chain plans. Arguably, however, this was the first approach that formally suggested collaboration had a role in successful supply chain planning.

Also in the 1980s, the Theory of Constraints (Goldratt, 1992) was applied to the supply chain planning problem. Concepts started to build that recognized the need to consider all 'variables' together to achieve feasibility in supply chain planning. Terms like 'bottleneck' appeared in master production schedules and just-in-time was a management catch-cry. A practical application manifested itself in kanban. Kanban is a mechanism based on 'fixing' the amount of stock physically held between activities within the supply chain and, when an item is consumed by the 'customer', the company needs to produce (make or procure) another to replace it. This approach logically 'ties' the dependent events together, manages the statistical fluctuations through the use of stock, and thus balances the flow. Kanban is traditionally associated with production control, but also has been effectively applied to balancing supply chain flow.

Technology caught up with the Theory of Constraints and enabled advanced planning systems. Companies could now consider all the 'variables' in supporting supply chain planning decisions.

However, unfortunately, it was not until around the turn of the decade when technology had 'caught up' with the Theory of Constraints concept and allowed for what is now known as advanced planning systems. The enabling technology meant that supply chain managers no longer had to wait for a database to read/write the hundreds of thousands of data elements to come up with a feasible plan. Memory-resident solutions could do the same thing in a fraction of the time. This technology-enablement was a real breakthrough in providing a way to solve the original supply chain planning problem. Companies could now consider all the 'variables' in supporting supply chain planning decisions.

That said, however, technology was not quite developed enough to allow all supply chain variables to be considered in one single memory-resident planning engine. Moreover, the evolution of advanced planning systems vendors, mainly because of their growth through acquisition, meant differing levels of technology, or perhaps their focus on different parts of the supply chain footprint, no one offering from one single provider could consider the supply chain planning activities listed above in one end-to-end solution: e-marketplaces conceptually came close to mimicking this, but the architecture behind it all was based on the 'break up the problem and re-assemble the result' approach with multiple planning engines, workflows and integration embedded in the solution.

The technology was also not advanced enough to solve the demand planning problem. By its very nature, or in any case, the way that we humans have approached the problem, it is dependent on historical facts to predict the future – at least at a statistical forecast level. Database technology lends itself to this by virtue of being able to hold weeks', months' and sometimes years' worth of data. Database technology has evolved through time and now allows sophisticated 'slice and dice' as well as multiple read/write arbitration, but has not evolved to the extent of having a single model that forecasts demand and determines the supply chain consequences based on capacity and material constraints.

With the advent of the Internet, these tools could be accessed from any Internet café in any part of the world, and while this ease of access is being touted as collaboration, real operational improvements in supply chain planning will only happen when things are done differently because of collaboration. Giving a customer access to the same order screen that your tele-sales team uses, or taking orders over your web site, or reverse auctioning to get a better price for materials, is not collaboration. Executing transactions more quickly may have a marginal effect on supply chain costs; true collaboration around supply chain planning will add significant value to those who understand it and master it.

Until the technology and protocols evolve that allow, say, a retailer to play supply chain planning 'what if?s' on the consequences in a suppliers' supplier, perhaps we will need to make and accept the inherent process dependencies, the statistical fluctuations and the break-it-down problem solving approach to help plan supply chains.

The practicalities of supply chain planning

Of course, we have come a long way in supply chain planning development through the implementation of new processes and technologies. The planning developments of past decades show that many of the problems in planning have been solved. Companies now recognize they can secure real competitive advantage by having supply chain planning processes and technologies in place. But why is it that customers still sometimes do not receive the 100 per cent quality service they expect? Why can't we get the products as we like them from even the most advanced producers with very progressive supply chains in place? The answer lies in the gap between the perfect supply chain and where we are today. In this section we will put a Utopian or

Why is it that customers still sometimes do not receive the 100 per cent quality service they expect? The answer lies in the gap between the perfect supply chain and where we are today.

perfect supply chain next to reality and compare them to explore this gap and derive some insight into future trends.

A Utopian supply chain

Think, if you will, of the day when supply chains can offer instantaneous fulfilment. The supply chain has evolved to such an extent that, when an order arrives unexpectedly, the supply chain is capable of delivering products to customers at the right time, quantity, quality, information and price, right there and then.

For this to happen, the supply chain needs to have evolved into an entity that exhibits some, and preferably all, of the following characteristics:

- a supply lead time tending to zero
- a very simple process with few links in the chain of supply
- little or no human involvement
- very understanding customers
- a very simplistic product offering
- sophisticated suppliers that have evolved on par with yourself and perhaps
- a fulfilment mechanism based on Star Trek technology.

Unfortunately, very few organizations can claim even one of these characteristics. In fact, any activity that involves human endeavor has characteristics that are in direct opposition to these nice-to-haves. Hence, in a quest to make do with what they have got, most businesses today do supply chain planning in one form or other.

So why can't the control of the supply chain be easy?

The reality of supply chains

The role of supply chain planning is to consider the multiplicative effect of all process dependencies and the inherent fluctuations within the supply chain.

If we put aside the ever-increasing complexity and volatility of operating environments, there are some fundamental principles that inhibit attempts at controlling supply chains. While other factors such as changing market demands, unreliable suppliers and unpredictable workforces all can be held responsible for foiled plans, there are two fundamental phenomena that confound most planning efforts.

First, supply chains, by their very definition, are processes that are linked somehow: processes that span departments, organizations, businesses, industries and countries. Once a simple activity, say 'Storeperson P, puts away item A into location Y' is part of a process, then it is 100 per cent dependent on the activities within the preceding processes. Moreover, the activities subsequent to it are at risk in terms of when and how they can happen because they are in turn dependent on this activity completing successfully on time.

So with the example of 'Storeperson P, puts away item A into location Y', the first level assumptions include: item A has been received; location Y is available; storeperson P is not doing anything else at that time. At an execution level, the consequences of these assumptions tend to be somewhat obvious, but put the assumptions in a plan at some point in the future either next hour, or next day, or next week, or next month, they become less obvious. Looking out through time, the thought of considering all such dependencies, with multiple levels of assumptions up and down the supply chain, becomes a rather daunting task.

Second, the law of averages plays havoc with supply chains. The statistical nature of the real world works against all attempts at getting control of the materials flow. On average, it may take three hours to change over the production line. Sometimes it could take two hours and other times it could take five hours. It usually takes overnight to get the product into stock, but sometimes it takes two days. The customer normally buys 100 of the products a week, but this week she wants 200. This line has a standard output of 1000 units per day, but some days we seem only to be able to get 850 units.

Again, at an execution level, this would seem a harsh reality that would need to be accepted or, at that level of detail, the variability seems to be less acute and precise data tends to be used. Once the line is set we always get 200 units per hour; the truck has just left and will not arrive until 3 p.m. It looks like we are achieving an 82 per cent yield on this batch. But remove yourself from the execution level to view what is required an hour, a day, a week, or a month from now and the variations become significant.

It was Eli Goldratt (1992) who suggested that, in the context of materials flow in production plants:

Dependent events + Statistical fluctuations = Unbalanced plants

It must be reported, however, that these two phenomena are alive and well and unbalancing the whole supply chain. The role of supply chain planning is to consider the multiplicative effect of all process dependencies and the inherent fluctuations within the supply chain. On top of this, add the ever-increasing complexity of doing business, while at the same time being able to determine the impact on customer fill rates and levels of working capital make a daunting task rather arduous.

Industry response: collaborative supply chain planning

The response from industry to supply chain trends and realities has been the recognition that much higher levels of collaborative planning are needed between supply chain participants. Depending on the characteristics of each industry, collaborative planning activity tends to focus on different areas of the supply chain.

Companies are recognizing that much higher levels of collaborative planning are needed between supply chain participants.

• *Design collaboration.* Companies involved in manufacturing complex equipment in such industries as consumer electronics, aerospace and defense have led the way in the area of collaborative design of new products. Nokia and Boeing respectively are examples of leaders in design collaboration in their industry.

- *Supplier collaboration*. Electronics and high technology manufacturers tend to focus on collaborative materials planning with key suppliers as they seek to ensure availability of critical components from their suppliers. Companies such as Dell Computer and Cisco Systems have led their industry in this area.
- *Manufacturing collaboration*. Electronics and high technology companies have also led the way in collaborative supply planning with third-party contract manufacturers. Original equipment manufacturers such as Ericsson and Nokia are leaders in collaboration with contract manufacturers, such as Solectron and Flextronics.
- *Logistics collaboration*. The existence of third-party logistics providers is not new and there has been widespread adoption of 3PL services across many industries. What is new, however, is the development of closer relationships with 3PLs as companies try to minimize cost and maximize the service they receive through collaborative transportation planning. Ryder, Fedex, DHL and TNT are examples of leading logistics companies forging closer relationships with their customers through collaboration.
- *Customer collaboration*. Consumer goods companies tend to focus on collaborative demand planning with customers as they seek to understand the true market demand for their products. For this reason collaborative planning, forecasting and replenishment initiatives (CPFR) have been high on the agenda of many consumer goods manufacturers. Companies such as Wal-Mart and Procter & Gamble have derived significant benefit from a close collaborative relationship between customer and supplier.

While the wide-scale adoption of collaboration has been slow, industry leaders are showing the way forward and reaping significant rewards for their efforts. As shown in Figure 3.3.3, the adoption of collaboration tends to be evolutionary.

Integration

Integrating functions internally within an organization is the first step to collaborative planning.

The initial step for companies embarking on collaborative supply chain planning is to integrate the functions within their own organizations. It is critical that before an organization tries to enter into collaborative planning with its business partners that it gets its own house in order, so that it can be confident of meeting the commitments it makes. Nothing could be more damaging to a developing collaborative planning relationship than if one party consistently fails to meet the commitments it makes to its supply chain partners. In this first step, internal business functions such as marketing and production must work together to develop mutually accepted demand and supply plans to ensure supply chain activities are agreed and correctly aligned.

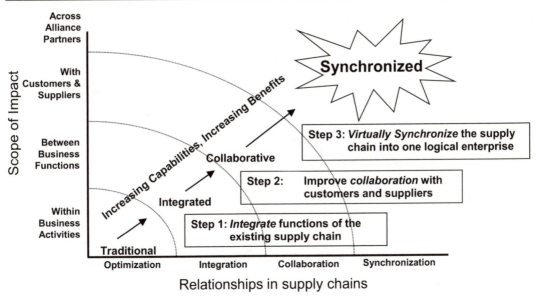

Source: Accenture

Figure 3.3.3
The evolution towards collaborative supply chain planning

Collaboration

Once the company has its own operations working effectively it can start to look outside it own four walls to find potential partners for collaborative planning. The easiest place to start is with its Tier 1 customers and suppliers although both parties obviously need an attractive value proposition to justify entering into a collaborative arrangement. Once that is agreed, however, the companies can begin to share supply chain information such as sales forecasts and materials and capacity availability in order to develop a mutually agreed supply chain plan. As collaboration requires each company to open up to the other, it clearly requires a high degree of trust between the parties. It may be said that the most critical element of collaborative planning is developing the relationship between business partners and getting the organizations to work collaboratively on a problem rather that competitively.

Companies build relationships with potential partners and share supply chain information as they start to work collaboratively.

Synchronization

The final stage of the evolution towards collaborative supply chain planning is the development of a network of supply chain partners who work together for mutual benefit. This network would encompass the extended supply chain and include outsourced service providers such as contract equipment manufacturers and 3PLs into an intelligent supply chain ecosystem. Much like an ecosystem in nature, the synchronized supply chain would be self-sufficient and self-sustaining.

A network of supply chain partners work together to form a synchronized supply chain that is self-sufficient and self-sustaining.

Competition in this brave new world would be between supply chain ecosystems, not between the individual supply chain entities.

Clearly, the synchronization stage is still some way off for most companies and requires a set of highly developed relationships between the parties involved. However, some leading companies are pushing this envelope today through close collaborative relationships with their supply chain partners..

What is apparent from this evolution towards collaborative planning in the supply chain is that the power focus has shifted. Efficient management of supply chain assets, the traditional focus of most parties in the supply chain, is no longer a source of competitive advantage. Rather, it is the movement of information in the supply chain that is increasingly important to manage and control.

The supply chain 'Kingmaker'

A Kingmaker is a company that creates value in the supply chain by creating an alliance of supply chain partners to work collaboratively to optimize service and reduce costs.

In every supply chain it is becoming evident that an opportunity exists for one of the supply chain partners, or perhaps even a third party with no physical presence in the supply chain, to take control of the information flows and decision processes across the extended supply chain for the mutual benefit of all parties. This is the role of the 'Kingmaker', as shown in Figure 3.3.4.

A broad definition of the supply chain 'Kingmaker' is a company that creates value in the supply chain by establishing an alliance of supply

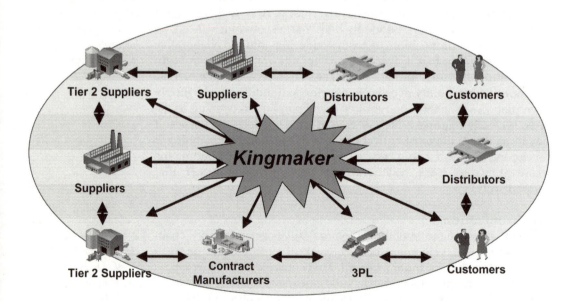

Figure 3.3.4
The supply chain 'Kingmaker'

chain partners to work through a series of collaborative arrangements to optimize customer service and reduce overall supply chain costs.

One of the major questions raised is 'Who will emerge as the supply chain Kingmaker?'. Will it be the original equipment manufacturer, the contract equipment manufacturer or possibly the 3PL? Perhaps the 4PLs of the future will become the ultimate Kingmaker, providing a central data repository, synchronizing planning processes and information flows between relevant parties?

In Europe, different models are developing and it is interesting that multiple Kingmakers appear to be emerging. The key characteristic of the Kingmaker is that it is a company that can create effective supply chain alliances to team the best supply chain partners together. However, no one Kingmaker is dominating the entire supply chain – rather, each Kingmaker recognizes and demonstrates its own supply chain competence, coordinating the supply chain decision processes within its sphere of control.

Take for example Infineon, a large global semiconductor manufacturer. Of the seven or eight discrete steps within the manufacturing process, Infineon itself now physically does very little, having outsourced all but a few of the processes. The company does not need to own the manufacturing assets; Infineon's key is to maximize the effectiveness of the information flow within the supply chain. By repositioning itself as a supply chain Kingmaker, Infineon aims to maximize its shareholder value by reducing time-to-market for new products (and hence time to profit) and minimizing inventory and production costs.

Supply chain planning impact on shareholder value

Supply chain improvements overall and especially along the path of sophistication in collaboration will affect all drivers of shareholder value, as shown in Figure 3.3.5.

Improvements to the supply chain will affect all drivers of shareholder value, particularly when collaborative planning is achieved.

Companies can achieve improved profitability through either increased revenue or reduced costs. On the revenue side, supply chain initiatives such as collaborative demand planning and implementation of real time allocated available to promise (AATP) can deliver improved customer service and a reduction in lost sales, leading to higher market share and gross margins. On the cost side, collaborative supply chain planning can deliver a reduction in costs such as transportation, warehousing, material handling and distribution costs. Further, process integration with supply chain partners in areas such as engineering and marketing enable the sharing of resources and skills with obvious cost benefits.

Companies can also create shareholder value by reducing fixed and working capital. As the aim of the supply chain Kingmaker is to

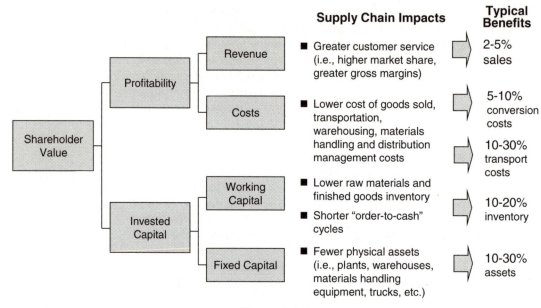

Figure 3.3.5
Supply chain impacts on shareholder value

control the information in the supply chain, not own the assets, it is possible for companies to outsource non-core activities and reduce their working capital tied up in physical assets. Collaborative supply chain planning can also deliver a reduction in working capital through reduction in the levels of raw materials, work-in-progress and finished goods inventory throughout the supply chain.

A good example of a company able to create significant shareholder value is Gambro, a leader in medical technology and healthcare. Due to pressure on profit margins, Gambro was forced to focus on cost-effectiveness and implemented leading supply chain planning software. As a result, Gambro was able to improve on-time deliveries by 30 per cent, while simultaneously reducing finished goods inventory by 40 per cent. Gambro also significantly, reduced working capital by streamlining warehousing operations from 52 warehouses down to 4 distribution centers and 2 satellites.

Accenture's own research has shown that significant benefits can be achieved in all areas of supply chain planning. Collaborative demand and supply planning can reduce production costs by around 10 per cent and inventory by around 2 per cent. Reductions in total inventories occur as increased forecasting accuracy lessens the need to carry large inventories or lengthen lead times. Collaborative logistics operations (including carrier and route management and transportation scheduling) improve supply chain responsiveness, resulting in a reduction in transportation costs of up to 20 per cent. Collaborative product design, incorporating innovation, new product development and design change management can reduce the time to market by up to 33 per cent. In an age where product life cycle is getting progressively shorter, this can result in an invaluable competitive advantage. Finally, the collaborative management of both suppliers and inventory can reduce inventory costs by about 10 per cent. Again, as the product life scale is so short, the timely and accurate flow of information can reduce the needless production of goods, which are immediately consigned to waste.

Barriers to achievement of the benefits

With all the stated benefits of supply chain synchronization, what is preventing the vision becoming a viable reality? Many of the issues hinge on the quality of data and the necessary technical infrastructure. For collaborative planning to be a success, all parties in the supply chain must have their own house in order. Data must be clean because collaboration excellence is not possible using redundant, duplicated or unstructured data. The old computer adage 'rubbish in leads to rubbish out' will always be true.

The quality of data and the technical infrastructure are critical to synchronization. Once these are resolved, then managing the people and process is vital.

Technology standards are critical to enable integration of the technical infrastructure required to support collaboration. While the underlying technology has not been a focus of this chapter, suffice to say that there are several emerging standards – and while standards are emerging there is still sufficient choice to lead to infrastructure chaos.

Another critical issue is the central collaboration mechanism – how should the data be managed? At a technology level there are multiple ways of managing the data. Two alternatives are the propositions:

- 'You come to my hub and pick up/deposit the required information,' and
- 'Pump out data to everyone' – with the resultant 'what and when' translation issues.

An answer to this data transfer issue may lie in the development of a prevalent information hub to support the intelligent supply chain ecosystem. An information hub would involve data being held in a central data repository and the technology designed so that each partner could interface seamlessly for the correct information. Management of this data repository could be a role for the Kingmaker of the future.

Once the data and technical issues have been resolved, it becomes clear that the principal barriers to successful collaborative planning are related to people and process. Collaboration is fundamentally about open business relationships – something of which many companies have proved wary. Traditionally, the buyer and supplier relationship has been a hostile one and over ten years of trying to change this through commercial partnerships, such as CPFR, many have failed to change the traditional behavior patterns.

Another issue, which the Kingmaker should resolve, arises because of the differing objectives of the partner companies. First, the supplier in a supply chain always intends to reach the most profitable outcome with every partner in the supply chain. The supplier is also not keen on sharing any type of price information with his customer. The objective of the Kingmaker is to maximize benefit for the entire supply chain. Second, partners in a supply chain rarely want to exchange competitive information and design or technological know-how so that they do not undermine their own technological competitiveness. Furthermore, with every new stage of collaboration, benefits are realized, but who is the beneficiary? The Kingmaker's role could help to overcome the above selection of possible misalignments by aligning the objectives and planning processes of the supply chain partners.

Conclusion

Increasingly, the best supply chain performers will team with the best partners to reduce costs, improve service and create value within a supply chain.

Supply chain planning excellence has advanced significantly in recent years, but a lot still has to be done before companies can capture the huge potential inherent in achieving collaboration across entire supply chains. Recent experience shows that manufacturers can be up to 70 per cent more profitable if they connect to all of their trading partners through the Internet. Executives will need to 'plan the work' and 'work the plan' if they are to achieve such increases in profit. Establishing performance metrics, for instance, and setting up a strong internal team will be necessary to achieve company objectives.

Supply chains can improve significantly if all participants are able to align their objectives and planning processes through effective collaboration. Some companies may be able to do this through their own dynamics. Or, more realistically, one or more Kingmakers will emerge within an industry to establish alliances of partners across the supply chain so that true collaboration is achieved. Increasingly, the best supply chain performers will team with the best partners to reduce costs, improve service and create value within a supply chain. In the future, the site for competition will be between whole supply chains, rather than between the entities that comprise them.

References

Goldratt, E. M. (1992), *The Goal*, 2nd edn., New York: North River Press.

Hewitt, F. (2001), 'After Supply Chains, Think Demand Pipelines', *SCM Review* (May).

Strategic sourcing and procurement

3.4

Jeffrey S. Russell and Neeraj Thukral

Purchasing has evolved significantly over the last few decades. Suppliers today are providing more of the value to the customer's product, making supplier relationships and flexibility more important than ever. Today, companies typically spend 60 per cent of their revenue on the purchase of goods and services. A 5 per cent reduction in the price of goods and services procured will therefore translate into a 37.5 per cent increase in profitability for the company. Also, purchasing decisions are in many ways now more complex than they used to be and the days of just selecting the supplier with the lowest quoted price are over. As organizations strive to differentiate themselves from their competitors, they must look to alternative methods to cut cost and improve services.

A paradigm shift is required to gain strategic advantage through procurement.

Procurement has appeared on the CEO's radar screen more than ever before as businesses realize that savings from purchasing contribute directly to the bottom line. By focusing on the total cost of ownership, including both quantitative and qualitative process or service improvements, strategic sourcing can also facilitate better internal or external customer service and in so doing increase revenue.

Although companies now have a better understanding of the importance of purchasing in their business, a paradigm shift is still required to gain strategic advantage through procurement. This chapter discusses how procurement professionals can achieve procurement excellence and secure a competitive advantage for their organization. A framework is provided to assess the current state of procurement and to help to develop a vision for a preferred future state. Key strategic sourcing concepts are outlined and the technology tools to enable strategic sourcing described in detail. Finally, trends are considered to help explore how sourcing and procurement will look in tomorrow's world.

Sourcing assessment framework

The terms 'purchasing', 'procurement' and 'strategic sourcing' are often used interchangeably in discussions about the buying activities of companies. However, they are not identical concepts. Purchasing applies to the transactional functions of buying products and services at the lowest possible price. Procurement is a broader activity: it involves the materials management of goods and services in addition to purchasing transactions. Strategic sourcing takes the process further, focusing on developing channels of supply at the lowest total cost to the company, not just the lowest purchase price.

Sourcing is a multidimensional discipline involving the following elements:

- *Aligned strategy.* An organization's sourcing strategy should be aligned with the overall business strategy. The business strategy will drive the kind of relationship that an organization should have with suppliers of a commodity. Also, the business strategy is the key driver of outsourcing decisions.
- *Coordinated processes.* Organizations need to drive out non-value added activities from their sourcing process. Significant time and resources are dedicated to purchase order processing and accounts payables. Process efficiency improvements in this area will have a direct impact on the bottom line of the company. Another non-value added investment in any value chain is inventory. Close relationships with suppliers can help to reduce the inventory carrying costs along the entire value chain.
- *Optimized organization.* Today's procurement has become a specialized function, requiring specialized skills and training. As a result, companies need to train their resources continuously and align their organization structure to deliver maximum value to their business.
- *Enabled technology.* Development of Internet technologies has brought a significant change in the way procurement functions are carried out. Technology has deeply influenced all the components of the procurement cycle, from product development to vendor management. Leading companies are extending information integration to their suppliers and leveraging these technologies. The new technology is increasing collaboration between channel parties and reducing the transaction costs involved.
- *Measured results.* Both internal and external performance management systems are critical to the management and monitoring of an organization's sourcing function. While supplier performance management is critical for relationship management and collaboration efforts, internal performance management is critical to ensure that the procurement function is indeed creating value for the business.

Table 3.4.1
Sourcing assessment framework

Sourcing dimension	Key drivers	Key assessment questions
Aligned strategy	• Strategic supplier partnerships • Global leverage • Product development involvement • Business strategy alignment • Supplier value added	• Is my supplier base too fragmented? • Should I source globally? • Are suppliers integrated with product development? • Am I partnering with key suppliers? • Is procurement a means to an end or a business strategy?
Coordinated processes	• Contract sophistication • Market analysis and hedging • Supplier process linkage • Proactive versus fire-fighting • Supplier replenishment process	• Is the purchase order/contract procedure a simple or difficult operation? • Do we currently hedge volatile/high value material? • Is more time spent fighting fires or engaging in proactive strategic initiatives? • Is inventory owned and managed by suppliers?
Optimized organization	• Continuous learning • Cross-functional involvement • Management talent • Global organization • Professional career track	• Does procurement operate in a functional silo or as part of a cross-functional team? • Is procurement recognized within the company as a 'stop' on the way to executive management? • Is there an atmosphere of continuous learning within procurement?
Enabled technology	• ERP leverage • Efficient data exchange • e-commerce/e-procurement • Procurement decision support • Supply chain planning	• How do I leverage Internet technology? • Is ERP right for my organization? If so, how do I leverage globally? • Are electronic market places used? • Are all key suppliers linked electronically? • Are plans created by using real-time data?
Measured results	• Total value focus • Balanced metrics • Supplier performance metrics • Organizational performance metrics • Value enhanced focus	• Is the performance of suppliers tracked regularly in order to facilitate better decision making? • Do metrics exist to track supplier performance to shareholder value? • Are supplier performance metrics tied to other functional metrics? • Should benchmarking metrics be used? If so, which ones and from what source?

Table 3.4.1 summarizes the key dimensions and questions that managers can ask to assess the performance of an organization.

Several dimensions can be used to measure the effectiveness of sourcing.

How can organizations use this framework to improve their procurement organization? Strategic sourcing provides the principles and practices that can be leveraged to improve the performance of a procurement organization.

Strategic sourcing

Strategic sourcing is about finding the highest value, highest service, and the lowest total cost sources of supply, while ensuring materials and services availability for value-adding activities. It is a disciplined process that buying organizations implement to purchase materials and services from suppliers. Strategic sourcing should embrace all activities within the procurement cycle, from specification of product to receipt and payment of goods and services. It is also about involving procurement earlier in the process to ensure that value and cost are considerations in every sourcing decision made. Above all, strategic sourcing should enhance revenues, not just reduce costs, something that has become increasingly important in ever-competitive markets. As Gattorna (1998) found, a strategic sourcing model can be aligned with business strategy to achieve business objectives.

The key principles involved in strategic sourcing are:

- total cost of ownership (TCO)
- fact-based negotiations
- supplier relationship management (SRM).

Total cost of ownership

TCO is the driver for delivering value through strategic sourcing. While the initial purchase price is a common starting point, it is imperative that organizations move away from their traditional focus on purchase price, towards minimizing TCO and enhancing supplier capability and flexibility.

Quality, price, delivery and service all contribute to the total cost of the goods and services procured. Costs other than purchase price are not as obvious. Table 3.4.2 identifies some of the cost elements assigned to these broad categories.

The TCO model must encompass the full cost of the commodity, including price, usage and administrative costs. Price is not only comprised of the actual price paid, but also includes volume rebates, gain sharing benefits, payment terms and delivery terms. Usage reductions can drive a lower TCO through standardization, elimination, functional equivalents, product redesign, specification changes and scrap reduction. Administrative and process costs are especially important for low-value, high-transaction commodities such as maintenance, repair and operating supplies. These costs can be driven down by automating purchase order processing, consolidated invoicing, stockless inventory and electronic data interchange.

Identifying total cost ownership involves quantifying all the relevant costs and setting targets for future performance. Some companies use activity-based costing and zero-based budgeting to set targets. Others set targets based on industry and competitive benchmarks.

Table 3.4.2
Components of total cost of ownership

TCO element	Cost elements	
Price	• Supplier cost structure • Guaranteed reductions • Volume leverage • Hedging	• Performance/incentive structure • Rebates • Gain sharing
Usage costs	• Product specification • Product design • Customer and product variations • End product cost • Standardization • Elimination	• Functional equivalents • Mix shifting • Extended life products • Scrap • Transportation • Recycle
Administrative and process costs	• Materials planning • Receiving • Performance reporting • Obsolete inventory • Payables • Store/ready to use • Purchase order processing	• Procurement card • Consolidated invoicing • JIT deliveries • Stockless inventory • Electronic ordering/ Internet technology • Quality

Best-practice companies understand and quantify the total cost of ownership. Mediocre companies are more likely to focus exclusively on price reductions, with the result that costs pop up elsewhere in the same way as air squeezed from one end of a balloon to the other. What, for example, is the point of buying in bulk at a low price if large warehousing costs are then incurred, or the goods become obsolete? Both eventualities affect overall expenditure. Similarly, poor forecasting can impose extra costs on suppliers by increasing their set-up expenses, which are eventually passed on as higher charges.

Fact-based negotiations
Successfully implementing strategic sourcing relies largely on the ability to undertake fact-based negotiations. This method, outlined in Figure 3.4.1, takes a TCO approach to selecting suppliers, rather than focusing on the purchase price alone. The fact-based approach achieves a win–win outcome as opposed to the win–lose result of more traditional supplier-buyer relationships.

To carry out fact-based negotiations, a team is assembled comprising people with experience in a range of business functions, from procurement, engineering and finance, to maintenance and R&D. Conducting specific industry and supplier analysis provides the team with strong knowledge about cost drivers and the unique capability of each potential supplier. Generally done as a first-stage screening, fact-based negotiations provide a high-level understanding of which suppliers are broadly aligned with the company's sourcing

SRM is a coordinated program of actions developed jointly by buyer and supplier to improve overall performance and reduce total costs in the supply chain.

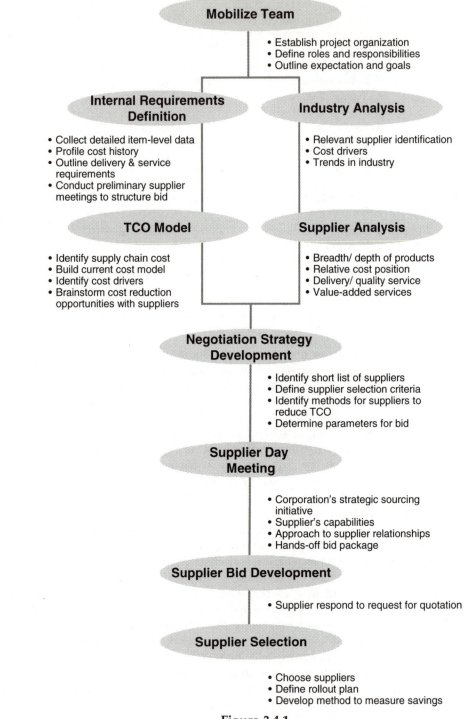

Mobilize Team
- Establish project organization
- Define roles and responsibilities
- Outline expectation and goals

Internal Requirements Definition
- Collect detailed item-level data
- Profile cost history
- Outline delivery & service requirements
- Conduct preliminary supplier meetings to structure bid

Industry Analysis
- Relevant supplier identification
- Cost drivers
- Trends in industry

TCO Model
- Identify supply chain cost
- Build current cost model
- Identify cost drivers
- Brainstorm cost reduction opportunities with suppliers

Supplier Analysis
- Breadth/ depth of products
- Relative cost position
- Delivery/ quality service
- Value-added services

Negotiation Strategy Development
- Identify short list of suppliers
- Define supplier selection criteria
- Identify methods for suppliers to reduce TCO
- Determine parameters for bid

Supplier Day Meeting
- Corporation's strategic sourcing initiative
- Supplier's capabilities
- Approach to supplier relationships
- Hands-off bid package

Supplier Bid Development
- Supplier respond to request for quotation

Supplier Selection
- Choose suppliers
- Define rollout plan
- Develop method to measure savings

Figure 3.4.1
Fact-based negotiation process

requirements. Organizations will need to consider issues such as whether the potential supplier has the required capacity and the necessary breadth of product lines and whether it can perform R&D to support new product development.

To conduct industry and supplier analysis, as outlined in Figure 3.4.1 above, the team can use various sources such as industry reports, trade publications, published work of industry associations and industry analysts and Internet research. Site surveys of suppliers may be undertaken and an analysis of raw materials pricing trends will be critical to understanding changes in commodity pricing over time.

Analytical techniques have to be focused internally as well. Companies will not have credibility with suppliers if they cannot demonstrate a detailed understanding of spending at the item level within a commodity group. Data on item purchase volumes, inventory levels, cost history and delivery and service requirements will help develop the quantitative portion of the request for quotation (RFQ) and begin to define the categories within the TCO model.

More time and effort spent up-front will drastically minimize issues when bids are evaluated.

Strategy development requires the team to consider issues such as: can we sole source?, should we index to a base raw material price?, how long should the contract run?, can we source globally? and should we qualify additional sources? In order to develop quantitative supplier selection criteria with weighting and scoring guidelines based on pricing, delivery, service, value-added service and overall supplier capabilities, the team will identify, with respect to the company's situation, the critical factors of each commodity. More time and effort spent up-front will drastically minimize issues when the bids are evaluated.

Communications between the sourcing team and prospective suppliers are critical throughout the process, ensuring that suppliers will fully understand the requirements. The team will have to decide the number of suppliers, the requirements for back-up capacity and percentage award to the suppliers if the bid is multisourced. Once the supplier is chosen, implementation planning with the supplier will ensure a smooth rollout. Communications throughout all levels of the organization are needed to resolve issues immediately. Follow-up meetings on a quarterly basis with the supplier will allow continuous total cost reductions and a successful longer-term relationship.

Supplier relationship management

SRM differs in two key respects from most other attempts to improve supplier performance, because these are usually based on measurement alone. Under SRM the improvement agenda and metrics are jointly owned and developed by both buyer and supplier. Moreover, they are backed by a commitment from both sides, which can include investments of capital, resource and time, to introduce the new, broader SRM philosophy. Both parties are working towards a common goal of improving the efficiency of the supply chain, and both have a direct financial interest in the success of the relationship.

SRM is a coordinated program of actions developed jointly by buyer and supplier to improve overall performance and reduce total costs in the supply chain.

A frequently quoted example of an SRM relationship is that between auto manufacturers and car seat suppliers, where the latter deliver made-up units to the line-side with a high degree of precision on a just-in-time basis.

The foundation of SRM is a process-based approach to improving relationships with suppliers by developing a detailed understanding of the operational issues that affect the relationship on a daily basis.

Implementation of SRM

SRM implementation consists of three main phases. These are, first, for the buyer to identify the relevant targets for cost savings, both in terms of the categories of purchase and the suppliers that are to be targeted.

The next stage is to develop a detailed bottom-up view of the relevant performance issues – taking a view across the entire supply chain, starting with the purchasing function of the supplier, through to the buyer's production line and the information flows back to the supplier.

Finally, supplier and buyer then need to validate and prioritize the areas which are to be the subject of the SRM program in a joint forum where they make a commitment to a coordinated program of action to achieve the intended results.

While SRM generally has a medium to long-term focus, it can also deliver immediate wins (in as little as one to two months) when channeled correctly. Indeed, short-term success is an important factor in driving a successful SRM program.

Benefits of SRM

SRM takes a 'nuts-and-bolts' view of the relationship and examines it from an operational perspective to identify improvement opportunities, many of which lie within the buying organization. It is only through an SRM program that many companies have learned the extent to which they have inadvertently 'engineered cost' into their supplier relationships, processes, and products.

SRM is also a key generator of cost-reduction opportunities and can be a significant driver of innovation within a company. Improvement opportunities identified range from new product development, through packaging, despatch, inbound inspection and line-side delivery to 'power-by-the-hour' deals, which support the product in operation. In this way SRM programs can touch virtually all parts of the supply chain through to the end user.

SRM also represents a fertile training ground for understanding customer requirements on both the buyer and supplier side by laying out the cost savings, improvements, and contribution to customer satisfaction of all opportunities identified, and importantly, also embeds responsibility for delivery of benefits at an operational level, and systematically encourages longer-term, supply-chain wide thinking. In this way it can be a good facilitator of other, deeper cross-company supply-chain wide initiatives such as collaborative planning, forecasting and replenishment (CPFR).

Leading practices in procurement

Most companies undergo an evolutionary journey towards maturity of their procurement function, with the typical stages being innocence, awareness, typical, adding value, and leading edge. Organizations increase their strategic value and capability as they develop with each procurement stage.

Companies increase their strategic value and capability as they develop with each procurement stage.

To embark on this journey, the first step an organization needs to take is to assess its current state of procurement practices. That is, whether it is at the innocence, awareness, typical, adding value, or leading-edge stage of maturity. Organizations could be at different stages of maturity across various sourcing dimensions.

The next step is to identify the stage where the organization wants to be. This will be driven by overall business strategy and imperatives. This is then followed with designing the path that the organization needs to take to achieve the desired stage. This will involve due consideration of the adaptability, skill levels, and change readiness of the personnel involved.

The following Table 3.4.3 provides an overview of the leading practices associated with the different dimensions of sourcing. It is important to remember that although organizations should always strive for leading practices, they need to undergo an evolutionary development process and manage the change in alignment needed for different business realities.

Table 3.4.3
Leading practices in sourcing

Sourcing dimension	Key driver	Leading practice
Strategy alignment	Strategic supplier partnerships	• Key suppliers contribute to strategic planning • Suppliers seen as extensions of internal business • Mutual respect permits free flow of ideas to ensure enterprise wide success
	Global leverage	• Mature global supplier base achieves consistent performance and quality across the entire network • Other functions operating globally further enabling coordination
	Product development involvement	• Suppliers effectively performing component development freeing engineering resources and enabling reduced development cycles and increased product innovations
	Business strategy alignment	• Metrics and procurement's actions are in harmony with business strategies • Competencies gained through supplier partner present new strategies and growth opportunities for business

Table 3.4.3 (continued)

Sourcing dimension	Key driver	Leading practice
	Supplier value added	• Most or all non-core business activities are outsourced to trusted world class suppliers, freeing up company assets to be devoted wholly to core competencies
Coordinated processes	Contract sophistication	• The purchase order is not necessary due to integration of supplier processes with buyer's • Procurement cards widely used • Terms of relationship may include continuous improvement technology
	Market analysis hedging	• Market intelligence is gathered, screened, and 'pushed' to management in real time • If no futures market exists for volatile, high value materials, management creates one
	Supplier process linkage	• Strategic supplier partners manage certain buyer processes as key part of business model • Suppliers paid on basis of services rather than materials shipped
	Proactive versus fire-fighting	• Process re-engineering and technology have enabled individual contributors to spend most time engaged in strategic activities and improvement initiatives
	Supplier replenishment process	• Supplier fully integrated into the production process while all inventory is owned and managed by suppliers • Payment is according to usage
Optimized organization	Continuous learning	• Continuous learning is part of the balanced scorecard and results in innovation and value • Clearly defined competency model • 'Plugged in' to best thinking through academic, other relationships
	Cross-functional involvement	• Procurement is more of a centre of excellence than a functional group • Personnel are aligned more with manufacturing cells or project teams (such as product development and source selection)
	Management talent	• Procurement is a 'stop' on fast track to executive management • Among peers, procurement is recognized as professional and a source of considerable management talent
	Global organization	• Global organization serves as a 'center of excellence' • Global group is able to deliver significant value on production materials due to other functions coordinating globally
	Professional career track	• Concern that procurement managers are targets for other companies and executive search firms • Individuals desire to work in procurement due to fast pace and promotion opportunities
Enabling technology	ERP leverage	• ERP leveraged on global basis allowing full data capture, common measurements, and decision support capability • Web technology used to link ERP to suppliers' systems

Table 3.4.3 (continued)

Sourcing dimension	Key driver	Leading practice
	Efficient data exchange	• Web technology has rendered EDI obsolete • Suppliers have access to internal demand/production plans, adjust their production, and replenish accordingly
	e-commerce/ e-procurement	• 'Middleware' used to link internal ERP to those of suppliers and exchange transaction data • Electronic marketplaces are used to purchase materials that are in short supply
	Procurement decision support	• Decision support tools passively gather relevant performance or market data • Information is customized and 'pushed' to user regularly or accessed when needed
	Supply chain planning	• Joint customer and supplier chain planning is performed on a 'real time' basis by leveraging ERP data, middleware, and/or web technology
Measured results	Total value focus	• Total value of ownership (TVO) analysis used to adjust supplier assessment and gain insight into supplier's ability to impact top-line revenue enhancement as well as total supply chain costs
	Balance metrics	• Balanced metrics package in place that drives value creation and includes measures that capture financial performance, process improvement, customer focus and innovation
	Supplier performance metrics	• Key supplier metrics collected automatically, and made available to decision makers on demand

Technology enablers

The technology enablers that have significantly influenced or are influencing the procurement landscape are: e-requisitioning, B2B e-markets and e-sourcing. e-requisitioning and e-sourcing are usually together referred to as 'e-procurement'.

e-requisitioning

e-procurement creates value through the combined impact of more efficient procurement processes and more effective supplier relationships. e-procurement leverages global electronic networks to integrate buyer and seller processes to provide a real-time platform for conducting business.

e-requisitioning has, until recently, been focused on indirect goods and services. Process savings have been achieved through eliminating inefficiencies in accounts payable and the 'lock-in' of negotiated prices for corporate contracts. Companies have targeted about 5–8 per cent in spend savings addressed by e-requisitioning.

e-requisitioning has introduced self-service purchasing to casual buyers in large organizations. The unique proposition of e-requisitioning is that it enables users to select pre-specified items from an electronic catalogue at better contracted rates than individuals could attain, and to process those orders with suppliers electronically in as efficient and cost-effective a manner as possible.

Some of the value generated by e-requisitioning includes:

- *Reduced administrative costs.* Time spent on requisition-to-pay activities is estimated at more than $100 per transaction. e-requisitioning enables corporate users to buy efficiently, remove non-value-adding steps in the procurement process, and eliminate the usual order and invoice error processing. The cost of an e-requisition is therefore comparatively low – estimates are in the $10 to $30 range.
- *Improved sourcing and supplier management.* Generally, an estimate of historical spends without any forecasting or segmentation of demand is used as a basis for contracting with suppliers, resulting in poor decisions. e-requisitioning plays an important role in improving sourcing performance.
- *Rollout and sustain sourcing deals.* Benefits that have been negotiated through better sourcing contracts typically phase in gradually. e-requisitioning accelerates the rollout of new deals by embedding the new arrangements in electronic catalogs or providing easy-reference contracts databases for those items or services that cannot be e-requisitioned. Terms become effective as soon as a new catalog is in place, ensuring that the benefits are achieved immediately.
- *Enable (and share) supplier benefits.* Most procurement departments aspire to have more strategic relationships with fewer suppliers. While this does not lead to a partnership in every case, it requires the procurement department to commit to professional and efficient daily operational contact with suppliers. e-requisitioning supports this goal with the ability to order accurately, deliver expected spend volumes and pay on time, thereby delivering financial benefits through shared savings.

It is true that with enough management attention and effort within the procurement organization, and enough external goodwill, each of these goals could possibly be achieved without e-procurement capabilities. However, the reality is that procurement generally is not a high priority for corporate users and the burden of administration has prevented many organizations from effectively implementing strategic sourcing programs.

B2B e-markets

B2B e-markets leverage the power of the Internet to bring many suppliers and buyers together to carry out transactions efficiently. In addition, e-markets endeavor to drive out inefficiencies from the market and provide value-added services to its participants.

There are primarily three types of e-markets:

Private exchange. This is a one-to-many connection between a company and its trading partners. Private exchanges typically offer a customizable interface and can support deep collaboration. They provide access to the company's qualified supplier base or known customers, but do not enable companies to look beyond the trading partners they already know.

Industry consortia. This is a some-to-many connection among industry members and their trading partners. Consortium e-markets might offer almost as much collaborative capability as private exchanges, but at the expense of standardizing processes across members. Consortium e-markets give individual members access to each other's trading partners. In addition, they might allow other companies to join e-market, which broadens access.

Independent e-market. This is a many-to-many connection among buyers and sellers through an independent intermediary. Independent e-markets have the widest variety of participants, which maximizes access but makes deep collaboration difficult.

In early 2000, independent e-markets looked like the wave of the future. Analysts predicted that as many as 10 000 e-markets would flourish by 2004. Clearly, the marketplace has entered a period of rationalization, selecting business models that work and eliminating those that do not. Ultimately, this is likely to result in about 200 major surviving industry consortia, 500 independent e-markets, and 2 000 private exchanges.

Euphoria around B2B e-markets in early 2000 has been replaced by a pragmatic approach towards supplier collaboration through private exchanges.

For a long time, companies have wanted to foster supply chain collaboration, but the tools to do so just have not been in place. Essentially, private exchanges have combined the tools and technologies that are supporting public exchanges with traditional supply chain management applications. This combination has created an opportunity to truly implement a collaborative supply chain.

Companies need to assess their capability to support a private exchange. The three facets of capability are: the degree of buying power, the strength of market position and the size of the company or business unit creating the market exchange. The companies also need to evaluate the strategic fit: the complexity of the supply chain, uniqueness of the design or product, and link to the product life cycle.

e-sourcing

The concept of 'e-sourcing' addresses the idea that tools can be used to complement the traditional strategic sourcing process. An emerging breed of software solutions is looking to transcend the transactional buying hitherto targeted by e-requisitioning systems and focus on enabling the high-impact, strategic activities of sourcing and supply management.

e-sourcing provides tools to identify potential suppliers and negotiate the lowest cost.

Starting with online bidding or e-auctioning, software is being developed at pace as vendors look to cover the entire strategic sourcing process from supplier identification and analysis, online RFPs and RFQs to ongoing supplier management and scorecard functionality, as shown in Figure 3.4.2 below.

Implementation lessons learned

As with any enterprise software installation or business initiative, organizations have to overcome cultural, process and technical hurdles to access the total value available. Organizations first need to develop a robust and realistic business case for their initiative. They need to take care to distinguish software hype from reality – technology should not be regarded as the cure-all for any problem, but the enabler of a wider strategy. Processes, people and strategy are all needed to support the best solution.

There is also no substitute for planning. Before the implementation, companies should spend time assessing and planning the implementation. This will involve understanding how much they want to spend, on which products, and with which suppliers. A

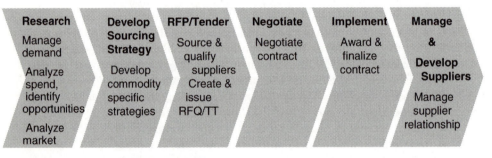

- e-intelligence from multiple buying tools
- Online market analysis, i.e. newsfeeds, market intelligence, corporate information
- 3rd party service capability, i.e. spend analysis supported by strategic sourcing services
- Online negotiation, sealed bidding and auction
    - multiple formats, languages & currencies
    - 3rd party services: event setup, training & facilitation
- Industry-specific marketplaces and online 'communities' and directories
- Online process tools based on best practices
- e-RFI creation
- e-RFP/Q creation:
    - Multi-line, multi-parameter
    - Automatic weighting of responses for assessment and elimination of suppliers
    - Collaborative tool/template creation allows group-wide re-use
- Weighing of bids to reflect total cost of commodity ownership & supplier track record
- Online confirmation of contracts

Figure 3.4.2
Applying new technologies to the purchasing cycle

preliminary spend analysis can identify opportunities for improving contract compliance, aggregating spending and rationalizing the supply base.

The level of success of an e-procurement initiative is inherently tied to the support it achieves from executives. Since e-procurement touches every aspect of the business, it is even more critical to have strong sponsorship and to manage change across the enterprise. e-procurement champions are typically pulled from the purchasing or IT departments and need to be responsible for driving system deployment and adoption, measuring results, communicating successes and repairing glitches.

The most successful companies always allocate time to do their homework. If they are looking to complete an auction, they need to research the market to find out what they are buying so that they can prioritize category-specific improvement projects. Generally, companies need to conduct market analysis so they can decide whether point solutions or an integrated suite of products is most appropriate. Technology will continue to develop and functionality will evolve but organizations need to consider the merits of delayed versus early adoption. They can use a pilot to test the concept and software before starting a full-scale rollout.

In most cases, achieving maximum participation by suppliers is a critical part of implementation and a significant key to success. Strategies to accelerate supplier adoption include educating suppliers on the value of e-procurement, providing tools and services for easing participation and driving additional business to participating suppliers. At the same time, suppliers not keen on adopting e-procurement can be penalized through fees or limiting the volume of business awarded to non-compliant suppliers.

Successful implementors ensure they establish a system for performance management. They set and monitor performance parameters such as user adoption, contract compliance, process improvements, and cost savings and supplier adoption. These measures help to demonstrate the value of e-procurement to all constituents and identify areas for improvement.

Overall, companies embarking on an e-procurement project need to be clear about what they want to achieve, how they want to achieve it and in what time-scale. They need to consider their strategy and opportunities for short and long-term value creation. Once they have identified priorities and needs, the choice of technology platform will become clearer.

What is the future of procurement?

Internet technology, collaboration imperatives and global competition are some of the forces that will be shaping the future of procurement.

The major trends we expect to see are outlined below; some may be already in planning or visible in some organizations today.

e-sourcing

While niche products will continue to emerge, economic realities and user demand for integrated suites will drive vendor consolidation. We expect to see:

- the development of deeper product functionality, especially in e-tendering and e-auctions,
- a new focus on less mature areas, including supplier development and advanced contract management, and
- the development of broader, integrated solutions, either proprietary or more likely through acquisitions/alliances.

Overall, no solution will suit all organizations. Some strategies enabled by sourcing tools – for example, reverse auctions – also might not be appropriate for all industries or organizations or indeed across commodities. Leveraging existing purchasing expertise and methodologies across industries, software vendors will need to provide an interoperable suite of online solutions that can be mixed and matched as required across an organization. Above all, historical barriers to e-sourcing are falling as client capabilities and technologies mature.

Outsourced procurement services

A market is emerging for outsourced procurement services in the same way that transportation, logistics, contract manufacturing and R&D have become large markets for third-party providers. A class of third-party sourcing providers will emerge to satisfy the needs of companies seeking to outsource part or all of their procurement efforts. Several local and global companies are already operating in this arena.

External intelligence aggregators

Companies will outsource procurement services and gain intelligence from third-party providers.

A market for the aggregation and warehousing of supplier information will emerge. This information will reach beyond product content information housed in the databases provided by companies such as Aspect Development (now a part of i2 Technologies), lists of suppliers by category (TPN Register) and supplier financial and credit information (Dun & Bradstreet). These third-party providers will be acting as the initial nucleus of supplier information – capturing all data such as performance and capacity information on a real-time basis. This means that commodity buyers can 'plug' into this hub when they need to make a sourcing decision, shortening the sourcing cycle considerably.

Increased collaboration across the value chain

Selection of suppliers will become more critical to companies in the future. Resources will be increasingly shared between interdependent firms that rely on each other as customer/suppliers in the supply chain to maximize value-added contributions and reduce the duplication of resources. Procurement managers will be required to study their supply chains and search for opportunities to achieve competitive advantage through their choice of supply chain partners, determination of core competencies and influence of design, manufacturing, operations and sourcing.

Greater collaboration will occur, placing more importance on the choice of partner.

Demand-pull purchasing

As indicated in the joint research conducted by CAPS, NAPM and AT Kearney, demand-pull systems will become a norm. With suppliers becoming more integrated and involved throughout the chain, the Internet is providing more information to facilitate this transition. The major challenge will lie in getting uniform systems across supply chain members to work together. These systems will be enabled by enterprise-based software and Internet technology. Already initiatives such as collaborative planning, forecasting and replenishment, and enabled uniform standards such as XML are being rolled out across the companies. This trend is expected to strengthen in the future.

Organizations will increase their focus on managing relationships with suppliers and customers.

Focus on vendor relationship management

Organizations will increase their focus on relationship management with suppliers and customers because of increasing global competitiveness, limited resources and the need for global reach while maintaining flexibility. The relationship focus will require trust building, communications and joint efforts, while planning will be increasingly studied and managed to achieve competitive advantage.

Global supplier development

The Internet is improving the availability of information on suppliers. At the same time, technologies such as e-auctions are eliminating the need for face-to-face negotiations. Consequently, companies are involving overseas suppliers in the sourcing initiatives. This is generating additional competitive pressure on the local suppliers to improve their performance and also helping the buyer organization in case of foreign market penetration.

Third-party purchasing

Companies will buy most non-tactical products and services under master contracts. Consortia that have leverage and buying expertise will negotiate some contracts. Other contracts will be with third-party companies that also have leverage and buying expertise.

Negotiation strategy

Negotiation strategy is continuing to move towards a win–win relationship. Companies are looking at total cost as a criterion, and a strong win–win relationship is critical to reducing total cost. Negotiations will become more complex and sophisticated and rely less on emotions.

Conclusion

Companies that can manage the virtual networks of tomorrow will be the winners.

Sourcing and procurement have undergone a paradigm shift in the last decade or so. Organizations are changing in three fundamental ways: they are integrating and collaborating with their suppliers; they are increasing their technology enablement of sourcing processes; and they are focusing on their core competencies and outsourcing their non-core capabilities. Internet technology is also continuously changing the way organizations conduct their sourcing and procurement. New procurement tools can enable strategic sourcing cycles to be conducted more often, more consistently and with less effort. All of these changes necessitate a change in the mindset from 'win–lose' to 'win–win' in all transactions with suppliers. Tomorrow, competition will not be between individual organizations, but among value chains and organizations. Those who have developed the capability to manage their virtual network effectively will be the winners.

References

Alaniz, S. and Shuffield, E. (2001), *Strategic Sourcing: Applications to Turn Direct Materials Procurement into a Competitive Advantage*, Stephens Inc. Internet Research.

Berger, A. J. and Gattorna, J. L. (2001), *Supply Chain Cybermastery*, Aldershot: Gower Publishing Ltd.

Carter, P. L. et al. (1998), *The Future of Purchasing and Supply: A Five- and Ten-Year Forecast*, A joint research initiative of CAPS, NAPM and AT. Kearney, Inc.

Gattorna, J. G. (1998), *Strategic Supply Chain Alignment*, Aldershot: Gower Publishing Ltd, pp. 285–301.

Krause, D. R. and Handfield, R. B. (1998), *Developing a World-Class Supply Base*, Centre for Advanced Purchasing Studies.

Minahan, T. and Degnan C. (2001), *Best practices in e-Procurement*, Boston: Aberdeen Group.

Phythian, P. and Allen, R. (2002), 'Back to basics', *Logistics Europe* (March), pp. 20–22.

Securing immediate benefits from e-sourcing

3.5

Brett Campbell and Anthony Du Preez

The powerful combination of logistics and e-commerce is expected to fuel significant changes in the business landscape. e-commerce will provide the ability for many companies to communicate and exchange transactions with each other, and logistics will provide the capability to use this information to manage business activities more effectively. Instead of two-way relationships between a supplier and a customer, business will increasingly revolve around supply chain networks made up of groups of suppliers and groups of customers.

Business leaders need to identify how their company will be affected by the emergence of dynamic supply chain networks.

e-commerce not only allows this connectivity of multiple companies in the form of a network, but also provides the flexibility for companies to join or leave the network at short notice and for the products and services to change and develop quickly. In this sense the trading conducted within the network will be more dynamic than supply chain executives are used to with the current generation of systems. This new form of commerce has been termed dynamic supply chain networks or simply *dynamic trading*.

This chapter looks at how a buying organization can use emerging e-sourcing technologies to achieve the best possible outcome – speedily and effectively. As e-commerce starts to have an impact on relationships with trading partners, supply chain managers need to consider which trading partners provide the best opportunity (or the greatest threat) to positively change the way they conduct business. From a supply chain perspective, partnerships fall neatly into two groups: either upstream trading partners such as suppliers, or downstream partners such as customers and consumers. Significant opportunities exist for developing competitive supply chains within both groups by using e-sourcing and associated techniques such as reverse alignment and e-auctions.

The chapter reviews the new paradigm of reverse alignment. It assesses new tools that are being developed for e-sourcing to respond to different sourcing needs of buyers. One of the most powerful of these new tools is e-auctions, which use real-time dynamic pricing environments to achieve maximum competition for buyers. Finally a forward outlook is given; integrating aspects of e-auctions, reverse alignment, and e-sourcing.

Aligning procurement strategy and e-commerce

Companies must realign their organization to maximize the opportunities presented by dynamic purchase networks.

The critical factor for dynamic purchase networks is to ensure that the procurement strategy and the new e-commerce-enabled approach to purchasing are aligned. One of the most common mistakes is to apply a 'one-size-fits-all' approach: choosing a strategy and forcing all procurement activities through that strategy. Supply chain professionals must reconsider the existing purchasing strategies for each commodity group in the light of new processes and technologies, then develop the most appropriate strategy to purchasing that best serves the objectives of the company. The type of commodity, number of

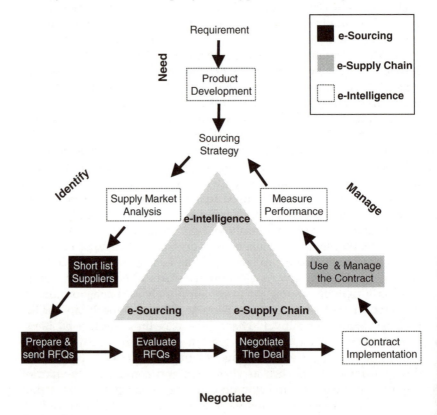

Source: Accenture

Figure 3.5.1
e-sourcing in the supply chain

potential suppliers, level of sophistication of suppliers and use of the commodity all have an impact on how to operate within dynamic purchase networks.

As part of cost reduction through purchase networks, many companies are attracted to the medium- to long-term benefits from e-commerce using B2B exchanges and other supply chain initiatives such as e-procurement. One of the most effective and readily adopted techniques has been e-sourcing, including electronic requests for quotation (e-RFQs), and e-auctions. As can be seen in Figure 3.5.1, e-sourcing is part of the identification and negotiation areas of the end-to-end sourcing process.

The benefits from supply chain initiatives can amount to tens of millions of dollars; however, the payback often exceeds 12 months. Companies spending time building participation in the new systems, and hence achieving the scale required to make these new systems viable, cause a time lag to occur between implementation and benefit realization. Participation itself is dependent on establishing contracts and agreements; these can take months to finalize using traditional static, or one-on-one, negotiation techniques.

To maximize the opportunities presented by dynamic purchase networks, companies must realign their organization to focus on efficiencies and cost reductions in their supply base. Most companies spend considerable time and energy on market alignment, through getting their revenue models correct, optimizing their sales channel strategies, developing partnerships with customers to lock out competition, and trying to establish differentiators that will sustain their customer relationships, as illustrated in Figure 3.5.2.

Traditionally, these activities have been based on one-to-one discussions in a static negotiation framework. Emotional, subjective relationships have been developed where the alignment of the buyer is tied as closely as possible to the supplier. Purchasing departments must find ways to balance the (often competing) demands of strong supplier relationships versus achieving the best price for commodities or services. In one-to-one negotiations the personality factor can influence decisions in ways that are not to the benefit of the buying organization.

The advent of e-commerce and dynamic trading is quickly making emotional, subjective relationships obsolete.

The advent of e-commerce and dynamic trading is quickly making these subjective relationships obsolete as increased volumes of information put all business and purchasing decisions under objective scrutiny. This focus back down the supply chain is called *reverse alignment*.

The traditional business focus has been on revenue models. In contrast, dynamic trading now allows an increased focus on cost models. Since organizations are suppliers to other organizations in the supply chain, the focus on costs is now ubiquitous. Organizational leaders must adapt and drive a capability which is responsive to market opportunities; this will be relevant in both sales and cost reduction efforts. Dynamic trading allows market factors such as

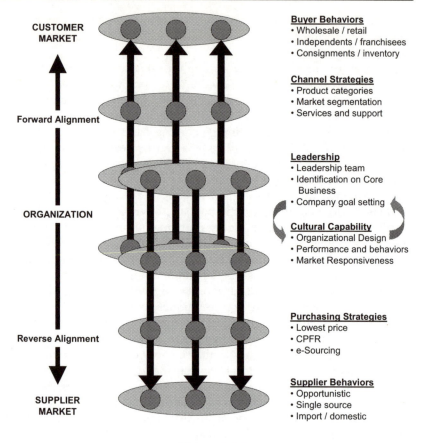

Figure 3.5.2
Forward and reverse alignment

supply and demand to be managed at the total market level as well as the individual organization level.

In much the same way as companies develop their forward alignment, leading companies are starting to embrace the concept of reverse alignment. The same foundations for success are required. The company's leaders must work hard and consistently to develop the appropriate cultural capabilities to realize the potential of reverse alignment. Just as forward alignment relies on an analysis of the customer market, reverse alignment begins with an understanding of the supplier market. Purchasing strategies must be developed for each different purchasing group, that is some indirect, non-strategic items are best bought on a purely 'lowest-price' basis, and more collaborative planning can be used to best manage the purchasing of inputs for products which have accurate and quick sales and forecast downloads from customers.

The combination of appropriate purchasing strategies and dynamic trading environments will provide organizations with immediate benefits. The quality and integrity of decisions will rise because of the transparent nature of the negotiation and the increased volume of data that can be managed. Reverse alignment will set the foundation for these higher quality decisions, and e-sourcing is the strategy to maximize the benefits.

e-sourcing

One of the most powerful strategies to emerge over the last few years has been e-sourcing. e-sourcing can dramatically improve purchasing decisions through techniques for rapid market and price discovery. Suppliers may see themselves in three ways: (1) they may be opportunistic, (2) they try to dominate the market as single-source suppliers, or (3) they attempt to develop long-term relationships. To take maximum advantage of purchasing opportunities and to continue to build shareholder value, leading companies must recognize and understand these different attributes in the supplier market. Companies can then apply reverse alignment thinking to their purchasing strategies to achieve maximum value from their supplier market.

e-sourcing can dramatically improve purchasing decisions through techniques for rapid market and price discovery.

e-sourcing uses a variety of tools to complement the traditional process for strategic sourcing. An emerging breed of software solutions is looking to transcend the transactional buying that has been targeted by e-requisitioning systems. e-sourcing focuses on enabling the high-impact, strategic activities of sourcing and supply management.

Software for online bidding or e-auctioning is quickly being developed as vendors look to cover the entire strategic sourcing process from supplier identification and analysis, online requests for proposals (RFPs) and RFQs to ongoing supplier management and scorecard functionality.

Software vendors normally predict that the use of sourcing tools will achieve savings of 40 to 70 per cent and a return on investment within three months. While this has not yet been proven on a significant scale, the true value lies in the ability of these tools to speed up existing manual processes and enable faster realization of the savings that are otherwise associated with strategic sourcing. Sourcing tools can also be used to counter some of the traditional weaknesses of strategic sourcing. The tools allow organizations to focus more on commodities or categories and repeat strategic sourcing cycles more frequently, thus achieving higher returns in the immediate term.

An analysis of e-sourcing tools shows the key areas where the tools can be used, the business needs that are driving them and the functionality they can provide to organizations, as summarized below.

e-tendering

e-tendering tools can enable speedy submission and evaluation of RFQs, improved fact-based negotiations and reduced cycle times.

e-tendering provides value in the following ways:

- allows users to quickly create, submit and evaluate RFQs and link to traditional negotiations or e-auctions
- centralized RFI/RFP/RFQ and e-auction applications provide a one-stop shop for the entire process
- makes tendering and negotiation more effective by moving the communication, comparison and negotiation of contracts online
- provides, stores and identifies critical information for effective fact-based negotiation
- reduces strategic sourcing cycle times – repeatable set-up process, stored templates and reduced costs
- provides enhanced, effective and efficient negotiation capabilities – using database data-mining capabilities,
- improves quality management through standardized and consistent processes and templates, and
- becomes an effective tool to reduce purchase costs when combined with e-auctions.

e-tendering tools include:

- *ERFI*. This tool captures supplier information electronically and enables online supplier qualification. To date, no vendors fully cover this capability, although Frictionless Commerce and Atlas Commerce are the closest.
- *e-RFP/Q*. These tools enable Web-based creation, distribution, tracking, and advanced analysis of requests for proposals or quotes with integration into other sourcing channels, such as sealed bids or e-auctions. The main vendors working in this area include B2Emarkets, Frictionless Commerce, Portum and Webango. For highly complex criteria selection, Hologix also have a deep relational database solution.
- *e-auctions*. These tools cover both online reverse and forward auctions between buyer and chosen suppliers. Current solutions typically focus on creating a dynamic pricing environment to maximize competition. New functionality is emerging to allow weighted averaging of results to permit a focus on price and all other significant decision factors. The main vendors working in this area include Moai, Portum, Ariba and Commerce One. An Australian vendor called BOMweb is also emerging with leading functionality. e-auctions provide the most transparent, dynamic environment for commercial transactions. They will become one of the most important elements of e-commerce, and e-auctions will be explained in more detail later in this chapter.

Procurement portals

Because of the complexity of the strategic sourcing process, it is critical that the individual tools related to the different sourcing steps are connected. Procurement professionals need easy-to-use tools and easy access to information at the point of need. Many clients are looking at Intranet and Internet portals as the important enabling factor to achieve this. Vendors working in this space include Plumtree and RadNet. Typically, such vendors provide:

Intranet and Internet portals can provide easy access to information at critical points in the sourcing process.

- *Easier access to information.* A single access point can be provided to all the supporting tools that procurement professionals need. Users can easily access tools and documents regardless of location and format. The portal can be personalized to deliver role-relevant external and internal information and contain the right tools for the job.
- *Increased collaboration and use of information.* Information-sharing tools can facilitate collaboration and support global standardization processes. They also provide the potential to connect and collaborate with suppliers and external partners.
- *Virtual communication space.* Portals can offer several virtual meeting tools, which can reduce travel time and costs while maintaining the speed of decision-making through close contact. This feature can also help foster buyer communities and maintain buyer–supplier relationships.
- *Flexible user and technology platform.* The use of flexible Internet-centric architecture reduces the 'cost of ownership' of IT systems. Portals can be easy to maintain and upgrade as business needs change.

While the majority of vendors are focusing on the up-front phases of a sourcing decision, few have paid more than cursory attention to the equally significant areas of supplier development and ongoing contract management. e-procurement tools can be used to enforce compliance to a contract and reduce maverick spending. However, once an agreement has been made, organizations must still continue to ensure that the actual terms of that contract are met and that supplier performance continues to meet expectations. While this need is widely recognized, it has received limited attention to date.

Organizations need to maintain thousands of contracts while also monitoring supplier performance against those contracts.

The opportunities for sourcing vendors are clear. Organizations continue to struggle both to maintain thousands of inconsistently or arbitrarily developed contracts and also to monitor supplier performance against those contracts. While some organizations have invested in customized databases to organize contracts, automation has largely concentrated on the call-off process only. Applications from vendors such as diCarta, Menerva and Frictionless Commerce focus on contract creation and management, including the impact of terminology changes. However, further opportunities to expand functionality and services exist across the following areas:

- improved contract visibility (to both buyers and suppliers)
- document management (including access to expired or cross-company contracts)
- standardization and classification of contract content (templates)
- contract generation and approval management
- supplier performance management against contract (including relationship scorecards, quality metrics, surveys and links to penalty and termination clauses for underperformance)
- record of purchasing history per supplier
- contract price compliance (including identification of overpayment), and
- automatic notification of contract expiry or milestone dates.

Other sourcing tools

e-intelligence
e-intelligence enables the buyer to access and analyze customized external market information via the Internet. This includes supply market research, competitor analysis, and industry/commodity trends and fluctuations. A complete e-intelligence solution would also seek to mine internal knowledge, information and data through searchable databases, discussion areas and specific repositories. This is a key area where a portal solution would be especially relevant. e-intelligence vendors working in this area include SAS Institute, Factiva, Hyperion and Dun & Bradstreet.

Collaboration
Collaboration enables formal and informal virtual collaboration at the intra- and inter-enterprise levels. Vendors working in this area include EAI and Supplybase.inc.

Procurement scorecards
Procurement scorecards enable data capture and reporting of supplier, contract and purchasing performance versus key performance indicators (KPIs). They also allow ongoing measurement of supplier performance. Vendors working in this area include SAS and Hyperion.

Online strategic sourcing tools
Online strategic sourcing tools that guide the buyer in determining and executing the type of sourcing strategy appropriate for the sourcing item according to best practice methodologies. Vendors working in this area include Accenture and B2Emarkets. As a subset of this, spend analysis enables the buyer to analyse and report internal spend data related to part numbers, suppliers and contracts. Vendors include Aspect Development (i2 Technologies), Mergent Technologies (Commerce One) and Sharemax.

e-auctions

As a part of e-sourcing, e-auctions are an efficient business tool that allows organizations to gain the greatest competitive advantage from prevailing market conditions. e-auctions fall under the wider umbrella of Dynamic Pricing Solutions. As the name suggests, one of the benefits of conducting an auction over a traditional RFQ is that it elicits a more dynamic and competitive response from competing bidders.

An online reverse auction allows suppliers to respond and counter-respond to each other's bids, creating a more dynamic response from bidders.

Typically, when the initiator of the RFQ receives responses, they are checked for conformance and supplier capability as part of the preliminary analysis. The bids may be then selected on the basis of price and non-price dimensions. The selected group then enters into further rounds of negotiations with the buyer. The respondents are usually narrowed down from the initial selection because of the high transaction and coordination costs associated with traditional negotiation with multiple suppliers. This contrasts with an online reverse auction where the negotiation proceeds simultaneously with multiple suppliers in real time. In the Internet environment, the marginal cost of including all conforming suppliers in a negotiation approaches zero. This is particularly attractive to suppliers since they are less likely to be culled on the basis of their initial bid. They can also see more information about the market via competitor responses and choose to keep their initial offer firm or make one or more counter-offers.

This new approach to negotiation for strategic and non-strategic goods and services is only possible with the advent of the Internet. Organizations who recognize the need to remove the inefficiencies and previously subjective methods of awarding contracts are embracing e-auctions as a key driver to improve profitability. CEOs of organizations will not be asking why they should be using reverse auctions, but rather why they should not be using them as a means of maximizing the opportunities to achieve supplier value and improve their competitive position.

Reverse and forward auctions

Procurement is concerned mainly with reverse auctions; however, if properly applied, forward auctions can give sales organizations considerably increased flexibility and margin. The differences between the two types of auctions are important. Reverse auctions are where the host uses an e-auction to buy a product or service, and forward auctions are where the host uses an e-auction to sell a product or service. e-auction providers will generally offer a number of service levels to cater for different levels of experience and capability in a client. The service levels generally fall within four groups, as shown in Figure 3.5.3.

Different formats for reverse and forward auctions have been developed for different industries, markets and individual buyers and sellers.

The different service levels are applicable to both forward and reverse auctions. In addition to the service level variants, different formats of forward and reverse auctions have been developed to suit

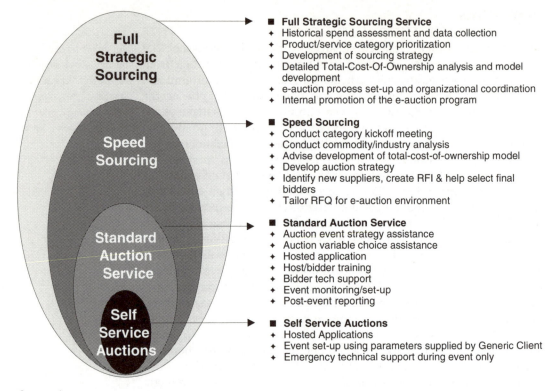

■ **Full Strategic Sourcing Service**
 ✦ Historical spend assessment and data collection
 ✦ Product/service category prioritization
 ✦ Development of sourcing strategy
 ✦ Detailed Total-Cost-Of-Ownership analysis and model development
 ✦ e-auction process set-up and organizational coordination
 ✦ Internal promotion of the e-auction program

■ **Speed Sourcing**
 ✦ Conduct category kickoff meeting
 ✦ Conduct commodity/industry analysis
 ✦ Advise development of total-cost-of-ownership model
 ✦ Develop auction strategy
 ✦ Identify new suppliers, create RFI & help select final bidders
 ✦ Tailor RFQ for e-auction environment

■ **Standard Auction Service**
 ✦ Auction event strategy assistance
 ✦ Auction variable choice assistance
 ✦ Hosted application
 ✦ Host/bidder training
 ✦ Bidder tech support
 ✦ Event monitoring/set-up
 ✦ Post-event reporting

■ **Self Service Auctions**
 ✦ Hosted Applications
 ✦ Event set-up using parameters supplied by Generic Client
 ✦ Emergency technical support during event only

Source: Accenture

Figure 3.5.3
e-sourcing applications: four levels of e-auction services

the needs of different industries, markets and individual buyers and sellers. The most popular formats are:

English auctions
In the procurement scenario the host (buyer) begins with an opening price, and the bidders (suppliers) place bids that decrease the price in set amounts (decrements). This reduction in price continues until the bidders are no longer willing to decrease the price and the winner supplies the entire lot. No real value is placed on these lots and the lowest bidder determines their worth. A variation on the English auction is the Kensington format, which enables suppliers to place their best bid even if it is higher than the current winning bid.

Dutch auctions
For procurement, the host offers lots from a low level, at which price the goods are unlikely to be bought. The price gradually increases at set increments and timings, with the first bidder to accept becoming the supplier. This model is often used where demand is likely to exceed the capacity of individual suppliers.

Yankee auction

This model has been developed to suit the buying of large numbers of lots of moderately priced items in small lot sizes. The lowest bidder wins the contract at its bid price. Bids are ranked firstly in order of price, secondly by quantity sought, then thirdly by the time of the initial bid. So if bid prices are the same, the bidder for the larger quantity takes priority, and if price and quantity are still the same the earliest bidder wins.

The increased competition and transparency of e-auctions create two compelling reasons to make the tendering and contract award processes more dynamic. However, applying reverse auctions without fully understanding some of their deficiencies can result in disrupting critical supplier relationships. Initially reverse auctions were applied to pure commodities, since they were seen as providing an efficient price discovery mechanism where decision criteria were based largely on price alone. Yet, as organizations have started to understand the power of running reverse auctions, and applied these tools to more strategic goods and services, it has become clear that negotiations based on price alone will not suffice. This is hardly surprising since in traditional tendering processes a detailed decision matrix is normally applied to competing bids once they are received from suppliers. Typically, this decision matrix involves applying weightings to various criteria, then scoring supplier responses against these criteria.

Even if decision factors are applied to the bidding results after the e-auction, suppliers can only guess the premium that the buyer is willing to pay them compared to the other bidders. While there is some competition under this approach, the result can be disappointing for buyers and suppliers alike. Rather than a truly competitive and dynamic event, this process is more akin to a multi-shot RFQ.

The open bidding format can allow competition between bidders, with non-price dimensions being taken into account. But the result can be disappointing.

BOMweb, an Australian e-sourcing software vendor, has developed the capability to incorporate non-price dimensions into a real-time bidding event. This requires procurement professionals to apply the same rigor that they would normally employ in post RFQ analysis, then the objective analysis is applied systematically to raw bids received during an online bidding process.

Using this approach allows buyers to conduct online auctions using a total-cost-of-ownership approach. Another strong benefit is that a definitive result is achieved at the close of the bidding event. Here the buyer is making a credible commitment to award the contract subject to the reserve price being reached. This represents a major step forward for buying organizations to embrace this approach, since it relies on the accuracy and veracity of their decision making matrix. Suppliers also benefit, as there is no post-event negotiation or arm wrangling offline. Subject to the reserve price being reached, the contract award decision is made automatically at the end of the bidding event.

Such an approach acts as a powerful incentive for suppliers to submit their best bids during the auction. The buyer makes a credible commitment by pre-factoring suppliers and allows competing market forces to determine the outcome. Suppliers too must make a credible commitment by offering their best combination of price and non-price components, as there will be no subsequent offline negotiations. This allows a negotiation process that has a high level of transparency, integrity and probity from both sides. In economics terms, we are approaching the efficient frontier associated with perfectly competitive markets.

Examples of e-auction successes

When e-auctions first began appearing, most organizations believed that e-auctions would only be suitable for indirect or non-strategic commodities. However, new techniques have been developed and refined so that virtually any purchase in a competitive environment can be managed through an e-auction. Following are four e-auction examples sourced from Accenture Australia's experience, covering direct materials, indirect materials, a large services contract, and material for a one-off construction project.

Direct materials purchase

A large Australian mining company uses sodium ethyl xanthates as an integral material in its ore processing plants. The reliable supply of high-quality xanthates is critical to achieving its productivity and profitability targets. A team from Accenture and Dynamic Pricing Solutions (DPS) worked with the client's contract manager to expand the supplier base, develop a total cost of supply (TCS) model, then design the auction event. One of the major considerations was to maximize the site managers' options so the client could choose the most appropriate combination of liquid or solid xanthates. The e-auction team was able to design an accurate TCS model, including the detailed storage and pumping facilities required for the various combinations, thereby enabling the buyer to select the most cost efficient supplier over the life of the contract. All participants were trained on this model, which encouraged new suppliers from Mexico and Europe to participate.

- Baseline spend: A$ 19 million (approx.)
- Savings ($): A$ 3.5 million
- Savings (%): 18 per cent

Indirect materials purchase

A major Australian company identified the 2000-plus line items it held in stationery and office products as one of its indirect materials for e-auctions. The stationery supplier market in Australia is restricted because of the locations and service demands of the mining sites. To generate the maximum competition the e-auction team divided the total requirements into three lots as follows:

- Lot 1 – Western Australia (four competitors, including a WA specialist)
- Lot 2 – eastern and South Australia (three competitors)
- Lot 3 – national (same three competitors as Lot 2, but twice the value).

To manage the large SKU count the team used the top 650 items comprising 85 per cent of the client's spend as the bidding basket. Suppliers' RFQ responses were based on this basket, and then a post-bid spreadsheet was required from the suppliers to confirm the discount percentage, which would be applied across all catalogues for the company.

- Baseline spend: A$ 4.5 million (approx.)
- Savings ($): A$ 0.55 million
- Savings (%): 10.9 per cent.

Services purchasing
An organization had issued an RFP for mining services, and then later decided to conduct an e-auction as a substitute for the price negotiations. The RFP included an elaborative pricing schedule running to over 60 pages. This was a large, critical service contract, so considerable efforts were made to train suppliers and get their buy-in to the e-auction process. This involved sending customized training packages to the suppliers, face-to-face training for software usage and bidding strategies. A decision matrix identified and included various quantitative and qualitative factors. The factors were used to award the contract after the auction had been conducted. Five suppliers participated in the final auction for six lots. The successful execution drove a paradigm shift in the sourcing process for the organization. e-auctions are now perceived as a re-usable tool, which are more open, transparent and efficient than the traditional, static one-on-one negotiations.

- Baseline spend: A$ 82 million (approx.)
- Savings ($): A$7.5 million (approx.)
- Savings (%): 9 per cent (approx.).

Construction purchasing
A global company had to source HDPE pipe for water drainage at their remote site in Indonesia before the start of the wet season. This constraint provided only four weeks for the contract to be awarded. The company had used three suppliers in the past and was not aware of any other supplier with the capability to supply the required pipe in the Asia-Pacific region. The e-auction team assessed the global market for HDPE pipe and was able to develop an initial list of 28 suppliers with the capability to supply required HDPE pipe to the client. The suppliers in the initial list were based in Australia (1), Asia (8), Europe (1), South America (11) and North America (7). These suppliers were

then issued with an RFQ specified for an e-auction. The suppliers were further qualified based on their response to the RFQ. Suppliers were invited and participated in the final auction, with the process taking three weeks in total.

- Baseline spend: A$ 5.2 million
- Savings ($): A$720 000
- Savings (per cent): 13.8 per cent.

Outlook – integrating tools and approaches

The advent of Internet technology such as e-sourcing and e-auctions to previously inefficient or cumbersome processes gives organizations the ability to benefit from more competitive supply chains. In order to see the new opportunities presented, the previous rationale for strategic sourcing needs to be examined.

One of the major initiatives coming out of strategic sourcing studies was the rationalization of supply chains. Since transaction and coordination costs were higher with a fragmented supplier base, and organizations were not able to exploit their collective knowledge and buying power across their entire organization, supplier rationalization was seen as a good starting point to decrease input costs. These costs were twofold: first, the transaction costs to deal with multiple suppliers would be decreased, such as through consolidated invoicing and processing. Second, buyers were able to benefit from scale or volume-related discounts via aggregation or standardization of products within and across organizations.

Figure 3.5.4 shows the procurement costs and trends under the two distinct regimes of supply chain rationalization and competitive supply chains. Before the Internet, the tools were not available and organizations could not extract the maximum benefits of negotiating more effectively with competing suppliers. In the end, important negotiations still came down to one-on-one interactions between buyers and suppliers.

While supplier rationalization brought about decreased procurement costs, some other trends also began to emerge. With a limited number of suppliers competing for business, the level of contestability trended downwards. In some cases this may have caused suppliers to exit the market. Where monopolistic or oligopolistic supply chains were created, this may have also caused supplier performance to decrease as incumbents and preferred suppliers had less motivation to innovate, improve or remain competitive. A related, albeit more latent, trend was that with a diminishing supplier base, the negotiation effectiveness of buyers remained about the same since it still relied on traditional tendering, negotiation and contract award processes.

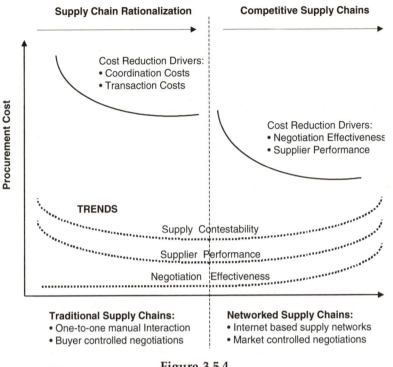

Figure 3.5.4
Competitive supply chain networks

Figure 3.5.4 shows two distinct cost curves, with the latter indicating a shift or disruption brought about with the introduction of Internet-based supply networks. The unparalleled reduction in transaction costs and coordination costs normally associated with manual tendering and traditional negotiation processes act to shift the procurement cost curve downward. Initially this shift can be attributed to a new dynamic afforded by running online reverse auctions, where suppliers are effectively negotiating market prices with each other rather than one-on-one with the buyer.

Conclusion

With the introduction of dynamic purchase networks, however, organizations now have the opportunity to keep reducing costs by driving change. Through the judicious use of reverse alignment, e-sourcing and e-auctions, sustainable increases in value from suppliers will be realized. By improving negotiation effectiveness on each strategic procurement occasion and collaborating with a more contestable supplier base to improve performance, organizations are directly improving their competitiveness and the competitiveness of their supply chain.

3.6 Industry-level collaboration through ECR

Garry O'Sullivan

The power of leading brands is creating a counterbalance to the normal domination of supply chain relationships by retailers.

Historically, retail supply chains have been characterized by an imbalance that has delivered disproportionate negotiating power to the major retailers. In any relationship where a power differential exists, it is rare to find real partnerships between the parties. Such a situation often leads to a relationship based on control, rather than one based on trust and cooperation. However, an interesting counterbalancing force is now at work – brand power. The strength of leading brands is such that branded goods retailers must stock them.

In a recent example in Belgium, a dominant supermarket chain decided not to stock a global food brand, due to the manufacturer's unwillingness to manufacture a house-brand product for the retailer. After a stand-off of some months, the chain was forced to invite the manufacturer back, on the manufacturer's terms. Shoppers had voted with their feet. The trading partners lacked the shared vision of what would constitute joint success and a lose–lose situation arose from the attempt by one party to use its power to coerce the other.

Unfortunately, this example is typical of many performance improvement initiatives taken by business; they are focused on securing a larger proportion of the existing profit pool, rather than on securing an equitable share of an enlarged pool. The reason is simple enough; senior management has a measure of control over functional areas within the business. Stepping across the corporate boundary into the territory of customers and suppliers is far more difficult and requires real insight into business practices and operational procedures right along the value chain.

Even within companies, cross-functional cooperation usually only occurs when the chief executive makes sure it happens. Individual managers tend to focus on creating islands of excellence within their organization, often to the detriment of the overall performance of the business. Pouring resources into a 2 per cent improvement in manufacturing performance may be far less effective than expending those same financial resources on distribution and marketing. However, to measure the gains of the latter initiative may require information that the company does not have – only the retailer may be able to provide the feedback needed to determine the effectiveness of particular market initiatives. Retailers are often reticent to provide the information in a timeframe that is useful, fearing loss of control.

This chapter explores the issues behind such sub-optimizing behavior in one industry and describes, in some depth, a global example of collaboration at the industry level among trading partners and competitors. The example shows how the grocery industry has tackled the breaking down of the walls of mistrust between trading partners to allow the focus of their joint activities to become delighting the consumer, more profitably.

While the examples are taken from a single industry, the principles are transferable. The grocery industry has recognized the critical importance of tackling some issues on a broad collaborative basis; many other industries could profit from a closer look at the paradigm.

The retailing scene

Even the casual observer of large retail businesses will notice certain key characteristics. Most notable, of course, is the increasing level of concentration in the industry at the retail level and among global brands. At the operational level in the retail sector, the buyer/seller mentality still dominates. Buyers are often trained to keep suppliers at arms' length, so as always to be able to extract the best pricing deal. Nor is the problem one-sided. Sellers, too, behave in a manner that is not conducive to developing trust. Commitments to supply are made and then broken, for reasons that include overcommitment of stock, internal production problems and attempts to minimize inventory, without adequate mechanisms to respond to demand.

Changing the culture of mistrust is the greatest challenge facing retail supply chain participants.

The Internet retailing phenomenon saw this situation reach crisis point. Internet retailers attempted to totally avoid holding inventory, without having the depth or strength of relationships with their suppliers to allow communications and logistics to become a realistic substitute for inventory.

At the heart of the problem is the lack of effective communications between retailers and manufacturers, from business planning down to short-term operational alerts and responses. To suppliers, the idea of working 'open book' with trade customers as a basis for developing closer partnerships with those customers is anathema to them. Their instinctive perception is that granting a customer visibility of cost and profit information will immediately lead to a squeeze on margins.

On the contrary, many customers are interested in establishing fewer, more robust relationships with suppliers, particularly at the raw materials stage and see continuing profitability of those suppliers as pivotal in ensuring a lasting relationship. However, the entrenched culture is one of mistrust. Changing that culture remains the single greatest challenge facing retail supply chain participants, if break-through improvements are to be achieved.

Notwithstanding these issues, the grocery sector provides an illustrative example of the way in which one value chain has tackled the challenge of inter-company collaboration at an industry level and on a global basis. This sector is unique, in terms of the sustained velocity of goods through the value chain. In contrast to department stores, where stock turns are measured in 'times per year', in the grocery sector, fast moving products will have stock turns measured in 'times per week'. In this environment, close collaboration is the only mechanism that offers the potential to overcome, or better, avoid availability problems.

An industry looks over its back fence

The North American grocery sector instigated ECR with the aim of delivering enhanced value to consumers, while improving profitability for all.

In the early 1990s, leading executives in the grocery sector saw their colleagues in the textile, clothing and footwear industry achieving real, bottom-line benefits through an industry-wide initiative called QR, for quick response. That initiative was shortening lead times, improving in-stock position and reducing working capital in a value chain characterised by long lead times and deep mark downs of surplus stock. No significant performance improvements were in sight for the grocery industry, where adversarial behavior continued to drive win–lose business relationships.

Drawing on the quick response experience, the North American grocery sector instigated a far-reaching collaborative initiative, called efficient consumer response (ECR). ECR was directed at delivering enhanced value to consumers, while improving profitability for all participants in the supply chain. The simple premise underpinning this seemingly contradictory pair of aspirations was that, by reducing the working capital tied up in the grocery value chain, retailers and suppliers could improve the return on funds employed, while delivering superior range and pricing to the consumer.

To achieve their dual aim, the ECR movement's founders, the retailers and manufacturers themselves, realized they must create a forum where competitors from both sides of the trading relationship would be prepared to work together to overcome structural hurdles to efficiency. It is the principle of collaborating on any issue where there is not obvious sustainable competitive advantage, which has kept the ECR movement alive and flourishing for a decade, at least outside North America. Indeed, the major momentum for this initiative now exists in Europe. The challenge of retailer–supplier collaboration is compounded by the existence of many national and, hence, cultural boundaries. Over the past seven years, the joint industry and trade body, ECR Europe, has undertaken a multitude of industry-level initiatives in the grocery sector to deliver practical, implementable standards and processes.

To illustrate the power of such work in the hands of industry participants, the remainder of the chapter explores just three of the many common processes developed by industry working parties comprising retailers and manufacturers, often direct competitors, and made available to any company as published guidebooks.

Nothing focuses the mind like a stock-out!

Lost sales due to stock-outs occurring at the retail shelf are costing retailers and manufacturers globally tens of billions of dollars a year. This is nowhere more evident than in the fast moving supermarket supply chain. Out-of-stocks on the supermarket shelf are not the result of fickle consumer behavior; they are the result of a failure of effective coordination between the retailer and the supplier. In markets where promotions are used to drive consumer buying behavior, up to 40 per cent of promoted items can be unavailable on the shelf at any time.

The absence of effective sharing of business plans undermines both retailers and suppliers' initiatives. Four out of five promotions fail to meet their objectives.

At the core of today's business relationships in the grocery industry lies category management, the process that creates the framework for retailers and manufacturers to build and execute joint business plans. The theory of category management is that by optimizing the mix of products on offer and managing location on the shelf, promotional activity and price, the retailer and supplier can maximize the financial yield of supermarket 'real estate' – the shelf – while satisfying consumer needs and wants. That is the theory.

However, retailers' approaches to category management tend to be proprietary and often poorly standardized between categories. It is therefore difficult to communicate category plans down through the retail organization to stores and across the trading relationship boundary to suppliers. In the absence of effective sharing of business plans throughout the value chain, the trading partners' agendas become mismatched, thereby undermining both parties' initiatives. Promotions that cannibalize others run concurrently, prominent advertising of promotions and last minute price changes are not communicated; the list of uncoordinated behaviors goes on. The result is that very few promotions meet their objectives.

As an example, (Accenture and ECR Europe, 2000) one sophisticated supermarket chain, with turnover in excess of $15 billion acknowledges that only 20 per cent of its promotions meet the target success criteria of a) not running out of stock and b) having less than 10 per cent excess stock at the end of the promotion. On these criteria, four out of five promotions are failures!

Further up the chain, the inability of manufacturers to obtain relevant, timely consumer sales forecasting and point-of-sale information, has led to demand management by manufacturers becoming 'just-in-case' rather than 'just-in-time'. This results in inventory holdings far greater than needed to meet actual demand, but often held in the wrong place to meet consumer offtake.

Compounding the ineffective communication of demand signals, the financial incentives driving buyer and seller behavior in the industry do not match the outcomes that maximize the profitability of the trading relationship. Buyers receive incentives based on gross margin achieved, plus additional promotional payments extracted from suppliers, while sales people receive incentives based on volume ordered. While current category management approaches use quite sophisticated measures to optimize product assortment from a consumer perspective, most still use relatively crude financial measures as the primary determinants of category performance. Neither party's key performance indicators reflect the total profitability of sales to the consumer. Trading terms (the basic financial arrangements) are, therefore, driven by parameters that do not adequately allocate costs where they fall. This skews the category financial management process, resulting in under-performing products receiving disproportionately high shelf space allocation at the expense of highly profitably lines, resulting in stock-outs and loss of sales.

The supermarket industry is tackling this largely self-induced problem in several ways.

Tackling the out-of-stock challenge

The solution to the out-of-stock problem lies in tackling the underlying behavior that causes poor collaboration.

The out-of-stock problem is by no means intractable. The solution lies in tackling the root causes and not the symptoms. For many years, throughout the fast moving consumer goods industry, companies have focused on better ways to move stock quicker, rather than to look at the behavior that causes the problem.

To make the links between retailers and manufacturers more effective, more collaborative operating practices are required at the merchandizing, sales and supply management interfaces. A more seamless, standardized way of doing business is required to optimize the whole value chain, based on joint visibility of planning and execution from manufacturer to checkout. More productive collaboration enables the value chain to be more responsive to consumer demand, at lower cost.

Three approaches developed in the grocery industry, effectively integrated, provide a practical framework to tackle the alignment of business planning and execution between retailers and manufacturers. These initiatives are:

- profit impact analysis
- Web-enabled collaborative category management and
- collaborative planning, forecasting and replenishment (CPFR ®).

Outlined below is a brief description of these three approaches. Companies can link these together into a structure that can be implemented progressively to yield measurable improvements for both retailers and manufacturers, in terms of stock-on-shelf and profit contribution.

Profit impact analysis lays the foundations

Central to effective collaboration is a shared view of the value chain and of each trading partner's costs and profit contributions. Recognizing this, an ECR Europe working group, comprising retailers and manufacturers, developed and published a simple methodology to allow trading partners, working together to show, using a time- and cost-effective mechanism, what is eroding margin, from the manufacturer's loading dock to the retailer's shelf.

Profit impact analysis provides trading partners with product-level visibility of costs and profit, encouraging partners to collaborate in areas of joint benefit.

Profit impact analysis, as the approach is called, delivers the factual information to help break through the trust barrier, which often hinders collaborative initiatives. By providing the trading partners with product-level visibility of cost and profit performance, rather than focusing solely on gross margin contribution, profit impact analysis directs collaborative efforts to areas of joint benefit. This visibility encourages business partners to rethink promotional and assortment strategies to best use scarce shelf space, without creating out-of-stock situations.

The elegance of the approach lies in its simplicity. While based on the use of activity-based costing and other related approaches, the power of the methodology lies in focusing on those issues relevant to the problem at hand. It is a bottom-up approach, driven from the business, not from the general ledger. The profit impact approach shifts the focus of financial performance away from cash flow measures of profit (cash profit), towards a measure called true profit. True profit takes into account the costs that accrue in generating category revenue. Those costs do not fall uniformly across all products and vendors in a category and therefore need to be allocated at the individual stock keeping unit (SKU) and vendor level.

Figure 3.6.1 shows a real supermarket category situation and illustrates the significant difference between cash profit, which accounts for all financial flows, including discounts, allowances, trade spend, etc., and true profit, which also factors in direct costs, such as finance, storage, transport, handling, shelf space use and support resources.

The graph shows that, while all SKUs in the category contribute to cash profit, the last 10 per cent are actually dragging down category true profit. The inclusion of these products in the category may be justified, but not on grounds of financial contribution to the category.

The shift to a true profit approach potentially shifts the focus of trading terms negotiation away from category revenue measures towards true category profitability measures.

This true profit-oriented approach has the potential to dramatically change the way in which retailers measure the financial performance of their categories and of products and suppliers within categories. This, in turn will shift the focus of trading terms negotiation away

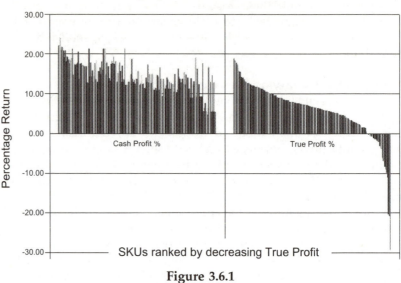

Figure 3.6.1
Category profitability profile

from category revenue measures towards true category profitability measures. It will also enable far more objective evaluation of promotional effectiveness by both retailer and supplier.

The real hurdle to be overcome will be the need to realign the reward systems in use throughout the industry, to reward profit creation, rather than simply sales and market share.

The approach is a breakthrough in three key respects:

- It bridges the gap between retailers' and manufacturers' views of performance, by providing a consistent approach to cost and profit measurement, end to end.
- It is quick to use and delivers action-oriented results.
- It is neutral, having been developed and validated by industry working parties.

With the financial foundation in place, category management is the next step.

Category management drives the relationship

The day-to-day approach to category management is inherently collaborative, based on sharing information and aligning objectives.

In the supermarket sector, category management is used to optimize the financial yield of a category, while meeting consumer needs. Prima facie evidence, however, would indicate that category management today is failing to deliver on its promises. With out-of-stocks at shelf running at up to 10 per cent in general and much higher for promoted items in the supermarket chains, the conclusion has to be that category management is not meeting the needs of the consumers, nor optimizing financial yield.

Whatever the immediate causes of the out-of-stock situation, the scene is set by category management decisions. It is category management that ultimately determines the product mix, the space to be allocated, the price points and the promotional strategy at the supermarket shelf. The category plan must surely take account of the realities of running supermarket operations, down to store level, in terms of replenishment strategies, available space, shelf restocking cycles, promotional demand and the other factors that contribute to providing the desired offer to the shopper.

Using a recent definition, category management is 'a partnership between retailers and suppliers to jointly manage categories as individual business units created to meet the needs of consumers'. Missing from most current approaches to category management are the notions of joint management and partnership. This again raises the issue of collaboration: joint category management should drive the collaborative process.

It is often said that category plans break down in the execution at store. The counter-argument is that many category plans are incapable of effective and sustained execution at store. The point is moot. The reality is that a fresh approach is needed, one that links retailer to manufacturer and head office to store, and one that takes category management from being a major periodic project to being a manageable day-to-day process.

The recognition that a fresh approach was needed to category management was the motivator for the development of the four-phase 'day-to-day category management' approach by another ECR Europe industry working party. Figure 3.6.2 provides an overview of the activities undertaken in each of the four phases of the process. Involvement by manufacturers in Phases 1 and 2 of the process is usually limited to the one or two leading suppliers in a category, the so-called 'category captains'. These phases are executed periodically, typically once or twice a year. Steps 3 and 4 potentially involve all category participants and are a real day-to-day process.

The day-to-day approach is groundbreaking in several respects:

- the process is inherently collaborative, based on sharing of information and alignment of business objectives between trading partners
- it uses standard templates, for wide deployment and ease of e-enablement
- it is capable of implementation at varying degrees of sophistication, depending on the capabilities of the trading partners, the availability of category data and the needs of the category
- promotional planning, the key to demand management, is integral to the approach
- the process has clear linkages with CPFR ®, to carry collaboration through to operational planning and execution, and

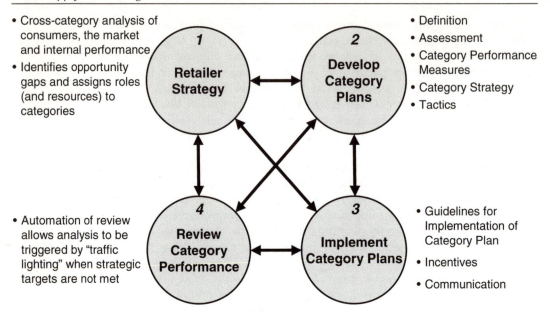

- Cross-category analysis of consumers, the market and internal performance
- Identifies opportunity gaps and assigns roles (and resources) to categories

- Definition
- Assessment
- Category Performance Measures
- Category Strategy
- Tactics

- Automation of review allows analysis to be triggered by "traffic lighting" when strategic targets are not met

- Guidelines for Implementation of Category Plan
- Incentives
- Communication

1 Retailer Strategy

2 Develop Category Plans

4 Review Category Performance

3 Implement Category Plans

Figure 3.6.2
The four phases of day-to-day category management

- the process easily supports the creation and use of shared performance measures, crucial to sustainable collaboration.

The day-to-day category management process, as its name implies, has been developed for use on an ongoing basis, to manage categories and portfolios of categories collaboratively to whatever level of sophistication the category demands and resources allow.

This approach allows all stakeholders in category management to have a common view of information. The approach can be implemented using minimal technology, such as email and spread-sheets, but really comes to life when Web-enabled, as illustrated in Figure 3.6.3 below. Through such a tool, all parties can focus on the critical issues, typically those relating to promotions.

Promotions – the root cause of demand variation

Trading partners need to understand which promotions actually create value, in net terms, and which do not.

In many markets, promotions are one of the key levers used by retailers and manufacturers to stimulate demand. In the absence of promotions, it would be possible to predict demand for most supermarket items to a high degree of accuracy months ahead. Promotions are the primary cause of out-of-stocks, due to the dramatic increase in consumer demand that they cause. Sales uplift by factors of five to ten are quite common. Shelves, dimensioned for non-promotional offtake, simply cannot be kept stocked during promotions.

Whatever the long-term financial outcome for the consumer from promotions, the outcome for most manufacturers has been the

File Edit View Favorites Tools Help
←Back • → • ⊗ ⊇ ⚏ | ⚏Search ⌷Favorites ⌷History | ⊡• ⌷ ▦ • ⌷ ⚏ ⚏

eCategory Management Dashboard

Retailer: *Hypermarkets*
Category: *Chocolates*
Category Manager: *Mr. González*

Date: *15-May-2001*
Time: *08.03:34 AM*

● Menu

KPI	Dimension	Indicator	Week 19 Value	Week 19 Target Value	Trend vs. Week 18
Sales	x 1.000 €	●	12.000	1.000	Going up
Sales/m2	€/m2	●	180	165	Going up
Margin %	%	●	24%	24%	Going down
Margin/m2	€/m2	●	43	40	Going up
Promotion up lift	index	●	200	300	Going up
% Sales to gold customers	%	●	67,0%	67,0%	Steady
% Basket penetration	%	●	1,7%	1,7	Going up
% Product availability	%	●	87,0%	89,0%	Going down

Figure 3.6.3
Web-enabled category management visibility

destruction of substantial shareholder value. To illustrate the point, in the United States market, it is estimated that $25 billion is spent on trade promotions annually to generate incremental revenues of only $2 to $4 billion (Kearney, 1999).

This does not mean that promotions should be abandoned as a selling tool. Promotional activity remains one of the easiest levers to pull to generate consumer response. To abandon this lever totally in favor of true everyday low pricing (EDLP) would be a brave move for any retailer and few, if any, full-range grocery retailers have done so, anywhere. Likewise, few branded products manufacturers would want to ignore the potential of promotions to support product strategies.

The issue, of course, is understanding which promotions actually create value, in net terms, and which do not. By focusing on the 20 per cent of promotions that work and adopting an everyday pricing approach for the rest, shelf space can be rebalanced to support the promotions that count. Unfortunately, neither the retailer nor the supplier alone has the information to determine which promotions are successful in terms of wealth creation.

The reason for this is that the costs and revenues associated with promotional activity fall very unevenly on the two sides of the trading boundary, hiding the true cost of promotions from both parties. From a cost-of-business point of view, it is tantalizing to consider the elimination of promotions, given the various negative impacts they have on the grocery value chain, including:

- vastly increased stock holdings, due to poor promotional forecast accuracy
- the high cost of expediting activities associated with promotional 'crises'
- loss of sales due to promotional offtake exceeding shelf capacity in store (that is, out-of-stock at shelf) and
- the high level of payments made by manufacturers to retailers for the privilege of holding the promotion.

However, sharing information to understand the true cost of promotions implies creating visibility of revenues and the associated costs, at the individual SKU level, from manufacturing to consumer trolley. This visibility of margin, together with sales performance information, also addresses the trade spend issue, by providing the facts to allow renegotiation of trading terms around true profit optimization for both parties.

For both sides of the trading relationship, the focus should be on understanding the financial impact of promotional activity on category and portfolio profit, end to end. The profit impact approach provides the product-level true profitability measures that allow these informed decisions to be made. Using this approach, both sides can pool their knowledge, allowing them to make informed decisions about promotional optimization.

Trading partners also need to consider the question of the increased inventories that occur for promoted products. The cause of the inflated inventory in the supply chain, at both retailer and manufacturer distribution centers, is not the promotions themselves; the cause is the poor forecast accuracy that is typically associated with promotions. This distinction is far from semantic. Forecast inaccuracy is a treatable condition and the treatment is collaboration. Collaborating on this issue involves pooling the knowledge of retailer and manufacturer to achieve substantially better forecast accuracy. The impact on inventory levels and, hence, working capital can be dramatic. In grocery, a standardized process – collaborative planning, forecasting and replenishment (CPFR ®) – has been introduced to achieve this outcome.

CPFR fosters 'day-to-day' collaboration

CPFR is a process that involves the collaborative sharing of information across the supply chain with the aim of achieving joint profit growth for all parties.

CPFR ®, developed by the US industry body Voluntary Interindustry Commerce Standards Association (VICS), and trademarked to protect its integrity, provides a mechanism for trading partners to share their respective views of consumer demand, and allow the execution of their joint plans. See CPFR (2001). To be effective, CPFR must be driven by effective, joint category management practices.

Briefly, CPFR is a best-practice nine-step process, which begins with the creation of a formal agreement on objectives between trading partners and the development of a business plan. This 'front-end' work then drives joint sales forecasting and order forecasting, based on shared information regarding sales. The operational focus of CPFR is on handling exceptions. The end-point of the process is efficient replenishment. The objective is joint profit growth.

Experience implementing electronic data interchange (EDI) between trading partners over the last 20 years shows that it has not been the message structures or content that have been the impediments to achieving benefits. It has been the lack of synchronization, between trading partners, of the business processes to which the messages relate. Most internal business processes have not been conceived for a collaborative connected trading environment. CPFR provides an opportunity to avoid a repeat performance in the connected world, by going beyond the message standards to address the business processes at the trading interface.

CPFR promotes standardization of the way in which companies interact with their trading partners at the process and message level, focusing on the joint management of exceptions to agreed plans. It is not about dictating how companies run their businesses. The CPFR process (Figure 3.6.4.) is the work of industry bodies in the US and more recently Europe, drawing on many years of experience with the frustrations caused by misaligned forecasts. It is intended to be both platform and vendor independent. It uses technical standards that are already in place, such as EDI and EAN/UCC numbering and has lead to the development of new XML messages to fully use the Internet and Web-enabling technologies.

The CPFR process is directed at frequent, event-triggered collaboration and is structured to support effective communication. A recently completed European industry survey, undertaken by Accenture as part of the ECR Europe CPFR project, found that the greatest benefits from CPFR were reduced out-of-stock items at the point of sale and improved promotional effectiveness to consumers.

By focusing on the creation of a single, shared forecast, CPFR provides the framework to allow each organization to contribute its knowledge of past and likely future consumer behavior, in formulating predictions of consumer demand. However, sharing bad information does not make it better. It is therefore critical, that in a collaborative forecasting situation, the parties first look to the quality of internal information. Often, in manufacturing organizations, manufacturing and sales each produce a forecast based on the department's own historical information and experience. In order to share a single forecast with the retailer, the departments must first pool their internal knowledge to achieve internal consensus. This process of internal collaboration is often a breakthrough in itself, forcing departments to understand the issues and factors driving behaviors elsewhere in the organization.

Companies that have introduced CPFR are experiencing improvements in absolute forecast accuracy of around 12 to 15 per cent.

While there are relatively few large-scale implementations of CPFR to date, those companies that have introduced the process are experiencing significant improvements in forecast accuracy and are

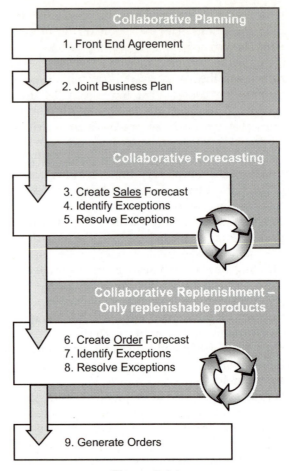

Figure 3.6.4
Day-to-day category management process

enjoying the benefits that this brings. Improvements in absolute forecast accuracy of 12 to 15 per cent are being regularly reported (Johnson, 1999). As a result, in-store out-of-stocks are being reduced and inventories are being reduced right along the supply chain, as supply is better matched to demand. The reduction of 'just-in-case' safety stocks means that techniques such as flow-through can be used to further reduce inventory levels, without pushing the level of stock-outs back up.

Flow-through is a supply process, whereby retailers order from manufacturers the exact quantity of stock required for supply to stores. The stock is received at the retailer's distribution centre, is broken down to individual store quantities and shipped, without any need for warehousing. Typically, this approach has been applied only to slow moving stock, where errors in quantities ordered have limited impact on sales revenues. However, with the introduction of CPFR ®, the same technique can be applied to faster-moving lines, due to the improved quality of the underlying forecasts.

As with profit impact analysis, the elegance of the CPFR process lies in its simplicity. CPFR does not require complex technology to pilot – e-mail and telephone have readily supported trials of the approach. However, to scale the approach to many products and potentially many trading partners does require system support, to allow process automation, for the many situations where forecasts from the two parties are within agreed limits, and hence do not require human intervention. Sharing forecasts and collaborating on the points of mismatch allow the trading partners to focus scarce human resource on those issues that will have an impact on performance.

Assembling the jigsaw

Figure 3.6.5 illustrates how profit impact analysis, day-to-day category management and CPFR fit together to provide the industry with a toolkit to support effective supply chain collaboration, from business planning through to the review of outcomes. To achieve the goal of minimizing out-of-stocks at shelf, trading partners require a practical pathway. It must involve manageable, measurable steps that build trust and deliver valuable performance improvements.

Experience indicates that a pragmatic first step toward resolving the out-of-stock problem is for retailers and manufacturers to jointly

A pragmatic first step is for retailers and manufacturers to jointly rethink performance, assortment and promotion strategies for commonly out-of-stock categories.

PROFIT IMPACT ANALYSIS	DAY-TO-DAY CATEGORY MANAGEMENT	COLLABORATIVE PLANNING, FORECASTING AND REPLENISHMENT
Assess category profit contribution for resource allocation across portfolio	STEP 1 Develop Retail Strategy	STEP 1 Develop Collaboration Arrangement
Efficient Assortment analysis; profit contribution of promotions; financial KPIs	STEP 2 Develop Category Plans	STEP 2 Develop Joint Business Plan
	STEP 3 Implement Category Plans	STEPS 3-9 Collaborate on Sales & Order Forecasting and Order Placement
Measure profit performance of SKUs & categories at net contribution level	STEP 4 Review Outcomes & Adapt	

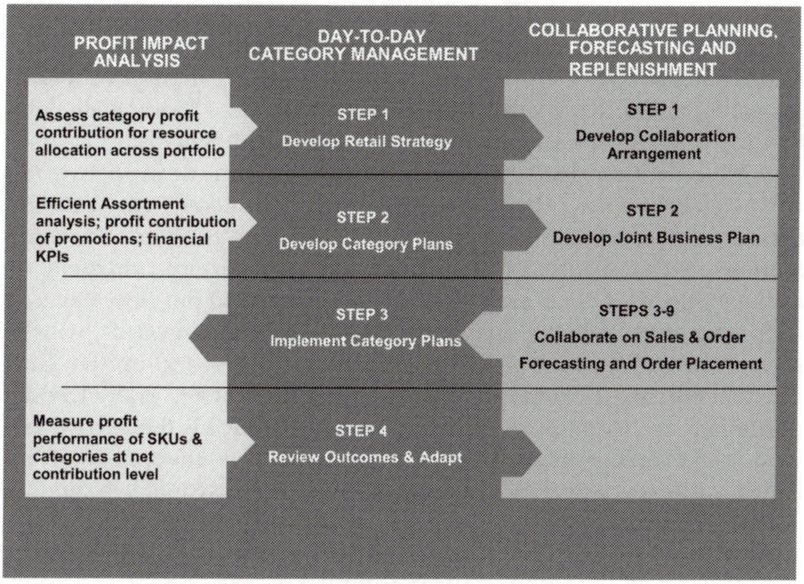

Figure 3.6.5
Value chain management jigsaw assembled

rethink performance, assortment and promotion strategies for categories that experience significant out-of-stocks.

Identifying the true profit contribution of SKUs within categories with high stock-outs, using profit impact analysis, generates great insight into the actions that can be taken to start improving performance at shelf. This leads to:

- joint fact-based assessment of assortment, with non-performing SKUs highlighted for potential removal, subject to meeting consumer needs
- development of promotional strategies within the category plan, around SKUs which deliver high profit contribution and have high price elasticity, to maximize yield and
- the planning of shelf layouts to support category plans, which adequately reflect the impact of the promotional plans.

This step can deliver significant stand-alone benefit, as well as being a foundation step in creating the collaborative value chain approach.

Conclusion

In the same way as the grocery industry borrowed the quick response concept, other industries have the opportunity to draw the essence from ECR and apply it their situations.

All of the approaches described in this chapter have been developed as a result of the cooperation fostered by the global ECR movement. While the integration of these approaches into an overall trading process is still in its infancy, progress is being made. To date it has been the leading retailers and manufacturers that have invested time and money into developing a better way to do business. They have recognized that they will reap the full benefit only when the industry, as a whole, adopts that better way, allowing duplication of processes to be eliminated. They know that as early adopters, already well along the learning journey, they will derive the greatest benefits.

Initiatives that lead to breakthrough outcomes in delivering enhanced consumer value, profitably, can only be taken to a successful conclusion through the joint efforts of manufacturers, distributors and retailers, with the support of logistics and other service providers. To achieve this level of cooperation, all parties need to develop a shared understanding of goals and a confidence that the rewards will be shared equitably among the participants. The work of the ECR movement has provided many tools and approaches to allow trading partners to develop this confidence, but ultimately it is the individuals who must change their thinking and recognize the potential for collaboration to deliver outcomes far beyond those available under the adversarial model.

In the seven years since the ECR movement was initiated in the US, ECR has steadily caught the attention of the grocery industry in every corner of the globe. It began by tackling supply issues and has progressed to tackling the demand-side issues explored in this chapter. But ECR is not just about taking cost out of the supply chain or about maximizing profitability; the aim of the ECR movement is to make the whole grocery industry more responsive to consumers' needs and wants. Quite a challenge! But the evidence is there – it can be done. ECR works, but only when there is a high level of cooperation and collaboration between trading partners.

The notion of enhancing consumer satisfaction and profitability, simultaneously, is not a contradiction. As a primitive example, if a company can reduce cost in its supply chain and pass on 100 per cent of that saving to its customers, it can improve profitability by maintaining constant dollar margin on lower working capital. A real win–win.

Of course, consumer satisfaction is not simply about lowering prices. It is about enhancing the whole shopping and consumption experience. A model of the path along which ECR should be leading the grocery industry is shown in Figure 3.6.6. Almost universally, ECR efforts have commenced at the supply chain level, with optimization initiatives, such as EDI and numbering standardization, the creation and maintenance of product data integrity, and the elimination of excess inventory from the total supply chain.

The leading-edge work in ECR is now moving to the less tangible, but ultimately more significant areas of consumer enthusiasm generation and consumer value measurement. These issues are as relevant to other retail formats as to grocery. It is therefore likely that thinking in these fields will be exchanged across many retail formats.

In the same way that the grocery industry borrowed the quick response concept and built upon it, so the opportunity exists for other industries to draw the essence from ECR and apply it as appropriate to their own situation. What is needed is industry leaders with the

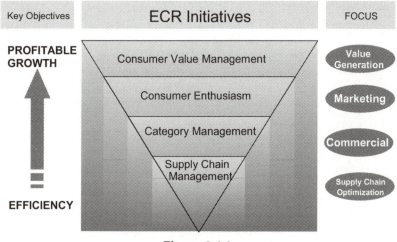

Figure 3.6.6
The ECR journey

vision to see beyond their own corporate competitive situation, to the real opportunities beyond. Those opportunities lie in the extension of value chain collaboration to involve the shopper and the consumer in a true exchange of value given for value received.

References

Accenture and ECR Europe (2000), 'The Essential Guide to Day-to-Day Category Management', *ECR Europe* (10 April 2000). <www.ecrnet.org>

Johnson, M. (1999), 'Collaboration Data Modelling: CPFR Implementation Guidelines', *CPFR*. <www.CPFR .org>

Kearney, A. T, and PAP (1999), 'Assessing the Profit Impact of ECR', *ECR Europe* (27 October 1999). <www.ecrnet.org>

CPFR (2001), *'About CPFR'*, Voluntary Interindustry Commerce Standards Association. <www.CPFR .org>

Collaborative product commerce

3.7

Alejandro Cuartero, Manuel Chaure and Stefano Lorenzi

It is February 2002. A project manager heading the construction of a new chemical plant detects a problem with one of the installations. He calls a meeting with his project team: the process engineer, the external engineering representative, the equipment purchasing manager, the production manager and the equipment supplier. 'Well', says the project leader, 'I think we've covered everything that might affect the completion date. Our priority is to check the detailed design of the hydraulic circuits to try to reduce the loss of pressure on the outlet. If it's not possible to redesign, we'll have to resize the equipment or find alternative energy supplies.'

Somewhat bluntly, the production manager adds: 'We must have the alternative solution by the end of the week. Otherwise we'll have a minimum delay of four weeks.' 'But if we do that', an economist working for the project manager pipes up, 'we may end up 15 per cent over our budget.' The project leader focuses on what must be done. 'I'm more worried about the deviation of four weeks in time than the deviation of 15 per cent in our budget,' he says. 'The time delay will have a potentially bigger impact. We have to get back on track – and quickly!'

This situation does not differ from any project meeting where a project leader checks progress with team members. However, in this case, the project manager is on site with his staff in China, the engineers of the technical department are in Germany, and the equipment supplier is in the United States. New technologies have enabled the company to set up a project team with the best qualified people – regardless of their location and whether they work internally or externally. Such is the power of collaborative product commerce (CPC), a business capability that enables fast product development across dispersed locations, systems and organizations. This chapter will describe trends in product development, the capabilities of

CPC is a business capability that enables products to be developed across diverse locations, systems and organizations.

collaborative product commerce and its impact on the competitiveness of different industries.

Major drivers of product development

Product development has been influenced by a range of forces over the last two decades – technological, economic, social and cultural. These forces have driven changes in the way organizations undertake product development. Product development has evolved from a relatively time-intensive, step-by-step approach to a process that involves a complex network of people, project partners and processes all working to develop a product within the shortest possible timeframe.

Globalization and market trends

Globalization has increased the competitiveness of industries dramatically, such as in the automotive, electronics and high technology, and electrical appliances industries. Globalization has put pressure on major companies to consolidate so that today many have operations in all regions of the world. The global reach of organizations has also created growing competition on a cost basis and generated a new approach to production and design. Corporations now need to introduce products at the same time and of the same quality around the world, regardless of local or regional adaptations to the products. Companies no longer have the luxury of keeping products on the market for long or extending their life cycle by introducing them in other geographical markets. Today, customers throughout the world are demanding similar levels of quality and sophistication.

Alongside globalization, technological and sociological changes have had a major impact on the competitive environment of companies. Markets are fragmenting as customers start to demand increasingly tailored products and services. The tastes of consumers are changing rapidly as people demand new and better products across the world. Technological innovation is also driving the capability of companies to deliver new products and services and the ability of customers to both access information and to buy products and services (Figure 3.7.1).

Other factors have been impacting business initiatives in the area of design and development of new products since the 1980s.

- *Mass customization.* Companies developed the ability to adapt products to the needs of customers by changing certain product characteristics and maintaining the product base. This strategy has been extensively applied in the car and consumer electronics industries.

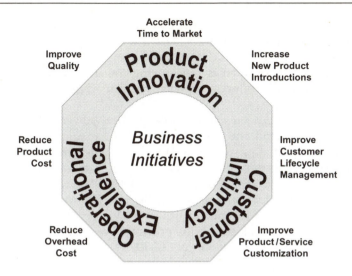

Figure 3.7.1
Impact of CPC on business initiatives

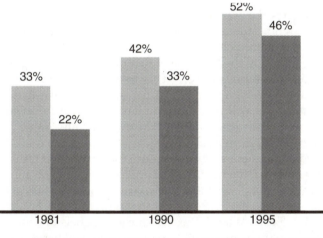

■ Revenues coming from products developed in the last 5 years
■ Profits coming from products developed in the last 5 years

Source: Cooper, 2001

Figure 3.7.2
Revenue and profits generated by new products

- *Modularization of products.* Organizations expanded products developed for mass markets by designing modules that provided different characteristics on a basic product design. The modules could be designed, industrialized and pre-assembled independently before being integrated into the final product. This strategy has made mass customization possible.

- *Focus on core capabilities*. With globalization, cost pressures and shrinking margins, companies started to concentrate on their core business of overall product design and integration of modules. This strategy led to companies outsourcing the design and complete manufacture of product components and modules to component manufacturers.
- *Profits flowing from new products*. The growing power of technology, consumer demand and market reach has led to a large increase in the number of new products launched on to the market. The proportion of revenue and profits generated by these new products is growing, as shown in Figure 3.7.2. In 1995, 52 per cent of revenue came from products developed in the last five years, compared with 42 per cent of revenue in 1990 and 33 per cent in 1981. Profits from products developed in the previous five years doubled from 22 per cent in 1981 to 46 per cent in 1995.

The importance of time

A second major trend driving product development is the question of time. Simply, there is not enough time to meet the needs of consumers. Those companies that can succeed in a faster product development cycle derive significant competitive advantages from their speed.

First, for each month cut off product development time, companies can add one month to the life cycle of the product, increasing revenue and reducing development costs. This benefit is all the greater for products that have a high change cost. Second, companies that launch pioneering products will win a larger market share at the expense of those that follow their lead. Market followers will always struggle to win over customers from a market leader.

A third advantage gained by getting products to market faster lies in larger profit margins. If a new product appears before the competition, the company may set prices more freely, especially in the first phases of the product life cycle, thus increasing the margins that may be achieved, as Figure 3.7.3 shows. When prices fall due to the effect of competition, the company will have managed to reduce its costs along the learning curve and will have a significant advantage over its competitors.

In the same way, a company capable of developing its products faster than the competition may use this advantage by starting the development process later than its competitors, enabling it to use advances in technology and incorporate these into its products.

Different studies have demonstrated the value of time as a major differentiator in the development of new products. A study on Collaborative Product Commerce conducted by Accenture (Cuartero and Lorenzi, 2001) revealed that companies may lose up to 33 per cent of their profits when they launch a product six months late on the market (Figure 3.7.4). If they spend 50 per cent more on the budget for the development of the product, the loss is just 3.5 per cent. The

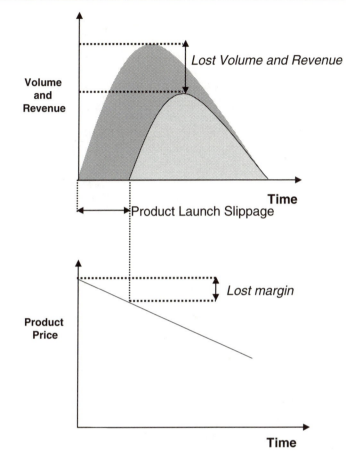

Figure 3.7.3
Impact of time on volume and revenue

project manager at the start of this chapter was wise, then, in wanting to push ahead with his project rather than suffer a four-week delay.

Concurrent engineering and the extended enterprise

Companies have responded to the competitive challenges of recent years by introducing a new way of structuring the design and development of new products using concurrent engineering techniques. Commonly known as 'simultaneous engineering', this method involves different departments forming multifunctional teams to collaborate in developing a new product. The team – made up of people from marketing, engineering, manufacturing and finance – is responsible for the cost and time of the project to launch a new product.

The traditional form of product development commonly involved separate areas of an organization being responsible for different stages of the project. The design engineering department normally made the major decisions about product characteristics, target costs and

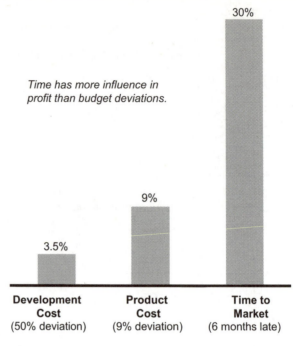

Source: Accenture

Figure 3.7.4

Impact of time and budget deviations on profit (% total profit loss)

prioritization of tasks, with limited input from marketing, finance, purchasing or manufacturing. Often delays occurred because of conflicting views or differing priorities of each functional area.

The formation of multifunctional teams addressed these flaws by taking into account all 'departmental voices'. The interaction of design and manufacturing engineers, for instance, helped to ensure the product can be manufactured at an effective cost and by the agreed deadline. Most importantly, the team structure ensured the focus and commitment of all members was on the new product rather than functional priorities. Overall, the multifunctional teams shorten a product's time to market through three major ways: commitment, communication and decision making.

Collaboration is not limited to the company boundaries; product development today extends to suppliers and customers in what is known as the extended enterprise. Supplier and customer collaboration helps to improve speed to market, as shown in Figure 3.7.5. Suppliers are involved through the joint development of some of the modules of the product, by the externalization of some phases of the detailed product design, and by contract manufacturing and product change management.

Customer collaboration is a new area of organizational interaction. Organizations understand and establish relationships with these

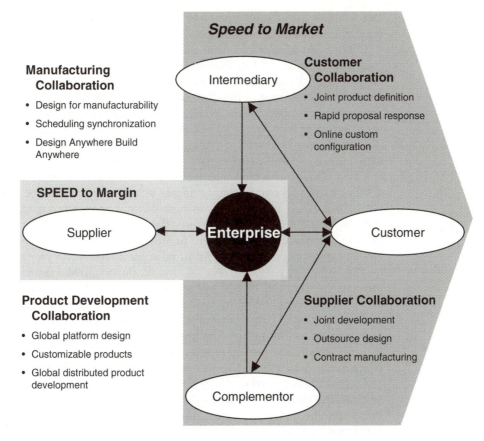

Figure 3.7.5
The role of supplier and customer collaboration

customers through one-to-one marketing and work with them on product definition, product proposals and product customization. Manufacturers gain direct feedback from selected groups of customers via the Internet, with customers from around the world giving their opinions on product features. In a globalized market, this helps organizations to tap into the views and needs of customers at a global level.

What is collaborative product commerce?

If collaboration via multifunctional teams is one stage in product development, the next stage in evolution is collaborative product commerce. CPC enables an organization to achieve fast and efficient product development across geographically dispersed places and across diverse organizations in the supply chain. CPC uses articulated information systems to capture the innovative processes, emerging

CPC captures processes, technologies and competencies across dispersed locations and organizations to accelerate product development.

technologies and competencies of all product team members. In this way, it accelerates the rate of product development.

CPC is distinguishable from its technology predecessor – product data management (PDM) systems – in that it is a business capability. Traditionally, PDM systems made it possible for people to share and store all data relevant to the development of a new product, including plans, bills of materials and engineering change approvals. However, these software tools were limited to the four walls of the company. As discussed, the extended organization of today needs to exchange ideas, processes and people with other companies in its supply chain.

CPC allows external partners to be added to the product development process, so that it creates virtual communities of people who are focused on the development of new products regardless of the time and the place. This captures the ideas, competencies and core capabilities of a larger number of organizations, resulting in the more efficient and faster development of new products.

The technology aspects of CPC are similar to PDM systems. Both pursue the creation of an integrated environment for product or project development and are based on the management of documents and the creation of data repositories, together with change management and product configuration. The most important difference is that CPC is built on Internet technologies and is thus able to connect all participants, albeit from the company or external, in virtual teams.

One of the areas where CPC tests its value is the management of engineering changes, a major capability needed for successful product development projects. CPC manages engineering changes with functions such as:

- *electronic workflow* – the capacity to automate the sending of documents for checking and approval of engineering changes
- *subscriptions* – elements of information that can be associated with specific people or departments, thus ensuring that suitable notifications reach the right people in time for action and
- *red-lining* – the capacity for all people participating in the definition or implementation of the change to visualize or add comments to an engineering document, regardless of whether they have access to the application in which the original document was made.

Engineering change management is being used by the contract manufacturers to establish closer relations with original equipment manufacturers, by accelerating the process of implementation of the engineering changes in products with the subcontracted manufacturing firms.

Another of the key applications is the management of product configuration in environments where greater customization of products is needed. The efficient management of configuration enables manufacturers to restrict the proliferation of configurations of the product falling outside standards and thus control the multiplication of components. Among other things, CPC enables the approval of processes associated with new products to be defined by encouraging the use of standard components and making use of existing platforms, thus reducing the product development costs derived from the principal.

Capabilities of CPC

Collaborative product commerce involves a set of applications, technologies and philosophies to achieve the most integrated product development, using the best knowledge and technologies of all product team members. As Figure 3.7.6 illustrates, CPC capabilities cross all stages of product design and manufacturing, from concept definition; to planning; to designing, building and testing; to production and ongoing manufacturing. The capabilities are important, therefore, to achieving the design-to-cost phase of the process and the management of product value. The CPC capabilities are summarized below.

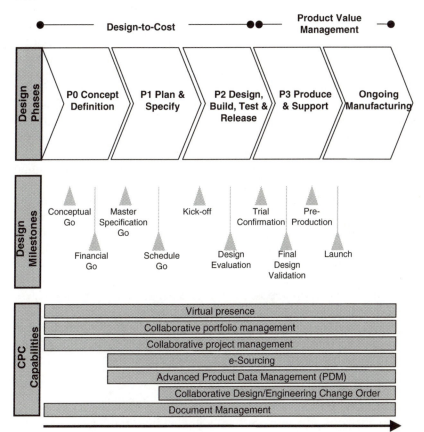

Figure 3.7.6
CPC capabilities in the product development process

- *Workflow management*: Web-based technologies for identifying work task and role-based work flow, task assignment and delegation, routing, notification and work-item tracking.
- *Product definition, configuration, and version control management*: a Web-based version of capabilities found in traditional PDM systems: product structure management, versioning, iteration and data configuration.
- *Portfolio management*: Web-based tools and resources to assess product portfolios and associated investments to determine their alignment with market trends, and company values and strategies.
- *Requirements definition and tracking*: the capture and storing of requirements from a variety of internal and external sources. Using Internet technologies, captured requirements can be tracked from conception to inclusion into final products.
- *Product life cycle/release tracking*: Internet technologies to manage the life cycle of products, from conception, to introduction, and through to retirement.
- *Component sourcing and supplier management*: management of component sourcing and supplier relationships using the Internet, including the procurement area in the product development process. The components already negotiated are available for the engineer to include them in the designs. Purchasing requisitions are created automatically when an engineer defines the specification and forwards it to the procurement representative in the team.
- *Engineering design and collaboration*: an Internet-based environment where design data can be shared and modified by engineers, customers, suppliers and internal company organization.
- *Program and project management*: Internet technologies to define program/project work plans, milestones, project status, and project estimates. Integration with workflows is a feature that helps the project manager control the advance of each of the task packages.
- *Personalized Web content delivery*: a customizable view of product and organizational information based upon the user's defined roles and responsibilities.
- *Document control, distribution and publishing*: Internet-based methods to provide a secure repository for the storage and controlled release of product documentation to all subscribers.
- *Product management training and knowledge management*: Internet technologies to customize and deliver product-centric training on an as-needed basis.

Benefits of CPC

Companies can achieve significant value by undertaking collaborative product commerce. Improving time to market, as mentioned, can generate higher revenues and increase margins. Costs can be reduced significantly, not only in product costs but the costs involved in product development and tooling. Achieving economies of scale through more efficient product development can also keep costs in check.

The application of CPC technologies, and the change in business processes this implies, can also provide an opportunity for organizations to differentiate themselves from their competitors. By implementing distinctive capabilities, companies can lock their customers into their business processes and create such an integrated environment that it is costly and inefficient for customers to change.

Despite the benefits that CPC can deliver across the entire product life cycle, the improvements can be difficult to evaluate for the following reasons:

- improving speed to market can be related to the company's characteristics and can change (in the amount or in time of achievement) according to the industry, market trends and pressure from the competitors and
- companies don't communicate data related to their CPC initiatives, not only because the initiatives are still running and so final data are not yet available, but also because the data involved in CPC processes is considered strategic.

However, Figure 3.7.7 below highlights the numerous ways that CPC contributes to value creation in an organization. As would be expected, CPC can increase sales growth, and therefore revenue, by decreasing time to market and time to volume. CPC contributes to the same revenue value lever by increasing customer satisfaction and the efficiency of research and development. Achieving greater engineering efficiency, volume leverage and more flexible infrastructure through CPC adds to value by reducing costs.

Case studies: applications of CPC in three industries

Many companies in industries such as automotive, electronics and engineering are deriving substantial competitive advantage from collaborative product commerce. The case studies of companies below describe the business issue faced by the company, the approach taken, the capabilities that CPC provided, and the expected qualitative and economic results.

Automotive supplier

A leading supplier of metallic components for car manufacturers wanted to improve its quotation process to clients. The automotive supplier had several divisions located in different countries and operated in a highly competitive environment. Generally, the quotation process was complex because several departments and

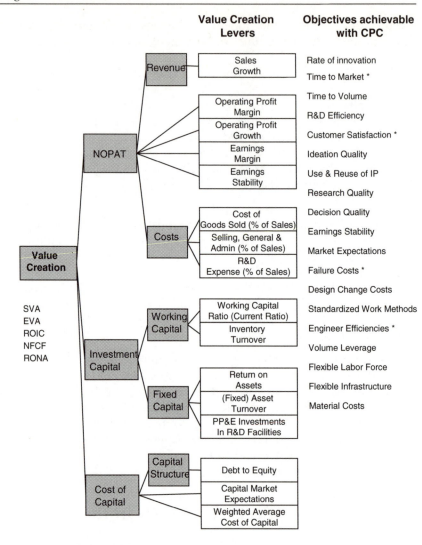

Value Creation Levers		Objectives achievable with CPC

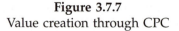

★ = Primary Value Creation Opportunities

Figure 3.7.7
Value creation through CPC

areas of the company had to contribute different types of information such as technical data, costs of the product and projected production capacity.

The manufacturer had several critical requirements in the quotation process. It needed to ensure the traceability of multiple versions of the quotation during the whole product lifecycle so that it could analyze the final results of product profitability compared to the initial client offer. The company also had to provide multiple formats for customer-specific quotations and use new channels such as Internet auctions and an automotive industry e-market.

Capabilities
The CPC solution produced several new business capabilities:

- *Communication.* CPC enabled the company to implement a single new collaborative environment that supported the various customer templates that were needed to record information during the quotation process. The integrated environment permitted different departments to contribute their information and views, with a quotation project manager managing the entire process. The team members could provide feedback based on their previous experience so the quotation had all the relevant information that was needed.
- *Workflow management.* The CPC solution enabled the standardization of the quotation process among plants and divisions, while maintaining specific differences. Various templates were established to record information needs for stamping and assembly, die tools and tailored welded blanks.

The solution also created a customized workspace for team members who were assigned different roles in the quotation process. The workspace enabled the company to implement workflows so that each member knew when to take part in the process and what to do in each step. This prevented inefficiencies and unnecessary delays and accelerated the process. Consequently, senior managers had enough time to review the quotation and make their decisions based on the commercial aspects of the quotation.

Benefits
By implementing these business capabilities, the company expects to obtain significant benefits such as:

- increasing sales volume and profit due to a more efficient quotation process
- increasing bidding capacity through a 50 per cent reduction in process lead time
- achieving a 95 per cent completion in on-time quotation, while improving delivered information quality
- assuring more adjusted prices and better margins, and
- improving sales visibility and projected capacity planning using more accurate sales forecast information.

Foundry company
The foundry company is a world leader in the production of iron, aluminum and magnesium castings for the automotive industry. With operations spread throughout Europe, North and South America and Asia, the company was being pressured by its clients to reduce its time to market and improve the reliability of its products. The company also needed to harmonize its product development processes at a global level.

Capabilities

- *Communication*. The company defined and implemented a CPC solution to manage and to circulate valuable technical information, such as documents and technical data, and distribute knowledge across the company.
- *Project management*. The foundry used a new PDM infrastructure to reduce the distance between the people involved in the product development process so as to improve the effectiveness of project management activities.
- *Workflow management*. The company reorganized and redefined company processes so that it could use a PDM system for structuring data workflow.

Benefits

The foundry expects to achieve the following benefits:

- reducing the time needed to retrieve and manage information
- reducing errors due to incorrect data entry
- reducing time in the development process due to re-using technical solutions, and
- learning time compression for technical resources.

Engineering and construction company

The engineering and construction company operates worldwide in the fields of refinery and gas plants, natural gas treatment and monetization, fertilizer and petrochemical plants, onshore and offshore pipeline systems, and power and environmental plants. The company had been experiencing fast growth in its markets, with growing clients and an increasing number of construction sites. However, the firm was also facing strong competition in its industry and pressure to reduce the time involved in its projects, so that it could increase the return on investment for its clients.

Capabilities

The CPC solution allowed the company to develop the following business capabilities:

- *Communication*. The company developed a knowledge management system that was based jointly on technical and economic analyses of engineering solutions. It also implemented a tool for the collaborative management of product documents.
- *Workflow management*. The firm also re-engineered the 'project start-up process' phase and implemented engineering change management.

Benefits

The company invested about 5 million euros in the CPC project, including hardware and software investments and the deployment of internal and external resources. The payback on the investment is expected to occur about 2.5 years after the system roll-out.

The main benefits expected by the company include:

- improved operating effectiveness (accounting for around 67 per cent of the total benefits) through:
  - reducing administrative activities, such as archiving, photocopying and postal services
  - reducing the level of reworking needed, and
  - increasing the level of reuse
- lower supply costs (28 per cent of benefits) through:
  - reducing the modification of equipment orders
  - cutting purchasing costs for bulk materials, and
- lower building costs (5 per cent of benefits) through:
  - reducing the level of reworking.

Future trends in CPC

With competition likely to increase in the future, organizations will be seeking to gain even greater value from their product development efforts. Industry leaders will need to meet the dual challenge of achieving earning efficiencies in the short term while freeing up critical resources to deploy to product innovation in the medium term.

Research commissioned by Accenture shows that European companies that have launched CPC initiatives have gained an advantage over their competitors. The survey of 100 leading firms across Europe was conducted in July 2001 to develop new insights into CPC in the key industries of automotive and trucking, engineering, high technology and aerospace, and manufacturing. About two-thirds (or 67 per cent) of respondents confirmed they are already rolling out a CPC project. Fourteen per cent of the companies have given their CPC projects top priority in order to maximize expected benefits.

At an industry level, the automotive and trucking sectors are more mature than others and are expected to move one step ahead of competitors by developing greater external collaboration between their suppliers and clients. The engineering sector, on the other hand, concentrates more on internal collaboration and in this way is not as advanced in its approach to product development. Despite these differences, CPC capabilities are set to expand in all industries, although at differing speeds and intensities. No company will want to be left behind.

To be successful, CPC has to be supported by two developments: strong cultural change and new technology infrastructures.

CPC as cultural change

Implementing CPC capabilities in an extended manner is an important change, as it requires strong integration of technologies, processes and strategy both inside and outside the company. For companies planning to launch a product development program, there are more than just technology considerations to factor in. In fact, only 20 per cent of the change impacts technological infrastructures, while 80 per cent of the change is related to cultural changes in the organization and business relationships with different partners.

Accenture's CPC survey (Cuartero and Lorenzi, 2001) feedback shows that the most important problems that companies face when implementing CPC projects are:

- lack of resources (skills and numbers)
- involvement or integration of the different stakeholders in each step of the process:
  - across business functions and processes, optimizing the organization structure
  - among clients and suppliers, by identifying mechanisms to share the benefits of collaboration.

Technological infrastructure

Like in a lot of company processes, also in the product development domain, technology is now ready to support terrific breakthroughs both in terms of performances in results and efficiency in work behaviors.

Due to the dramatic growth of enterprise resource planning, customer relationship management, supply chain management, business-to-business e-commerce, and other packaged application implementations, nearly all Accenture technology engagements contribute some element of application integration.

Conclusion

As the competitive landscape has changed, organizations have changed their approach to product development. The driving forces of globalization, the need to get products to market quickly, and the emergence of concurrent engineering have expanded the role and capability of the development process. Collaborative product commerce is the next stage of product evolution, giving organizations the power to develop products quickly and efficiently across diverse geographic locations and across different companies in their supply chain.

They held a videoconference to check the latest versions of the plans, specifications and the budget together, using Internet technology to share the information. They logged the technical notes at the meeting in real time and made them available for the detail engineers to use later. The equipment supplier even attended part of the meeting from his headquarters in the United States, when he explained the characteristics of the equipment and the modifications that could be made to optimize the system.

References

Cuartero, A., and Lorenzi, S. (2001), *Pan-European Collaborative Product Development Survey*, Accenture.

Baldwin C. Y. and Clark K. B. (1997), 'Managing in an age of modularity', *Harvard Business Review*, (September–October).

Bartezzaghi, E. et al. (1998), 'Managing Knowledge in Continuous Product Innovation', paper presented to the 5th International Product Development Management Conference, Como, Italy, 25–26 May.

Brown, H. K. and Eisenhardt, K. M., (1995). 'Product Development: past research, present findings and future directions', Academy of Management Review, Champaign, Ill.

Clark, K. B. and Fujimoto, T. (1991), *Product Development Performance: Strategy, Organization and Management in the World Auto Industry*, Boston, MA: Harvard Business School Press.

Cooper, R. G. (2001), *Winning at New Products: Accelerating the Process from Idea to Launch*, 3rd edn, Cambridge, MA: Perseus Books.

Imai, K. et al. (1985), 'Managing the New Product Development Process: How Japanese Companies Learn and Unlearn' in Clark, K. B. et al., *The uneasy Alliance: Managing the Productivity–Technology Dilemma*, Boston, MA: Harvard Business School Press.

Robertson, D. and Ulrich, K. (1998), 'Planning for Product Platforms', *Sloan Management Review*, Cambridge, MA.

Ulrich, K. (1995), 'The role of product architecture in the manufacturing firm', *Research Policy*, Vol. 24, No. 3, pp. 419–440.

3.8 Integrated fulfilment

Jon Bumstead, Sara Ford and Roger Gillespie

New business practices may have emerged, but some of today's supply chain problems are all too familiar.

Invent a time machine. Travel back to the late 1980s, kidnap a supply chain executive and bring him/her back. Some of what the executive would see of today's supply chain world would look frighteningly different: Web-based public and private marketplaces, third- and fourth-party logistics providers (3PLs and 4PLs), and collaborative planning and forecasting. New thinking, enabled by new technologies, has resulted in the emergence of some very different business practices.

However, some other aspects of today's supply chains would look all too familiar – worryingly so, perhaps. The supply chain executive would see many of the same problems that he or she had wrestled with 15 or so years earlier. Reverse logistics is still the messy process it was previously, even if it has been given an impressive-sounding name. The wrong inventory still piles up in the wrong places. And far too much time, money and energy are invested in business processes because companies assume their supply chain partners are unreliable, or not to be trusted.

What has been happening? Many of the priorities lay with optimizing – sometimes to a fine pitch of perfection – aspects of the supply chain that often were not the prime cause of inefficiencies. Simply put, organizations optimized these areas because they had the tools to do so. Any improvement was better than no improvement, even though the areas were not high priority. Valuable cost-savings often accrued, but the result did not do much to improve the performance of the supply chain.

More recently, the focus of many supply chain operations has changed. Where supply chain executives were often inward looking, they became increasingly focused on the external links between their part of the supply chain and other parts. 3PLs, 4PLs, collaborative planning, e-procurement: these and other developments are extensions

392

of the traditional supply chain that advances in technology have made possible. To an unprecedented degree, the management of supply chains today is down to creating, understanding and optimizing relationships with other entities.

Integrate, integrate, integrate

However, has this really done much to solve today's supply chain challenges? Are companies any better at reverse logistics, for example, even though the ability to bring back or redirect goods from the marketplace is emerging as a core requirement in new business models? Has the enormous investment in Internet-based technology and elaborate new business systems actually improved essential business metrics such as debtor days, cash flow and working capital ratios?

Traditional approaches to fulfilment often have been overly focused on the physical flows of goods or on optimizing the technology.

Often, the answer is 'no'. And that, too, to our time-traveling supply chain executive would come as no surprise, because he or she rarely saw much improvement in those things anyway. Fulfilment may be incrementally better, but it still has not crossed the chasm to become truly integrated.

One reason is the simple fact that traditional approaches to fulfilment have often been overly focused on the physical flows of goods, rather than on the flows of data that underpin those physical movements. Take, for example, the effort that has gone into determining the 'optimal' solution for where to locate a central distribution facility that is replacing a dozen facilities scattered around Europe. Achieving the best location is a worthy goal, of course, and a number of sophisticated tools have been developed to aid businesses in making those decisions.

But in reality, much of that endeavor has been misplaced. Whether or not a location close to Eindhoven or one of the other favored spots is the ideal physical point from which to distribute goods around Europe is immaterial. What matters more, experience now shows, is the flow of orders *through* to the warehouse, not the flow of goods *from* the warehouse. And if a company has ten different ERP systems to contend with, automatically they have to tackle a three-year integration project first – and one with a very questionable business case.

Likewise, a lot of the focus on optimizing the technology of fulfilment and distribution has been equally wide of the mark. Sophisticated picking faces, highly automated packaging and sorting lines, and finely honed distribution networks are all useful. However, they fail to tackle some real underlying business problems. As countless companies' experience in implementing ERP systems shows, the cultural barriers to transformation are harder to surmount than the technological ones. Nirvana is always 'just around the corner', and surely the organization will get there once the technology is ready or matures. Somehow, this never quite happens.

Supply chain event management

Is there a better way? Assuredly. But again, this is not quite the question. Companies have spent billions developing their fulfilment operations to their present degree, and no one can imagine that businesses will simply throw away their investments overnight and hurtle down some other road to perfection. A better question is this: taking the organizations already in place, what will move companies to the next level of fulfilment best practice? The answer lies in viewing the supply chain as a series of *events* that the organization must manage. This holistic approach is the central idea behind what is coming to be termed supply chain event management.

Conceptually, supply chain event management can be thought of as four layers, each of which must be in place for the supply chain to be able to manage this holistic process of integrated fulfilment, as illustrated in Figure 3.8.1.

Connectivity and data translation

The first layer comprises connectivity and data translation. The warehouse in Eindhoven, for instance, has to be connected to the dozen or so ERP systems that want to send it orders. The organization has to forget the three-year integration program. It needs a way for all of the ERP systems to communicate flawlessly in real time with each other and with some central warehouse and transport management

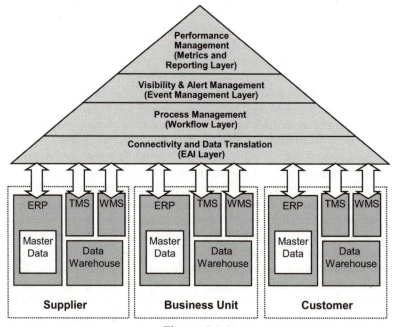

Figure 3.8.1
Supply chain event management solution framework

system at the warehouse. Such a simple-sounding requirement is actually an ambitious undertaking.

The problem is not in the wiring – or the cost of the wiring; the problem lies in the lack of common standards and data protocols. The Internet and other advances in telecommunications have provided the raw capability, but organizations still lack a way to put data in one end and have them understandable at the other. 'We need common standards' is the normal demand. However, standards take time to hammer out and are prone to dilution or debasement. Java and Unix, for example, started out with lofty goals of cross-platform standardization, but then incurred less-than-ideal variations.

Another – albeit crude – solution is to have the same system at both ends. This is certainly possible, but expensive and time consuming to achieve. EDI tried to do this, and did so very successfully for those relatively few businesses that adopted it. Inevitably, however, this solution would fall foul of the problem that repeatedly tripped up EDI: only 20 per cent of those companies that needed it could afford to do it properly. The remaining 80 per cent achieved a limited scope of application or sub-optimal performance. The alternative is a universal translation mechanism, which is beginning to emerge.

Process management

Data translation, however, is not the entire answer. Just as in human languages, concepts do not always translate or map on to one another exactly. Anyone who has implemented different enterprise systems will know that while the systems may appear to offer the same capabilities, in reality, large differences of definition exist. What 'allocated' or 'dispatched' or 'received' means in one system might mean something slightly different in another. In today's commercial environment, such slight differences are simply not permissible.

Defining a universal process will clarify what is taking place and prevent important information being lost. The definition must be flexible and capable of evolution.

There is another problem, too. With a stream of data transferring from one commercial entity to another, the system at the receiving end of the transfer has to do something with the incoming data. Each piece of incoming data needs to be correctly identified as a forecast, order, dispatch, cancellation or deferment, and inserted into the correct place within the receiving location's system.

The best way organizations can optimize data is to define a universal process, by which they reference the inferred processes in all other systems. Defining a process not only clarifies exactly what is taking place at each stage, but also prevents the possibility of pieces of data 'falling between the cracks'. In this way, information being sent or received will have a corresponding slot at the other end.

Such a process definition must be flexible and capable of evolution. Today a company might wish to incorporate a 'receipt' stage in the process, recognizing that a supplier might want to have some formal acknowledgment that the company has received its dispatch. The inclusion of a receipt stage enables invoicing and other procedures to recognize that a transfer of ownership of the goods in question is underway. However, there is no guarantee the company will want this same information tomorrow. Alternatives such as vendor managed inventory, for instance, render the need to issue a receipt unnecessary.

Visibility and alert management

A third layer of communication is necessary to create the framework for supply chain event management. Simply put, it is the need for some kind of 'control channel' to achieve an integrated fulfilment process. Think of it as a battlefield communications system, or the Unicom frequencies found at airport control towers. Each party in the supply chain constantly puts out messages signaling an order's current status and how this might affect others.

The level of granularity in such communications can be high. Messages might be transmitted to say that orders had left the factory, or raw materials had been satisfactorily received. A little thought reveals that the Unicom analogy yields another benefit, too: just as in aircraft traffic control, where the sequence of messages reveal the position of each aircraft at a point in time, so can the sequence of event alerts provide a picture of where inventory is within the supply chain, and how orders are progressing through to fulfilment.

This high degree of granularity, however, has given rise to a misleading belief by some supply chain commentators that these kinds of emerging communication channels might best be used to provide 'alerts' that things are going wrong. So they might. Just as readily as reporting that things are going right, it is obviously possible to communicate that events are going awry. Such exceptions, though, are almost inherent in the very act of forecasting: no forecast can ever be 100 per cent correct, and one party's forecast variation may well be another party's 'error exception'.

The critical issue is that communicating knowledge of forecast variation in advance can help an organization react and respond to the information so as to prevent a variation being a problem. The process of steering a car, for example, is a series of minute responses and reactions to variations from the intended path: no car ever goes precisely where it is steered, and second-by-second driver intervention is constantly required. The 'alerts' that the driver receives to say that the current path is not the one that was intended are a perfectly normal part of the process.

This is not to say that the proponents of the 'alert to exceptions' school of thought are wrong. Simply, a more useful approach is to regard alerts as a way of communicating necessary information, certain in the knowledge that thanks to the process definition and connectivity layers, the information will be intelligible and meaningful.

Performance management

The final layer satisfies the need for a metrics and performance-monitoring layer within the supply chain. In part, this is necessary in order to provide an assurance of acceptable service levels from parties within the supply chain. Consider, for example, the highly detailed vendor performance statistics produced by the automotive giants and major grocery retailers. Quality, invoice accuracy, delivery reliability and packaging conformance are all measured, leaving their suppliers in no doubt as to the adequacy of their performance relative to peers and potential competitors.

Performance monitoring across the whole supply chain will identify the cause of failures and also highlight the overall consequences of change.

However, such measures presently fail to distinguish between failures arising from aspects of a given supplier's own performance, or failures at least partly predicated on shortcomings upstream in the supply chain. If a supplier failed, was this the company's fault, or the fault of a raw material supplier two levels along? Arguably, any failure is ultimately the responsibility of the immediate party within the transaction, and this is true. However, the point of conceiving of a series of linked transactions as a supply chain in the first place is to be able to distinguish each party's role in the entire linkage. Applying a set of consistent metrics across the supply chain achieves this.

The same set of metrics has another role to play, too: identifying the impact of changes in one area of the supply chain on the performance of other areas. Consider the consequence of reducing inventory in one part of the supply chain. Here, the metrics will show such results as an improved working capital ratio, fewer days of inventory, less money tied up in stock, and so forth. Under conventional performance measurement systems, this will be good news. Only subsequently – and often accidentally – will it transpire that the inventory reduction has had a harmful effect on service levels in another part of the supply chain. Without a framework of performance measures, such linkages are very difficult to either identify or prove. Once again, a layer of measures, operating across the whole supply chain, can demonstrate such consequences beyond doubt.

From fantasy to fact

But how far away is a framework for supply chain event management becoming a reality? Five years? Ten years? Fifteen? The answer is perhaps surprising: in large part, it is here already. By 'here' we mean the technology described above exists. However, use of the capabilities is only beginning.

A framework for supply chain event management is, in large part, a reality. The technology exists; however, use of the capability is only beginning.

For proof, look no further than Figure 3.8.2, which shows examples of how each layer in the supply chain event management framework is being addressed by software system vendors' existing solutions. For each layer, a number of vendors already have offerings on the market

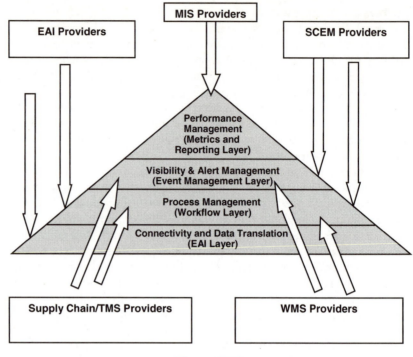

Figure 3.8.2
Supply chain event management solution landscape

that substantially match the required capability. Soon, that number will grow, as will the overlap between the ideal capability requirement and the commercially available software that companies can buy and implement.

Some of the names are extremely familiar to experienced supply chain executives – McHugh Software International (WMS), Manugistics (SC/TMS), Viewlocity (SCEM), Manhattan Associates (WMS), and i2 Technologies (SC/TMS). Leading-edge companies are today buying these solutions, using them and exploring their capabilities.

The reason for the growth in technology solutions is not hard to determine. Analysts such as ARC Advisory Group in 2001 reckon that the entire supply chain software and service market is currently growing at 11 per cent a year – reaching over $7 billion by 2005 (Figure 3.8.3). However, the growth in tried and trusted application areas such as supply chain planning and supply chain execution is slowing. Not so long ago, for example, the supply chain planning solution sector market was growing at 40 per cent a year – now, ARC predicts growth of 12 per cent per year. The market for supply chain execution is even more sclerotic; growth is expected at around 9 per cent a year.

However, the market for supply chain event management is set to soar at 33 per cent per annum, according to ARC. While the sector will still be just a fraction of the more mature supply chain planning and

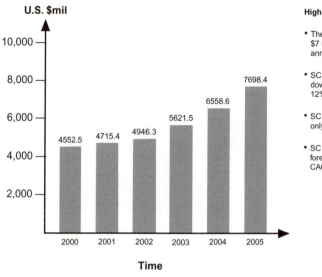

U.S. $mil

Year	Value
2000	4552.5
2001	4715.4
2002	4946.3
2003	5621.5
2004	6558.6
2005	7698.4

Time

Highlights:-

• The total market will top $7 billion in 2005 with an annual growth of 11%

• SC Planning will slow down from recent 40% to 12% CAGR

• SC Execution will grow at only 9% CAGR

• SC Event Management is forecast to grow at 33% CAGR

Source: ARC Advisory Group (2001)

Figure 3.8.3
Total shipments of supply chain management software and services

supply chain execution markets in size by 2005, it will be growing at more than twice the rate.

This matters for two reasons. First, it is the adoption of new and leading-edge applications that give companies their competitive edge – not the more mature and stale applications that are already well embedded within the industry. Second, because the interests of supply chain software and services vendors are aligned with those of their customer base, leading-edge applications that let a company stand out from the crowd soon find buyers.

'Leading-edge' means 'leading-edge': the mainstream of the user community is likely to be at least five years behind in adopting such applications, and perhaps closer to ten. If that seems a remarkable time lag, consider that some companies are implementing ERP systems for the first time – 15 years after leading-edge companies began the transition from mainframe-based SAP R/2 to ERP systems.

The parallel with ERP is worth pursuing a little further. The biggest barrier to the effective adoption of ERP was not the availability of the technology, but the need to manage the change process effectively. Repeatedly, ERP implementations ran foul of cultural hiccups that would set back the go-live date by months or years. Although this same lesson arguably needed to be re-learned when the same companies began adopting e-procurement technology, the underlying principle is clear. In these kinds of application areas, the technology develops faster than the cultural climate within many of the adoptive organizations.

Leading-edge companies adopt new applications at least five to ten years faster than their competitors.

There is another barrier, too, with parallels to ERP. Few, if any, of these suppliers have put together a coherent and compelling marketing message that explains to CEOs and CIOs exactly what their solutions offer. Often jargon and acronyms can confuse and obscure far more than they illuminate.

The answer? An end to the proliferation of long-winded explorations of 'the possible' and a shift to the delivery of some pioneering examples of what actually can be achieved. Although the growth statistics for the supply chain event management market assume either that marketers will sharpen their messages – or that customers will somehow divine the selling proposition anyway – it would be reassuring to see more clarity. Even so, this is more of a niggle than a barrier; ERP survived the same confusion, and went on to become a 'category killer'.

Where to start?

So what might those compelling propositions comprise? Several possibilities suggest themselves.

Globalization

A small but growing slice of the supply chain event management market comprises solutions for global direct sourcing.

Take, for example, the rise in direct sourcing from Far East nations and other low-cost economies. The gains, both for niche discount retailers and manufacturers alike, can be substantial. But so can the headaches: company after company compares the European-sourced ex-works cost with the Far Eastern ex-works cost and assumes that the difference is all potential profit. In fact, a common mistake is to forget how long can be those physical supply chains, how poor are the communication links, how difficult to interact with people in other time zones and languages, and how crude are the planning and scheduling tools sometimes deployed by Far Eastern manufacturers.

Succeeding in direct sourcing can create a ready-made solution ready for others to exploit. This is starting to happen already: a small but growing slice of the supply chain event management market comprises companies providing solutions to do just that. The message to retailers and manufacturers wanting to open such direct trade links is whether they want to do so with or without the time, resources and risks involved. Inevitably, companies will adopt such solutions. They will regard the price of doing so as a worthwhile ' insurance premium' against the potential of further margin erosion through the sheer complexities of trying to import price-sensitive and sometimes time-sensitive items from the other side of the world.

Collaborative freight management

Another opportunity waiting to be seized is collaborative freight management. Again, the basic facts have not changed since the 1980s. Despite the resources that have gone into solving the problem, many trucks are still running empty. Official statistics, in fact, show that 30 per cent of all vehicles in Europe run empty – and that may understate the true figure. British statistics, based on distance traveled and proportion of carrying capacity utilized, have shown a figure closer to 50 per cent.

A collaborative Web-based community of fleet owners would develop synergies through sharing information and trading loads.

This is a significant waste in both environmental and financial terms. Around two-thirds of the cost of a typical logistics operation is transport-related and only one-third warehouse-related. Therefore, the consequences of such inefficiency manifest themselves forcefully on the bottom line. That bottom line is increasingly precarious, affected by higher taxes, higher fuel bills and environmentally based restrictions. Hauliers' margins, already tight, are under renewed pressure.

However, extra loads can not just be magically conjured. Or can they? The allure of collaborative freight management is the potential it offers to match empty vehicles traveling in one direction with a load going the same way. Solutions such as this have been tried before, the most successful being long-term fixed arrangements designed to take advantage of regular trucking runs. However, other attempts at filling empty vehicles have found little favor.

Imagine a collaborative Web-based community of fleet owners, in conjunction with the four layers of the supply chain event management framework outlined earlier. Now imagine them sharing information about where their trucks were going to be, and what loads or part loads they needed to get to particular destinations. Almost inevitably, synergies would emerge and loads would be traded.

Spanish transportation management and optimization service provider Agoratrans, for example, has successfully developed a business model aimed at unlocking the potential of empty backhauls among its member companies. Nistevo, another transportation management and optimization service provider reckons to have saved General Mills in the United States some four to seven per cent in logistics costs. Transplace, used by Transora, claims to have reduced less-than-truckload (LTL) shipments from 85 per cent to less than 2 per cent through load consolidation technologies for one particular client.

RFID: silent commerce

Many companies, however, are unwilling to entrust their freight shipments to others despite the allure of the potential gains. They are not so much worried about the threat of theft, loss or damage, as the potential for confusion and lack of transparency. In an era of tightly specified delivery slots and online vehicle tracking, a company has to pinpoint where its shipments are at a moment in time. Inevitably, this tends to be simpler and easier when those shipments are within a company's own freight network, or that of known and trusted partners.

Radio frequency identification tags make it possible to know where everything is in the supply chain, in real time.

Imagine, however, a facility to locate and interrogate shipments. Such a facility could ask the shipments, in effect, 'Where are you?' and ask that question not only at the truckload or pallet level, but if necessary at the individual item level on the pallet. The effect on the supply chain would be substantial indeed. With the ability to know where everything is along the supply chain, such 'integration pull' would make integrated fulfilment a real possibility.

Far from being the stuff of science fiction, radio frequency identification (RFID) tags make this capability a supply chain fact. The tags are beginning to become both cheap and ubiquitous. Requiring no batteries or external current, they sit passively attached to whatever they are stuck to, holding the same information as a barcode – and much more besides. A radio transmission is enough to activate the tags, providing them with enough power for read/write operation at some distance. Unlike barcodes, RFID tags do not rely on line-of-sight operation and are readily interfaced to ERP systems in much the same way as today's generation of barcodes (Figure 3.8.4).

All this functionality comes at a price, however. RFID tags are more expensive than barcodes – at least for the time being. Their prices have fallen over the past few years from between $1 and $2 to around 30 cents or so today. Once the major retailers – who have the most compelling business case for using RFID – start to exploit their potential in earnest, volumes will rise. With that rise will come economies of scale, leading to significant cost reductions. If an RFID

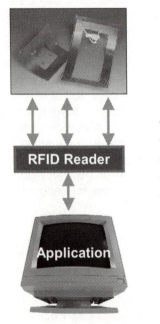

- Non-line of sight
- Simultaneous reads
- Updateable
- Unique object standard
- Decreasing cost

Figure 3.8.4
Silent commerce – RFID will have a greater impact than bar codes

tag costs 30 cents today, a figure of around 3 cents can be expected in five years' time.

Putting it all together

Put all these propositions together and the case for integrated fulfilment appears compelling. Like a jigsaw, though, the art lies in piecing the parts together. However affordable individual pieces of the puzzle might be, many companies will be wary of trying to complete the picture too quickly. The attractions sound wonderful, but in reality, they suspect that as before they will find themselves struggling to complete the process and be left with a half-finished project that delivers only a fraction of its promise.

The new generation of service providers need to be strong in IT and systems integration. Many 3PLs do not have this capability.

Worse, expectations of supply chain performance constantly get higher. Around the world, companies have spent billions on improving their supply chain management and they have achieved much. But a company that scored an 'average' grade on its supply chain management systems a decade ago is likely to score the same today. The company's performance may be better than it was, but so too is the performance of its competitors. The company has spent a lot of money simply to stay where it was in the race.

A better solution is to outsource the task to an organization for which piecing pictures together holds no fears. The emerging generation of would-be 4PLs seems to provide obvious candidates for this role. However, while 4PLs possess much of the required experience in manipulating the physical infrastructure of the objective, they are often weak when it comes to IT and systems integration. True, a party with this capability can be invited to join the 4PL consortium, but, this is precisely where the heart of the integrated fulfilment challenge lies.

Worryingly, too, as research carried out by Accenture in 2001 highlights, many of the present 3PLs have no intention of rushing in and acquiring that capability (Figure 3.8.5). Sixty per cent are planning to hold back from Internet-based developments and learn from the experiences of others. It is an alarming attitude for a group of companies who at the same time professed to recognize that those same Web technologies would be core to their growth.

A new kind of service provider

This gap gives rise to an opportunity for a new kind of service provider to address these challenges. Imagine, for a moment, the attraction to companies struggling to move towards integrated fulfilment of a service provider who offered to take on the task of putting the pieces together. They would not manage a typical systems integration project, where they put together systems then leave the client to operate and maintain them. Instead, the arrangement would be similar to Web hosting or application service provider (ASP)

A fulfilment service provider would not only integrate the systems, but also undertake the operation and maintenance.

September 2001

e-fulfilment: The Future Awaits
Pan-European Logistics Service Provider Survey 2001

Introduction

Customers are increasingly demanding a greater service from their Logistics Service Providers (LSPs) that deliver their goods, in a word – e-fulfilment. The term itself is all embracing, but essentially comprises eight or so familiar value-adding services, many of them electronically enhanced. From Order Capture and Processing, Planning & Optimisation, Service Support Centres and Track & Trace – all these and more fall within the e-fulfilment spectrum.

To find out how Europe's Logistics Service Providers are prepared for these new demands, Accenture commissioned 101 in-depth interviews with senior executives within some of Europe's leading LSPs. The interviews took place in June and July 2001, and included both large and medium-sized LSPs. The distinction between the responses did differ according to size – with a significant bearing on the future of e-fulfilment within the LSP sector.

Country	Number of Interviews
UK	21
Germany	11
Italy	8
France	14
Spain	19
Benelux	15
Nordic	13
Total	101

Key messages from 100 European 3PLs:-

• 72% of companies believe that Web technologies will be core to their future growth

• 40% were unaware of the term e-fulfilment and had not assessed the new Web technologies

• After the dotcom boom and bust, 60% plan to wait and see and learn from others

• A gap is appearing between the leading firms and the rest in terms of attitude, readiness and activities underway

• The clear differences by country provide interesting pointers as to who may dominate the European industry in the Web enabled future (Spain & Italy)

Source: Accenture (2001)

Figure 3.8.5
European logistics service provider survey results

software 'rental', where the provider not only does the integrating, but also undertakes the operation and maintenance as well.

Such ventures are an obvious extension to the ASP concept and will prove compelling to companies who are still scoring the same 'average' grade for their supply chain management as they were a decade ago. These companies want to use the emerging integrated fulfilment model as a way of genuinely gaining ground, rather than spending money simply to stay in their present position in the race. A fulfilment service provider offers client companies three key advantages as shown in Figure 3.8.6.

A fulfilment venture aims to sell transportation management and optimization services to the CPG industry at scale, clearly distinguishing itself from the competition in three ways.

First, properly integrated systems will be able to take a centralized view of demand. Impossible? Think back to those four layers. There will be no more forecasts, guesses and over-reliance on buffer stocks. The gains that come from this will be immense, as companies can reduce inventory levels while at the same time improving service levels.

Second, the service providers will be able to integrate existing solutions, rather than re-inventing the wheel. At a stroke, this reduces

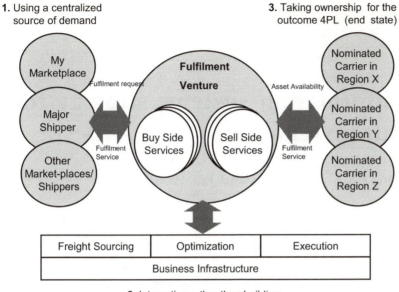

1. Using a centralized
source of demand

3. Taking ownership for the
outcome 4PL (end state)

My
Marketplace

Fulfilment request

Fulfilment

Venture

Asset Availability

Nominated
Carrier in
Region X

Major
Shipper

Fulfilment
Service

Buy Side
Services

Sell Side
Services

Fulfilment
Service

Nominated
Carrier in
Region Y

Other
Market-places/
Shippers

Nominated
Carrier in
Region Z

Freight Sourcing	Optimization	Execution
Business Infrastructure		

2. Integrating rather than building
Best of Breed Solutions

Figure 3.8.6
A new kind of fulfilment service provider

acquisition cost, reduces risk and reduces implementation lead time. Impossible? Again, think back to those four layers.

Third, the providers will be able to take ownership of the outcome – and will want to do so, to differentiate themselves from transport-led 4PLs. Assuming a greater degree of responsibility for the execution processes will balance the risks and thereby provide value to both carriers and to shippers. By doing so, they will be able to fulfill the promise inherent in the name that is emerging to describe this class of service provider: the managed supply chain operations provider.

Conclusion

A time machine is a handy thing – and too good to just use once and throw away. If we sneak a trip to the future, rather than the past, and look at fulfilment in ten years' time, will it look the same? Will the same failings of traditional fulfilment operations still be in place? Somehow, we think not.

Reference

ARC Advisory Group, (2001), Dedham, MA.

3.9 Information systems strategy for supply chains

Donald S. Puckridge and Ian Woolsey

Organizations have been striving for a Utopian supply chain, where data flows across the organization in real time to provide visibility wherever it is required.

Many successful firms have used information technology to support their business strategies and to enhance their supply chains. To a degree, organizations have been striving for the Utopian dream – a magical supply chain where data flows across the organization in real time to provide visibility wherever it is required. In this perfect place, analysis, insight and technology ensure seamless execution free of market imperfections. Enterprises effortlessly link with their trading partners to provide a synchronized supply chain, eliminating waste and delays, and creating a demand-driven, mean, lean and agile network.

Each wave of new technology theoretically brings organizations closer to Utopia. Enterprises have often used a number of 'point' solutions that addressed specific components or issues across the supply chain. An increasing number of initiatives have been using information technology to integrate the supply chain and logistics 'point' solutions and to achieve greater collaboration across the elements of the supply chain. Initiatives such as efficient consumer response (ECR) and collaborative planning forecasting and replenishment (CPFR) have demonstrated the benefit of sharing plans, inventory and forecast information between partners.

Success in supply chain integration and collaboration is easily defined. It is simply a matter of excelling at design, manufacturing, procurement and logistics and synchronizing those activities across the supply chain. This chapter will look at the current state of information systems (IS) underpinning today's supply chains, where vendors have been promising a supply chain Utopia in which millions of dollars will be saved. We will consider what comprises an effective IS strategy and what steps are needed to align the strategy with overall business objectives. Finally, we consider the important role of organizational leaders in translating IS strategy into success.

Why is Utopia so difficult to attain?

Functional, business unit and technology boundaries within enterprises diminish the organization's ability to build strong relationships within the organization or externally with customers and suppliers. Disparate IT systems and multiple databases blur the organization's focus and ability to collaborate. The greater the decentralization within a business, the greater the degree and cost of fragmentation that it creates. For many organizations, the existing systems functionality and the internal fragmentation make it impossible to support the required responsiveness and capability demanded by their customers.

Disparate IT systems and internal fragmentation make it impossible for many companies to support the required responsiveness and capability demanded by their customers.

Organizations also face challenges arising from the shrinking of key business cycles. Shortening timeframes increase pressure for supply chains to be more responsive, and for the IT systems that support them. As the level of external complexity increases, organizations are driven towards shorter implementation cycles of information systems and are seeking shorter payback periods in an attempt to stay in touch with, or in front of, their competitors in synchronizing their supply chain.

A further complication is introduced by the increasing diversity of IT offerings. New entrants and established vendors are providing new products, extending existing products and providing a breadth and depth of sophistication and functionality that was not previously possible. Such an explosion of technology is becoming exponentially more complex to manage. Some of these emergent market offerings provide the desired capability but are not capable of being used within the organization's current environment.

Across the software systems market, there are significant overlaps in functionality as well as conflicting offerings that do not necessarily integrate in a logical function. Organizations need to understand which systems support, or oppose, their environment and strategic imperatives. Without an effective information system strategy the risk of disparate and fragmented information flow across the supply chain is real and effectively fragments the supply chain itself.

What steps are needed?

Unfortunately, this chapter provides no magical map to reach Utopia. However, there are a few pragmatic steps that can be taken to ensure that an organization's IS strategy underpins logistics integration and supply chain collaboration.

An IS strategy outlines a plan for developing the information systems needed to achieve the company's business goals and to attain its future vision.

What is an IS strategy?
The purpose of an information systems strategy is to bring together the business aims of a company with an understanding of its information requirements. The IS strategy outlines the applications

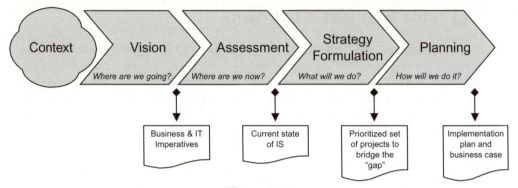

Figure 3.9.1
IS strategy process

and technology needed to support the organization's business goals as well as the required implementation path. The strategy provides a plan for the development of the information systems towards some future vision and provides a clear understanding of the role information systems have within the organization.

IS strategy can be considered both an activity (once-off or frequent) and an outcome.

When viewed as an activity, a classic IS strategy involves four clear phases of work, as shown in Figure 3.9.1.

As an outcome, an IS strategy is a document or set of deliverables that clearly articulates the answers to the following questions:

- Where is the business heading, and how can information systems enable this journey?
- What is the current state of information systems (from a business process support, internal IS function and expenditure perspective)?
- What is the gap between vision and reality, and how can these gaps be bridged?
- What is the program of prioritized activities that must be undertaken, and what value will they deliver or enable for the business?

IS strategy lessons learned

Executives need to understand the business context and define the vision before formulating their IS strategy. The gap between vision and reality also must be understood.

When undertaking the IS strategy, experience has shown that several activities help to ensure success. These 'lessons learned' include:

- Spend time up-front to understand the business context. Ensure you understand the business issues, have gained appropriate business sponsorship and have defined the focus or 'centre of gravity', for the IS strategy. Is the focus on IS architecture, or on business-focused change programs?
- Define the vision. The outcome from the visioning phase is a set of business and IS imperatives that articulate where the business is heading and how information systems can become an enabler of

this business change. Workshops and referencing leading practice are valuable tools.

- Perform a comprehensive on-site assessment. The IS strategy is built on rocky foundations if a company does not understand the current level of IS application support for its business processes, the state of the IS function's skills, processes and organization, and the current and planned levels of IS expenditure.
- Understand the 'gap' between the vision and reality. This gap defines the starting point for the strategy formulation process, and it is worthwhile thinking through the value versus effort trade-off for closing any gaps.
- Developing an IS 'blueprint' model is useful to define how to close the business capability gap. An IS blueprint should show the IS infrastructure layer, applications layer, information layer and business process layer, which together show how information systems will support the new business capability.
- Iterate through the strategy formulation and planning phases on a project-by-project basis. Identify the projects required to close the identified gaps, describe each project in terms of the IS blueprint, then map out project timelines and resources requirements. The iterative process and the link back to the blueprint ensures that projects are considered as a whole, rather than as separate initiatives which risks fragmentation.
- Develop a business case (with costs and benefits) by project. The business case is the key to an IS strategy being owned by the business.

In developing the IS strategy, different audiences will have different expectations. The business community will expect more of a business process focus, with a compelling business case, whereas the IS community will be more interested in the target application and technical architectures (the 'boxes and wires'). Balance and compromise with respect to the breadth and depth of what the IS strategy is delivering will therefore be required.

Integrating the IS strategy with the supply chain

By the nature of the environment the information strategy is not a static document, but is constantly evolving. This is most apparent within the area of the supply chain. Each industry or organization will have a separate and evolving vision for their supply chain and this will be reflected in its IS strategy.

Regardless of the industry or the strategy that an organization undertakes, there are three key elements required to ensure that the IS strategy is capable of underpinning logistics integration and supply chain collaboration. These are:

- alignment of the IS strategy with the organization's strategy
- underpinning the supply chain with an effective architecture, and
- management and leadership.

Alignment with the organization's strategy

The development of an effective IS strategy must occur within, and support, an enterprise's overall strategic context and be guided by an appropriate vision of a future state.

In the 1990s, companies devoted considerable effort to unlocking process potential through process innovation or reengineering. Information technology was used as an enabler and an implementer of process change. However, in some instances the focus was on identifying IT-enabled strategies rather than ensuring that IT was used to implement strategies. One problem that organizations faced was the absence of a process context or structured approach for achieving improvement.

The challenge that emerged from the period of process innovation still exists: the IS strategy cannot exist in a vacuum or be effective amid chaos. Organizations need to ensure that the development of an effective IS strategy does not occur in isolation from the enterprise's overall strategy. It must occur within and support the overall strategic context and be guided by an appropriate vision of a future state.

Executives can achieve a tighter connection between corporate strategy and IS strategy through using a framework, such as the Value Diagnostic Framework (Figure 3.9.2), developed by Accenture in partnership with the ANZ Banking Group. Such a model provides a critical bridge between the overall strategy and a practical business blueprint. The three levels of the framework illustrated are:

- *Vision or intent* – the context and the objectives, strategy and value proposition needed to 'win'.

Source: Accenture

Figure 3.9.2
The value diagnostic framework – blueprint elements

- *Capabilities* – the multiple enterprise capabilities needed to realize, deliver and sustain the strategy. Critical linkages within the business and with external businesses require consideration.
- *Business blueprint* – the integrated business architecture and assets that deliver the full range of required capabilities. A comprehensive operational blueprint encompasses the total supply chain as relevant from sourcing through to manufacturing, distribution and customer management.

The IS strategy is derived and driven from many of the key elements at the blueprint level. Key among these is the information knowledge and the associated technology that support the business. Information technology should not only support the current environment but should also provide opportunities that were not previously present. More and more organizations are using IT in innovative ways to enable new business strategies. Indeed, most chapters in Part 3 of this book depend on supply chain technologies to achieve expected benefits. There is a cyclical relationship between business requirements and emerging technologies. Based on 'Moore's law', companies will be able to leverage increasingly faster and cheaper processing capability as technology continues to evolve. This enables organizations to identify new opportunities to enhance business functionality across their supply chain. As the business continues to evolve, technology is also being developed and applied to enable new business functions.

Information technology should not only support the current environment but should also provide opportunities that were not previously present.

For the IS strategy to complement the corporate strategy, organizations must clearly identify what capability must be adapted and implemented to create value now. Organizations also need to be clear on how they will create value in the future.

The current direction of supply chain strategies and their continuing evolution is considered throughout this book. However, one common element that executives need to consider in the development of IS strategy is that both current and future business models are based on the concept of internal collaboration and external collaboration with trading partners.

Strategic collaboration begins with the alignment of business objectives. The understanding and discussion of cost and service tradeoffs, critical constraints and cost drivers in the supply network are required. Internal and external collaboration partners can reach agreement on the boundaries that need to be supported. These boundaries define the policies, targets, rules and the flow of information that monitors and enables each supply chain network. These boundaries move and need to continue to evolve with any changes in the environment.

In considering the need to align IS strategy with corporate strategy, companies need to be increasingly sensitive to the turbulence that is occurring in markets. The rise and subsequent rationalization of dot.coms and e-marketplaces, the explosion of supply chain software offerings, and today's rapidly evolving business environment clearly means that business models must change.

The same forces that are requiring supply chains to become agile – the ability to respond rapidly to unpredictable changes in the market – also require the same agility in the organization's IT capability. Success will be defined by those organizations that are able to adapt and evolve their IS strategy to meet the future requirements across their supply chain.

Underpinning the supply chain with an effective architecture

Neither the IS strategy nor the technology provides the solution – companies need to have the right processes and organization in place to make collaboration a success.

Many organizations use a combination of ERP systems and a range of best-of-breed technology to support and run their supply chain. The technology requirements are complex, given the scope of business functions within the internal supply chain and the need to integrate processes and provide visibility across the extended supply chain. However, the capability is continuing to evolve. True collaboration technology is still a new market with many relatively immature products. No vendor alone is offering a complete solution, but a combination of several tools. Vendors provide the best options at present. This is unlikely to change in the future. At this point, it is worthwhile being reminded that neither the IS strategy nor the technology provides the solution – companies need to have the right processes and organization in place to make collaboration a success.

The first step is for an organization to 'put its own house in order' and ensure that there is effective internal integration across the organization. This means streamlining processes and technology across all of the supply chain functions, from sales to planning to manufacturing. The core processes need to be well designed and operating effectively or the technology will merely formalize poor processes and practices. A clear vision is required across the supply chain model, encompassing all the relationships needed to integrate all components of the supply chain, as shown in Figure 3.9.3.

Internal integration

The objective of internal integration is to make organizations permeable rather than uniform. The way that groups interact within the organization and the way that information is managed across the organization need to be optimized.

Every organization will continue to have functional, geographic and organizational silos in some form or fashion. The objective of internal integration is to make organizations permeable rather than uniform. However, different strategic imperatives and processes are required across the supply chain functions. People also require different skills, they work across different processes and they are measured and rewarded in different ways. Imposing uniformity eliminates the differences that provide optimization. The way that groups interact within the organization and the way that information is managed across the organization need to be optimized. The first step in this

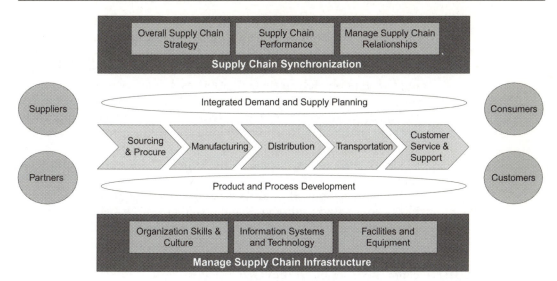

Figure 3.9.3
The supply chain model – identifying and integrating the components

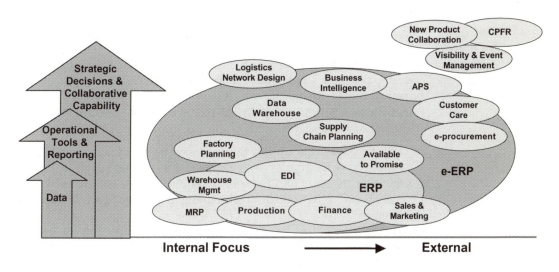

Figure 3.9.4
Evolution of application systems and tools

process is to ensure that the organization has synchronized the internal IT architecture.

In the past, particularly over the last decade, organizations have focused on this internal IT architecture and have attempted to achieve synchronization in several different ways. These include integrating in-house development, data warehouses, integrated business reporting and ERP implementations. In reviewing the ERP approach, organizations invested large amounts of money in complex systems with a number of interlinked applications based on an integrated infrastructure layer, network and databases. In most instances the ERP implementations solved several problems, but focused predominantly on the core transactional processes. The implementations often included interfaces to legacy systems or best-of-breed solutions to provide additional functionality outside of the processes enabled within these core systems.

Figure 3.9.4 reviews some of the supply chain systems and tools that have developed over the last few years.

In the development of an IS strategy, a clear understanding of the business process requirements and how they will be enabled is critical. Developing an operating model and a supporting target systems architecture assists in defining the business processes, which will drive the information requirements needed to support the supply chain. An example is provided in Figure 3.9.5.

IT architecture now exists in three layers. Top: the application services or customer layer. Middle: the middleware layer of legacy systems. Bottom: the infrastructure of networks, standards and protocols.

An end-to-end view across the supply functions in most organizations would continue to find a hodgepodge of linked and standalone systems. The implementation of ERP systems themselves has in some instances created problems; they tend to lock organizations into rigid business processes and it becomes hard to adapt quickly to changes in the marketplace. ERP implementations by themselves have not been able to deliver the internal integration required.

In response to this inability to integrate the organization through the development of a single organization-wide system, a new approach to viewing the IT architecture is required. The IT architecture across organizations is now generally described as three separate layers, as depicted in Figure 3.9.6.

- The *top* layer, the application services or customer layer, is the visible layer for employees, customers and trading partners. This is the layer that provides the services and solutions that are used on a daily basis from production scheduling to generating a collaborative forecast.
- The *middle* layer, or 'middleware', is the collection of legacy applications, products or utilities that can be aggregated and assembled to support and provide the 'tailored' business functions that are required across the organization.
- The *bottom* layer is the infrastructure layer, the network, standards and protocols that allow information to be exchanged and understood. Within an organization this also includes the databases and the legacy systems.

The decoupling of the infrastructure from the employee or customer-facing layer is to allow organizations to be more responsive, support new initiatives faster and to allow the focus to be on developing and enhancing functionality for servicing the employees or customers.

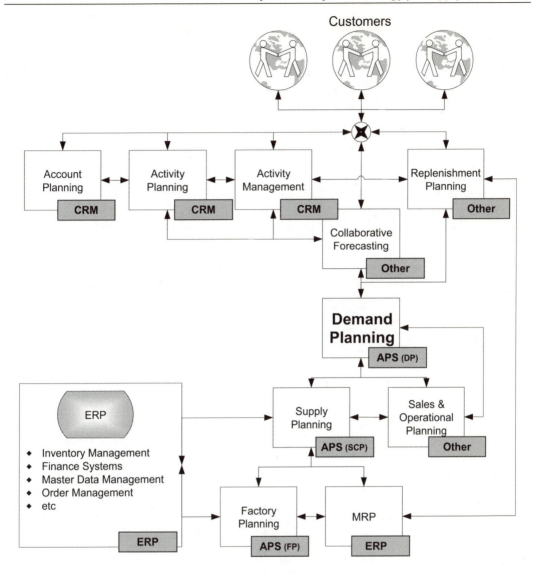

Figure 3.9.5
Overview of an integrated demand planning operating model and corresponding system architecture

To enable this decoupling process, and more importantly to enable the collaboration process, the technology supporting the organization needs to be modular and flexible and have several characteristics:

- It must enable the integration of applications and business processes, while providing full data visibility.
- It must be adaptable, allowing its evolution into a fully collaborative process.

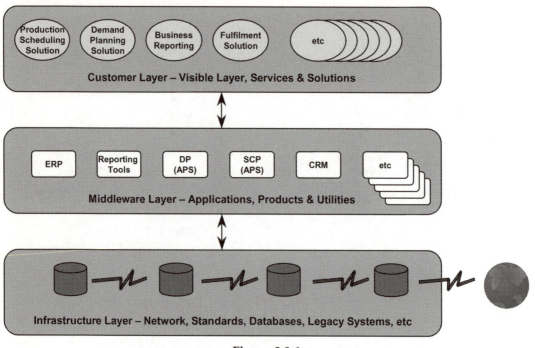

Figure 3.9.6
IT architecture layers

- It needs to be flexible, so that it can be configured for each business-to-business (B2B) relationship, whatever collaboration level or business terms are required.
- It should be open, allowing interoperability through extensible mark-up language (XML) standards.
- It should be 'plug and play', allowing the business to extend outside of the organization and to build on strong e-integration frameworks to bring businesses together in a simple manner.

Underpinning all of the different applications is the enterprise integration (EI) connection layer, or 'the glue'. The EI infrastructure provides the backbone for organizations focused on supply chain integration, customer relationship management and internal integration.

Finally, internal shortcomings are easy to hide when 'barriers' are in place. But when external parties have access to a company's systems and data, they may see a very different picture that is impossible to hide. With the internal house 'in order', organizations are then able to open up to external trading partners without any fear of appearing disorganized or inefficient.

Connecting to the extended enterprise

One challenge that organizations face is that supply chains are becoming more complex as companies choose to focus on their core competencies and outsource other functions to third parties. A prime example of this trend is the electronics and technology sector, where disintegration has steadily increased during the last few decades. The semiconductor industry has seen a transition from the full integration of the 1960s, outsourcing manufacturing operations in the 1970s and 1980s and silicon intellectual property in the 1990s.

By extending links across organizations, companies can operate potentially as one logical, fully linked and optimized supply chain.

The trend has led to the blurring of boundaries of the traditional, fully integrated supply chain as more functions have been taken outside of the enterprise. Many more business partners are acquired in addition to the traditional suppliers and customers. From a practical perspective, a high degree of integration is required with third-party provider systems across contract, co-manufacturing or manufacturing service providers as well as transport and logistics providers. However, connecting to the extended enterprise allows forward thinking companies to effectively collaborate with their trading partners, despite this disintegration, both up and down the supply chain.

By extending links across organizations, companies can operate potentially as one logical, fully linked and optimized supply chain. Fortunately, the explosion in technology and e-commerce tools and methods has provided significant opportunities for synchronizing organizations across the extended supply chain.

Without question, technology is an important enabler of this integration, but technology alone does not provide collaboration. Organizations need to determine the business process that is driving the sharing of information and define the key areas of its business where it will enable collaboration. It needs to identify the approach that it will use and the companies that it will deal with, for each specific area and its overall strategy.

Organizations have five major areas of logistics integration and collaboration:

- *Demand* collaboration – the synchronization of a company's manufacturing outputs with its customers and their demand.
- *Logistics* collaboration – the synchronization of transportation and fulfilment with supply, manufacturing and demand. This includes the organizations, suppliers and third-fourth-party logistics (3PL/4PL) providers.
- *Supplier* collaboration – the synchronization of manufacturing needs with suppliers and their capacity to meet the material requirements.
- *Manufacturing* collaboration – the synchronization of the supply needs for the manufacturing of finished and part-finished goods with demand from customers, where third parties or internal capabilities perform manufacturing.

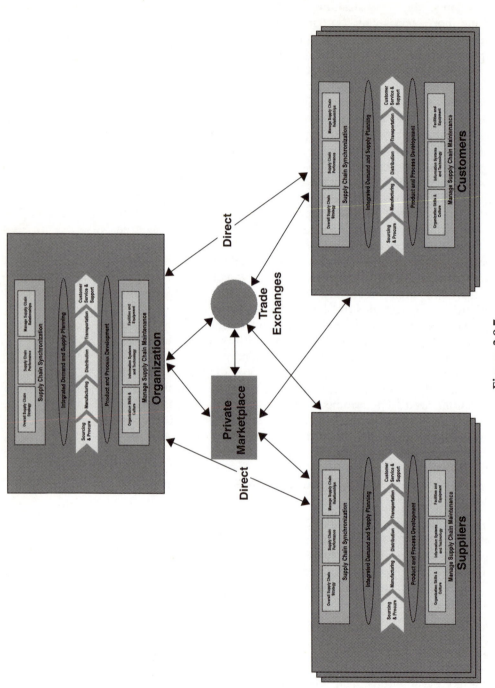

Figure 3.9.7
Extending the supply chain

418

- *Design* collaboration – the collaboration of manufacturing and supply chain partners with research and development to allow integration of the design process across the supply chain and to allow feedback and resolution of design issues.

Achieving demand collaboration

Demand collaboration provides an example of how an information systems strategy can enable the sharing of information and support collaborative processes. Two supply chain trends – demand-driven planning and trading-partner integration – come together in demand collaboration. Both need and support each other. A greater focus on market demand allows large stocks of inventory to be eliminated from the supply pipeline; however, eliminating buffer stocks requires companies to have greater agility in responding to any variability in the supply chain. Integrating manufacturers and customers through demand collaboration provides the capability for real-time visibility; and integration into the supply chain enables organizations to respond faster and more effectively.

Organizations must first identify the solution concept, design the business processes and systems that will support it, and then build the solution.

To do this, organizations must first identify the solution concept, design the business processes and systems that will support it, and then build the solution. A demand collaboration process is provided in Figure 3.9.8.

If it is that simple, where are the challenges in developing an effective architecture?

The first challenge is the size of the task. Integrating with trading partners is a significant business initiative that involves time, effort and a large degree of investment. The timing of building infrastructure, the development costs of shared infrastructure and the governance process for areas where infrastructure is shared require careful consideration and management.

The second challenge is determining the approach that will be taken. The traditional approach has been to develop point-to-point connections, linking each individual system with every other system. The one-to-one connections progressively become more complicated as the number of systems increases and makes the overall system expensive to maintain and change. The Internet has complicated the approach by making it 'cheaper and faster' to add and change new partners. However, at some point the cost and effort to build and maintain a point-to-point basis for collaboration becomes prohibitive.

To overcome these problems some organizations are using an approach called 'the integration hub'. Just as EI was used to decouple the infrastructure from the applications within the organization, EI is used to create a middle layer between the internal and external applications. When a new system needs to be linked in, it can be

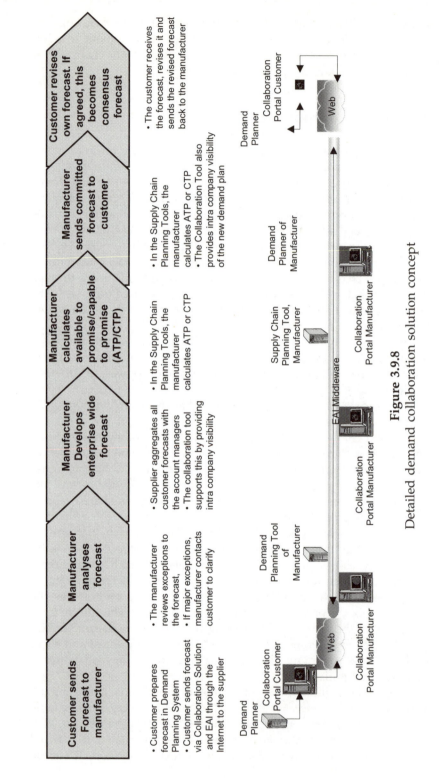

Figure 3.9.8
Detailed demand collaboration solution concept

simply connected to the EI layer, rather than integrated to all of the affected internal systems.

The integration hub, or collaboration portal, is one of the keys to achieving collaboration excellence as it provides B2B data exchange visibility. This integration occurs within the company via the corporate intranet as well as between companies using the Internet. The different applications such as the ERP, SCP/DP and the portal, are linked using an EI connection layer as 'the glue', as shown in Figure 3.9.9.

EI is also used to create a common data model, allowing data from the new systems to be mapped once rather than to all of the systems that use it.

The challenges ahead

However, a number of challenges are still outstanding. The biggest issue is the lack of a common language; we are living in a modern-day Babel rather than Utopia. Speed and accuracy of information transfer is increasingly critical and must be achieved through the establishment of shared language, standards and protocols. Until common standards are fully implemented and accepted within organizations, across organizations and even industry wide, true collaboration is likely to remain difficult with EI software shouldering most of the work.

Speed and accuracy of information transfer is increasingly critical and must be achieved through the establishment of shared language, standards and protocols.

One of the developments that holds the promise of moving towards a common language is through the development of Web services (the approach is also known as network services, open network services, and a number of brand names). Like any new wave of innovation that promises early adopters Utopia, the marketing concepts can be treated with a degree of scepticism. However, substantial investment from all major organizations is ensuring that the development of technology standards is very real (including XML, Java, .Net, UDDI, Soap and WSDL).

How is this relevant to developing an IS strategy and achieving integration and supply chain collaboration?

Web services allow information to be exchanged with other applications across the organization, as well with external applications. Web services assist in reducing the costs associated with accessing and transporting information. One caution is that although the technology provides the grammar for talking and translating information transferred between organizations, companies still need to ensure that the information transfer is underpinned by an agreed business strategy.

Two other areas of opportunity are also becoming increasingly feasible and affordable. One is visibility and event management; the other is the effective integration of the inter-business network.

Visibility and event management are enabled through access to information that was previously too difficult or too expensive to access within a timeframe that enabled organizations to respond. In tandem

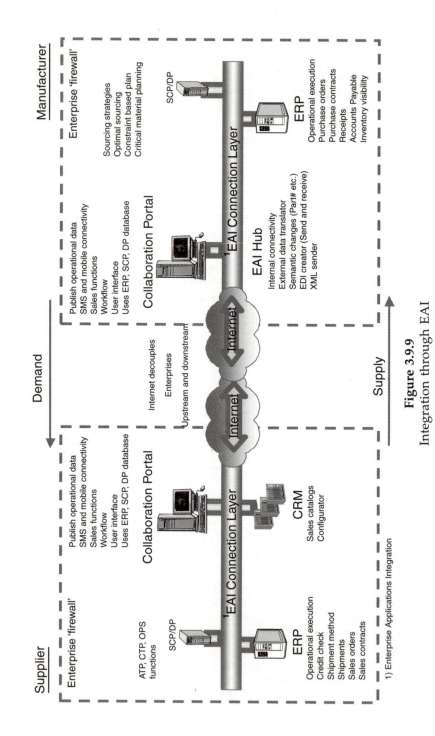

Figure 3.9.9
Integration through EAI

with visibility, organizations now have the ability to intelligently monitor and notify event-based alerts or triggers. These provide the organization with the ability to optimize its supply chain in ways that it could not previously.

Another advance centers on communicating with partners across the extended supply chain. In outsourcing, automated processes were often cut and became manual. Technology now provides organizations with the capability to use specialist providers for processes where appropriate and still retain visibility and the efficiency that comes from the integration and automation of processes. Organizations have an increased number of options to consider on how they will implement their business strategy, as well as whom they involve across the network. The IS strategy can assist to underpin and support those choices.

Management and leadership

The final challenge for organizations to be successful, is to convert the information systems strategy into reality. With complexity across the supply chain increasing, only organizations with excellence in leadership and management will achieve the opportunities offered by integration and collaboration.

Only organizations with excellence in leadership and management will achieve the opportunities. Leaders set the direction and inspire and motivate the organization. Managers provide the structures for coping with complexity.

A number of influences need to be considered. First, management needs to ensure that the information technology provides benefits. They must also understand the relationship between each of the elements and how each piece of the IT jigsaw enhances the overall outcome. A clear understanding of the relevance, importance and priority for each of the pieces of the architecture is required. Second, they need to manage the priorities and conflicts in a dynamic environment. They need to drive the appropriate use of resources and they must extract value from their assets.

Finally, the successful management of the complex relationships across the value chain network requires a high degree of connectivity, trust and cross-organizational support. Every member of the value chain must be committed to achieving the same levels of operational excellence and continuous improvement. Each must bring measurable value to the competitive entity. The identification of where relationships will be developed and the ongoing management of those relationships is critical.

Leadership provides the vision that enables the organization to cope with rapid change. Leaders set the direction and inspire and motivate the organization. They need to clearly demonstrate a compelling requirement for change in terms that are easily understood and that are quantifiable. Organizations need to have a clear vision of where they are going and the mechanism for identifying how each change program or potential change relates to the others over time.

Leaders will regularly review and reassess the priorities for each change program against the overall business architecture. External and internal context factors need to be monitored to ensure that the programs remain relevant. The organization needs to focus on achieving the overall business goals by setting and adjusting the appropriate course of action to reflect the business context.

The role of management is to provide the structures for coping with complexity. Managers simplify the implementation of complex programs in order to produce predictable and orderly results. This is essential in business transformation programs that are likely to be driven by the IS strategy. High-quality management is needed at the earliest point in business transformation, from the business case and planning stages. Managers will create the plan and budget, maximize quality and minimize risk, coordinate interrelated projects and ensure that interdependencies are addressed. It assesses and interprets the progress of the change journey. It is the guide to the success of the journey.

Conclusion

The IS strategy articulates the vision, outlines the applications and technologies that are needed, and details the path for transforming the vision into a reality.

Organizations striving for a Utopian supply chain are seeking synchronization within their organization and across the supply chain network. Many have disparate IT systems and decentralized structures that create fragmentation, rather than the responsiveness and capability that customers are demanding. Developing an information systems strategy is a way to plot how to get from today's unsatisfactory state to a future organizational capability – or even Utopia. The IS strategy articulates the vision, outlines the applications and technologies that are needed, and details the path for transforming the vision into a reality.

Strong leadership and management are essential to navigate the conflicts and complexities that will inevitably arise. The IS strategy needs to be clearly aligned with the organization's business goals and underpinned by an effective IT architecture that facilitates internal and external collaboration. Finally, IS strategy requires continual guidance. The strategy must support the ongoing delivery of business capability through multiple projects and releases. Organizations with a clear vision of where they are going and strong management have shown that it is possible to use technology, through the use of an appropriate IS strategy, to achieve synchronization across the extended supply chain.

References

Anderson, D. and Lee, H. (2001), 'New Supply Chain Business Models – The Opportunities and Challenges', ASCET Achieving Supply Chain Excellence through Technology Volume 3, Montgomery Research, Inc.

Arntzen, B. C. and Shumway, H. M. (2002), 'Driven by Demand: A Case Study', *Supply Chain Management Review*, January/February.

Bradley, J., Suwinski, J., Thomas, J. and Thomas, D. (2001), 'What Has Not Changed in Supply Chains Because of E-Business?', ASCET Achieving Supply Chain Excellence through Technology Volume 3, Montgomery Research, Inc.

Davenport, T. H. (1992), 'Process Innovation, Reengineering work through Information Technology', Harvard Business School Press, Boston, MA.

Forbes, S. and Herzberg, C. (2001), 'Achieving Collaboration Excellence', Accenture POV, June.

Hagel III, J. and Seely-Brown, J. (2001), 'Your Next IT Strategy', *Harvard Business Review*, October.

Kotter, J. P. (1999), 'What Leaders Really Do', Harvard Business School Press.

Oliver, K., Chung, A. and Samanich, N. (2001), 'Beyond Utopia The Realist's Guide to Internet-Enabled Supply Chain Management', *Strategy & Business*, 2nd Quarter, http://www.strategy-business/special/01209.

Quinn, F. J. (2001), 'Collaboration: More than Just Technology', ASCET Achieving Supply Chain Excellence through Technology Volume 3, Montgomery Research, Inc.

Sawhney, M. (2001), 'Don't Homogenize, Synchronise', *Harvard Business Review*, July–August.

Simchi-Levi, D. and Simchi-Levi, E. (2001), 'The Dramatic Impact of the Internet on Supply Chain Strategies, ASCET Achieving Supply Chain Excellence through Technology Volume 3, Montgomery Research, Inc.

Wleklinsk, J. M. (2002), 'Webservices', Viscera , Accenture Technology Labs, Issue 28, May 2002.

Part 4
Virtual Supply Chains

In Part 4 we extend our discussion of supply chains in the context of recent developments in technology. Supply chains have been affected by the 'new economy' and the advent and maturation of e-commerce solutions. However, major changes still lie ahead.

Chapter 4.1, 'e-commerce and supply chains – breaking down the boundaries', suggests that developments in supply chain technology and software have to be evaluated against their potential to deliver business benefits and practical approaches for delivering supply chain improvements through e-commerce.

Using technology and management techniques to achieve best-of-breed supply chains is the subject of Chapter 4.2, 'Best-of-Breed supply chains'. The chapter discusses the challenges and opportunities of modern supply chains. Three new factors have an impact on the creation of 'master' supply chains: the widespread availability of information on supply chain best practices and metrics; the emergence of Internet-based technologies (including e-commerce) to improve connectivity between enterprises; and the emergence of new software technologies to support more complex supply chain transactions.

In Chapter 4.3, 'Supply chains as vehicles for transformational change', the proposition is put forward that supply chain management is ideally placed to act as 'change agents' within the firm. However, even though in many cases the main levers for change are well known, many companies still appear to lack the structure and discipline to master and drive purposeful change. Indeed, very few enterprises seem to have the necessary frame of reference to understand what they should be aspiring to. The chapter describes the mechanics by which change can be understood and managed.

Chapter 4.4, 'Third- and fourth-party logistics service providers', puts the focus on supply chain partners outside the organization. The authors explain the meaning and role of third-party logistics (3PL) providers, fourth-party logistics (4PL) providers, lead logistics providers (LLPs) and other emerging new types of business models in this domain.

Chapter 4.5, 'Emerging requirements for networked supply chains', suggests readers take a forward-looking view of supply chains and their capability requirements. It is argued that most supply chain managers today are stuck in an 'efficiency trap': they focus inwardly, on 'getting their house in order', rather than on creating supply chains for the future. To establish new competitive operations, supply chain executives need to implement customer service strategies that utilize new technologies and introduce the principles of collaboration and networking.

Chapter 4.6, 'Strategic transformation and supply chains', extends the view of supply chains into the boardroom. CEOs are being forced to focus on value creation. The way ahead, it is argued, is for supply chain strategy to be strategically transformed to create radically new operating models that are more capital efficient and less demanding in terms of up-front investment requirements.

e-commerce and supply chains – breaking down the boundaries

4.1

Andrew J. Berger

Internet technologies have already had a dramatic impact on the way that people around the world think and act. In the six or so years since the World Wide Web's inception, its speed of acceptance has been unprecedented. The first two years of the 21st century have seen a boom and a bust in predictions of the impact of technology on supply chain management. For instance, a recent study conducted by the Momentum Research Group found that United States organizations currently deploying Internet business solutions had realized cumulative cost savings of $155 billion over a three-year period, starting on average in 1998. Furthermore, the study estimated that US organizations deploying Internet business solutions expect to realize $0.5 trillion in cost savings once all Internet business solutions have been fully implemented by 2010. I suspect that these estimates are probably realistic for the potential of 2010 but over generous in their assessment of benefits being delivered to current supply chain.

Supply chains have been affected by this new economy of e-commerce solutions, but I believe the major changes that are possible will take a lot longer to happen. To use a showbiz phrase: 'you ain't seen nothing yet!' Organizations have experienced a period when many people involved with supply chain technology and software lost the plot when it came to the potential delivery of business benefits. People commonly confused the potential for very significant supply chain benefits, with the capacity of a technology solution to deliver those benefits. For a period, it seemed that causality between benefits and solutions had become unnecessary. Many companies learned the expensive way that supply chains are complex beasts to tame; there are rarely 'magic bullets' for success. However, we are now seeing more practical and effective approaches to delivering supply chain improvements through e-commerce. With

Many companies learned the expensive way that supply chains are complex beasts. More effective approaches to improving supply chains through e-commerce are now emerging.

429

time, these new approaches have a big potential to address the clear performance gap that exists between what companies are achieving in their supply chains and what they could achieve.

This chapter will address the five major questions:

- Why will e-commerce have an impact on the supply chains of companies?
- Where will e-commerce affect the supply chain in the future?
- How is e-commerce affecting supply chains already?
- When will the major impact of e-commerce on supply chains emerge?
- What is the future impact of e-commerce that we should be preparing for?

Why will e-commerce have an impact?

e-commerce has the capacity to have an impact on the physical, information and financial flows of supply chains.

e-commerce can be defined as the conduct of business communication and transactions over networks and through computers or as the buying and selling of goods and services, and the transfer of funds, through digital communications. It can include all inter-company and intra-company functions (such as marketing, finance, manufacturing, selling and negotiation) that enable commerce. e-commerce uses communications such as electronic mail, EDI, file transfer, facsimile, video conferencing, workflow, or interaction with a remote computer. e-commerce has also become associated with solutions and tools such as portals, e-marketplaces, e-auctions or virtual inventory. The last few years have seen a dramatic increase in the capabilities of e-commerce as hundreds of millions of dollars were invested in building new solutions and in fighting a marketing war for apparent first mover advantages.

So why should all this investment in technology and communication have impact on the supply chains of companies? At a simplistic level, supply chains are typically made up of three major flows – physical, financial and information. e-commerce has the capacity to affect all three.

- *Physical flows* can be affected by using information to avoid physical movements and to make product information available through virtual ways. In essence, e-commerce can give companies access to more markets and customers without the physical need to move the levels of product and inventory that were required in the past.
- *Information flows* can be affected by the capacity of e-commerce solutions to provide '24 x 7 x 365' access to information and to eliminate traditional paper-based approaches to working and company interactions. e-commerce is also particularly well suited to providing information such as product tracking and tracing.

- *Financial flows* can be affected by the capacity for e-commerce solutions to offer faster payment and settlement solutions at all stages of the supply chain.

At a more sophisticated level, e-commerce will have an impact on supply chains for five main reasons:

- *The performance gap can no longer be hidden.* An undoubted impact of the last few years has been the way that dot.com companies have helped to highlight the gap between the level at which companies' supply chain could and are performing. It is now clear that major companies can no longer afford to be complacent about under-performance. Given that companies now know they need to change, e-commerce-related solutions are the logical enablers of new levels of performance.
- *Companies have new capabilities that are not yet fully exploited.* Most major companies have implemented new capabilities as a result of concerns over Y2K and the e-commerce revolution. For instance, many companies now have major ERP systems that integrate data between functions, locations and countries. They have the capacity to manage operations at a different level not only internally but also with customers and suppliers. In addition, many companies have bolted on best-of-breed software applications, such as e-procurement, demand and supply planning and e-logistics, to these ERP systems. Most companies are still at an early stage of exploiting these capabilities but will increasingly use e-commerce to deliver the benefits from these existing investments.
- *Technology companies have invested heavily in new e-commerce solutions.* The last few years have seen an unprecedented investment by technology companies and their financial backers into new supply chain technology. There has been an acceleration of the development of new software technology to support supply chain management. This has been particularly evident around procurement, market-place, planning, and event management and fulfilment software. The casualty rate among software companies has been high. However, supply chain software now exists that software companies need to sell to get a return on their investments. We can expect them to remain aggressive in continuing to develop and sell new e-commerce solutions.
- *The supply chain is one of the last major areas of business benefit.* Supply chain change is hard work. Many companies have avoided addressing some areas of the supply chain because they have been too difficult physically or politically. e-commerce will help to break down this reluctance to address supply chain opportunities in two ways: by providing new solutions to old problems and by helping to reduce the political barriers to cross-functional, cross-company and cross-country changes.

> *e-commerce has significant potential because its capabilities have not yet been fully captured, it is one of the last areas of business benefit and is the site for future global competitiveness.*

- *The future competitiveness of companies will be fought out between value chains of partners on a global basis.* The world is shrinking and the supply chains of companies are having to become more integrated between customers and suppliers and across geographies. e-commerce will be a key enabler of this integration and collaboration. The ability to use e-commerce to work with business partners quickly and effectively will also be a key differentiator between value chains of multiple companies. Business partners will become increasingly demanding of their supply chain partners and particularly their e-commerce capabilities.

Where will e-commerce have an impact?

e-commerce will not change what needs to happen in the supply chain, but how it is done.

e-commerce will not change what needs to happen in the supply chain, but how it is done. Business processes rarely disappear, they just get done differently. The impact of e-commerce on the supply chain will be felt in how work is done, including how areas of the supply chain interact, and in how supply chains operate between company and geographic boundaries.

e-commerce and how work is done

e-commerce will have an impact on all major areas of supply chain work in companies from design, through buying to fulfilment and service support. The major areas of work inside companies can be illustrated using a simple process map of a supply chain, as shown in Figure 4.1.1. The process map shows the high-level flows and interactions between suppliers' suppliers and customers' customers. It can also be used to show where e-commerce will have its greatest impact:

- *Indirect procurement.* e-commerce will have a direct impact on both indirect and direct procurement of goods and services. e-procurement applications, such as CommerceOne, Ariba and Rightworks, are being used to bring greater efficiency and effectiveness to the buying of indirect goods such as travel and stationery. The major benefits from such programs, which are typically in the 5–15 per cent range, will always come from effective strategic sourcing. e-procurement will have its greatest effect on change management and compliance. In some cases, indirect procurement will be shifted to e-marketplaces or outsourced procurement services using e-procurement solutions
- *Direct procurement.* Direct procurement represents a bigger prize for most companies than indirect spend simply because of the size of direct spends. In this area, the combination of e-commerce procurement solutions with existing ERP and MRP systems has the capacity to provide large efficiency savings. The level of these

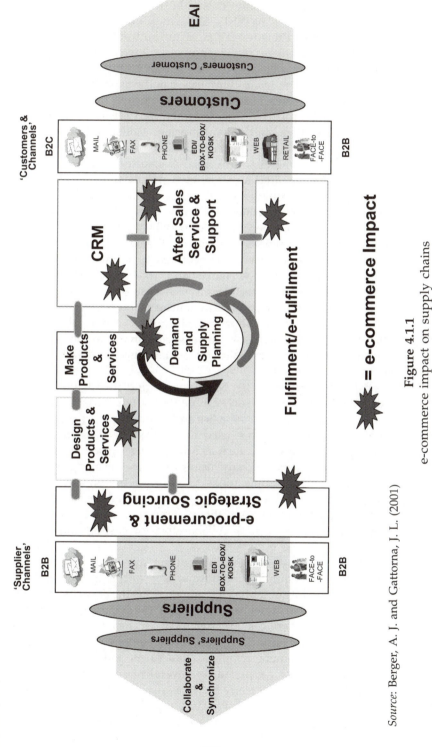

Source: Berger, A. J. and Gattorna, J. L. (2001)

Figure 4.1.1
e-commerce impact on supply chains

433

savings will clearly depend on how well direct procurement is currently managed. In some cases, the major benefits will come from the integration of ERP, MRP and demand and supply planning systems. Procurement is, at the end of the day, a matter of visibility and business intelligence. e-commerce has the capacity to make buyers smarter and cost saving opportunities more visible.

- *Product and service design.* e-commerce has the capacity to improve the quality of product design, reduce design time-scales and fundamentally improve the interaction between designers, engineers, suppliers and manufacturing. Collaborative product commerce (CPC) is a term that is often used to describe the potential of e-commerce in this area. A great deal of the thinking and capabilities required for CPC have already been developed in the automotive, aerospace and electronics industries. We can expect these capabilities to be rolled out across many other industries as e-commerce solutions become more widely accepted.

e-commerce can help manufacturing become more flexible and responsive, and ensure demand and supply planning are more effective.

- *Manufacturing.* e-commerce solutions will also have an impact on manufacturing as companies are required to be more flexible and responsive in what they make and in the levels of mass customization that manufacturing systems can deliver. e-commerce can, in some ways, be seen as a mechanism for customers to become more demanding of their suppliers. However, it can also be seen as a highly effective mechanism for ensuring that manufacturing is ultra responsive to the reality of actual customers rather than intermediary demand.

- *Demand and supply planning.* Most people find it difficult to cope with planning when it involves more than a few variables. This is an area where computers, statistics and e-commerce will always be more capable – if they are used in the right way. Demand and supply planning systems, such as Manugistics, Aspen Tech and i2 Technologies, are increasingly using e-commerce alongside their traditional software applications to improve the effectiveness of planning solutions. e-commerce is also expected to allow much greater interaction between the planning systems of multiple companies in areas such as collaborative forecasting and replenishment (CPFR) and e-marketplaces.

- *Fulfilment and e-fulfilment.* Fulfilment remains an area of great promise for e-commerce solutions, but one that has largely underperformed its potential. e-commerce has the capacity through information, such as tracking and tracing, to revolutionize the way that goods and services are delivered. It has the capacity to virtualize inventory and to change fundamentally the relationship between end customers, retailers, wholesalers and manufacturers. As yet, this has not happened for several reasons. First, it is not clear that customers are ready but it is only a matter of time before this changes. Second, most logistics suppliers are under intense margin pressure, making investments in fulfilment technology difficult. Third, retailers and wholesalers are unclear about how their role will change if e-commerce allows greater interaction between customers and manufacturers. The potential for e-fulfilment is huge – it is just a matter of time before e-commerce revolutionizes this area.

- *Service and support*. Service and support is another area where e-commerce has made some impact but there is still potential for greater change. e-commerce has the capacity to transform the effectiveness of field service forces and to change the way that returns and repairs are managed. Like fulfilment, this is an area where the value proposition will drive radical change, but it will take time.
- *e-working*. e-working is an area that will have a more immediate impact on the supply chain. Most companies have already given thousands of their workers access to intranets and the Internet. They have given them e-working tools such as employee portals, knowledge management systems and computer-based training. Through e-mail they have revolutionized the way in which people work across boundaries of time and space. E-working capabilities are already having a significant impact on the working of supply chains and on the ability of employees to manage complex events and issues in the supply chain.

e-commerce and company boundaries

The impact of e-commerce is already being seen on the boundaries between companies, particularly in industries where great value is placed on inter-company collaboration. e-commerce will be a key enabler of this breakdown of boundaries, because it provides not only the solutions required for inter-company transactions but also the standards that will enable companies to connect and communicate. The breaking down of inter-company boundaries is likely to be a slow process. This is because it takes time to build trust in business partners and competence in new ways of working. By establishing common standards for data connectivity and content, e-commerce solutions have the capacity to eliminate a great deal of unnecessary duplication of effort in companies. The breaking down of inter-company boundaries can be seen in at least three areas:

e-commerce provides not only the solutions required for inter-company transactions but also the standards that will enable companies to connect and communicate.

- *Inter-company collaboration*. Collaboration is the logical next step in the process of breaking down barriers. Collaboration can happen without e-commerce, as already seen in famous case studies such as Procter & Gamble and Wal-Mart. However, a new phase of inter-company collaboration is now being enabled by e-commerce. Cisco and Flextronics provide a good example of how new levels of collaboration are being achieved between 'best partners' almost 'one supply chain at a time'.
- *e-marketplaces*. A vast investment of money and time has been made in the building of e-marketplaces whether they are private,

independent or consortia. Despite the predictions of industry outsiders, these marketplaces generally have failed to make a significant impact on industries. However, following an inevitable consolidation of the number of marketplaces it is likely that a small number will play an active and effective role in promoting collaboration between companies across the supply chain. Some of these e-marketplaces will focus on areas such as indirect procurement or industry data standards and connectivity. Others will endeavor to balance industry discontinuities like excess demand and supply. In a more focused way, they will help to break down a number of inter-company boundaries.

- *Supply chain event management*. The number of software vendors offering event management solutions has also risen. These e-commerce solutions set out to improve overall inter-company transactions by highlighting and sorting out problems in the supply chain. This technology has great promise, although it is still early days. Event management technology also offers the possibility that true intelligent fourth-party logistics companies could emerge soon. These companies have the potential to become 'magic clouds' of data and transaction monitoring and decision-making. Much still needs to be done before this is ready for prime-time supply chain management, but there is significant potential.

e-commerce and geographic boundaries

e-commerce has the potential to breakdown many of the traditional barriers to supply chain management caused by geography. Greater integration is already occurring through NAFTA and the European Union and greater integration can be expected among some Asian nations in future. e-commerce is helping to establish the standards for cross border cooperation and collaboration. Such standards are needed to smooth supply chain operations across countries and enable companies to avoid managing inventory simply at a country or regional level.

How is e-commerce affecting supply chains?

Many examples indicate the e-commerce future is already here. However, the roll-out of e-commerce capabilities is patchy. A lot more needs to be done.

e-commerce solutions for the supply chain have been available for some years, so it is reasonable to assume that there are already good examples of its potential to deliver significant business benefits. Indeed, this is happening and there are some excellent case studies showing the impact of e-commerce on supply chain effectiveness. Leading these case studies are companies such as Dell Computer and Cisco that have the advantage of being relatively new, strongly versed in e-commerce technologies, growing rapidly (and hence attracting flexible new talent to solve new challenges) and unencumbered by traditional supply chain constraints.

More traditional companies have also embraced e-commerce rapidly and effectively in their supply chains. GE is a much quoted example. Its combination of 'destroy your business' thinking, Six Sigma and e-business execution have seen the successful introduction of new capabilities, including e-ordering, e-procurement, e-marketplaces, such as GE Polymerland, and new retail business models using virtual inventory, such as GE Appliances. Jack Welch, the former CEO of GE, has used the word 'boundaryless' to describe the corporate culture that emphasizes the removal of any boundaries within and external to a company to encourage idea sharing and team working.

Even industries traditionally slow to change such as chemicals and oil have seen the partial implementation of radical new uses of supply chain e-commerce solutions. Shell and BP have championed, until recently, indirect e-procurement marketplaces such as Trade Ranger. e-auctioning has become common using internal and external providers. Dow has been a leader in the chemicals industry in linking Six Sigma, a single ERP system and new supply chain solutions together into a coherent supply chain strategy. British retailer Tesco has been highly effective in combining traditional supermarket logistics with online ordering and local deliveries. In many ways the future is already here – just unevenly spread!

However, amid these examples the overriding impression is one of unfinished business. Few companies have completed the roll-out of these capabilities. Few software providers can honestly claim to have completed their products so that they can be effectively implemented. A great deal still has to be done before the causality between potential for supply chain benefits and e-commerce solutions can be proven on a significant scale.

Case study – Dell Computer

Dell is an excellent example for breaking the boundaries. Dell Computer Corporation is the world's leading direct computer systems company, with more than 16 000 employees in 33 countries. Dell has completed a supply chain program called DSi2 to rapidly develop next-generation capabilities in supply chain management for the organization.

Dell Computer is breaking the boundaries between departments to develop next-generation capabilities in supply chain management.

The new capabilities are focused on breaking the boundaries between departments through:

- redesigning materials requirements planning (MRP) processes and configuring i2's Supply Chain Planner (SCP) tool
- enabling collaboration with suppliers regarding forecast and purchase information and configuring i2's Rhythm Collaboration Planner (RCP) tool
- assimilating and summarizing global demand and supply data from each of Dell's regions and providing the business community visibility to this much sought-after data

- automating factory scheduling processes to create build schedules based on materials availability and configuring i2's Factory Planner (FP)
- enabling collaboration with third-party distribution hubs for materials replenishment pulls every two hours into Dell manufacturing sites, including the configuration of i2's RCP tool.

During the 12 months after project initiation, the project paid for itself with more than $32 million in measurable benefits and a 500 per cent plus return on investment. Factory utilization has increased by more than 5 per cent, with considerable factory headcount and space savings, reduced factory inventory and expedition costs, improved shipping to target and increased efficiency for materials planners and procurement.

The globally consistent processes for demand fulfilment and supply planning have improved inventory visibility across the supply chain (for Dell and its suppliers), providing a proven large-scale program methodology with a reusable framework. Automation of previously manual processes has led to a reduction in error introduction points, contributing to lower factory employee attrition rates.

When will the major impact of e-commerce emerge?

The timing of the impact of e-commerce on the supply chain will vary by industry, but it is likely to occur in three distinct phases.

A central theme of this chapter is that organizations are generally underestimating the impact that e-commerce will have on supply chains and overestimating how quickly change will happen. These are common mistakes that are made when dealing with disruptive technologies. Many companies have certainly had a tendency to be better at starting supply chain initiatives than rolling out and completing their delivery. It was not uncommon to find senior executives losing interest in supply chain initiatives that they had sponsored after the first few implementations. e-procurement initiatives in some companies, for instance, are still to be delivered across all geographies and for all major commodities. The timing of the impact of e-commerce on the supply chain will vary by industry. It will also take companies much longer to deliver the full benefits of current e-commerce solutions and capabilities. The likely impact of e-commerce can be divided into three distinct phases over the next five to ten years.

Early stage impacts (up to 2004)

In the early stage, companies will focus on getting the basics right while experimenting with some new solutions.

This period is likely to be characterized by two developments. First, companies will focus on getting the basics right and rolling out existing solutions, such as ERP, e-procurement, e-order management, and demand and supply planning, across organizations. Second, there will be a period of limited experimentation around new solutions, such as e-fulfilment, tracking and tracing, collaborative design, and between supply chain partners. Some companies, for instance, could experiment with one-to-one collaboration between trusted partners. The early roll-out of new types of supply chain models could also occur. These would be aimed at new retail models and in connecting manufacturers (such as automotive) more closely to their customers.

We expect the early stage to be a critical time for the leading companies of the future to establish dominance around operational excellence and continuous innovation. While this might sound like simply getting the basics right, it is much more. This is a time when companies will succeed or fail in establishing whether they are the most attractive supply chain partners for others to collaborate with. The key differentiators will be whether companies are very good at their part of the supply chain, whether they are easy to partner with, and whether they understand what the key priorities in e-commerce and the supply chain will be in the future.

Medium stage impacts (2004–07)

In the medium term, we can expect to see the rollout of a much broader range of robust and sophisticated e-commerce solutions in the supply chain. e-marketplaces are likely to take a limited but important role in industry-level connectivity and in logistics solutions. The 'one supply chain at a time' solutions are likely to broaden as best supply chain partners gradually start to include a wider range of partners in their value chains. There will also be a much more robust range of e-fulfilment and service and support solutions using e-commerce. Much greater experimentation will occur between leading supply chain partners around supply chain synchronization solutions. During this period a shake-out of poorer performing companies is inevitable as they will be forced by economics to either focus on niche areas of supply chain excellence or to rescale their businesses to reflect their diminishing supply chain power.

A range of robust and sophisticated e-commerce solutions will be rolled out, while leading partners will experiment with synchronization solutions.

Later stage impacts (2008 and beyond)

By this late stage, we can start to expect to see the increasing impact of supply chain synchronization initiatives in major companies. Supply chain synchronization is in many ways the 'Holy Grail' of current supply chain thinking. It will require e-commerce to work. It represents a world in which machine-driven decision-making, combined with very, very smart human analysis will be able to synchronize and re-synchronize multi-regional (if not global) supply chains on a real-time basis. The potential for this technology is huge. However, it is not simple. The first live simulators of synchronization were being built five years ago – and the technology worked then. However, the sheer scale of the changes in boundaries that are required suggests that effective implementation by 2008 is still very ambitious!

Major companies will achieve success in their supply chain synchronization initiatives, unlocking huge potential.

What is the future impact of e-commerce?

With use of the Internet growing, the design and execution of local supply chains within cities will change significantly.

e-commerce will not only have an impact on the supply chains of medium to large companies. It will also change the way we live and work in our cities and communities, it will change government at both a local and national level and it will affect the way that we build contingency into our lives.

Internet technologies have grown out of a range of standards that are based on the need to communicate and interact openly. As such, we can expect to see day-to-day activities such as shopping, ordering, booking tickets and personal services increasingly moving online. This will have a dramatic impact in cities. More than 90 per cent of all telephone calls are local. Most people spend most of their income within a small radius (less than 50 miles) from where they live. It seems logical to predict that the design and execution of local supply chains within cities will change significantly.

Local distribution will change, as will the role of the city centre. Local and national government will need to adapt to new realities such as taxation, voting patterns, education levels and payments as people question the need for fixed assets and locations such as buildings. Government and local supply chains will need to be more responsive or companies and people will be increasingly willing to circumvent their authority and control. While e-commerce will make us more efficient it is also likely to make our supply chains more vulnerable to shocks. After 11 September 2001, we are all more aware of the need to be prepared for catastrophic changes in business conditions. This does not mean a return to high levels of company-level safety stocks, but a more mature approach to contingency between companies and geographies based on greater cooperation around mutual interests.

New e-commerce technologies will also emerge and have an impact, including wireless data communications such as 2.5 and 3G and radio frequency identification (RFID). This will give us the very real prospect of being able to not only track products and to transfer data using mobile communications but also the possibility of managing products and deliveries to the individual product level in real time. The amounts of data involved could be huge and will require significant enhancements to current ERP systems. Companies will see the benefits and penalties involved in giving all their products an individual personality!

Conclusion

e-commerce is already having a significant impact on supply chain management in some companies. In this chapter, we have outlined how that impact will increase over time as companies adopt e-commerce solutions more broadly and increasingly collaborate between companies and across countries. The broadening of e-commerce will be a gradual process, phased in over time; it will involve a lot of hard work. The benefits of supply chain improvements will be considerable, however, representing 5–15 per cent of overall supply chain costs. Leading supply chain operators are likely to achieve collaboration with their key value chain partners far more speedily and effectively than their slower competitors. Overall, we can expect a ten-year period of fundamental restructuring of the way that companies collaborate and synchronize their supply chains. The benefits of cost savings and performance improvements will accrue to the companies that are the best at harnessing e-commerce solutions.

The broadening of e-commerce will be a gradual process. It will involve a lot of hard work, but the benefits will be great.

References

Berger, A. J. and Gattorna, J. L. (2001), *Supply Chain Cybermastery*, Aldershot: Gower Publishing.

Brooks, J. and Dik, R. (2001), 'B2B – the Smart Path Forward' Internal paper, Accenture.

Davenport, T. et al. (2001), 'The Dynamics of e-commerce Networks', internal paper, Accenture.

Porter, M. (1999), 'Rethinking competition' *in Rethinking the Future*, Nicholas Brealey Publishing.

4.2 Best-of-breed supply chains

Andrew J. Berger

Leading companies are able to synchronize people, assets and technology for best-of-breed supply chains

An internationally recognized best-of-breed supply chain is the aspiration of most supply chain executives and managers. However, history shows that very few will be able to deliver on this aspiration. The reason for this is the size, geographic dispersion and complexity of modern supply chains. It is not a question of not wanting the outcome enough, it is a question of who has the capability to synchronize and continuously improve the large numbers of people, assets and complex technology involved in major supply chains. The good news is that there are people out there who have achieved and sustained best-of-breed status. They have achieved this through a smart combination of clear strategic thinking, excellent execution, relevant use of technology, engagement of the right people and partners, and by embedding continuous innovation into everything they do.

The ability of companies to build best-of-breed supply chains has been enhanced by the emergence of three new factors:

- the widespread availability of information on supply chain best practices and metrics
- the emergence of Internet based technologies (including e-commerce) to improve connectivity between enterprises
- the emergence of new software technologies to support more complex supply chain transactions.

These new factors are helping to break down many of the barriers that made supply chain excellence difficult for companies. In this chapter, we analyse the characteristics of best-of-breed supply chains and set out to answer four questions:

1　What are the characteristics of best-of-breed supply chains?
2　Which companies have succeeded in building best-of-breed status? And how?

3 Why is it difficult to achieve and sustain best-of-breed status?
4 How can companies learn from the best?

Characteristics of best-of-breed supply chains

Supply chains can be a bit like automobiles. You can't answer the question about a best-of-breed car until you understand what you want to use the automobile for (for example, speed, luxury, utility, off road and so on). In the same way, supply chain is used to describe a whole range of buying, making, fulfilling and servicing activities, where success will require many different types of configurations depending on the ongoing sources of profit. Even in highly focused companies there can be radically different supply chains. For instance,

Each company's or business division's competitive situation requires different best-of-breed approaches to supply chain.

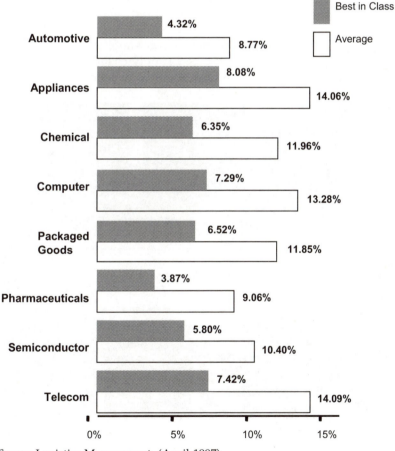

Source: Logistics Management, (April 1997)

Figure 4.2.1
Logistics costs as percentage of sales

in a telecommunications equipment company like Nokia, the supply chain for mobile handsets (a fashion item) is very different to the one for base station installation and management (design configuration and project management).

The concept of best-of-breed supply chains is difficult to define for several reasons. First, we need to have a common definition of what a supply chain is. For some people, it is just about physical distribution and logistics. For others, it covers all the areas of buying, making, fulfiling and servicing. Second, we have to recognize that different factors drive supply chain success in different business situations and geographies. Finally we have to recognize that most companies have more than one type of supply chain spread over multiple suppliers, customers and business partners. However, it is relatively easy to illustrate that some companies appear to do much better than others at supply chain activities such as logistics (see Figure 4.2.1 above). The chart shows the level of variability between average and best in class logistics across a range of industries. The gap in performance averages between 4 and 7 per cent. It appears to give support to the idea that there is a significant gap between the best and average supply chain performers.

The characteristics of best-of-breed supply chains can be divided into two levels; those characteristics required to achieve basic supply

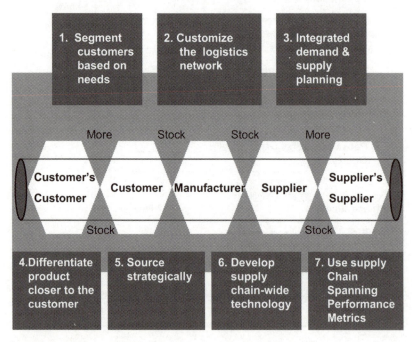

Source: Accenture

Figure 4.2.2
The best-of-breed entry level – the seven principles of supply chain excellence

chain excellence and those characteristics required to build and sustain best-of-breed status Figure 4.2.2).

The seven principles of supply chain excellence have been around for many years in various forms depending on who claims authorship. They are a well-recognized set of best practices that (if followed) should help a company to assess the gap between the actual and potential performance of its supply chains. The principles have the potential to improve the average performance of companies supply chain activities and to reduce the level of variability (the spread between the best and worst performances) in any company or supply chain. They emphasize the need to base supply chain performance on customer needs as well as the other factors that should be addressed in any excellent supply chain. However, it is now no longer sufficient just to focus on the seven principles. They can help to deliver operational excellence and continuous improvement. They cannot, by themselves deliver best-of-breed success. For best of breed, more is required. What is required is an embedded culture of value chain competitiveness that combines excellence in operations and technology with the engagement of large numbers of people and the best strategic brains in the organization.

The future of best of breed – the eight cultures of value chain competitiveness

The eight cultures of value chain competitiveness recognize the seven principles as one of the cultures – operational excellence and continuous improvement. However, they also set out the other cultures that should be present in best-of-breed supply chains. The level of sophistication of these cultures will depend on the state of evolution of supply chains in an individual industry, market or geography.

The concept of best-of-breed supply chains combines eight cultures of value chain competitiveness that go beyond operational excellence and continuous improvement]

1. Operational excellence and continuous innovation

As with the seven principles, we strongly believe that the basis of any best-of-breed supply chain is sustained operational excellence (Figure 4.2.3). In recent years, companies like GE, Dow and Motorola have shown the value of initiatives like 'Six Sigma' in building this culture in their companies. Six Sigma has gone well beyond the rather mechanistic quality approaches of TQM and has shown value through engagement of people and champions such as Black Belts and Green Belts. Six Sigma uses a simple DMAIC method (Define, Measure, Analyse, Improve, Control) for process improvement and DMADV (Define, Measure, Analyse, Design and Validate) for new process design. Six Sigma initiatives are highly likely to spread fast in major companies as the value of their impact and their engagement of people becomes recognized. GE's successes have already led directly to Six

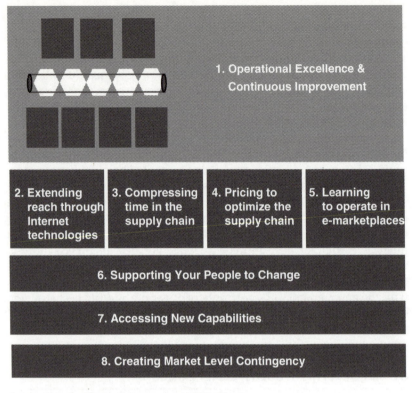

Source: *Supply Chain Cybermastery*, 2001, Ch. 1.

Figure 4.2.3
Typical components of sustained operational excellence

Sigma initiatives in other companies such as 3M, Home Depot and Bechtel.

2. Extending reach through Internet technologies

Best-of-breed supply chains are based on ease of communication between suppliers, customers, partners and manufacturers. Increasingly, this communication is based on Internet technologies backed up by ERP systems. It is not the Internet itself that is so important; it is the acceptance by multiple supply chain participants that they need to use simple, common standards to be able to work together. This use of Internet technologies allows much greater access and reach to all participants. Dell and Cisco have pioneered many of the best examples of Internet technologies for internal and external supply chain effectiveness.

3. Compressing time in the supply chain

Best-of-breed supply chains recognize the cost of time in the supply chain and have adopted new approaches to eliminating unnecessary bottlenecks and inventories. Increasingly, best-of-breed supply chains are introducing advanced planning systems to constantly re-optimize flows and inventories in the supply chain. Advanced Planning Systems (APS), such as i2, Manugistics, SAP APO and others, recognize that there are too many variables present in a supply chain for the average human to optimize. What is required is complex mathematical and statistical analysis of optimization options. Once in place these advanced planning systems can be used strategically and tactically to optimize time and resources across an extended supply chain. Such approaches require sophisticated participants and rapid decision-making. They change the role of the planner from one of a 'spreadsheet jockey' to one that can require high levels of mathematical and statistical competence. They can change yearly/monthly/weekly planning cycles into weekly/daily/hourly cycles. Their overall effect is to squeeze inefficiency out of extended supply chains. However, they do require excellence from all participants, particularly in the areas of process discipline, rapid decision making and action.

4. Pricing to optimize the supply chain

Pricing is a discipline more often associated with marketing and sales rather than with the operators of supply chains. However, there is an increasing recognition that price can be used in the supply chain as an effective lever to switch demand up and down. This is important because it is often easier to switch demand than it is to fulfill demand that cannot be easily met by current supply chain resources. Some best-of-breed supply chains have recognized this effect and implemented sophisticated pricing systems that are designed to increase yield and to 'head-off' potential supply chain problems (such as stock-outs, late deliveries and customer complaints). Use of advanced pricing systems in the supply chain (e.g. Talus) is still relatively new but growing. It represents a much more sophisticated approach to managing supply chains. It recognizes that many problems in supply chains can be eliminated by recognizing imbalances between supply and demand and using price to help correct the balance.

5. Learning to operate in e-marketplaces

e-marketplaces have emerged in recent years as a new mechanism for correcting market level inefficiencies in supply chains. Different e-marketplaces have focused on different functional areas and industry issues (for example, procurement, spare parts, excess assets and so on) The performance of most e-marketplaces has been generally unimpressive. They have taken a long time to create, cost a lot of money and have often struggled to gain supplier and user acceptance/usage. In part, this can be blamed on over-optimistic expectations, software problems and an unrealistic level of ambition. However, with all the resources at their disposal it is inevitable that some e-marketplaces will achieve some of their market positioning ambitions over time. Best-of-breed supply chains have recognized the need to operate with these e-marketplaces and to take advantage of their successes. For instance, in the chemical industry in 2001, Chemconnect (an online commodity chemicals exchange) was used by some of the major chemicals companies to buy chemicals that they could not produce profitably, thereby avoiding losses and contractual difficulties. Best-of-breed supply chain operators are recognizing that there can be value in e-marketplaces if used appropriately. They are cautiously experimenting to establish the best role for the different types of e-marketplaces.

6. Supporting your people to change
People will always be a key component in supply chains regardless of the increasing levels of automation and automated decision-making. Best-of-breed companies recognize that as the supply chain becomes more complex and time critical, it is important that people are engaged and fully trained to understand their role. Supporting people to change is about training, performance measurement and leadership. Best-of-breed supply chains are most often characterized by people who know what their role is, what their performance targets are and how they are doing.

7. Accessing new capabilities (buy, build, borrow)
Best-of-breed supply chains recognize that access to the best supply chain capabilities is more important than ownership of those capabilities. The key questions are: what to buy in? what to build internally? and what to borrow from others? The best supply chains share resources between partners that are best at doing their particular piece of the supply chain. This may often involve competitors working together to create products and services (for example, Toshiba parts in Dell laptop computers, British Airways engineers servicing competitors' aircraft). The key to success in best-of-breed supply chains is efficiency and effectiveness, not ownership and pride.

8. Creating market-level contingencies
As 11 September 2001 has shown us, we live in an uncertain and sometimes dangerous world. In the past, companies and governments coped with uncertainty by building in high levels of stock and redundancy to provide security of supply. Over the last 15 years (and particularly with the fall of Communism), there has been a significant reduction in contingency in almost all supply chains. This has been driven through a desire for efficiency as well as the breaking down of trade and other barriers between countries. However, this now leaves us vulnerable to a range of supply chain shocks that will test the brittleness of our super-efficient supply chains. In some cases, this may be bad luck as with natural events such as earthquakes and fires. In other cases, we may see deliberate attempts to sabotage vulnerable

supply chains. Best-of-breed supply chains will recognize that there is a need to build in contingency to deal with the unexpected. However, this should not mean a return to country- or company-level reserves. The most logical place to build contingency is at the market level, sharing contingency planning across markets and industries, for instance, by 'building in' shared contingency at the industry/market level for chemical plants producing PTA and PET (key to plastic bottle making) rather than at any individual company level.

Which companies have succeeded in building best-of-breed status?

No company is perfect but some are much better than others. Those that appear to have the best supply chains have not created them overnight. They have evolved supply chain excellence over many years in what can be seen as waves of differentiation. We have picked out a number of companies as examples and recognize that there are many others that we have not mentioned. We have attempted to show in the examples that best-of-breed status comes from a combination of the eight cultures of value chain competitiveness that build and sustain best-of-breed status over many years.

It is these continuous waves of differentiation that help best-of-breed companies to constantly renew their supply chains ahead of their competition.

Dell

Dell has established itself as the best-of-breed assembler of personal computers and servers over a number of years. Its initial source of competitive advantage came from adopting a direct channel model using Internet and call center technologies when its competitors were committed to an indirect model. Through the direct channel and low R&D expenses, Dell was able to create a much lower cost/higher margin position. In addition it created a distinct supply chain advantage based on a make-to-order/postponement approach, supplier-held inventories and state of the art manufacturing facilities. It has added to this model continuously over the years. Its planning systems, based on i2 Technologies, allow it to re-plan factory output plans every two hours. It has learned to use its Web site sales and pricing tools to switch demand, thereby avoiding stock-outs and customer satisfaction issues. It has learned how to supply peripheral products such as printers, PDAs and scanners through the Dell supply chain. It has worked hard to engage and train its people around a small set of accepted principles and performance measures. It has put real customer demand and satisfaction at the center of its supply chain operations. It has recognized the cut throat nature of competition within the PC world and worked hard with suppliers (some of whom are competitors) to ensure that it has the most cost-efficient position. In the middle of all these successes, it has also recognized its vulnerability to changes in the market. There have been times in their past when Dell was close to failure and the lessons have not been forgotten. Dell is well aware that the PC is not the only device that will be used for Internet access and working. The test of Dell's supply chain in the future will be its ability to adapt to a new world of multiple Internet access devices and miniaturization of PC and communications devices.

Cisco

Cisco Systems has risen from obscurity to world wide recognition over a very small number of years. It has established dominance in the market for routers at a time when a huge amount of infrastructure building took place over the Internet. Cisco, like Dell, established the Internet as a major sales channel at a time when most companies did not believe that it could be possible. Like Dell, Cisco had to make a lot of changes happen by itself and through its supply chain partners. Cisco recognized at an early stage that it needed supply chain partners for manufacturing and logistics excellence. Cisco needed to concentrate on customer relationships and product excellence. It built up an impressive network of contract manufacturers to build its routers while maintaining a small number of internal plants (mainly for development and to understand costs). In addition, it employs contract logistics providers to deliver routers to customer locations. Cisco was able to rapidly reach a position by 2000 where over 40 per cent of orders that were received by Cisco were satisfied without any employee touching the product (this percentage is still rising). Cisco was very innovative in its use of Internet and other ERP technologies in the supply chain. The basis of Cisco's IT infrastructure was a single Oracle ERP system and widespread usage of the company's intranet. In addition, Cisco was an early adopter of employee portal technologies, e-procurement systems and integrated planning systems using Tibco and Manugistics. Cisco is another example of a company where a strong internal culture of excellence, clear performance measures, responsive information systems and strong supply chain partnerships are used to create best-of-breed supply chain performance.

Flextronics

Flextronics has focused on being excellent in one part of the supply chain – contract manufacturing. It has recognized the need of other best-of-breed supply chain companies for excellent outsourced manufacturing capabilities. Flextronics's focus had been on building manufacturing facilities in low-cost economies. This requires the skills of building not only the facilities but also the base of next tier suppliers around these facilities. Flextronics has also been building up its capabilities to integrate seamlessly with the demands of companies like Cisco and those of contract logistics providers like UPS.

Flextronics has demonstrated the key role that contract manufacturers can play in best-of-breed supply chains by constantly building its presence around the world (for example, new plants in Mexico and Hungary).

GE

GE has been highly successful at running autonomous business units and supply chains with common objectives. Each of the GE business units has been driven by a philosophy that focuses on annual cost reductions, integrating new acquisitions and speed of decision making and results. GE has become the leading proponent of operational excellence and continuous innovation through its Six Sigma culture. Jack Welch has claimed that this has saved GE over $1billion. In addition, GE has driven continuous supply chain and e-commerce innovation through its 'Destroy Your Business' (DYB) program. In DYB, each business unit has been required to put together an e-commerce strategy that shows how it could reinvent its business to stay ahead of traditional and new competitors. GE has also produced some of the most successful e-commerce initiatives and e-marketplaces. In its plastics business, GE Polymerland has been set up as one of the strongest private plastics e-marketplaces. GE appliances has brought the use of Internet technologies into stores using kiosks, thereby reinventing the dynamics of order management and logistics in appliance sales. GE Medical Systems has used e-marketplaces to open up whole new markets that they have not traditionally served through its second hand market capabilities. GE has a strong philosophy of autonomy within a shared (but light touch) business support framework. This framework allows cross-business unit efficiencies (such as in the area of procurement) without building internal empires.

Dow

Dow has established itself as one of the leading chemical companies without having the backing of a major oil company. It has demonstrated a very strong capability to combine the need for operational excellence and continuous innovation with the need to respond effectively to the supply chain needs of e-commerce and the new economy. Behind Dow's success has been integrating initiatives such as a single SAP ERP system and a widely implemented Six Sigma program. In addition to this Dow has taken a lead in the chemicals industry at internal e-commerce initiatives as well as industry consortia solutions. By combining this with a well thought through business unit strategy Dow has been able to establish industry leadership as well as to cover most of the likely future migration paths of the industry. Its approach has recognized that supply chain excellence is required both at a product level (for example, polyethylene) as well as at a functional level (for example, logistics, HSE, storage).

Starbucks

Starbucks may be an unlikely choice for best-of-breed supply chain, but it has created a globally successful retail concept in a relatively short number of years. Its supply chain can be viewed at a number of levels; in the stores it has replicated a retail model in multiple countries with great success. In the product area, it has established an integrated supply chain for its own brands of coffee, tea and other products. In technology it is now working with Compaq and Microsoft to implement a wireless Internet access capability. The combination of these supply chains will be a unique source of competitive advantage for the next few years. Starbucks has been highly successful by integrating the delivery of multiple supply chains, using e-commerce around the needs of its customer base.

Why is it difficult to achieve and sustain best-of-breed status?

Although the characteristics of world class supply chain management are well known, they are complex to implement and it is difficult to keep processes best in class over long periods of time. Supply chain management and associated IT are often not the priorities of executive teams and this makes it difficult for companies to build and sustain best-of-breed supply chains.

Examples of factors that make world-class supply chain management difficult are:

- history – few companies have the luxury of the greenfield supply chains of Cisco and Dell. This does not mean that they cannot build best-of-breed status, just that it takes more time
- size and complexity – most supply chains cover multiple processes, organizations and geographies
- relevance – in some markets, such as mobile phones, profits and priorities have meant that there has been more emphasis on customer acquisition rather than supply chain effectiveness
- too many changes in priorities in many companies' change programs, and lack of long-term stability in objectives
- over-focus on technology and belief in 'magic bullet' solutions
- too little focus on supply chain relationships and change management in building new levels of supply chain performance
- lack of engagement of people in multinationals that are increasingly destructuring and restructuring to increase shareholder value
- confusion in recent years about whether new e-commerce technologies could replace the need for disciplined supply chain processes
- many companies are stuck between a world of traditional and new e-commerce technologies
- increasing complexity and infrastructure costs.

All these factors are within the control of management teams. The major difference between best-of-breed and other supply chains can often be the determination of management to take tough decisions and to stick to long-term improvement goals.

It is often surprising how little many companies have done to close the performance gap between their supply chains and the best-of-breed competitors. There is certainly no shortage of information on what can be achieved and how. The key learning seems to be the need for a plan that has a realistic probability of successful delivery.

The building of best-of-breed supply chains requires a balanced response of multi-year plans to deliver on operational excellence, well-tested new supply chain capabilities and innovative new solutions. It requires the implementation of three key elements: the seven principles of supply chain excellence, the eight cultures of demand chain competitiveness and the engagement of people at all levels in supply chain excellence and innovation. Achieving this is not simple and it requires a coordinated portfolio of change projects.

Supply chain change projects can be divided into three types depending on the time horizon and level of complexity (Figure 4.2.4).

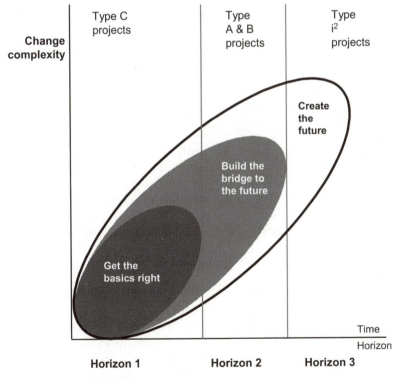

Source: CI-Culture Ltd (CI-C.com)

Figure 4.2.4
Managing a portfolio of change projects

The most important factor is the integration of the delivery of new capabilities and benefits with a simple framework as we have seen at companies like GE, Dow, Cisco and Dell.

- A&B projects are the projects that gain most management attention. They typically cost more than $1million and companies assign the best internal and external resources to manage and deliver new capabilities.
- Most companies managing a portfolio of A&B projects are remarkably similar given the free flow of information on company activities within industries and functions. The major difference between companies is the level of successful delivery and the fit between different projects and an overall strategy. Despite their resources and importance, the probability of real success (measured by ROI) on A&B projects is generally not much above 50 per cent.
- C projects are the most numerous and are generally focused on incremental improvement targets. In the best companies, they engage large numbers of people, deliver 40–45 per cent of annual benefits in the change portfolio and they are the breeding ground of Six Sigma Black Belts and future project managers for A and B projects. In most companies, C projects are under-managed, under-resourced and under-rewarded. As a consequence, projects that should deliver a success rate of 90 per cent often fail to deliver even 50 per cent. For most companies this is a major source of their failure to deliver best-of-breed supply chains.
- Innovation and incubation (i^2) projects are designed to create the future supply chains. They are risky, experimental and require careful support and control. They have a low probability of success but a high return if they can create genuine supply chain innovation.

Best-of-breed supply chains are full of people who are actively engaged on operations as well as change projects and who understand the role of their work in creating meaningful change. They are probably not working any harder than people in other companies but they are almost certainly more focused on delivering their benefits targets in a shorter timescale with greater management support.

Conclusion

There is a clear performance gap between what best-of-breed and average supply chains achieve. This performance gap has been highlighted over the last few years, particularly by the growth of e-commerce, the availability of benchmark data and the increasing need for integration between extended supply chain partners. A few companies have emerged strongly in this period as drivers of excellent supply chain performance. Most companies are still struggling to catch up. The solution is within the grasp of most companies.

However, it is hard work, it takes time and it requires ongoing management commitment to a portfolio of change projects that will deliver tangible benefits. The real challenge for most companies is keeping that dedicated focus and grinding out the results, particularly in the smaller continuous improvement projects.

Reference

Berger, A. J. and Gattorna, J. L. (2001) *Supply Chain Cybermastery*, Aldershot: Gower Publishing.

4.3 Supply chains as vehicles for transformational change

John L. Gattorna

The whole area of change and change management has drawn a lot of attention over the last few decades as organizations have sought to extract more value for the effort and resources poured into this activity. However, too often, change initiatives have not been attached to business strategy and therefore have been entirely meaningless exercises that have done little more than agitate the organization for no real gain. Indeed, although the main levers for change have been known for some time, and more recently diagnostic tools have been available, one gets the impression that most change initiatives have been a somewhat 'trial and error' affair. The reason for this is that very few organizations have had a *frame of reference* to help them understand what they should be aspiring to. This and the fact that those same organizations have had little or no idea of their own existing *cultural capability*, means that they have been going through the motions of change, not knowing either the starting point or the end point! No wonder most change initiatives have delivered little more than frustration and a very agitated workforce. The time has come to end all that. We can now see into an organization and measure its 'dominant culture' and subsidiary sub-cultures, and we can do likewise in the marketplace to measure the dominant sub-cultures there too, otherwise called behavioral segments, which become the frame of reference for guiding the change referred to above.

The relatively recent close examination of supply chains and, within these, logistics operations, has led to the conclusion that they represent excellent vehicles for change, because all logistics and supply chain processes by definition cut across the organization and bridge between organizations, in both cases breaking down the silos of yesteryear.

As developments in supply chains have moved rapidly to a focus on value creation, we have begun to recognize that different types and

456

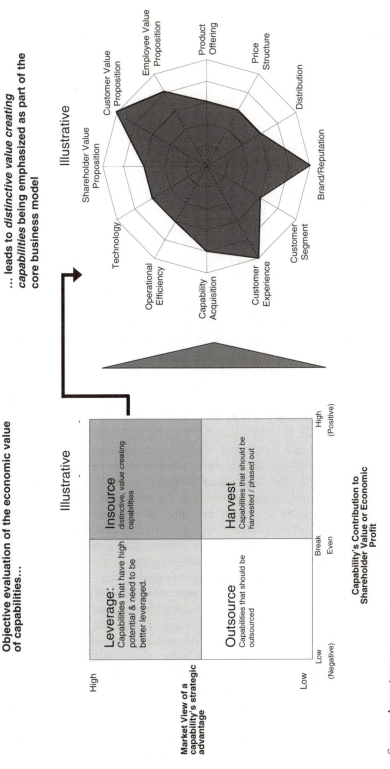

Objective evaluation of the economic value of capabilities...

... leads to *distinctive value creating capabilities* being emphasized as part of the core business model

Illustrative

Market View of a capability's strategic advantage

High

Leverage:
Capabilities that have high potential & need to be better leveraged.

Insource
distinctive, value creating capabilities

Outsource
Capabilities that should be outsourced

Harvest
Capabilities that should be harvested / phased out

Low

Low
(Negative)

Break
Even

High
(Positive)

Capability's Contribution to Shareholder Value or Economic Profit

Illustrative

Product Offering
Price Structure
Distribution
Brand/Reputation
Customer Segment
Customer Experience
Capability Acquisition
Operational Efficiency
Technology
Shareholder Value Proposition
Customer Value Proposition
Employee Value Proposition

Figure 4.3.1

Framework for evolving differentiated business models

Source: Accenturre

degrees of change are possible and necessary depending on the repertoire of new capabilities required to underpin the chosen supply chain operating strategy; the four possible business models which may be found in any combination, are indicated in the matrix of Figure 4.3.1.

For the purposes of this chapter, we are mainly interested in the 'Insource' model, because this involves re-inventing the organization from the inside out to better align with the operating strategy; the options for leverage and harvesting are generally considered in conjunction with the question of what to retain inside the organization, and what to outsource. In Chapter 4.6 we will address the 'outsource' option in more detail by introducing the notion of creating change outside the body of the organization. In our experience in dealing with large, complex organizations, achieving successful change is comparatively easier in the latter case although it is often suggested, quite wrongly, that this is the more difficult and risky route to take. By 'outsource' we mean a full transformation, not just some incidental contracting-out of certain functions to 3PLs.

The point of Figure 4.3.1 is to illustrate that the decision to Insource and grow certain capabilities internally is usually made because these capabilities are distinctive, that is, the external marketplace views them as strategic, and the internal view is that they contribute significantly to economic profit.

Multiple supply chains

In the early chapters of this book we introduced the notion of 'alignment' with a number of dominant customer segments. This in turn implies that the equivalent number of cultural groups will necessarily have to exist inside the organization if differentiated responses are to be delivered into the marketplace, rather than a lowest common denominator solution as in the past. Or indeed, the other extreme, which was to 'overcustomize' and try to meet everyone's expectations, which generally proved very costly and in any case impossible with the way most organizations are configured. So in a situation where four (or less) clear market segments were found to exist, four supply chains with different operating characteristics are required for complete alignment and corresponding optimum financial performance. This case is depicted in Figure 4.3.2.

So when we talk of change we mean the complete portfolio of coordinated actions that have to be undertaken in order to move the organization from one state of *cultural capability* to another desired state to support the chosen strategy. These initiatives may include changes in organization design; the introduction of re-engineered processes, new KPIs; new ways of communicating with, and training, the workforce, and new approaches to recruitment in an attempt to

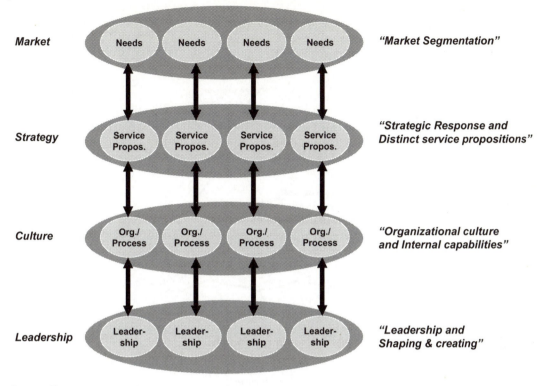

Source: Gattorna

Figure 4.3.2
Multiple strategic alignment drives distinct responses to customer segments

'genetically engineer' the new organizational cultures. We will now explore the fundamentals of this vital ingredient to business success.

Organization culture – the hidden engine

In the overall four-tiered alignment model (refer to Figure 1.3.2 in Chapter 1.3), perhaps the most important interface is that between Levels two and three, that is, strategic response and cultural capability. This is because the sub-cultures buried deep in an organization largely determine which parts of any operating strategy will actually be delivered into the marketplace; 'realized strategy', compared with what the words in the business plan say, otherwise known as 'emergent strategy'. Often there is up to a 60 per cent slippage, and the biggest reason for this is cultural resistance within the organization. So a better understanding of how this 'organizational engine' actually works is vital to improved operational performance.

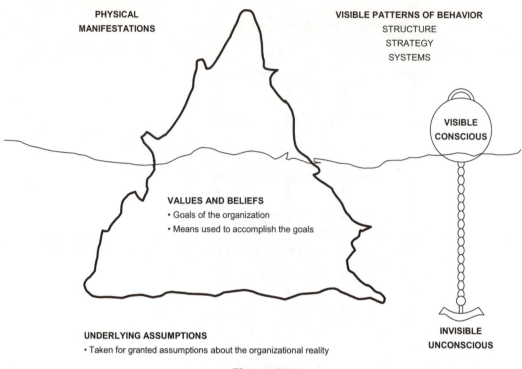

PHYSICAL MANIFESTATIONS

VISIBLE PATTERNS OF BEHAVIOR
STRUCTURE
STRATEGY
SYSTEMS

VISIBLE CONSCIOUS

VALUES AND BELIEFS
• Goals of the organization
• Means used to accomplish the goals

UNDERLYING ASSUMPTIONS
• Taken for granted assumptions about the organizational reality

INVISIBLE UNCONSCIOUS

Figure 4.3.3
Culture defined

'Culture' may be defined as the way of life in an organization; *the way we do things around here*. It is a set of shared meanings within the organization, and the way an organization sees and responds to its operating environment. Closely associated with culture is the climate of the organization, that is, *the way we feel about the way we do things around here*. Climate is relatively easy to change, but culture is much harder because we are dealing with deeply held values, beliefs and underlying assumptions. Perhaps the best way to represent this difficult intangible concept is with an iceberg picture in Figure 4.3.3. The real 'forces of darkness' inside an organization reside below the surface, out of sight and difficult to detect. That is why passive resistance to change is the most insidious form; it is very difficult to detect and therefore to manage.

The dominant cultural forces are listed in Figure 4.3.4 below. Every organization will have some combination of these four forces, P, A, D, and I, as previously defined in Chapter 1.4, 'Operating Strategy'.

Before going any further on the topic, it is best that we introduce the normative model of culture as depicted in Figure 4.3.5 below. Essentially, there are four main subcultures as depicted by the four quadrants of the model, P, A, D, and I. However, depending on the organization, there are up to 16 different combinations of sub-cultures

"P"
- Emphasis on action
- Goal directed, results count
- High environmental awareness
- Productivity valued

"A"
- Traditional, administration
- Process is more important than content
- Strong internal orientation – what is good for the company
- Stability and order are valued

"D"
- Creativity and innovation abounds
- A focus on broad concepts and the hypothetical
- Proactive orientation toward the environment
- Inspiration and entrepreneurship are encouraged

"I"
- An emphasis on people and teamwork
- Decisions are based on consensus
- Internal, individualistic orientation
- Loyalty and commitment to the group are highly valued

Source: Strategy Spotlights, 1991

Figure 4.3.4
Dominant cultural forces

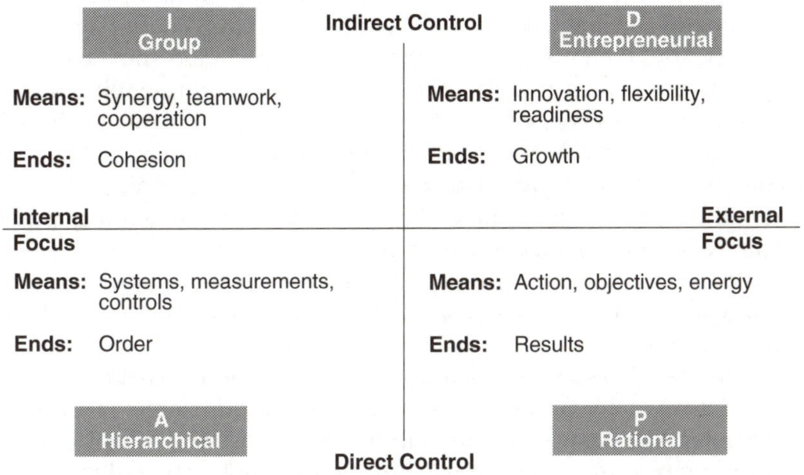

I Group	**Indirect Control**	D Entrepreneurial
Means: Synergy, teamwork, cooperation		**Means:** Innovation, flexibility, readiness
Ends: Cohesion		**Ends:** Growth
Internal Focus		**External Focus**
Means: Systems, measurements, controls		**Means:** Action, objectives, energy
Ends: Order		**Ends:** Results
A Hierarchical	**Direct Control**	P Rational

Figure 4.3.5
Culture framework in Strategic Alignment Model

possible; it all depends on where the center of gravity falls that defines the 'dominant' or resident culture.

Firstly, a brief word about each of the four quadrants. The 'D' or entrepreneurial culture is characterized by individualism, creativity, growth and flexibility. There are open, informal communications which are shared with whoever happens to be around at the time.

Control is achieved via commitment to the agreed vision and management leads by inspiration. Individuals are empowered to perform their roles and rewards are based on creativity and entrepreneurial behavior. Deviant behavior is tolerated, as long as it is goal directed.

The 'P' or rational culture values action, energy, meeting objectives and results. Here the emphasis is on analysis, guidelines and sustained high levels of activity. Communications are open but more formal. Control is achieved by focus on results, and management support emphasizes planning. Individuals are given structural authority to perform their roles, and rewards are based on formal standards and relevant results. No deviation from plans or performance standards is tolerated.

The 'A' or hierarchial culture is internally focused, and values analysis, systems, control and measurement, Communications are closed and formal, and information is only shared on a 'need to know' basis. Control is achieved by focus on process, and management support emphasizes procedures. Individuals' tasks are established by precedence, and rewards are based on formal standards and the ability to maintain internal cohesion and good administration. No deviation from approved processes is allowed.

And finally, the 'I' or group culture is one where the key values are loyalty, commitment, teamwork and consensus. Communications are closed and informal, and shared by the 'inner circle' only. Control is achieved by commitment to common values, and management support emphasizes the internal climate and working environment. Individuals' tasks are negotiated by consensus, and rewards are based on informal standards and the ability to be good team players. Deviant behavior is tolerated provided it adheres to consensus values.

So, these are the four main cultural types that will be found in every organization in some combination or other.

Because culture is so deeply embedded in an organization it is usually the most difficult and slowest to change of all four levels of the alignment model.

So the real question is: what do we change, and in what sequence, in order to achieve better alignment with our target customer segments? The answer to this question becomes self-evident once a culture map is made of the existing organization. The culture map looks at multiple factors such as change tolerance; performance/ reward system; internal organizing; knowledge capability; autonomy; identity; conflict; informal standards; and others as part of a very detailed mapping process.

The final culture map comprised of all the various layers of detail can then be compared to the external 'cultures' (or buying values) identified in the respective customer segments. From that point the change process is best explained by way of the following typology of change possibilities as depicted in Figure 4.3.6 below.

EVOLUTIONARY   **REVOLUTIONARY**

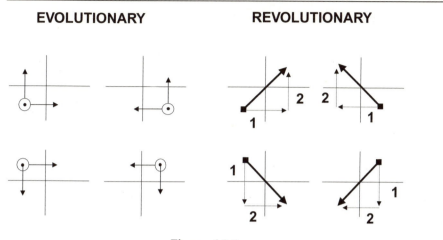

Figure 4.3.6
Typology of cultural change possibilities

Why change occurs

Change can be either evolutionary or revolutionary, as depicted in Figure 4.3.6. Clearly, Evolutionary change requires only crossing from one quadrant to the next adjacent quadrant, whereas Revolutionary change means moving to the diagonally opposite quadrant, a much more complex task.

Evolutionary change involves an incremental modification of organizational behavior, and does not require immediate alteration to the organization's 'sub-conscious'. It may be planned, but often occurs 'naturally' as the organization adapts to its marketplace.

But revolutionary change means fundamental changes to the underlying assumptions, values, and beliefs previously held, causing a significant change to manifested strategic behavior. It is usually planned, but often occurs when the organization is a 'victim' of changes in its operating environment.

We will now look at an example of each type of change. In Figure 4.3.7a below, we have an example of where the current culture has been diagnosed as Rational, and evolutionary change is required to move either towards a Hierarchial or Entrepreneurial culture. Or indeed stay in the same position. The point of this diagram is that once the current and desired cultures are known, the change process is quite deliberate and fairly mechanical.

In the case of a revolutionary change as depicted in Figure 4.3.7b, the process is a two-step one, and for this reason is obviously more difficult and usually takes longer to achieve. And it sometimes takes nerve to hang on to the whole change program when the change is so visibly slow, which is often the case in very large organizations.

Culture Diagnosed As Rational – Evolutionary change required

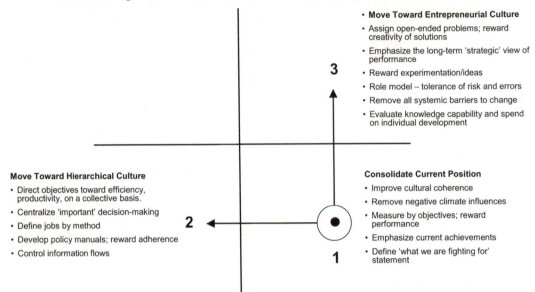

Figure 4.3.7a
Culture diagnosis outcome and sample Evolutionary change approach

Culture diagnosed as Hierarchical: best fit Entrepreneurial - Revolutionary change required

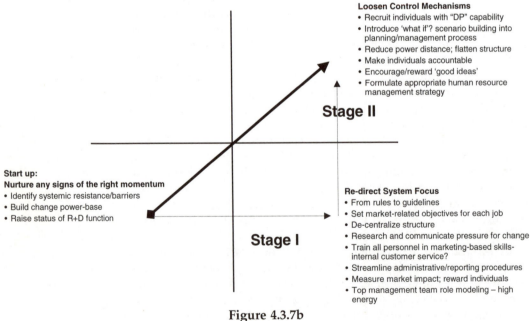

Figure 4.3.7b
Culture diagnosis outcome and sample Revolutionary change approach

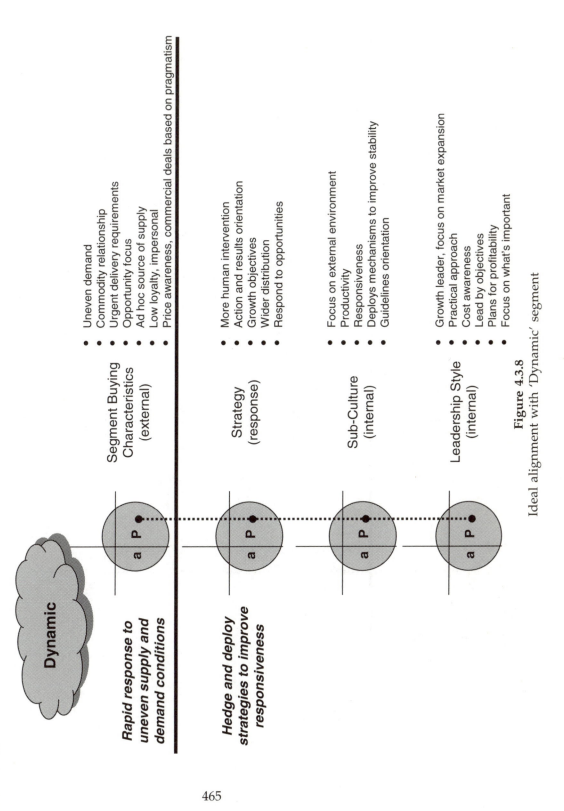

Dynamic

Rapid response to uneven supply and demand conditions

Hedge and deploy strategies to improve responsiveness

Segment Buying Characteristics (external)
- Uneven demand
- Commodity relationship
- Urgent delivery requirements
- Opportunity focus
- Ad hoc source of supply
- Low loyalty, impersonal
- Price awareness, commercial deals based on pragmatism

Strategy (response)
- More human intervention
- Action and results orientation
- Growth objectives
- Wider distribution
- Respond to opportunities

Sub-Culture (internal)
- Focus on external environment
- Productivity
- Responsiveness
- Deploys mechanisms to improve stability
- Guidelines orientation

Leadership Style (internal)
- Growth leader, focus on market expansion
- Practical approach
- Cost awareness
- Lead by objectives
- Plans for profitability
- Focus on what's important

Figure 4.3.8
Ideal alignment with 'Dynamic' segment

465

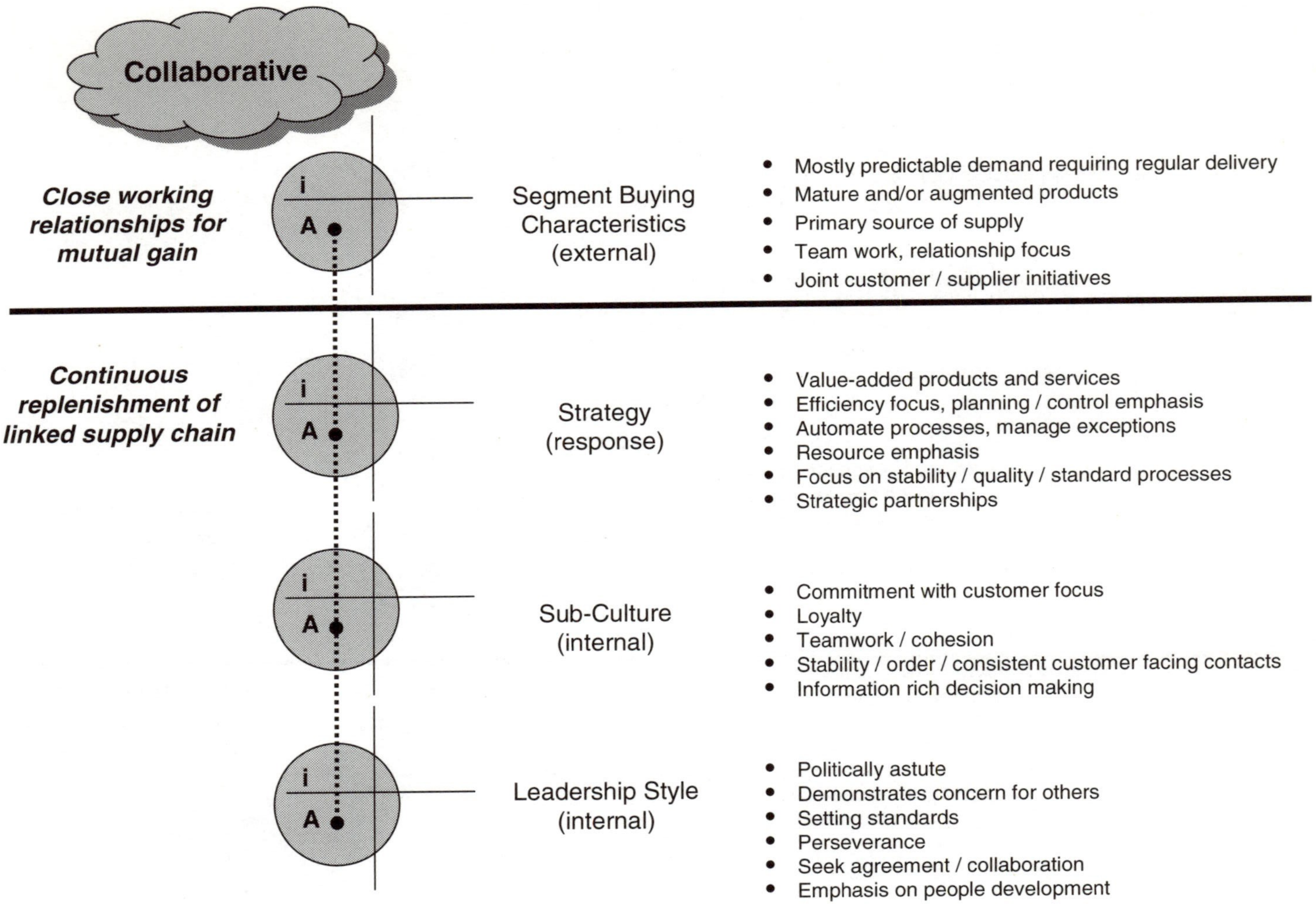

Collaborative

Close working relationships for mutual gain

Continuous replenishment of linked supply chain

Segment Buying Characteristics (external)
- Mostly predictable demand requiring regular delivery
- Mature and/or augmented products
- Primary source of supply
- Team work, relationship focus
- Joint customer / supplier initiatives

Strategy (response)
- Value-added products and services
- Efficiency focus, planning / control emphasis
- Automate processes, manage exceptions
- Resource emphasis
- Focus on stability / quality / standard processes
- Strategic partnerships

Sub-Culture (internal)
- Commitment with customer focus
- Loyalty
- Teamwork / cohesion
- Stability / order / consistent customer facing contacts
- Information rich decision making

Leadership Style (internal)
- Politically astute
- Demonstrates concern for others
- Setting standards
- Perseverance
- Seek agreement / collaboration
- Emphasis on people development

Figure 4.3.9
Ideal alignment with 'Collaborative' segment

What true 'alignment' looks like

Let's assume we have carried out a full alignment analysis in a particular market in which we identified two major behavioral customer segments 'Dynamic' and 'Collaborative' – see also Table 1.3.1; these become the 'frame of reference' for future change initiatives. The corresponding ideal strategic responses, cultures and leadership styles which underpin these two supply chains are as depicted in Figures 4.3.8 and 4.3.9, respectively.

It then remains to assess and map the existing cultures and compare these with those above in order to gain an accurate understanding of the size of the required change, and exactly what the journey will be in terms of the range of initiatives required to achieve the 'ideal' fit with these target market segments.

Core cultures in supply chain management

Apart from developing the capability for multiple responses across a range of market segments, the supply chain function in the enterprise must also nurture and grow some basis or core capabilities, which in themselves require careful development of specific sub-cultures. These three core cultural capabilities are depicted in Figure 4.3.10 below.

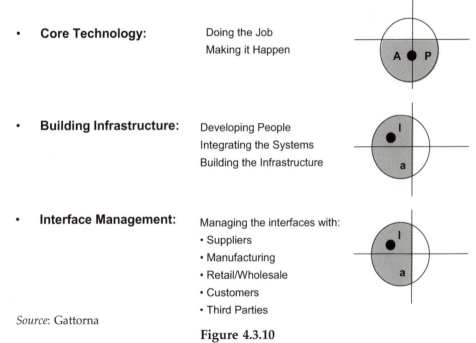

- **Core Technology:**   Doing the Job
                                    Making it Happen

- **Building Infrastructure:**   Developing People
                                    Integrating the Systems
                                    Building the Infrastructure

- **Interface Management:**   Managing the interfaces with:
                                    • Suppliers
                                    • Manufacturing
                                    • Retail/Wholesale
                                    • Customers
                                    • Third Parties

Source: Gattorna

Figure 4.3.10
Core cultural capabilities of the supply chain function

Conclusion

The good news is that we now have the tools and the precise knowledge to undertake successful transformations of organizations, and the supply chain executive are in a lead position because of the natural cross-functional, cross-company characteristics of logistics and supply chain processes. The bad news is that too few companies are taking advantage of the obvious opportunities to re-engineer their businesses, and it can only be a matter of ignorance and/or lack of will and leadership – for which there is no excuse. It is to be hoped that as the operating environment becomes even more unforgiving in the years ahead there will be no alternative other than to adopt the alignment principles enunciated in this book. In this situation it is to be hoped that managements will undertake well thought through and orchestrated change programs to perfect the alignment of their respective supply chains and sales forces with the marketplace. In turn this will surely be a rich new source of potential improvement in operational and financial performance.

Reference

'Alignment and the Concept of Strategic Fit,' in *Strategy Spotlight*, J. L. Gattorna (ed.), Vol. 1, no. 1, February 1991, pp. 4–7.

Third- and Fourth-party logistics service providers

4.4

Mark Bedeman and John L. Gattorna

Over the last few years we have been asked many times about the role and meaning of a fourth-party logistics (4PL) provider (Fourth Party Logistics® and 4PL® are global trademarks of Accenture). Indeed there is general confusion in the marketplace about the differences between 4PL and third-party logistics (3PL) providers, lead logistics providers (LLPs) and other types of business models. Clients have asked us: 'How would I know a 4PL if I saw one?' and 'How can I transform my operationally adequate asset-based company into a virtual 4PL?'.

The aim of this chapter is to clear up the confusion and Table 4.4.1 below is a good start. Specifically, we will present some understandable definitions of 3PL and 4PL organizations, identifying the critical factors that define their differing roles and responsibilities. We will look into the capabilities and skills outside of the obvious technical requirements that distinguish a 4PL from other service provider operating models, and re-establish a clear mission statement for 3PL providers. Finally, we will set the scene for the next generation of outsourced supply chain service companies in the wider context of business transformation outsourcing.

This chapter will outline the role and capabilities of 3PL providers and 4PL providers and look at the next generation of supply chain service companies.

Historical perspective

The concept of a 4PL was first introduced by Accenture circa 1996, reflecting the demands of clients in the United States for substantially better operational performance than they had been getting from 3PL providers. At the time, 3PL providers considered themselves at the 'top of the tree', having evolved from road transport companies and warehouse managers into distribution companies before becoming logistics companies. While a lot of the early transformations took place

The 3PL providers were trapped between narrow margins and customer demands for new and innovative solutions.

Table 4.4.1
Different types of supply chain outsourcers

Types	Key Characteristics	Examples
4PL	• Supply chain visionary • Supply chain planner and optimizer • Deal shaper and maker • Supply chain re-engineers • Project management • Service, system and information integrator • Continuous innovation	UPS/Compaq Exel/Samsung Danzas/Ericsson
Lead logistics provider (LLP)	• Experienced logisticians • Optimization engines • Decision support • Manage multiple 3PLs • Continuous improvement	Exel/Ford
3PL	• Integrated warehousing and distribution • IT infrastructure provision and support • Localized data tracking • Asset owner and asset buyer • WMS systems	Tibbett & Brittain TNT Geodis Schenker
Prime asset provider	• Transportation asset provider, any mode • Warehouse, cross dock, property facility • Manufacturing (outsourcing) • Packaging products	DBCargo Lufthansa Cargo P&O, TDG Norbert Dentrassangle

in the US, similar developments unfolded elsewhere. In the United Kingdom, Exel Logistics was born of British Road Services in an attempt to create a new industry brand that would generate customer interest.

Most, if not all, the contracts let for physical logistics operations in the first half of the 1990s relied on the twin value propositions of externalizing industrial relations issues and reducing capital employed. However, the 3PL providers became caught in a cycle of continuous downward cost pressure caused by annual negotiations and competitive RFQs. From the shippers' viewpoint, they were becoming increasingly disenchanted with the low value-adding nature of traditional contract outsourcing arrangements with 3PL providers. The providers themselves had become commoditized over time because of their ever-reducing margins and their few strategic investments. The missing 'gene' to transform the 3PL providers was continuous improvement. Such improvement needed an innovation-friendly operational environment to survive and thrive – a condition that did not exist in most 3PL providers.

However, some of the newly created 3PL providers had enough intelligence to be aware of the need for significant IT investment, research and development (R&D) and high-calibre management. But, they did not have, and still do not have, the necessary profit margins to proactively develop the required new service offerings that would add value to their customers' logistics networks. The 3PL providers, so it seemed, were trapped between narrow margins and the increasing demands from customers to bring new and innovative solutions to bear. All this was being played out in a world that was getting larger, faster and more complex.

In the second half of the 1990s, the Internet was 'discovered' by industry and commerce, and a whole plethora of new software companies emerged to launch the e-commerce era. Performance expectations on 3PL providers went up a few more notches. One of the prime fallacies of this era was the belief by 3PL providers that buying high-profile expensive supply chain software would somehow miraculously transform them into 4PL organizations. In fact, many have not even taken their expensive 'toys' out of the box.

The ERP phenomenon

About the same time, major investments in enterprise resource planning (ERP) systems were taking place, mainly driven by concerns about Y2K. For the first time, transactional data was becoming available because it was a necessary pre-requisite for the next generation of operating models, including 4PLs. Hitherto, there had been much talk but sadly little action in terms of 4PL development, with a few notable exceptions mentioned later in the chapter. Upon reflection, the reasons for this slow roll-out appeared to be a lack of uniform data; multi-country operations; silo or divisional organizational designs; and lack of any semblance of an innovation subculture. Just about any European company that tried to tackle its logistics and supply chain opportunities in the late 1990s was confronted with one or more of these barriers.

ERP systems provided a partial solution, but they did not have the capacity to deliver sustainable value over time.

To embellish the point, they had no data, no common data definitions and no corporate understanding of the key supply chain levers present in their businesses. In addition, many companies had for years been building a complex pan-European network, often via acquisitions, which were not well integrated, and where geographical differences and independence were tolerated and indeed flourished. Also, these companies had been working to a traditional formula involving the creation of powerful business units with strong independent leaders, working in silo divisions, for whom any form of shared services or cross-divisional planning, resource optimization and collaboration was anathema. And to top things off, managements at the time took the intuitively attractive point of view that managing internal change was easier than setting up arrangements that move the center of gravity for change outside the organization.

The widespread adoption and implementation of ERP systems provided a partial solution. But it has taken most companies far too long to bed these down and apply the next layer of application systems that have the capacity to deliver sustainable value over time. It is here that 4PL organizations come into their own, with a 'virtual management' role to play.

Also not addressed by the ERP developments at the time was how to rebalance value creation within the supply chain at the corporate level – over and above the sum of the individual business units. 'Now that there is common data, can there be shared services?' was the typical question, pinpointing an organizational, rather than technical, issue. The new CEO of Philips, Gerard Kleisterlee, described his plans in *The Economist* in February 2002, to shift performance bonuses from divisional to corporate levels in order to motivate business unit leaders to deliver corporate results Such a shift is likely to release opportunities to create value in Philips' complex, multi-divisional supply chains. This type of strategy is fertile 4PL territory, as it involves forging alliances between the best internal resources, best-of-breed 3PL providers and technology implementers, in combination with change and project management experts.

3PL providers defined

The character and shape of 3PL organizations can be defined in terms of some combination of the following attributes:

- owns/leases and operates a vehicle fleet, and may also use a substantial contracted fleet
- owns/leases and operates warehouses
- employs a large number of blue-collar workers
- provides a range of added-value services around labor or capital intensive tasks, for example packing; labeling; and sub-assembly
- can manage international movements
- has operational IT mostly in the form of point solutions for WMS, routing and scheduling
- pricing is based primarily on task-oriented tariffs, with some open-book arrangements, and
- involves a combination of fixed-income and benefits-sharing relationships at or below the level of supply chain director.

Issues surrounding 3PL providers

Even as 3PL providers emerged as a hybrid solution there were problems. For instance, once they had contracted all or part of their logistics tasks out to one or more 3PL providers, customer companies found they still had to spend significant time managing them. Meanwhile, 3PL providers tended to focus on maximizing the utilization of their own assets, sometimes at the expense of additional cost to their clients. Also, the relatively narrow operational focus of 3PL providers meant they tended to be short of senior management attention on the broader supply chain issues that were important to their clients. Finally, they underinvested in R&D, information technology and project management.

LLPs are the same as 3PL providers but they also have extra visibility tools and access to optimization modeling.

Some of these flaws were overcome via the introduction of the lead logistics provider, a variation on the traditional 3PL. This occurred as manufacturing and retailing companies with deep experience in outsourcing contracts in different regions and across different product ranges and operational functions, began to realize the potential synergy through improved 'oversight management' across several 3PL contracts. In practice this meant appointing one 3PL to take on the additional lead role of improving productivity across a network of providers.

So, LLPs are 3PL organizations as defined above, but they have some additional visibility tools to work with, and access to optimization modeling for decision support purposes. Such an organization is rewarded by a fee or tariff linked to some mathematical modeling of cost and corresponding benefits.

Another 'wall' that the LLPs hit was that they were not designed, motivated or sufficiently integrated into the business to push through their synergizing agenda, in the face of the still all-powerful regional and plant management determined to retain their 'local' arrangements.

The LLP approach has worked to some extent, but customers were still clamoring for more performance, hence the invention of the 4PL concept and its subsequent variants.

The 4PL business model

Accenture's 1996 definition of a 4PL organization is: 'A 4PL is an Integrator that assembles the resources, capabilities, and technology of its own organization and other organizations to design and run comprehensive supply chain solutions.'

A true 4PL organization comes to life around a focused problem or opportunity, whose scope defines the required combination of capabilities.

The definition has stood the test of time well, although the number of new 4PL organizations operating today is still disappointing, given the substantial value that they can potentially deliver, as shown in Figure 4.4.1.

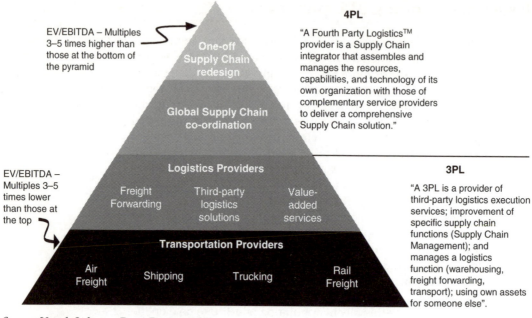

Source: Vogel, Lehman Bros. Report, 2001

Figure 4.4.1
Value generated by 4PL providers

Notice that we do not mention 'assets' or 'no assets' in the definition. The truth is that applying correctly dedicated assets, fully utilized, is and must be an essential part of an effective solution. Ownership is not the issue, productivity is. Similarly, the word 'partnership' is not explicitly included. But the definition is very clear – it is a combination of resources, capabilities and technology from in-house in the shipper's organization, combined with the best available from outside the firm, which creates the 4PL.

Under this definition, 3PL providers can be part of the 4PL organization, either as one of the capabilities brought in to manage the operation and/or as a contractor to the 4PL provider carrying out much of the physical task. It is also possible for a large 3PL organization to set up a separate 4PL sub-organization within itself that can target new opportunities outside its normal general contracting operations. Examples of this are Ryder Logistics in the US and Danzas in Europe. In fact Deutsche Post (DPWN) has created a dedicated 4PL company, called XPL – Excellence in Partner Logistics, clearly highlighting the essential concept behind this form of outsourcing. XPL incorporates the capabilities of DHL and Danzas and other resources within DPWN and at time of going to press, an investment from Lufthansa Cargo. Now with this name, we should have exhausted the use of the '4PL' name. Establishing the internal rules of behavior between the 3PL and 4PL family members is indeed a highly critical business issue and one that is often overlooked.

The reference to 'technology' in the definition is fundamental. Unlike 3PL providers, which have little free cash to invest in world-class supply chain technology applications, 4PL providers use technology as their prime capability. Because of the infinite number of combinations and permutations in configuring a 4PL provider, the best way to create one is around a real client or clients. A true 4PL organization only comes to life around a focused problem or opportunity, whose very scope helps to define the specific combination of capabilities that are required and become part of a final design. Too much time has been wasted in many boardrooms, asking 'what are the capabilities of a 4PL organization?' instead of 'what are the capabilities I have to assemble to solve this problem?'.

Another area of development for the 4PL model has been the growth and survival of a few e-marketplaces. Figures 4.4.2 and 4.4.3

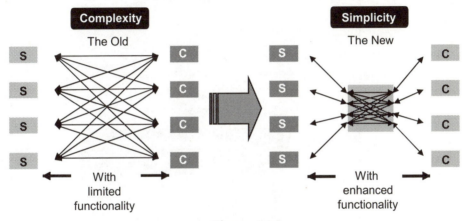

Figure 4.4.2
Collaborative supply chain solutions

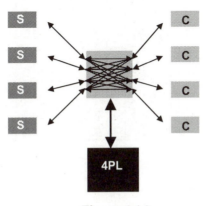

Figure 4.4.3
4PL attached to a collaborative network

depict a conceptual model developed for the fast moving consumer products industry.

Equally important in the 4PL definition is the reference to 'comprehensive supply chain solutions'. By 'comprehensive' we mean much more than the physical logistics activities of planning, forecasting, order management, inventory management, product development, design and procurement, to list a few. By 'solutions' we mean to ensure that it is understood that a single 4PL can be configured at the outset to exploit cross-industry, multi-client synergies that can multiply and sustain the ongoing creation and delivery of vast financial benefits. How these benefits are calculated and shared among the constituent members of the 4PL service company poses some challenges and is indeed one of the biggest obstacles to the formation of this type of business model.

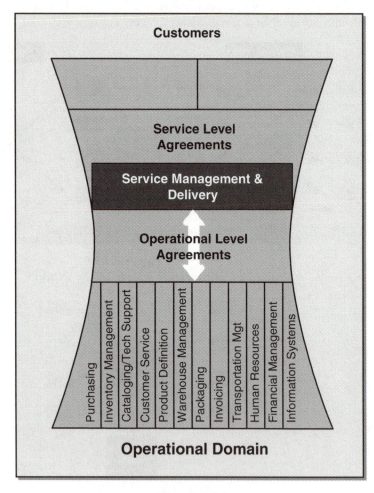

Figure 4.4.4
The core capabilities of a 4PL

Outsourcing model 1: 'sell–manage–buy'

Any 4PL must contain three basic core capabilities: to 'sell', 'manage' and 'buy', as depicted in Figure 4.4.4.

In our model, to 'sell' means to really understand the value proposition and to develop a commercial offering that fits the needs of all the various buyers/users of the 4PL. Understanding the 'value proposition' is one of the most under-developed skills within this whole arena. Too much time has been spent on technology and not enough time on understanding the 'deal'. The 4PL needs not only to articulate but to write into the contract what will be delivered in terms of key performance indicators (KPIs), milestones, costs, service levels and other tangible measures, and by when, how they will be measured and how the costs and benefits will be shared. In other words, a world-class service level agreement (SLA)!

KPI design will be a crucial component of any successful participation in a 4PL structure. The 4PL/outsourcing KPI map in Figure 4.4.5 demonstrates how superior management of total logistics costs and service level agreements inexorably lead to a 'win–win' or 'reward zone' where continuous improvement flourishes.

In the model, to 'buy' means to identify suppliers of all the supporting operational and functional services, entering into supply contracts, administrating in order to pay, and – the most demanding – to manage these suppliers against written operational service level agreements. These SLAs, of course, must be aligned with those offered to the client.

To 'manage' means to have the technology to deliver visibility across all the managed supply chain components, a means of

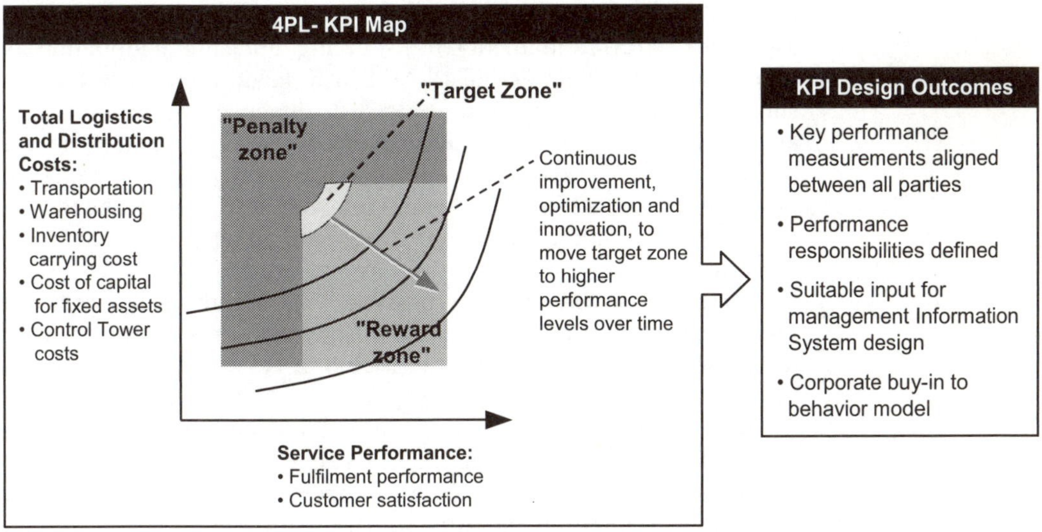

Virtual management means to really understand the value proposition, identify all suppliers of operational services, and use technology to deliver visibility across the supply chain.

Figure 4.4.5
Creating a motivated SLA

controlling performance, and the balancing of resources across different networks. This then is the 'virtual management' concept, and which we often refer to as the 'control room or control tower' overseeing the entire outsourcing service management.

Outsourcing model 2: 'find–enable–extract–share'

The people- and behavior-related issues are now at the core of successful outsourcing developments.

Finding the value is a recurrent theme throughout this book because it is so important to business success in general, and the impact on operational supply chains in particular. The emphasis is not only on finding the value, but also on extracting value and then sharing the value. All are vital considerations in the formation and successful operation of a 4PL organization. As mentioned, in our experience finding an acceptable formula for sharing the value is perhaps the most difficult issue to resolve up front.

In terms of finding the value, various supply chain valuation models are available, such as the supply chain operations reference model (SCOR) and Accenture's supply chain value assessment (SCVA). Irrespective of what model is used, we are looking to assess the full economic value added (EVA^{TM}) impact of any new business model in terms of such parameters as revenue lift from improved shelf fill, and lower cost of inventory holding, perhaps offset by higher transport costs, to mention just a few.

Perhaps one of the more stressful issues facing the development of 4PL opportunities comes from within the organization, rather than from outside. Creating the right environment internally to accept the very principle of substantial and deep outsourcing needs astute message creation and delivery. Handling the blue- and white-collar industrial relations issues associated with change is a vital ingredient, and policies have to be well thought out. Even the managerial issues associated with fundamental outsourcing and the elimination or reduction of fear are critical. At board level there needs to be substantial 'buy in', not only to the clear financial opportunities, but an understanding of those 'soft' enhanced revenue gains that would be deliverable. These upsides have to balanced against managing the negatives perceived in the industrial relations field, and perhaps even the possible negative impact on the brand image, associated with outsourcing.

Extracting the value is now possible. We have the technology; we have implemented new supply chain software successfully; we have the project management skills, and while it is very hard work – it is 'do-able'.

The real problem after creating the enabling environment is and has always been, the negotiating and agreeing how to share the value internally across the divisions and functions, and externally amongst the various partners and suppliers. Shaping the 'deal' so that company managements feel compelled to transform and change their organizations, and manage the attendant risks along the way, is the real challenge. These 'people' – and behavior-related issues are now seen to be at the core of successful outsourcing developments. This has prompted us to amend our definition of a 4PL, adding one more element: 'and which has the cultural diversity, political and communication skills and the commercial acumen to not only find value, but to create motivating and sustainable deals that offer incentives to all the parties involved'.

So a true 4PL unlocks value in customers' supply chains by offering services that go beyond pure aggregation of the underlying 3PL services. Indeed, it is fundamental that the 4PL generates 'new money' to share. It cannot live off the backs of the asset owners and 3PL providers!

A true 4PL unlocks value in customers' supply chains by offering services that generate new revenue for all partners.

The 4PL organization must create and release value and thus generate fee and transaction income from the following areas:

- increased asset productivity, not lower prices, from optimization and operational innovation
- improved planning from the visibility of forward orders
- lower transaction costs, through enhanced IT and e-commerce solutions
- lower inventory costs, not lower space rental, from managing 'why' not 'how'
- less obsolescence
- better packaging management, and
- high sales from improved service.

As mentioned, negotiating this type of value proposition and gain sharing are the difficult issues for 4PL organizations to resolve. The complexity is depicted in Figure 4.4.6, along with the types of questions that would distinguish a 3PL from a 4PL provider.

Figure 4.4.6 contains many messages. The degree of outsourcing is portrayed from left to right, and from bottom to top, the degree of complexity, synchronization, and information, rather than asset management, being tackled. Many companies have completed a high degree of outsourcing, arrow 1, to the 3PL providers, in the physical area of blue-collar work, industrial relations management and asset reduction. Arrow 2 shows where many leading companies are now, with ERP programs beginning to be effective, and the supply chain planning systems, and cross-business collaboration and planning under development now. While there is a clear set of potential outsourcing partners for step 1, the traditional 3PL providers, the move to partnering and outsourcing of these complex processes, arrow 3, is not so obvious. This is the 4PL box. Many 3PL providers, arrow 4, consultants and dot.com pure plays have seen this as their domain – their 'Holy Grail'. All wrong. This is the place for the next generation of innovative partnering of all the players.

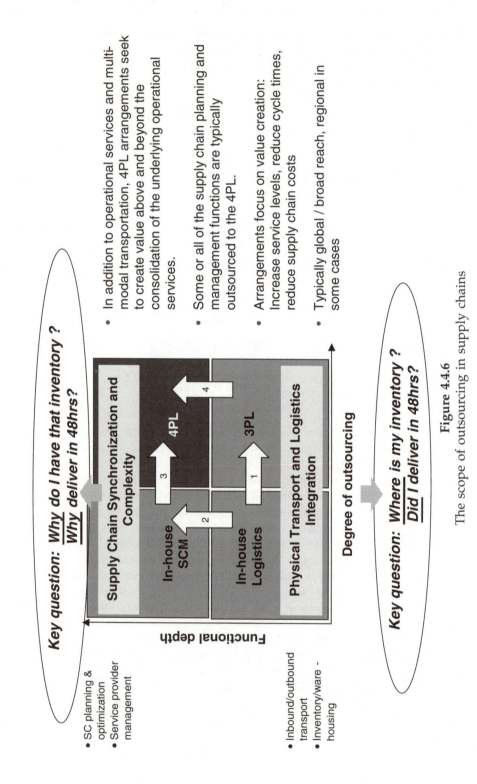

*Key question: Why do I have that inventory ?
Why deliver in 48hrs?*

- In addition to operational services and multi-modal transportation, 4PL arrangements seek to create value above and beyond the consolidation of the underlying operational services.

- Some or all of the supply chain planning and management functions are typically outsourced to the 4PL.

- Arrangements focus on value creation: Increase service levels, reduce cycle times, reduce supply chain costs

- Typically global / broad reach, regional in some cases

Supply Chain Synchronization and Complexity

4PL

In-house SCM

In-house Logistics

3PL

Physical Transport and Logistics Integration

Degree of outsourcing

Functional depth

- SC planning & optimization
- Service provider management

- Inbound/outbound transport
- Inventory/ware - housing

*Key question: Where is my inventory ?
Did I deliver in 48hrs?*

Figure 4.4.6
The scope of outsourcing in supply chains

Examples of successful 4PL providers

In the early 1990s, one of Accenture's first examples of a solution that went beyond the capabilities offered by 3PL providers was the creation of New Holland Logistics. This company was owned 80 per cent by the Fiat agricultural machinery subsidiary and 20 per cent by Accenture. In addition to operating a 3PL provider, the company was also responsible for planning and inventory management, and procurement. Both parties to the deal were rewarded in a combination of ways, including task-related tariffs, and benefits sharing according to equity.

Market examples show that a 3PL provider can successfully dedicate part of its organization to a 4PL capability.

The Thames Water 4PL organization, known as Connect 2020, was created by Thames Valley Water Authority and Accenture under a gain sharing arrangement. A more current example is Vector Logistics in the US, which is a joint venture between Menlo Logistics/CNF and General Motors. The ownership structure in this case is 20 per cent GM and 80 per cent Menlo Logistics, but with GM holding the key voting shares.

Vector Logistics is an interesting example because it demonstrates, as in the case of Ryder Logistics, that a 3PL provider can successfully dedicate part of its organization to a 4PL capability. The division is necessary because the larger organization, in its 3PL configuration and mindset, would not otherwise be considered for the more complex supply chain operations required by GM in this particular case. As it stands, the new, jointly owned company has the task of managing the entire global transportation requirements of GM, involving spending in excess of $5 billion. Some further examples of 4PL providers are given below, and the success rate is gradually increasing with experience. 'Learn by doing' is the mantra here.

Kuehne and Nagel, at the beginning of 2002, announced they were taking over and managing the Nortel Global supply chain activity. The deal is certainly gain sharing in nature, but does not have the ownership of the joint venture model as seen in Vector Logistics.

Neither of the two early models, New Holland, nor Thames Water, ever reached out beyond the single founding client operation, though both were planned to do. We will see over the next few years 4PL organizations delivering value to the initial client, and then extending horizontally, into other related, even competitive clients' situations to sustain value creation for all. The problem remains one of defining a mutually acceptable deal to share the value.

Reviewing these examples and other experience leads us to believe that a 4PL is in effect the 'brains' or central nervous system of the participating organizations. Specifically, a successful 4PL must have the following elements and the full revised definition would read as outlined in the sections below.

4PL providers defined

A 4PL is an Integrator that assembles the resources, capabilities and technology of its own organization and other organizations to design, build and run comprehensive supply chain solutions and which have the cultural sensitivity, political and communication skills, and the commercial acumen, not only to find value, but to create motivating and sustainable deals that offer incentives to all the parties involved.

Using this definition, a 4PL organization comprises a combination of the following attributes:

- an organization with direct access to 3PL resources and capabilities and clearly articulated business behavior rules between the 3PL and the 4PL providers if owned by the same corporation, such as 'neutral', first refusal and last bid, or other defined limitations
- an assembly of organizations with the full spectrum of required capabilities
- extremely strong IT capabilities, in all aspects of design, build and execute and manage
- can manage information flows
- employs only a few management and white-collar workers
- characterized by a culture of innovation
- can find and extract value through world-class project management
- has extraordinary capabilities to construct value-sharing deals within and across divisions and companies
- has a pricing scheme based predominantly on value creation and sharing mechanisms, with some fixed overhead support infra-structure component, and
- relationships at or above supply chain director level.

The 3PL provider mission – revisited

Strategically positioned 3PL providers who excel in operations and customer management will successfully increase their market value.

As already mentioned, there is a continuing and vital role for 3PL providers despite the emergence of the 4PL business model. If this is the case, then what does it take to be the 'best of the best' 3PL? The answer is those players who are strategically positioned within the industry landscape and who excel in operations and customer management will be the 3PL providers who will increase their market value. The diagram below (Figure 4.4.7) describes the four essential ingredients for success.

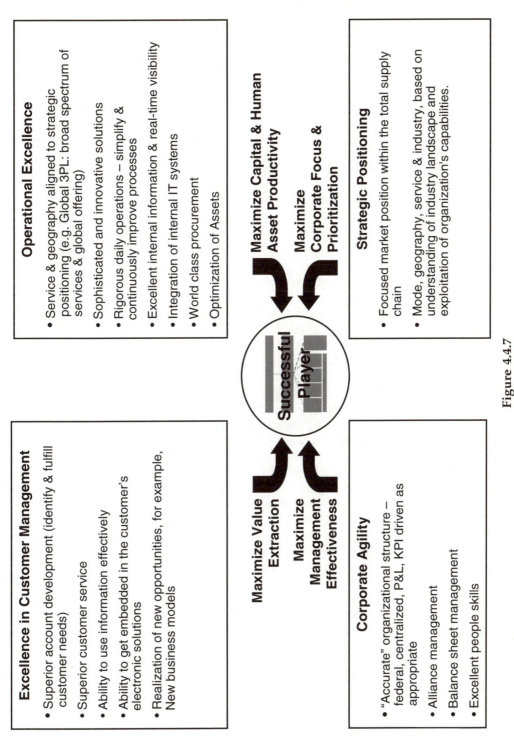

Figure 4.4.7
Ingredients for 3PL provider success

483

Setting the scene for the next generation of outsourcing

In the last 25 years, outsourcing has steadily grown in most first world countries, but not at the high rate initially expected. This is because the expectations of the customer base have stayed ahead of the capability of 3PL providers to develop the required performance, and the ability to demonstrate that the perceived risks are unbiased.

However, customers still have at the back of their minds when they enter new outsourcing contracts with today's 3PL providers, that they just may have to take the business back in the future, and this reversal will be expensive. The 4PL option offers a third alternative whereby the main players continue to have emotional, financial, and operational interest in the outcome. Beyond this there is only a complete transformation into a multi-party jointly owned services company, where scale in business volumes and critical mass in competencies are developed across many geographies of a single global business and eventually across several global businesses.

The UK is one of the leading countries in outsourcing transport, warehousing, and distribution operations, mainly due to the business coming from major UK retailers. Across Europe the penetration of outsourcing varies by country, but there is still a trend to outsource the more traditional asset intense operations. Some newer forms of relationship-based outsourcing are appearing, with open book accounting and shared benefit commercial arrangements based on risk, meeting agreed milestones and KPIs, but still largely based on the core asset based operations within the supply chain.

As companies have started to see their ERP systems coming together across the business, they are beginning to seek ways of outsourcing some of the information-based supply chain processes to a new breed of intelligent 3PL providers with strong IT capabilities and innovative relationship ideas. But despite this trend, most companies are still fundamentally about outsourcing non-core processes. Looking ahead, the 'best' companies are reaching out to partner and outsource even those core capabilities in which they believe they can find yet greater improvement from scale and leverage.

Conclusion

The next generation of supply chain providers will be able to 'transform' the businesses for whom they act as outsourcers.

The next generation of supply chain providers will be able to 'transform' the businesses for whom they act as outsourcers. They will be the outsourced supply chain management companies of the future. Business transformation outsourcing, addressed in detail in Chapter 4.6, 'Strategic transformations and supply chains', will offer companies a way of quickly achieving transformational outcomes. And, 3PLs and 4PLs will each have a vital role to play.

References

Accenture (2001), 'A program to transform the way a business works, enabled by outsourcing to achieve a rapid, sustainable step change in enterprise-led performance', White Paper, Institute for Strategic Change.

Kleisterlee, G. (2002), 'Struggling with a Super Tanker', *The Economist* (9 February 2002).

Vogel, J. (2001), Report on 4PLs, Lehman Bros., London (March 2001).

4.5 Emerging requirements for networked supply chains

Robert Ogulin

Supply chain management capabilities link a corporation's strategy and the needs of the customers it serves. Today, capabilities that help companies to consistently keep delivery promises and commitments have become the essence for success. New technologies and new management styles change traditional and often adversarial business relationships in the supply chain leading often to more collaborative models.

These trends pose new capability requirements in the supply chain and are changing the way companies create value and sustain competitive advantage. Many companies today do not know which capabilities will become critical to execute their strategies. Others might start to identify emerging advanced capabilities that will impact their organizations but they are not able to leverage them for value creation.

Often companies are also not quick enough to identify and deploy new supply chain capabilities. The reason is that they are paralyzed by the increasing complexity that these strategic and business changes induce. So today, the typical supply chain continues to be a sequence of disconnected activities both within and outside the organization. This lack of cohesion destroys value in the supply chain.

A forward-looking approach of the supply chain is needed that aims to bring the company in line not only with today's requirements, but with relevant emerging capabilities. Most supply chain managers today are stuck in an 'efficiency trap' that is, they focus inwardly only, on 'getting their house in order', rather than on creating supply chains that include customer service strategies that utilize new technologies and introduce principles of collaboration. As Michael Porter (1999) puts it, 'companies need to find ways of growing and building advantages, rather than just eliminating disadvantages'. However, defining and implementing such advanced and sustainable supply

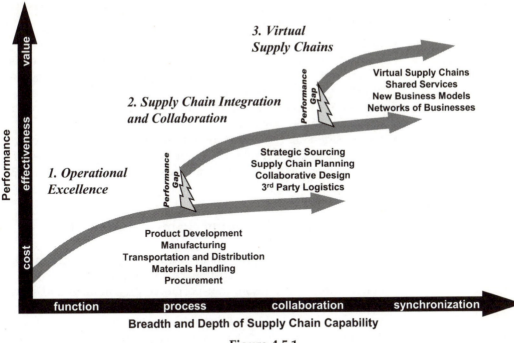

Figure 4.5.1
The supply chain management performance/capability continuum

chain capabilities that are hard for competitors to imitate also requires new approaches to managing opportunities and risks.

Previous chapters in this book discussed operational excellence, aspects of integration and collaboration and different ways to take advantage of new business models along the supply chain continuum (Figure 4.5.1). This chapter will extend this discussion and focus on how companies need to address emerging requirements for the networked supply chain along the entire supply chain management spectrum.

Emerging requirements for the networked supply chain

Successful advanced supply chain management is characterized by 'frictionless' coordination of product, financial, and information flows between supply chain partners. Hence, supply chain capabilities that address the requirements in a networked world are determined by the company's ability to identify and combine the necessary processes, technologies and intra- and inter-organisational competencies to create new value for customers and all participating stakeholders – shareholders, suppliers, service providers and employees.

Companies will need to develop the ability to identify and respond to four emerging requirements:

- include the customer and end consumer in your supply chain
- utilize new technologies and management techniques opportunistically to take advantage of quick value opportunities; and strategically, to extract greater value from superior service to their customers
- develop the capability to participate and manage a diverse portfolio of relationships
- foster leadership styles that are responsive to constant change while maintaining competitive levels of operational efficiencies. The phenomenon 'agile' versus 'lean' was described in Chapter 3.1, 'Creating agile supply chains'.

End-to-end customer supply chains – the base for competitive advantage

A company's typical supply chain (Figure 4.5.2) integrates multiple areas of the organization – customer service, product development, manufacturing, distribution, transportation, procurement and service management. Supply chain leaders excel in conducting basic operational activities in all of these areas with efficiency, consistency, and accuracy. These disciplines and best practices that lead to such world-class performance are not only a source of competitive advantage; they are a competitive necessity. World-class product quality, accurate inventory tracking, lean operations, customer-focused service, and a rationalized supply base all will be respected by the customer and envied by the competition.

And it has already begun to change in the sense that supply chains have started to interact more tightly with their customers. Supply chain management begins with insightful market segmentation and

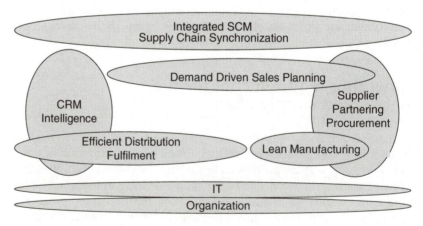

Figure 4.5.2
Integrated supply chain capabilities

interaction with these segments. Successful companies carefully define both target customers and, equally important, accounts that do not fit with their supply chain strategy. Starting with selecting the right customers and offering distinct value propositions, a company can create an appropriate set of core operations capabilities. The capabilities are rooted in the core business processes, the execution of which puts the focus on emerging supply chain management capabilities.

Traditional improvement initiatives in the supply chain focused on cost and functional excellence and integrating such activities as purchasing, manufacturing, distribution, spares management, and customer service within a single enterprise. Increasingly, companies are trying to find solutions to the demands caused by one-to-one marketing, shorter product lifecycles, increased customer demands, and more complex supply chain networks and technologies.

When Hewlett Packard designed the integrated processes and systems for their new order fulfilment platform they included key customer representatives and their logistics service providers in the process design teams. This lead to shared value propositions and service levels that approached 100 per cent, increasing overall supply chain efficiencies and bottom line results (Sherman, 1996).

An increased focus on customer- and consumer-centric business models will keep the pressure on supply chain management. The Internet provides an opportunity to increase supply chain visibility and provide organizations with real-time information across various points in their value chain. It promises reduction in costs and improved productivity through better data and information exchange. Now, Internet-based supply chain business models are evolving into a more cost-effective and powerful way to do business.

An example is the area of supply and demand matching. At the core of defining a value proposition for a supply chain segment is superior knowledge about the customer's value creation process. This cross-functional and cross-organizational task of identifying the right value drivers and priorities include such functions as demand planning, forecasting and capacity planning. If not aligned well with the customer it highlights inefficiencies in basic supply chain performance leading to poor performance, waste, and inadequate service levels. Excellent end-to-end customer supply chains will require organizational, procedural, technical, and strategic capabilities applied across organizations to address:

- time compression (from product development to manufacture; from order to delivery)
- agility and flexibility with regard to changes in demand, schedules, and strategic plans
- ability to handle different levels of details and keep them interconnected (propagation of plans in real time; multi-echelon planning)

- ability to handle geographic planning (global capacity and demand planning).

The availability of Internet-based communication and collaboration has enabled changes in new product development across the supply chain, reducing costs, cutting cycle time for new product introduction, and better matching new products to consumer preferences. For example, software companies routinely release development copies of their software to the public. The role of the customer in that process is to use the new software and in so doing to assess its usability and identify problems in the program. By providing beta versions to the public, companies enlist the input of knowledgeable users to perfect the product. The Internet provides a real-time mechanism for the software companies to stay in touch with their "beta" testers.

While information sharing and customer orientation changed the game many companies still find themselves struggling to collaborate, even on the more basic business issue of delivering products and services. Companies seem to be reluctant to share plans and reduce 'gaming' between the partners.

Collaboration between business partners and customers can induce simplification as it reduces the uncertainties in the supply chain and allows all participants to use their resources more efficiently. Traditional rules of adversarial supplier management and cost-driven transaction processing generally do not apply anymore. Collaboration encourages co-operation and trust instead of costly arm's-length contracts and control. Paradigm shifts in management since the beginning of the 1990s slowly changed how products are planned, designed, produced and delivered to the customers involving multiple supply chain partners. Information is not proprietary but shared, using technology that enables a more seamless flow of information across company boundaries.

Technology – the driver of new business architectures

Technology, and in particular mobile commerce and the Internet, have led to a virtualization of different aspects of moving product through supply chains. Physical features of the process, from paperwork to product attributes have been transferred into virtual space. The management of information flows has become more important and more critical than optimizing the physical parts of the supply chain.

Increasingly, companies are relying on networked-based solutions because the impact can reach throughout an enterprise, enabling faster inventory turns; reduced asset and production costs; fewer write-downs and better customer service. Technology provides the 'architecture' that drives supply chain innovation.

Indeed, the Internet, mobile commerce, and other networking technologies have created great scope for corporations to improve the efficiency of just about every business process yet again.

However, a significant constraint to creating the synchronized supply chain is the shortage of other organizations who have integrated architectures. Few have developed the sophisticated collaborative capabilities required, that is, do not use open standards. But those organizations that are ready to move to this level of sophistication have a powerful incentive to seek companies among the less advanced and assist them along this journey. Once a critical mass has been achieved, the pace will accelerate – and the laggards will be shut out.

A quite significant evolution can be observed, from spreadsheet-based planning of inventories and manufacturing runs in the 1980s and the beginning of the 1990s, to MRP and ERP, which focused mainly on the integration of information to streamline the planning and transacting of one company. However, not all business practices can be easily integrated across multiple enterprises. The widespread introduction of ERP systems has provided shared data and operational processes across the supply chain functions that are the basis of integration. While complex systems like SAP R/3 can achieve significant results 'within the four walls' of a single enterprise, the complexities of implementing such a solution across multiple organizations are quite forbidding.

Building on this foundation, supply chain optimization techniques have become the catalyst for integrating each functional area of the enterprise into an orchestrated operation. Supply chain planning (SCP) introduced advanced logic and algorithms that simultaneously integrate demand, supply and resource constraints from multiple partners in the supply chain all the way to the customer. When correctly implemented, these systems provide the decision support and planning tools to manage the complexity of an integrated global supply chain. Today, there are a large number of tools available for collaborative planning, sourcing, collaborative design, collaborative manufacturing, and other emerging areas such as supply chain event monitoring referred to in previous chapters.

The Internet impacts for example; supply and demand planning processes through new processes and applications such as collaborative planning, forecasting and replenishment (CPFR), efficient customer response (ECR), and vendor managed inventory (VMI). These and similar initiatives, coupled with the extension of supply chain planning software functionality in this area, promises to unlock new value, as discussed in Chapter 3.6, 'Industry-level collaboration through ECR'.

In manufacturing, Internet-based applications will allow many companies to evaluate their build-to-order capabilities and to differentiate themselves by customizing products to each customer's needs. In fact, traditional build-to-stock models are becoming obsolete for some product types because of the massive inventories required to support constant SKU expansion. The build-to-order model and its variations have arisen as a mechanism for reducing inventories while increasing flexibility of manufacturing operations. Dell's build-to-order business is based on leading the deployment of new capabilities on an ongoing basis, and tight integration of suppliers.

In the product design arena, new Internet tools allow a variety of parties to participate in a concurrent collaborative design process. Electronically linked in real time, key suppliers, manufacturers, engineers, marketers, designers and customers will be able collaboratively to design products faster. In a world of shortening product life cycles, it is crucial that products be rolled out faster – without the 'silo' issues inherent in traditional sequentially-oriented design activities.

In the automobile industry, which has used proprietary networks since the 1980s, the networks have enabled the use of platform teams that cut across all departments, from design to manufacturing, as well as in-house and outsourced service providers, in order to reduce dramatically the cost and cycle time of new car design and introduction.

In addition enterprise application integration (EAI) provides the technology platform for linking best-of-breed supply chain applications. The breakthrough to collaborative relationships requires an open, economical, and flexible communications medium. Whereas EDI has found only limited uses, the Internet has created a wealth of potential for enhancing many supply chain processes. Further technical innovations such as XML (Extensible Markup Language), the development of broadband communications, and ubiquitous access through 'Internet appliances' will continue to drive progress. These developments will increasingly impact every functional area of the supply chain by enabling new business processes and capabilities.

Technology capabilities and business needs will drive the Internet in other new directions. Internet functionality will move from enabling information-based processes (that is, order management transactions, payment flows) to enabling physical aspects of the supply chain (that is, the virtualization and integration of vehicles and buildings). New mobile devices and Internet-enabled instrumentation will allow the Internet to be used to manage and monitor real-world machinery and conditions.

The benefits achieved for all stakeholders through integration and collaboration are significant. Products begin to appear that use networking technologies to augment the attributes and capabilities of the products and, thereby, to differentiate them in the market. For example, a General Electric subsidiary sells plastic to manufacturers who use it in their products. The plastic is stored in silos with sensors linked to an Internet connection. When the inventory of plastic drops to the point at which replenishment is needed, the sensor identifies the need and the silo automatically orders more inventory over the Internet.

General Motors already offers an active safety and security monitoring system for its cars, combining sensors, a cell phone, and a global positioning satellite (GPS) receiver to provide a new range of services. If the system senses, for example, that the airbags have inflated, the system will automatically call to report the possibility of an accident and the car's location, so that help can be dispatched, if needed.

Cemex, a Mexico City cement manufacturer, builds global positioning sensors into its trucks to determine their location and whether they're stuck in Mexico City's traffic. That allows Cemex to narrow delivery times – the company promises to deliver cement – to 30-minute windows, compared with competitors who can only promise a three-hour delivery window.

The Internet can also be used to upgrade and modify products after they are in customers' hands. Cisco Systems, a leading producer of Internet equipment, sells products that consist of both hardware and software. Their products can be upgraded over time with new software. The company enhances the value of its product to its customers by providing software upgrades free if they are accessed over the Internet. That approach adds value for the customer while imposing minimal additional distribution costs on the seller.

Networks – connecting and managing for value
The proliferation of capabilities related to information in the supply chain has also allowed companies to revise their relationships. Business relationships and networks emerged that are based on the integration and exploitation of information advantages, rather than controlling a physical supply chain. Internet-based business architectures have a profound impact on the underlying assumptions and principles upon which traditional supply chains have been built. This includes Internet-based markets, exchanges, and third- and fourth-party service providers. Figure 4.5.3 illustrates how supply chain relationships developed.

As far as Internet-based service providers are concerned, that is, marketplaces and exchanges, they will need to offer distinct value-adding capabilities in order to be attractive to partner with and to be viable as a business. Operators are realizing that simply providing a transaction mechanism is not perceived as added value. Sophisticated buying of direct materials, collaborative planning, and synchronized supply chains require processes and information flows that are developed, disseminated, and maintained across multiple organizational boundaries. In addition, as routine transaction processing becomes more automatic and 'hands-off', getting information to the decision makers in the supply chain becomes even more challenging.

Information is further replacing physical aspects of supply chain management. New models have started to emerge that fundamentally change existing inter-enterprise supply chains and intra-organizational operations. Companies review their capabilities and, as traditionally with transportation and warehousing, other supply chain capabilities are being outsourced to third parties. The reasons for outsourcing in

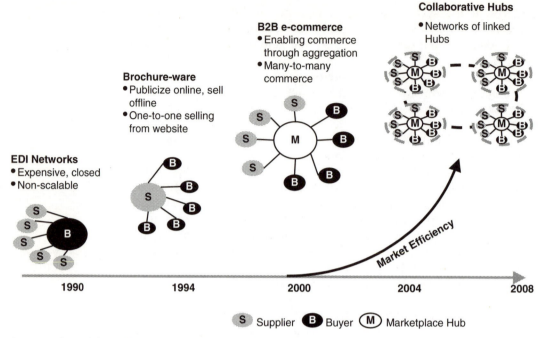

Source: Adapted from Morgan Stanley Internet Research

Figure 4.5.3
Evolution of business-to-business relationships in the supply chain

the supply chain are not new, albeit they are different from the current context:

- move activities and workflows that are no longer part of a company's core set of capabilities to another company, and now achieve additional benefits by connecting the supply chain through virtual processes
- engage in new business models in the supply chain, that is, markets and exchanges, third- and fourth-party arrangements now in order to achieve a performance advantage relative to your competition and
- build and manage a networked supply chain now because a portfolio of relationships with customers, suppliers and service providers opens new opportunities while minimizing risks.

These approaches enable process and product innovation and provide opportunities to enhance operational efficiencies and to identify new growth opportunities.

Moving low-value capabilities outside

Over the past few years, outsourcing in different areas of the supply chain has swept through many industries. As companies consider ways to improve their asset and resource utilization this trend is likely to continue. However, transferring a business capability outside the company to a third party is not trivial. Companies must upgrade their capabilities to collaborate with current partners appropriately. This does not only include technology and processes but also the ability to form and maintain relations with new players as they emerge. And, of course, each company needs to be aware of its own potential and capabilities to take the lead in building a new business model itself.

For example, a trend toward collaborative manufacturing can be observed in the electronics and high tech and automotive industries. Here collaborative manufacturing is largely financially driven. It allows a corporation to reduce its fixed capital assets (its manufacturing facilities); reduce its ongoing personnel and equipment costs; and 'focus' its business on its core competencies – specifically selling its product and managing its brand. For the manufacturing services providers, it allows companies to allocate costs across multiple clients; maximize utilization of their facilities; reduce component costs and improve margins.

But, for companies that may be considering whether to outsource parts of their operations, there are also significant pitfalls to consider. It's not just a matter of handing responsibilities 'over the wall' to a logistics services provider. More often than not, outsourcing creates new levels of complexity when it comes to operational execution. Design, engineering and manufacturing must stay synchronized, regardless of where the corporate boundaries lie.

Managing the relationships with its customers becomes key for the outsourcer. Collaborative relationships must address the interests of all companies that are part of the supply chain rather than just one. Collaborative supply chain management requires fair and equitable contract deals, which create 'win–win' situations for all parties. It works best when all companies benefit from the process.

Outsourcing also works best when the complexity of a product is relatively low, as in consumer electronics and wireless devices (personal computers, PDAs, and handsets). As the product becomes more complex and the customer–supplier relationships become more idiosyncratic the process of successfully managing the relationship becomes more difficult.

Network business models in the supply chain

The new business models that foster virtualization and synchronization of supply chains are based on advances in technology and organization. Networked supply chains lead to new bases for competition among firms as they compete not just on their own internal capabilities but also on the breadth and service depth of the networks to which they belong. Executives of networked firms will be forced to identify their core competencies and to eliminate functions that can be more efficiently performed elsewhere by network partners.

To extend capabilities and provide comprehensive solutions, more and more alliances are being formed among supply chain partners and include traditional manufacturing organizations and third and fourth parties that provide virtual supply chain capabilities. The resulting networked applications help companies synchronize activities such as product design, procurement, transportation planning, production planning and marketing. Eventually such processes have the potential to be synchronized and coordinated within entire industries. In the automotive industry, for example, synchronized industry coordination implies the coordinated flow of resources from the plant to the dealership, resulting in lower inventories, better forecasts, faster return on capital and more timely responses to market changes.

As a consequence, the ability to manage a supply chain efficiently outside the confines of a single company is giving rise to new organizational forms. Command and control is divided up between supply chain partners and distributed in relation to the value created. The forces of competition ensure that at every stage of the value chain resources are allocated efficiently.

The most competitive companies are doing just that. Cisco Systems' core competency revolves around the design of new products and the managing of customer relations. It is a $10 billion-dollar-a-year company with only about 500 production workers. Half of Cisco's products are produced and shipped to customers without Cisco ever seeing or touching them. Product quality at supplier plants is monitored by Cisco using a network.

Large, worldwide, express package delivery companies have developed complex logistics management processes and systems in order to excel in their core business – the picking up, routing, tracking, delivering, billing and verifying of millions of packages a day. Once they have developed these capabilities, many realized that they had an asset that was of great value. The capability for managing supply and distribution chains far more efficiently than any manufacturing business had become the most valuable core competency, so whole new lines of businesses were started, taking over the integrated supply and distribution chains of manufacturing companies.

The consolidation of the Internet and associated new technologies has enabled the spread of business-to-business commerce moving supply chains into virtual space. The result is a networked form of supply chain organization. These networks, or groups of companies collaborating over the Internet, have the potential of bringing revolutionary advances to the efficiency and responsiveness of business. Before the Internet, integrating supply chain operations was limited to companies that could afford private communications networks. With the Internet, inter-organizational technology is no longer an obstacle.

Managing a portfolio of supply chain relationships

For established firms that buy and sell large quantities of goods and services, networked supply chains, that is, markets are simply one channel model among several possibilities. As they do with offline channels, companies that are moving quickly into Internet-based commerce are choosing from a mix of channels those that best fit their strategic priorities and operational demands. The Dow Chemical Company, for example, uses several different Internet-based channels, similar to those illustrated in Figure 4.5.4, through which it buys product, collaborates on product design and sells to, various channels through various supply chains (Davenport et al., 2001).

The Dow Chemical Company uses a corporate-level Electronic Business and Commerce team to hone its strategic e-commerce vision, and to drive implementation throughout its widely dispersed organization. The team collaborates with Dow's independent global businesses, balancing the benefits of a unified strategy and single infrastructure against the demands of each business's specific market. This arrangement provides a controlled environment in which Dow's organization can learn by doing and pilot test capabilities. The company can then leverage robust capabilities across the organization (where appropriate) to maximize benefits.

A key success factor in Dow's portfolio approach is that the expected goals and possible benefits are articulated clearly to all partners. Participating in the exchange requires linking the exchange's functions by service level agreements and incentives for ongoing

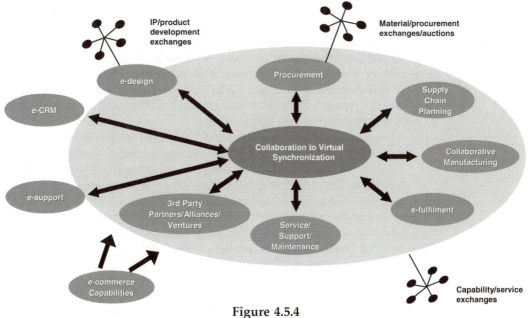

Figure 4.5.4
Portfolio of network capabilities in the supply chain

improvements. The supply chain partners are encouraged to share business plans and previous experience.

Participation is further ensured when the network linkages are easy to set up and use, both from a process and technology perspective. This can be done by using common templates, having common or standardized part numbers or by adopting a flexible architecture using best-of-breed solution providers with pre-built connectors and adapters.

New capabilities – new leadership styles and cultures

In the past the vertically integrated firm was dominant in its era because of its ability to manage and process information efficiently in the context of a complex production process, and it survived as an efficient organizational solution as long as the costs of acquiring, managing, and processing information did not change.

The advent of networked business models changed this equation. The Internet and other networking technologies dramatically lowered the cost of exchanging information within and between firms. If it is cheaper to conduct transactions internally, the organization grows; if the opposite, then it shrinks. The industrial era leveraged internal transactions, but networks reduce the value of central control and expensive bureaucracy.

Companies now realize that command and control slows down supply chain performance. Command and control requires that data climb a ladder of supervision and then step back down a ladder of approval. Companies realize that skills are needed to utilize new tools and methods to speed up supply chains. And companies realize that they cannot do it on their own, and that partnerships are crucial. As the boundaries of the firm crumble, so does control have to be shared among supply chain partners. Collaboration and communication among supply chain partners will replace command and control simply because it is faster. Skills, collaboration, communication will create greater functional integration of the supply chain. This integration will create greater speed.

Supply chain collaboration and integration requires changes that affect key aspects of a company's business model. Companies must restructure their organizations and behavioral drivers, such as compensation and budgets, to ensure all departments are aligned towards overall supply chain optimization – which might even mean a temporary sub-optimal performance for individual supply chain partners. Organizational skills, processes, technologies all need to be learned and assembled anew to meet the requirements of the networked economy. The complication is that most organizations have to first 'unlearn' their old practices before they can learn for the new.

New business models and paradigms have emerged and change the way people think about competition, business partners, employees and shareholders and how work is performed within and across companies. Leadership skills are required to break out of current frames of thinking and to change inflexible organization in order to capitalize on new opportunities.

In a highly dynamic and collaborative supply chain the critical success factor for deploying new capabilities is organizational and leadership capability. All too often, organizations fail to consider the costs and effort involved in realigning their people to new, collaborative business practices. Not only must people throughout the organization be appropriately trained to internalize and work with new processes, they also need to be involved in their development.

Design engineers for years sourced parts by referring to catalogs. Now, those catalogs are online and the company may even soon implement a 'build-to-order' environment. The role of the design engineer has changed dramatically, going from sourcing existing parts to working with selected manufacturers to build new ones. When tasks change, people must change and learn and identify with their new roles.

Although many organizations are struggling to assemble all the capabilities that make an integrated supply chain happen, those companies that are figuring it out typically share several characteristics: they usually have a well-developed ability to collaborate within their own organization, and have extended that ability to achieve similar levels of collaboration with other organizations. In addition, they are enthusiastic innovators, adopting Web-based technologies to increase internal and external information sharing, and readily migrating to new technologies and processes that increase business effectiveness.

Conclusion

Some basic steps should be considered when integrating and collaborating in supply chains and business networks.

- *Master supply chain fundamentals.* The key success factor of companies such as Cisco Systems and Dell is the excellence of their conventional operations and integration of customers and supply chain partners. Unfortunately, this is not the strong suite of most companies, not because they lack awareness of this requirement but because of their inability to force through change.
- *Learn to operate in the Internet-based world.* Achieving tight integration has much to do with implementing on the Web what the organization already has developed to achieve operational excellence. The caveat is that, without operational excellence, virtual processes are likely to cause chaos rather than enhance performance.

- *Build networks and capabilities around relationship management.* A consequence of the Web's ubiquity will be a loosening of long-term relationships between organizations in favor of shorter-term liaisons. In the integrated world corporations will come together in a series of brief cooperative engagements as expediency dictates. The key to success in this environment will be an ability to attract and assemble a portfolio of network partners.
- *Embrace change.* Management's traditional role was to plan around the expected and then deal with the unexpected. More and more, however, the expected has become rare and the ability to optimize around the unexpected has become paramount.
- *Manage complexity in real time.* No company can sidestep the challenges of increasing complexity and decreasing time scales. This requires that traditional companies learn new ways of operating. Making the transition demands an ability to learn in teams rather than as individuals, develop the skills required to collaborate with customers and suppliers, and to be prepared to experiment liberally and learn from those experiences.

References

Berger, A. J. and Gattorna, J. L. (2001), *Supply Chain Cybermastery,* Aldershot: Gower Publishing.

Brooks, J. and Dik, R. (2001), 'B2B – the smart path forward', internal paper, Accenture.

Davenport T. H. et al. (2001), 'The dynamics of e-commerce networks', internal paper, Accenture.

Porter, M. (1999), 'Rethinking competition', in *Rethinking the Future,* Nicholas Brealey Publishing.

Sherman, S. (1996), Secrets of HP's 'Muddled' Team, *Fortune,* 18 March 1996.

Strategic transformation and supply chains

4.6

Michael A. Donnellan

Stock markets around the world have unprecedented access to the underlying drivers of corporate performance. Analysts regularly meet with CEOs and executive managers, they are given a clear view of corporate strategy and, following US changes in the relationship between investment banking and research analysts, now have access to penetrating, realistic investment information. This is a far cry from the days before US corporate giant Enron collapsed, when executives were obsessed with managing earnings and repeatedly beating EPS expectations by a penny. In the pre-Enron era, results were engineered using a variety of financial mechanisms such as 'cookie jar' accounting, eyebrow-raising revenue practices and changing assumptions on pension fund valuations to inflate underlying trading profit. Corporate accounting was opaque, and in many instances deliberately designed to mislead.

Back to basics: manage the business not earnings.

Today, the message is clear: investors, media commentators, regulators and governments now insist on transparency, honesty and trust. Those that continue to play by the old rules of the game will find their share prices severely punished. Computer Associates, IBM, Cisco and WorldCom are notable examples of corporations that have experienced the wrath of Wall Street during the early part of 2002 as a result of the post-Enron world order.

The new agenda for CEOs and their top teams is to address the challenges posed by:

- investors' views of the competitive landscape, including their tough, independent assessment of the corporate strategy for growth, profitability and investment returns
- the requirement to secure the confidence of the investment community in management's ability to execute, and
- the market's expectations for employing capital resources in an efficient way.

Companies are being forced fundamentally to re-structure their operating models and to adopt policies that are more consistent with creating rather than destroying value.

The collapse of corporate earnings following the terrorist attacks of 11 September 2001, together with the exposure of questionable corporate accounting practices, has led to a complete re-appraisal of why and how investment capital is allocated across equity and bond portfolios. Executive management teams around the world are now in fierce competition for the scarce investment resources needed to pay off the corporate debt binge, re-capitalize companies, and fund the next phase of growth. CEOs now face altered rules regarding the way corporate assets are deployed and the conditions under which investors provide investment capital. Former darlings of the stock markets such as ABB, Bristol Myers–Squibb, Tyco Industries and WorldCom have found that dramatic downturn in fortunes that awaits companies who treat capital as a free lunch.

With such challenges ahead, this chapter explores how CEOs are being forced fundamentally to re-structure their operating models and to adopt policies that will create rather than destroy value. The market's thirst for returns is driving the search for new sources of value creation, and particularly, to change the vertically integrated operating model that has serviced corporations around the world for the past two decades. We argue the way ahead is for supply chain strategy to be strategically overhauled to create new operating models that are more capital efficient and less demanding in terms of up-front investment requirements. We advocate wholesale reinvention of traditional supply chain models to new forms that redistribute assets and resources across the value chain.

The thirst for returns

Healthy returns are driven from a combination of top-line revenue growth, good margins and, critically, healthy growth in the asset base.

The question CEOs now have to answer is: what steps will drive decent investment returns in the future? The answer is in stark contrast to the accepted assumptions of the past and has two parts. First, managers at all levels have to be made responsible for the capital they consume as well as the profit they generate. Increasing profits in the absence of investment returns that fail to beat the cost of capital is a fruitless exercise. Second, executives need to deploy an operating model that is capital efficient in terms of its ability to consistently generate returns in excess of the cost of capital.

ABB, the global industrial engineering conglomerate, is a prime example of a company that has consistently produced a trading profit and a constant flow of dividend payments. Superficially, ABB's corporate performance looked steady throughout the 1990s; however, when changes to the asset base of the business are taken into account, a different story emerges. The reality has been an asset base that has progressively shrunk smaller and a business that rarely delivered investment returns above its market discount rate. The end result has been several years of relative share price underperformance to the

Swiss Market Index. Clearly, companies cannot sell off the family silver forever.

Healthy returns are driven from a combination of top-line revenue growth, good margins and, critically, growth in assets. To illustrate this, consider the flaws emerging in some of the following examples of conventional corporate wisdom:

- *A singular focus on relentless cost-cutting is good for profits.* Coopers Industries is one company that has a well-publicized discipline in budgeting, cost control and financial management. Yet its share price has only managed to outperform the S&P 500 in two of the last ten years. So much for cost-cutting!
- *Growth driven by mergers and acquisitions is good for shareholders.* The reality has been revealed by major companies such as WorldCom, AOL Time Warner, and Tyco Industries, who have all written off huge amounts of goodwill (investor capital) as their plans failed to deliver pre-deal aspirations. Tyco Industries went, in a matter of months, from espousing the virtues of scale and leverage emanating from being a globally diversified industrial conglomerate to the merits of break-up and focus around four separately quoted entities. Tyco's share price nose-dived as a result, causing debt financing to strain under the load. The same situation has emerged at ABB which has had to re-negotiate new and more costly forms of financing as short-term debt funding contracts came up for renewal.
- *Growth and cost containment will add value.* The experience of Ford Motor Company is far different. Ford has been at the leading edge of globalization, developing new markets and relentlessly driving growth, raising revenues from $100 billion in 1992 to $162 billion ten years later. Management has constantly sought new ways to manage costs downwards, practising just-in-time techniques, total quality management, target design costing plus an array of in-vogue management philosophies. Despite these efforts, the share price has barely budged from $12.72 at the end of 1992 to $15.72 at the end of 2001.

The fundamental issue in many businesses today is that they are simply too capital intensive. Industry growth rates and cash margins are too low to generate adequate cash flow returns on the capital invested in the business. An analysis of four randomly selected industries in Belgium, shown in Table 4.6.1, illustrates this alarming fact.

Many businesses are simply too capital intensive. Industry growth rates and cash margins are too low to generate adequate cash returns on the capital invested in the business.

The capital driver

Capital consumption can be both a corporate killer and a liberator at the same time. Historically, capital consumption has not been something that troubled management too much, particularly middle managers who have had little or no finance training. The CFO and his team were expected to worry about this issue. For companies such as

Table 4.6.1
The gap between ROI and the cost of finance

Industry	Cash flow return on investment (CFROI)	Cost of finance (market discount rate)
Brewing	4.65%	6.30%
Chemicals	3.26%	7.65%
Electrical and gas utilities	4.09%	6.05%
Insurance	5.64%	5.43%

Source: Accenture

Barr Laboratories, Nokia and Nestlé, asset efficiency and how this is achieved lies at the heart of business strategy and the creation of shareholder value. It is the operating model that companies choose to use that is a principal determinant of the asset intensity of the business. Dell Computers uses a vertical supply chain model that consumes a fraction of the investment capital of competitors such as Compaq and Toshiba.

Our research tells us that capital-efficient operating models combined with sound investment in the expansion of profitable top-line growth, together with a sustained investment in net assets, is the best recipe to out-perform all comers. Companies such as Microsoft, Pfizer and enterprise software maker Sybase, for instance, have consistently generated growing cash flow returns from sustainable profitable growth. They have successfully reinvested this cash back into further expansion of their core business, creating a perpetual cycle where 'cash flow return on investment' is in excess of the market discount rate (see Figure 4.6.1). The reinvestment is an annual event that repeats itself over a prolonged period of time.

Companies such as Novo Nordisk, a Scandinavian pharmaceutical company, General Dynamics, a US defence business, and Nestlé, a Swiss-based global food company, are winners who have become adept at the new rules of the game. The current losers in the corporate performance stakes such as Kellogg and Campbell Soup, two US food companies, and South African Breweries seem to be playing a different game where below-average asset efficiency acts as a drag on shareholder value.

New operating models

Evidence of the success of a new class of operating model can be seen in the size of the premium – or the discount – given to a company's share price.

The winning companies provide compelling evidence to support our assertion that the traditional operating model for the vast majority of companies is past its 'sell-by' date. Strategic transformation and innovation of the old business model has emerged to produce a new class of operating models that are lean in asset consumption and heavy on growth in revenues and cash margins.

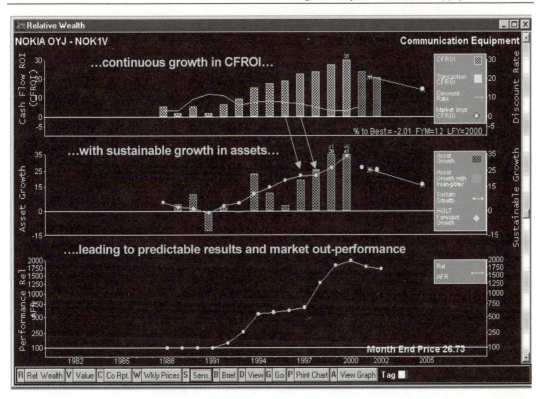

Figure 4.6.1
Nokia's recipe for outperformance

Evidence of the importance of this can be seen in the size of the premium – or the discount – that the market gives to a company's share price. A premium is awarded by the market in the expectation of growing cash flow returns; it is a vote of confidence in management's credibility and track record. Kraft, for instance, commanded a 49 per cent premium in the market at the end of February 2002, as shown in Table 4.6.2 below. This was based on investors' belief that management would deliver an 18 per cent improvement in inflation adjusted gross cash flow alongside revenue growth (increased volumes rather than price) from their strategic change programs by the end of fiscal year 2003. US food manufacturer Archer-Daniels Midland, at the other end of the scale, had 93 per cent of its value tied to investments already made, an acknowledgment by the markets of a lack of faith that incumbent management could deliver attractive returns to investors.

The pressures on CEOs are all the greater when considering that product companies are operating in a world of deflation. Year after year, the automobile, food, consumer and high-technology manufacturing industries suffer from relentless price erosion and a loss of power relative to the retailers of their products. The power gap is

Table 4.6.2
Valuations based on existing and future investments

Company	% Valuation based on future investments	% Valuation based on existing operations	% Cash flow return on investment net of discount rate	NYSE Ticker symbol
Archer–Daniels Midland Co	7	93	−1.29	ADM
Pilgrims Pride Corp	5	95	−1.42	CHX
Corn Products	4	96	−3.19	CPO
General Mills	52	48	12.93	GIS
Kraft	49	51	12.53	KFT
Sara Lee	55	45	22.36	SLE

Source: CS First Boston Holt, Accenture Analysis, April 2002

growing. Global retailers, offering customers tailored products and services at lower and lower prices are exerting enormous market power and posing commercial challenges that many organizations are struggling to meet. Superior performance is increasingly elusive in such an environment.

Figure 4.6.2 illustrates how Wal-Mart aggressively improved its cash conversion cycle by pushing inventory and costs back up the supply chain.

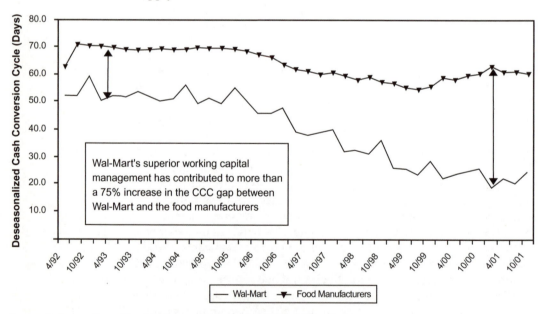

Source: Lehman Bros. Food Industry Report, March 18, 2002

Figure 4.6.2
Widening cash conversion cycle between Wal-Mart and the food industry

Table 4.6.3
Working capital requirement for every $1 of sales revenue

Company	5-Year Avg CCC (days)	1-Year Avg CCC (days)	2-Year Working Capital/Sales
General Mills	5.9	28.1	4.3%
Danone	20.3	5.0	2.8%
Kellogg	45.9	41.7	7.4%
Campbell Soup	53.3	36.6	0.2%
Unilever	53.7	48.3	6.7%
Kraft	n/a	63.0	3.4%
Nestlé	70.5	67.4	8.3%
Heinz	83.8	93.3	16.0%
Hershey	95.2	106.1	19.0%
Wrigley	106.9	100.4	25.6%

Source: CS First Boston Holt, Accenture Analysis, April 2002

Even the best-performing companies such as Danone are suffering, but relatively less so than other firms such as HJ Heinz. In fiscal year 2000, Danone required only a third of the relative working capital requirement compared to HJ Heinz. The difference in lower financing costs provided Danone with $71million of extra investment dollars available from lower borrowing costs. Across the consumer goods industry some companies require up to seven times the working capital requirement for every one dollar of sales revenue compared to the industry leaders, as shown in Table 4.6.3. This performance gap not only harms cash flow but also acts as a drag on competitive capability allowing the leaders to reinforce their market position via higher levels of investment.

In Europe, the top five retailers including Tesco, Arhold and Metro already have a combined market share of between 63 per cent and 83 per cent. By 2007, these mega-retailers are expected to capture more than 80 per cent of the consolidated European market. By that time they will also possess advanced supply chain management capabilities such as collaborative planning, forecasting and replenishment (CPFR). This poses major challenges to conventional supply-chain strategies, asset models and execution approaches. Core competency thinking has truly come of age with a vengeance; it's no longer Harvard Business School theory but reality baked into the share price models of the investment community. This is the wake-up call to management.

Despite this, thousands of overcapitalized companies are trying to hang on to the ownership of non-essential, non-strategic assets. The smart companies are moving quickly to take advantage of this lapse. Innovative new entrant Dell Computer has become famous for its make-to-demand supply-chain model that produces inventory turns greater than 30. At the start of 2002, Dell had a sales-to-asset ratio of

3.57 compared to the 2.14 ratio of industry rival Gateway. Dell stock outperformed the NASDAQ by 29 per cent during the previous 24-month period compared to an underperformance of Gateway's stock of 92 per cent over the same period. What an investment this has been for shareholders. Those who bought the stock at the time of Dell's IPO will be the proud owners of shares that have outperformed the NASDAQ by 4000 per cent.

The share price outperforms when investment returns grow asynchronously with asset expansion

CEOs must intensify investment to build cutting-edge competitive capability; the problem is that many businesses are locked into a low-growth, diminishing margin business where the downturn of 2001–02 has ravaged corporate balance sheets.

Companies using more conventional, asset-based strategies, where for example they create from scratch new Web-based e-commerce solutions face a double-edged sword. On the one hand, they are using operating models that are exceptionally capital intensive (lower asset turns relative to sales). On the other, they also face the challenge of having to increase the level of investment year-on-year in order to be able to acquire the rapidly evolving IT capabilities that enable them to compete against global competitors. How do they do it? We believe they need to think about innovation in a completely different way if they are serious about delivered transformed businesses that are highly distinct from their competitors and provide compelling reasons for customers to make them their number one choice. Dell, Easyjet, Nokia and Microsoft are examples of companies who have accomplished this to date.

Our research supports our thesis that there is a direct correlation between those companies investing at close to what is sustainable economic rates and those who achieve an outstanding share price performance relative to their peers. We have found this relationship holds true across industry sectors. Table 4.6.4 illustrates how this analysis applies for a number of randomly selected companies.

Nestlé and Unilever have both been investing at 60 and 80 per cent of their relative sustainable rate; correspondingly, their stocks both have outperformed the FTSE and Swiss Index. In contrast, companies investing below the sustainable rate have seen their share price lag. Kellogg and Campbell's have significantly underinvested, shrinking their asset base, and their share prices have underperformed the index by between 20 to 40 per cent. Peter Doyle (2001) commented that '... if companies over-invest in traditional branding activities, they under-invest in other tangible and intangible resources. For example, an under-investment in new technology and lack of genuine innovation appears to have played an important part in the decline of Procter & Gamble and H.J. Heinz' through the late 1990s.

Accenture's research underlines the challenge that CEOs today face. They must find a way to release greater funds to fuel a strategy to

Table 4.6.4
Relationship between asset growth and share price

Company	Average annual actual asset growth (%)	Average sustainable asset growth (%)	% Sustainable investment deployed (%)	Relative share price performance (%)	Ticker
Barr Laboratories Inc	23	17	130	370	BRL
Nokia	31	26	115	198	NOK
SAP	28	23	123	108	SAPG
Pfizer	23	15	153	89	PFE
Novo Nordisk	6	10	65	83	NVOB
General Dynamics Corp	23	26	89	60	GD
Nestlé	6	7	77	44	NESZN
Unilever	8	9	95	18	ULVR
Associated British Foods	−1	1	−104	11	ABF
British American Tobacco	12	12	102	8	BATS
JR Wrigley Co	6	11	60	6	WWY
Rockwell Intl Corp	−16	2	−1003	−4	ROK
Kerry Group	4	4	107	−5	KYGA
General Motors	0	3	−4	−19	GM
HJ Heinz	2	12	20	−23	HNZ
Daimler Crysler	18	2	982	−34	DCXGN
Cooper Industries	−2	9	−19	−41	CBE
South African Breweries	−11	6	−176	−51	SAB
Campbell Soup Co	−7	20	−37	−52	CPB
Kellogg Co	4	9	41	−56	K

Source: CS First Boston Holt, Accenture Analysis, April 2002

build competitive capability, and they must do so in an environment of close share market scrutiny, diminishing operating margins, and relentless competitive pressure. Too many firms are simply playing catch-up. Incremental change is not enough to solve the fundamental problem we are discussing; companies have to outleap their competitors and in the process, change the rules of competition.

Speed of execution

Once CEOs have answered the asset-based strategy question, they face a further difficulty. In the e-business world, corporations have to acquire new IT-enabled capabilities faster than their organization can actually absorb both the technology and the investment. Traditionally, such companies built new capabilities in-house, from scratch. But such an approach simply cannot deliver the necessary pace at which organizations need to acquire these new capabilities. Today it could take three years to get a major enterprise resource planning (ERP)

Traditionally, companies have built new IT capabilities in-house, but this approach cannot deliver the required pace or breadth of capabilities.

system in place and operating effectively. But after such time, effort and resources, the system might only deliver common data; the more sophisticated application systems still needing to be built.

Clearly, the traditional operating model just does not stand up to the task. A study by research firm Metadata (1999) investigated the success of 200 of the largest ERP implementations in the world. Looking at projects that had been fully implemented and operational for at least two years, the study found that 60 per cent of ERP projects resulted in negative net present value (NPV). Clearly, the ERP projects had not delivered on their promise. Peter Burns, senior vice-president and co-research director of *Metadata*, is quoted as saying that:

> implementing ERM/ERP solutions requires an enormous commitment, is an understatement. They are expensive, time consuming and require change in virtually every department in the enterprise. With so much at stake, META Group wanted objective market information. What we found through our broad-reaching study was eye-opening and in some instances, shocking.

This is sobering given the huge commitment corporations make to continually reinventing the application of IT to their businesses.

The other difficulty facing CEOs lies in re-building capability against an ever-shortening half-life of leading-edge technology. The next generation of technology can be developed and a competitor down the road can start installing it before a company has even finished installing the last generation. Clearly, corporations cannot afford to keep upgrading their IT systems in this way. One global resources company spent $100 million putting in an SAP system. As the CEO said, 'we'd just finished the implementation, and then we were being told to upgrade it'. Therein lies the problem of traditional operating models.

Companies continually have to acquire technological capabilities across a broad range of competencies. The problem lies not in whether to acquire the technology, but how to acquire the capability across such a broad spectrum. They have to get a broader range of competencies on a scale they have never encountered before, faster, and they are trying to do this organically, using a delivery model that has already proven to be a failure in 60 per cent of the 200 documented cases analyzed. In reality, many of the capabilities that companies are seeking to build already exist outside their organization. They are trying to re-create assets – a costly exercise consuming scarce investment capital that ultimately destroys shareholder value. Once CEOs start assessing whether to develop a capability internally or to find a strategic partner who is capable of helping them strategically transform themselves they quickly discover the latter option is faster, cheaper and has greater benefits and less risks. In making such a decision, they soon find that creating capability using traditional methods is no longer an option.

New execution model

In investigating how to acquire IT capabilities, CEOs need to consider the issues of speed and scale. Dell Computer created its supply chain model using leading edge IT capabilities in collaboration with Accenture. AT&T, Danone and DuPont have announced long-term strategic business transformation partnerships with Accenture that have similar aims. Such companies excel because they do not approach outsourcing with a narrow view. In too many cases, companies have handed over their systems to external providers through outsourcing without paying attention to how they retain innovation or continuous improvement in the area they outsource. They use business partners that not only help them wring out excess costs, but also grow the business while creating a more efficient asset-based solution. This takes them to the next level of business performance.

Strategic transformation involves a company working in a strategic partnership to reinvent their operating models. In doing so, they can reset the rules of the game in their industry.

Connect 2020 is a prime example. Following privatization, Thames Water, one of the largest UK water utilities, faced the regulatory challenge of a severely regulated price regime and was having to step up to tough targets to improve efficiencies and reduce prices to consumers. Connect 2020 was set up as a procurement and logistics services entity where the best assets and resources from both Thames Water and Accenture were combined to create new capabilities at speed. This resulted in hundreds of millions of pounds sterling being cut from the spend on goods, services and capital. This is a new, collaborative co-sourcing model that is wholly owned by Thames Water, but whose profits are shared with the strategic partner. The benefits are compelling: 11 per cent annual savings, 10 per cent service cost reduction, 40 per cent inventory reduction, 97 per cent customer service levels and a 70 per cent reduction in back orders. Says Les Williams, Senior Finance Manager, 'the co-sourcing arrangement has enabled us to redeploy our scarce resources to competitively critical areas, knowing full well that what we've left with our strategic partner is being run in an extremely professional fashion'.

AT&T Consumer business provides a further example of how collaborative asset powered supply chain models are being used to address every day business challenges. AT&T provides a broad range of communications options to consumers, including transaction-based services such as prepaid phone cards. Over the last few years, AT&T's prepaid card business has grown dramatically – in size as well as complexity. While highly skilled at delivering telecommunications services to customers, AT&T had minimal experience in the supply chain management processes needed to bring tangible, packaged goods such as prepaid cards to channels such as grocery stores, convenience stores and mass merchants. AT&T made a strategic business decision to outsource its prepaid card end-to-end supply chain management functions in an effort to enhance business performance, improve operational efficiency and obtain significant cost savings.

Accenture teamed with AT&T to develop an innovative, customer-focused supply-chain operating model that integrates all supply-side business processes. Next, they created a new organizational role that provides comprehensive management of the entire customer life cycle by assigning responsibility for customer-facing supply chain functions to individuals or small teams, rather than multiple individuals across organizations. This unique, strategic approach was a key step in transforming AT&T PrePaid's supply chain processes from a functional view across many organizations with many hand-offs, to a customer-focused approach that optimizes the end-to-end supply chain. To help accelerate results, warehouse operations were also integrated into the overall solution architecture. By integrating procurement and other decisions that impact the cost of warehouse or other operations across the supply chain, the new service entity reduced costs while supporting increased volumes with improved service levels. Recognizing an opportunity to transform purchasing and inventory decision-making processes and substantially reduce inventory levels and cost, the service entity also initiated a strategic sourcing approach for prepaid card production. Lastly, the two partners worked together to enhance existing and establish new contractual service level targets and to develop methods for tracking, measuring and reporting them.

DuPont is a third example of the new, asset-powered execution model at work. DuPont is an icon in the global chemical industry, with 92 000 employees serving customers in 65 countries. DuPont's IT organization had long been viewed as being highly capable, having successfully supported the company's business objectives while reducing IT costs by 45 per cent in just four years. Yet, IT is not a core business for DuPont, nor did the company want it to be. However executive management recognized the need to accelerate progress in equiping the business with new, IT-enabled capabilities.

Rather than turn IT into a core business, DuPont preferred to focus its attention on the business of science – delivering science-based solutions that make a difference in people's lives in food and nutrition; health care; apparel; home and construction; electronics; and transportation. DuPont's IT organization would need to be flexible enough to support a changing mix of businesses, and sophisticated enough to keep delivering innovative solutions – without adding costs. DuPont began to see the new sourcing model as a way to strategically and effectively move the organization forward towards its ambitious goals.

DuPont decided to take an innovative step and enter into a groundbreaking co-sourcing relationship with Accenture. This 10-year, $4 billion 'alliance partnership', as DuPont calls the relationship, combines the business process management expertise of Accenture with DuPont's chemical leadership to ensure overall IT and business performance success. As part of this growing relationship, about 400 DuPont employees transferred into the new service entity.

Understanding how to bring value through co-sourcing, Accenture is providing proven business solutions that are critical to the support of DuPont's global manufacturing, marketing, distribution and customer-service functions for the chemical business, including management of applications such as:

- materials and resource planning
- order processing
- manufacturing and engineering systems, and
- safety, health and environmental analysis and reporting.

The alliance partnership is proving to be a smart move for DuPont. The company is reaping increased variability in spending, greater flexibility in responding to business needs, and access to diversified state-of-the-art business solutions, methods, skills and techniques. 'On-demand' IT support is available, allowing DuPont to bring on new businesses quickly, or to get out of a market without being left with the residual costs of an IT infrastructure that is no longer tied to a business. Furthermore, the alliance partnership has improved DuPont's ability to stay on top of evolving technology and a changing business environment. Through the partnership, DuPont is confident that its own technology will not only keep pace with the company's growth and changes, but will also speed up the creation of new systems while reducing IT costs.

Market leaders are thus developing innovative arrangements to build capability externally while also re-inventing their own business models. Through the use of traditional outsourcing arrangements, companies were primarily motivated by the need to simply deliver better service at lower cost. Strategic transformation on the other hand involves a company working in a strategic co-sourcing partnership with a higher order ambition of wholesale reinvention of their historic, vertically integrated operating model to a virtual business design where the very best assets and resources are combined with a partner to create a service entity that creates value greater than either party could do alone. In doing this, they reset the rules of the game in their industry leapfrog their competition; and deliver growing investment returns from expanding assets resulting in share price outperformance.

These new operating models are created through a joint venture company owned equally by a company and its strategic partner. The company only has one customer, the client. Unlike normal third party service arrangements such as traditional outsourcing, where work is often awarded competitively and monitoring is sometimes conducted in an adversarial way, the joint service entity is based on successful partnering and a new, stand-alone dedicated services company. The co-owned, co-directed management structure creates ongoing emotional

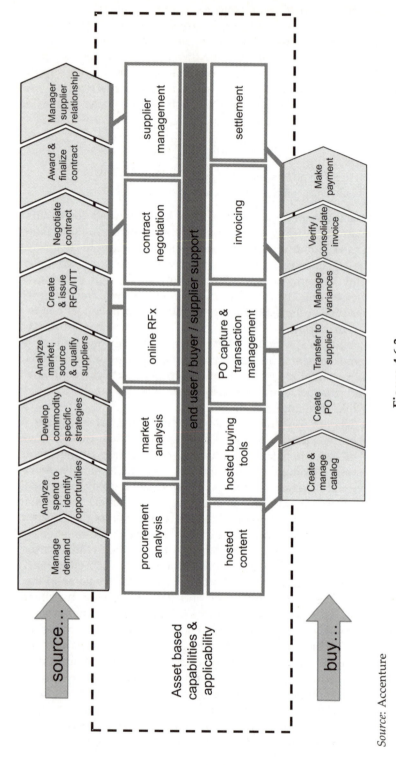

Figure 4.6.3
Web-based procurement, from requisitioning to settlement

Source: Accenture

514

and financial interest in the venture, so that both parties have a greater stake in its success.

It uses a co-governance model to ensure that there is continual alignment to the strategic imperatives of the client organization. The governance model is flexible, adapting to the changing needs of the client and provides for a formal management structure and process that enables the service entity to be managed at the strategic, tactical, and operational levels with management positions shared between the two parties and alignment to the critical success factors for the organization. Unlike traditional outsourcing where services are provided via rigid contracts, the joint service entity deploys a far more flexible service arrangement where both the client and the startegic partner are incentivized to continually extend competitive capabilities with elevated performance and service levels as prime motivations.

The benefit for the CEO is that he or she gains a world-class execution capability from the provider partner, without the complexity of trying to create and maintain the capability in-house. The arrangement is far more flexible and far more aligned to the business's corporate strategy. This is what we call a network-of-businesses capital-asset model. This is somewhat different to the conventional notion of a joint venture in that the joint service entity model has an exclusive service focus on a single client where the aim is to truly transform the competitive positioning of the client organization.

To illustrate the power of this, consider the area of procurement. Many executives consider procurement to be simply negotiating with suppliers, placing an order and waiting for the goods to arrive. It is far more complex than that, particularly if CEOs want to access dramatic cost savings and efficiency gains of up to 40 per cent in their organization. Corporations such as Sara Lee, General Electric and Thames Water have moved swiftly into Web-based procurement where the end-to-end process of requisitioning to financial settlement has been digitized. They have collaborated with Accenture to take advantage of the existing 'plug and play' assets being used to lower the total cost of ownership of these solutions. An example of this is illustrated in Figure 4.6.3.

One of the powerful attractions of strategic transformation is its potential to reinvent even so-called mature industry models. Figure 4.6.4 shows the position of different companies and industries at different stages of their growth life cycles; with returns on investment anywhere between high and discount. Ryanair in air transportation and Centrica in the energy business are good examples of companies in mature industries that have reinvented themselves, with dramatic results.

Nestlé and Ocean Spray are further examples that demonstrate the power and far-reaching competitive effect of adopting this new, network-based asset model. Announced in January 2002, the two companies have formed a collaborative supply chain services company in North America that brings together the best combination of assets

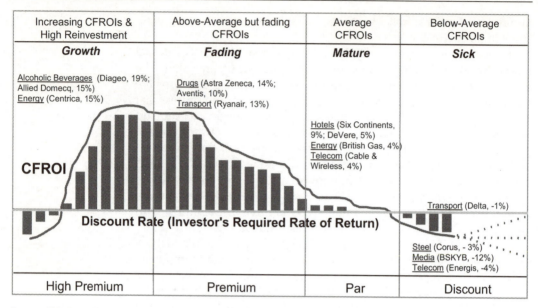

Increasing CFROIs & High Reinvestment	Above-Average but fading CFROIs	Average CFROIs	Below-Average CFROIs
Growth	*Fading*	*Mature*	*Sick*

Alcoholic Beverages (Diageo, 19%; Allied Domecq, 15%) Energy (Centrica, 15%)

Drugs (Astra Zeneca, 14%; Aventis, 10%) Transport (Ryanair, 13%)

Hotels (Six Continents, 9%; DeVere, 5%) Energy (British Gas, 4%) Telecom (Cable & Wireless, 4%)

CFROI

Discount Rate (Investor's Required Rate of Return)

Transport (Delta, -1%)

Steel (Corus, - 3%) Media (BSKYB, -12%) Telecom (Energis, -4%)

High Premium	Premium	Par	Discount

Source: CS First Boston Holt, Accenture Analysis, April 2002

Figure 4.6.4
Cash flow ROI and the industry life cycle

and resources from both companies. The press release announcing the venture included a compeling statement that demonstrates why the world's leading food company entered into such an arrangement – 'both businesses find value in each partner's assets, we send the best people to run the joint service company and we stay vigilant as to how to improve the partnership on an ongoing basis'.

Case study 1 – Asian food company
Figure 4.6.5 (below) illustrates the main differences in the business case contrasting a digital procurement solution hosted in-house and a solution provided through a joint service company (JSC) execution model. The JSC provides the client company with greater scale, reach and depth of efficiency that are five to one better than the company could achieve on its own. It achieved a $1 billion incremental stream of margins compared to a baseline trading profit of $2.6 billion. Translated into shareholder value this adds more than $5 billion to the market capitalization of the group company. This provides dramatic evidence that the strategic transformation of supply chain management has arrived.

Case study 2 – J. Sainsbury
Figure 4.6.6 (below) illustrates the difficulties faced by leading UK grocery retailer J. Sainsbury when it found that Tesco had overtaken its

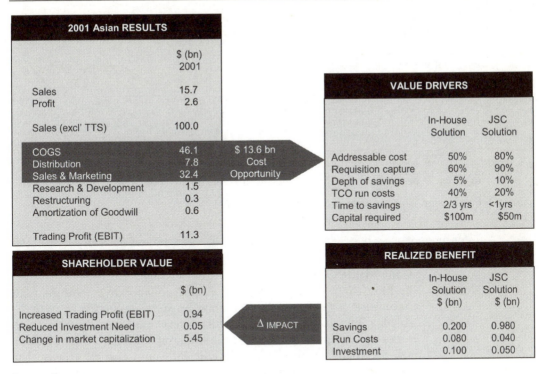

Figure 4.6.5
Benefits of using a joint service company execution model

premier market position. By 1998, revenue growth had stalled, under-lying profitability was static, investment in the business was being squeezed and the share price had declined substantially, leading to the appointment of Sir Peter Davies as CEO in March 2000. Sir Peter quickly concluded that J. Sainsbury needed to transform itself strategically. The company embarked upon an accelerated program of investment in IT-enabled leading-edge capabilities, together with storefront and service innovation aimed at creating an exciting shopping experience for the consumer.

This ambitious program is being executed at a pace leading to the creation of substantial shareholder value and a share price performance that has outperformed the FTSE All Share Index. The company has strategically refreshed its operating model out of the fading/mature stage of the cash flow return-on-investment life cycle, (see Figure 4.6.6 below), to an exciting phase where returns are increasing on the back of asset-efficient, margin-rich, top-line growth. J. Sainsbury has restored its profitability, recaptured its number one position in grocery retailing in the UK, and increased revenue growth as a result of gains in market share.

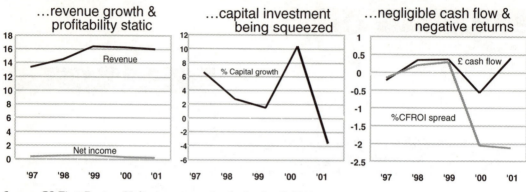

Source: CS First Boston Holt, Accenture Analysis, April 2002

Figure 4.6.6
Interdependencies between revenue growth, investment and cash flow

Case study 3 – eBay

In May, 2002 eBay announced a new collaborative venture with Accenture that connects its 46 million consumers who use eBay to the surplus inventories of US manufacturers and retailers. The new service is designed to help retailers, manufacturers and distributors sell merchandise on eBay more efficiently and cost-effectively. The new service, called 'Connection to eBay' combines eBay's marketplace of nearly 46 million registered users with Accenture's technology and management services and technology assets. The new service, which will be owned and operated by Accenture, allows sellers to tap into a wide range of enhanced tools and services including sales strategies, high-volume listing capabilities, customer service and support, checkout, payment and fulfilment processes.

'Connection to eBay' will expand the eBay trading platform by offering buyers a greater choice of merchandise while presenting new distribution options for businesses looking to sell excess inventory. Research reveals that US businesses process nearly $80 billion in excess or 'end-of-life' inventory. But selling this inventory is inefficient, often involving multiple distribution points, intermediaries and numerous physical and transactional steps.

> '"Connection to eBay" creates a new alternative to cumbersome and costly liquidation channels for companies to achieve a greater return by selling inventory through eBay's efficient marketplace. The asset based solution provides scalable tools and services that help companies tightly integrate their business within the eBay platform allowing them to more quickly reach eBay's extensive online commerce community.'

The two companies conducted extensive market research and field trials and found that merchants often earn up to twice as much, and sometimes more on each transaction, by selling on eBay as compared to traditional liquidation channels.

Conclusion

The thousands of companies around the world that are using traditional business operating models are failing to equip themselves properly for the increasingly intense battle to deliver attractive shareholder returns. Their excessive consumption of capital is not beating the cost of providing that capital, cash margins are inadequate and in many cases, there is a shortfall in revenue growth rates. They are under-realizing their IT productivity potential and are also unable to develop new IT-enabled capabilities at speed. In short, competitiveness is flagging and their share prices are underperforming their smarter competitors. Incremental change cannot address these structural deficiencies. Companies need to achieve scale, speed and new capabilities that they are unable to acquire on their own.

Companies that undertake strategic transformation gain immediate access to scalable, proven solutions that can accelerate a turnaround in corporate performance.

The new generation of operating models discussed in this chapter is characterized by being:

- value led, underpinned by continual growth in investment returns and share price outperformance
- asset powered, underpinned by the re-investment of growing surplus cash flow and ready availability of investment funds
- part of a network or constellation of leading-edge businesses that lowers start-up costs and minimises ongoing operational costs
- co-owned, co-directed joint service entities
- possessing cutting-edge competitive capabilities
- delivered at speed
- transformational in terms of market leadership and a change in the rules of the game.

Under transformed operating models, assets and resources distributed across the value chain are no longer hosted inside the client organization, but are reconfigured and redeployed within a broader network created with a strategic partner. By following such a path, companies gain immediate access to scalable, proven solutions that can accelerate a turnaround in corporate performance. CEOs that fundamentally re-structure their operating models through strategic partnerships are re-writing the rules of their industry play and delivering high returns for their shareholders. This is the reality of the post-Enron era.

References

Doyle P (2001), 'Shareholder-value-based brand strategies', *Brand Management*, Vol. 9, No. 1, September, Henry Stewart Publishing.

Wilderman, B. (1999), 'ERM Solutions and their Value', Meta Group, April, www.metagroup.com.

Part 5
Regional and Global Supply Chains

Here we introduce relevant aspects of regionalization and globalization as they impact on supply chains. Chapter 5.1, 'Globalization and regionalization of supply chains', introduces a general framework to evaluate the alternative positioning of global, regional, and local supply chains. As physical, informational and financial aspects of infrastructure continue to drive comparative cost advantages, an understanding of individual strengths enables companies to take a distinct position in their respective supply chain environments. Factors that go beyond the usual operational issues need to be considered; these include political, legal and regulatory drivers as well as business cultures and variations in leadership styles.

Chapter 5.2, 'Supply chains in Europe', extends the discussion and provides concrete examples of how European supply chains are growing as new consumer markets emerge and cross-border trade and investment develops at pace. In Europe, the formation of a single currency and a unified market have accelerated competitive pressures across the Continent. This in turn has led to the requirement for pan-European order taking and processing at centralized customer care facilities.

Chapter 5.3, 'Supply chains in Asia – challenges and opportunities', examines the peculiarities of supply chains in Asia. Supply chains are often imprisoned by Asia's diversity in language, culture, infrastructure, tax regimes and customs regulations. Companies doing business in Asia also need to be aware of the gaps in supply chain performance across the region. Business practices place pressures on supply chains in this region as well, and demand responsive, agile and low-cost behaviors. Indeed, many businesses now believe that the 'sweet spot' for cost reduction in Asia lies within logistics and the supply chain.

The importance of supply chain management becomes especially evident in the case of China, as discussed in the Chapter 5.4, 'The changing face of supply chains in China'. Significant differences exist between metropolitan and rural areas. Underdeveloped infrastructures create major operational challenges, and much effort is needed to improve overall logistics operational performance.

Globalization and regionalization of supply chains 5.1

Robert Ogulin

In today's globalized world, supply chain management is emerging as one of the keys to generating value and contributing to a company's bottom line. Virtually all companies are now part of more or less complex supply chains spanning multiple countries, regions and continents. They interact, transact and collaborate on activities ranging from product development to the delivery of products to customers. In such environments it becomes important that supply chain partners understand their individual strengths and sources of value creation. This enables a clear positioning of supply chain partners on global, regional and local playing fields.

In a strategic sense companies – large and small, local and multinational – need to secure competitive advantages from their supply chains to ensure sufficient revenues and profits individually, as well as for the entire supply chain. Companies that understand the relevant structures and drivers as well as their core competencies and distinctive strengths will be better able to carve out their position.

On tactical and execution levels, companies bring to bear their capabilities. These are based on process excellence, technology sophistication and management skills. The degree to which companies can – or want to – combine their existing capabilities to collaborate with their international business partners will vary. This means, companies will need to know about and take advantage of their distinct supply chain management capabilities to 'play' successfully in the supply chain game of the future.

Organizationally, companies need to learn to trust their business partners in the supply chain and to build enduring partnerships. For companies used to regarding other enterprises in a combative fashion, this can involve a substantial cultural hurdle. The hurdle is even higher when strategic and operational challenges are applied

Understanding individual strengths enables companies to take a distinct position in local, regional and global supply chains.

globally. Interpretations of what constitutes 'partnership' differ throughout the world hence appropriate management responses are needed.

The following chapter introduces the underlying context and starts with the structures and drivers for local, regional and global supply chain management. A framework is used to structure the analysis and to provide the reference for determining a company's position on the global supply chain 'playing field'. Based on this, we discuss different ways of extracting value out of the supply chain from positioning along a capability and global reach continuum.

The chapter also introduces the discussion of rationalization and globalization in the supply chain. Subsequent chapters will further discuss the peculiarities of supply chain management in different regions of the world

Positioning in local, regional and global supply chains

An understanding of country and region-specific supply chain drivers is critical, regardless of whether the company is a multinational purchasing from Asian countries or a European firm selling to North American partners. Companies wishing to operate beyond their home bases will need to analyse the different factors that create complexity and drive supply chains in different regions, even if they are highly uncertain and difficult to predict.

The degree, to which a company can then internalize or respond to global and regional drivers in combination with its supply chain capabilities will eventually determine its position and ultimately its ability to achieve competitive performance. Figure 5.1.1 provides a framework for categorizing players in the global supply chain arena. As with any other frameworks, it does not intend to prescribe a course of action, but rather help the supply chain practitioner think through the implications and alternatives ahead of appropriate responses. The categories that define the two dimensions in this framework are 'degree of supply chain capability' and 'reach into global supply chains'.

Supply chain capabilities

Previous chapters in this book have addressed the importance of supply chain capabilities in terms of operational excellence, integration and collaboration and synchronizing through new business models. For companies, the significance of capabilities in a local versus regional and global context is to analyze capabilities relative to other companies in their industry.

Capabilities are the link between a company's strategic intent and the needs of the customers served. Hence, a company that knows its

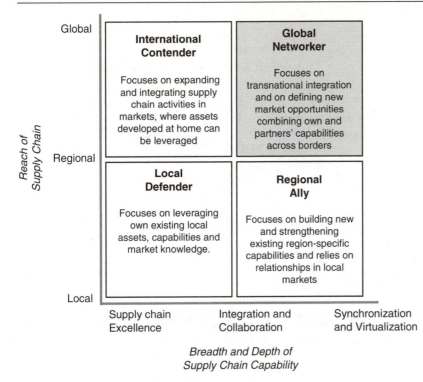

Figure 5.1.1
Local, regional and global supply chain plays

particular breadth and depth of supply chain capabilities will be able to determine where they can best create value and sustain competitive advantage, and where the constraints are.

The extended view of the supply chain (Figure 5.1.2) represents the focus companies should have when they compete at local, regional and global levels. Implementing the appropriate supply chain capabilities according to a chosen strategy is the key to success. And, excellence in the execution of it will make it hard for competitors to imitate.

On the dimension 'supply chain capabilities,' a company would consider:

- Continuously striving to improve existing capabilities peculiar to its markets. This includes a focus on understanding market requirements and the ability to respond to these demands.
- Integration of, and collaboration with, supply chain partners across core processes allows companies and their partners to extract greater value from superior service to its customers.
- Advanced business models allow exploitation of new value creating opportunities through synchronized network capabilities and virtualization of supply chain operations.

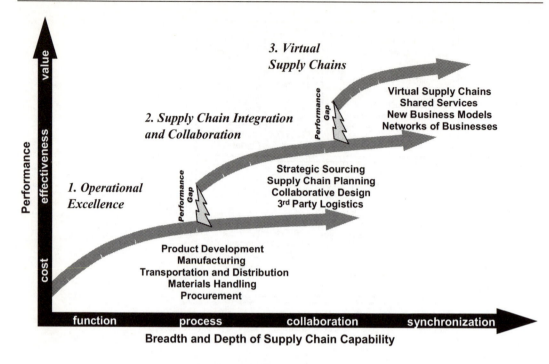

Figure 5.1.2
The supply chain management performance/capability continuum

The dimension of 'local, regional and global reach' shows how successful supply chain management will require new abilities, either to fend off new entrants or to realize opportunities through international expansion.

Local, regional and global reach of supply chains

This second dimension includes aspects that are to a large extent out of the control of the company itself. They are the underlying structures and environments within which the company defines its strategies and conducts business. Supply chain performance here will be determined by such factors as

- political, legal and regulatory drivers (that is, export/import regulations, taxation)
- physical (that is, roads, harbors), information and communication infrastructures (that is, access to the Internet, spread of mobile communication technologies)
- industry-wide developments and trends, and
- business cultures.

Political, legal and regulatory drivers

Competing successfully through global supply chains requires the awareness and support of public policy makers. Impediments to foreign ownership, imports and exports, for instance, will slow the adoption of advanced business practices by individual companies, potentially slowing down the country's economic and business development. In contrast, nations with low barriers to trade, stable currencies, and flexible capital markets provide hospitable environments for business and will encourage economic growth.

A liberal and forward-looking political, legal and regulatory environment enables companies to better integrate into global supply chains.

With increasingly globalized trade and technology, regulators in less-developed countries need to speed up the liberalization process in their markets. For example in India and Indonesia, the liberalization of the telecommunications sector has been slow and has hindered the uptake of new business models. These behaviors reflect the fact that some countries place more importance on controlling their network infrastructures rather than seeking to realize the economic opportunities that can flow from liberalization and internationalization (Poon, 2001).

Other governments promote local development initiatives through a range of incentives to attract foreign direct investment, such as subsidies, tax relief, access to capital and policies for foreign ownership. The Singapore Government introduced a program called the 'Content Hosting Scheme' to attract international companies to set up facilities for product development, which put Singapore at the center of many regional supply chains, for example in the electronics and high technology industry.

Regional free-trade zones such as NAFTA, ASEAN and MERCO-SUR increasingly have collaboration on their agendas and have started removing barriers between member countries. Of course, free trade agreements and falling customs duties are accelerating globalization. However, international logistics remains a challenge. For example, many purchasing managers insist that all purchase orders, sales contracts, and invoices be quoted only in US dollars to avoid the trouble and risks of currency exchange. Subsequent chapters on European and Asian supply chains will provide further insight into these issues.

Infrastructure drivers

As the majority of international trade continues to be based on comparative cost advantages, it will be crucial for countries and companies not to fall behind in the adoption of new technology and associated processes. Countries that have traditionally relied on low-cost labor to attract trade will see their competitive advantage diminish if they do not also adopt new technology to generate value beyond cost savings and efficiencies. Technology infrastructure is one of the main drivers for supply chain participation and value creation and the stakeholders increasingly recognize the opportunities of the Internet as a 'space shrinking technology'.

Physical, informational and financial aspects of infrastructure drive comparative cost advantages in supply chains.

Regions and nations will not have the same technology adoption rates and timeframes. Government and regulatory bodies provide incentives or disincentives for local and international businesses to build and operate advanced solutions, for example e-commerce based models, in their countries. In China, for example, the lack of infrastructure sophistication and skilled resources means that solutions for the emerging new supply chain business models might not be as quickly deployed as elsewhere in the region (EIU, 2001).

Korea is an example of an early adopter in the Asian region, where private and public stakeholders have coordinated their efforts to achieve e-commerce readiness. Significant investments in broadband have given Korea a comparatively sophisticated infrastructure. The Korean Government initiated strategies to increase the use of e-commerce in industries such as electronics, automobiles, ship building, steel, machinery and textiles (*Korea Times*, 2001). While the Korean approach might not be applicable in all cases, it illustrates that countries cannot remain complacent if they do not want to be left behind.

Bureaucracy and uncertainty about the allocation of development funds can set the precedence for other companies operating in the country. Recent research (Pike, et al., 2000) into manufacturing in China found that 'the central government focuses its support and supervision on 1,000 of the largest enterprises', with a substantial portion of new bank lending in 1996 going to 300 large enterprises selected as the 'best performers'. Funds and resources are hence concentrated on selected enterprises. This will no doubt accelerate the uptake of supply chain capabilities in China, especially for larger conglomerates and state-owned enterprises. They will be able to run or participate in new business models, and to create enough scale and throughput for a sustainable business. On the other hand, small and medium-sized companies might be left out in the short term.

In Mexico, distribution systems are still inefficient because of 'structural factors, such as inter-provincial and inter-ministerial relationships, the level of relatedness between industries, inefficient administration procedures and overlaps in the roles and functions of different administrative organizations' (Dawar and Frost, 1999).

Industry drivers

Industries are increasingly global and scale drives developments in the supply chain.

Different influencing factors can be observed at industry level. Certain vertical industries are often early adopters of global supply chain practices, while others are followers. Presently, the most sophisticated and most globally oriented supply chains fall into three vertical industries: the high-technology/electronics industry, the automotive industry, and the retail/consumer packaged goods (CPG) industry. As a result, these industries are on the cutting edge of global supply chain management. They are also the early adopters of advanced information systems in global logistics.

Multinational corporations in these industries have realized above average benefits through the extension of advanced supply chain capabilities on a global level. These companies have successfully established networks of virtually synchronized global supply chains by outsourcing manufacturing and assembly work to overseas contract manufacturers. They retain only the core design, development and marketing functions at headquarters. In a similar fashion multinational corporations in the retail/CPG industry import a large portion of their merchandise from global sources for distribution in their home markets.

These industries will be the testers and co-developers of advanced global supply chain systems. Others will follow their lead, adopting and customizing the systems to suit the demands of their own vertical industries.

The above examples show that supply chain leaders identify key success drivers and turn them into an advantage. For example, as global companies are aggressively seeking to gain operational efficiencies and identify new profit opportunities, they will also try to dictate standards and rules of business.

Nike's multi-echelon supply chain partners in several Asian countries manufacture apparel that needs to be coordinated and delivered globally. Nike will lead growth and supply chain innovation in these countries because each country will continue to strive for better integration and synchronization of global product and supply flows. Global firms such as Nike will leverage the Internet to streamline processes and move significant portions of their trade transactions and information online to achieve further efficiencies. Such moves will result in networked commerce solutions being built, in which firms will form relationships, share information, set standards of communication that will tie them together and leave others outside.

Business culture impacting supply chains

All companies part of a multinational supply chain need to accept that business rules and practices differ by country. The implementation of effective global and regional supply chain architectures needs to consider business cultures, organizational change constraints and leadership styles that empower a diverse workforce.

Companies in Asia need to manage the fact that many business relationships depend on personal networks. Rather than ignoring this difference, success is more likely when companies address the cultural barriers appropriately. For instance, *guanxi* agreements in China are made face-to-face between parties who know each other and rely on informal rather than contractual relationships. On the one hand, this emphasis on personal relationships might be a barrier to the uptake of new business models that are technology heavy. Internet-based solutions include standardized processes and business

Business cultures and large differences in leadership styles continue to be a challenge for implementing integrated and collaborative global supply chains.

rules, reducing the opportunity for personal negotiations and practices.

However, Internet technology can provide a pervasive communication medium to strengthen collaboration and enhance understanding between trading partners around the world. Internet-enabled collaboration will not replace traditional face-to-face deals, but companies will need to adjust to new global business standards in the supply chain. In addition, such an environment may offer highly valuable opportunities for knowledge exchange and organizational learning, which increases the likelihood of companies in the region to upgrade their capabilities, faster.

Business boundaries are becoming permeable and communities are converging across organizations, regions and industries. Electronic commerce and communication transcends time, geography and culture. This creates new challenges for many leaders. Building networks is a matter of organizational design, and involves issues such as alliance structure, roles, performance measures and integrating mechanisms. The design work needs to take place at three levels: across the network, within individual organizations, and between work units. Organizational culture affects how people perceive what they do and how they behave. New business models in the supply chain should consider support tools such as frequently asked questions and Intranets to enable the communication of information. Communication is a major way to build readiness and support for change and helps to defuse resistance, including culturally based resistance.

The implementation of supply chains and the establishment of organizational goals must be linked to performance. Performance measurement involves assessing the extent to which organizational activities are moving the organization closer to its goals. Performance measures need to be understood and accepted by all participants within and across the supply chain. Departments or business partners that try to maximize their individual performance will inevitably jeopardize the outcome for the entire network. In this respect, it is critical for all participants to design a performance measurement system that reinforces desired behaviors.

Many organizations often regard global supply chain implementations as a technology driven exercise and hence delegate leadership to a senior IT manager or chief information officer. Others see the setting up of collaborative business models as a new trading platform and therefore a significant driver of financial performance. These companies get their senior executives from finance or operations to take the lead on achieving a return on investment. This yields short-term results, that is, through e-procurement or the reduction of back-office costs to create long-term advantages.

Extracting value in a global supply chain context

Local contenders

'Local contenders' represent the most basic supply chain strategy. These companies focus on sustaining competitive advantage in their home markets by concentrating on excellence in selected capabilities. Many conglomerate models, particularly throughout Asia, grew on a strategy of serving very specific local market needs and exporting only on an opportunistic basis. Some commodity products that are specific to the customer needs in a particular country or region might lend themselves to such a strategy. Foreign challengers could not break into the markets because of idiosyncrasies in market demands (that is, languages and tastes) or availability of resources. Many niche markets of that nature remain in regions around the world.

In Mexico, Grupo Industrial Bimbo is the largest producer of bread. They leverage their local knowledge of buying behaviors (most Mexicans buy their bread in small 'mom-and-pop' type corner stores) and an extensive local distribution network to fend off foreign competition. They have established an extensive network of 14 000 drivers to make 420 000 deliveries of bread daily to 350 000 clients. This supply chain strategy is focused on deepening local skills and execution for sustaining competitive advantage.

A strategy of local focus that works well for some companies today might have some significant limitations for the future. Any advantages based on highly idiosyncratic practices and cultures are at risk of being eroded over time when economies open up and become more global. In many countries, for example in South America and emerging economies in Eastern Europe, both private and state-owned corporations were often able to hide operational inefficiencies such as overstaffing, low profitability and low productivity shielded by cultural and protectionist barriers. Now, political, economic and cultural barriers have been lifted to expose the inefficiencies of those companies.

Regional ally

Chaebols in Korea, family-owned conglomerates in Indonesia and Malaysia and state-owned enterprises in Latin America share certain common characteristics such as a concentration of power and wealth, advantages of scale and scope, strong ties to regulatory bodies and governments, and long-term relationships with customers, suppliers and service providers. Undoubtedly these strengths build a basis for the creation of advanced local and regional networks, even when supply chain capabilities are not considered. Once the companies begin to expand their relationships into networks, for example foreign business partners and supply chain services providers, they will have the opportunity to thrive.

Supply chain service providers, for example international freight forwarders and trading houses, have been highly instrumental in facilitating international trade. International trade processing puts a heavy burden on multinational corporations and local partners through simple challenges like maintaining the accuracy of all transactions. For example, it is important, even required by trade laws, to maintain detailed and accurate customs records. All companies must be able to demonstrate, through historical records, their compliance with any country's rules and regulations. The impact of failing to do so could lead to fines, export/import restrictions or other penalties.

Regional freight forwarders will leverage their physical fulfilment facilities, established customer base and operating experience. In 1994 Tesco, a European retail giant, had the opportunity to purchase a stake in Global, a troubled Hungarian grocery retailer. Assessing an engagement in Hungary, Tesco managers saw a very different retail picture than existed at home. But, in the region generally, they also saw the kind of growth prospects Tesco was seeking. Central Europe had a newly affluent population that was clearly open to fresh shopping experiences. The region only had a few large domestic retailers, leaving the field wide open to foreign competitors. In the same year, Tesco purchased a significant stake in Global. The next year, the retailer moved into Hungary in full force, then followed quickly with stores in Poland, the Czech Republic and Slovakia.

Tesco was opting for a strategy of depth – leveraging existing capabilities in contiguous countries – rather than the global breadth other retailers have sought. By forming clusters of shared costs, Tesco built regional economies of scale. Geographic proximity maximizes efficiency by enabling stores to share resources, even if they don't operate in the same country. Tesco stores in Slovakia and the Czech Republic, for instance, import up to one-third of their products from each other.

Another example are trading houses taking advantage of the relationships, for example, Hong Kong based Li & Fung. The company has started to connect with new business models, i.e., e-marketplaces in the Asian region, and potentially can act as a partner, adopting a critical role in order fulfilment. When business-to-business online exchanges first emerged, Li & Fung took the opportunity to become involved early. Instead of competing with e-marketplaces, Li & Fung collaborated with them. They provide an interface that enabled companies to access Li & Fung's offerings for sourcing, trading and distributing diverse products throughout the Asia–Pacific region. Li & Fung leveraged its large established customer base and successfully shifted the power to its own advantage. Li & Fung also leveraged its network and became the regional fulfilment house for exchanges.

International contender

Many companies will seek to leverage their own existing assets abroad. They do not focus on building regional or global alliances, but rather want to excel in a similar international market in 'what they are doing best'. This strategy is feasible if products and/or capabilities are easily transferable to other countries. In many cases this will mean that companies need to find particular niches in the market where they are immune against the size and power of larger multinational competitors. With regard to appropriately leveraging local competencies a company might choose to concentrate on a selected aspect of the supply chain, for example access and knowledge of regional distribution.

The integration of global supply chains fosters specialization of capabilities that can be leveraged internationally. Differentiating capabilities like development of succinct brands generates enormous scale effects, for example the cost of creating world-class drugs, software, movies and the like varies little with volume, and companies like Pfizer capitalize on this fact.

Cemex, Mexico is another example of a company that expanded into international markets and kept the focus on their core competencies (Dawar and Frost, 1999). Cemex, expanded into the Spanish market focusing on two core supply chain competencies: the combination of its logistics network capabilities and its advanced information systems for scheduling and routing cement trucks to construction sites. Cemex has become one of the low-cost producers of cement. And instead of becoming a take-over target for other giants in the construction industry, Cemex has itself acquired companies in its industries and is focusing on continuously strengthening its position.

Global networker

'Global networkers' characterize organizations (companies and groups or networks of organizations) that successfully manage capabilities in both dimensions, 'supply chain capability' and 'reach into global supply chains'. Organizations operating as global networkers extend their involvement into global supply chains and use their influence to dominate.

Companies extending into global supply chains leverage their assets and capabilities (that is, skills and resources) and seek to achieve scale to improve the utilization of their operation. In doing so they identify supply chain inefficiencies, that is, deliver products and services faster than local competitors and find advanced collaborative solutions. In many cases this might mean partnering with local service providers. The benefits are best achieved in integrated supply chains, where all interdependencies between the supply chain players are understood, integrated and optimized for the whole network.

The players in integrated multinational supply chains assume different roles. In supply chains that produce and sell labor-intensive goods, as is the case with apparel, local firms, manufacturers and contract manufacturers, assume the ownership of manufacturing processes. Large retailers, logistics services providers and trading houses take ownership of information and financial flows because they are able to manage the complexities of multi-level flows.

Originally, low labor costs were offset by long lead times. Ongoing pressures to eliminate supply chain cost and at the same time increase the speed of responsiveness means this is no longer acceptable. In agile supply chains this trade-off can be reduced and value creation increased. New Internet-based business models and supply chains that are complemented by advanced optimization tools and electronic marketplaces promise tighter integration and more value extraction for all global supply chain partners.

Global companies adapt their supply chain approaches to succeed with local, regional and global partners. In many emerging markets, the desirable supply chain assets and distribution systems are managed by only a handful of attractive partners. Getting access to those and including them into the network will provide a barrier for other competitors to liaise with the same supply chain partners. 'Global network extenders' take a joint approach to building not only their own but also network partners' capabilities.

Leading 'global networkers' in other industries have shown how to enter partnerships without losing control of the business. Starbucks, for example, extends its reach at home and abroad through alliances with United Airlines, Barnes & Noble, and other partners. Internet companies – amazon.com, for instance – build alliances with companies like LiveBid, Drugstore.com, and HomeGrocer.com to get leads, enhance their distribution systems and build brand equity in new markets.

Coca-Cola (Ashwin et al., 1997) is another example: because it expanded geographically and invested in customer access through a number of channels, it continues to accumulate advantages of scale and capability. The company now claims a significant lead in market share for the global soft drinks market, has superior operational performance (that is, comparably lower costs-of-goods-sold and selling, general and administrative expenses than its competitors) and specializes in the less asset-intensive parts of the value chain – in fact, it is transforming into managing supply chain information. This strategy permits the company to deepen its expertise in areas such as product development and branding. In 1999 Coca-Cola launched an intensive effort to penetrate southern and eastern China (see also Chapter 5.4.). After surveying local retailers the company approached local independent wholesalers to work with them. Coca-Cola offers training and management assistance to its wholesalers, and maintains control over order management and inventory. By 2001 Coca-Cola had enlisted a large percentage of its wholesalers in its program.

Consortia of industry players and software services providers have set up advanced business models in the supply chain. Commerce One and SAP, for example, together with General Motors were involved in building one of the biggest global industry-led public exchanges for the procurement of automotive parts (Covisint). More sophisticated marketplaces offer collaborative e-commerce technology that encompasses tools and features that allow enterprises to better optimize their supply chains across multiple players. The underlying idea is to allow trading partners to globally communicate in real time, so as to react quickly to each other's demand and schedules.

Supply chain technology vendors and consultants are 'global networkers' themselves and often play an important role in globalization of companies and entire industries. Being global, they must develop their products to cater to local requirements. The obvious ways to customize are translations into local language, multi-currency capabilities and cross-border trading functionality. However, other more complex customizations might be necessary to include local business rules into the core functionality, that is, the division of supply chain activities across multiple partners including trading houses.

An example is SAP, the German global leader in the provision of ERP software. It started in 1972 with a few people. In 1997 it was operating in over 50 countries; SAP made pretax profits approaching US$ 1 billion, with the majority of sales generated abroad. SAP has been known to invest a comparatively high percentage of its profits in research and development – a testimonial to its belief in the value of intangible capital. In this way, SAP continues to leverage its specialty into international markets. Because the company's brand is perceived as one of the industry's best, SAP is often the supplier of choice. It thereby benefits from enormous advantages of scale and can invest its savings in efforts to sustain its competitive edge.

Conclusion

The ability of an enterprise to survive and succeed in today's turbulent international environment depends on its ability to find the appropriate position in local, regional and global supply chains. Traditionally, the world has been split into countries with supply chain partners that provided labor-intensive production resources and countries with companies that could deploy advanced capital-intensive assets.

However, in a globalized world, the supply chain takes on new complexities and the degrees of freedom for supply chain partners have shifted. Now it's up to the individual to determine how to best fit supply chain capabilities and supply chain positioning strategy. By adopting advanced technology-enabled capabilities and integrating into global processes they can become global networkers. There is nothing wrong, however, in continuing to concentrate on serving local markets in superior ways.

References

Accenture (2001), 'The Evolving Role of Executive Leadership', Institute for Strategic Change.

Ashwin et al. (1997), 'Emerging market alliances: Must they be win-lose?', *The McKinsey Quarterly*, (no. 4), pp. 120–137.

Dawar, N. and Frost, T. (1999), 'Competing with Giants – survival strategies for local companies in emerging markets', *Harvard Business Review* (March–April).

EIU Research Report (2001), 'Beyond the Bamboo Network – Successful strategies for change in Asia', London: www.eiu.com.

Gerreffi, G. (1999), 'International trade and international upgrading in the apparel commodity chain', *Journal of International Economics*, vol. 48 (no. 1), p. 37.

Ghoshal, S. (1993), 'Horses for Courses: Organizational Forms for Multinational Corporations', *Sloan Management Review* (Winter).

Ghoshal, S. (1987), 'Global Strategy: An Organizing Framework', *Strategic Management Journal*, vol. 8, pp. 425–440.

Hemerling, J., Entwistle, L., Wetenhall, P. and Desmarais, S. (2001), 'Arming for e-combat in Asia pacific: the new rules of engagement', The Boston Consulting Group (February), www.bcg.com.

Korea Times (2001), 30 April 'Government's five strategic for B2B'.

Pike, D. et al. (2000), 'Manufacturing and Supply Chain Management in China', Working Paper, Tuck School of Business, Dartmouth College and The University of Auckland (June).

Poon, A. (2001), Yankee Group, Asia–Pacific regulatory update: part 2 (Feb.): <www.yankeegroup.com>

Porter, M. E. (1990), 'The Competitive Advantage of Nations', New York: Free Press.

Prahalad, C. K. and Hamel, G. (1990), 'The Core Competence of the Corporation', *Harvard Business Review* (May–June).

Supply chains in Europe

5.2

Jaume Ferrer

With the creation of a single currency, the formation of a unified market and the virtual elimination of trade barriers between EU countries, companies operating in Europe have experienced dramatic changes in the past ten years. Once a region sharply divided between east and west, Europe is now experiencing substantial change as new consumer markets emerge and cross-border trade and investment accelerate.

Forces such as consumer market integration, cross-border trade and investment is driving change in European supply chains.

Companies striving to achieve supply chain excellence in Europe need to tap into the opportunities made available through SC network consolidation and streamlining, process and IT integration, while also being aware of the challenges particular to the region. Levels of deregulation, tax regimes and rates of technology adoption vary markedly between countries. Also, growing traffic congestion is impacting supply chain effectiveness in specific regions of Europe.

This chapter is an attempt briefly to introduce the main forces that drive change in European goods markets and to illustrate the main supply chain responses to meet increasing challenges in service and productivity.

Such SC responses refer to: product and package harmonization, production, distribution and intermodal freight networks, 'operational excellence' in distribution and manufacturing, procurement transformation, integrated demand and supply planning across markets and customers and supplier collaboration. Finally, the chapter briefly describes solutions being discussed by experts in order to reduce road congestion in Europe.

Market forces driving change

Forces driving change in Europe vary by industry and even by company and product. However we believe there are a few key forces driving change in European supply chains.

Market unification

The formation of a single currency and a unified market have accelerated competitive pressures across the Continent.

The creation of the European Union has been probably the most important single event driving change in European supply chains. The formation of a single currency and a unified market have accelerated competitive pressures across the Continent, serving to cut costs and improve service standards to unprecedented levels.

The virtual elimination of trade barriers has resulted in cross-border trade within Europe growing significantly faster than the European Union's GDP. Both manufacturing and distribution companies have accelerated the restructuring and relocation of their production and distribution sites and networks. Such companies have been able to reap the benefits of economies of scale while improving service levels to customers and consumers.

A North-Central axis linking south England, the Benelux, northern France, most of west Germany and northern Italy has become rapidly congested (main residential, manufacturing and distribution hubs), the Benelux having become a hub area for pan-European distribution centers (EDC) as well as an important gateway for transatlantic traffic. The German ports in the North Sea are also key gateways and logistics hubs. In parallel a new Mediterranean axis is becoming increasingly competitive (city ports of Valencia, Barcelona, Marseille and Genoa-Liguria) in attracting manufacturing and distribution-logistics related investments (gateway for Far East traffic) and is expected to increase its competitive advantage in the coming years, for several reasons (for example high-speed train connections, lesser congestion, recent investments in infrastructure, quality of life).

During the 1980s countries such as Spain and Italy benefited from attracting strong manufacturing investment due to their lower production costs. This same trend is now benefiting Eastern European nations as trade and investment barriers fall. The Czech Republic, Hungary, Poland, Slovakia, Slovenia and the Baltic States are expected to join the EU by 2007, which will open new manufacturing opportunities. Already the growing consumer markets in these countries have attracted an impressive flow of investment in multiple industries since the early 1990s. Other remaining Eastern European countries, such as Croatia, Romania, Bulgaria and Ukraine, are seeking to become attractive industrial zones. Some have already achieved limited success as they follow the path of reform and sign free trade agreements with the EU.

Despite recent progress, there are important barriers to EU market unification as a result of differing competition regulations and tax legislation. Prices for popular car models vary markedly, for instance. In countries such as Denmark, Ireland, the United Kingdom, Finland, Netherlands, Germany and Austria, one popular car model was selling in December 2001 for anywhere between 5 000 and 12 000 euros, another popular car for between 8 000 and 11 000 euros and a third car for 8 000 to 12 500 euros.

Consumer values, product harmonization and time-to-market

Although consumer values differ significantly across Europe, in general consumers are increasingly attaching more importance to values such as: quality, health, respect for the environment and value of time spent in activities such as leisure and family.

Manufacturers and retailers are responding to increasingly sophisticated consumers with pan-European product and marketing strategies, including country-specific adaptations.

Manufacturers and retailers have responded by building consumer loyalty through product and marketing strategies that are based on such changing consumer values. In parallel most are also striving to cut costs, especially in low-growth industries such as fast moving consumer goods (FMCG), automotive and white goods. For example, one global consumer goods company has engaged in a brand simplification strategy while reducing its number of key sites to 150 (with additional local ones). Another FMCG leader, in turn, refers to 'power SKUs' to drive growth.

Several consumer product companies are moving to partially harmonize product and packaging across Europe, although this is occurring at a much slower pace than originally planned. Consumer barriers to such harmonization are much more severe in some industries, such as food and personal care, than in others, such as consumer electronics, white goods, automotive, home equipment and fashion for young people.

Needless to say, achieving significant levels of harmonization is a prerequisite for fully effective pan-European procurement, manufacturing and distribution. Producers also face the challenge of formulating product development and time-to-market strategies in order to reconcile the contradictory goal of effectively meeting diverse consumer needs while achieving economies of scale through consolidation. Meeting such a challenge requires an optimum mix between mass customization, make-to-order, and production postponement.

Time-to-market is increasingly becoming a strategic issue in almost all industries. According to a survey on pan-European 'collaborative product development' (CPD) by Accenture in 2001, 67 per cent of the interviewed executives said their companies were involved in CPD initiatives mostly aimed at improving time-to-market and cost-baseline reduction. The survey covered a cross-section of industries: automotive, consumer and professional, electronics, high technology, aerospace, engineering, and their respective suppliers (refer to Chapter 3.7, 'Collaborative product commerce', for more detail).

Retail consolidation and expansion

Increased retail competition has resulted in cross-border expansion, improved assortment, on-the-shelf availability, and decreasing prices in most European markets.

The retail industry has experienced a process of inter-company consolidation and search for efficiency in mature markets, as well as intense cross-border expansion. For example, there were more than 1600 cross-border moves involving retail companies during the 1990s.

French grocery retailers have expanded mostly into southern and eastern Europe, British companies have moved into central Europe, German retailers have largely shifted to neighbouring countries, while Dutch companies have expanded in a variety of regions. Leading specialized retailers from Spain (specializing in fashion), Italy (fashion) and Denmark (high street retail) have also shown strong cross-border expansion during recent years. The cross-border expansion has also benefited the first ring of Eastern European countries where western retail formats, such as hyperstores, supermarkets and discount stores, are already common.

In general, increased retail competition has resulted in improved assortment, on-the-shelf availability, and better prices in most European markets. Supply chain executives have faced strong challenges to attain the required levels of service with reduced total costs. As a result, the main retail chains have re-engineered their supply chains to much higher levels of efficiency or are in the process of doing so in most markets.

B2C takes off

A significant percentage of orders placed via the Internet have deficiencies in the fulfilment process, but e-fulfilment capability is improving at a rapid pace.

Business-to-consumer business powered by the Internet has become more than a testimonial reality in Europe, although European markets are still two to three years behind the United States. For example, key 'bricks and mortar' chains have planned a one-digit share of total sales from their Internet business, and some retailers have attained this goal already (UK and Northern Europe). In the grocery and in some key category markets, traditional bricks and mortar stores seem to be winning the B2C battle against new entrants, some of the latter being successful in very specialized segments.

Internet sales have been slower to take off in Europe than in the US for several reasons. The level of Internet penetration into homes is lower in Europe, there are fewer truly European B2C Web sites, and language barriers across the Continent inhibit use of the Internet as an information and trade channel. Key successful B2C players from the US for instance, have specific web pages for each European country. Nevertheless, Internet consumer businesses are following a steady path of growth in Europe in all markets, with Nordic countries recording the highest share, followed by the UK.

e-fulfilment was certainly underestimated during the initial stages of the B2C boom as a fundamental enabler of successful business launches and consolidations. As a result, many e-business ventures failed, especially among start-up companies.

A global survey of Internet retailers by Accenture during the Christmas seasons of 1999, 2000 and 2001 revealed that a significant percentage of orders placed via the Internet showed deficiencies in the fulfilment process. The 'eSanta' survey (Accenture, 2001) investigated 392 orders from customers in London, Barcelona, Frankfurt and Paris, placed with 81 online retailers, and found a lack of confirmation to the consumers, long order-taking times, late deliveries, and incidents with returns.

Nevertheless, the most recent season in 2001 showed improvement in some aspects of e-fulfilment, such as availability confirmation to consumers, improved range of products, improved quality and information on the websites. A problem remains, however, in the fact that a significant number of European sites still do not allow cross-border shipments. A positive sign for the future is revealed by a further survey by Accenture 2001, of pan-European logistics service providers, which found that building solid e-fulfilment capability was widely recognized as critical to the success of any future B2C business.

Privatization and deregulation of public services

During the 1990s and early 2000s, most European countries have privatized government services as well as partially removed the umbrella of regulatory protection for several key service industries. Industries such as communications (fixed and mobile), gas, electricity, petrol, and water provision have been subject to varying degrees of privatization and liberalization, depending on the country and industry. Many companies have had to face competition for the first time, albeit to different degrees, since often privatization has not led to genuine competition. The newly privatized companies have responded by introducing new management cultures based on the principles of cost-effective service provision to the consumer, quality and return on investment.

Recently privatized public service companies are mostly now beginning to streamline their supply chains, often by creating a logistics and procurement organizations from scratch.

Given the prior lack of focus on supply chain management, most of the deregulated companies have had to start from scratch, often by creating a logistics and procurement organization. In the mobile telecom industry, new entrants have been the quickest to grasp the strategic importance of integrated supply chain management and have generally resorted to third-party providers to accelerate the implementation of their logistics capabilities. Despite huge efforts, the task is largely unfinished and potential remains to reduce inventories significantly.

Zero deficit with better government

Government services such as health, education, defence and public transport are gradually being put under the imperative of managing public resources according to objective scorecards. They are coming under pressure from two opposing forces: public demand for improved service, and constraints on public funding. Government agencies have identified sourcing and logistics as two key areas with the potential to both reduce costs and improve services.

Public demand for better service coupled with constraints on public funding are placing pressure on governments.

In the case of the health and pharmaceutical industries, the single market does not yet exist. Progress towards a unified licensing regime in the EU is very slow and hence full product harmonization has not yet been rendered possible. Prices show significant variation between countries and sometimes between regions of the same country. Service levels to pharmaceutical outlets are very high and often supply chains are long and inefficient. Public health services most often have not yet implemented centralized procurement, warehousing, inventory management and deliveries to hospitals.

New and more efficient national, regional and local administrations in Europe have started to evolve, such as the national and regional health services of several European countries. However, most of the potential for improvement and the change has yet to materialize.

A congested Europe

Specialists argue that a 24-hour economy and better intermodal transport would ease traffic congestion.

Although a more unified market has brought increased trade and prosperity the spectre of a massive pan-European traffic jam is haunting citizens and businesses. Road freight traffic is growing at very high annual rates, by 2.1 per cent above GDP growth between 1992 and 1997 and by 3.5 per cent from 1997 to 2001. The traffic explosion is forecast to continue, with an expected increase of 2.6 per cent above GDP growth between 2001 and 2003.

Congestion not only penalizes citizens through more time spent on roads and more accidents, but it has a very high economic toll, representing roughly 0.5 per cent of European GDP. The economic toll is expected to represent up to 1 per cent of GDP by 2010 if no steps are taken to reduce the traffic.

The problem is made worse by the combination of several factors. A high percentage of deliveries are made during peak daytime hours of 9 a.m. to 5 p.m. There is a low share of rail versus road transport, due to the slow pace of deregulation of the railroad industry in key nations. Inadequate transportation regulations and pricing hinder effective transport management. A lack of adequate infrastructure also limits home deliveries in urban areas.

EU and industry specialists argue these problems necessitate several changes:

- the introduction of a 24-hour economy
- a strong commitment to more economic transport, such as inter-modal rail-road-sea transport
- more efficient integration of transport operations in supply chains
- clearly defined and separate transport management models for urban and non-urban networks, and
- the right balance between economic, environmental and social objectives.

For example, costs could be reduced substantially by introducing 24-hour distribution, as the extended hours would allow the removal of whole fleet segments. A simulation exercise executed on pan-European road networks has shown that transferring 10 to 20 per cent of total daily traffic to night-time significantly changes levels of congestion, average speed and pollution emissions. A UK retailer has estimated that extending 24-hour deliveries to the 42 per cent of stores currently under curfew regimes would reduce costs by 20 per cent. A major barrier to such changes is the issue of noise to residents. However, specialists argue that significant environmental and economic benefits have been achieved when night delivery schemes have been introduced with adequate regulations and technologies for noise minimization.

Supply chain responses

The market forces driving change in European supply chains are leading to several strategic responses.

Pan-European SC network optimization

The restructuring of supply chain networks is taking place in almost every key industry in Europe in order to generate the economies of scale that are made possible by the unified market. Networks based on European distribution centres and supplemented by local trans-shipment and delivery centres (often third-party managed) are already common. Typically, the networks comprise three to six distribution centers for high-volume goods and one to two centers for high-value goods, such as spare parts.

The move to fewer, larger and more specialized pan-European plants and distribution centres is becoming a reality in several key industries.

Across Europe, advanced retail chains have achieved significant benefits through inventory and warehousing centralization and for example in the UK third-party logistics companies are being encouraged to create multi-retailer relay centers near to the source trans-shipment points, to serve the single-retailer regional distribution centers. They hope to take more inventory out of the regional centers as the multi-retailer centers render even more frequent deliveries possible, without increasing transportation costs. Nevertheless, moving inventory back to nearby point-of-use locations – such as plant distribution centers or regional distribution centers – is also a new reverse trend in some companies due to road congestion and unreliable delivery.

The move to fewer, larger, and more specialized pan-European plants is also becoming a reality in several industries, such as automotive original equipment manufacturers, white goods, FMCG, and consumer electronics. The trend raises challenges in distribution center networks, such as establishing mixing centers, new layouts and the right technology, making it necessary to rethink manufacturing and distribution networks in a coordinated way.

Key issues and challenges
Further progress in supply chain network optimization will require the following:

- further product and package harmonization across markets
- more effective network management through advanced pan-European logistics partnerships
- inter-modal freight networks
- integrated pan-European process and IT capability for order processing, inventory (available-to-promise) and shipment management
- pan-European demand and supply chain planning and execution.

Bear in mind that today multiple legacy ERP systems in different subsidiaries of the same company continue to represent a major barrier to integrated planning and execution in the early 2000s.

Operational excellence in distribution and manufacturing
Achieving operational excellence is a never-ending challenge in a context dominated by the need to restructure wider SC networks, to accommodate a wider variety of products in manufacturing and distribution, and to ensure shorter and more reliable lead times to consumers. These efforts are leading to an avalanche of new investment in operational improvement and IT in several industries.

Warehousing and distribution challenges

Pan-European order management and centralized customer care facilities are still a challenge. So are appropriate warehousing and distribution automation strategies to each market situation.

Some of the major challenges in warehousing and distribution are listed below.

- Achieving integrated capability in order taking and processing. More precisely companies need to ensure integrated product and client masters, order pricing, credit checking and inventory assignment, as well as available-to-promise, substitution management, and integration with distribution center activities such as: picking, order status tracking and delivery confirmation.
- Establishing centralized customer care, such as rapid response front-office, multi-lingual and back-office links with legacy ERP systems in each country or centralized system.
- Ensuring flow-through and productive layout design and technology choices for pan-European multi-purpose facilities. These centers are more than warehouses and often must include activities such as: cross-docking, kitting, pre-assembly, product tagging, storage, receiving, picking, load planning.
- Adopting appropriate levels of automation for the new, centralized European distribution centers. Currently there is considerable debate about the desirable degree of automation. Even though economics alone may justify automation, the centers must retain a

level of flexibility to meet changing product and demand profiles. However, automated warehousing becomes more attractive when other issues are considered, such as the shortage of low-cost labor under flexible contracting to support traditional warehousing. (typically in northern and central European markets)

As a result, modular and flexible semi-automated solutions are becoming increasingly accepted, including full or partial auto-mated storage together with mixed levels of automation in receiving, order picking and packing. Supporting economic and other factors include costs of land and labor, interest rates, the need for 24-hour service, audit trail requirements, and low variations in demand and product profiles. The technology alternatives available today, such as automatic sorters, light picking and mini-loads, also allow for much more flexible and modular automation than the earlier fully automated options

- Implementing seamless integration with carriers, ensuring shared information is available on load status and delivery confirmation. Web-enabled e-transportation firms are facilitating tracking and tracing for loads and vehicles, as well as optimization services. This is discussed in more detail below.

Manufacturing challenges

Some of the major challenges in manufacturing include:

Companies are seeking a balance between customization and increased efficiency as plants have to cater for increasingly wider product and packaging ranges in increasingly more reliable and shorter timeframes.

- Re-engineering products and component bills of materials to ensure the success of production strategies to serve pan-European and/or global demand. For example, industries such as engineering, industrial equipment, automotive and white goods, are re-engineering their production processes in order to ensure maximum pre-configuration through increased component and product commonality, whilst allowing for flexible consumer customization through modularised option availability.
- Ensuring customized and flexible plant operations, including realigning plant processes and layouts, to allow for example: a wider mix of packaging options, build-to-order (B2O) and engineer-to-order (E2O) strategies. Also facilitation of frequent changeovers and plant logistics with maximum productivity ability to change.
- Introducing new metrics, values and training to enable a swift transition from a 'manufacturing productivity' culture to a 'manufacturing responsiveness' culture with an increasing focus on 'compliance to order/plan/schedule'.
- Similar change management approaches are helpful in educating plant managers and teams in accelerating the transition from serving local markets to serving wider European or global markets.

Procurement transformation

Companies are quickly trying to grasp the opportunities being generated by the consolidation of European procurement. A significant number of European players in different industrial, services, and even government sectors are involved in efforts to rationalize and transform sourcing through practices such as the following:

- supplier-base segmentation by type of relationship depending on criticality and market situation
- consolidated supplier bases for key direct and indirect materials
- strategic partnerships, with the more critical suppliers including long-term agreements for product development, continuous improvement in quality and cost, and integrated processes for collaborative design, quality testing, replenishment, receiving and payment
- use of fact-based negotiation principles, tools and methodologies
- use of Internet-enabled tools (via e-markets or through direct use) for e-sourcing (e-RFI, product and supplier search, e-tendering and e-auctioning) and e-requisitioning (catalog ordering-thru-payment), and
- achieving consolidated visibility of raw materials and packaging requirements (via shared supply chain planning and ERP systems), order tracking and tracing from suppliers.

Although many of the advanced procurement methods and tools were introduced initially in the manufacturing and retail industries, such practices are now becoming widespread, including in recently deregulated utilities and government services.

A survey of pan-European procurement by Accenture in 2001 found evidence of an increasing adoption of e-sourcing support tools, particularly for a wide range of purchased products such as specific raw materials, packaging and indirect goods. Half of those interviewed were using specialist e-sourcing service providers and around a third using category specialist e-markets, such as in energy, metals, and chemicals. Another third relied mostly on industry consortia (for example in the CPG industry). Most companies were at the early stages of introducing e-requisitioning as it presented deeper organizational and integration challenges.

Key issues and challenges

Despite recent progress, important change management challenges lie ahead in achieving the successful transformation of procurement practices. First, organizational cultures are struggling in the transition from adversarial to more collaborative models. Second, organizations are also struggling to overcome the significant fear and lack of understanding that surrounds e-enabled sourcing and requisitioning tools. Significant efforts are needed in skills acquisition and training.

Third, many issues still surround IT integration, including pan-European purchasing and replenishment requirements, visibility, ordering track and trace and e-requisitioning tools integration.

Integrated demand and supply planning

Integrated demand and supply initiatives at the national and pan-European levels are common, aiming to improve forecasting accuracy and delivery compliance at reduced costs in a more complex (that is, cross-border operations) environment.

The following are just a few examples of the challenges faced by pan-European SC planning efforts:

Effective pan-European SC integration requires integrated planning. Although efforts are being made, organizations often underestimate the change management and IT challenges involved.

- product proliferation, including products options, kits and promotional packs making forecasting accuracy
- ever-increasing service requirements in on-the-shelf product availability and committed lead times to customers
- need to reduce inventory and improve asset utilization (plant, warehouse and vehicles) to meet cost reduction targets in an increasingly 'intermarket' environment
- increased risk of obsolescence because of increasingly reduced product life cycles
- increased physical distances between production, supply and demand locations because of pan-European network consolidation.

Key issues and challenges

Companies are meeting such challenges by working simultaneously to achieve operational excellence and implement integrated demand–supply planning and execution process and IT capabilities across Europe.

While such planning integration initiatives are prevalent in many industries, organizations often underestimate the change management challenges involved. Cross-departmental and intermarket challenges need to be addressed early and with adequate top management support and resources, in order to avoid failure. In addition efforts to establish a new culture based on intermarket and horizontal collaboration tends to require new metrics, roles and skills.

Still today some key global and European players do not have in place fully empowered supply chain organizations that integrate demand and supply planning processes, and this leads directly to resulting strife and inefficiency in cross-market operations.

Collaboration with customers and suppliers

Despite recent progress and some frequently highlighted cases, supply chain collaboration is in its infancy in Europe. Examples of developments in key industries are outlined below.

Food retailers are focusing on consumers and value chain efficiency through improved collaboration.

FMCG and retail industry

Vendor-managed inventory (VMI) and other supply chain execution collaboration initiatives are occurring widely across Europe.. The initiatives have an increasing focus on delivery customization and efficiency agreements. The new frontiers are collaborative promotions planning and execution (e-promotions) and 'collaborative planning, forecasting and replenishment' (CPFR). Key UK retailers have launched supply chain and collaboration initiatives with their suppliers. Four leading European retailers together with 19 manufacturers have launched a CPFR initiative in Europe, including manufacturer suppliers, under the sponsorship of ECR Europe. Other retailers are also piloting CPFR and e-promotion initiatives.

FMCG retail collaboration

Again the main challenges lie in change management, as companies have to shift from old to new retail–manufacturer relationships. Standards definition is well under way, including the Global Commerce Initiative and projects by ECR Europe. Another key challenge is e-market leverage. It is difficult to conceive collaboration becoming effective beyond pilots without the support of public or private e-markets in order to ensure connectivity and data synchronization. Store replenishment, planning and procurement capabilities and integration with legacy systems are also key success factors to be addressed.

Non-food retail collaboration

Retailers in some European markets are sharing point-of-sale information with non-food suppliers, such as white goods manufacturers. Examples exist in different industries (for example, a Danish consumer electronics manufacturer and its 2 300 retail clients, and a Spanish fashion retailer and its collaborative approach with more than 1 000 store outlets). However, there is significant room for improvement in reducing lead times to consumers and cutting inventory and transport costs through supplier collaboration in multi-category traditional retailers.

Automotive collaboration

Automobile manufacturers are focusing on improved demand visibility, reduced product proliferation and improved production responsiveness to demand.

During the 1990s, the automotive industry in Europe (as elsewhere) focused on achieving high levels of supply chain synchronization and quality in-flows from suppliers as well as reducing manufacturing costs. Limiting the supply chain synchronization approach only to suppliers often resulted in pushing inventory from manufacturing back to Tier 1 or Tier 2 suppliers.

The issues then and often now are:

- improving consumer demand visibility
- reducing the proliferation of models, options and colors

- reducing the rigidness in production capacity (labor agreements and practices), leading to wide cycles of inventory accumulation when demand dropped and 'lead time to consumer' crises (at least for popular models) when demand picked up
- reducing inventory sitting in dealers (and poor tracking and feedback of real customer demand), and
- moving from a 'push' to a 'pull' philosophy in vehicle supply to consumers.

Recently the main global automotive OEMs have begun to transform their supply chains. They have made significant process, IT and human resource investments in improving demand planning and achieving higher levels of flexibility and synchronization between demand, inventory and production planning. Consequently, they are seeking to extend the existing 'pull' philosophy applied to inbound materials management to the management of finished vehicles demand and inventory.

Collaborative product development (CPD)
A survey on CPD in Europe, undertaken by Accenture in 2001, found that companies believe that collaboration needs to occur throughout the whole product development process if time-to-market is to be improved and costs reduced. Collaboration is necessary not only across internal departments, but also with suppliers and third-party providers. Web-enabled collaborative design tools help to support internal and external communications, document sharing and concurrent planning. Most of the executives interviewed identified CPD as fundamental to reduce time-to-market, cut the cost baseline in the design stages, and to improve quality and innovation. The study shows that a significant share (70 per cent) of European industry are undertaking CPD initiatives, or will be doing so by 2005 (refer to Chapter 3.6 for more detail).

Transport collaboration
The emergence of Web-enabled load and fleet exchange, and optimization capabilities has paved the way for opportunities in collaborative transportation management, allowing shippers to share transport capacity along specific lanes in dynamic short window environments. Third-party logistics companies, and new entrants such as Agora-Trans are offering multi-party optimization under partnership agreements with and between shippers. Benefits include reduced empty returns, increased asset turnover, and improved service, information and carrier ratings.

Advanced logistics partnerships

The rapid growth in outsourcing is transforming third-party logistics. Mergers and acquisitions are accelerating, companies are investing in offering value-adding services, and the scope of contracts is increasing.

The trend to outsource logistics services in Europe is growing as companies seek to accelerate the building of European networks and focus on time-to-market, core business, total cost reduction and new market development. Outsourcing in 2000 accounted for between 25 and 30 per cent of total logistics spending, according to some estimates, with the UK having the highest spend at 35–40 per cent.

The rapid growth in outsourcing is transforming third-party logistics in Europe. Mergers and acquisitions are accelerating as companies seek to offer wider, more comprehensive services. Leading logistics companies in Europe have engaged in mergers and acquisitions as a means to combine assets and increase their ability to offer customers integrated end-to-end services in warehousing, handling, value-add activities, transportation, courier services. Virtually every important UK and US logistics provider has moved into Continental Europe. French, German, Spanish and Italian third-party players have also increased their cross-border activities dramatically.

Growth and competition in the market has led to companies value-adding their services beyond warehousing and distribution, in ways such as network optimization, e-fulfilment, contract manufacturing and replenishment. In contract manufacturing, for instance, a leading UK contract logistics company is managing a plant for laser printers in the Netherlands serving a global high tech company.

Europe has also seen expanded roles for service providers through the creation of 'Lead Logistics Provider (LLP)' , 'lead service provider' (LSP) or 'fourth-party logistics' (4PLs) providers. For example, two key global automotive OEMs have given the responsibility to manage global logistics budgets to newly created logistics consortiums in turn managing numerous third party contracts. Also, Thames Water created Connect 2020 with Accenture to manage procurement and logistics under a gain-sharing contract. More about this trend in Chapter 4.4, 'Third- and Fourth-party logistics providers'.

The scope of contracts is also growing as companies seek to have a single point of contact for their logistics services. In 2001, more than 20 per cent of contracts signed were global, 20 per cent were European and 60 per cent were regional or country-specific. Consequently, the value of contracts has grown dramatically in the last five years, from Euro 10 million for a typical single distribution center contract to Euro 100 million per year for a contract consisting of the management of a logistics budget across Europe.

A new transportation model for Europe

Given the challenges raised by congested traffic and increasing transport costs in Europe, the EU has developed a strategic framework and specific initiatives, including:

The fight against congestion requires a combination of 24-hour transport, new regulations and new investment incentives.

- Euro freight corridors, comprising freight freeways: north–south and east–west
- a 'Combined Transport Trans-European Network' (CTTN) with Stage 1 involving the creation of a pan-European distribution network for road, rail and port, and Stage 2, a national and regional distribution network, and
- infrastructure management schemes. These include, for example: upgrading public transport, introducing heavy transport management regulations, reserving lanes for buses and taxis, and setting up vehicle location centers and special multi-client urban delivery centers. For example, La Rochelle in France has created a multi-shipper urban distribution center that also uses electric vehicles for delivery runs to urban stores.

Experts believe that the fight against congestion requires a combination of a 24-hour transportation philosophy, modified regulations, and new investment incentives to be jointly funded by both public and private sectors. Regulations should affect: night delivery norms, vehicle technology noise reduction devices, and fuel emissions. Some experts point to the inevitability of some form of road pricing to tackle Central European road congestion and even higher fuel taxes to better reflect the opportunity costs of lost time and infrastructure. Such measures could lead to the recalculation of optimal network solutions and recommend the reintroduction of regional stockholding locations in order to counter increasing delivery lead times.

Important barriers to be overcome still remain. For example: rail monopoly deregulation and pan-European rail standards, (especially for traction services), zero-deficit constraints hindering long-term public investment in infrastructure, adequate taxing policy and incentives, harmonized national, regional and local government regulations, public–private cooperation for inter-modal and 24-hour transport regulations, and funding.

Conclusion

European supply chains are being transformed by a combination of forces including global and European-specific trends. In several industries a combination of contradictory forces is in place on one hand seeking to reap the benefits of operational consolidation whilst on the other, ensuring product SC customization and flexibility to win new customers and increase sales. Both objectives are being made possible through simultaneous and persistent efforts in improving operational excellence (in design, procurement, manufacturing and distribution), and in process and IT integration (affecting SC planning and execution)

Yet the drive towards consolidated leveraged and integrated operations across Europe faces obstacles ranging from structural market and product diversity to cultural and legal regulation diversity (for example, labor laws and competitive practices).

Finally, some key 'European' challenges in supply chain management are shared with those being faced by companies in other developed markets; such as, the establishment of truly advanced logistics partnerships and extended e-enabled supply chain collaboration with customers and suppliers.

References

Accenture (2001), 'Pan-European e-procurement Survey', Internal Paper.

Accenture (2001), 'eSanta Survey: 1999–2001', Internal Paper.

Accenture (2001), 'Pan-European Logistics Service Provider Survey', Internal Paper.

Accenture (2001), 'Pan-European Collaborative Product Development Survey', Internal Paper.

Accenture (2001), '24-hour Economy, 24-hour Transport. Nightmare or Solution?', Distribution Forum, AgipPetroli, Sole 24-Hore, Iveco. Contributions for a better use of existing capacity of transport infrastructure. Baveno, Italy, September 2001.

ECR Europe, Accenture and Industry members (2001), 'A Guide to CPFR Implementation', *ECR Europe*, 2001.

Bedeman, M. (2001), 'Is 4 More than 3?', *Logistics Europe*, February 2001.

Supply chains in Asia – challenges and opportunities

5.3

**Robert Easton, William Thurwachter and
Tian Bing Zhang**

Supply chain excellence has become a driver of value and competitiveness across most industries and many nations around the world. Yet in Asia, with few exceptions, supply chains in multinational corporations and in local private or state-owned companies are more fragmented and less competitive compared with those in the United States and Europe. In fact, some would argue their performance level lags three to five years behind that of the West.

Companies doing business in Asia need to aggressively address gaps in supply chain performance.

Companies that do business in Asia – or want to do business in this critically important region – need to address this performance gap aggressively. The first step is to clearly understand the supply chain challenges facing the region. Some of these, such as the continuing economic slowdown in the US and Europe, have affected markets everywhere. Others, such as the huge market and regulatory diversity, culture, and complex distribution networks, are unique to Asia. By understanding these challenges, companies can take the action needed to enhance their supply chain efficiency in the region and reach the levels of supply chain competitiveness achieved elsewhere in the world.

This chapter highlights the major supply chain challenges facing companies operating in Asia. It then lays out seven opportunity areas that have the potential to improve supply chain performance and competitiveness dramatically. CEOs and CFOs need to pursue these opportunities as a top priority. In Asia, perhaps more so than in other parts of the world, supply chain excellence can be used as a competitive weapon to deliver market advantage and achieve quantum leaps in cost and revenue performance.

Characteristics of Asian supply chains

To be competitive, a supply chain must be cost efficient, responsive, flexible, agile, 'right' (in terms of product, quantity, place, time and quality) and easy to do business with, while maximizing safety. Yet achieving these qualities can be difficult in Asia, a region of great diversity in language, culture, currency, regulations, taxes, infra-structure, business practices, organizational forms and stages of economic development. Complicating matters, this diversity exists not only between countries but also often between cities within the same country, particularly in China. As Figure 5.3.1 suggests, these factors act individually and collectively to make supply chain competitiveness a difficult goal even for the best-run companies.

The supply chain challenges in Asia can be broadly categorized into five areas: market and regulatory diversity; supply chain network complexity; uneven market penetration; organizational models; and cultural mindset.

Market and regulatory diversity

Supply chains are often imprisoned by Asia's diversity in language, culture, infrastructure, tax regimes and customs regulations.

Great diversity and complexity in markets and regulatory environ-ments exist across Asia. In particular, there is a growing gap between the developed economies such as Singapore, Hong Kong, Japan and South Korea; developing economies such as China, Indonesia, Malaysia, the Philippines, Thailand and Taiwan; and emerging economies such as Cambodia, India and Vietnam, as shown in Figure 5.3.1. The diversity in language, culture, transportation infrastructure, tax and duty regimes, and local customs regulations combine to make the collaborative movement of goods within and across borders difficult at best and typically leads to increased supply lead times. In effect, supply chains are often imprisoned by this diversity and national borders. Compounding the difficulty of developing compe-titive supply chains in Asia are the capability gaps in terms of the people, technology and third-party logistics providers available across the region. Underdeveloped e-commerce infrastructure and the historical tendency to organize and plan at the local rather than regional level also constrain supply chain development.

Supply chain network complexity

One outcome of the market and regulatory diversity across Asia is the resulting supply chain network complexity. Distribution channels, for example, are often multi-layered, as illustrated in Figure 5.3.2, with three to four intermediaries between manufacturers and customers being the norm. In the US and Europe, one or two intermediaries are the norm. Further, a localized approach to business, even among the multinationals and conglomerates, has led to a massive duplication of supply chain infrastructure, operations, and organizations across the region.

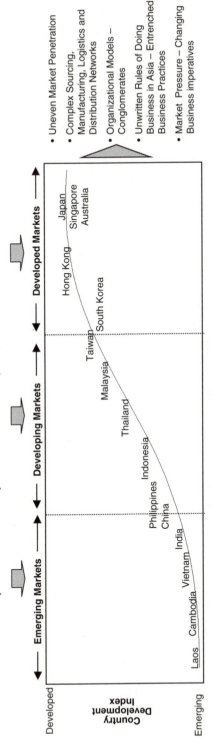

Market and regulatory diversity

- Economic development, political stability
- Customs duties and taxes (some free trade zones)
- Differences in language – complexity of documents, country specific branding and packaging
- Currency differences and stability
- Varying taxation and regulatory systems
- Logistics and communication infrastructure
- Varying banking practices incl. cash-based transactions
- Sophistication of consumers, customers and vendors

- Uneven Market Penetration
- Complex Sourcing, Manufacturing, Logistics and Distribution Networks
- Organizational Models – Conglomerates
- Unwritten Rules of Doing Business in Asia – Entrenched Business Practices
- Market Pressure – Changing Business imperatives

Country Development Index

Developed / Emerging

Emerging Markets → Developing Markets → Developed Markets →

Laos Cambodia Vietnam India China Philippines Indonesia Thailand Malaysia Taiwan South Korea Hong Kong Singapore Australia Japan

Key characteristics for supply chain management

- Poor infrastructure and distribution
- Limited data, low levels of automation
- Fragmented industries
- High degree of government involvement
- Resistant to third parties, low third party capability
- Very low Internet uptake
- Focus on fire-fighting

- Mix of traditional and modern distribution channels, emerging channels e.g. super/hypermarkets
- More demanding customers, increasing competition, consolidation and rationalization of industries
- Difficult to access sophisticated supply chain capabilities
- Technology but varying levels of integration
- Low to medium Internet uptake
- Moving from reactive to collaborative

- Modern distribution channels
- Intense competition
- Demanding consumers
- Availability of sophisticated capabilities and technology
- Easier to attract quality labor
- Greater propensity to outsource
- High Internet uptake
- Processes and infrastructure which supports collaboration

Source: Adapted from Figures 1.0 and 2.0 in Gattorna, J. L., (2000)

Figure 5.3.1
Factors impacting supply chain competitiveness in Asia

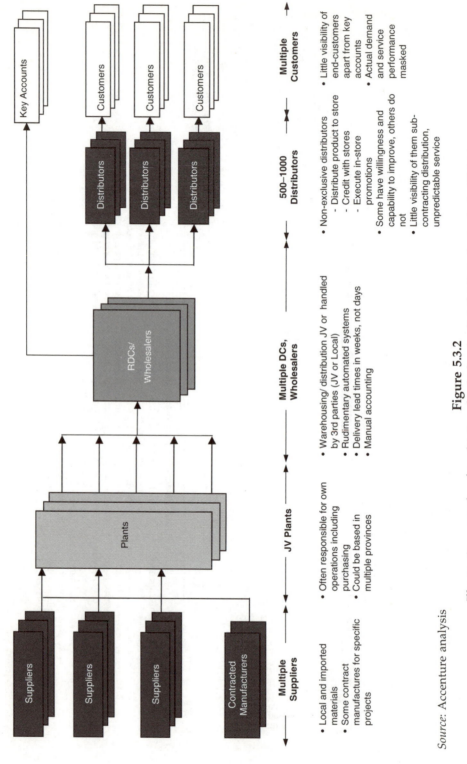

Figure 5.3.2

Illustrative sample of multi-tiered wholesale distribution channels in China

Source: Accenture analysis

Uneven market penetration

For many companies in Asia, market penetration is concentrated regionally around the more developed countries such as Japan, Singapore, Korea, Taiwan and Hong Kong, as well as at country-specific urban centers such as those along China's east coast. In general, supply chain networks and infrastructure have been developed to support these areas of greatest penetration. This poses a considerable challenge for achieving future supply chain efficiency. As countries such as China, Indonesia, India and Vietnam emerge as key markets or points of penetration, existing supply chain networks and infrastructure will have to be reconfigured and new capabilities developed.

The conglomerate organizational model

While conglomerates are declining as an organizational form in the West, many vertical and horizontal conglomerates continue to dominate and shape markets in Asia. In spite of the efficiencies that Asian conglomerates might derive from their scale, scope, wealth and longstanding relationships, this organizational model actually inhibits supply chain efficiency. That is because the entities within most conglomerates take a portfolio approach to investment decision-making which encourages the development of disparate technology systems and architectures that inhibit company-wide transparency of information. The result is fewer enterprize performance metrics and less opportunity to collaborate at the group level, for example by leveraging aggregated spend; rationalizing and sharing supply chain assets; jointly developing and sharing forecast and planning data; and leveraging core competencies across entities. Finally, family values and consensus decision-making hinder collaboration and the use of outsourcing as a vehicle to transform the supply chain.

The conglomerate organizational model traditionally runs counter to supply chain efficiency.

Cultural mindset

The cultural mindset and established business practices in Asia can have a negative impact on supply chain efficiency. One example is an ingrained 'win–lose' way of thinking, which many Asian companies perpetuate by their reward structures. This mindset is particularly evident when it comes to dealing with suppliers. A survey of 582 companies from five Commerce Net Asian members (China, Japan, South Korea, Singapore and Taiwan) provides revealing support for the prominence of this thinking. The survey found that while most companies in Asia wanted their suppliers to add Internet capabilities for obtaining product prices, searching and comparing product features and conducting online price negotiation, few planned to add such capabilities themselves (Manion 1999).

A lack of trust also inhibits supply chain efficiency. Trust is the foundation for open sharing of information and collaboration between supply chain parties – yet trust remains a major issue in Asia. When combined with a tendency to stay within boundaries and 'mind your own business', this lack of trust can have a crippling effect on achieving supply chain efficiencies because it inhibits coordination between functional departments and trading parties. Finally, unwritten rules and entrenched practices or 'off-book' transactions, which vary across the region, can be major sources of resistance to change.

Further exacerbating Asia's supply chain challenges

Business imperatives are placing pressure on the supply chain to be responsive, agile and cost-efficient.

Consumer demands for 'better, faster, cheaper' are a worldwide phenomenon, as well as a major incentive for supply chain improvements. But in Asia – a global hub for the manufacture of consumer products (and particularly electronics) – the pressures are even greater (Figure 5.3.3). On the one hand, a global economic slowdown left many Asian companies holding excess inventories, while local spending on their goods also has dropped. However, the region's astonishing diversity and complicated distribution network schemes makes responding to these pressures even tougher than it might be in the United States.

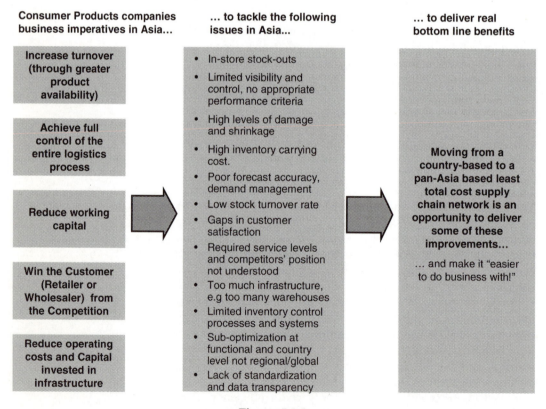

Consumer Products companies business imperatives in Asia...

- Increase turnover (through greater product availability)
- Achieve full control of the entire logistics process
- Reduce working capital
- Win the Customer (Retailer or Wholesaler) from the Competition
- Reduce operating costs and Capital invested in infrastructure

... to tackle the following issues in Asia...

- In-store stock-outs
- Limited visibility and control, no appropriate performance criteria
- High levels of damage and shrinkage
- High inventory carrying cost.
- Poor forecast accuracy, demand management
- Low stock turnover rate
- Gaps in customer satisfaction
- Required service levels and competitors' position not understood
- Too much infrastructure, e.g too many warehouses
- Limited inventory control processes and systems
- Sub-optimization at functional and country level not regional/global
- Lack of standardization and data transparency

... to deliver real bottom line benefits

Moving from a country-based to a pan-Asia based least total cost supply chain network is an opportunity to deliver some of these improvements...

... and make it "easier to do business with!"

Figure 5.3.3
Business imperatives and supply chain responses for consumer products companies in Asia

The opportunities – recipes for competitiveness

As the previous overview of challenges makes clear, realizing supply chain improvements in this part of the world is not easy. Yet it can be done. As summarized in Figure 5.3.4, the remainder of this chapter profiles seven ways that companies operating in Asia can significantly improve their supply chain efficiency and competitiveness. Obviously, Asia's diversity complicates the task of prescribing solutions that successfully relate to more than one group or business context; which is why many of the cited opportunities need to be addressed on a country-by-country, company-by-company or supply-chain-by-supply-chain basis.

Each opportunity needs to be addressed country by country, company by company, and supply chain by supply chain.

It also should be noted that the numbering sequence of opportunities in Figure 5.3.4 is deliberate – an attempt to proffer a logical order to approaching supply chain tasks and determining what is achievable. For companies dealing with underdeveloped infrastructures and tough regulatory constraints, just exceling at the basics would be a major achievement. For others (operating in more sophisticated environments), the task of synchronizing supply chains and connecting networks of e-markets might be a reasonable goal. The greatest likelihood, however, is that multinational companies operating throughout the region will have to address both scenarios.

As already indicated, the numbering of the opportunities in Figure 5.3.4 is intended to give a sense of logic to determining the best sequence to attack supply chain issues in the region.

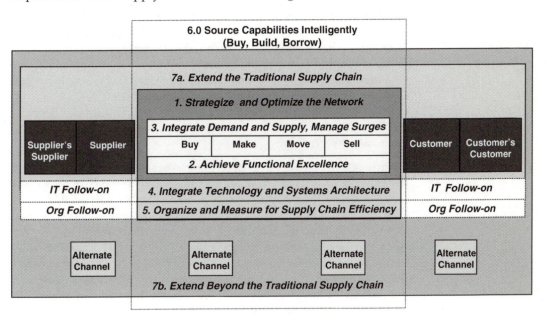

Figure 5.3.4
Supply chain opportunity areas in Asia

There is also a clear path that companies need to follow in their quest for supply chain effectiveness. This is particularly true in Asia, where operating environments can be varied and unsophisticated, and basic systems and capabilities are of utmost 'infrastructural' importance. In effect, the development and mastery of core capabilities – consistent processes and procedures; integrated I/T; accurate and reliable data; straightforward metrics; and thoughtful management of people – are even more important to companies doing business in Asia. Thus true leaders and innovators do not question the need for a logical, evolutionary approach to supply chain improvement. Instead, they look for ways to do it quicker and smarter.

Opportunity 1. Strategize and optimize the supply chain network

Companies need to determine what drives real advantage in their supply chain and what delivers real value to the customer.

Organizations in Asia often embark on an array of supply chain projects without a coherent guiding supply chain operating strategy – in reality, few in the region have such a strategy. The problem with this approach is that it results in incremental improvements at best. Unless these projects are implemented within the context of a broader, clearly defined operating strategy – supported by an optimized supply chain network – their impact will be diluted and localized. Strategic considerations like localization versus regionalization (for factory, warehouse and so on), revenue versus profit maximization, role and relevance of each location or each country in the overall strategy need to drive decisions about issues such as:

- What is the least-cost sourcing strategy?
- How many 'make' sites do I need and where should they be located; what is the least-cost conversion strategy?
- Where should products be made?
- Where should finished goods be sourced from to get lowest total cost?
- Where should stock be held across the network?
- What new infrastructure is required?
- What are the cost-to-serve and service trade-offs for particular customer segments?

Companies in Asia need to determine what drives real advantage in their supply chain and what delivers real value to the customer – and then configure their supply chain accordingly. As part of this effort, they need to align supply chain capabilities, processes, and structures to an overall strategy. Sourcing, conversion, distribution and replenishment planning should be coordinated within the overall network design to ensure optimal spread of resources, assets and lower cost-to-serve, as shown in Figure 5.3.5. Complexity in algorithms caused by the impact of tax regimes and regulatory diversity on make–buy decisions, justifies use of robust optimization tools. Yet to date, limited use has been made of network optimization tools in Asia – so the use of these tools is a big area of opportunity for Asian companies.

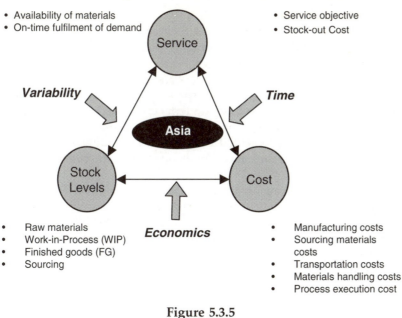

- Availability of materials
- On-time fulfilment of demand

- Service objective
- Stock-out Cost

Variability

Time

- Raw materials
- Work-in-Process (WIP)
- Finished goods (FG)
- Sourcing

Economics

- Manufacturing costs
- Sourcing materials costs
- Transportation costs
- Materials handling costs
- Process execution cost

Figure 5.3.5
Strategizing and optimizing the network

This is a far bigger deal in Asia than in other parts of the world but, to date, few broad-scale efforts have been undertaken. Network and inventory savings ranging from 10 to 40 per cent have been realized by companies in Asia who have focused on developing a strategy and optimizing their network. More importantly, companies have experienced improvements in revenue and market share of between 2 and 5 per cent from aligning and optimizing their supply chains to customer segments.

The diversity of geography, language, culture, customs, regulations and tax and tariff regimes makes 'postponement' strategies particularly relevant in Asia. In fact, the lack of local packaging, labeling, region-specific parts or multi-language documentation routinely adds cost, complexity and bloated inventories to the supply chains of companies that perform final configuration at their manufacturing sites. Asian-based companies that have implemented postponement strategies have realized inventory savings in the range of 10–30 per cent. Additional savings have resulted from higher fill rates and lower product obsolescence.

Opportunity 2. Achieve functional excellence
Functional and operational excellence – improving the supply chain performance of a company's buy, make, move, and sell processes – should be a core goal of every company with business interests in Asia. Following are some examples of the opportunities that exist in each of these areas:

Buy

Strategic sourcing and procurement transformation are expected to grow across Asia.

Asian companies tend to lag behind their counterparts in the US and Europe in consolidating and leveraging purchasing activities across the enterprize. Similarly, they have been hesitant to adopt strategic sourcing practices where the suppliers are embraced as true partners of a supply chain team and transparency is brought to the total process. Organizations that have undertaken strategic sourcing using techniques such as e-auctioning have realized immediate benefits. The leaders have also implemented e-procurement solutions to improve productivity, transparency and compliance so that the benefits will be sustained over time.

Excellence in sourcing offers multinational corporations (MNCs) and particularly conglomerates tremendous opportunities for immediate supply chain improvements and value creation through leveraging and transforming cross-entity procurement activities and capabilities. Strategic sourcing and procurement transformation are expected to grow across Asia. With such attractive opportunities, companies must find ways to overcome the challenges of unwritten rules, trust, and transparency to remain competitive.

Make

Manufacturing dominates in Asia; cheap labor has led to the region becoming the 'workshop of the world'. Operationally, there are pockets of manufacturing excellence in Asia. A number of companies, led by multinationals, are fairly advanced and widely apply such principles as 'lean' manufacturing and Six Sigma. However, conversion processes are basic in many large local companies and state-owned enterprizes (SOEs) in developing nations such as China, but opportunities to improve abound.

Many of those opportunities involve make-versus-buy decisions and plant rationalization. As noted earlier, for example, outsourcing is seriously under-represented in Asia, despite its potential to help companies (particularly small and medium enterprises, SMEs) realize huge production and cost efficiencies.

Move

The 'sweet spot' for further cost reduction in Asia now lies in logistics and distribution.

With much focus in Asia having been on squeezing costs out of production, the 'sweet spot' for further cost reduction now lies in logistics and distribution. In Korea, for example, costs for transportation, storage, unloading and packaging account for 16.3 per cent of GDP compared with 9.9 per cent in the US and 9.6 per cent in Japan. The important opportunity is to minimize costs and damage, while maximizing service across distribution networks. Presently, distribution center productivity, layout and operations, in most of the developing countries, are basic at best. Technology offers opportunities to improve this situation.

To cite one example in Malaysia, Mayne Logistics, in support of Unilever, implemented EXE's supply-chain executive software and saw on-time performance rise from 75 per cent to its current level of 99.8 per cent (Bowman, 2000). Additionally, as the number of inventory holding points are reduced through network optimization and centralization, transport costs will probably become a much larger element of the logistics budget and hence demand fresh attention. Given the amount of movement in Asia, transport is a significant number on the bottom line.

Sell

In the US and Europe tailoring supply chain responses to customer requirements has delivered revenue increases of between 3 and 5 per cent, along with market share gains. In Asia, the 'one-size-fits-all' approach to providing supply chain services is common – herein lies a major opportunity. Leading companies, understand the cost-to-serve each customer, the service customers require, and the price they are prepared to pay. They use this understanding to align their supply chain culture, capabilities, infrastructure and people with the specific response required. Other opportunities in this domain arise from the lack of recognition given to the link between line fill and revenue, the linear relationship between poor service and cost, and the failure to measure customer satisfaction from a customer perspective. Many simply fail to ask their customers what they think on a regular basis, preferring instead to rely on internal measures of service performance.

Opportunity 3. Integrate demand and supply, manage surges

Effective integration of supply and demand across the enterprise is a cornerstone of supply chain success. Leaders such as Wal-Mart and Dell Computer have demonstrated this convincingly for years. Many organizations in Asia have a problem in being very silo based. Moreover, companies that have implemented some form of integrated planning often end up back in silos because they lack the measures to drive full integration. Complicating the task of integrating demand and supply is the fact that forecast accuracy, in Asia overall, is poor.

Companies should start with the basics before embarking on integrating demand and supply chain planning.

To lay the groundwork for integrated demand and supply chain planning, companies should start with the basics: an effective sales and operations planning process. That means getting marketing, sales, logistics, manufacturing and procurement people talking with one another, planning together and identifying every opportunity to replace inventory with information. With that foundation in place, demand/supply planning software from companies such as i2 Technologies, Manugistics, SAP and Oracle can help them make complex operating decisions, ensure process consistency, adhere to key metrics and increase data integrity and transparency. The extensive use of demand and supply planning software in the US and Europe has not been emulated to the same extent in Asia but we expect to see a sharp growth in the use of these tools as companies re-engineer their processes and improve their technology and data integrity.

Opportunity 4. Integrate technology and systems architecture

If basic operational data is far off best practice, getting the best software solution may only succeed in automating a mess.

Leading organizations have demonstrated the value of developing an end-to-end supply chain view by integrating a range of advanced planning and scheduling software solutions with their enterprize resource planning (ERP), customer and supplier systems, as shown in Figure 5.3.6. In Asia, however, particularly in developing countries, many companies have yet to implement ERP systems and are faced with integrating an array of legacy systems. Regardless of the level of development, the key opportunity for all is to achieve as much integration of systems, data transparency, and data integrity as possible. Without integration in these areas, the use of more advanced technology solutions will be ineffective.

The availability of enterprise applications integration (EAI) or middleware provides companies with a real opportunity to achieve enterprise-wide integration and, in doing so, accelerate the journey to data transfer and transparency across entities. In approaching this opportunity, the challenge for Asian companies is to be wary of focusing on IT when the problems are more operational than technical. If basic operational metrics – forecast accuracy, make adherence, line fill, inventory accuracy, inventory turns, operating cost and delivery accuracy – are off base, it's unlikely that any software package will provide much relief. Companies must recognize that, in general, 30 percent of the benefits to be derived from a software solution will come from the software and technology itself, the remaining 70 per cent will come from process re-engineering. Without the appropriate level of process re-engineering a company may merely be speeding up or automating their current antiquated processes.

Opportunity 5. Organize and measure for supply chain efficiency

CEOs and CFOs need to move their supply chains from a localized to a regionalized orientation.

Companies striving for supply chain competitiveness must first organize for efficiency. That means optimizing the whole, not the constituent parts. Asian organizations, however, have historically done the opposite: They have organized their supply chains around local markets, functions and business units. As a result, there is a deeply ingrained legacy of duplicated and inefficient supply chain infrastructures, technologies, operations, processes and people.

Following are four ways that Asia business leaders can rationalize the whole of their supply chain operations to increase efficiency:

1. Regionalize supply chain functions and processes

Several high-tech and consumer goods companies operating in Asia have adopted regional manufacturing, distribution and marketing

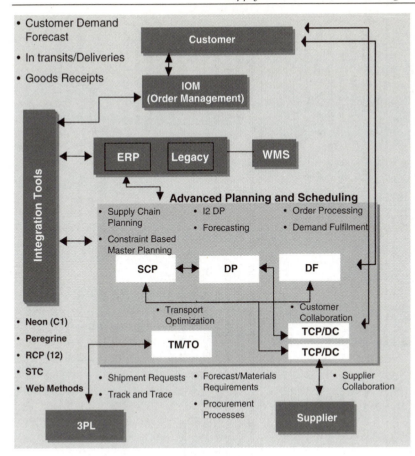

• Customer Demand Forecast

• In transits/Deliveries

• Goods Receipts

Customer

IOM (Order Management)

Integration Tools

ERP   Legacy   WMS

Advanced Planning and Scheduling

• Supply Chain Planning
• Constraint Based Master Planning

• I2 DP
• Forecasting

• Order Processing
• Demand Fulfilment

SCP   DP   DF

• Transport Optimization

• Customer Collaboration

• Neon (C1)
• Peregrine
• RCP (I2)
• STC
• Web Methods

TM/TO

TCP/DC

TCP/DC

• Shipment Requests
• Track and Trace

• Forecast/Materials Requirements
• Procurement Processes

• Supplier Collaboration

3PL

Supplier

Figure 5.3.6
Illustrative examples of integrated IT

strategies. However, the area's exceptional diversity makes it nearly impossible to prescribe a single pan-Asia operating model or regional solution. Figure 5.3.7 summarizes Accenture research into what various companies have done to organize for efficiency.

Perhaps the most important centralization/regionalization effort companies can make is consolidating the supply side to reduce variable costs and improve economies of scale. Several companies have successfully centralized demand and capacity planning, while still executing locally. Similarly, various intra-country logistics (move) efforts now are planned and executed locally, but are centrally planned when materials movement is between countries.

These important efforts currently are being pursued by multi-divisional MNCs, conglomerates and regional companies, and are showing strong potential not only to reduce costs and increase efficiencies, but to:

Product Development	Procurement	Manufacturing	Logistics & Distribution	Demand Management	Trends
• Most of the product innovation is handled centrally • Modification or customization is performed regionally or locally to ensure customer preference and needs are met	• The procurement of direct or strategic materials is mostly handled globally or regionally • Other indirect or non-strategic purchases handled locally • Very strong on regionalism	• The manufacturing process may be handled regionally or locally-depends on the nature of the products and the degree of configuration required.	• Most of the logistics and distribution is handled locally as the market in different countries varies	• Most of the demand planning is performed regionally • Product planning is executed locally based on the regionally/ centrally planned demand	• Regionalization is a trend for all companies to lower their variable costs and achieve economies of scale • There is no one solution for a Pan-Asia operating model
Possible Configuration: • Country center handles localization of formula • Regional centers responsible for regional harmonization	**Possible Configuration:** • Handled regionally possibly globally for direct materials (major contracts negotiation, supplier rationalization) • Handled regionally for indirect & packaging materials • Demand aggregated regionally	**Possible Configuration:** • Handled regionally • Planning to outsource some activities, e.g assembly / packaging outsourced to third parties and co-packers	**Possible Configuration:** • Handled and planned regionally when between countries • Handled and planned locally when within countries, often by the manufacturing entity	**Possible Configuration:** • Regional S&OP • Regional scheduling of production at local factories	**Possible Configuration:** • Major Regionalization on supply side to lower variable costs and achieve economies of scale • Some regionalization on R&D and product development • Limited regionalization on sales and marketing, local factors dominate
Rationale: • Ensure consistency & meet local customer needs	**Rationale:** • Cost reduction • Ensure regional consistency • Provide flexibility in scheduling at factories	**Rationale:** • Cost efficiency through economies of scale • Maintain locality of management • Provide flexibility in scheduling at factories	**Rationale:** • Limited benefits and practicality in regionalizing local activities	**Rationale:** • Optimize regional production • Maintain supply chain in balance	**Rationale:** • Optimization of facilities and resources

Source: Accenture research

Figure 5.3.7

Summary of operating models and trends in regionalization of supply chains

- standardize processes
- adhere to best practices and create 'centers of excellence'
- develop tighter controls
- improve access to higher-quality management
- leverage scarce skills
- build critical mass
- clarify management's focus on areas of value creation
- provide sophisticated capabilities to less developed markets which, if looked at in isolation as independent markets, would be constrained to the supply chain capabilities that characterized their stage of development: see Figure 5.3.8.

2. Rationalize across business units

Regionalization/centralization increases the transparency of a company's supply chain and planning requirements, while helping it develop a more consolidated view of customer requirements across

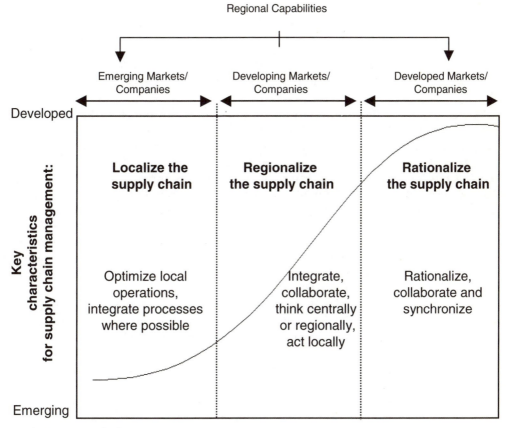

Source: Accenture analysis

Figure 5.3.8
Organizing for efficiency versus market development

regions and divisions (see Figure 5.3.7). This, in turn, can help the organization recognize and realize opportunities to rationalize assets, infrastructure, people and operations across business units. As the Asian market grows and matures, the likely result will be more supply chain shared services centers and greater supply chain visibility in executive boardrooms.

3. Elevate people and structures

Regardless of geography, sustainable increases in efficiency can only be achieved if companies 1) can successfully develop, attract and retain key talent, and 2) migrate from a functional or sub-process orientation to one where direct, high-level accountability is established for each supply chain process. Boundary issues, resource conflicts and divergent opinions about the need for change naturally increase when higher levels of regionalization and centralization are embedded. Without talented people and a single, cross-boundary process owner, most initiatives will not increase the effectiveness of the company as a whole. New cost-effective options for rapidly building supply chain talent and capability across a dispersed supply chain organization are emerging which provide an immediate infusion of infrastructure and virtual supply chain training which can be tailored to individual and corporate needs. These options also provide companies with the ability to rapidly transfer best practices across divisions and markets.

4. Focus on performance measures and benchmarks

The best firms in Asia recognize that performance metrics provide the link between strategy and operational reality.

We know of no organization that has achieved high levels of supply chain efficiency and effectiveness without an effective performance measurement and benchmarking capability. In fact, Michigan State University's multi-year study of supply chain excellence cited 'performance metrics and benchmarking' as one of the top four drivers of supply chain excellence. However, Accenture's research and case experience in Asia reveals that many companies are 'flying blind' when it comes to this capability. Capture and reporting of data across the region is inconsistent. In addition, in most cases, no common performance measurements exist across countries, business units, plants, or distribution centers.

The best firms in Asia, by contrast, recognize that performance metrics provide the link between strategy and operational reality. They use monthly, weekly, and daily scorecards to focus supply chain activities on what is important. These leaders apply rigorous metrics based on data with integrity, instead of relying on rules of thumb. They use uniform scorecards that set common goals, clearly communicating what is required of the supply chain partners to achieve total supply chain efficiency and competitiveness. No organization has achieved high levels of supply chain efficiency and effectiveness without a strong performance measurement and benchmarking capability.

Opportunity 6. Source capabilities intelligently

The choices – build, borrow, buy

Many opportunities exist for companies that are smart about sourcing supply chain capabilities. Three main options exist – build, borrow, buy – and each has its own merits. The ability to assemble and coordinate a large, complex network of supply chain capabilities quickly provides an opportunity for building a supply chain-based competitive advantage.

Dell Computers offers an excellent example. When tasked with setting up two assembly plants in Malaysia and China, Dell obtained various supply chain capabilities using a combination of options (see Table 5.3.1). To overcome gaps in the capabilities of their people, they used consultants, thus providing velocity in implementing short-term projects. At the same time, they invested heavily in training their supply chain personnel to assure strong management capabilities going forward. To help solve gaps in the technology capabilities of local suppliers, Dell provided access to demand information via the Web so that suppliers only needed access to a Web browser to link to Dell's system and check actual demand information. Recognizing the logistics infrastructure constraints, Dell outsourced elements of transport and distribution to third-party providers. The result: Dell has successfully implemented its direct sales model across Asia.

Trend towards outsourcing in Asia

Dell's actions highlight the opportunities that arise from recognizing that access to the best supply chain capabilities is more important than ownership of the capabilities. In the US and Europe, borrowing (or outsourcing) has emerged as a preferred way of obtaining supply chain capabilities because of its multiple benefits. These include speed to implement and create impact; low capital investment; conversion of previously fixed costs into variable; and flexibility to change, upgrade, or manage surges in demand.

Like Dell, companies such as Agilent, Colgate, Danone, Compaq, Hewlett Packard, Motorola, Ericsson, Nokia, Lucent, Herman Miller, Johnson & Johnson, Procter & Gamble and Sun Microsystems have all outsourced portions of their supply chains in Asia. Accenture research shows that a number of factors will drive more companies towards outsourcing in Asia. Thus, growth in outsourcing opportunities should be anticipated, particularly in transportation, warehousing, and inventory management. IDC, for example, predicts the business process outsourcing market for logistics to rise from $8.6 billion in 2002 to $29.2 billion in 2005, with the most opportunities in Greater China, Singapore and Malaysia (Jaffe et al. 2001).

The ability to assemble a complex network of supply chain capabilities can quickly build competitive advantage.

Access to the best supply chain capabilities is more important than ownership of the capabilities.

Table 5.3.1
Dell's supply chain capability sourcing strategy

Capability gaps	Build	Borrow	Buy
People	Invested in training supply chain personnel	Used consultants to help with high-impact projects	Recruited key supply chain managers
Technology	Developed small proprietary software together with their supply chain partner	Licensed software and influenced the software vendor to change product specs to meet Dell's need	Bought off-the-shelf application software
Logistics infrastructure	Built the assembly plants	3PL	Nil

Transformation – not 'tinkering' – the new wave
The unique challenges in Asia and the need for organizations to transform themselves rapidly, combined with a lack of capability, will work as a catalyst for outsourcing models that will 'transform' rather than 'tinker with' supply chains. Following examples of successful supply chain transformational outsourcing ventures in the US and Europe, a number of Asia's key business players and some large conglomerates are considering developing solutions that first provide quantum leaps in the supply chain performance of their individual business units or markets, and second, provide a capability that can be marketed to other players in the industry. Selling supply chain services to other players clearly helps the originator build scale and synergies, which may be leveraged by selling services to the numerous small and medium enterprises that might be unable to achieve scale in more conventional ways. In fact, there is every reason to believe that in some industries these 'NewCos' may eventually sell services to their competitors.

In Asia, there is a strong rationale for creating an independent 'SupplyCo' as a vehicle to help a company rapidly transform itself from independent management of the supply chain across business units or markets, to consolidated management of the entire supply chain, including:

- accelerated savings and release of cash
- overcoming resistance to change in regions, countries, and functions; overcoming strong organizational inertia that many companies attempting to rationalize and centralize face in Asia
- creating an independent 'SupplyCo' provides a reason and rationale to change.
- rapid development of people and skills
- providing an infusion of instant capability and infrastructure
- enables centralization of savings to be directed to areas where highest economic value add.

Watch this space.

Opportunity 7. Extend the supply chain

Across Asia, major opportunities exist to build collaborative supply chain capabilities that span multiple business entities. If issues relating to trust, data capacity and win–lose thinking can be overcome, this could make companies' regional and national supply chains significantly more competitive and cost efficient. Here are two basic extension opportunities:

Overcoming the issues of trust, data transparency, and 'win–lose' thinking can contribute significantly to making supply chains much more competitive.

7a. Extend the traditional supply chain

Extending the traditional supply chain refers simply to collaboration with suppliers and customers – a strategy with three principal permutations:

Industry collaboration Thus far, industry-level collaboration across Asia has only been approached informally. Moreover, there are few organizations working towards standardized rules, protocols or accepted practices. There are two exceptions, however: Singapore and Hong Kong. In the latter, there are several initiatives underway to increase collaboration levels, including the formation of the Hong Kong Logistics Development Council in 2001, comprising key industry and government leaders. There also are some indications that the Association of South East Asian Nations (ASEAN) may spur on collaboration efforts in the near future.

Supply chain collaboration for dispersed production Dispersed production refers to the process of developing goods and materials at a sequence of facilities. According to Magretta (1998), for example, yarn purchased from a Korean producer is being shipped to Taiwan, where it is woven and dyed. And zippers produced in Japan are purchased through a Chinese manufacturer. Then, because of quotas and labor conditions, woven yarn and zippers are shipped to Thailand, where garments are made in one of five factories.

Not surprisingly, this movement of raw materials, semi-finished goods and finished products poses a significant supply chain challenge, particularly to smaller businesses. However, many Asian players are working hard to fill the void. A premier example is Li & Fung, Hong Kong's largest export trading company, which works with more than 7500 suppliers across 37 countries. Working primarily over the Internet, this innovative firm coordinates the Pan-Asia supply chain efforts of numerous suppliers, manufacturers, wholesalers, retailers and customers. And it collaborates with virtually all of them on forecasts, capacity management and resource availability, thus enhancing each party's flexibility, responsiveness and agility.

In addition to overall cost savings, value is realized in the reduction of delivery cycle times, from months to weeks. Plus, Li & Fung uses information – not assets – to create competitive supply chains. And its adroit use of e-commerce helps to counteract the threat of major retailers going directly to suppliers, which might cut Li & Fung out of the loop (Magretta, 1998).

Collaborative planning and synchronization   Collaboration among supply chain partners (that is, customers and suppliers) can involve vendor-managed inventory, collaborative demand planning, joint capacity planning or synchronized order fulfilment (which involves the most risk because it makes parties dependent on each other). In any context, however, collaboration represents a new way of thinking for many Asian companies. It also involves several prerequisites: First, companies must re-engineer and integrate their internal supply chain planning processes and technologies prior to involving themselves in collaborative activity. They also must be able to ensure that the data produced by their respective supply chain technologies is valid, consistent, and transparent. Lastly – because real collaboration means sharing information on demand – companies must develop a trust-based 'win–win' perspective. When these requirements have been met, it becomes possible for trading partners to understand each other's basic operating mechanisms and thus develop unified processes that drive down costs and increase the effectiveness of both parties.

7b. Extend beyond the traditional supply chain
Extending beyond the traditional supply chain speaks to the creation of new revenue channels and cost-reduction opportunities by interacting in new or less conventional ways. Here are four examples:

Synchronization of 'trade chain' participants provides the key to making trading hubs more efficient.

Trading hubs   The establishment of logistics and distribution trading hubs is a hot topic in Asia. China, Hong Kong, Malaysia, South Korea, Taiwan and Singapore are all competing to develop supply chain hubs that will control and shape the movement of goods in and around the continent. Making the hub concept work involves the development of solutions that move synchronization beyond supply chain participants to 'trade chain' participants – connecting customers, suppliers, enterprises, bankers, third-party logistics services, air and sea ports, freight forwarders and customs/tax officials. In places such as Hong Kong, there is no more important supply chain imperative, even though overcoming hurdles relating to trust, data standardization, language, currency, security, bureaucracy, ownership and leadership will also pose major challenges.

Even further out, the distributed nature of Asian manufacturing, and the subsequent trade flows that occur among Asian countries, suggest that a major opportunity may exist to connect several hubs into a network of co-opetition (cooperation and competition at the same time). In the long term, this sort of synchronization could help make Asian supply chains a formidable global business force.

'One World' alliance for logistics service providers Seeking to leverage new market opportunities and the growing popularity of hubs are the logistics arms of several nationally backed conglomerates. These forward-looking organizations desire to use their logistics capabilities to develop a network or alliance of national supply chain services providers. This network would likely resemble the 'OneWorld' and 'Star' alliances developed by the airline industry, which bring together a number of previously competing national flag-carrying airlines. Just as competing national airlines collaborate on (and synchronize) the flow of passengers to optimize capacity utilization, an alliance of logistics providers could synchronize the complex flow of goods into, out of, and across Asia.

An opportunity exists for a hub to connect and synchronize the activities of e-marketplaces.

e-marketplaces Most of Asia's e-marketplaces are focused on procurement: Sesami in Singapore, BayanTrade in the Philippines, Cyberlynx and CWOptus in Australia and Pantavanij in Thailand. However, no pan-Asia e-procurement marketplace yet exists – and the market and regulatory diversity makes development of such an entity unlikely in the near term. However, there is an opportunity for a hub that connects and synchronizes the activities of multiple e-marketplaces. Toward this end, Sesami recently announced that it has linked six of the most active e-marketplace operators in the world to form the Global Interoperability Group (GIG). A network of horizontal marketplaces within the Global Trading Web Association, GIG will move e-commerce transactions seamlessly around the world. The theory is that companies working with any of the participating e-marketplaces will be able to use GIG to interact online with trading partners around the world – with one consistent business contract and no concerns about technical compatibility.

Horizontal conglomerates With superior supply chain capabilities developed within and/or across verticals, companies doing business in Asia can further leverage their scale, efficiency and knowledge by improving information flows among horizontals. The goal is to 1) provide a simpler, more integrated one-stop service to customers by synchronizing the delivery of services, and 2) make services available to others – particularly Asia's myriad small-to-medium-size businesses.

Conclusion

Asia is one of the world's most dynamic and diverse markets, and certainly will remain so well into the future. From a supply chain perspective, it is also one of the most challenging markets; and that, too, is unlikely to change any time soon. In fact, different (and generally divergent) cultures, business practices, regulations,

With Asia's supply chain challenges come powerful supply chain opportunities.

technology capabilities and transportation infrastructures often combine to make effective Asian supply chain management seem more like a lofty ideal than an achievable objective.

Certainly, the seven opportunities discussed in this document will not alleviate the basic differences or conflicting priorities that characterize the Asian marketplace. But they do constitute a viable framework for reaching levels of supply chain efficiency and competitiveness that might otherwise be unattainable. Various companies will obviously position those opportunities in varying ways and contexts. – while some will need to focus on mastering the basics, others will be able to move quickly into more advanced optimization and synchronization opportunities. But in all cases, the time to act is now. If you do not begin to capitalize on these opportunities in Asia, rest assured the competition will.

References

Bowman, R. J. (2000), 'Despite Obstacles, Shippers Score Success in Asia', *Supply Chain Brain* (July).

Chee, W., Harrison, C. and Jaffe, D. A. (2001), 'Taking Logistics into the 21st Century – A study of Logistics in Asia/Pacific (Excluding Japan)', IDC, www.idc.com.

Dhawan, R. and Padhi, A. (2000), 'The Asian difference in B2B', *McKinsey Quarterly* (no. 4), pp. 39–47.

The Economist (2001), 'Link in the Global Chain – A surprising world leader in supply-chain management', (2 June).

EIU – Regional Economic News (2001), 'Asia industry: Redefining the pharmaceutical supply chain', 15 October, www.viewswire.com.

Gattorna, J. L. (2000), 'The E-Supply Chain Reaches Asian Shores', in *ASCET*, vol. 2, pp. 335–339, Montgomery Research, Inc., San Francisco, 2000.

Hemerling, J., Entwistle, I., Wetenhall, P. and Desmarais, S. (2001), 'Arming for e-Combat in Asia Pacific: the New Rules of Engagement', The Boston Consulting Group (February), www.bcg.com.

Kim, M. (2001), 'LG Electronics' Global Supply Chain Management System Goes Live', *Business Wire* (5 September).

Lim, June (2001), 'Malaysia continues to improve logistics infrastructure', *MHD Supply Chain Solutions* (Nov–Dec), p. 14.

Magretta, J. (1998), 'Fast, Global, and Entrepreneurial: Supply Chain Management, Hong Kong Style', An Interview with Victor Fung', *Harvard Business Review* (September–October), pp. 103–114.

Manion, D. (1999) 'Asia Pacific Supply Chain Survey', CommerceNet, (19 November).

The changing face of supply chains in China

5.4

Robert Easton

Supply chains in China are on the edge – the edge of spectacular development. China's current supply chain infrastructure and operational paradigms restrain social and economic development and limit the profitable performance of local and foreign companies. Nowhere else in the world will the development of infrastructure and capabilities play such a critical role in achieving the aspirations of a nation and individual companies over the next five to ten years.

China has long been hampered by poor infrastructure, a fragmented and chaotic distribution system, local protectionism, a lack of third-party capabilities, cash flow and accounts receivable problems, and anachronistic and restrictive laws. These conditions mean there are few efficient supply chains in China and improvement in these areas will take time. China's accession to the World Trade Organization (WTO) in 2001 and the increasing liberalization of government regulations, together with huge government investment to upgrade China's logistics and transport infrastructure, brings the modernization of China's supply chains one step closer. Overall, the future directions of China's supply chains are promising, but moving forward a number of issues, such as the pace of regulatory change and the shortage of skilled people will need to be managed with patience, tact and care.

This paper assesses the current state of China's supply chain infrastructure and identifies the major challenges to achieving supply chain efficiency. The results of these inefficiencies are summarized. The paper then describes current drivers fueling change such as market growth, liberalization of government policies and China's accession to WTO. Likely future directions for China's supply chains are discussed and the issues to be managed going forward highlighted.

'The quickest route to failure is the assumption that experience in other markets will translate to China. On the ground, unexpected gaps – in infrastructure, commercial law and the business expertise of local partners – foil the equation.' (EIU, 2001)

Change is inevitable for China's supply chains. Given current capability levels, the changes portend huge opportunities for all supply chain participants.

The challenges of China's supply chains

The reality of China's supply chains today is characterized by five important challenges: geography, infrastructure, customs inefficiency and transparency, regulations, culture and unwritten business practices.

Geographic dispersion – the tyranny of geography

Demand is greatest in China's major cities, the developing urban areas of the south and the eastern coastal provinces. Business is more difficult in central and western China.

China is a country of multiple, self-reliant provinces. The principle of self-reliance, itself a legacy of the post-1949 Maoist doctrine, resulted in duplicated industrial infrastructure, over-capacity in manufacturing and distribution, little synergies between provinces, complex and inefficient bureaucracies, and local protectionism. Demand is concentrated around the developing urban areas of the south and along the coastal provinces in the east and the major cities of Beijing and Tianjin, Shanghai and Guangdong. These regions contain China's major logistics infrastructure, including ports and hubs, and have the highest per capita income in the country.

The interior, northern and western part of China offer significant opportunities since two-thirds of the population live there. However, the challenges are great. Low per capita incomes, local protectionism, and a lack of infrastructure makes doing business in these areas difficult, particularly because of poor access.

Distribution and transport infrastructure

Standard supply chain theories cannot be applied because of an incapacity to ship and receive product in a timely manner.

China lacks adequate road, rail, air, port and technology infrastructure; of the seven world's most highly industrialized nations, China is last in development of infrastructure. China's national logistics network is significantly underdeveloped. Companies entering the Chinese market have found standard theories of supply chain management simply cannot be applied in a region that does not have the physical capacity to ship and receive product in a timely manner. Each mode of transportation will be briefly reviewed below.

Rail

A lack of rail sidings at ports and plants and no inter-modal links makes use of rail inefficient or impossible for carriage of many commodity types.

Rail is the cheapest method of distribution in China but is used predominantly for moving bulk materials, including chemicals, coal and grain. Many constraints, however, exist for using rail efficiently. Our research indicates that between 25 and 30 per cent of demand for cargo space on railroads cannot be met and about 2000 towns are inaccessible. Also, a lack of rail sidings at ports and plants and no inter-modal links makes use of rail inefficient or impossible. For these and other more service-related issues, moving finished goods by rail is problematic, including inflexible schedules and pilferage. Together, all these problems lead many companies to opt for alternative distribution methods. HAVI Food Services who distribute for McDonald's continue to use refrigerated truck fleets for distribution in China when rail would be ideal if it could provide a reliable cold chain service at a competitive price.

Rail is controlled by the MOR (Ministry of Rail) who have embarked on a number of projects to upgrade the rail infrastructure and to increase both capacity and travel speed.

Road

Although costs are generally higher than rail and water, road transport is the preferred option for moving packaged finished goods in China. Road transport offers foreign companies greater flexibility and control over delivery times and the delivery condition of goods. Like rail, there are many challenges to achieving efficiencies in road transport. While China is investing billions of dollars in upgrading its road transport infrastructure, development cannot keep pace with the demand for road freight traffic and the overall network remains severely inadequate. Urban areas are highly congested, placing limitations on delivery times and movements for vehicles in cities such as Shanghai and Beijing.

Road transport is the preferred option for moving packaged finished goods, providing greater flexibility and control.

From a structural point of view, the road transport industry in China is extremely fragmented. There are over two milllion registered trucking providers and 5.4 million trucks registered in China, of which only 187 000 are registered heavy duty vehicles. Regional, provincial and local fleets continue to dominate the market and do so with inefficient, aging and inappropriate fleets. Ultilization is low, pricing cartels exist, overloading is common, service is poor, preventative maintenance is lax, damage is common due to bad roads and poor equipment, and huge inefficiencies exist. Empty miles, for example, average about 50 per cent for Chinese trucks at an estimated loss of over US$8 billion each year. Only one-fifth of China's freight trucks are containerized, meaning that goods are frequently damaged as they sit in open-back vehicles. Local providers are not reliable, maintenance is poor and quality control lax. Moreover, there is limited finance available for upgrading equipment and investing in new technology.

Trans-provincial movement remains problematic due to local protectionism and complex licensing. Some provinces and munici-palities make it so onerous for outside trucking firms to secure licenses, that shipments must be reloaded onto the next jurisdiction's trucks. Many cities will not allow trucks to enter without licensing, which can often take hours to obtain. Toll roads also pose a major challenge for road transport in China with some provinces levying additional tolls on out of province trucks. According to Shaw and Wang (2001), tolls amount to as much as 20 per cent of trucking costs in China. Security remains a major concern with road transport and it is still necessary to use escorts in some interior provinces.

Air

Airfreight is predicted to grow considerably in the long term but today use of air cargo suffers a host of problems. Prices are high, routes are fragmented, information exchange between airlines and forwarders is problematic; cargo capacity is limited due to a heavy focus on passengers by major Chinese airlines; and airport networks are inadequate. Moreover, freight forwarders rarely provide basic value-added services that are the norm in the United States or Europe. Despite the limitations, foreign service providers are restricted from expanding capacity. Over the next 10 to 15 years China plans to spend billions of dollars on airport construction, including a super-hub for air cargo at Guangzhou to rival Hong Kong's Chek Lap Kok airport.

The air express sector, particularly, faces problems from short hours and sudden closures of relevant departments at cargo terminals. Same-day outbound services are problematic unless goods are picked up from customers early in the morning. Tax regimes also demand higher taxes as a service industry than the tax bracket for the rest of the transportation industry

Ocean and inland water transport

Shipping is China's most developed distribution sector and significant investment is being made in upgrading the infrastructure. The top ten ports in China account for 40 per cent of all domestic and international cargo. China's shipping companies rank among the world's largest. The China Ocean Shipping Group (COSCO) is the seventh largest shipping company in the world. China's ports, however, face many inefficiencies, including: an inability to process and manage cargo at international standards of efficiency; intermodal operations often require multiple crane moves causing bottlenecks; bureaucratic delays in customs processing; high pilferage and damage rates relative to other modern ports; over capacity; and an inability to take larger cargo vessels.

Inland water transport for domestic distribution of goods is cheap but is underutilized due mainly to the many problems and inefficiencies – schedules are inflexible, and deliver reliability is an issue, with delays experienced due to storms, 'lost in transit' or damage. While not suitable for moving finished goods and time-sensitive freight, shipping and inland barges are a good solution for moving bulk commodities, particularly over long distances. Until infrastructure is developed, this mode will remain relatively under-utilized.

Warehousing

Access to modern warehousing is a necessity in China; however, current warehousing is rudimentary with limited use of automation, inefficient designs, low ceilings, unreliable temperature controls to manage humidity and cool chains, and a lack of pest control. Goods are handled and stacked manually, often without the use of racking, and they are mixed indiscriminately regardless of the risk of contamination. Automation and use of information technology is rare in China. Consequently, warehousing operations are characterized by poor inventory controls and discrepancies, limited ability to track orders, and high incidences of obsolescence, shrinkage, pilferage and damage. Improving warehousing infrastructure and operations is a major focus for many companies and China is witnessing improvements in building design and structures, and increasing use of warehouse management systems and automated materials handling equipment.

As more modern warehouses are built, access to higher quality services at lower rents in close proximity to other services will result. The development of a number of logistics hubs with sophisticated warehousing and other supply chain capabilities have been announced by national and provincial authorities. EIU (December, 2001) reported that by 2005 the government aims to build 30 modern distribution and logistics centers around the country. Two modern logistics centers are being built in Shanghai today where, the local government is investing US $15 billion to build a world-class logistics business; one is also being built in Beijing. Some companies like HAVI have constructed their own purpose-built distribution centers and are achieving productivity levels which are comparable to the best in the West.

Information technology and the Internet

Information technology and particularly e-commerce infrastructure in China are in their infancy, relative to the US and Europe. Some attempts to take logistics online in China have been made. However, use of IT and penetration of the Internet is poor. A 2001 International Data Corporation paper rates China's electronic logistics services as 'very poor'. Many organizations still conduct their operations manually so the number of participants required to complete a supply chain transaction is significantly higher than would be found in a developed economy. Data on customer needs and preferences are hard to obtain, cargo tracking is poor, communication with supply chain participants within the four walls difficult, and beyond them patchy. According to a survey by the China Storage Association (CSA), 61 per cent of Chinese logistics providers do not even have a logistics information system (Ho and Lim, 2001).

Most companies in China have been cautious in embracing leading-edge technologies. Indeed, many SOEs and local Chinese companies have not undergone re-engineering and have only just started to implement enterprise resource planning (ERP) systems. Yet it is impossible to embark on more advanced supply chain initiatives, for which data and process re-engineering are a prerequisite.

Customs inefficiency

Inefficiency of customs is a major issue for many businesses. A multitude of different bureaucracies are involved in customs clearances, paperwork is daunting and processing inefficient. Clearance can only be achieved during business hours, which themselves are short, and closures are common during public holidays. This compares to other Asian ports where customs officials operate 7 days a week, 24 hours a day. If disputes arise over documentation, duties or valuations, customs officials will impound goods until such disputes are settled. For many foreign organizations in China, delays in clearance procedures rank among their biggest concerns. Electronic processing is being developed but is not yet working effectively. Manual methods remain in many cases. Based on the attention this issue is being given by both government and business, significant improvement in the efficiency of customs is anticipated in the short to medium term.

Government agencies – complexity and coordination

Multiple government bodies divide responsibilities for different sectors of the industry.

Multiple government bodies divide responsibilities for different sectors of the industry. Many firms, both foreign and domestic, find it difficult identifying the agency handling their sector. Meeting the different sets of approval requirements for working in multiple sectors of the industry is also difficult. Overlapping jurisdictions coupled with the scope of business restrictions and non-transparent regulations further hinder market access. Lack of coordination between agencies reduces the Government's ability to plan and develop the infrastructure that is necessary for logistics.

Regulations – implications and impacts

The current rudimentary state of China's supply chains results a lot from the regulatory controls, which have severely restricted distribution rights for foreign companies (see Figure 5.4.1) and inhibited the development of service based rather than asset based logistics enterprises. Regulations have impacted the development of supply chain capabilities, efficiencies and costs in three critical areas: distribution channels, the ability to consolidate across MNC entities, and third party and non-asset based logistic providers.

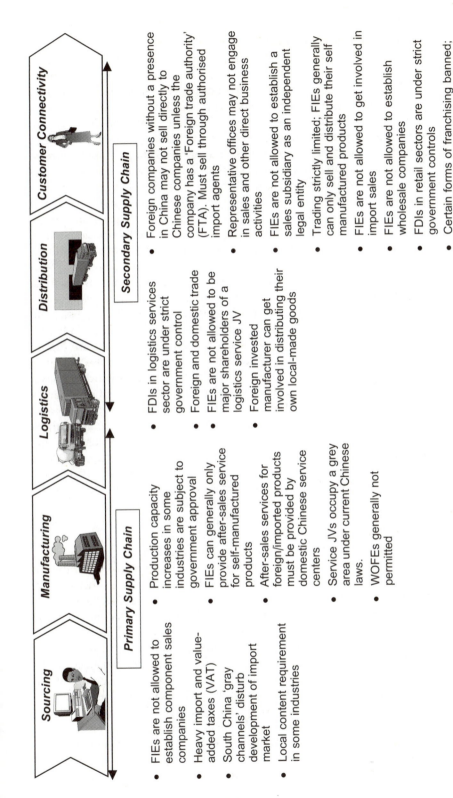

Sourcing | **Manufacturing** | **Logistics** | **Distribution** | **Customer Connectivity**

Primary Supply Chain

Secondary Supply Chain

Sourcing
- FIEs are not allowed to establish component sales companies
- Heavy import and value-added taxes (VAT)
- South China 'gray channels' disturb development of import market
- Local content requirement in some industries

Manufacturing
- Production capacity increases in some industries are subject to government approval
- FIEs can generally only provide after-sales service for self-manufactured products
- After-sales services for foreign/imported products must be provided by domestic Chinese service centers
- Service JVs occupy a grey area under current Chinese laws.
- WOFEs generally not permitted

Logistics / Distribution
- FDIs in logistics services sector are under strict government control
- Foreign and domestic trade
- FIEs are not allowed to be major shareholders of a logistics service JV
- Foreign invested manufacturer can get involved in distributing their own local-made goods

Customer Connectivity
- Foreign companies without a presence in China may not sell directly to Chinese companies unless the company has a 'Foreign trade authority' (FTA). Must sell through authorised import agents
- Representative offices may not engage in sales and other direct business activities
- FIEs are not allowed to establish a sales subsidiary as an independent legal entity
- Trading strictly limited; FIEs generally can only sell and distribute their self manufactured products
- FIEs are not allowed to get involved in import sales
- FIEs are not allowed to establish wholesale companies
- FDIs in retail sectors are under strict government controls
- Certain forms of franchising banned; direct sales and multi-level marketing banned

Figure 5.4.1

Factors impacting supply chain competitiveness in Asia

Complexity and sophistication of distribution channels

Historically supply chains have been at the mercy of local protectionism, unfair competition, and an excessive number of government regulations at both the national and provincial level. Distribution channels in China today evolved from the three-tier command and control structure that existed in the 1970s and much of the 1980s. Within this structure distributors, who were not able to import products, provided basic distribution services but no marketing or sales support. Foreign trade corporations (FTCs) by law were required to sell goods through a distributor and were forbidden from owning distribution channels and logistics infrastructure. State distributors were not required to be commercially minded nor innovative, they were simply required to transport goods from producers to local distribution points.

Today, regulations still prevent foreign companies from distributing products directly to retailers, other than those they make in China, and from owning or controlling their own distribution channels. In some industries, restrictions are very strict. Foreign companies are forced to rely on local companies with sub-standard capability to distribute product through multi-tiered wholesaler channels, as shown in Figure 5.4.2. Consequently, many distribution channels in China are highly inefficient, fragmented and costly. Wholesalers, for example, lack scale and financial strength – receivables often extend beyond 90 days. Their transport, warehousing and inventory management capabilities are poor, leading to damage and excess inventory; sales and merchandising is almost non-existent; the quality of their management sub-standard; and they rarely have a defined strategy. Only a few companies like HAVI have the ability to distribute nationally, so there is a plethora of small and medium-sized local players. The Economist Intelligence Unit (EIU) reports there are 16 000 wholesalers in the pharmaceutical industry in China. This compares with the US where there are only eight, of which half distribute 80 per cent of the product with margins of 3–5 per cent (EIU, October 2001).

The multi-tiered structure also results in a lack of control of both logistics service levels and at the point-of-sale, because a number of sub-contractors are used by distributors. In reality many manufacturers cannot control delivery times or condition, and control at point of sale poses significant challenges for sales and marketing. A company who pays for shelf space, for example, will not know if the goods are stocked in the shelf space paid for unless additional staff are used to check this. Moreover, wholesalers are often unable to provide information on customer demand or preferences and they are not in a position to, or not willing to, solicit feedback from customers. So access to up and down-stream information is limited, making management of sub-contractors very difficult. Worse still is the common practice of cross-boundary selling where wholesalers exploit differential pricing strategies in one place by buying up large and selling in another region at a profit.

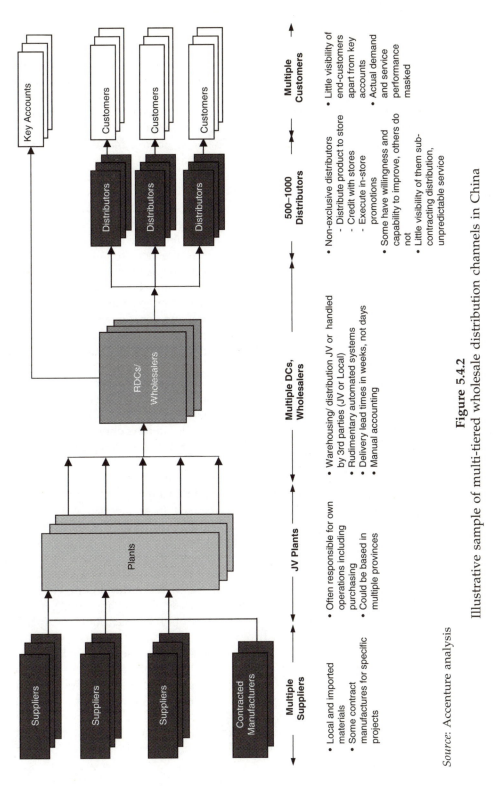

Figure 5.4.2

Illustrative sample of multi-tiered wholesale distribution channels in China

Source: Accenture analysis

The consumer goods industry provides a good example of distribution issues and practices in China. Ninety per cent of the retail outlets are 'mom and pop' stores that have floor space of about 10 square meters and capacity for one to two days' stock of fast-moving goods. While some companies have tried distributing direct to retailers with varying degrees of success, no one has achieved this at a national level – the economics simply do not justify it.

Within the multi-tiered wholesaler structure, many second- and third-tier wholesalers operate on slim margins of 1–2 per cent, yet they provide the service face to the customer. Some manufacturers of strong brands have found they have been able to eliminate one or two layers from this distribution system by working with bottom-tier wholesalers directly to service the tail and dealing directly with selected key accounts. The increase in physical distribution costs has been more than offset by the margin retained from the layers eliminated.

Regulations together with the rudimentary state of distribution infrastructure have and will continue to compel foreign companies to adopt creative distribution solutions which enable them to get product to customers while preserving margins and control over information, inventory, and point-of-sale services. For Coca-Cola, this meant developing an independent distribution network in China. Coca-Cola hires its own distributors to service an area within a 50 km radius of each bottling plant and outsources distribution in remote areas. In cities such as Shanghai, the company uses elderly 'street committee' members whose privileges enable them to distribute in hard-to-reach areas and thus achieve ubiquity. These distributors only sell Coca-Cola and do so out of refrigerated push carts and cycles stocked straight from the bottling plant.

In 1999, Swire Beverages launched an intensive effort to penetrate southern and eastern China down to township level. After surveying local retailers, the company approached local independent wholesalers to work with them. Swire's program, called Partnership 101, offers wholesalers training, management assistance and still enables the company to control order management and inventory. By 2001, Swire had enlisted 1000 Partnership 101 wholesalers (Weisert, 2001).

Other companies that have been successful in developing effective distribution networks in China. HAVI and Tricon have done so by owning their own fleets to direct supply key accounts or major retailers and selected distributors in urban areas that fall within a defined radius of regional factories or warehouses, and using local distributors in outlying regions. High levels of business are used to compel local operators to meet minimum capability requirements and service levels, albeit in most cases the local operation needs consistent and time consuming monitoring. For companies who do not have regional plants or warehouses to operate a base from, the common practice is to appoint regional distributors to handle relationships with wholesalers.

For a number of companies in China today, however, the biggest challenge facing them is how to migrate to the untapped market in the west, where many more people are now in a position to buy a hamburger or a piece of chicken and drink a Coke. Reaching remote areas in the northeast, northwest, west and southwest is difficult and arduous. Even the best companies are finding that the effort required to create their distribution infrastructure and systems in the east have to be repeated all over again in the west.

There are two major lessons learned to date about distribution in China:

- There is no single right answer to developing distribution channels in China. However, a step-by-step approach seems to have been most successful – city by city, region by region, province by province.
- Heavy investment in distribution channels pays off. The companies that have invested, such as HAVI, Coca-Cola, Swire, Tricon, Haier and Legend, usually develop the most reliable and efficient networks. Moreover, in doing so these companies are also getting closer to gaining control over where and how their products are marketed to consumers. Of course, strong brands and high volumes were essential determinants in making these distribution models successful. There may also be opportunities for lesser brands to build an attractive proposition for distribution partners, through coalescing with complementary brands and partners. Since operating in China cheaply and efficiently is so difficult, companies who can create efficient distribution solutions have a huge advantage. To take advantage of partnering opportunities, however, companies will need to break the mindset that a capability must always be owned; so they must be able to make the leap from asset-based logistics to service-based logistics.

Constraints on consolidating across MNC entities

Current regulations are particularly constraining on foreign companies with multiple entities or ventures. One of the biggest challenges facing multinational corporations in China is how to consolidate the supply chain and back-office functions across their entities. For many, regulations have resulted in duplicated structures, assets, operations and contractual relationships. While each plant may sell its own production in China it cannot sell or distribute product from a sister plant or entity, nor finished goods imported into China. Moreover, parent holding companies in China are restricted from selling the products from any of the plants. This prevents foreign companies from consolidating shipments and issuing consolidated invoices and statements for shipments going to the same customer.

For foreign logistics providers to offer total supply chain solutions to clients, they need a relaxation in regulations, the ability to source and retain key talent, and the ability to offer non-asset based services.

Constraints on third-party and non-asset based logistics providers

Foreign logistics providers in China rate dealing with government restrictions as their biggest single challenge. The lack of reform by state distributors and transport operators combined with regulatory blocks has created a massive void in sophisticated third-party logistics providers. Currently, only four wholly owned foreign companies offer logistics outside of special zones and within China. Regulations have prevented foreign third-party providers from owning logistics distribution resources, except through joint ventures. Technically, foreign firms are limited to a 49 per cent stake in logistics ventures. But joint ventures have not worked well nor led to the major developments in capability that China's government had hoped for. Many foreign firms find themselves in direct competition with their joint venture partner when bidding on contracts. Many partners have also enjoyed a protected position without making an effort to modernize or improve their services. A recent survey by Accenture of a number of logistics executives in China found that joint ventures have not delivered – quite simply partners are not motivated to improve.

The inability to control downstream distribution and thus unmask one of the major sources of supply chain inefficiency restricts their ability to help customers achieve the type of efficiencies they might otherwise enjoy. Worse still, foreign logistics providers cannot compete on price, local knowledge, relationships or domestic network coverage and still have to use local operators, thus undermining their offer of 'value-added services'. Their hope lies in being able to offer a 'one-stop-shop' or total supply chain solution to clients. For this, however, they need a relaxation in regulations which permits the establishment and operation of non-asset based service providers and the ability to source and retain key local talent.

Indeed, for China the inability of companies to establish non-asset based logistics operations places a major logistics cost impost on supply chains. Regulations act against companies setting up non-asset based logistics, and the mindset in China for most companies, both foreign and local, is that ownership of assets is a prerequisite to having a logistics capability. This contrasts significantly with the West where third-party logistics providers are solution architects rather than asset providers. In the West a third-party logistics provider avoids asset ownership unless that asset is tied directly to a contract and even then it tries to get assets off balance sheet. Failure to address this issue will significantly impact the competitiveness and attractiveness of investments in SOEs such as Sinotrans and COSCO, amongst other local companies, as they seek to list on the stock market. More importantly, unless focus moves away from asset ownership towards a service-based mentality, there will be a severe backlash from customers and consumers whose expectations are rising at a rapid pace.

Constraints on culture and business practices

In China, three culturally based factors can have a crippling effect on supply chain efficiency; and these will be difficult for MNCs to overcome. First, 'win–lose thinking' dominates business, especially when dealing with suppliers. The road transport industry in China is a classic example of this type of thinking, where the delivery of the lowest-cost solution is given priority, without regard to service. Second, trust is the foundation for open sharing of information and collaboration between supply chain parties, yet trust remains a major issue in China. Third, people often 'mind their own business': they stay within their own boundaries and avoid challenging the way those outside those boundaries do business, especially those they perceive as superiors. This mindset inhibits coordination between departments and trading parties and in doing so can prevent value being unlocked from the supply chain.

Business behavior arising from cultural beliefs can have a crippling effect on supply chain efficiency.

In addition to these cultural traits, 'off-book' transactions such as incentive payments are common in China. These practices affect specific supply chain initiatives, particularly those that will result in transparency of these transactions, such as initiatives to improve the buying of materials and services and the development national logistics infrastructures.

Constraints on human resources

Finding and keeping people with skills in supply chain management poses one of the most difficult challenges facing companies in China today. People with the relevant capabilities do exist, as third-party logistics providers, the People's Liberation Army (PLA), and a number of MNCs have trained people over time. However, the resource pool is limited. As one supply chain director at a leading MNC in China noted, 'China lost its entire middle-level generation of managers due to the cultural revolution'. In the command economy, striving for transportation or logistics functional excellence, received little attention. For many companies, their people have little concept of functional or service excellence and they do not understand how value-added services will help the business grow.

People have little concept of functional or service excellence and they often have little incentive to perform.

In addition, many people are looking for short-term gains and often make impulse decisions to leave if they are offered a better salary or if change programs are poorly perceived. The human resources director of one MNC in China noted that 'staff have a lower sense of career; they are just embracing the market economy'. Staff members also have little incentive to perform because seniority is valued over performance, there is often little connection between job responsibilities and reward structures and benefits are overly complex. Moreover, a 'passive aggressive' attitude towards change is the norm in China and there is a propensity to refuse to take responsibility or ownership of issues.

Outcomes – inefficient supply chains

The challenges posed by doing business in China should not be underestimated. Supply chains in China are costly, inefficient, unreliable and limit the ability to understand and interface with the customer. These challenges are summarized in Table 5.4.1. This table is supported by some key statistics taken from a 2001 EIU report. For example:

- working capital turnover in China ranges from 1.2 times for manufacturing SOEs to 2.3 times for commercial SOEs – compared with 15 and 20 times respectively in the US and even as high as 30 times for some MNCs in the US
- on average, 90 per cent of a Chinese manufacturer's time is spent on logistics, with just 10 per cent on manufacturing (EIU, 2001)
- many commodities in China cost 40 to 50 per cent more to transport than they would in the US

Table 5.4.1
Challenges facing China's supply chains

Cost	Efficiency	Reliability – Service performance	Customer contact and management
• High comparative costs – 30% to 50% higher than in the west • High national costs • High fixed costs, duplication of assets and infrastructure • Large accounts receivable, poor credit control • Pilferage, shrinkage, damages are high • High provincial protectionism increases costs	• Inefficient supply chain operations • Double and triple handling common • Little collaboration • No industry/national standards • Regulatory limitations on centralization and consolidation • Restrictions on vehicle movements in cities • High dependence on manual systems	• Poor service performance • Unpredictable pick up and delivery of goods • Re-prioritization of cargo • Dissatisfied customers, unfulfilled needs • Reliance on sub-contractors who have little sense of quality and service • No transparency in the shipment process; limited track-and-trace • Preventative maintenance, unreliable and poor • Poor forecasting and inventory accuracy • Poor sales and operations planning processes	• Lack of sophisticated market intelligence • Limited systematic feedback from distributors and retailers • Major gaps in understanding customer needs and contact points • Limited direct contact with end customers and consumers • Limited control of sales, marketing and merchandising • Demand data is inaccurate • Masking of actual demand • Published data is inconsistent • Complex customer segmentation • No understanding of cost-to-serve

Source: Accenture

- transport and warehouse costs in China equal 30–40 per cent of the total cost of goods sold, and up to 80 per cent for chemical products.

There are structural reasons for higher costs, but the principal drivers of the inefficiencies are the challenges and shortcomings of China's supply chain reality, discussed earlier.

The winds of change – trends and drivers fueling change

Despite the challenges to achieving competitive supply chains in China there are three strong factors fueling change: first is market growth and changing customer requirements; second is liberalization of government policies, and third is China's accession to WTO.

Market growth and changing customer requirements

China's population of 1.2 billion is expected to keep growing rapidly, by some 15 million people per year. Current GNP of $816 billion is also forecast to increase by 8–9 per cent per year. Four hundred of the world's top 500 enterprises have invested in China between 1995 and 1999, $230 billion has been invested in China. As a byproduct of this strong growth, the consumer goods market is expanding at an increasing pace as the spending power and aspirations of consumers rise. Industries are consolidating and modern retailers are penetrating second and even some third-tier cities These trends are fuelling the drive to modernize China's supply chain infrastructure and creating demand for more sophisticated supply chain solutions. Domestic distributors will be unable to meet the levels of service demanded by companies in an increasingly competitive market, leading to a long overdue restructuring of the logistics services sector.

Strong population growth and increases in consumer spending power are fueling the drive to modernize China's supply chain infrastructure.

The emergence of modern retailers, including foreign retail chains like Carrefour, for example, are generating demand for more efficient and reliable services. These demands from retailers have sent a wave of requirements back along the supply chain and forced shippers, manufacturers and distributors alike to upgrade their capabilities.

Liberalization of government policies

The Chinese Government has been very public about its recognition that the lack of development in the logistics and transportation sectors is a major impediment to industrial growth. Encouraged by central government, state and provincial governments continue to commit to huge investments to upgrade infrastructure and build logistics centers or hubs to promote consolidation and collaboration between logistics players and capabilities.

In addition to developing infrastructure, the Chinese Government announced its intention to:

Table 5.4.2
Post-WTO regulations

	By 2002	By 2003	By 2004	By 2005	By 2006	By 2007
Trading restrictions	• Minority ownership/JVs to engage in wholesale of both import and domestic products • FIEs can distribute products made in China	• Lifting of foreign majority, geographical and quantitative restrictions • In retailing some geographic restrictions	• Lifting all restrictions • Establish WOFE • All geographic restrictions lifted for retailing		• Books, chemicals fertilizers, crude oil and processed petroleum phased in over 3–5 years • Few limitations • No restrictions for retailing	
Shipping and freight forwarding		• Majority ownership			• Wholly owned subsidiaries • Foreign companies not limited in ownership percentage	
Maritime cargo handling, customer clearance	• Foreign – PRC ventures permitted					
Rail transportation	• Minority ownership/JVs		• Majority ownership			• Wholly owned subsidiaries
Road transport	• Minority ownership/JVs	• Majority ownership		• Wholly owned subsidiaries		
Warehousing and storage	• Minority ownership/JVs	• Majority ownership		• Wholly owned subsidiaries		
Courier services	• Minority ownership/JVs	• Majority ownership			• Wholly owned subsidiaries	

- promote third-party logistics and the use of modern information technology, particularly among its state-owned enterprises and local manufacturers
- provide education and training in logistics, and
- establish a legal and regulatory environment that supports development of the logistics sector in China.

There also appears to be a degree of relaxation in some regulations in a bid to accelerate the modernization process. For example, the Ministry of Rail recently announced changes in regulations to encourage foreign firms to invest in railway infrastructure.

China's accession to WTO

Accession to the WTO, granted in December 2001, complements China's own economic reform process and reinforces the reform movement. Under China's WTO agreement, it will progressively remove the restrictions that prevent foreign companies from participating in the logistics and transportation sector, as summarized in Table 5.4.2. The WTO agreement will stimulate China's economic growth by opening the economy to competition and encouraging collaboration between local and foreign companies.

The WTO agreement will stimulate China's economic growth by opening the economy to competition and encouraging collaboration between local and foreign companies.

The important point to remember is that while membership will be phased in over several years, a key change taking immediate effect is that foreign firms will be able to distribute all products made in China, and within a year be able to distribute imported products. They will be able to hold a majority share in a logistics joint venture within a year and operate without restrictions within three years. Within three to four years of accession, all restrictions on logistics primary and ancillary services will be phased out, eventually enabling foreign companies to set up 100 per cent foreign-owned subsidiaries covering warehousing, refrigeration, freight forwarding, road transport, rental and leasing, rail, express delivery, air courier, advertising, sorting and grading of bulk lots, breaking bulk lots, packing services, testing and analysis, and installation and after-sales services including maintenance and repair.

Future directions and opportunities

The sustained growth, favourable government policies, and entry to WTO will drive significant changes in China's supply chain landscape over the next five to ten years in a number of key areas.

Supply chain status

The expanding market and increasing customer demand is positioning the supply chain as a competitive differentiator. Retaining the status quo is no longer an option. Businesses now clearly recognize the size of the performance gap in China's supply chain and see it as an inhibitor to progress and efficiency. Furthermore, the poor supply chain is not only constraining the performance of local and foreign companies, but development of the nation.

Delays should be anticipated, competition will be regulated

The WTO accession will stimulate major changes to China's economy; however, delays should be anticipated. The extent of liberalization of China's distribution and logistics service sector will depend a great deal on how committed the Government is to expose the domestic players to open competition in a free market. China is likely to manage the opening of the logistics and distribution sectors carefully and in a way that maximizes the opportunities to pass management and operational expertise to local companies. Foreign investors must anticipate that the Chinese Government will enact new rules to regulate competition and bring order to the WTO transition. Delays due to structural factors should also be anticipated.

Increase in efficiency and transparency of customs

There will be an increase in the professionalism and transparency of customs requirements and operations. Service at customs points will become more efficient.

Hard commercial reality will challenge the existing order of Guanxi

With such rapid changes in China's business and consumer world, hard commercial reality will eventually challenge the existing order of Guanxi. Strong networks and relationships are important throughout the world, but in China business traditionally has been based on relationships, often at the expense of harsh commercial reality. This will change.

Intensifying competition and industry consolidation

Many sectors exposed to foreign competition are consolidating rapidly, particularly in the fast-moving consumer goods sector. Significant consolidation has already occurred in the home appliance, television, and beer sectors to name a few. Since under the planned economy even the smallest manufacturer had its own truck fleet and warehouses, massive duplication of logistics assets exists. With consolidation comes the opportunity to eliminate unnecessary assets and create scale and efficiencies in supply chain operations.

Consolidation of Hong Kong-based foreign traders

Pressure to increase margins and exert greater control over channels, together with the need to reach deeper into China's heartland will lead to the consolidation of Hong Kong-based traders. The closure of EAC and sale of Inchape to Li & Fung are evidence that this trend is already underway.

Increased efficiency in ports

Bigger trade flows, more intense competition, and increasing demands from shippers for better service, together with a rise in foreign investment, will lead to changes in the port sector. Since the efficiency of the port sector is considered one of the biggest obstacles to global competitiveness, major involvement of foreign companies in infrastructure joint ventures is anticipated. Foreign firms will be able to take a 49 per cent stake in shipping JVs upon accession and participate in port development projects.

Bypassing inefficient and non-value adding third parties – delayering distribution channels

Established firms will be able to bypass third parties such as state import–export corporations and wholesalers unless they can provide some true value-added service. These parties will be forced to upgrade their capabilities to be attractive outsourcing alternatives. Inevitably, unnecessary layers of bureaucracy and the non-value adding participants in distribution chains will be eliminated. For example, in the pharmaceutical industry, where multiple layers of distributors exist, only one layer is expected to survive in the future (EIU, October 2001). Consolidation in the retail industry already is leading to manufacturers selling direct to retailers and this trend is likely to continue as online systems are implemented. By taking the middlemen out of the supply chain, Dell Computer, for example, has achieved price points 10–25 per cent lower than its foreign competitors. Dell is able to reach more than 300 cities in China within nine to ten days, seven of which are attributed to delivery time (EIU, 2001).

Development of distribution channels

Will there be a mad rush by shippers to develop their own distribution channels and wholesale networks following China's accession to the WTO? Unlikely, as eliminating wholesalers and relying on foreign logistics providers, or even attempting to bring distribution in-house, could be costly and time consuming. Time taken to establish a network could lead to lost sales or market share foregone to competitors – exited distributors will react against attempts by a shipper to develop their own network. So even after all clauses take effect, establishing an independent nationwide network will remain a dream for most foreign distributors who will continue to rely on local partners to reach outside major cities and into second tier cities and remote regions.

Integration, centralization and rationalization of supply chain functions and assets

Significant growth in integration, centralization and rationalization of supply chain functions, assets, infrastructure, people and operations is expected. This trend will be fueled by removal of regulatory restrictions together with rising customer demands for a 'one-stop' service and the recognition that significant cost savings are achievable. For example, by integrating and centralizing its procurement, raw materials distribution and finished goods distribution functions, previously scattered across dozens of product centers, Haier achieved significant reductions in cost, assets and major gains in service performance (Ho and Lim, 2001). Given the size of the potential benefits, we predict a rise of supply chain shared service organizations across both foreign and local companies in China.

Consolidation and development of third-party logistics providers

The opportunity to incorporate wholly owned foreign enterprises (WOFEs) within three years from accession should attract foreign firms to an industry, which is currently growing at over 30 per cent per annum for the next five years, willing to invest in infrastructure projects necessary for a modern national logistics transportation network. The entry of foreign providers as WOFEs will place great pressure on local distributors to develop competitive capabilities over the next three years. Competition is already intensifying in the third-party logistics market. This competition will force a consolidation of the logistics and distribution industry as a whole in China, just as it did earlier in the US and Europe.

Restructuring of ministries, SOEs and local logistics firms

China's accession into the WTO will have a more profound effect on local Chinese companies than on China-based MNCs. WTO membership will provide consumers, customers and shippers with choice, and choice means more competition. Accession to the WTO will therefore create impetus for ministries such as the Ministry of Rail, SOEs and local firms to develop efficient capabilities. The current thinking is that China has a three- to four-year window in which to restructure its companies and industries before foreign providers become a significant force. A number of local companies are readying themselves for battle. Sinotrans, for example, is positioning itself to become the first company in China to offer total transportation and logistics solutions for countrywide door-to-door services and the leading logistics provider in China.

Other SOEs and local firms have ambitious aspirations as well, for example:

- COSCO, China Post and China Rail are in the process of transforming themselves into value-added third-party logistics service providers. China Chengtong Group, a US $1.2 billion company plans to become one of the top five logistics service providers through a process of acquisitions and alliances.
- There is a set of new emerging local players like ST-Anda, EAS and PG Logistics who are developing a portfolio of value-added

services in a bid to gain a leading position in the market. These companies have limited assets but focus on delivering solutions and extending their services to cover the full supply chain. They are also targeting MNCs as key clients but have some way to go before they will be able to offer the total solution the MNCs are looking for. ST-Anda already has a network of 20 distribution centers throughout China covering 600 cities, and claim to be able to deliver goods to over 300 of these cities within 48 hours by either rail or road (Ho and Lim, 2001).

- Finally, new entrants to the third-party logistics market have emerged from in-house distribution divisions of local manufacturers, for example Haier Logistics. For Haier, the fast-growing 3PL industry is a lot more attractive than the commoditized appliance industry.

Outsourcing

The shortage of key talent and supply chain capability will force companies to rethink their strategies to acquire capabilities, that is, whether to build, buy or borrow the capability. Outsourcing is underdeveloped and highly fragmented in China, with no player achieving more than two per cent market share. According to Morgan and Stanley, third-party logistics providers currently have a penetration rate of only 2 per cent of China's overall logistics business, compared with 8 per cent in the US, and 10 per cent in Europe (Ho and Lim, 2001). This is likely to change significantly over the next five to ten years, fueled by:

- an increase in MNC operations which will create more demand for third-party services
- pressure on Chinese companies to reduce costs and increase service. Legend and Haire, for example, both believe that third party providers cannot achieve lower costs, better service, and better control than their own in-house capabilities. However in the case of Legend, its in-house capability has only been able to get inventory days to 28 against Dell's 6 (Ho and Lim, 2001). As local companies like Legend observe falling ratios in its competitors, outsourcing will be put back on the agenda.
- realization among Chinese companies they do not need to own the assets in order to gain the capability.

Third-party logistics providers, on their own, however, will not be able to provide the broad supply chain capability required by the market. Based on experiences in the US and Europe we will see a rise of alliances and JVs as the 'best of the best' in China get together to build competitive supply chains. Today, there are few international standard market based capabilities to align with, so many companies still see ownership of logistics assets as critical to their strategy; as capabilities emerge this will change. When this happens service-based rather than asset-based logistics will grow and this will change the face of supply chains in China.

Information, not assets will be King

Information is likely to come of age as Chinese companies shift their focus from assets to information. Logistics in China will become more and more reliant on the flow of information than the physical movements of vehicles and consignments. Chinese local companies have assets, but they lack information and knowledge. In the short to medium term, a strategic stock of assets will remain necessary for foreign companies to secure trust and ensure quality of service. Over the longer term, a convergence of local and foreign companies is likely to occur to create solutions that leverage both information and assets and in doing do will bring service-based logistics to life.

Information technology

Businesses seeking a superior supply chain will need to take up supply chain technology to achieve optimal decisions, integration and end-to-end synchronization. More implementations will occur, and fewer 'installations'. The International Data Corporation forecasts that the annual growth in China's information technology market will increase from 24.4 per cent in 2001 to 28.1 per cent in 2002.

The laggards will die

Those companies that cannot change, or who tinker rather than transform, will be left behind to wither and die.

Issues to manage going forward

The changes taking place in China portend a number of wide ranging reforms which will create great opportunities for supply chain performance improvement once thought impossible. However, in moving forward a number of issues will need to be carefully managed.

Regulatory uncertainties and the pace of change

Some restrictions in China will remain. Companies will still need to gain a license for establishing a presence in China.

There is a danger that the impact of China's membership of the WTO has been oversold. A number of gaps exist in the present protocols. They do not, for example, map out the path for migrating from being a minority stakeholder in a joint venture to a wholly owned foreign enterprise (WOFE). Companies still need to gain a license for establishing a presence in China. The Government, therefore, could issue some licenses to satisfy the WTO and then refuse to issue more. Indeed, the biggest potential gap permitted within the WTO is that Chinese law may impose restrictions as long as they apply to all enterprises.

Some current restrictions will not change. For example, foreign companies will still be restricted from distributing goods in China, either wholesale or retail, without a presence in China. While established foreign investment enterprises (FIEs) will be able to import or export third-party goods, they will not be able to distribute them. Finally, China will retain its regulations that prevent foreign companies from both making sales through representative offices and establishing sales branches in China.

There is also a danger that unrealistic predictions of demand and market growth rates could lead to poor commercial decisions, such as creating excess capacity in anticipation of demand. The beer industry in China provides a telling case study of this phenomenon. MNCs, in particular, should be mindful to remember that just because of China's membership of the WTO, one billion people do not automatically become one billion customers!

Lack of compliance at provincial levels
While change may be fully embraced at the national level, compliance at the local and provincial levels may not occur. Rules may be mandated in Beijing but by the time they get to the municipalities, cities and towns, it is likely that they will be watered down if not ignored for some time.

Skill levels and capacity of people
Finding and keeping people will pose a major barrier to building competitive supply chains. The costs of foreign experts is prohibitive so the capability has to be developed in China and this will take time. Even if you make the appropriate investments in technology, infrastructure and other capabilities, people's capacity to change remains an issue. The other people-related difficulty lies in the capacity to change. A number of expensive technology implementations in China have not been successful. Some observers argue that 85–90 per cent of supply chain initiatives fail in China due to the people factor. Training staff to utilize new capabilities, particularly more sophisticated information technology solutions remains a fundamental problem, as does the lack of incentive to change.

Some observers argue that 85–90 per cent of supply chain initiatives fail in China due to people issues.

Cultural mindsets and entrenched practices
The culture of organizations also needs to change to achieve supply chain efficiencies. All participants in the supply chain must learn the benefits of developing closer relationships built on trust and embrace win–win principles.

Difficulties in translating best practices in China
The quickest route to failure in China is to assume that experience in other markets will translate to China. Best practices from the West may not be achievable in the short term given the size of the gap between

the current state and the best practice state. Plans for achieving best practices need to face the reality of current infrastructure, systems, business practices, and people capabilities.

Lack of understanding of cost structures

A robust, fact-based business case provides a strong catalyst for change; however, few manufacturers in China understand their baseline supply chain costs. A few local companies track their transport and warehousing costs but not their inventory, order management, and other administrative costs. Few, if any, have an integrated view of their total supply chain costs.

Conclusion

Speed, coordination and commitment, grounded in a robust strategy, will be the key to exploiting China's substantial market.

China's accession to the WTO in December 2001 means that China's marketplace will become accessible for the first time, from a regulatory point of view. Companies seeking to capture the growing customer base will need to build a national supply chain capability. China poses vast challenges of geography, infrastructure, regulations, culture and talent. Seeking to develop a national supply chain capability from scratch – or attempting to jump from basic to leading capabilities without first mastering the basics – is fraught with danger and likely to fail. Organizations need to start small, think big, scale fast and focus. As the Chinese like to say, the 'thousand mile journey commences with the first step'. Speed, coordination and commitment, grounded in a robust strategy, will be the key to exploiting China's substantial market.

Companies choosing to establish efficient supply chain solutions need to focus on building functional capabilities and operational excellence; controlling the network and the information not the assets; building and retaining capability; and forming alliances with the best providers of critical capabilities. There is no easy path. Going it alone, however, would be a recipe for disaster – working with local capabilities has proven a successful formula for many MNCs to date. As seen elsewhere in the world, few companies can build or provide a full suite of supply chain services alone; partnerships and alliances are still the keys to success.

In China the value of networking or Guanxi is well understood. Extending this concept to creating networks of capabilities between the best local and best foreign firms will be a winning formula in China. The challenges are daunting, the risks great, but the opportunity huge – supply chains in China are on the cusp of something great. In closing, it would be timely to remind ourselves that in China 'nothing is impossible, but everything is difficult'. Simplicity and mastery of the basics will remain the keys to supply chain competitiveness for many years to come.

References

Baldinger, P. (1998), 'Distribution of Goods in China: Regulatory Framework and Business Options', The US-China Business Council, *China Economic Quarterly* (2001); Dragonomics Ltd.

Dresdner Kleinwort Wasserstein (2001), 'China Distribution Networks – Chinese Companies' Most Valuable Asset', *China Investment Strategy* (2 February).

The Economist (2001), 'A surprising world leader in supply-chain management' (6 June).

EIU (2001), 'China Hand – The Complete Guide to Doing Business in China', Chapter 12 (December).

EIU (2001), *Regional Economic News*, (2001), 'Asia industry: Redefining the pharmaceutical supply chain', (15 October).

Gates, Robert (2001), 'Beyond Sinotrans: China's Distribution Infrastructure', *The China Business Review* vol. 28, (no. 4) (July–August), pp. 14–17.

Ho, Henry and Lim, Chin (2001), 'Spot the Early Bird', Morgan and Stanley. (5 October) p. 56.

Jong, A. and Gruetzner (1997) 'Distribution in China, Charting a Course to Profit', The Economist Intelligence Unit Limited.

Manion, D. (1999), 'Asia Pacific Supply Chain Survey', CommerceNet. (19 November).

Mann, Ainsley (2001), 'Dry Packaged Goods: Overcoming Logistical Hurdles', *The China Business Review*, vol. 28 (no. 4) (July–August), pp. 24–29. *The McKinsey Quarterly* (2000) (no. 2).

Powers, Patrick (2001), 'Distribution in China: The End of the Beginning' *The China Business Review*, vol. 28, (no. 4) (July–August), pp. 8–12.

Shaw, Stephen and Wang Frank, (2001), 'China's Evolving Logistics Landscape', McKinsey and Company, Greater China Office, (30 August).

Sinotrans (2002), Various discussions with Sinotrans. Particularly thanks to Mr Fanduanwei for his guidance, advice and input into this paper. I had many discussions with Mr Fanduanwei and his colleagues on the challenges facing China and the efforts Sinotrans is making to change to make itself more competitive.

Weisert, Drake (2001), 'Coca-Cola in China: Quenching the Thirst of a Billion', *The China Business Review* vol. 28 (no. 4), (July–August), pp. 52–55.

Part 6

Other Practical Considerations in Supply Chains

The last part of the handbook considers a range of important practical considerations related to the transformation of supply chains.

Chapter 6.1, 'Achieving supply chain alignment through behavior change', points out that only by changing the behaviors of those who are required to 'live and breathe' the change program will changes be successful and sustainable. The fact that more than 60 per cent of initiatives are either not implemented as planned or not implemented at all highlights the need for strong leadership to sustain change initiatives. The chapter discusses three principles of change: creating awareness, reinforcing change and refining change.

In this context Chapter 6.2, 'The role of knowledge management in supply chains', expands the discussion into the subject of knowledge being one of the most important assets that companies need for the future. Most companies are at risk of failing to capture the value of knowledge and as a result will not be able to build, support, and optimize superior supply chain activities. Companies that recognize and use their knowledge capital are more likely to create new value, apply appropriate management processes and technologies, and maintain an open culture.

Chapter 6.3, 'Education and skills training requirements in the supply chain', covers the fact that the speed of change and the emergence of new technologies have further complicated how employees cope with rapidly increasing skills requirements. The challenge for companies is to respond by rapidly building the requisite skills in their workforce to prepare employees not just for today, but for the challenges of tomorrow, so that they can shape the future of collaboration and competitive advantage in their industry.

Finally, Chapter 6.4, 'Building successful consulting relationships' discusses how consultants are being used to complement skill gaps and accelerate the pathways to value realization. Using consultants is a way for organizations to secure the right skills and capabilities during critical periods of transformational change. The model of the 'value-based consultant' is introduced, underlining the need to align expectations and goals to deliver expected solutions.

Achieving supply chain alignment through behavior change

6.1

Jamie M. Bolton and Karen Dwyer

The advent of e-commerce and the creation of new business models have given organizations an enormous opportunity to change their supply chains fundamentally. However, organizations often fail to realize the changes are unsustainable in the long term. A new supply chain capability or improvement idea might be attractive to executives in the planning stage, and supported by a sound business case, but realizing the innovations can be elusive.

Only by changing the behaviors of those who are required to 'live and breathe' the change program will the changes be successful.

Organizations need to undertake a long journey before their changes come to fruition; many do not make it. One of the most common reasons is that organizations lack alignment between the value proposition and the work and beliefs of individual employees of the organization – the people responsible for making the changes happen. Many staff members are not able to see how their daily tasks and responsibilities contribute to realizing the value proposition and business case.

Only by changing the behaviors of those who are required to 'live and breathe' the change program, will organizations be able to implement the changes successfully. This chapter discusses how organizations can harness the energy and support of people through an integrated approach to behavior change. The approach identifies and aligns the required behaviors at the individual level to the processes, the business case, and ultimately the value proposition of the change project.

Key elements of the integrated behavior change approach include:

- identifying and defining the supply chain value proposition
- defining clear process outcomes (value drivers) and aligning these with the value proposition
- identifying the supporting behaviors required to realize the process outcomes and

- determining the appropriate change levers to build and reinforce these behaviors and understanding the likelihood of success of these levers having an impact on individual behavior.

This chapter describes a model for integrated behavior change to provide a framework for aligning the value proposition, process outcomes, change levers and individual behaviors required to embed the change. Individual change levers are also discussed; these levers can create the awareness of behavior change, reinforce the need for behavior change and provide a refinement mechanism for when the required behaviors are not initially realized.

Upwards and onwards – the drivers of change are relentless

Change will not be slowing. Organizations will face increasing demands to manage and absorb changes generated by new technologies.

Undoubtedly, technology advances during the last ten years have fundamentally changed the way commerce is performed and the way transactions occur throughout the supply chain. The ever-demanding search for speed, efficiency and increased effectiveness within supply chains is resulting in an increasing reliance on technology and, in particular, new business models, to deliver an increase in performance.

Analysts' forecasts of the penetration of e-commerce within business have been revised downward since the dot.com crash in 2000 and the slowdown in the global economy. However, the expected resurgence of e-commerce in the next five years means technology will continue to be a major driver for change. Organizations will still need to manage technology effectively.

Research by Accenture (2001) has found the use of e-commerce to drive improved business and supply chain performance remains high on the agenda for CEOs around the world. Trends in European organizations demonstrate that e-commerce continues to penetrate business functions beyond sales and marketing and into purchasing, logistics and human resources, as indicated in Figure 6.1.1. European businesses are endeavoring to shorten the process time associated with not only capturing and processing customer orders, but also in procuring supplies, moving goods and improving the skills of staff. They are seeking to create a real 'step' change in their overall supply chain performance.

However, it will not only be e-commerce driving the change in supply chains. The Accenture research found that 81 per cent of European executives expect to experience even greater change between 2001 and 2004, mainly from m-commerce (mobile commerce) and u-commerce (ubiquitous commerce) technologies, such as wireless, television and voice commerce, as shown in Figure 6.1.2. Hence, more organizations will be using increasingly sophisticated

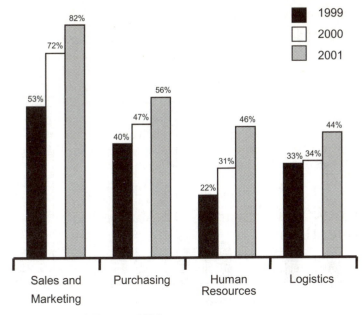

Source: Accenture (eEurope, 2001)

Figure 6.1.1
e-commerce penetration in European businesses (% of respondents)

technologies to develop new ways of doing business and identify new opportunities to improve the performance of their supply chains.

Certainly, change will not be slowing. Organizations will be facing increasing demands to absorb and manage the change the new technologies will be generating. Whether it be e-, u- or m-commerce driving the changes in how business, customers and suppliers interact and how supply chains are managed, the trend represents the next wave to advance the way business is done. To be successful, the organizational change needed to make these technologies effective and to ensure the full value is extracted will be large and must not be underestimated.

Why doesn't change last?

The prospect of more change can be daunting for many organizations, be it changes to technology, business process, policy, or people, or a combination of these. Further, the magnitude of what is required within an organization to implement sustainable change successfully is not always fully understood.

In a time-poor business environment, organizations face demands for quick returns, one-year paybacks and limited capital budgets. Based on Accenture experience, these organizations also face the

More than 60 per cent of initiatives are either not implemented as planned or not implemented at all.

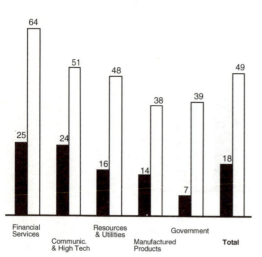

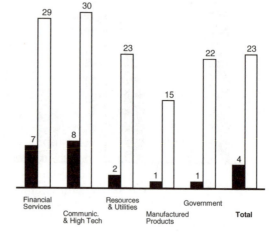

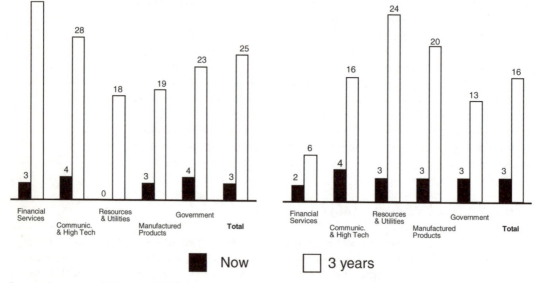

Now   3 years

Source: Accenture (eEurope, 2001)

Figure 6.1.2
Adoption rates of e-enabling technologies

business reality that more than 60 per cent of change initiatives are either not implemented as planned or not implemented at all. There are many reasons why organizations may not succeed in either getting their supply chain initiatives started, or, once started, ensuring their supply chain changes are sustainable so that they deliver the full business benefits.

Before developing an integrated approach to behavior change, it is critical to understand the common reasons why change initiatives fail.

Inadequate change leadership

- *Lack of executive sponsorship.* Without senior management and executive support for change, the initiative will either not start, or if it does, will not receive the appropriate level of people and financial resources to be successful. Supply chain initiatives should not begin unless the sponsorship for the project is clear and unreserved. This point is consistent with our Strategic Alignment Model introduced in earlier chapters.

Strong leadership is needed to start and sustain a change initiative.

- *Losing leadership attention.* A common misconception is that once the project has finished, the system is installed and the people are doing their new job, that is it. Senior managers can get on with their other projects. Wrong. Indeed, the challenge has just started! Change leaders must ensure that everything is working as planned, the change initiative is delivering as promised, benefits are being realized, people are doing their jobs correctly, and people are exhibiting the behaviors required to make the change sustainable. Reinforcing and refining the changes is needed before, during and after the change program takes place.

Poor understanding of what's ahead

- *Underestimating the change effort.* Many organizations are over-whelmed by the magnitude of what needs to be done, in terms of the timeframe and the required resources to embed the changes. In addition, organizations do not fully understand all the elements of a successful change program that they need to address. Based on Accenture client experience, to be successful, change management should be not less than 25 per cent of the total project effort and resource. Without adequate resources, there will be frustration within the organization.

Organizations need to understand the magnitude of the task and to devote adequate resources to it.

- *Lack of understanding of the reason for change.* Quite often, there is simply a lack of understanding of why the change is taking place at all. If people do not understand the logic or rationale for the change, they have no apparent reason to change from the way they currently do things. Unless the compelling reason for the change is articulated then those required to implement it and those affected by it will not be fully committed.

Failure to harness people

People need to be involved in, trained for, and informed about the changes ahead.

- *Insufficient people involvement.* Organizations need to ensure that people are committed to the change process in two main ways. First, all stakeholders in the initiative need to be involved, including those required to participate, those who will be directly and indirectly affected by the change, and those who will be required to support and lead the change. Second, people should be involved at the start of the change process rather than at the end when the changes take place. Frequently, the involvement of people is either underestimated or implemented too late.
- *Lack of training and skilling.* For a change initiative to be sustainable, it is paramount that the people have an opportunity to build the required skills, knowledge and capabilities required to perform effectively in the 'new world' that is being created. Frequently in the push to deliver results quickly or in an attempt to reduce costs, the training and skilling component of the change project is forgotten. Consequently, people are inadequately skilled for their new tasks and feel anxious about their role, so that they revert to their 'comfort zone' of old habits and processes.
- *Lack of communication.* People must be told about change initiatives. Failure to communicate with people who are directly or indirectly affected will result in failure to build awareness and ownership of the change. In addition, without communication, people may become suspicious and anxious about their position in the organization.
- *Loss of momentum for change.* Sometimes, people become 'change weary' – it just gets too hard, there are too many projects! This is particularly the case when other initiatives or people's day jobs are simultaneously sapping resources and demanding attention. Unless an organization provides the right resources in the right quantities and people are able to dedicate their time, there will be insufficient momentum for the initiative.

Inadequate change implementation

Change leaders need to assess the readiness for change and realize benefits early in the implementation.

- *No measurement of business readiness.* Sometimes an organization will start an initiative with no real understanding of the readiness, mindset and the attitude of the business in undertaking change. Unless the 'starting point' is known, it is impossible to understand how far an organization must be moved during the change, what is likely to stop the change being effective, and who are the key stakeholders to manage during the process.
- *No quick benefits.* Change is most powerful for an organization when benefits are quickly realized and the organization begins to see a rapid return on the effort invested. The reason for the change becomes clear and people understand that any short term 'pain' experienced is for the good of the organization. Failure to realize benefits quickly can be a significant cause for motivation to be lost and, hence, for the momentum for change to wane.

- *No performance measurement.* Performance measures provide the mechanism by which the intent and business case underpinning the supply chain change initiative is translated into a specific set of performance objectives at the organizational, functional, process and individual levels.

  Tracking performance will help to confirm that the change initiative is delivering benefits.

  Rigorous performance measures and a robust performance measurement and benefits tracking system is required to ensure benefits are being delivered as planned and that people are being measured and managed in a way that is aligned with the intent of the supply chain initiative. Without this, there is no way that an organization can confirm that the supply chain initiative has delivered the promised benefits or that people are behaving in a way that will result in the desired outcomes.

A common theme among all these reasons for why change does not last is lack of alignment. For change to be sustainable, the people of an organization must behave on a day-to-day basis in a manner that is consistent with the intent and expected outcomes, or 'value proposition', of the supply chain change initiative. Unless an individual can see how their daily tasks and responsibilities contribute to delivering the supply chain value proposition, there is little motivation for behaving in the required way.

With ongoing and increasingly relentless change having an impact on organizations' supply chains, with chequered change history and many points where change initiatives can fail, how does an organization make sure its changes are sustainable? The remainder of this chapter proposes a way to align individual behavior with the value proposition of a supply chain initiative and provides an example of how this can be achieved with a typical supply chain process.

Integrated behavior change model

Why should an organization focus on changing the behavior of individuals who either will lead or be affected by the change? Simple. It reduces the risk of failure and therefore increases the likelihood of achieving the desired returns on the investment in the supply chain initiative.

Supporting behaviors are matched with the supply chain value proposition.

The Integrated Behavior Change Model (Figure 6.1.3) ensures alignment is achieved by identifying the specific 'supporting behaviors' required by each individual and ensuring these behaviors are aligned with the supply chain value proposition, or outcome of the initiative. Refer also to Chapter 1.3, 'Developing an aligned supply chain operating strategy' for more information on strategic alignment.

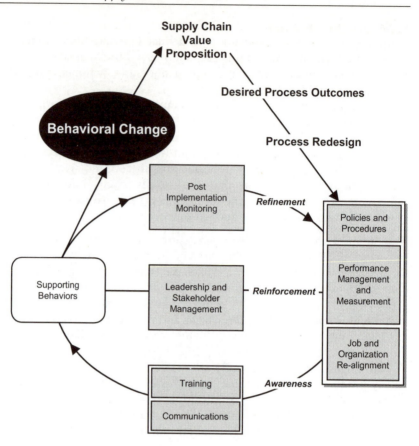

Figure 6.1.3
Integrated Behavior Change Model

The three principles of change are: create awareness; reinforce change; and refine change.

Using the supply chain value proposition as its anchor point, the Integrated Behavior Change Model is built around three key change principles:

- create *awareness* of the need for change and how people and the organization will be affected
- *reinforce* the need for change through the organization's leadership and key stakeholders, and
- *refine* the organization and change approach if the desired supporting behaviors are not realized and if the supply chain value proposition is not fully delivered.

Behavior change levers

A range of levers can be used to change the behavior of individuals.

Specific 'change levers' – all the tactical 'tools' that an organization possesses – must be used by an organization to bring about the change in behavior required at an individual level. The role of each lever in a change project is outlined below.

Policies and procedures

Policies and procedures are the business rules that define the 'way we do business around here'. They can include operational procedures, for the execution of a specific task, as well as written policies, which help to guide decision-making. This lever is important for building awareness and reinforcing the new behaviors in people by supporting them in their day-to-day work.

Performance measurement systems and performance management

Performance measurement systems and performance management are often confused. On the one hand, performance measurement refers to the system of key performance indicators (KPIs) in place to measure the performance of a process. Sometimes the process being measured is 'end to end' in nature, such as DIFOTEF (delivered in full, on time and error free), and other times it is a sub-process, such as forecast accuracy. KPIs also contribute to diagnosing the causes of positive or problematic performance, which includes behavioral change. In this way, performance measurement drives and reinforces the new behaviors, because 'what gets measured gets done'.

Performance measurement drives and reinforces the desired new behaviors.

Performance management, on the other hand, refers to the way in which the performance of individuals is incentivized, measured and rewarded. Again, this is a powerful lever to reinforce the required behaviors, because people respond to the way in which their efforts are viewed and rewarded. People must know that their performance is being measured and if they behave and act appropriately, they will be rewarded.

Organization and job realignment

Organization and job realignment is the lever associated with restructuring and, in some cases, redefining job descriptions and reporting lines. This lever is important in building the required behaviors for achieving change over the long term. To achieve this realignment, organizations need to define and link the appropriate roles, accountabilities, behaviors, performance measures, reporting lines, incentives and rewards to the right individuals.

The structure of organizations and jobs needs to be aligned to the right individuals to achieve process outcomes.

If this lever is not activated, people continue to function in the old way using their old habits, making the new or revised tasks impossible to introduce. At the extreme, changes to organization structure will be required to ensure alignment with supply chain processes and clear responsibility for specific process outcomes. For example, organizations can nominate 'process owners' to be responsible for changes to particular processes, such as the demand chain planning process, the order-to-cash process and the procure-to-pay process.

Training

Training is the lever most commonly associated with change management, but sometimes the most neglected or the first to be abandoned when the project strikes difficulties. In an effort to generate awareness of the required behaviors, as well as build the appropriate skills and knowledge for individuals, training must be directed at the right people, using the right delivery mechanism at the right time. Many forms of training must be considered in a change program, depending on the audience and the message, such as instructor-led training, e-learning and on-the-job training.

For example, it may be appropriate to deliver on-the-job training in the use of radio frequency equipment to staff in a warehouse, just before the equipment is switched on. The customer service team may require intensive hands-on training for a couple of weeks with the guidance of a coach prior to interacting directly with customers. e-learning training, however, may be appropriate where users are required to become proficient in new portal technology (which can deliver the training), particularly if many users are in remote locations. Whatever the approach, the training needs to explicitly or implicitly outline the behaviors that are required to make the change successful. Performance support tools introduced in training, such as job aids or 'cheat sheets', are also useful in sustaining the right behaviors well after the change has occurred.

Communications

Failure to communicate, as outlined earlier, will result in failure of the change initiative. Communication and key messages must be targeted and tailored to each stakeholder group and can take many forms, such as newsletters, workshops, posters, visits from a senior sponsor, demonstrations and pilots, even placemats in the canteen. If the communications are not executed effectively, an informal 'grapevine' can emerge instead, which has the potential to destroy the initiative. Regardless of how communications are delivered, messages from a credible source must be consistent across the organization and stakeholder groups, frequent in delivery, and raise awareness of the required behavior change.

Leadership and stakeholder management

This lever is useful in reinforcing the required behaviors after awareness has been established. Leadership – from the senior sponsors of the initiative to managers throughout the organization – is paramount in sustaining change through difficult times. The change leaders, including process owners, must exhibit the required behaviors in their 'walk and talk' well after the changes have taken place.

In addition to the role of the leadership team, it is important that this lever includes using stakeholders to help sustain behavior change.

Stakeholders will behave in response to how they see the change will have an impact on them. In the early stages, stakeholders must be identified, their 'stake' in an issue understood, and their role, accountabilities and incentives structured so that they will support the initiative fully. Once identified and supportive of the process, stakeholders can become staunch allies of the change leaders and be encouraged to exhibit, and hence reinforce, the required behaviors of successful change implementation.

Post-implementation monitoring and support

The monitoring and support lever involves reviewing the success of the change initiative after its implementation. Organizations need to put in place a system for monitoring the achievement of the supply chain value proposition, delivery of business benefit and required process outcomes. As appropriate, the change leaders need to adjust the levers to ensure sustainability after the change has taken place. This lever needs to be factored into the work plan and given adequate resourcing from the start of the project.

Monitoring and support needs to be factored into the work plan and given adequate resourcing.

Post-implementation monitoring and support may include:

- a team to offer performance support to individuals who are directly affected by the changes on the job
- a formal review each month, using tools such as a balanced scorecard, to check the achievement of benefits, and
- process owners to 'refine' the organization's behavior accordingly.

The post-implementation support may or may not include the original project team members, but should include those who have ownership and accountability for the initiative, and hence, are advocates of the required behaviors.

If the organization designs and implements the change levers successfully, it will have the capacity to institute significant behavior change and, thus, achieve the targeted step change in supply chain performance.

Implementing the Integrated Behavior Change Model

How does an organization implement the Integrated Behavior Change Model? A step-by-step approach is outlined below to provide details of the tasks an organization must follow to increase the likelihood of change being sustained.

Implementation needs to include a series of steps in order to ensure the change is sustainable.

Step 1. Define the supply chain value proposition

The first step in any supply chain initiative must be to define specifically the value that will be created for the business. This definition must be described in two ways:

- a detailed business case must be defined where the hard benefits from the supply chain initiative are calculated, owned by specific individuals within the business and are directly linked to specific projects and processes
- a qualitative description of the value delivered must be developed, so that the business understands the overall supply chain 'outcome' that will be delivered by the initiative and how the business will be different.

Step 2. Determine the processes that need to change

Change will not be realized in an organization unless specific processes in an organization change and unless people change the way that they work. All the necessary processes that must be redesigned to deliver the value proposition must be identified, scoped and agreed within the business.

Step 3. Identify the outcomes required from each process

Once the supply chain value proposition is determined and the specific processes that need to be changed have been identified, the outcomes of each process can then be determined. Focusing on specific outcomes at the process level provides the mechanism to create alignment. As a check, if all the specific process outcomes were delivered, there should be no doubt that the overall supply chain initiative outcome will be delivered. If there is doubt, then either processes have not been fully identified or the process outcomes are not correct.

Step 4. Define the supporting behaviors for each process outcome

The organization needs to identify the supporting behaviors for each process and each role affected within each process. Supporting behaviors describe the way that people executing the process must act and behave so that the process outcome is delivered. In identifying the supporting behaviors it is useful to first understand the current 'detracting' behaviors of people – those behaviors that are not desired and cause processes to be executed ineffectively. Once the organization understands what it does not like about the way people currently execute the process, it is then relatively straightforward to identify preferred behaviors.

Step 5. Identify the change levers available

Most organizations access an array of change levers as outlined earlier, and use them with varying degrees of success to support a change initiative. All the available change levers, including any organization-specific levers, must be identified before assessing how effective each lever will be in changing the way people act and behave. The key to using these levers successfully is to assess, understand and focus on those that are likely to work best in the business and those likely to be most effective in changing the way people behave.

To determine the effectiveness of each lever, some simple questions can be asked:

- Does the organization document and reference business rules or policies frequently? Are they used by people regularly to ensure they are doing their job correctly? Are they reinforced by the organization's leaders (and therefore strongly reinforce 'the way business is done around here')?
- Does the organization respond well to the way in which people are measured and rewarded? Are there consequences for poor performance?
- Does the organization have strength in the way it builds skills and knowledge, and therefore would tend to focus on building awareness during transformation.
- Does the organization pride itself on the credibility and influence of its leaders (again, an ingredient for powerful reinforcement for the change)?
- Is the organization stringent in monitoring the capture of business benefits and refining change after it occurs, or does it 'declare victory' and assume that because the project is finished it must have been successful.

Whatever the strength of a lever, it must be identified and resources directed to it. This is not to say that other 'less influential' levers and criteria should be ignored. Organizations can jeopardize the sustainability of their change effort by neglecting one of the key change principles of awareness, reinforcement and refinement. Organizations should retain the less influential levers by directing fewer resources to them throughout the transformation period. If needed, leaders can develop these levers at appropriate times.

This step is similar to a football or military strategy that is prepared to help a team succeed. The team leader needs to assess the levers available, rank them, and identify which are the strongest. Are we good at building awareness of change, reinforcing it, or refining it? The team leader will focus limited resources on the strongest levers, but to maximize chances of embedding the changes for the long term, all three change principles need to be covered.

Step 6. Design each change lever

Once the levers have been assessed and understood, the organization needs to design and develop the levers according to the required supporting behaviors. This will involve:

- revisiting and updating policies and procedures
- creating or extending the performance management and measurement systems

- assessing the organization for realignment activities and training needs
- designing and developing training, performance support and communications
- identifying and understanding the perspectives of leaders and stakeholders and
- designing the post-implementation support activities.

Step 7. Ensure levers are activated

Assuming the sponsorship team is familiar with the integrated behavior change approach, the task of ensuring each of the levers is activated should become part of the regular project milestone check and part of post-implementation monitoring and support. The approach to ensuring levers are activated should be underlined by considering that supply chain initiatives are, in essence, change management programs with technology issues, not technology programs with some change management.

Example of a change implementation

To illustrate the integrated behavior approach, Figure 6.1.4 (below) shows a simple example of a supply chain planning initiative. To guide the change project, the supply chain value proposition has been translated into specific process outcomes and individual behaviors.

Once the individual supporting behaviors have been identified, the change levers can be designed to drive these behaviors. Table 6.1.1 (below) shows how the behavior of 'challenge the need for manual intervention' for the forecast customer demand process can be delivered through the various change levers.

Conclusion

Defining the strategy is only half the journey; making change sustainable is what creates and delivers value.

Defining the supply chain strategy is only half the journey for an organization; executing the strategy and making change sustainable is what creates and delivers value. To be successful, the executive agenda should not be dominated by the question of whether to embark on a new journey or implement a new supply chain strategy or business model. Nor can an organization wait, continue to function traditionally and hope that competitors and business partners still want to function that way too.

Today the agenda must be balanced with the critical question of 'how do we ensure this journey will deliver the expected improvement in performance and how do we minimize the risk of failure?' While the risk is undeniable, integrated behavior change provides a practical and rigorous way to mitigate it. Only by changing the

Table 6.1.1

Integrated behavior change approach – forecast customer demand behavior: 'challenge the need for manual intervention'

Change lever	Delivery mechanism	Example
Training	Forecast customer demand overview training module	**Training key messages** 'We should focus on *trusting* the statistical forecast and as a result, *challenging* the need for manual revisions to this forecast' **Evidence provided in training** Quantitative analysis comparing statistical forecast accuracy with manually adjusted forecast accuracy to clearly show manual intervention reduces accuracy
Job alignment	Role descriptions and job information packs	**Role description – Demand Manager** 'This position is responsible for maintaining the company forecast using a statistical forecast and incorporating promotions and causal information supplied by the business for the region each week'
Performance management	Individual accountabilities and bonus criteria	**Documented accountability – Demand Manager** 'Challenge the need for contributors (to the forecasting process) to manually alter the statistical forecast' **Bonus criteria – Demand Manager** 25% of annual bonus is dependent on meeting defined forecast accuracy targets
Performance measurement	Key performance indicator	**New KPI – manual changes:** The number of agreed changes that are made in the forecast consensus meeting which do not reflect any new promotional activity (i.e. manual changes) – Target=Zero changes **New KPI – statistical forecast accuracy:** Forecast accuracy generated by the system prior to manual review **New KPI – manual forecast accuracy:** Forecast accuracy following any manual changes from the S&OP process
Policies and procedures	Policies and procedures	**Policy updated to reflect the new required behavior – *reduce manual changes*** Reduction in manual changes to system generated forecast (target=0). Changes must be made by exception and captured though comments in RDP
Communications	Process champion workshops	**Specific workshops conducted** Process champion workshops conducted to raise awareness of process specific behaviors and emphasise their criticality in achieving stickability of process outcomes
Leadership	One-to-one meetings and performance reviews	**Performance reviews** Leaders use *one-on-one meetings* and *performance reviews* to reinforce the importance of these behaviors, impact on achieving process outcomes, measure their achievement and assess individual KPI targets. Leaders also measured through accountabilities and expected to *lead by example*
Post-implementation monitoring	Support structure	**Dedicated post-implementation support team established** Post-implementation capability support team implemented to measure capture of business benefits, measure achievement of business case and assess degree of behavior change achieved

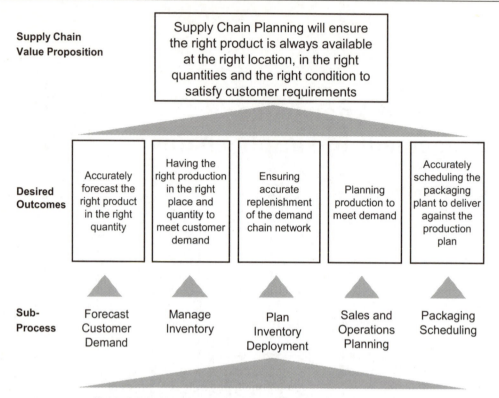

Figure 6.1.4
Supply chain planning value proposition and supporting behaviors

behaviors of those who are required to 'live and breathe' the new strategy or solution will the changes required to deliver the business case and expected outcomes be implemented successfully.

Reference

Accenture (2001), 'The unexpected Europe: The surprising success of European e-commerce'.

The role of knowledge management in supply chains

6.2

Wanda S. Brown

Knowledge management can be a significant source of value for companies if they can successfully capture, share, and leverage knowledge across their global enterprise. Unfortunately, most companies are at risk of failing to capture this value. Hard-won knowledge often resides only in the minds of employees, many of whom could be made redundant at any time, or worse, defect to a competitor. Organizations could be making poor decisions because of gaps in corporate knowledge and intelligence. Today, organizations need to implement solutions to minimize the inefficiencies of continuously re-creating knowledge. Instead, they are in danger of forgetting what their employees know.

Most companies are at risk of failing to capture the value of knowledge.

Technology research group International Data Corp. estimates that poorly managed knowledge costs Fortune 500 companies about $12 billion per year (Stewart, 2002). Some of the drivers for these huge financial losses include substandard performance, intellectual rework and a lack of available knowledge management resources. Despite its potential impact on the bottom line, the concept of knowledge management is only beginning to get the attention of senior managers. Many organizations neglect knowledge management efforts for two reasons. First, knowledge management is difficult to do, and second, the return on investment from knowledge management is even more difficult to quantify. This has caused some companies to scale back formal knowledge management activities or abandon programs altogether.

For supply chain leaders, the ability to capture and share knowledge is important to improve supply chains, or even to help to redefine supply chains to create new sources of value. The core focus of supply chain operations is on designing, buying, making, moving and selling products to customers. However, just as important is managing the knowledge that builds, supports, and

Knowledge helps to build, support and optimize supply chain activities.

optimizes these supply chain activities. Those companies that develop the right processes to capture and share knowledge across organizational boundaries will be in a better position to increase process efficiencies, maximize strategic effectiveness and improve innovative capabilities.

To manage knowledge across the supply chain, companies have to learn faster by creating a culture that rewards knowledge sharing across the enterprise. Organizations need to continuously capture and share both implicit and explicit knowledge. This chapter offers six principles to help organizations to develop a knowledge management strategy that supports supply chain effectiveness:

- Principle 1. Expand the concept of knowledge management
- Principle 2. Ensure senior management support
- Principle 3. Form a dedicated knowledge management team
- Principle 4. Build strategies based on core business processes
- Principle 5. Perform a knowledge gap assessment
- Principle 6. Use multiple technologies and tools.

Principle 1. Expand the concept of knowledge management

Two types of knowledge are important to capture: explicit and tacit.

Knowledge sharing in organizations is not a new concept. However, the field of knowledge management is concerned with helping companies to optimize the value of what people in organizations know. This means expanding the concept of knowledge management to include more than just collecting information in repositories. Knowledge managers are concerned with two types of knowledge: *explicit* knowledge, which can be codified, written in reports or white papers or audio or video taped; and *tacit* knowledge, which includes peoples' experiences, undocumented expertise and know-how.

Core knowledge management initiatives usually focus on processes and tools to enable a company to identify the organization's tacit and explicit knowledge. Companies need to leverage knowledge to enable 'those with the knowledge' to link with 'those with a need'. Not surprisingly, a major challenge of knowledge management is to convert tacit knowledge into explicit knowledge. This distinction between the two types of knowledge is a powerful one and may partly explain why companies can be aware of the same best practices, but realize very different results in the marketplace.

Knowledge management enables companies to define processes effectively to create, capture, and share the knowledge that is critical to the success of the enterprise. Seven major activities and technologies form the core of knowledge management, as shown in Figure 6.2.1 and summarized below.

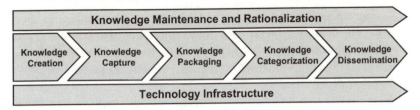

Figure 6.2.1
Core knowledge management activities and enabling technologies

- Knowledge *creation* – how organizational intelligence is derived from employees' day-to-day work, employee networks and discussion groups, and interactions with other supply chain partners.
- Knowledge *capture* – the process of codifying knowledge.
- Knowledge *packaging* – the process of refining and presenting content in ways that will be most useful to the user community.
- Knowledge *categorization* – how knowledge is organized to facilitate easy retrieval and use by people in the organization. This includes establishing the appropriate taxonomy to enable users to find the knowledge and content they are seeking.
- Knowledge *dissemination* – the myriad of ways in which both explicit and implicit knowledge is shared across organizational boundaries, such as forums, communities of practice, training and development programs, storytelling, and knowledge portals.
- *Maintenance and rationalization* of knowledge – the process of updating documents to ensure that content reflects the organization's most current practices. This covers all stages of knowledge management and includes the critical process of archiving documents and purging documents.
- *Technology infrastructure* – the enabling technologies that underpin all knowledge management activities, from knowledge creation through to knowledge dissemination.

Knowledge management helps to define processes that create, capture and share knowledge.

Principle 2. Ensure senior management support

Creating a culture that supports and promotes knowledge sharing starts at the top. Corporate executives who want employees to share knowledge must communicate their expectations in corporate policies, meetings, mission statements and other formal and informal channels. Executives must exemplify the behaviors that they want employees to emulate by attending forums and discussion groups that focus on sharing knowledge, and encouraging their staffs to do the same.

Company leaders should also support creative incentives and rewards that encourage functional experts to share tacit knowledge that can be converted to explicit knowledge. At BP, for example, not

Creating a knowledge culture in an organization starts at the top.

only are business unit managers, 'judged on their ability to meet specific performance targets for their unit', but the company also rewards and promotes managers according to how effectively they – and their staff – share knowledge with people outside their units (Hansen et al, 2001).

Executives can take a range of steps to embed knowledge sharing as part of company culture.

- designate a chief knowledge officer who can act as a credible sponsor of knowledge management and training and development programs
- establish a formal charter for the knowledge management process which defines the knowledge management team's roles, responsibilities, objectives and success metrics
- view knowledge sharing as everyone's responsibility and reward people for sharing knowledge within and across functional boundaries
- demonstrate the importance of sharing knowledge by inclusion of knowledge management topics in meeting discussions, job descriptions and promotion criteria
- solicit executives to teach or actively sponsor a training and development session
- encourage employees to participate in communities of practice where employees from different functional groups share information, experiences and challenges about specific business processes to help to solve problems and identify new opportunities (Burtha, 2001)
- understand that effective knowledge management requires attention and focus on a combination of elements to ensure that the right knowledge is effectively linked with the business need. Some elements include: willing and knowledgeable people, technology, organizational structure, management support, culture and metrics
- allow some flexibility when establishing programs to share tacit knowledge. Adjustments may be required as the organization learns what is most effective.

Principle 3. Form a dedicated knowledge management team

Knowledge teams act as facilitators, packagers, organizers and distributors of content.

Knowledge management, like other organizational functions, requires dedicated resources such as capital and people to meet the needs of the business. Effective knowledge management demands that a dedicated group take full, day-to-day responsibility for capturing, refining, categorizing, and enhancing the organization's knowledge infrastructure and tools. Such a knowledge management team also needs to be responsible for continuously updating the business's knowledge repository so that it reflects the organization's most up-to-date thinking across critical business capabilities.

The purpose of establishing a centralized knowledge management group is not to implement a strategy through command and control. The knowledge managers act as facilitators, editors, packagers, content organizers and content distributors to help users gain efficient access and greater use of the knowledge that resides in the organization. They also help the business to monitor who gets access to confidential or sensitive knowledge by using technology to establish access rights for documents.

Principle 4. Build strategies based on core business processes

Before starting to develop a knowledge management program, the management team should agree on the core business processes that characterize how the company designs, manufactures, sells and delivers its products and services. Senior managers should use this collection of processes to define the structure, and act as a guide for, developing knowledge management strategies.

Business processes will define knowledge management strategies.

Core business processes within an enterprise might include the following components:

- *research and development* – the process of exploring new products and processes for development and use by the business
- *procurement* – the process of developing strategies for how critical and non-critical goods and services will be sourced and to put in place the processes and tools to execute against those strategies
- *manufacturing* – the process of building and assembling product
- *fulfilment* – the process of warehousing and transportation of product to the customer
- *sales and marketing* – the process of customer identification, service and retention; market analysis, promotion development
- *finance and accounting* – includes the processes of accounting, accounts payable, accounts receivable, profit and loss analysis, balance sheet analysis, and
- *human resources management* – includes the processes of benefits administration, payroll administration, recruiting, staffing, training and development.

The knowledge management team should work with internal experts to build detailed process flows. These process maps need to show which group is responsible for each business process, identify the major inputs and outputs of the process, and show how the processes are linked together. The knowledge management team can use the process flows as a powerful tool for collecting information for the knowledge repository.

Process flows are a powerful tool for collecting information.

For organizations interested in improving supply chain performance, it is critical to think in terms of integrating core business processes. Examples include:

- order cycle management, from order receipt and order entry to production and distribution and payment
- product life cycle management, including all phases of the product life cycle – from market research and concept development through to design, launch and product retirement and
- customer relationship management, including activities from initial customer contact through to sales and after-sales support.

The knowledge management team, with the help of content experts and executives, can start to identify areas where knowledge and intelligence can help to improve the company's supply chain performance. Knowledge management leaders can ask themselves a series of questions in order to help prioritize where to focus or enhance their organization's current knowledge management efforts.

Examples include: What are the company's business strategies and goals? What are the major issues or areas of the business that are capturing the CEO's attention? Where is the organization at risk in the marketplace? Are manufacturing costs higher than competitors'? Are customer service levels being met? Is product quality declining? Are costs of critical materials too high? Is the business losing market share? Is the organization developing new products and innovations at the rate that it should? Answering these types of questions will help the team to determine which processes are most in need of an infusion of knowledge and intelligence.

Knowledge managers should work with process and content experts.

Attacking these high-priority areas should be a two-pronged approach. The knowledge management team should work with the process experts or content owners to understand the requirements that are needed to enhance performance of core business processes. They can also focus on gathering explicit knowledge and information from content experts and external sources that they can share across the enterprise.

The knowledge management team should also establish discussion forums, face-to-face meetings and voice-to-voice opportunities for employees to share and discuss tacit knowledge related to challenges in critical business process areas. Knowledge management can help to link individuals in organizations by creating easy access to a list of subject matter experts that includes a brief profile of their experiences and areas of expertise.

Principle 5. Perform a knowledge gap assessment

Conducting a knowledge inventory will identify current knowledge stocks as well as gaps in knowledge.

Once the team agrees on the high-priority business processes, it should assess the knowledge and expertise which already exists in the organization. For routine activities, such as fabrication and assembly, it is possible to find a plethora of knowledge capital. The job of the knowledge management team is to rationalize the information, keeping only the best content for organizational sharing via the knowledge repository. Through the process of helping to determine the types of knowledge capital that are evident in the organization, knowledge management will also begin to identify knowledge gaps.

According to Richard Kesner (2001), knowledge managers can undertake an initial knowledge assessment using a simple framework, shown in Figure 6.2.2. The framework enables companies to take an inventory of the knowledge that already exists in the company and helps to identify knowledge gaps. Note that each business process will require a different emphasis on the knowledge capital required by the organization. The inventory assesses the following types of knowledge:

- *Content* knowledge (know-what). Content knowledge is primarily explicit knowledge that focuses on helping users to understand the company's products and market offerings. The inventory of content knowledge is all about capturing knowledge related to what the company sells, the product performance histories, list of experts, intellectual capital, and other physical assets.
- *Process* knowledge (know-how). Process knowledge is knowledge that relates to methodologies and step-by-step procedures concerning how the company manufactures or assembles products and how it packages and delivers its services to customers. Knowledge capital in this area can be either tacit or implicit and relates to how the organization performs key business processes such as procurement, manufacturing, or sales and marketing.
- *Marketplace* knowledge (know-where). Marketplace knowledge is content related to the company's customers, competitors and the market in which the organization competes. It includes customer

Business Process	Process Definition	Content Knowledge	Process Knowledge	Marketplace Knowledge
Research and Development				
Procurement				
Manufacturing				
Fulfilment				
Sales and Marketing				
Finance and Accounting				

Source: Kesner, 2001

Figure 6.2.2
Knowledge capital inventory sheet

profiles, lead generation profiles, market data, competitor actions, and company opportunities and threats.

The Supply Chain Practice Aid makes knowledge available to 75 000 people worldwide.

Accenture's knowledge repository, the Supply Chain Practice Aid, is an example of a document database that includes all knowledge areas. Summarized in Figure 6.2.3, the repository provides access to leading supply chain practices and intelligence for more than 75 000 people worldwide and is available on Lotus Notes and via the Internet.

This repository provides users access to selling materials, client engagement profiles, market intelligence, external research, thought leadership and other materials that help individuals understand the supply chain-related products and services that the company sells. It also contains links to process knowledge, methodologies, project deliverables, alliances and centers of excellence that detail how Accenture packages and delivers its services.

In addition to codifying explicit knowledge, the repository contains a list of subject matter experts, employee photos and other information designed to help link individuals with individuals who can help solve problems by sharing both tacit and explicit knowledge. The repository also provides centralized access to e-learning courses, other training and education programs, and information about marketing initiatives.

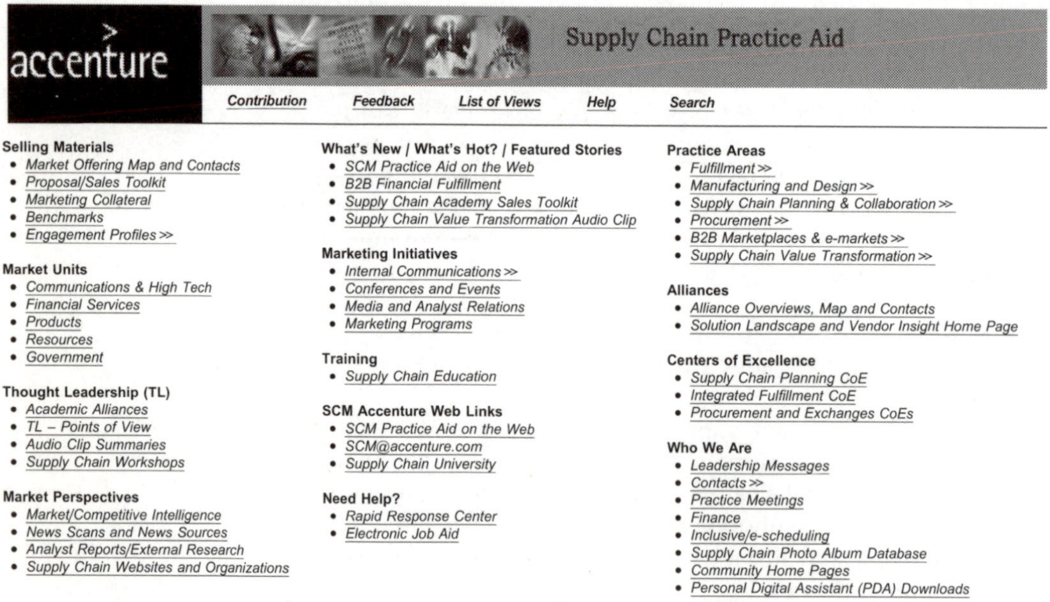

Source: Accenture

Figure 6.2.3
Accenture's supply chain Practice Aid

Principle 6. Use multiple technologies and tools

For most companies, their most valuable knowledge by far is tacit. The best way to share tacit knowledge is through face-to-face meetings, discussion groups, networking sessions and communities of practice. While technology cannot replace the human interactions required to transfer tacit knowledge most effectively, it can assist with a broad range of communications that help to facilitate employee knowledge sharing. Several technologies are on the market to help companies to collect, categorize and disseminate knowledge. The question is how to choose the right ones.

Technologies can help to collect, categorize and disseminate knowledge.

A range of technologies are available to help facilitate the interplay of explicit and tacit knowledge. These technologies are especially valuable for global organizations that are highly dispersed geographically.

To support knowledge management activities effectively, technologies must be able to support both explicit and tacit knowledge transfer. Groupware and workflow management systems are two types of IT systems helping organizations to achieve this knowledge sharing. For business problems that are not well defined, discussion groups or newsgroups may be required to gather the right knowledge.

Groupware is a class of IT system that supports interactions among individuals and groups either simultaneously or at different times. Groupware can help to facilitate bringing the right individuals together to solve problems or share ideas. Groupware, as described by Marvin Manheim (1999), comprises a variety of IT systems:

- e-mail, which is the most basic type of groupware, can support one-on-one and broad dialogues between groups. For example, a strategic sourcing interest group, consisting of more than 300 employees worldwide, uses e-mails to ask procurement-related questions or to request project deliverables. Within minutes, users can get answers or ideas on where to find the information they need.
- Document databases are repositories where multiple documents, contact lists and templates are made available for copying and use by authorized viewers.
- Discussion forums can support asynchronous and synchronous dialogue. For asynchronous communications, individuals post questions and issues called 'topics' that others can view and discuss by posting 'sub-topics'. Alternatively, chat discussions are an example of synchronous dialogue in which participants can interact in real time.

Workflow management systems (WFMS) are a second type of IT system that can help companies to gather knowledge. WFMS support interactions among people where the processes have been previously defined. These types of systems enable the efficient execution of pre-defined, standard business processes such as receiving a shipment at a warehouse, routing approvals for a capital expenditure or handling a routine customer inquiry.

WFMS tools help companies to automate business process logic and execute it repetitively. While WFMS enables efficiencies in process execution, these tools also create audit trails and valuable historical information related to the processes they automate. Over time, the historical data represent a body of knowledge that can provide pointers for process improvements. For example, a process may operate more efficiently with specific customers, vendors or employees, or a process may operate more efficiently during certain times of the day or year. Through data analysis and tacit knowledge sharing, companies can identify improvement areas and use these to refine business processes.

Conclusion

Companies that leverage knowledge capital are more likely to create new value.

Companies have to expedite their learning capability if they are to master the increasing complexities of today's supply chains. They need to create a culture that rewards the sharing of knowledge across the enterprise while also continuously developing, capturing and sharing explicit and implicit knowledge. Many management techniques are available to organizations to help them to share and leverage their knowledge. Companies can introduce best practices in knowledge management to increase their chances of success.

Top management support should be gained, for example, to create a mandate for knowledge sharing and to establish a knowledge culture in the organization. Companies need to leverage and continuously refine strategies to share implicit knowledge and introduce ways to recognise the social side of knowledge transfer – the source of most sharing of implicit knowledge. Explicit knowledge can be transferred through enterprise document management, enterprise portals, community portals and other shared repositories. External knowledge can be sought through competitive intelligence and market intelligence. Overall, knowledge maps can be developed to make knowledge easy to find.

Companies that succeed in leveraging their knowledge capital are more likely to improve process efficiency and create new value in the organization. They can enhance or enable their competitive advantage in their supply chain operations by supporting collaboration and learning across the enterprise. Essential people talent, expertise and product knowledge will stay with the company through knowledge management strategies, rather than be lost to competitors. Effective knowledge management also increases the use of 'best in breed' supply chain practices across the organization and improves product and process innovation. Companies will spend fewer resources 'reinventing the wheel' through effective knowledge management, enabling people to devote their time and talents to achieving the organization's corporate goals.

References

Burtha, M. (2001), 'Working with Leaders', *Knowledge Management Review*, (September/October), p. 7.

Donoghue, L. P. et al. (1999), 'Knowledge Management Strategies that Create Value', *Outlook*, (no. 1), 48–53.

Hansen, M. T. and Oetinger, B. (2001), 'Introducing T-Shaped Managers: Knowledge Management's Next Generation', *Harvard Business Review*, (March), pp. 107–116.

Kesner, R. (2001), 'Preparing for Knowledge Management: Part I, Process Mapping', *Information Strategy: The Executive's Journal*, vol. 18 (Issue 1).

Manheim, M. L. (1999), 'Integrating People and Technology for Supply Chain Advantage', *Achieving Supply Chain Excellence Through Technology (ASCET)*, vol. 1, (April) pp. 304–313.

Stewart, T. A. (2002), 'The Case Against Knowledge Management', *Business 2.0* (February).

6.3 Education and skills training requirements in supply chains

John L. Gattorna and Richard S. Clarke

The challenge is to rapidly build a workforce with the skills not just for today, but to shape the supply chain and gain the competitive advantage for tomorrow.

Supply chain management has evolved from a functionally oriented discipline in materials management, manufacturing, warehouse and distribution management to a discipline dealing with complex flow issues related to the global movement of products and information. The supply chain discipline has matured beyond logistics and found its way on to the executive agenda, where it now contributes to the generation of company value. Similar to the uptake of information technology as an enabler for process change in the 1980s, supply chain management has become an enabler for transformational change in the way products and services are developed and brought to market to satisfy customers' needs. With this 'growth spurt' to new levels of maturity, effective supply chain management demands new levels of human performance. In a recent survey (Wirthlin Worldwide and Accenture, 2002), 150 C-level executives from Fortune 1000 companies identified 'world-class programs to build and maintain the right skills in their employees' as the single most important driver for supply chain improvement.

The imperative for doing so is now. The complexity of the supply chain, illustrated in Figure 6.3.1, and the need for innovation is increasing exponentially compared with the steady state of the past few decades. The speed of change and emergence of new technologies are driving the demand for broader skill sets; workforce diversity and employee turnover are further complicating the people issue for organizations. The skills shortage is already being recognized. A study by the University of Michigan (Masters, 1998) highlighted the shortage of fully trained supply chain managers – a shortage that would have since increased. The challenge for companies is to rapidly build the requisite skills in their workforce to equip them not just for today, but to prepare them to shape the supply chain and gain the competitive advantage for tomorrow's markets.

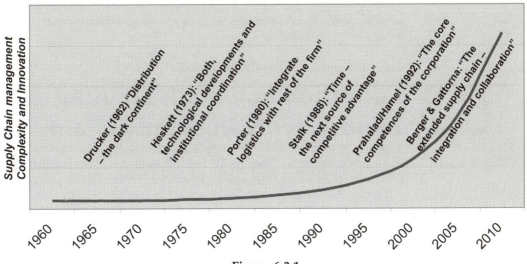

Figure 6.3.1
Increasing supply chain complexity

To address this challenge, traditional learning programs alone will not be sufficient. A review of the academic offerings of some of the world's most esteemed universities and professional schools shows that most are still locked into functional silos such as finance, transportation/logistics and operations management. Training curricula do not account for the more recent developments in the way supply chains are evolving, including the demand for collaboration, negotiation, channel design, and e-commerce.

This chapter suggests some practical steps to identify, develop and measure the supply chain skills necessary to ensure success in this dynamic business environment.

A practical guide to skills development

Step 1. Defining what supply chain competency means to the organization

The first step is for senior managers to agree which skills are relevant to their company's supply chain. Most companies have defined a set of 'core competencies'; however, these tend to be generic across the entire workforce rather than articulating the specific skills required to run effective supply chains. Creating a supply chain competency model is one way of clearly defining the capabilities that an organization requires. This competency model not only defines what skills need to exist or be developed, but also provides a profile for company recruiting and a framework for performance management.

Creating a supply chain competency model is one way of clearly defining the capabilities that an organization requires.

Depending on the business's aspirations for the levels at which the supply chain should operate, a company can define a competency model for each level.

Level 1: Functional supply chain skills

Functional skills in the supply chain are the basis for operational excellence and include expertise in the more traditional areas of procurement, manufacturing, distribution and warehousing. These skills will help a company to achieve operational excellence and continuous improvement in areas of the supply chain that are fundamental to a company's success. They will help differentiate the company's performance of a core competence as superior to that of competitors.

Figure 6.3.2 shows an example of a supply chain planning competency model used by a global food ingredients manufacturer. This model defines the whole-of-job competencies required for supply planners, including behaviors, processes, systems and industry factors.

Level 2: Integration and collaboration skills

Companies put significant effort into integrating their supply chain activities within their own organizations and across business partners. The supply chain is not only about moving products through some sort of transformation process. It is about optimizing physical, informational and financial flows to achieve optimum output for all entities involved, from the start of the transformation process through to the delivery of goods and services to the end consumer. Indeed, the best supply chain leaders try to put themselves 'in the shoes of the customer' and attempt to anticipate customers' needs, and translate these needs into appropriate supply chain responses. All this requires a supply chain skill-set that goes far beyond the original focus of functional excellence.

For example, Hewlett Packard's computer products organization has identified the key functions they are good at, such as product development. Many of HP's other functions are outsourced where the company believes other parties have more expertise, such as in contract manufacturing, and distribution. Some of these processes are shared with other divisions but remain within the organization. Others are outsourced to service providers, which in turn have to be managed as well – creating yet another critical skill. Suffice to say that it certainly is a challenge to technically integrate product, information, and financial flows. Consequently, Hewlett Packard has set out to address this issue of building the skills necessary to maximize value extraction from its supply chains, focusing on three components:

- *integration skills*: technical, process, and organizational
- *management and leadership skills*: tactical and some strategic
- *organizational skills*: trust, collaboration, negotiation, and partnership.

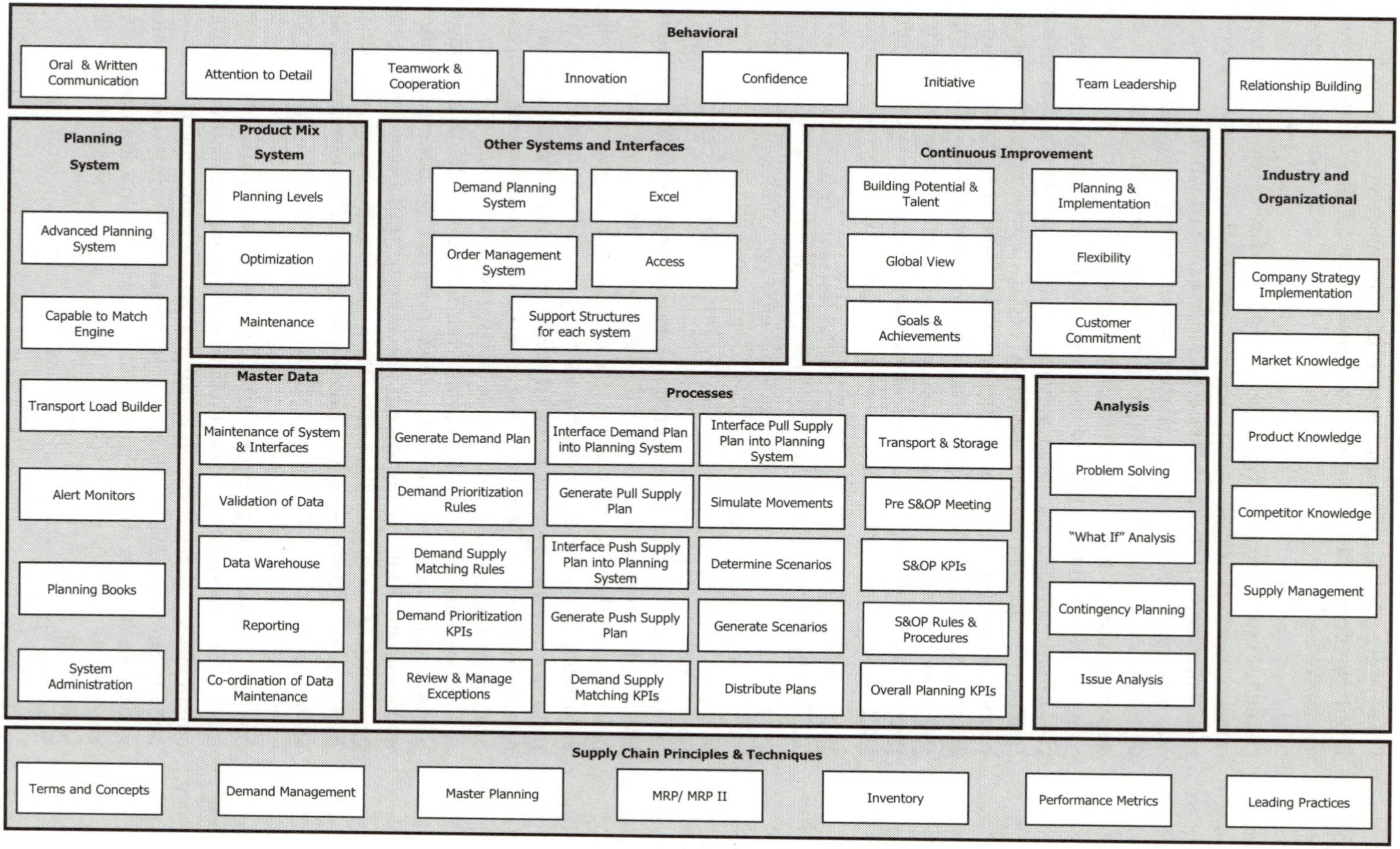

Figure 6.3.2
Supply chain planning competency model

Level 3: Synchronization and new business models

While the concept of a supply chain assumes that one company has the power to control most of the activities, it is the emerging new business models that truly take advantage of the Internet and challenge existing paradigms of supply chain organization and management. Networks of businesses have emerged where business partners connect for the purpose of driving new quantums of value creation for all parties to share. For example, Cisco Systems operates in a network of several hundred suppliers and service providers to deliver products and services to their customers.

Networks of interconnected exchanges and marketplaces will give rise to entirely new business models in time, despite the somewhat flawed start to the e-commerce era. The best companies continue to probe the boundaries, looking for ways to use this virtual phenomenon; others are just hoping it will all go away – which it will not. With this new virtual world comes the difficulty of learning to manage people in a distributed operating environment across the globe: a new skill indeed. The types of skill required to operate at this level are:

- *synchronization skills*: using platforms for collaboration and synchronization, adopt new technologies and business paradigms
- *leadership skills*: entrepreneurial – developing value propositions for new initiatives, energizing others to buy-in, mentoring
- *organizational skills*: innovation and alliance management.

While all this is true, it is important to recognize that the different levels of complexity associated with the three-level continuum described earlier in this book in *Introduction and frameworks* requires a corresponding level of appropriate sophistication in terms of the response. As Ashby's Law (1956) tells us, for a complex system to adapt to its external environment, its internal systems must adapt to and incorporate variety. We can be sure of one thing: that the demand for more sophisticated supply chain management skills will continue to rise, particularly as e-commerce continues to have an impact on the supply chain. The Gartner Group, the International Data Corporation and Morgan Stanley Dean Witter all predict that the rapid increase in B2B services driven by e-commerce will have a direct impact on the supply chain.

Step 2. Matching people with the required skill levels

Once the organization has a starting definition for the required competencies, executives can determine which teams and individuals need to have which skills. Usually performance levels will be defined within each competency. This provides a yardstick for measuring current capability and setting targets and timeframes, at the individual, team, business unit, and company levels.

If the supply chain is operating at multiple levels of the performance versus capability framework then managers are likely to target different people to obtain the skills appropriate to each level. For example, most of the workforce will have the skills to deliver operational excellence, while a select few will have the higher-level skills needed in areas such as collaborative planning and third party negotiations.

When operating at the integration/collaboration and virtual supply chain levels, companies should also consider the skills requirements and education of those outside the organization, such as suppliers and franchisees, as they are fundamental to the success of the supply chain. For example, a large US automobile manufacturer provides training on its models and parts to its network of dealers via an Internet-based learning management system. They are also looking at providing technical training for suppliers through similar media.

Step 3. Developing the skills-building curriculum

Organizations are often faced with a plethora of constraints in terms of budget, time and location, all of which pose barriers to skills development. Although its importance is given 'lip service', in reality education and training often ends up low on the company's priority list. This means that developing a workable skills-building curriculum for supply chain workforces requires creativity and pragmatism.

Education and training often ends up low on the priority list. Developing a workable skills-building curriculum, therefore, requires creativity and pragmatism.

Flexibility is key. While it would be nice to send everyone on a training course for a few weeks each year – facilitated by industry experts and providing networking opportunities with co-workers or peers from other companies – this is unlikely to happen for the majority. Managers need to select a practical mix of internal and external content, 'build versus buy' training, delivery via classroom and electronic media, and dedicated training time versus on-the-job coaching.

An example of a training curriculum implemented recently for a supply chain operations team is shown in Table 6.3.1.

This example demonstrates the way different training approaches, mediums, and providers can fit together to cover the needs of a supply chain team for whole-of-job skills development.

Step 4. Make the delivery commitment

As mentioned, the gap between the intention and the reality of training is usually big. Even with the best intentions, either training budgets get cut or the perceived day-to-day pressures of work mean that the training does not happen.

The benefit of planning skill development activities is that companies can increase the chances that they actually happen.

The benefit of planning skill-development activities is that companies can increase the chances that they actually happen. Many business cycles are seasonal, which provides times when it is easier to allocate time to be 'off the job'. Planning ahead also allows the chance to notify customers and other stakeholders who may be affected. As

Table 6.3.1
Sample supply chain training curriculum

Introduction to supply chain principles	Self-paced, Internet-based – external provider
Seven critical processes and procedures	Workshop – led by supply chain managers – company specific
Order management and inventory system	Instructor led, hands-on systems training – internal IS trainers
Product knowledge	Presentation and discussion – led by product technical managers
Market knowledge	Presentation – led by customer service managers
Managing relationships	Scenario-based workshop – external facilitator
Customer service techniques	Self-paced, Internet-based – external provider
Product specification systems	System demonstration – internal IS trainers
Product safety program	Presentation – compliance manager
Order to delivery	One-on-one 'shadowing' with experienced peer

service performance is ultimately improved due to improved job performance, staff training can be positioned as a benefit to customers.

Skill-building activities can also be positioned as a reward or employee benefit. In the worst cases, last-minute offers of training are a knee-jerk reaction to a valued employee's resignation. When appropriate training is planned ahead and commitments kept it can become a powerful motivator. The combined result of a more highly skilled and motivated employee will undoubtedly increase job performance. When this is applied to the team or unit it translates to enhanced business performance.

The combined benefit of skill development and team building is another compelling reason to keep training commitments. A good example of this combination is the supply chain simulation – 'The Beer Distribution Game' (Forrester, 1961; Sterman,1988). In this game, participants play the roles of manufacturer, distributor, wholesaler and retailer. Players make ordering decisions that trigger certain volumes of inventory moving through the chain. Costs of inventory holdings and back-orders are tracked and participants learn the value of communicating demand signals and of creating information transparency up and down the chain. They experience the benefits of collaboration and have a lot of fun in the process. After the fun, staff can make the experience more real by discussing how it is relevant to their daily work in the company.

Many learning technologies are now available and these provide a variety of delivery options and access to great content. 'e-learning' is a method of improving performance that incorporates the power of the Internet and integrated knowledge management with personalized features that shift control to the learner. e-learning is being used increasingly by organizations as a viable solution for supply chain education needs. The benefits of e-learning over traditional approaches to training include reduced operating costs, increased speed of meeting learning needs, improved learning and business outcomes, and higher quality standards.

e-learning is being used increasingly by organizations as a viable solution for supply chain education needs.

Examples of eLearning technologies include advanced search engines, which not only locate specific pieces of information and people, but also provide quantitative assessments as to the appropriateness of these resources in addressing a particular need. Virtual coaches and intelligent tutors are 'smart tools' that can step in to provide guidance when needed – either as part of a formal performance improvement initiative, or to support the informal improvements that occur on the job every day.

Personalized Web-based employee portals are another tool that provide workers with point-of-need access to the information they require most – for example customer profiles, product specifications, contact lists, pricing guidelines, transport schedules. Finally, expert-led chats, online laboratories and collaborative workshops allow employees to hone their skills in a team environment on an ongoing basis. This can be used to inject external perspectives as well as improve knowledge sharing between decentralized supply chain teams.

Step 5. Evaluate and improve

The last step closes the continuous improvement loop. All training should be evaluated in terms of its effectiveness, not just at the point of delivery, but later in terms of the actual impact on job performance. This way, companies can actually measure the return on investment for their skill development dollar, which in turn will provide a strong case for continuing investment. The best way to measure on-the-job performance is by self- and manager assessments. Use an assessment tool that is based on the supply chain competency model.

All training should be evaluated in terms of its effectiveness, not just at the point of delivery, but in terms of impact on job performance.

Table 6.3.2 is an extract from an assessment tool used to measure the increasing proficiency of a supply chain team during the implementation of an advanced planning system.

Using a quantitative method the assessment tool enables organizations to attach dollar values to performance levels, such as increased sales, reduced inventory, and reduced third-party transport and storage costs. Remember that achievement of these business improvement benefits always comes back to the skills of people.

Accenture is a company whose prime assets are the knowledge and skills of its people and for this reason it has always invested heavily in

Table 6.3.2
Supply chain skills assessment

Demand management	My level
0 I do not have current knowledge in this area.	
1 I understand that a forecast and demand plans exist but cannot explain the difference between them.	
2 I understand and can explain the difference between a forecast and a demand plan. I know where these are generated and what system they are stored in.	
3 I can convert a forecast into a demand plan and understand the purpose of demand management. I am aware of the link between forecast accuracy and safety stock requirements. I understand the company's application of forecasting, demand management and forecasting accuracy measures.	
4 I understand and can explain the difference between a forecast and a demand plan and am familiar with the management of demand. I understand the impacts of forecasting, demand planning and management on the company's supply chain. I understand the use of various forecasting methods and techniques.	
5 I can teach forecasting, demand planning and management and can explain the impacts of these on the company's supply chain. I am sought after within the company for the depth of my forecasting, demand planning and demand management knowledge and experience.	

developing skills and so increasing the value of those assets. The supply chain practice of Accenture is no exception and many internal courses have been developed to train consultants in supply chain best practices and practical approaches. Recently, as the demand from client organizations for similar levels and types of skills has increased, Accenture has responded by making many of these learning assets available via the Internet. The final section of this chapter discusses the approach to educating supply chain practitioners used by Accenture's Supply Chain Academy, released in November 2001. This example demonstrates many of the features and practical steps for developing supply chain skills.

A comprehensive approach – the Supply Chain Academy

With courses available across different delivery formats, professionals can tap into materials depending on their required skill type, time flexibility and level of sophistication.

The Supply Chain Academy, launched globally by Accenture in November 2001, delivers fundamental knowledge and skills to develop foundational supply chain capability via all functional disciplines. By offering a portfolio of courses across different delivery formats, the Supply Chain Academy provides a flexible program allowing professionals to easily tap into the appropriate materials depending on their required skill type, time flexibility, and level of sophistication. A large array of e-enabled training via e-learning modules and Web-casts are available for functional skills, while interactive classroom and workshop events can be scheduled for more advanced topics. Industry and functional news feeds, articles, and white papers are also available on demand to disseminate knowledge at any time.

The training materials capture the many years' of experience that Accenture has recorded in developing and delivering training to mobilize and develop a global management consulting workforce of more than 75 000 people. In addition, Accenture has also extended its relationships with leading academics and consultants from more than 20 university and research institutions, such as Professors Hau Lee at Stanford University, John Langley at Georgia Tech and Martin Christopher at Cranfield University, to establish an ongoing program to develop and deliver new course materials.

The program covers the full breadth of supply chain management at three different levels, as shown in Figure 6.3.3. In addition, tailored learning solutions can be developed to address the specific needs of clients, and programs can be integrated into existing client programs.

Delivery mechanisms for ongoing learning

Five different formats are used to provide a portfolio of training to meet the requirements of individuals and groups with different time, skill and level needs. These include: e-enabled training, e-enabled distance learning, simulations, e-enabled knowledge, and executive forums.

Level 1: Common Foundation

Supply Chain Analyses, Tools & Techniques
Supply Chain Concepts & Processes

Level 2: Specialty Areas

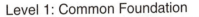

Supply Chain Planning

Product Development	Procurement & e-Exchanges	Manufacturing	Fulfilment	Service Management & Customer Support

Level 3: Leadership Skills

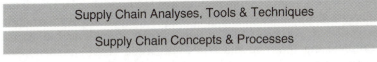

World Class Supply Chain Expertise
Value Creation & Realization
World Class Supply Chain Expertise

Source: Accenture

Figure 6.3.3
Supply Chain Academy framework

e-enabled training

The Supply Chain Academy presents a comprehensive collection of focused one- to two-hour e-learning modules and longer e-courses that are designed to build specific skills and knowledge online. They may be assembled and taken together as a course or taken individually, depending upon the users' needs and ability.

e-learning modules range from introductory subjects such as the fundamentals of procurement to skill-building subjects, such as capacity planning, through to advanced subjects such as strategic sourcing. The modules, which normally take one hour to complete, are comprised of a structured set of text materials which is broken down to digestible sections on each screen and supported by pictures, diagrams and video clips to bring the subject to life. Interactive exercises are included in each section to test understanding and improve retention along the way. Students can move through the material at their own pace and go back to previous sections as required.

For example, 'Fundamentals of Procurement' provides an overview of the procurement business function and serves as a foundation for advanced courses in the fields of supply chain management, strategic sourcing and e-procurement. It is made up of six one-hour modules, such as 'Procurement Concepts' and 'Procurement Processes'.

Advanced e-courses are designed to build further mastery of supply chain management skills. These are conducted over a two to three weeks timeframe using a combination of recorded presentations, team-based case study exercises with live faculty debriefs, Web-based community discussions, and a Web-based simulation. Students need to be available for set Web-cast or teleconference sessions, but are free to complete the recorded materials and team-based case studies at convenient times to suite their individual schedules. They can also interact with faculty or fellow students at any time through e-mail, Web-based community discussions or telephone.

For example, 'Integrated Supply Chain Management', taught by Professors Hau Lee of Stanford University and David Pyke of Dartmouth College, focuses on the interrelationships and interdependencies of sourcing, production and delivery across supply chains. Five of the most fundamental supply chain principles are covered in the presentations and exercises, including:

- plan according to market demand signals
- design and differentiate the product closer to the customer
- customize the logistics network
- develop supply chain-wide information technology and
- use supply chain-spanning performance measures.

e-enabled distance learning

Distance learning programs at the Academy include regularly scheduled Web-casts, video conferences and audio conferences. Students log on to these live presentations made by leading academics and management consultants from wherever they are around the world, as long as they have access to the Internet and a telephone. Presentation slides are transmitted via the Internet to the student's computer screen, while the voice goes through a traditional teleconferencing hook-up. An online chat room allows students to ask questions or respond to questions initiated by the facilitator or faculty. The faculty can see the questions and responses and adapt their presentation accordingly or give real-life examples.

Students can log on to live presentations made by leading academics and management consultants from wherever they are around the world.

Multiple sessions can be run to suit different time zones and each session is recorded and made available for playback at any time.

One subject, 'Logistics and Financial Performance', is an example of a two-hour audio conference, presented by Professor Doug Lambert of Ohio State University. He explores how the understanding of logistics costs and the impact of logistics on revenue can drive decisions that can provide significant opportunities for both revenue generation and cost savings. Another subject, 'The New Wave of Supply Chain Management', is an example of a web-cast video presentation, by Professor Hau Lee, in which he explores the future issues likely to impact efficient supply chain management.

Simulation

Team-based competitions and individual simulations involve participants in solving supply chain problems using a computer simulation tool. These simulations give participants a chance to apply their skills and supply chain knowledge in a realistic environment.

Computer simulations give participants a chance to apply their skills and supply chain knowledge in a realistic environment.

In the Global Supply Chain Simulation, for example, participants play the role of global manufacturers who must make multiple rounds of decisions involving such factors as procurement, manufacturing, distribution/warehousing and transportation. Performance is measured by a series of financial and operational reports. Like the e-courses described above, the simulation can be conducted virtually, with teams located at different locations around the world. Each team can set their own schedule to review the situation and formulate their response, as long as they submit their response by a pre-agreed time. Teams can interact with other teams and the faculty through e-mail, Web-based community discussions or telephone.

e-enabled knowledge

The Supply Chain Academy also provides a suite of supply chain thought leadership, news and reference materials, such as news feeds, articles, white papers and industry reports. These are available on demand from a variety of sources, including industry analysts, Accenture experts, research institutions and university academics.

Supply chain thought leadership is made available through news and reference materials.

News feeds are delivered every business day on topics selected by the client from more than 2 000 options. Sample topics include: freight transportation logistics and distribution; European pharmaceutical regulatory regimes; tobacco; Asia Pacific semiconductors overview; and IT in Government.

Executive forums

The Supply Chain Academy hosts live executive seminars designed around current thought-leadership topics affecting today's supply chain executives, or issues that are specific to a client's current needs. Lasting one to two days, seminars are developed and led by leading academics, industry experts and Accenture's industry and functional leaders. The seminars include executive roundtables and opportunities for networking with peers and world-class experts.

Deployment of learning services

The one e-learning portal can be used to provide full training requirements to a disparate workforce in a cost-effective way.

Based upon a client's needs and interests, the Supply Chain Academy can provide services to support the development, delivery and management of the supply chain education program. The academy can be customized to include access to the company's in-house training materials, leadership messages or schedule of classroom courses. In that way, personnel have access to their required training on operational procedures such as safety or maintenance specific to their site situation, while being able to access leading supply chain training through the same channel.

In this way, the one e-learning portal can be used to provide full training requirements to a disparate workforce in a cost-effective way. The Supply Chain Academy works with organizations to identify, assess and define learning solutions to improve their capability to compete. Based upon identified requirements, the Supply Chain Academy will assemble curricula for each relevant area of the business, drawing upon both existing and custom developed learning solutions.

The Supply Chain Academy builds a more proficient workforce at a lower cost, leading to greater organizational responsiveness and superior supply chain performance. The multiple e-learning formats adopted provide a direct cost savings over traditional classroom methods through lower per student cost and reduced travel expenses. Enquires should be directed to Mike Mikurak at Accenture (2001): *michael.g.mikurak@accenture.com.*

Conclusion

In the end, it will be the strong recognition by C-level executives of the importance of the supply chain that will force the pace of supply chain capability and skills development. With fully trained supply chain managers already in short supply, companies need to start establishing skills-ready workforces to ensure they will be at the leading edge of supply chain competition. Clearly, the way forward is to forge broad partnerships within and across industries, and with other stakeholders such as academic institutions and leading consultants in the field. Companies need to focus on knowledge transfer from 'best' companies and consultants and start to be more selective about which academic institutions they should embrace as partners, such as those that have a history of close ties with industry and lead the way in supply chain education. In this way, business, commerce and industry will have access to the talent they need to take advantage of the opportunities that surely lie ahead.

The way forward is to forge broad partnerships within and across industries, and with other stakeholders such as academic institutions and leading consultants.

References

Accenture (2001), Supply Chain Academy. Contact M. Mikurak, St Petersburg, FL. (michael.g.mikurak@accenture.com).

Ashby, W. R. (1956), *An Introduction to Cybernetics*, London: Chapman and Hall.

Forrester, J. W. (1961), *Industrial Dynamics*; Cambridge, MA: MIT Press (contains a description of an early version of the Beer Distribution Game).

Masters, J. M. (1998), 'Removing the barriers', Proceedings of the Twenty-Sixth Annual Transportation and Logistics Educators Conference, Chicago, Il, October 1997, Oak Brook: Council of Logistics Management), pp. 1–28.

Sterman, J. D. (1988), 'Modelling Managerial Behaviour: Misperceptions of Feedback in a Dynamic Decision Making Experiment', *Management Science*, **35** (3), pp. 321–339 (contains a detailed analysis of Beer Game results).

Wirthlin Worldwide and Accenture (2002), Executive Omnibus Survey of 150 Fortune 1000 Executives, (December), New York.

6.4 Building successful consulting relationships

Ken Davis and Jamie M.Bolton

Using consultants is a way for organizations to secure the right skills and capabilities during a critical period of transformational change.

Achieving transformational change across the supply chain or the performance of any part of an organization is often a significant and difficult task. To ensure the right change is made – and that the change is sustainable – all aspects of the transformation agenda must be appropriately addressed. Strategy, process design, technical design, implementation, change management, communications and stakeholder management, training, support, and project and program management must all be present for successful transformation. Each of these areas requires a significantly different skill-set.

However, given the broad range of skills and capabilities required to realize successful change, organizations may not be able to fully undertake this change alone with internal resources. The primary reason is that organizations often do not possess the people with the right skills and capabilities at the right time.

The targeted use of consultants is a way to apply the right skills and capabilities at each stage of the change program. This chapter provides a client perspective on how to successfully use consultants and describes the attributes of a successful consulting relationship. The overall premise is that a successful relationship is not solely the responsibility of the consultant; the client organization needs to devote significant effort to make the relationship work, and the project successful.

This chapter is designed to be a 'checklist' of success factors that both the consultant and the client must exhibit to ensure a successful relationship. Many of these may appear to be simply common sense; however, experience suggests that it is often the simple factors that if not executed successfully can often be detrimental to the relationship. Furthermore this checklist is not intended to be a list from which the consultant or client can pick; these factors must be executed as a total package to be successful.

Characteristics and key success factors of a value-based consultant

What makes a consultant value-based? Typically, there are three categories of consultants:

- *Bookshelf decorators* – the consultants who produce voluminous reports, filled with insightful analysis of what is going on in the organization, what is wrong with the organization and how much can be saved by solving all the problems. Unfortunately, a practical, clear and agreed path forward is rarely presented to the organization: no executable plan for unlocking value and no consultant resources with the capability or experience to deliver the solution. Overall, these consultants are long on insight, but short on the ability to implement.
- *Body shop workers* – the consultants who provide the people resources to help on project teams. These consultants can be given a workplan and are able to execute against it, as long as they are provided with sufficient direction. Once the body shop workers are aimed in the right direction they are able to move forward. However, if the aim is slightly off-target they will efficiently work in the wrong direction until 're-aimed'.
- *Value prospectors* or *value extractors* – these consultants are able to work with an organization to diagnose a business problem, identify the underlying causes of poor performance, ascertain the specific value that can be gained from rectifying performance issues and develop pragmatic solutions that can be executed within the constraints of the organization and quickly deliver value to the business. These consultants are value-based. They know how to look for value within the boundaries of a business problem, they can develop executable strategies to capture this value, and they can provide experienced resources with implementation skills capable of unlocking such value.

Some consultants provide great insights, but lack the ability to implement. Others can execute a workplan, but need close direction. Value-based consultants, in contrast, identify problems and develop and deliver solutions.

How does a client recognize a value-based consultant? Many success factors differentiate a value-based consultant from the rest. If any one factor is missing, the client has a high risk of engaging a consultant who cannot develop the type of relationship required for lasting success.

Bias for action

The consultant must be a catalyst for driving momentum in an organization and overcoming any current inertia the organization possesses. But, equally important, the consultant must have a partner in the client organization who is also passionate about creating the change. This 'bias for action' is absolutely critical if a project is to be delivered fully and successfully on time, at the right quality levels, and with barriers to successful delivery rapidly removed.

A bias for action will create momentum and drive the project through to delivery.

The principal way a bias for action can be delivered is through developing and executing rigorous plans and milestones on the consulting engagement. Progress against these plans and milestones needs to be highly visible and communicated to the client and project team, frequently. Defining these deliverables, milestones and out-comes with the client early in any engagement and agreeing responsibilities for delivering them (both for the consultant and client) is critical to ensure a common understanding is reached between both parties and that roles and responsibilities are clear. A detailed plan provides a very clear roadmap from which the expectations of both parties can be managed and against which both parties are held accountable.

The early definition of project risks and development of a comprehensive and actionable risk management plan is important, and ensuring the plan remains visible to all key stakeholders, and current, will minimize barriers to successful implementation. A bias for action will create project momentum, build team morale, and generate confidence within the business that the project is on track to deliver.

Contagious passion for the business

A shared passion for a client's business will help to build an effective partnership.

Clients want consultants who embrace their business as much as they do, who understand their industry, business model, culture and what creates value in the business. Unless there is 'contagious passion' the ability of a consultant to deliver on an engagement will be compromised.

Contagious passion can be demonstrated simply by having a clear understanding of the organization's structure, businesses, keeping current with industry trends and the positioning of the client within the industry and engaging frequently with the client on these. Where possible, simply using the organization's products or services is a personal demonstration of this passion. Conversely, if strong personal beliefs are held against the client's products or services it is difficult to sincerely demonstrate a passion for their business.

Developing a contagious passion for the business is one of the most effective ways for a consultant to ensure that any 'us and them' boundary is removed or reduced and will help build an effective partnership between both parties.

Sharp focus

Consultants with sharp focus will not be distracted by side issues.

A sharp focus is required to know what is important to deliver the project and what is not. The consultants should not be overly concerned about issues they have no ability to influence and which are unlikely to have an impact on the project outcomes. Sharp focus is required to ensure the consultants remain targeted on the 'end game' and do not get distracted by side issues. For example, consultants should not lose sight of the facts and deliverables and over-react to issues, organizational noise and individuals' agendas unrelated to the project. Nor should they overtly look for the next opportunity while failing to deliver on the current project.

Strong knowledgeable and fact-based leadership is required from both parties, to manage key business stakeholders and insulate the project team where possible from side issues. They also focus the project team on tasks, deliverables and outcomes and regularly track their performance against these. Furthermore, if any issues have an impact on team performance, the change leaders must rapidly act to provide direction to minimize distraction and ensure the team remains focused.

Sharp focus will help ensure the consultant successfully delivers on an engagement and builds a proven track record with the client for the long term.

Pragmatic commerciality

A strong client and consultant relationship is built upon consistent and successful delivery of measurable value. The delivery of value must be proportional to the commercial arrangements for the engagement. Consultants must always ensure that the commercial arrangements for a project ensure the client achieves a fair return on the consulting investment (measured either quantitatively or qualitatively).

The commercial arrangements must be fair to both parties, and ensure the client achieves a fair return on their consulting investment.

The true test of pragmatic commerciality will be the business case. Unless the business case meets the relevant hurdle rates for the client, such as IRR, NPV and payback periods, and costs can be covered within the available budget, the project is unlikely to proceed. There are, however, options that both parties can explore to improve the attractiveness of the project financials. These include:

- re-shaping project scope to focus on the most valuable initiatives
- adjusting the resourcing mix and levels between the parties to reduce costs
- developing gain-sharing arrangements where the consultant reduces costs in return for payments from the future benefits stream, and
- risk-sharing arrangements where payment is linked to successful delivery of milestones and capability.

Pragmatic commercial arrangements that are fair and equitable to both parties and meet the client's financial requirements are necessary to gain project approval and are the first step to mobilizing the project.

Active listening skills

This may seem self-explanatory but it is frequently one of the most under-developed skills of a consultant. Listening to the client is critical to ensure the client problem or issue, and its business context, is fully understood. One of the most common complaints about consultants is

Listening to the client at all stages of the project is critical to ensure the problem is fully understood.

that they have a preconceived idea of the solution to the problem before fully understanding the problem and the situation. Consequently the solution is not tailored to the client situation and does not fully solve the problem. Listening is the critical skill that overcomes this issue.

Effective listening is achieved by first identifying the key stakeholders across the business who understand the problem and are able to provide insights. Second, the consultant needs to listen carefully to these people early in the engagement to capture their points of view. Third, the consultant needs to use their collective knowledge as an input to diagnosing the business problem, validating and gaining ownership for the solution.

The principal outcomes of active listening skills are that the client is confident that the consultant has understood the business problem, feels engaged throughout the project and agrees to and owns the recommended solution.

Pushback

Consultants should aim to stretch the thinking of a client so as to provide a new perspective on business problems.

One of the most critical roles of the consultant is to provide objectivity and an informed 'point of view'. This may often require the consultant to present an opinion significantly different to that of the client, creating an environment of constructive tension. The best outcomes are delivered when the client and consultant challenge – or push – each other's thinking to deliver superior results.

The most effective and constructive way for both parties to pushback in this way is to always challenge the viewpoint by posing questions with the ultimate objective of stretching the thinking rather than threatening the individual. Simple questions to create this tension include:

- Haven't you considered …?
- Why do you think that …?
- What leads you to that view?
- What is your rationale for that solution?
- What stops you doing it sooner?
- What would you need to do it faster?
- What would happen if you also …?

Depending on the level of respect and trust in the relationship and knowledge of the other party, both parties should be able to move from probing questions to more provocative statements as a means of creating constructive tension without having a negative impact on the relationship. These statements could include:

- Convince me.
- That approach won't work.
- I don't believe that solution fully addresses the problem.
- The business won't buy into it.

For constructive tension to be effective, consultants must recognize that they must earn the right to pushback. Consultants can build trusting one-on-one relationships by delivering outcomes over time and demonstrating an understanding of the client's business environment and culture.

Pushback provides new perspectives on business problems, new opportunities and solutions and ultimately creates greater value through stronger relationships.

Skills transfer

Transferring skills from consultant to client is perhaps the best spin-off of any consulting engagement. Not only does the client have a significant opportunity to learn through the engagement, the consultant should also see the project as a learning opportunity. By ensuring skills transfer throughout the engagement, the client builds capability and the consultant builds a greater awareness of the client's business, organization, industry and processes, which will be beneficial on future engagements.

Consultants can build the capabilities of their client's people while improving their own knowledge of the client's business.

To achieve this, the client must ensure that the project is staffed with appropriately skilled people who are receptive to building their knowledge and capabilities through working with consultants. The consultant has the responsibility of staffing the project with people that have the appropriate skills and are willing and able to spend the extra time necessary to coach and train the client's people. Where possible, each consultant should be partnered with at least one full-time staff member so that they can work along side each other, build their relationship, and create the 'one-team' environment required for effective skills transfer.

The project team should measure and track capability building throughout the engagement by determining the skill and capability opportunity areas through a baseline skill level measurement for the whole project team (client and consultant) at the start of the project, and by continually monitoring this throughout the engagement. To ensure the client team focuses on skills building, the client must recognize the benefit of integrating this into the company's own employee performance management process.

Effective skills transfer will increase the capability across all members of the project team, increase the effectiveness of the client team members returning to the business and encourage other members of the client's staff to participate in future initiatives. It will also build the capabilities of the consultant and their understanding of the client organization and its business.

Building a partnering environment

A partnering environment involves all client and consultant team members working together as 'one team' to achieve a shared goal.

A 'partnering environment' is required to ensure that maximum benefit is gained from the participation of both parties which is key to delivering a successful project outcome. A partnering environment exists when all members of the project team feel their contribution is valued and their view is listened to and respected. The project team works in a highly constructive manner as 'one team' – the strengths, weaknesses and working styles of each team member are known and respected and all members of the team are open to coaching, mentoring and constructive feedback.

There is no 'silver bullet' to build a partnering environment. Several leadership behaviors, organizational fundamentals and basic team-building activities are, however, necessary prerequisites.

Leadership behaviors

Leaders need to stress the value of one team and build a common understanding of the project.

Some of the leadership behaviors required to create a partnering environment are:

- recognize the value to be gained from building an effective partnering environment
- ensure a common understanding of the outcomes of the project across all team members and how their role contributes to the outcomes
- continually stress the theme of 'one team'
- ensure the client meets all members of the consulting team prior to project commencement to outline the success factors for working in the client environment, communicate the organization's vision and core values and to develop a point of view on the cultural fit of the consultant team members.

Organizational fundamentals

Organizations should develop a team charter with shared principles.

The organizational actions that need to be undertaken are:

- understand the work styles of the people from both parties to ensure they are not in conflict
- develop a team charter to ensure shared operating principles for the project team, and
- develop clearly defined roles and responsibilities for every team member and stakeholder to ensure accountability for delivery and elimination of avoidance behaviors.

Team building

Some of the activities that can promote team building are:

- holding off-site events such as team dinners or social sports
- staging on-site events such as casual dress days or theme days
- recognizing and celebrating special project successes and milestones and

- developing a weekly measurement process for team effectiveness to continually gauge the mood of the team and quickly react to any issues.

The development of a partnering environment is essential to create synergy among team members. It will ensure ideas are created and freely shared and respected among all team members. Ultimately a team operating in a partnering environment will deliver significantly more than the team's individual members could achieve in isolation.

Understand the client culture and values

The ability of consultants to assimilate with the client organization is vital to ensure the project members work as one team. By understanding the client's culture and values, the consultants demonstrate respect for the organization and will help them to develop a passion for the business.

Understanding the client's culture and values will help the consultants to develop a passion for the business.

The simplest way to achieve such understanding is to live and breathe the client's core values and demonstrate these values daily through the behavior of every project team member. For example, a client's core value of 'facing reality' can be demonstrated by ensuring project plans, timelines and milestones are realistic and achievable within the resources and skills of the project team. Where this is not the case, it is naïve to continue to push the team to meet unrealistic deadlines. 'Facing reality' can also be used to ensure business benefits are realistic and achievable.

A value of 'respect for the individual' can be demonstrated by accepting team members' strengths and weaknesses and organizing and managing the team so that strengths are leveraged and capabilities are built to overcome any weaknesses. Furthermore, if the client's culture is direct and confrontational then the project team should recognize this in its behavior. Similarly if the culture is one of syndication and socialization then again this must be recognized. This does not necessarily mean that the project team must model the client culture exactly (as this will, at times, remove the ability to be objective) but a recognition of this culture must be clearly demonstrated.

The outcome delivered by the consultant understanding the client's culture and values is the team working as one team and not adopting an 'us and them' mentality. The client sees a visible demonstration of the consultant seeking to understand the values of the organization, which is critical to developing a consulting relationship based on partnership.

In addition to the success factors, the consultant must avoid demonstrating other behaviors as follows:

- A consultant must never play politics or become involved in the politics of the organization. Doing so may impair the consultant's ability to provide a fair and objective perspective on the business problem.

- A consultant must not be the 'prophet of doom' and scare the organization into believing *all* is not well. There are many positive aspects in all organizations and these must be incorporated into any recommendation to provide a fair and balanced view of the situation.
- A consultant must not prescribe a solution, or have a preconceived idea of the solution before thorough diagnosis of the business problem. Beginning the project with this frame of mind will only cloud the judgement of the consultant.
- A consultant must never double count benefits. This requires the consultant to understand all other initiatives occurring in the business, and their business cases, to ensure a realistic and pragmatic business case.
- A consultant must not overtly sell the next job. The consultant has been engaged for a specific purpose and looking for future opportunities will only distract from delivering on the current project. While it is understandable that the consultant will seek to win further work, the best way to guarantee this is to build a successful track record of delivery.

Key success factors for the client

It is not just the consultant who must demonstrate key success factors to ensure the consulting relationship is successful. Equally important are the characteristics and behaviors of the client that contribute to the success of the relationship.

Visible top-down ownership and accountability

Visible commitment and ownership from senior managers will greatly increase the likelihood of a project's success.

Unless there is visible commitment from the senior levels of management in the organization the project has little legitimacy and is at a high risk of failure through either inadequate sponsorship, resource commitment or just visibility within the organization. Senior management commitment is required so that responsibility for the project success is shared not only among the project team, both consultants and client, but also with client management.

Visible commitment can be achieved through significant and active representation on project steering groups and acting as a 'consult' for the project team for a specific content area or area of the business. Leaders can assist with identifying and allocating suitable resources to ensure the project team has the right mix and level of skills and capabilities to perform the work. Alternatively, they can ensure appropriate funding is available so that the project team can deliver as planned with manageable risk.

Visible top-down commitment and ownership will greatly increase the likelihood of project success. By having the senior management of an organization commit resources, funds, time, and by structuring a component of their remuneration around successful project delivery, their support for the initiative will be highly visible to the project team and across the organization. Furthermore, the ownership of senior management created by these actions will also result in a group of stakeholders who can assist the project team to overcome roadblocks and issues rapidly.

Full-time resourcing with 'A' team members

The successful delivery of the project is directly determined by the quality of the resources allocated to it. Staffing the project with the client's best people is one of the most effective ways of minimizing risk for the project, increasing the probability of successful delivery and clearly demonstrates the value of the project to the business. People need to be assigned to a project full time to create individual accountability and ownership for the project deliverables and outcomes. Where people are part time there is always a reason for not completing a project task, deliverable or activity or attending a project meeting. With full-time resources, allocated clear roles, responsibilities, tasks and deliverables, there is little reason for non-delivery.

Creating a high-quality, high-impact team for the project, before the project starts, is the most critical task for project mobilization.

Staffing the project with the right people is also key to eliminating 'outside forces'. Outside forces are things or people that have the ability to create barriers or impediments to the successful and efficient delivery of the project. To best control these forces it is desirable to have them on the project team or in the project scope rather than outside the project where they may have the potential to do significant harm.

The key to securing the right resourcing on the project (and all future projects) is to demonstrate there is no disruption to the ongoing business from people being seconded to work on project teams. Project work often may not be viewed as a critical part of ongoing business operations, in which case it will not get the profile required to be successful. Despite spare capacity at certain times of the year, organizations often do not want to release quality staff. However, businesses need to look upon the project as an opportunity for people to grow through gaining new capabilities and assuming extra responsibilities. Projects also provide an organization with a way of creating new and challenging experiences for people.

However, where the organization does not have the people to staff the project, it must consider contracting workers as appropriate. Although adding cost to the project (and these costs must be included in the business case to reflect the project's true cost), backfilling should be considered as an effective way to ensure the right resources are made available to the project, full time.

Significant effort to appropriately and fully resource the project team before project commencement is the most critical task for project mobilization. It will result in the creation of a high-impact, quality team with the legitimacy to implement change within the organization.

Contagious passion for the business and the project

The client must also have a passion for the project, believing in how the outcomes will benefit the organization.

Similarly for the consultant, the client must also have a contagious passion for the business and equally important must have a passion for the project. The client needs to believe in the outcomes to be delivered by the project. Failure to do so may result in the client not committing to provide appropriate resources or failing to empower the team.

The key to deliver contagious passion is to use this as a selection criterion for inclusion in the team. In addition to looking at people's skills and capability levels, the organization needs to select those people who firmly believe in the project, agree with the way the project is to be conducted, and believe that the project outcomes will benefit the organization.

With both parties being passionate about the business and the project, the creation of a cohesive work environment is enhanced and the ability to build one team is greatly increased.

Ability to challenge current work practices and paradigms

Unless the project team has the ability to challenge current ways of operating and thinking, provide new perspectives on existing business practices, and openly challenge key stakeholders, only incremental change will result.

Challenging current business practices and paradigms can be achieved by developing informed views of how things can be done differently, leveraging the knowledge capital provided by the consultant to present different perspectives on the business problem, in particular gaining insights from similar problems across a wide cross-section of industries.

Challenging prevailing work practices and paradigms should result in a 'step change' in performance for the organization – an improvement or business outcome over and above that initially expected at the beginning of the project. Furthermore, it will result in increased value being delivered from the consulting engagement and hence an improved return on the consulting investment.

Migration path for people back into the business

Creating a clear migration path will encourage people to view project work as a valuable way of building skills and experience.

Project personnel need visibility and clarity about their roles and responsibilities at the conclusion of the project, as early as possible. Unless people know there is a 'plan' for them when the project finishes they are unlikely to seek the project work in the first place, and the project leaders will have even less chance of securing the best people for the task.

The most effective way for ensuring a migration path for people is to ensure their position is held open for them at the conclusion of the project, and that this position is budgeted for. Where the position has been backfilled through a contractor this becomes less of an issue. Where positions are filled by internal staff, a new role needs to be clearly defined for the individual that takes advantage of the skills and capabilities they are expected to build through the project.

By ensuring a clear migration path, people will view project work as a valuable experience that provides them with an opportunity to build skills they would not typically have in their day-to-day roles. A migration path will enable them to return to the business, apply their newly gained skills and increase their performance. Projects then cease being viewed as an 'end point' in careers or as a sideline responsibility from the day-to-day operations of the business. Changing the perception of project work will give organizations a larger pool of people from which to draw for future endeavors.

Ability to remove roadblocks quickly

Removing obstacles and roadblocks is critical to successful and timely delivery on a project and vital to maintaining project team momentum.

At the outset a governance structure should be established, including project management, key stakeholders, steering group, key advisers and project champions. A sharing of risk and responsibility through the structure will help to insulate individual team members from the 'noise' created by barriers to change that might emerge. In this way, roadblocks can be removed quickly so that the team can continue to focus on project delivery.

The rapid removal of roadblocks will help to create a focused and effective project team that is able to minimize any time spent reacting to or managing issues that do not relate to delivery on their day-to-day tasks.

Timely access to the right stakeholders

At the outset, the project team members should be given access to the people or champions in the organization who have the best process knowledge. These stakeholders create an important channel for team members to resolve project issues, provide business input to solution design, and most importantly, to agree to and signoff on final project deliverables and outcomes.

The project leaders can identify the right stakeholders by developing a stakeholder map at the start of the project to pinpoint all those who will be critical to review, approve, support the creation of, and inform about, key tasks and deliverables across each project area and project initiative. The leaders need to clarify the stakeholders' roles and responsibilities and gain their commitment to contribute their time and knowledge to the project.

Securing access to the right stakeholders and developing sound relationships with them will help to resolve issues quickly, gain sign-off on deliverables, and reduce the possibility of the project being disrupted by unforseen issues.

Conclusion

The effort required to create a successful client–consultant relationship is relatively small compared to that needed to manage the consequences of a failed project.

Delivering a successful consulting project is challenging and many consulting engagements fail to meet expectations and to deliver outcomes. A significant amount of planning, preparation, thought and structure is needed to establish an effective, credible and highly skilled project team. Following project mobilization, there is further ongoing effort and discipline required to ensure the team remains focused, delivers against the plan and meets expectations, while simultaneously building team capability and enhancing the client–consultant relationship.

This chapter has sought to provide a practical guide to increasing the likelihood of project success by identifying the success factors that need to be addressed by both the consultant and client. While meeting all the necessary success factors and criteria may seem to be a daunting task, or even an excessive task for some, the effort required to implement these recommendations is relatively small compared to the effort required to mitigate and manage the consequences of a failed consulting engagement.

Reference

George Georgitsis, Discussions with Lion Nathan Technical Director, 1995–2000.

Finale: The future is here at last

John L. Gattorna

The world changed forever on 11 September 2001, but things were already changing for supply chains. Indeed, the e-commerce revolution that broke some five years earlier brought with it all the technology capabilities needed to operationalize the concept of supply chain management.

A much clearer picture has emerged of the migration path for companies that take the potential of supply chain management seriously.

Yet, as we launch this book in early 2003, many old and familiar problems remain. High inventories, poor forecasting accuracy, high logistics costs, and a poor understanding of customer buying behaviors are still plaguing many enterprises. In addition, few organizations have achieved any significant improvement in systems integration within, and collaboration between, parties in the supply chain. The relatively rapid progress in the first years of the e-commerce era has now given away to the dogged pace of earlier years. Indeed, we have regressed after what seemed a promising start; so maybe the future as we would like to design it has not yet arrived after all.

What we do have though is a much clearer picture of the migration path for companies that take seriously the huge potential of supply chain management to extract value for shareholders. As Figure F.1 depicts, the increasing complexity that is experienced along the value path is offset by increasingly sophisticated solutions, where leading companies can extract the exponential increase in value (VEX) that is available across a network of supply chains. We are talking in the plural because it is now widely recognized that most enterprises are involved in multiple supply chains. Supply chain executives these days have to think in terms of several 'conveyors' running in parallel, all with different operating characteristics, and carrying products to customer destinations determined by different customer buying behaviors.

And it is also equally clear that those enterprises that seek to follow the value path must demonstrate exceptional leadership and willingness to undergo whatever level of transformation that is

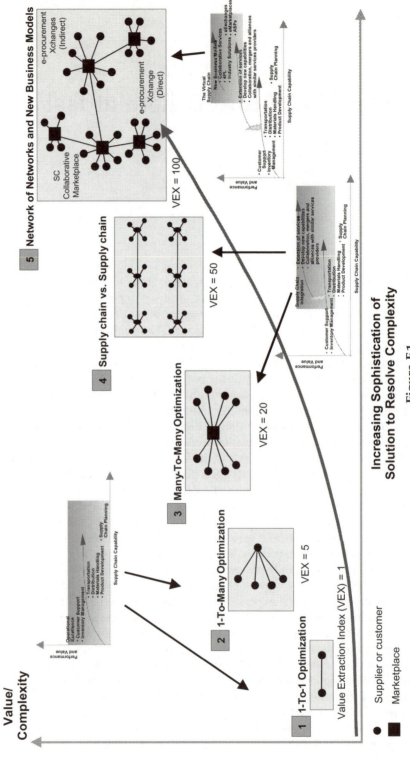

Figure F.1
The value path in complex supply chains

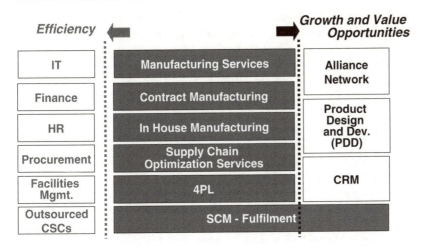

Source: Berger, 2001

Figure F.2
Destructuring and restructuring corporations

required to capture maximum value, at speed. For many organizations who will be unable to build the required portfolio of capabilities fast enough, the only option will be some form of business transformation outsourcing, which in turn means learning to manage risk of a different kind. Even before embarking on this course, organizations will need to diagnose their degree of alignment with the marketplace and use this as the basis to plan the change journey. In the process companies will 'destruct' and 'reconstruct' themselves, as shown in Figure F.2, and management teams will re-invent or remove themselves, depending on the degree of change involved.

As this process of fine-tuning supply chains continues, it will inevitably make them more vulnerable to unforeseen shocks in the operating environment; witness the devastating impact of the market collapse in 2000 on the hitherto successful electronic high-technology companies. This experience has led to a significant re-think about how to assess and manage the risks inherent in operating supply chains in volatile markets. New tools and techniques are actively being sought for this purpose. The Cranfield Centre for Logistics and Transportation has established a new research program to study the causes and consequences of supply chain vulnerability (Cranfield, 2002).

Coincidentally, the war for talent will reach a crescendo as companies realize that competent human resources will be the major variable in the competitive equation in the future. In addition, multinational corporations will institute large-scale e-learning programs as they seek ways to increase the skills of their workforces quickly and cost-effectively.

Ultimately, the best-of-breed companies in the most competitive industries will be the first to recognize that the rewards for designing

Best-of-breed companies will recognize they have to unleash the reservoir of human energy and competence inside and outside their organizations.

and operating high-performance supply chains will only come to those who discover how to unleash the reservoir of human energy and competence inside and outside their organizations. Companies that are able to successfully make the transition to this new hybrid style of organization will be the big winners in the future.

Reference

Berger, A. J., part of a presentation delivered at the SMART 2001 Conference, Sydney, May 2001.

The Cranfield Centre for Logistics and Transportation, Cranfield School of Management, *Supply Chain Vulnerability*, Executive Report on Behalf of Department for Transport, Local Government and the Regions, Home Office, Department of Trade and Industry, January 2002.

Notes on contributors

Douglas W. Allvine is an experienced Manager in Accenture's Supply Chain Practice, based in Atlanta, Georgia. He is a leader in Accenture's supply chain assessment offering and is a key contributor in its ongoing development. Mr Allvine has led numerous supply chain assessments for Accenture clients. He also regularly provides guidance and assessment training to other Accenture personnel around the world. In addition to assessment experience Mr Allvine has considerable experience in manufacturing strategy and operations, process re-engineering, and implementation management. He has a Bachelor degree in Industrial Engineering from the Georgia Institute of Technology.

Mark Bedeman is an Executive Consultant providing Accenture's Supply Chain Practice and European products industry group with 25 years' plus experience in logistics and the 3PL marketplace. In particular, he has helped with the development of the 4PL concept and the emerging supply chain management outsourcing model, as well as supporting the preparation of an extensive 'point of view' of the issues facing today's 3PLs. He worked previously for Danzas in the Basel headquarters for two years, and before that was a founding Director of Exel Logistics, where he had worked for BRS and the NFC for over 23 years.

Mr Bedeman held Divisional Board level roles in line management in the UK and mainland Europe, and was responsible in turn for strategic planning, acquisitions, operational IT, new product design and international business development. He is the Vice Chairman of the Global Supply Chain Council, and Director of the European Digital Solutions Council both of the Conference Board, and a Fellow of the Institute of Logistics and Transport. He has a BSc (Hons) degree in Mathematics from the University of Manchester, and lives with his wife and daughter near Barcelona, Spain.

Brooks A. Bentz is an Associate Partner in Accenture's Supply Chain Practice, based in Boston. His expertise is in transportation strategy and operations, shipper/carrier management and private fleet management as well as strategic transportation procurement. Mr Bentz has extensive expertise in the transportation industry, holding a variety of positions with companies large and small during a career spanning 31 years. He currently co-manages the Transportation Skill Group within the Supply Chain Practice.

Before joining Accenture, Mr Bentz was CEO of a regional motor carrier. Prior to that, he was a vice president with Burlington Northern Railroad, responsible for the creation and development of BN AMERICA, the company's domestic container business unit, and before that he was CEO of a 3PL company based in Philadelphia and founder and COO of a truckload carrier based in Boston. He is also Past President of the National Railroad Intermodal Association and former member of the AAR's Intermodal Steering Committee. He currently serves on the Board of Directors for the University of Denver's graduate transportation program and on the Program Committee for the Intermodal Association of North America and International Intermodal Expo.

Andrew J. Berger is CEO of Continuous Innovation Culture, an independent provider of integrated Six Sigma software solutions, based in the UK. Mr Berger has many years of project experience through his previous role as a partner at Accenture. He is well known for his work on supply chain and is the co-author of *Supply Chain Cybermastery* with Dr John L. Gattorna. Mr Berger has conducted projects for over 25 major multinationals, in 24 countries and 13 different industries. He has extensive experience of sponsoring projects and conducting quality assurance reviews. He left Accenture following a successful IPO to pursue entrepreneurial ventures. Mr Berger has a BSc degree in Economics from Bristol University and an MBA with Distinction from London Business School.

Jamie M. Bolton is a Partner in Accenture's Asia Pacific Supply Chain Practice based in Shanghai. Previously, he was based in Sydney. His experience is in working with consumer and industrial product companies in the areas of supply chain strategy, management and integration, supply chain network modeling and optimization, demand management, e-procurement, strategic sourcing, distribution and inventory management.

Prior to joining Accenture Mr Bolton worked with Pacific Power in Australia. He holds a Bachelor of Mechanical Engineering degree from the University of Technology, Sydney, and an MBA from the University of New England, Australia.

Wanda S. Brown is an Associate Partner in Accenture's Supply Chain Practice, based in Atlanta, Georgia. She has experience working with food and consumer packaged goods companies, energy companies and book publishing companies in the areas of strategic sourcing, supply chain management and supply chain planning. She was also the Americas lead for the Supply Chain Knowledge Hub, which was a compilation of groups that provided knowledge management tools and services, conducted virtual workshops, developed extensive thought leadership studies and provided proposal development support.

Prior to joining the company she held positions in engineering and sales and production planning for Corning Asahi Video. She also worked as a Production Engineer for Shell Western E&P.

Ms Brown earned an MBA from the Wharton School at the University of Pennsylvania and a BS degree in Mechanical Engineering from North Carolina A&T State University.

Jon Bumstead is a Partner in Accenture's UK and Ireland Supply Chain Practice, responsible for the Integrated Fulfilment practice area across Europe. He has extensive experience in procurement, manufacturing and logistics in the consumer products and retail industries.

Mr Bumstead has deep experience in B2B e-commerce from his participation in e-markets and more recently in the emerging e-fulfilment space and is frequently asked to speak on these subjects and contributes numerous press articles. Jon graduated from City University, London with a first class honors degree in Mechanical Engineering and, before joining Accenture, worked for Mars and Redland in a series of production and logistics management roles.

Brett Campbell is an Independent Consultant. Previously, he was Senior Manager in Accenture's Supply Chain Practice, based in Sydney. Brett specializes in logistics strategy development and operations, strategic sourcing, e-procurement, and e-sourcing. He initiated the Accenture Dynamic Pricing Solution (DPS) team in Sydney which focused on key procurement strategies and tactics for major Australasian and Asian companies.

Mr Campbell led the Accenture DPS team through a number of successful sourcing engagements with major companies in Australia and SE Asia. Prior to joining Accenture, he worked in senior logistics management roles such as the Regional Logistics Director for Black and Decker Australia, and National Operations Manager for Avon.

Mr Campbell is a Past President of the National Logistics Association of Australia, and he holds a Masters degree in Transport Management from AGSM and a Bachelor of Science degree from the University of NSW.

Manuel Chaure is a Senior Manager in Accenture's Southern European Supply Chain Practice, located in Madrid. He is the Manufacturing and Design Practice leader in Spain where he develops supply chain activities across industrial equipment, automotive and travel and transportation industries. Mr Chaure has broad experience in manufacturing and in product development, focusing on manufacturing strategy and operations, productivity and performance improvement and concurrent engineering process and organization design.

Mr Chaure has a Masters degree in Industrial Engineering from Madrid Polytechnical University, is CPIM by APICS and has a Postgraduate degree in Business Administration from IESE.

Dr Martin Christopher is Professor of Marketing and Logistics at Cranfield School of Management in the UK. His work in the field of logistics and supply chain management has gained international recognition. He has published widely and his recent books include *Logistics and Supply Chain Management* and *Marketing Logistics*. Dr Christopher is also co-editor of the *International Journal of Logistics Management* and is a regular contributor to conferences and workshops around the world.

At Cranfield, Dr Christopher chairs the Centre for Logistics and Transportation, the largest activity of its type in Europe. The work of the Centre covers all aspects of transportation and logistics and offers both full-time and part-time Masters degree courses as well as extensive management development programs. Research plays a key role in the work of the Centre and contributes to its international standing.

In addition to leading a number of ongoing research projects in logistics and supply chain management, Martin Christopher is active as an advisor to many organizations and is non-executive director of a number of companies.

Dr Christopher is an Emeritus Fellow of the Institute of Logistics and Transport on whose Council he sits. In 1988 he was awarded the Sir Robert Lawrence Gold Medal for his contribution to logistics education and in 1997 was given the USA Council of Logistics Management's Foundation Award.

Richard S. Clarke is an Associate Partner in Accenture's Australia and New Zealand products industry practice, based in Sydney and is an industry expert recognized for his work in human performance and e-learning.

Mr Clarke works with consumer products and entertainment companies to deliver superior business performance through improved human performance. He has also worked in financial services, government and utilities industries in Australia, New Zealand and Malaysia since joining Accenture in 1989.

Mr Clarke has significant experience in managing large-scale, technology-enabled change projects in addition to project management expertise in multimedia and CBT development. He also has training delivery and coaching experience in both classroom and virtual learning environments.

Mr Clarke has a BA Hons (Psychology) degree from the University of Sydney and is a member of the International Society for Performance Improvement and the Australian Human Resources Institute.

Alejandro Cuartero is a Partner in Accenture's Supply Chain Practice, based in Madrid. Leading the Manufacturing and Design Practice area in Europe, he has extensive experience in different industrial sectors – automotive (suppliers, manufacturers and distribution), transportation (airlines and logistics operators), industrial equipment, aerospace and electronics. He has commanded significant transformation projects in the manufacturing and procurement side for large companies involving many countries in Europe and Latin America, developing specific methodologies and tools for manufacturing improvement. The product development practice has expanded in recent years and Mr Cuartero has led the European design survey conducted with over 100 companies presented in Fall 2001. Mr Cuartero is Industrial Engineer by the ETSII of Madrid, member of APICS since the first promotion in Spain and represents Accenture in different logistics fora and associations. Before joining Accenture in 1984, he worked for Ramsey Ingenieros and Land Rover.

Greg Cudahy is the Global Director of the B2B/Supply Chain Global Service Line for Cap Gemini Ernst & Young, based in the United States. Mr Cudahy was previously with Manugistics where he was Executive Vice President responsible for the company's Pricing and Revenue Optimization line of business. Prior to Manugistics Mr Cudahy was a Partner at Accenture where he was leader of the North American Supply Chain Practice.

Mr Cudahy holds an MBA from the Fuqua School at Duke University, a Bachelor's degree in Electrical Engineering/Economics from the University of Dayton, and has pursued graduate studies in Elecro-Optics at the University of California, Los Angeles and International Business at the University of International Business and Economics, Beijing, China.

Alister Danks is an Independent Consultant, researcher and writer. Previously, he was a Senior Manager in Accenture's Supply Chain Practice, based in Melbourne. He has worked with clients in Australia, New Zealand, Singapore, Malaysia and Thailand in several industries including electronics, pharmaceuticals, consumer goods, construction materials and logistics. Mr Danks's interests are in supply chain strategies, inventory management, fulfilment operations, e-fulfilment and third-party logistics.

Mr Danks holds a Bachelor of Civil Engineering (Hons) degree from the University of Melbourne and an MBA (Distinction) from the London Business School.

Ken Davis is the Business Services Director at Lion Nathan Australia and has worked in a variety of finance roles for Lion Nathan across New Zealand, China and Australia. Mr Davis' area of expertise is in the financial management of organizations and he has a successful track record of project managing and delivering large-scale organization change initiatives for Lion Nathan. As Lion's Project Controller for the construction of their Suzhou Brewery in China, Ken was a key contributor to ensuring the brewery was commissioned on time and under budget.

Over the past four years Ken has partnered with Accenture across a number of projects, including project managing the implementation of a new ERP system and roll-out across five regions, the re-design and implementation of LNA's finance organization, development of their collaborative business services organization and the design, development and roll-out of Lion's Finance and Management Information Portal. He is currently leading the implementation of e-procurement across the Australian brewing business. Mr Davis holds a Bachelor of Commerce degree in Accounting from Otago University and is a member of the New Zealand Society of Accountants.

Michael A. Donnellan is a Strategy Partner in Accenture's UK and Ireland Products Industry Consulting Practice. Originally a time-served engineer in the UK Ministry of Defence armaments manufacturing division, he joined the consulting industry in 1984, implementing manufacturing techniques such as just-in-time, flexible production, cellular assembly and supply-chain scheduling solutions. In the early 1990s he joined Pricewaterhouse-Coopers, founding their European pharmaceutical industry practice. He subsequently became a lead partner in PwC's global finance and cost management group, launching the value-based management practice. From this background he co-authored the highly successful book *CFO – Architect of the Corporation's Future* which led to award-winning innovation in the field of strategic financial management. He returned to his supply-chain roots in late 1999, becoming a lead partner in PwC's e-market/e-supply-chain practice.

In July 2001 Mr Donnellan joined Accenture where he holds a leadership position in the area of Transformational Outsourcing, a solution that enables major organizations to move to radically new operating models that change the competitive rules of play creating substantial shareholder value. He has extensive international experience working with the boards of global corporations such as Johnson & Johnson, Unilever, Novo Nordisk, Bristol Myers-Squibb, Caterpillar and the governments of Saudi Arabia and Japan.

Stephen F. Dull is the Partner lead for Accenture's Brand Practice, based in Miami, USA. He has served a number of global companies on brand and marketing strategy over the last 19 years, and is quoted frequently in such publications as *USA Today*, the *Financial Times* and *Investor's Business Daily*.

He recently completed a landmark study on B2C and B2B e-branding and a study of how CRM capability drives financial performance, earning him Accenture's Thought Capital Award two years in a row, and will appear shortly in a book to be published by McGraw-Hill.

Prior to Accenture, Mr Dull spent eight years at McKinsey and started the Business to Business Marketing Center at that firm. Prior to McKinsey, Mr Dull spent five years in marketing at Pillsbury. He holds an MBA in marketing from the University of Michigan.

Anthony Du Preez is founder and Managing Director of a 'new economy' Australian company, BOMweb Pty Ltd. He has an engineering and business background in major defense projects with the Australian Air force and Honeywell. In these roles he has worked on several multi-billion dollar tendering projects in the US and Europe. His experience in these roles led him to develop a new approach to online negotiations at BOMweb to leverage the inherent efficiencies and ubiquity of the Internet.

Mr Du Preez holds a first class honors degree in electrical engineering, and is an MBA graduate from Melbourne Business School. He is a regular speaker at the Australian Institute of Purchasing and Materials Management (AIPMM) conferences. He also lectures on e-business models and web economics at the Royal Melbourne Institute of Technology Masters of e-business Program.

Karen Dwyer is a Consultant in Accenture's Australia and New Zealand Supply Chain Practice, located in Sydney. Karen is currently taking time out travelling and working in Scandinavia. Her consulting experience is in Sales and Operations Planning in industrial equipment businesses, and she has also worked extensively in Organization and Human Performance. She has also managed *change efforts* (particularly behavioral change) on large-scale business process re-engineering and ERP implementation projects for consumer goods and industrial products clients. Ms Dwyer has an Honors degree in Economics from the University of Sydney.

Robert Easton is Managing Partner of Accenture's Asia Pacific Supply Chain Practice based in Hong Kong. He is also a member of Accenture's Global Supply Chain Executive Leadership Team. Mr Easton has supply chain experience in both military and commercial organizations in Australia and Asia, focusing on supply chain strategy, supply chain transformation, distribution operations, supply chain planning systems, performance measurement and supply chain performance improvement.

Mr Easton has a BCom degree from Victoria University, a graduate diploma in psychology from Massey University, a Master's in Defence Studies from Deakin University and an MBA from the Macquarie University. He has also completed the US Army's logistics executive development course and graduated from the Singapore Command and General Staff College.

Jaume Ferrer is the Partner leading Accenture's Supply Chain Practice in Continental Europe which includes more than 250 professionals working in areas such as supply chain pan-European strategies, integrated supply chain management, supply chain planning, sourcing and e-procurement, B2B marketplaces, e-fulfilment and distribution operations and fourth-party logistics (4PL) alliances.

Mr Ferrer has had direct responsibility over supply chain and procurement projects in consumer goods, retail, pharmaceutical, transportation and automotive industries, as well as for B2B e-markets and in B2C e-fulfilment. Before joining Accenture in 1988 he worked as a supply chain consultant for another consulting firm and also for a public transportation planning organization.

Mr Ferrer obtained an MSc degree in Operational Research from the London School of Economics and Finance and a graduate diploma in Systems Analysis from the University of Aix-en-Provence. He graduated with a BSc degree in Business Management and Economics at the University of Barcelona and studied Transportation Engineering at Imperial College London.

Sara Ford is a Manager within the Integrated Fulfilment group of Accenture's Supply Chain Practice located in the UK. Ms Ford has over six years' experience of supply chain consulting, with industry expertise in the energy and consumer packaged goods sectors. Ms Ford's areas of focus include supply chain strategy, collaborative logistics technologies and transportation optimization. Over recent years, Ms Ford has managed Accenture's UK-based Integrated Fulfilment Centre of Excellence and has been heavily involved in the start-up of a number of new organizations operating within the fulfilment space.

Ms Ford holds a BSc degree in Business Economics from Durham University, with a specialization in labor economics.

Dr John L. Gattorna recently retired from Accenture after 6 years building and leading the Supply Chain Practice in Southern Asia, and was one of the firm's most respected thought leaders. Previously, he operated his own consulting firm for over a decade, specializing in marketing, logistics, and channels strategy, servicing an international clientele. John is generally regarded as one of the world's leading thinkers in the supply chain arena, and is much sought after as a speaker on the international circuit.

John has authored/co-authored 10 books and numerous articles on marketing, marketing planning, pricing, customer service, channels strategy, logistics, and supply chain management. His most recent book, co-authored with Andrew Berger, *Supply Chain Cybermastery,* was released at the height of the e-commerce boom in 2001, and has since been translated into Chinese. His previous book, *Strategic Supply Chain Alignment,* published in 1998, was the first book to bring a behavioral dimension to the task of building high performance supply chains. This book has since been translated into Japanese and will shortly be published in the Chinese language.

Although John originally came from industry he has a strong academic pedigree having taught undergraduate, post-graduate, and executive programs at the University of New South Wales and Macquarie University in Sydney; and Oxford and Cranfield universities in the UK. He is currently Visiting Professor of Supply Chain Management at Cranfield, and a Professorial Fellow at the Sydney Business School, University of Wollongong.

John developed the highly reputable Effective Logistics Management (ELM) program which is offered through the Sydney Graduate School of Management, University of Western Sydney. In 2003, this will be supplemented with the all new Effective Supply Chain Management (ESCM) program.

In 2001 John received the Smart Conference Award for Excellence in recognition of his outstanding contribution to the supply chain management profession.

John's email address is john@gattorna-alignment.com.au or visit his Web site at www.gattorna-alignment.com.au.

Roger Gillespie is a Senior Manager in Accenture's Supply Chain Practice, located in London, and is a specialist in e-procurement and strategic sourcing with more than 20 years' procurement management experience in blue chip companies. Mr Gillespie's procurement background includes a variety of line management roles in a major petro-chemical company where he was responsible for developing best practice strategic sourcing strategies and processes for their manufacturing, retail and commercial businesses.

Mr Gillespie holds an MBA from Leicester University in Supply Chain Management and is a Member of the Chartered Institute of Purchasing and Supply.

Scott F. Githens is a Manager in Accenture's Supply Chain Practice, based in Sydney. He specializes in supply chain planning with specific interests and experience in demand management and sales and operations planning. Mr Githens also has experience in the areas of distribution resource planning, warehouse design and management, transportation planning and execution, and experience in the planning and implementation of a number of Tier One advanced planning and scheduling tools including SAP APO, Manugistics and i2. Prior to joining Accenture he was a Logistics Analyst with Alcatel Australia and then a recruitment consultant specializing in supply chain professionals.

Mr Githens has a BA degree from the University of New South Wales majoring in Logistics and Human Resources Management and is Certified in Production and Inventory Management (CPIM) by the American Production and Inventory Control Society (APICS).

Dr Trevor Gore is an Independent Consultant, specializing in Manufacturing Strategy and Supply Chain Operations. Previously, he was an Associate Partner in Accenture's Australia and New Zealand Supply Chain Practice, based in Sydney. Dr Gore has over 25 years of professional supply chain experience gained throughout Europe, North America, Japan, and South-East Asia as well as Australia and New Zealand. His industry experience has covered heavy and light engineering, FMCG, Retail, Pharmaceuticals and Financial Services. Dr Gore was a major contributor to the development of Accenture's Supply Chain diagnostic methodology, the Supply Chain Value Assessment (SCVA) tool, and led the pilot.

Dr Gore was educated in the UK, gaining BSc (Engineering) and PhD (Bio-engineering) degrees from the University of Durham. After spending some time teaching at Cambridge University Department of Engineering, he began his industrial career, ultimately holding senior positions in design and development, manufacturing, and operations management. He returned to academia to gain an MBA from Cranfield School of Management.

Cameron H. Hall is pursuing a range of entrepreneurial interests in the Logistics and Supply Chain area. He was previously a Senior Manager in Accenture's Australia and New Zealand Supply Chain Practice, located in Sydney. Mr Hall's expertise is in designing and implementing process and organizational change across the supply chain with FMCG companies. He has logistics and customer management experience in commercial organizations in Australia, focusing on supply chain strategy, logistics transformation, trading terms redesign, performance measurement and achieving supply chain performance improvement.

Before joining Accenture Mr Hall was a key member of the supply chain management team at Australia's largest food manufacturer and a key contributor to the Australian grocery industry supply chain association. Mr Hall has a BBus (Economics) degree from Queensland University of Technology, a Graduate Certificate in Logistics, Supply Chain and Transport Management from Sydney University, and an MBA from Macquarie University.

Geremy J. Heath is a Consultant in Accenture's Supply Chain Practice, based in Hong Kong. He has experience in both the CPG and chemicals industries in supply chain planning applications, inventory management systems, performance management systems, supply chain performance improvement, working capital reduction and Accenture's Dynamic Pricing Solution (DPS) market offering. He has worked throughout Australia, Asia and the UK. While in the UK he worked in Accenture's Supply Chain Planning Center of Excellence, London. He was responsible for the development of Accenture's Inventory Rebalancing Model (IRM) which has been used to identify and deliver inventory reductions to organizations across multiple industries throughout the world.

Mr Heath holds a Bachelor of Engineering Degree – Civil (Hons) from the University of NSW Australia. He also has completed the APICS Certification in Production and Inventory Management qualification and was a member in the winning team of Accenture's Global Supply Chain Simulation competition for both the Asia Pacific Region and the World Championships held in Colorado, USA.

David Kennedy is a Principal with the Adexa Business Partner in Australia and New Zealand and is instrumental in bringing the iCollaboration suite to the region. Adexa's APS solution focuses on enabling manufacturers and distributors to accelerate time-to-market for products, improve customer service, reduce inventory, compress cycle times, and synchronize information and material flow across their supply chains. His current responsibilities include building the Adexa business in the region by ensuring successful delivery of projects. He is well known in the Australasian supply chain management arena, having overseen the implementation projects of i2 Technologies solution during his time as Consulting Director with the US-based APS Solution provider. Prior to his i2 work with clients in retail, CPG, steel and soft goods, Mr Kennedy was a Principal Consultant with Price Waterhouse. The time spent there as a supply chain practitioner ensured that he had the opportunity to build a significant reputation working in several industry sectors, including agri business, CPG, textiles and automotive.

Mr Kennedy's APS solution knowledge is underpinned with supply chain line management experience with companies such as Toyota and Lucas Diesel Systems. Mr Kennedy holds a Bachelors degree in Mechanical Engineering from the University of Glasgow and a Master's in Manufacturing Systems Engineering from Warwick University.

Stefano Lorenzi is a Senior Manager in Accenture's Supply Chain Practice, based in Milan, Italy. During his career, he has managed major change management programs in the automotive, food, consumer electronics and aerospace industries in the areas of product development, supply chain, mergers and acquisition and corporate strategy.

The early years of his career were spent with Philips Electronics where he worked as Program Manager to launch new products. Later, he opened his own consulting company prior to joining Accenture. Mr Lorenzi has recently co-authored a number of articles on the Product Development Process with CERIS, a Turin-based organization focused on economics.

Mr Lorenzi graduated from Milan Polytechnic in 1989 with a degree in Mechanical Engineering. Postgraduate studies led to a Master in Business Administration from the Kellogg University of Chicago in 1999.

Michael G. Mikurak is a Leadership Partner in Accenture's Global Supply Chain Practice, based in St Petersburg, Florida. He is a leader in supply chain activities across a number of industries and is responsible for Accenture's Supply Chain e-learning programs which includes the launching of a new supply chain e-learning market offering: Accenture's Supply Chain Academy.

Mr Mikurak specializes in supply chain strategy, procurement, materials management, distribution operations, logistics information and systems planning and implementation. Before joining Accenture, Mr Mikurak was a partner at KPMG Peat Marwick LLP and held logistics managerial positions with a major consulting firm, Textron Lycoming and GTE.

Mr Mikurak holds a BSBA Degree from Rider University and a certificate from the product development and manufacturing strategy program at Stanford University Graduate School of Engineering. He also has 25 pending US patents in the area of Collaborative B2B operations.

Craig Millis is a Senior Manager in Accenture's Supply Chain Practice, based in London where he manages the Supply Chain Planning Center of Excellence. He has extensive supply chain and general management experience across a range of industries including consumer products, oil and gas, high-tech and government. He specializes in supply chain planning systems in which he has extensive experience working for a range of clients in Australia, South-East Asia, Europe and the USA.

Mr Millis holds a Bachelor of Engineering degree and a Graduate Diploma in Integrated Logistics Management from RMIT University and an MBA from Deakin University.

David N. Morris is a Senior Manager in Accenture's Customer Relationship Management Practice, located in Sydney. Mr Morris's expertise is in business strategy development and operational engineering with particular focus on customer relationship management (marketing, sales and service) and supply chain management. Mr Morris has experience in the products, pharmaceutical, financial services and utilities industries in Australia, Asia and Europe.

Mr Morris holds Bachelor of Business in Accounting and Bachelor of Applied Science degrees in Computing from Monash University, Australia. He has also completed the Advanced Business Management Program at Northwestern University, USA.

Linda Nuthall works for Continuous Innovation Culture in London, developing new Six Sigma software. Previously, she was a Strategy Manager in Accenture's Australia and New Zealand Supply Chain Practice, based in Sydney. Ms Nuthall has experience working with consumer and industrial products companies in the areas of demand management, distribution, inventory management, supply chain modeling and optimization, customer segmentation and strategic alignment.

Ms Nuthall authored the 'Supply Chain Management Tools' chapter in *Strategic Supply Chain Alignment* (Gower, UK, 1998) as well as conducting much of the research for *Supply Chain Cybermastery* (Gower, UK, 2001).

Ms Nuthall holds a Bachelor of Applied Science degree in Industrial Mathematics and Computing from the Charles Sturt University, Bathurst, NSW and a Master of Science (Logistics and Supply Chain Management) degree, Cranfield University, UK.

Robert Ogulin is undertaking Doctoral Research in the Supply Chain area at Sydney Business School, University of Wollongong, and also works as an Independent Consultant/Adviser. Previously, he was a Manager in Accenture's Australia and New Zealand Supply Chain Practice, based in Sydney and was also affiliated with the global electronics and high-tech practice. Mr Ogulin has experience in supply chain management with a focus on strategic supply chain alignment, collaboration and integration in supply chains. He has worked with major electronics and high-technology clients on supply chain engagements in North America, Europe, Asia and Australia. His recent research centers on the impacts of regionalization and globalization in the supply chain.

Mr Ogulin has a Diploma in Economics from Hamburg University and an MBA from the Australian Graduate School of Management. He is certified in APICS and an active member of the Logistics Association of Australia (NSW).

David R. Olson is a management consultant specializing in warehousing and distribution and is based in Dallas, Texas. Previously he was an Associate Partner in Accenture's Supply Chain Practice. He has over 20 years of industry and consulting experience in facilities planning, material handling and performance improvement for manufacturing and warehousing operations. Prior to joining Accenture, he held executive positions with PricewaterhouseCoopers, Tompkins Associates and General Electric Company.

Garry O'Sullivan is a Grocery Industry Advisor, based in Sydney, working both independently and with Accenture to assist grocery industry clients develop collaborative initiatives to drive joint profitability. For the past ten years, he has worked in the grocery industry at the interface between trading partners. Mr O'Sullivan's special interest has been the creation of a trust-based environment, in which trading partners can develop break-through value chain initiatives to drive profitable growth.

Mr O'Sullivan has worked with retailers, manufacturers, material suppliers and intermediaries, to re-engineer their business processes across the trading partner interface, thereby allowing enabling technologies to support major collaborative initiatives. He has over ten years' experience in B2B e-commerce, working with suppliers and retailers in both grocery and apparel. Prior to entering the grocery and retail field, he worked for 15 years in the communications industry.

Mr O'Sullivan is an active participant in the Efficient Consumer Response movement and led the introduction of Profit Impact Analysis into Australia and its adoption as a best practice approach to creating visibility of net profit contribution along the supply chain, from raw materials supply to retail shelf. He writes a regular column on ECR in *Retail World* magazine.

Mr O'Sullivan holds Bachelor of Engineering and Bachelor of Science degrees from the University of New South Wales and an MBA from Deakin University. He is an Associate Fellow of the Australian Institute of Management.

Greg Owens, Manugistics' Chairman and Chief Executive Officer, is the driving force behind the company's marketplace momentum – leading the company to record annual revenues and doubled annual license fees in its most recent fiscal year. The company's impressive growth under Mr Owens' leadership was recently recognized by *Bloomberg Personal Finance* magazine – ranking the company 11th on its *The Bloomberg 100*, the exclusive annual ranking of its hottest stocks for 2000, and Manugistics was listed as one of The *Wall Street Journal*'s 'Best Performers' for 2000.

Strategically, Mr Owens has positioned Manugistics as the premier provider of Enterprise Profit Optimization (EPO) solutions – the first solutions to optimize both the supply- and demand-side functions simultaneously, utilizing the powerful combination of supply chain management and pricing and revenue optimization – for enterprises and e-marketplaces.

Since joining Manugistics in April 1999, Mr Owens has invested aggressively in strengthening and growing its sales organization, marketing initiatives and technology innovations globally. Manugistics' differentiated, strong, ROI-based solutions championed by Mr Owens are helping deliver profitable growth at eight out of top ten Fortune 500 companies. His strategic vision and balanced sales approach across key industry verticals – targeting companies across all industries and geographies – have enabled Manugistics to team with an impressive array of clients including US and European governments and industry leaders such as BP, Compaq, Cisco Systems, DaimlerChrysler, Geodis, IKEA, Japan Airlines, Maersk, Mitsui Chemicals, SwissAir, Target Stores, Texas Instruments and Vodafone.

Mr Owens is an active member of the Washington, DC metropolitan area community, and was recently honored as a 'Titan of Business' by the Washington, DC Leukemia and Lymphoma Society; recognized as Maryland's 2001 'Entrepreneur of the Year' for software and was also a finalist for the '2001 CEO of the Year' for the DC region.

Mr Owens graduated from the Georgia Institute of Technology in 1982 with a BSc degree in Industrial Management.

Mark Pearson is a Partner in Accenture's Supply Chain Practice, based in London. He has responsibility for the European Supply Chain Planning Practice and championed the development of Accenture's Intelligent Supply Chain Model. Mr Pearson also manages our alliance relationships with supply chain planning solution providers including i2, Manugistics, SAP and Oracle. He has worked extensively across industries, with a recent focus on the high-tech and consumer goods sectors.

Donald S. Puckridge is an experienced Manager in Accenture's Asia Pacific Supply Chain Practice, located in Melbourne. He specializes in manufacturing, advanced planning systems, supply chain performance improvement, inventory management, and systems planning and implementation. Before joining Accenture, Mr Puckridge held manufacturing, project and IT managerial positions with a leading automotive supplier.

Mr Puckridge has BSc and BE (Hons) degrees in Chemical Engineering from the University of Adelaide and graduated as a member of the Dean's List on completion of an MBA at the Adelaide University Graduate School of Management.

Mark Reynolds is an Associate Partner in Accenture's Australia and New Zealand Supply Chain Practice, based in Sydney. He has more than 25 years of operational and consulting experience in manufacturing, distribution and supply chain management across a wide variety of industries including automotive, food, beverages, dairy, basic metals, consumer and industrial products.

Mr Reynolds has worked in the UK, Australia, New Zealand and Asia on supply chain strategy, design and implementation projects at all stages from initial opportunity assessment and business case development to hands-on operational change and benefit realization. Most of his recent projects have involved development of new operating strategies and advanced supply chain planning and execution processes, with a particular focus on fulfilment processes.

Mr Reynolds has Bachelor of Mechanical Engineering and Master of Engineering degrees in Industrial Electronics from the University of Auckland.

Jeffrey S. Russell is Managing Partner of Accenture's Southern Asia Supply Chain Practice, based in Melbourne, with responsibility for products, communications and high-tech industries in Australia/New Zealand. Mr Russell also takes an active role in supporting leading global consumer packaged goods clients across Asia Pacific. He has 13 years' consulting experience in supply chain management in North America, Asia, Australia and New Zealand. Prior to his consulting career, he gained line management experience in the heavy industrial equipment sector, in manufacturing management and technical sales roles. Mr Russell specializes in supply chain strategy, channel alignment and business-to-business collaboration.

Mr Russell holds BSc and MSc in Mechanical Engineering degrees from the University of Manitoba in Canada.

Olaf Schatteman is a Manager in Accenture's Australia and New Zealand Supply Chain Practice, based in Sydney. He is also a member of the Australia and New Zealand Electronics and High-tech leadership team. Mr Schatteman transferred from the European practice where he serviced clients in the Electronics and High-tech and other industries through the design and implementation of large-scale technology enabled business transformation projects.

Mr Schatteman's interests are in strategic supply chain management and in designing and implementing supply chain planning strategies and strategic sourcing capabilities.

He holds Masters degrees in Economics and Business Administration from the University of Maastricht in the Netherlands and the University of Seville in Spain.

Dr Richard D. Schleusener has over 20 years of technical, quality and management experience in manufacturing and service processes. He has extensive experience leading line and staff personnel in Six Sigma and quality improvement efforts. In addition to his manufacturing expertise, Dr Schleusener has led several human resource initiatives both at the site level and at the corporate level.

Dr Schleusener worked for Eastman Kodak for several years before joining Six Sigma Academy. While at Kodak, he held various positions, including Black Belt instructor, consulting statistician, process engineer, product engineer, and department manager, among others. He was the project champion for a lean manufacturing effort for a major product flow. He spent several years as the Diversity Manager for the Kodak Colorado site.

As a Black Belt instructor for Kodak, Dr Schleusener achieved 30 per cent project cycle time reductions that resulted in inventory savings of over $5 million, throughput improvements of 27 per cent for a professional film process, and quality conformance improvements of 16 per cent. He delivered quality improvement programs that resulted in keeping customer accounts worth over $500K.

Dr Schleusener is currently the Vice President for Curriculum Development at Six Sigma Academy. He holds a BSc in Mathematics from South Dakota State University, an MSc degree in Statistics from Colorado State University and a PhD degree in Education and Human Resource Development from Colorado State University.

Timothy Stephens is a Senior Manager in Accenture's Customer Relationship Management Practice, based in Boston. Mr Stephens specializes in helping companies improve their CRM strategies by helping organizations become more customer-centric, understand their market opportunities, and develop and take to market new products.

Mr Stephens has worked across many industries including consumer and industrial products, communications, government, retail, and natural resources. He is also an active author and thought leader in the area of CRM. His articles have been published in *Beverage Marketing*, *Siebel Magazine* and *Software Strategies*. Additionally, Mr Stephens was a co-author of the Accenture-sponsored report 'How Much are CRM Capabilities Really Worth? What Every CEO Should Know'. He obtained his BA degree from Amherst College and his MBA from the Amos Tuck School of Business.

Ming Tang is a Senior Manager in Accenture's Supply Chain Practice, based in Sydney. She has experience working in consumer, healthcare and industrial products companies. She specializes in supply chain management, strategy formulation and new business development and has worked extensively with global organizations in Europe and the United States.

Prior to joining Accenture Ms Tang worked for a large global pharmaceutical company in a range of supply chain and customer-facing roles. Ms Tang holds an MBA from Warwick Business School and a BSc degree in Pharmacy.

Dennis Theis is a Manager in Accenture's European Supply Chain Practice. He has extensive experience in supply chain management with a focus on supply chain planning processes, technologies, collaboration, consensus forecasting and demand planning.

Mr Theis has worked on large supply chain planning technology implementations utilizing Manugistics, SAP-APO and i2. He has worked with major multinational corporations in various industry segments on supply chain management engagements in Europe and is an integral part of Accenture's Global Supply Chain Planning Solution Center Network.

Mr Theis has a diploma in industrial engineering from the Fachhochschule Wedel, Hamburg and the Budapest University of Economic Sciences.

Geoffrey Thomas is a Senior Manager in Accenture's Australia and New Zealand Supply Chain Practice, based in Sydney. During his career in consulting and industry, from a base in Australia and Europe, he has developed supply chain solutions for major organizations in the UK, most of Continental Europe, the US, as well as North and South-East Asia. He has worked across the fast moving consumer goods, retail, and pharmaceutical industries for several world leaders in these sectors, with an emphasis on integrating global or complex supply chain operations. He focuses on supply chain strategies to enable performance transformation, demand and supply chain planning, inventory management strategies, logistics network configuration, distribution operations, and strategic sourcing.

Mr Thomas has a BE Honors degree from the University of NSW in Sydney, and an MBA from the European School of Management (EAP) in France.

Neeraj Thukral is a Manager in Accenture's Supply Chain Practice, based in Sydney. He specializes in supply chain strategy, strategic sourcing, e-procurement, e-auctions and advanced planning and scheduling solutions planning and implementation. He has developed a number of diagnostics in the area of strategic sourcing and e-procurement and has been instrumental in establishing Accenture's e-auctions delivery capability in Australia.

Mr Thukral has wide industry and consulting experience in Asia and Australia. Before joining Accenture, he worked with CGEY in Asia and Australia. He has completed a Bachelor of Technology degree in Mechanical Engineering from the Indian Institute of Technology, Delhi (IITD) and an MBA from the Indian Institute of Management, Bangalore (IIMB).

William Thurwachter is a Senior Practice Partner in Accenture's Supply Chain Practice, based in the United States. His practice area for nearly 30 years has been operations management.

Mr Thurwachter has worked in many industries, including aerospace, automotive, PC, computer, semiconductor, paper and telecommunications. His area of specialization is supply chain management. For the last two years, his primary practice territory has included Japan, Korea, and Taiwan, assisting global semiconductor companies with the implementation of APS SCM capability.

Having attended the University of Wisconsin – Madison, Mr Thurwachter holds a BS degree in Mechanical Engineering as well as an MBA in Operations Research. He is a founding executive committee member of the Association for Manufacturing Excellence (AME), an organization whose purpose is to cultivate world-class productivity through improved manufacturing practices. He currently serves as a member of the Dean's Advisory Council of the Arizona State University School of Engineering and is the former Co-chairman of the Computer Integrated Manufacturing System Research Center at ASU. In 1997, Mr Thurwachter was recognized by the University of Wisconsin – Madison, College of Engineering, with a Distinguished Service Citation.

Stephen N. Wagner is President of Analysis Dynamics, LLC and is a partner of SLIM Technologies, Inc. He is an expert in the creation and application of Decision Support Systems (DSS) to address business issues, especially in the area of supply chain management. He has overseen the utilization of optimization based network modeling systems to address strategic and tactical planning supply chain management issues for over 15 clients in the US, Australia, Canada, Indonesia, and New Zealand spanning many different retail and manufacturing sectors.

Prior to his involvement in DSS/SCM consulting, Mr Wagner held executive positions in logistics management at Catenation, Inc. and at Federal Express. Mr Wagner holds a BS degree in Mathematics and a BA degree in Business Economics from Benedictine University, USA, and an MBA in Finance from DePaul University, USA. He is a frequent lecturer at the Massachusetts Institute of Technology on DSS and supply chain management topics.

Dr David Walters is Professor of Business and Head of the Business Department in the School of Economic and Financial Studies at Macquarie University in Sydney, Australia. Prior to joining Macquarie University he held posts at Cranfield School of Management, Templeton College Oxford, Stirling University, and the European Business School.

Dr Walters has published 14 textbooks in marketing subjects. In addition he has published over 30 articles in professional journals. Dr Walters is the Australasian editor for the *International Journal of Physical Distribution and Logistics Management*. He has teaching experience in a wide range of continents including North America, the Middle East, Europe, Asia and Africa.

Dr Walters is the Director of the Center for Strategic Operations Management at Macquarie University. The Center has been set up to investigate emerging business models that focus on enhancing customer value through the integration of supply chain efficiencies with demand chain strategies. Dr Walters' book *Strategic Operations Management: A Value Chain Approach*, was published in late 2002.

Dr Walters has acted as a consultant for a number of international companies, including Harrods, Laura Ashley, The Kingfisher Group, Storehouse, British Oxygen Company, Marks and Spencer, Tesco and a number of others.

Dr Jonathan D. Whitaker is an Associate Partner in Accenture's North American Supply Chain Practice, located in Atlanta, Georgia. He focuses on supply chain value transformation, supply chain outsourcing, supply chain strategy, B2B e-markets, and achieving supply chain benchmarking. He led the development of Accenture's supply chain value targeting approach and methodology. Prior to joining Accenture he was employed by General Motors and UPS.

Dr Whitaker has an MBA, a PhD and a law degree. He has written numerous articles and been published in both business and refereed academic journals. He has given numerous presentations to a variety of groups.

Mark T. Wolfe is the Strategy Lead Partner in Accenture's Customer Relationship Management Practice, based in Atlanta, Georgia. His areas of specialty include growth and customer strategies, product development, product development and sales and marketing. He has particular interest in brand and consumer marketing and direct customer relationships. He has more than 25 years of combined management consulting, operations and sales and marketing experience, having worked for major consumer goods companies including The Coca-Cola Company, Kodak and General Foods as well as McKinsey & Company.

Mr Wolfe recently completed a year-long study which focused on determining which customer relationship management capabilities mattered most in creating financial return for a business. This research has been cited in *Business Week* and will soon be the subject of a book being published by Montgomery Research.

Mr Wolfe holds a BA degree from Yale and an MBA from Columbia University. He is a member of the Technology Association of Georgia and serves as a Trustee for the Marketing Science Institute.

Ian Woolsey is an Associate Partner in Accenture's Strategy and Business Architecture Practice, based in Sydney. Mr Woolsey's expertise is in the information technology enablement of business change, and he has worked extensively in Australia and the Asia Pacific region in the petroleum (upstream and downstream), retail, consumer and industrial products industries.

Most recently, Mr Woolsey led a Shared Services program for a leading Australian 'blue chip' corporation. This program encompassed the design and implementation of a multi-function shared services organization, as well as a number of e-procurement and e-business initiatives. Previously, Mr Woolsey spent five years living and working in Asia, helping national and multinational corporations formulate their information technology strategies.

Prior to joining Accenture ten years ago, Mr. Woolsey spent four years in technical and account management roles with IBM Australia. He holds a Bachelor of Engineering (Electrical) degree, and a Master of Commerce (Economics) from the University of New South Wales.

Jonathan Wright is a senior member of the Accenture's Supply Chain Practice, based in London. He has worked with numerous pan-European and International clients in the area of after-sales and support. Mr Wright has concentrated on the electronics, communications and aerospace industries and is currently involved in developing and implementing a pan-European distribution strategy for a global music company.

Tian Bing Zhang is a Manager in Accenture's Northern Asia Supply Chain Practice based in Shanghai. He previously worked in the ANZ Practice based in Sydney and specializes in supply chain opportunity assessment, regional supply chain strategy, network optimization, strategic sourcing, procurement, inventory management, modeling and simulation. Prior to joining Accenture, he worked in a regional supply management role for ABB Transformer Business Area and as a senior consultant for Ernst & Young Australia.

Mr Zhang has a BSc degree in Physics from Tongji University, Shanghai, and an MBA from the Australian Graduate School of Management with an exchange program to the Graduate School of Business, University of Chicago.

Index

Awesome Purpose

Nigel MacLennan

Only the best businesses achieve the level of success that comes from aligning every member of their team behind some worthwhile goal. Few achieve such success, few become world class. Creating that alignment is not simply a matter of drafting a mission statement, but of understanding and placing each of the elements of the culture behind a single awesome purpose. Nigel MacLennan presents a definitive 'how to guide' to changing and aligning organizational structures.

For the first time a clear framework which incorporates all the elements of organizational culture, and how they relate to each other, is presented. The relationship between purpose, values, vision, mission, strategy, objectives, tactics and so on is presented in the Corporate Alignment Model (CAM).

Taken as a whole, this book provides a step-by-step guide to achieving culture change and alignment through the application of three innovative models – the CAM, the 9R Model and the 6P Model.

Business leaders and organization development specialists alike will find clear and innovative material in this book to stimulate and inspire them. They will find that they are provided with the tools to align their organization and inspire their staff to performance levels not possible without an awesome purpose.

GOWER

Activity Based Management

Improving Processes and Profitability

Brian Plowman

Product and particularly customer profitability are black holes in most managers' understanding of their business. Identifying customer revenue is easy but identifying what they cost – so we can understand whether or not they are profitable – is difficult. In a world in which competition, regulation and the increasing use of the Internet put ever greater pressure on margins it is vitally important to understand both product- and customer-profitability. *Activity Based Management* (ABM) enables you to do this.

This book explains the power of using ABM to increase the profitability of your business. It provides step-by-step guidance on basic principles, comparisons between traditional methods, definitions of processes, activities and cost-drivers as well as details of data collection techniques and implementation steps. Through the book's numerous detailed examples a logical picture builds up of how to obtain the benefits that ABM can deliver. On its own ABM will change management decision-making: by showing how ABM also supports other profit improvement initiatives such as Business Process Reengineering, Shareholder Value Added and Customer Relationship Management, managers will learn how they can use the best possible toolkit to put their business firmly on the road to leaps in profitability.

GOWER

Purchasing Scams and How to Avoid Them

Trevor Kitching

Purchasing scams are not a high profile topic in the boardroom or indeed in the purchasing department – victims don't like to talk about their experience. They don't want to admit that they were gullible enough to be fooled by a fake invoice or a plausible appeal for a bogus charity. And yet scams cost companies thousands of pounds every year!

Purchasing Scams and How to Avoid Them provides a comprehensive and practical guide to avoiding scams in the first place: any initiative in relation to scams must focus on prevention rather than cure. It contains descriptions of all of the most common scams including bogus directories, over-priced office consumables and business consultants who are too good to be true. It also describes how the infamous and ubiquitous Nigeria scam works. Advice is given on how to avoid each and, most importantly, how to establish a purchasing function that will provide effective defences against the perpetrators of such operations. Looking to the future the book considers the impact of e-commerce on the way that scams may develop and be dealt with in the years to come.

No one with the power to commit a company's money is safe from the attention of scam merchants. This book provides you with tools to ensure that your purchasing function is impervious to such approaches.

GOWER

Best Practice Procurement

Public and Private Sector Perspectives

Andrew Erridge, Ruth Fee and John McIlroy

In association with IPSERA (International Purchasing and Supply Education and Research Association)

Best practice procurement is a key contributor to any organization's strategic goals, but requirements and experience differ between sectors: this book provides a range of perspectives on subjects central to improving purchasing performance across public and private, manufacturing and service sectors.
The book consists of five parts:

- Supply chain management.
- Outsourcing and partnership.
- Organization and management.
- Electronic commerce.
- Performance evaluation.

This book comprises a range of cutting-edge, refereed contributions from the 1999 International Purchasing and Supply Education and Research Association meeting. The authors combine both leading academics and key professionals from organizations leading the way in challenging current approaches to procurement practice. The bringing together of both the world of research and business provides the opportunity to present evidence grounded in valid theory and methodology in order to develop better practice as transferable strategies and techniques, rather than one-off, quick fix 'solutions'. *Best Practice Procurement* will appeal to anyone working or studying in a procurement-related function to whom a deeper understanding of how to improve procurement's contribution to the achievement of organizations' strategic goals is important.

GOWER

Gower Handbook
of Purchasing Management

Third Edition

Marc Day

Published in association with the
Chartered Institute of Purchasing and Supply

The revised third edition of the *Gower Handbook of Purchasing Management*
views procurement as standing on the boundary of the firm, looking outwards
and scanning the environment for new opportunities and threats. In this respect,
as in many others, the new edition is quite different from the previous two,
reflecting the many changes that have taken place for businesses over the years.
In particular this edition has been slimmed down and focused to assist the reader
by working systematically outwards using a purchasing lens to view the wider
business world. The aim is to show the potential contribution that purchasing
can make as a driver for organizational efficiency and business development.
It is this latter requirement, the need for purchasing to generate revenue,
that has been identified as being ever more prominent as a demand on purchasing
directors' time and effort.

The book is now split into three sections. Part I lays the foundations for building
the organization of purchasing in a corporate environment. Part II overlays further
applications on the foundations of purchasing organization. The assumption is
made that the purchasing activities of a firm are proactive in outlook, gathering
knowledge and measuring their current corporate purchasing performance, while
also looking to generate revenues for the business. Finally Part III provides case
studies which bring to life some of the learning achieved through the framework
laid out in the previous parts.

Written by leading practitioners and academics, and published in association
with the Chartered Institute of Purchasing and Supply, this book is destined
to become a classic in the field.

GOWER

Supply Chain Cybermastery

Building High Performance Supply Chains of the Future

Andrew J. Berger and John L. Gattorna

Supply Chain Cybermastery is inspired by the eCommerce revolution, which has changed the world forever and reignited interest in the supply chain as a source of wealth creation. Chief executives and their management teams must re-invent themselves and adjust their leadership and management styles to cope with the new realities. Indeed, some are already emulating companies like Sun, Cisco, Intel, Oracle and Microsoft to get their more traditional multinationals back on the growth agenda. Their new focus is the supply chain and enabling technology, both areas previously delegated to functional specialists.

The underlying theme in this book is the huge potential that eCommerce has unleashed in supply chains. But is a bit like being asked to jump straight into a Formula 1 racing car, so we must first learn to drive this new phenomenon to extract maximum benefit.

Collaboration in the truest sense of the word is now technically possible throughout the length and breadth of the supply chain; all that is needed is the will to make things happen. Relationships will be everything in the future. And, with lessened conflict will come the opportunity to explore new ways of working smarter for mutual benefit.

The competition across all industries, in both the old and new economies, will be relentless, coming in waves, and often from unexpected directions. In turn the responses will often be unnatural alliances, within and across industries. The rules of the game are changing, and nothing should surprise. Innovation and creativity will be at a premium.

So whichever way you look at the first decade of the new millennium, speed and scale will be the key ingredients of success – and this is exactly where the new high performance supply chains will shine.

In keeping with the speed of the phenomenon that has so rapidly transformed the way business is transacted, the book is structured around the key areas of change in the B2B world. The objective is to give a 'work in progress' overview and to forecast how business might evolve as the initial flush of activity settles down.

GOWER

How to Forecast

A Guide for Business

James Morrell

Forecasting is an essential discipline in the planning and running of a business: not only for the business plan and annual budget but for the appraisal of investment projects, the commissioning of research as well as the appraisal of the competition and the feasibility of making acquisitions. Managers are continually confronted with the need to take decisions, and being able to construct a route map of the future is a key way of determining a course of action. This book provides a practical guide to forecasting the environment in which a firm operates.

James Morrell, with 45 years of experience as a forecaster to draw on, goes through the key areas which can affect a business. He includes those which are out of the firm's control such as fiscal and monetary policy, population levels and the labour market; and those under the firm's control such as costs, prices, profits and product development. By understanding the issues surrounding these varied subjects any manager will be able to better analyse the data they are given and construct practical and useful forecasts from them.

Forecasting is an art as well as a science – this book helps to unlock its secrets.

GOWER

Making the Connections

Using Internal Communication
to Turn Strategy into Action

Bill Quirke

Companies know that communication with their people is important. However, the road to incoherence is paved with good communications. Internal communication is often less than the sum of parts, because the parts do not fit together. This book looks at what a business needs from its people to succeed, what gets in the way, and the role of communication in helping to bridge the gap. It is designed to help companies link the components of their internal communication together for a more effective result.

Making the Connections examines how businesses can use internal communication to achieve differentiation, to improve their quality, customer service, innovation and to manage change more effectively. It describes the why, the what and the how of internal communication – why business needs better communication to achieve its objectives, what internal communication needs to deliver to add value, and how organizations need to manage their communication for best results.

Based on extensive international experience of one of the most knowledgeable and leading authorities on internal communication, this book provides a step-by-step approach for creating best practice.

GOWER